PRINCIPLES OF ENGLISH COMMERCIAL LAW

2 New York Street
Manchester
M1 4HJ

PRINCIPLES OF ENGLISH COMMERCIAL LAW

Edited by

PROFESSOR ANDREW BURROWS QC, FBA, DCL

Professor of the Law of England, University of Oxford, Fellow of All Souls College

CONTRIBUTORS

Michael Bridge FBA

Malcolm Clarke

Richard Hooley

Ewan McKendrick QC

Norman Palmer QC CBE FSA

Francis Reynolds QC FBA DCL

Francis Rose

Lionel Smith

OXFORD
UNIVERSITY PRESS

OXFORD
UNIVERSITY PRESS

Great Clarendon Street, Oxford, OX2 6DP,
United Kingdom

Oxford University Press is a department of the University of Oxford.
It furthers the University's objective of excellence in research, scholarship,
and education by publishing worldwide. Oxford is a registered trade mark of
Oxford University Press in the UK and in certain other countries

© Oxford University Press 2015

The moral rights of the authors have been asserted

First Edition published in 2015

Impression: 1

Crown copyright material is reproduced under Class Licence
Number C01P0000148 with the permission of OPSI
and the Queen's Printer for Scotland

Published in the United States of America by Oxford University Press
198 Madison Avenue, New York, NY 10016, United States of America

British Library Cataloguing in Publication Data
Data available

Library of Congress Control Number: 2015949487

ISBN 978–0–19–874622–5

Printed and bound by
CPI Group (UK) Ltd, Croydon, CR0 4YY

CONTRIBUTORS

Professor Michael Bridge FBA
*London School of Economics and
National University of Singapore*

Professor Malcolm Clarke
St John's College Cambridge

Professor Richard Hooley
Fitzwilliam College Cambridge

Professor Ewan McKendrick QC
University of Oxford

Professor Norman Palmer QC CBE FSA
3 Stone Buildings Lincoln's Inn

Professor Francis Reynolds QC FBA DCL
Worcester College Oxford

Professor Francis Rose
University of Southampton

Professor Lionel Smith
*McGill University Montreal and
King's College London*

INTRODUCTION

This book reproduces the chapters in *English Private Law* which are concerned with commercial law, namely agency, sale of goods, carriage of goods by sea, carriage of goods by air and land, insurance, banking, bailment, security, and insolvency. *English Private Law* seeks to provide a high-quality overview of the rules and principles that constitute English private law and the intention in producing a student paperback edition is to make particular parts of that work more accessible to students. The benefit of such an overview is that it enables students to see the overall picture of the law and hence to understand how its various parts may be regarded as fitting together in a coherent whole.

The authors are acknowledged experts in their respective subject areas and their brief has been to produce as clear, simple and accurate an overview as possible of the relevant rules and principles. What one has here, therefore, is the product of many years of learning in each particular area.

It is believed that all students, whether studying for undergraduate or postgraduate law degrees, or on professional courses to qualify as barristers, solicitors or legal executives, and taking commercial law papers, will find this book invaluable.

Much of commercial law is built from the law of contract and indeed deals with specific types of contract. This book therefore assumes that one has already taken a course on the law of contract. The general law of contract is covered in chapter 8 of *English Private Law* which is replicated in chapter 1 of the student paperback *Principles of the English Law of Obligations*.

It is important to appreciate that, with the exception of changing the chapter numbers and making corresponding amendments to the cross-references, this book essentially replicates the relevant parts of *English Private Law* which stated the law as at 30 January 2013. However, some light updating has been undertaken to reflect developments up until 30 April 2015 (and it has been assumed for the purposes of the updating that the Consumer Rights Act 2015 is in force although at the time of writing that is not so).

The reference 'EPL' refers to the main work *English Private Law*, edited by Andrew Burrows (OUP, 3rd edn, 2013).

Chapters 1–6 of this book correlate to EPL chapters 9–14, chapter 7 to EPL chapter 16, chapter 8 to EPL chapter 5, and chapter 9 to EPL chapter 19.

CONTENTS

TABLE OF CASES

TABLE OF LEGISLATION, TREATIES AND CONVENTIONS

TABLE OF STATUTES

TABLE OF TREATIES AND CONVENTIONS

1

AGENCY

A. General Considerations

(1) Introduction

An obvious meaning of the word 'agent' is 'someone who acts for or on behalf of another'. **1.01**
The law of agency, not surprisingly, deals with situations where one person acts for another.
The common law of agency is based on extremely general principles. The paradigm reasoning, on which much of the rest of agency law is based, is that one person, usually called the
principal, can give authority to, or authorize, another, the agent, to act on his behalf; and
that the giving of authority confers on the agent a power to affect the legal position of the
person who gave the authority. The principal may therefore become bound and/or entitled
as against persons with whom the agent deals: such persons are usually referred to by the
title 'third party'. To distinguish this situation from other applications of agency reasoning,[1]
which will be explained below, authority when conferred in the way above described is called
'actual authority'.

(a) Messenger and agent

No special principles are required to accept the notion that if one person sends a messenger **1.02**
to another who simply repeats a message from the person who sent him, a contract may arise
(or other legal consequences follow, in property or even in tort) between the sender and the
person to whom the message is given. Such a messenger is in such a case no different from a

---

[1] In particular apparent authority: see 1.60ff.

1

letter sent by his principal, and no one doubts that legal transactions can normally be accomplished by letter. It does not take much, however, to vary this situation to a point where the person to whom the message is directed is not found, and the agent has to take a decision as to what to do; or where the message is obviously, as the facts turn out, inappropriate, and the messenger varies it. It has to be accepted in general that the agent may himself, within limits, decide what to do. Here we begin to require a fuller law of agency.[2]

(b) Generality of agency reasoning

1.03 Agency reasoning is obviously most commonly employed in commercial situations, but in common law there is no reason of principle whatever why it cannot be used elsewhere. There is in common law no requirement that the agent pursue a recognized type of occupation as a commercial intermediary, or a recognized commercial occupation, or indeed any occupation at all. Many commercial relationships which might not in civil law countries easily be regarded as examples of agency at all can trigger off agency reasoning. Thus agency reasoning is used in connection not only with auctioneers, brokers and the like, but also in regard to some of the functions of solicitors, captains of ships, employees, directors of companies and so forth. It can also be used in completely non-commercial contexts: in connection with parents and children, or husbands and wives and cognate relationships. In all of these one person may act for another. There is (or may be) agency (of a very complicated sort) if one employs a Lloyd's broker; there may be agency if one sends a child to buy a lottery ticket.[3] Agency reasoning is not, however, in general used in common law to deal with official representation of persons lacking capacity such as minors and mental patients.

1.04 A result of this approach is that the question 'Is he (or she) an agent?', perhaps with the addition 'and if so of whom?', which is often asked of lawyers, does not often, at any rate in common law, form the basis for a useful approach to a legal problem. One person may have agency authority for another in some respects and not in other respects. A solicitor, eg, is in some respects merely a person who provides commercial services to clients. But in other respects the solicitor can act for the client, as by signing documents, commissioning the provision of services, or settling claims. Employees have agency powers in some respects but not in others: some can agree a price, some can sign receipts, some can place orders, some can receive payment, some can do none of these things. Employment law regulates much of their activities, but not, in general, their agency functions, which are for the law of agency. The fact that someone is called or describes himself as an agent does not mean that there is in law any agency power at all: eg, many distributors of particular goods, such as cars, may describe themselves as agents when in law they are really sellers on their own account—though they may have minor agency functions in respect to manufacturer's warranties and the handling of complaints. Equally, some persons who do not describe themselves as agents—even some who purport to state that they are not agents—may actually be able to act as agents, or at least have some form of authority. In common law an agreed description of a person by some particular title does not of itself establish or exclude agency functions.

(c) An exception: commercial agents

1.05 The common law does not in general, therefore, work by identifying types of agent, though there are a few which are regulated by statute and hence may require definition in the regulatory legislation.[4] To this there is now one exception, which, significantly, comes from the civil law.

---

[2] See G McMeel, 'Philosophical Foundations of Agency' (2000) 116 LQR 387.
[3] A problem of capacity could arise in such a case.
[4] eg, estate agents, regulated by the Estate Agents Act 1979, but even here the regulation is directed at 'estate agency work'.

An EU directive[5] deals with the relationship between persons called 'commercial agents' and their principals, and inter alia confers certain protections on such agents. The category means nothing in common law: to see whether the prescribed incidents of the relationship apply, it is necessary to look carefully at the definition of 'commercial agent' provided in the directive and in the regulations which implement it in the United Kingdom.[6] Before a common law court the situation is therefore not one where special incidents have been attributed to the position of a person pursuing a known occupation (which appears to be the intention behind the directive). Rather, it is necessary to see whether a particular person's mode of commercial operation comes within the definition laid down in the UK regulations. If so, but not otherwise, that person is a commercial agent within them and their special regime applies in accordance with its terms.

The definition given of a commercial agent is 'a self-employed intermediary who has con-   **1.06**
tinuing authority to negotiate the sale and purchase of goods on behalf of another person ("the principal"),[7] or to negotiate and conclude the sale and purchase of goods on behalf of and in the name of that principal'.[8] It will be seen that this excludes employees and persons authorized for one transaction only; however, it includes agents who have no authority to contract (referred to below as 'canvassing agents')[9] as well as those who have. It also uses the civil law terminology of acting 'in the name of' another, a phrase which has no clear meaning for a common lawyer. There is a (rather obscure) exception for those for whom commercial agency is a secondary activity.[10] What is clear however is that an intermediary who purchases for resale is not a commercial agent.[11]

---

[5] Council Directive 86/653, [1986] OJ L382/17.

[6] Commercial Agents (Council Directive) Regulations 1993, SI 1993/3053, as amended by SI 1993/3173 and SI 1998/2868. The Regulations apply to the actitivtes of commercial agents in Great Britain (reg 1(2)) (*Fern Computer Consultancy Ltd v Intergraph Cadworx & Analysis Solutions Inc* [2014] EWHC 2908 (Ch), [2014] Bus LR 1397, [108]ff). They have overriding status in that they apply even though the contract of agency is governed by the law of a non-EU country: *Ingmar GB Ltd v Eaton Leonard Technologies Ltd* (C381/98), [2000] ECR 1-9305, [2001] 1 All ER (Comm) 329. On this specialized topic see R Christou, *International Distribution, Agency and Licensing Agreements* (6th edn, 2011); F Randolph and J Davey, *European Law of Commercial Agency* (4th edn, 2011); S Saintier and G Scholes, *Commercial Agents and the Law* (2005); *Bowstead and Reynolds on Agency* (20th edn, 2014), Ch 11.

[7] This includes multiple principals: *Rossetti Marketing Ltd v Diamond Sofa Co Ltd* [2011] EWHC 2482 (QB), [2011] ECC 28; further proceedings not on this point [2012] EWCA Civ 1021, [2013] 1 All ER 308.

[8] Regulation 2(1). In the UK the definition is confined to agents for sale and purchase of goods. For a recent decision as to whether software ranks as 'goods' see *Fern Computer Consultancy Ltd v Intergraph Cadworx & Analysis Solutions Inc* [2014] EWHC 2908 (Ch), [2014] Bus LR 1397, [61]ff). In some other countries its protection has been extended to persons providing services.

[9] See 1.15ff. See *Invicta UK Ltd v International Brands Ltd* [2013] EWHC 1564 (QB), [2013] ECC 30; *Fern Computer Consultancy Ltd v Intergraph Cadworx & Analysis Solutions Inc* [2014] EWHC 2908 (Ch), [2014] Bus LR 1397).

[10] Regulation 2(3), added as a special definition for the UK which was criticized in the *AMB Imballaggi* case, n 11. See however *Tamarind International Ltd v Eastern Natural Gas (Retail) Ltd* [2000] Eu LR 708; *Gailey v Environmental Waste Controls* 2003 GWD 40-1068 (OH), [2004] Eur LR 423; *McAdam v Boxpak Ltd* 2006 CSIH 9, 2006 SLT 217, [2006] Eu LR 901. The power for a state to make special provision to this effect is affirmed in *Crane v Sky-in-Home Services Ltd* [2007] EWHC 66, [2007] 1 CLC 389. For further criticism of this provision see Saintier, 'The Interpretation of Directives to Suit Commercial Needs: a Further Threat to Coherence' [2012] JBL 128.

[11] *AMB Imballaggi Plastici SRL v Pacflex Ltd* [1999] 2 All ER (Comm) 249, CA; *Mercantile International Group plc v Chuan Soon Huat Industrial Group Ltd* [2002] EWCA Civ 288, [2002] 1 All ER (Comm) 788, CA; *Sagal v Atelier Bunz GmbH* [2009] EWCA Civ 700, [2009] 2 Lloyd's Rep 303. Nor is a *commissionnaire* (see 1.18): *Mavrona & Sia OE v Delta Etaireia Symmetochon AE* (Case C-85/03) [2004] ECR I-1573.

(2) *Internal and External Aspects of Agency*

(a) Basic division

1.07 It is a well-known principle in the civil law that the agency situation can be analysed as having two aspects, the internal (the relationship between principal and agent) and the external (the relationship between principal and third parties) and that these are to be regarded as conceptually separate. This holds true for common law also. But within the internal relationship, the grant (or conferral: the two words are usually interchangeable) of authority, which enables the agent to affect the position of his principal as regards third parties in the external world, should be treated strictly as a unilateral juristic act separate from the other internal arrangements between principal and agent, which may but need not be contractual. This is shown, first, by the basic institution of a power of attorney, the juristic significance of which is not always recognized. It is a grant of authority to another, or a conferring of authority on another, but need not be accompanied by any contract at all[12] (though the holder might be subject to fiduciary duties arising from the general law). Secondly, it is a general principle of agency law, directed to the protection of the principal, that the authority may be revoked at any time even though it may be a breach of the internal contract to do so. Thirdly, the rules governing capacity to act as agent are wide and not necessarily the same as those governing any internal contract. Lastly, the invalidity of an accompanying contract by reason of mistake (rare in common law) need not affect the grant of authority. This distinction between the grant of authority and the other features of the internal relationship has not, however, been put by the common law to any systematic use,[13] and the external authority is in common law usually rather loosely treated as simply deriving from the internal relationship, which is assumed normally to be contractual, or at least based on agreement. A failure to distinguish the two aspects of the internal relationship can be found in some civil law systems also.[14] The distinction can be significant in the context of the conflict of laws, where the grant or conferring of authority may require a different governing law from that governing the accompanying contract, though here again the point is often overlooked.[15]

(b) External aspect only: apparent authority

1.08 Like other legal systems, common law then extends the paradigm reasoning whereby agency powers derive from a grant or conferral of authority to situations where the principal has not, even on the most objective interpretation, conferred authority—he may even have forbidden the act in question—but where the third party is reasonable in a belief that he has. All legal systems must accept liability of the principal to the third party in some such circumstances. Here again the agent has a power to bind his principal, but this time it stems from what is called 'apparent' or 'ostensible' authority, as opposed to the 'actual' authority already mentioned. It is dealt with more fully below.[16] It relates initially to the external relationship only, and only imposes liability on the principal: if he has rights also, it is by virtue of other reasoning, especially ratification.[17] As regards the internal relationship, the agent may even be in breach of contract towards his principal in acting as he did.

---

[12] But the notion of contract is in common law narrower than that of civil law because of the requirement of consideration.

[13] R Zimmermann, *The Law of Obligations: Roman Foundations of the Civilian Tradition* (1996) 58.

[14] See M Graziadei, U Mattei and L Smith, *Commercial Trusts in European Private Law* (2005) 48–52, 'A Note on Terminology'.

[15] It appears in the Rome I Regulation, art.1.2(g) of which excludes 'the question whether an agent is able to bind his principal...in relation to a third party.'

[16] See 1.60.

[17] See 1.33ff; 1.71 as to estoppel.

If the distinction between the two aspects of the internal relationship is borne in mind, the **1.09** justification of the external relationship accounts for the power of the agent not only as regards apparent authority, but also in what common law calls actual authority, and it is possible to concentrate on the theoretical nature and justification of the power conferred in both these two cases. For common law however, actual authority is, as stated in 1.07, usually simply attributed to the agreement or consent of the principal, and for apparent authority other reasoning is found, as explained below. The two can ingeniously be reconciled on the basis that for both actual and apparent authority the principal is still manifesting a grant of authority, in one case to the agent, in the other to the outside world, or at least to the third party. This reasoning is not entirely satisfactory and there are difficulties, as in other legal systems, in reconciling the notion of apparent authority, essential though it is, with basic theory.[18]

(c) Features of the internal relationship

(i) Fiduciary obligation

Where authority is conferred, because of the importance of the external power, special rules **1.10** apply to the internal relationship. They may but need not arise from a contract between principal and agent. They are due to the fact that the person who holds the authority, or external power, is able to affect his principal's position. If there is a contract between principal and agent, he is therefore, even though paid for his services, regarded as a contracting party who is bound to act in the interests of his principal. In most commercial contracts the two sides have adverse commercial interests: each hopes to profit from the other. The paradigm example is that of buyer and seller. The internal relationship of principal and agent is however not commercially adverse: even if he is employed on a commercial basis the agent must in general act in the principal's interests. The internal relationship therefore imposes, whether or not there is a contract, fiduciary duties on the agent which support that position. Such duties apply outside the law of agency also, but agency relationships constitute a prominent example of them. They are discussed below.[19]

(ii) Payment by commission

Another feature of the internal relationship also arises out of the non-adverse nature of the **1.11** agent's function. The agent operating under a contract with the principal is in general not entitled to take his own profit on the 'turn' as would one who bought and resold to another: this would be a secret profit and hence inconsistent with his fiduciary duty. Rather, he charges a fee or commission for his services. There may be difficulty in distinguishing between these situations where the 'commission' includes or even comprises extra amounts calculated in special ways, but the distinction is clear in principle and commission (in the sense of the type of payment made) is one of the hallmarks of agency.

(iii) Duty of care only

There is another feature of the agent's position which is related to special features of common **1.12** law reasoning. In common law the starting point as regards many contractual duties is that of strict liability; that is to say, the contracting party does not merely undertake to exercise due care in performance of his functions, but prima facie guarantees a result. This is true, eg, of sellers. It is not of course true of most of those rendering personal services; hence it is (unless in specific cases) not true of agents. Since much agency arises in the context of buying and selling, this test provides a good way of distinguishing an agent from one who buys from

---

[18] See 1.60ff; T Krebs, 'Agency Law for Muggles: Why there is No Magic in Agency' in A Burrows and E.Peel (eds), *Contract Formation and Parties* (2010) 205ff.
[19] See 1.138ff.

or sells to another. The seller owes the strict duties, eg as to quality, associated with sale; the agent simply undertakes reasonable endeavours to carry out the principal's instructions.[20] However, the agent owes one strict duty, ie not to exceed (what reasonably appears to him to be) his authority.[21]

(iv) Control

1.13 We may then ask whether there are any other features of the internal relationship which must be regarded as typical. An obvious candidate is the power to control: the agent acts under the principal's control. The traditional relevance of control in law is to justifications for imposing liability in tort for the acts of employees. It can be said that it is the degree of control exercised over an enterprise and those involved in it that makes it appropriate to place the risks arising from the enterprise on the person exercising the control.

1.14 Agents are often independent contractors, who will not accept complete control over the way in which they do things for their principals; and some will only accept instructions to act in accordance with the usages of their own market. Others may be authorized to do particular things only, as when a stockbroker has specific instructions:[22] no further control is possible. In many such situations the principal's only control lies in his power to revoke the authority, a power which agency law assumes he must (with some exceptions) have at all times.[23] It might seem therefore that control is not a significant feature of the internal relationship. Nevertheless, if a principal gives up all control of his agent, either this amounts to a revocation of authority, or, if this is not so, the relationship was always only doubtfully one of agency. This is one of the problems with some of the arrangements at Lloyd's, which are purportedly based on agency. For these reasons it seems right to retain the principal's control as a feature of agency;[24] but the idea is certainly not used in the same way as in vicarious liability in the law of tort.

(3) The Boundaries of Agency

(a) Internal relationship only: canvassing agents

1.15 From these internal features of the agency relationship as expounded above, a further problem, certainly of exposition and probably of priority in analysis, now arises. There are a number of commercial and other intermediaries who act for others and hence must owe fiduciary duties, are remunerated on commission, owe duties of care only and are subject to some form of control, but have been granted no authority or power to do things that alter their principal's legal position. A standard example is the real estate agent, who (though practice varies) may be engaged only to introduce customers, with whom the principal then deals direct. He is also remunerated by commission, and undoubtedly owes fiduciary duties, eg not (at any rate without disclosure) to take commission from the other side to a transaction or potential transaction, and not to conceal from his principal offers made to him.[25]

---

[20] To the third party, however, he owes a strict duty, to warrant his authority. See 1.112.

[21] See 1.136. There may of course be argument as to how far the authority extends, and whether it has been exceeded.

[22] eg *Volkers v Midland Doherty* (1985) 17 DLR (4th) 343.

[23] See 1.100.

[24] Considerable stress is, however, placed on it by *Restatement, Third, Agency* §1.01 and comment. Such reasoning can be useful when the question of one company as agent of another arises.

[25] It may be queried whether such a person may validly undertake no more than a commercial duty as 'finder', to match potential buyers and/or sellers without attracting any fiduciary duties whatever. It must be possible in principle; but a court might find it difficult to accept that such was really the intention of the parties.

Is such a person to be brought within the law of agency, or are we to say that no external **1.16** relationship being possible, whatever he calls himself, the person concerned is not an agent, but merely one performing services who owes fiduciary duties and is remunerated on commission? Here again we have a doctrinal choice and the answer to it is not dictated by any legal rule or rules. The problem would not arise if agency was regarded as a branch of law attaching to certain specific occupations: persons such as real estate agents would be governed by their own special rules regardless of whether they came within any definition of agency. The generality of the common law approach, however, creates a problem of how to apply the general principles. Should the external or the internal aspect of agency be regarded as primary for definitional and analytical purposes?

The current trend has been to say that since such persons call themselves agents, and since **1.17** their internal relationship with the person on whose account they are acting is so clearly assimilated to that of those with external powers, it is right to regard them as coming under agency law, and it would indeed be misleading to exclude them. This has the result that it becomes necessary to give the internal aspect of agency analytical priority over the external. The fiduciary nature of the relationship, though it applies to other relationships also, then becomes a key definitional factor. This is the approach taken in the American *Restatement, Third, Agency*,[26] and also in some English books. Older writings may confine agency to persons who have the power to alter their principal's legal position.

(b) Indirect representation

The exposition so far has referred to agents who have the power to alter their principal's legal posi- **1.18** tion, who are involved in both internal and external relationships, and to those who have no such power but are governed by the internal relationship only. Civil law countries may however recognize another institution, that of indirect representation or agency. An indirect representative is one who acts for another, but on the basis that while internally he is an agent, externally he deals on his own account, with the result that the third party cannot (usually) proceed against the principal, nor can the principal proceed against the third party.[27] This is so even though the agent is known to act on this basis, and so is known to be very likely or even certain to have a principal: indeed, the actual name of that principal might be known to the third party. This role is performed by persons conducting certain types of commercial activity (which may vary from country to country), and is often referred to by the French word *commission*, or some parallel to this in another language, the agent being a *commissionnaire* (the word referring to the task undertaken rather than the method of remuneration). If this type of representation is taken into account, it can then be said that there are two types of agency or representation, direct and indirect.[28] To classify this arrangement with other forms of agency again involves giving priority to the internal relationship.

Like the (more specialized) commercial agent, this type of representative does not constitute **1.19** a category of agent known to the common law. Since the law of agency is general, and draws

---

[26] §1.01: 'Agency is the fiduciary relationship that exists when one person (a "principal") manifests assent to another person (an "agent") that the agent shall act on the principal's behalf and subject to the principal's control, and the agent manifests assent or otherwise consents so to act.'

[27] There are exceptions to this in some jurisdictions: see 1.20.

[28] This distinction forms the basis of the Agency section of O Lando and H Beale (eds), *Principles of European Contract Law* (2000); see art 3:102. See also the Draft Common Frame of Reference (2009) IV.D.1:102. The UNIDROIT *Principles of International Commercial Contracts* (2004), however, do not employ this distinction and indeed more or less eliminate the significance of the notion of indirect representation (together with the common law doctrine of undisclosed principal). On the *Principles* see T Krebs, 'Harmonization and How Not to Do It: Agency in the UNIDROIT Principles of International Commercial Contracts 2004' [2009] LMCLQ 57.

upon general principles, and if it is correct, as has been argued above, that it is the internal aspect that predominates from the expository point of view, there can be no objection to such an arrangement, nor to the description of a person exercising such functions as an agent. However, although there are dicta of the great nineteenth-century commercial judge Blackburn J, later Lord Blackburn, recognizing and explaining this mode of operation,[29] there are few decisions going any further. Even where the agent operates in a market (such as the London Stock Exchange as it formerly operated) where agents (in this case brokers) deal with each other on the basis that all transactions are between members only, the courts have often ignored this and assumed that the brokers were ordinary agents known to be acting for unidentified principals; and though they were personally liable on their transactions, their principals were in some cases held liable and entitled also.[30] The only alternative has been seen as that of an intermediary buying for resale.[31] Litigation on the internal relationship, which might have clarified matters or encouraged new analyses, is hard to find.[32] As often, there is probably a pragmatic reason for this. Such agents in the United Kingdom often acted for overseas principals, and litigation between agent and principal (as compared with principal and third party) would be likely to occur, if at all, in overseas jurisdictions.

1.20 Systems accepting this institution frequently have to make exceptions which allow the principal to sue the third party, and less easily the third party to sue the principal, especially in situations of insolvency. Some may make the indirect agent in some sense a guarantor of the third party. Civil law commentators are apt to assume that the undisclosed principal doctrine, to be discussed later,[33] constitutes a simpler way of dealing with this mode of operation, and that (subject to limits) it simply makes the principal of an indirect agent liable and entitled as if the agent were a direct agent—thus rendering this way of operating ineffective to insulate principal from third party. It is arguable that this is an oversimplification of the undisclosed principal doctrine.[34] In any case, this mode of operation becomes confused in the cases with other commercial figures such as del credere agency, *compradors*, confirming houses and later, moving further away, export guarantees and demand guarantees in general.[35]

(c) Use of representative terminology

1.21 In this connection, a warning is necessary as to wording which may be used to indicate that one person acts for another (to use about the most neutral phrase possible). There is no stability of terminology in this area. Civil lawyers tend to use wording which usually appears translated into English as 'acts in the name of another'. The phrase 'in the name of' has however no agreed meaning in English law and indeed such wording is not often used in an agency context. A common lawyer is puzzled in particular as to whether an agent who is known to

[29] *Robinson v Mollett* (1875) LR 7 HL 802, 809–810; another famous judgment on this type of function is *Ireland v Livingston* (1872) LR 5 HL 395, HL. It is found also in *Mildred, Goyaneche & Co v Maspons y Hermano* (1882) 9 QBD 530, CA, (1883) 8 App Cas 874, HL.
[30] eg *Hodgkinson v Kelly* (1868) Lr 6 Eq 496; *Scott and Horton v Ernest* (1900) 16 TLR 498.
[31] See the different analyses (esp that of Diplock LJ) of the position of a 'confirming house and shipping agent' in *Anglo-African Shipping Co of New York Inc v J Mortner Ltd* [1962] 1 Lloyd's Rep 610, CA. *Triffit Nurseries v Salads Etcetera Ltd* [2000] 1 All ER (Comm) 737, CA appears to concern an agent operating in such a way: this is clearer in the first instance judgment, [1999] 1 All ER (Comm) 110.
[32] A freight forwarder was held to be (in effect) an indirect representative in *M.Bardiger Ltd v Halberg Spedition Aps*, QBD (Comm Ct) 26 February,1990 (only available on LEXIS). In *Aqualon (UK) Ltd v Vallana Shipping Corp* [1994] 1 Lloyd's Rep 609 it was said that such an interpretation, while not impossible, would require very clear evidence of intention.
[33] See 1.72ff.
[34] And probably of indirect representation: see further 1.74.
[35] See 1.24.

have a principal but does not give that principal's name should be regarded as 'acting in the name of' that principal. It seems that he usually should, though there may in civil law be specific requirements as to disclosure of the principal's name on demand.[36] Other phrases are 'on behalf of'; another 'for (or 'on') account of', 'for the benefit of', 'in the interest of'. The mere 'for' (as in 'acts for') is completely equivocal. If any such representative formulation is used, it is necessary to examine the facts carefully to see in what legal role the person referred to must be analysed as acting.

(d) Companies: agent and organ

This leads finally to special reasoning which may be deployed in the area of company **1.22** law. Since a company has no physical existence it is easy enough to say that it must act by human agents, and that agency law is the key to problems of attribution of rights and liabilities to companies. This can be said to have been the dominant common law approach in the nineteenth century. The direct use of such reasoning did not prove entirely satisfactory, however, and in some areas special company law doctrines have been developed[37] while in others the law has been changed by statute.[38] A line of reasoning which regards the acts of certain persons as the acts of the company itself (rather than as those of an agent acting under normal principles on behalf of the company) has fairly recently become more prominent. As often in law the possibility has come to the fore in rather miscellaneous contexts: the shipowner's overall right to limit his liability except where he was seriously at fault,[39] offences under criminal law,[40] the personal liability of directors in tort,[41] and the attribution of knowledge or notice to companies.[42] Its overall significance may however be limited.

(e) Agent and trustee; agent and bailee

There are however in common law other legal roles the attributes of which are more clearly **1.23** worked out, and comparison of these with agency is instructive in showing the overlap between categories, and also the flexible nature of agency reasoning. The most obvious are those of the trustee and the bailee. A *trustee* holds property for another which may be regarded as the property of the beneficiary in equity; he is not normally subject to control or revocation of his powers by the beneficiary. A trustee may have agency powers for a beneficiary in certain circumstances; and an agent may hold money received for the principal on trust in certain circumstances.[43] But a trustee may have no agency powers, and an agent may hold no property for his principal at all: he may simply be a debtor to his principal. A *bailee* possesses goods owned by another: he may have agency powers, eg to take steps to preserve them.[44] An agent may hold goods for his principal as bailee (as did the factor), but may hold no goods at all. These various notions are not mutually exclusive.

---

[36] See 1.108.
[37] See eg *Royal British Bank v Turquand* (1856) 6 E & B 327, 119 ER 886; 1.69.
[38] eg Companies Act 2006, s 40; see 1.69.
[39] eg *The Lady Gwendolen* [1965] P 294.
[40] eg *Tesco Supermarkets Ltd v Nattrass* [1972] AC 153, HL (regulatory offence). See also *Odyssey Re (London) Ltd v OIC Run-off Ltd* [2001] LRLR 1, CA (perjury), and in general EPL 3.17ff, EPL 3.51ff.
[41] See 1.115.
[42] eg *El Ajou v Dollar Land Holdings plc* [1994] 2 All ER 685, CA; *Meridian Global Funds Management Asia Ltd v Securities Commission* [1995] 2 AC 500, HL; *Stone & Rolls Ltd v Moore Stephens* [2009] UKHL 39, [2009] AC 391, HL; *Jetivia SA v Bilta (UK) Ltd* [2015] UKSC 23, [2015] 1 WLR 1168.
[43] See 1.147.
[44] eg *Tappenden v Artus* [1964] 2 QB 185, CA (repairs).

(f) Lack of significance of types of agent

1.24 Since the law of agency does not rely on analysis by means of named types of intermediary function, there is in common law no difference of principle between one sort of agent and another, eg between a real estate agent and a shipbroker, though of course they may act in different ways legally. Names of types of agent are not of much significance in common law: what one needs to know is the way in which the agents work. However, a few names should be mentioned, if only to dismiss them. The phrases 'general agent' and 'special agent' were used in the nineteenth century and occasionally still are: the difference is (obviously) between one with wide authority and one with more specific authority.[45] It was once toyed with as a basis for what is now called apparent authority, but in common law this reasoning did not prove equal to the task.[46] Nineteenth-century cases often concerned factors and brokers.[47] The factor was a person who held goods, often from overseas, which he might or might not own: he dealt with them without mentioning a principal and raised a problem as to whether he was to be regarded externally as contracting for himself, or as agent for another, and internally whether he acted as agent or bought for resale. His function was obviously similar to that of the *commissionnaire*, and cases on factors are associated with the growth of the undisclosed principal doctrine;[48] but it is dangerous to draw too dogmatic conclusions as to his mode of operation, which is in any case largely a matter of legal history, the use of the word in this sense being largely obsolete. Brokering was a function which developed later: a commodity broker did not hold goods but simply negotiated contracts between others, normally dropping out of the transaction once it was agreed. A number of other types of agent may be mentioned. Del credere agents are agents who guarantee the liabilities of buyers or sellers to their principals: this function is similar to that of the *comprador*, a functionary formerly found in the Far East. Many of the cases from which early law on agency is derived concerned also masters of ships, auctioneers and solicitors. Other categories of agent have required definition because of statutory regulation placed upon them. As already stated, this is partly true of estate agents[49] and is now true of commercial agents.[50]

(g) Agency law outside its central context

1.25 It is of the nature of law, or at any rate of common law, to extend an established and agreed notion to perform other purposes. Agency reasoning has been particularly prone to this, and the trend continues. Assignment of a right of action achieved by means of appointing an agent to bring suit on one's behalf is ancient; there are of course parallels in the *mandatum* of Roman law. Agency has also been used under the heading of 'agency of necessity' in what would now be regarded as a restitutionary context, to justify the granting to persons of powers to act for others in situations of emergency, and then to deploy the internal rules to entitle the person concerned to some form of indemnity or reimbursement.[51] Attempts have also been made to prolong the effects of a reservation of title on sale into proceeds of resale by seeking to create an agency in the non-paying buyer who resells;[52] and quite recently

---

[45] eg *Smith v M'Guire* (1858) 3 H & N 554, 119 ER 886; *Barrett v Irvine* [1907] 2 IR 462. It occasionally still comes up in specialized contexts even now: eg *Dun & Bradstreet Software Services (England) Ltd v Provident Mutual Life Assurance* [1998] 2 EGLR 175, CA (notices between landlord and tenant).

[46] But see I Brown, 'The Significance of General and Special Authority in the Development of the Agent's External Authority in English Law' [2004] JBL 391, arguing that it did.

[47] See in general SJ Stoljar, *Law of Agency* (1961) 242–247.

[48] As to which see 1.72.

[49] See 1.04, 1.15.

[50] See 1.05.

[51] See 1.94.

[52] The '*Romalpa* clause', so called because of the case which first drew attention to the problem, *Aluminium Industrie Vaassen BV v Romalpa Aluminium Ltd* [1976] 1 WLR 676, CA. It has given rise to an extensive jurisprudence of its own: see, eg, RM Goode, *Commercial Law* (4th edn, 2009) 648ff.

problems of corporate identity, where the real argument is that the corporate veil ought to be pierced, have been attacked by (mostly unsuccessful) agency arguments.[53] Finally, and rather improbably, a form of the *commission* contract has been used in an attempt to establish a framework of operation directed towards favourable tax results. The law of agency, however, carries baggage with it, largely in the shape of fiduciary duties, (to some extent) powers of control, and certainly powers of revocation. All such invocations of agency law may sometimes therefore carry unexpected and inappropriate consequences.

(h) Agency and tort

The account so far given has confined itself to agency in connection with contract. It may **1.26** then be asked whether the reasoning is equally applicable to tort situations. If so, new and broader basic reasoning would probably be required. On one view it must be so: there must be general principles governing the liability of persons for, and the extent to which they are bound by, the acts of others, whether in a way that triggers off one type of obligation or the other, and also in the law of restitution and in the law of property. For many years agency courses based on this assumption, taking in vicarious liability in tort as well as agency in contract, were common and indeed traditional in the United States. There is a choice here as to technique of exposition and as to selection of linking factors, on which views are not right or wrong, but rather, preferable or less preferable.

The view put forward in this chapter is that whereas restitution for unjust enrichment and **1.27** (with more difficulty) the law of property can be taken into basic agency law, the assimilation of the law of tort is for the most part unproductive.[54] There may be an exception in connnection with tortious misrepresentation (the torts of deceit and negligence) where it may seem appropriate to deploy agency reasoning.[55] In contract situations, the idea of conferring authority on others to act represents the general justification for binding and entitling those for whom they then act: and apparent authority is a modification of this approach geared also to the deliberately undertaken relationships on which contract is based—the third party entering into a transaction is justified in assuming that there has been a conferring of authority on the person with whom he is dealing. The agent does not normally commit a breach of the main contract himself. Something similar, though with some reservations[56] can be said of property transfer. Liability for the wrongs of others on the other hand normally requires a tort committed by the intermediary and is, at least in common law countries, normally based on different considerations directed to the spreading of loss. Where a person is run down by a truck, the claim against the company owning it and employing its driver is not appropriately based on the idea that its driver was authorized, or apparently authorized, to commit torts. Indeed, a claim against the employer may be justified where the driver was not authorized to drive the truck at all. Also, in tort one speaks only of liabilities: contract involves rights also. The difference is fairly plain in the case law, and though efforts have been made to locate inner principles which would justify rights and liabilities acquired through others across all private law, nothing satisfactory has yet been found. As Lord Wilberforce said:

> It may be that some wider conception of vicarious responsibility other than that of agency, as normally understood, may have to be recognised in order to accommodate some of the more

---

[53] eg *Yukong Lines Ltd v Rendsberg Investments Corp (The Rialto)* [1998] 1 WLR 294 (person 'behind' company not undisclosed principal to its acts). See also nn 214, 250.

[54] But see 1.129 for a limited exception.

[55] See 1.128.

[56] See 1.120.

elaborate cases which now arise when there are two persons who become mutually involved or associated in one side of a transaction.[57]

But the gauntlet thus thrown down has not been picked up over a period of 40 years, and acceptable techniques of absorbing the two lines of reasoning have not been found. Marginal situations certainly occur, however, and these will be discussed below.[58]

B. Formation of Agency

(1) *Conferring of Authority*

(a) Significance of agreement

1.28 The most obvious way of making someone one's agent is by granting to, or conferring authority on, him (the wording is interchangeable); and the internal relationship normally requires that there be consent to the arrangement (in an objective sense) on both sides.[59] This can also be referred to as an agreement. The grant or conferral may be accompanied by a contract, and in a commercial situation normally will be, but it need not be: there can be gratuitous agents, operating in situations where at common law no consideration can be found and there is hence no contract.

1.29 A minor theoretical difficulty can arise because the pure granting or conferring of authority (as opposed to creation of the full internal relationship) is, as stated above, best regarded as a unilateral act. The principal may confer authority and not require the agent to manifest acceptance of it directly to him (for instance, he may send the agent a power of attorney and go on a journey). Normally, of course, the agent will accept, and agree to the internal relationship, by acting on behalf of the principal; and the principal may have waived notice of acceptance. In this sense agreement is required to establish agency. But it may be asked what happens if the principal sends an agent authority, which the agent does not receive: the agent then acts for the principal (perhaps because he erroneously thinks that his authority covers the act in question, or because he has forgotten that his authority has lapsed, or because he simply decides to take a risk that the principal will ratify). The unilateral model (as opposed to the agreement model) would suggest that in such a situation (admittedly difficult to construct plausibly) the principal has put himself on risk by the conferral of authority and is liable and entitled *vis-à-vis* the third party.[60]

(b) What can be done by an agent

1.30 The generality of principle again leads to discussions of what acts can be done by an agent. The starting point is that any act can; but there are of course restrictions where a power is conferred on the principal which he must exercise personally, and where statute or other instrument requires acts to be done personally. Proxy signatures are usually admissible.[61]

---

[57] *Branwhite v Worcester Works Finance Ltd* [1969] 1 AC 552, 587, HL.

[58] See 1.83.

[59] 'The relationship of principal and agent can only be constituted by the consent of the principal and the agent': *Garnac Grain Co Inc v HMF Faure & Fairclough Ltd* [1968] AC 1130n, 1137, HL, *per* Lord Pearson (a case distinguishing between agency and purchase for resale in a string contract).

[60] And it was so held in the United States in *Ruggles v American Central Insurance Co of St Louis* 114 NY 415, 76 NY Supp 787 (1889), US. But this case is strongly criticized in *Restatement, Third, Agency*, Reporter's note b. See however the dictum of Diplock LJ cited at n 115.

[61] There is a recent discussion in *General Legal Council v Frankson* [2006] UKPC 42, [2006] 1 WLR 2803, PC.

(c) Formalities not usually necessary

The starting point is that, consistent with the generality of agency principles, no formality is **1.31** needed for the creation of agency. Sometimes however there are specially imposed requirements that authority be conferred in writing, eg in connection with land;[62] and sometimes appointment must be by deed. This is true of powers of attorney, an undefined term covering formal documents conferring (usually) general powers,[63] and of powers to execute deeds generally. Such documents are normally used when the circumstances require a clear conferring of authority for important matters, with indications of its extent.

(d) Capacity

The interaction of agency with rules of capacity can be complex, because the rules of capacity can **1.32** themselves be complex. In general the principal needs to have capacity to do the act to be done on his behalf by the agent, but the agent, who is a mere instrument, does not need formal legal capacity as regards the external function: he merely needs to understand the nature of the acts which he does (though contractual liability on the internal relationship would require contractual capacity). There is no objection of principle to one party to a transaction acting as agent of the other in whole or in part, nor to one agent acting for both parties; but care has to be taken in such situations, as there may be a breach or potential breach of the internal fiduciary obligation.[64]

(2) Ratification

(a) General principle

Most legal systems accept the convenience of the idea that where a person acts for another **1.33** without authority, the principal can nevertheless by ratifying the act put himself in the same position as that in which he would have been had he authorized the act in advance. Agents must often act without authority on the basis that their principal, when he learns the facts, is likely to approve. Sometimes this can in fact be dealt with by a generous interpretation of the existing authority, or an assumption that the principal authorizes special acts in unforeseen situations: but not always. The idea of ratification as a solution to cases where there is no antecedent authority is accepted in English law and indeed has even been applied in respect of liability for torts (where its justification is normally in fact quite different).[65] A ratification, like a conferring of authority, appears to be a unilateral juristic act, and as such, though the person ratifying must know, or be attributable with knowledge of, the relevant facts, it seems that the ratification, so long as it can be proved, need not be communicated to the person whose act is ratified or to the third party.[66] It may be express or implied from conduct. It is normally said that there can be no ratification in part: either an act is adopted or it is not. This is true at least in the sense that the principal cannot by partial ratification secure for himself a transaction which is not that which the third party had intended.

Ratification, which is more likely to be invoked against rather than by a principal, must be **1.34** clearly distinguished from other notions such as estoppel, which to be effective would require communication to the third party and some degree of reliance; election, a decisive choice between alternative courses available at law, which would also require communication; and

---

[62] eg Law of Property Act 1925, ss 53, 54 (certain instruments relating to land).
[63] Powers of Attorney Act 1971, s 1(1) (as amended).
[64] See 1.138ff.
[65] The cases are mostly old and concern matters such as unlawful distress, and the tort of conversion, which moves into property law.
[66] *Pagnan SpA v Feed Products Ltd* [1987] 2 Lloyd's Rep 601, 613; *Shell Co of Australia Ltd v Nat Shipping Bagging Services Ltd (The Kilmun)* [1988] 2 Lloyd's Rep 1, 8, 11, 14.

from novation, or substituted contract. There can of course be estoppel as to whether there has been a ratification. But a purported ratification in advance (quite common in certain types of document such as powers of attorney) cannot in principle be a ratification: the starting point is that it can be no more than a promise to ratify.

(b) Void acts

1.35 Further discriminations have to be made in the case of acts which can be said to be void. It is said that a void act cannot be ratified as there is nothing to ratify; hence there can be no ratification of a forgery in the sense of a counterfeit signature[67] (as opposed to an unauthorized signature, which can also rank as a forgery in criminal law). A person may however be estopped from setting up a forgery in appropriate cases.[68] But as elsewhere in the law the notion of voidness has to be treated with care. Any unauthorized act on behalf of a principal could be said to be void as an act of the principal; but it is precisely such acts to which the doctrine of ratification may apply.[69]

(c) Who may ratify

1.36 Obviously, the only person who may ratify is the person on whose behalf the act was done. Two problems arise here. The first is whether a person who lacked capacity when the original act was done, or was not born, or was a company that did not yet exist, or was a person or company which existed but was not at the time within the description of the principal given at that time (eg, a subcontractor not yet nominated at the time a liability insurance policy was taken out) can ratify and so take advantage of the doctrine. The answer is fairly clearly that this cannot be done: the purpose of the doctrine is to correct the situation at the time of the act purported to be ratified.[70] A query can however be raised when the contract appears from the start to contemplate future principals: eg, the insurance contract above might be stated as made on behalf of all present and future subcontractors.[71] It seems appropriate that clarity of theory should be maintained: rights to sue in such a case could be conferred when appropriate by trust law, which has no objection to future beneficiaries, by rules on insurable interest,[72] and by rules allowing third parties to sue on contracts.[73]

1.37 The second problem relates to unidentified principals at common law.[74] It is clear that an agent can contract on behalf of a principal whom he does not at the time of contracting name or identify, so long as probative material can be adduced in case of dispute to show who that person was.[75] Such a person is called an 'unidentified principal'.[76] This rule obviously creates the possibility in practice of an agent contracting on such a basis and in effect allocating

---

[67] *Brook v Hook* (1871) LR 6 Ex 89.

[68] eg *Greenwood v Martins Bank Ltd* [1933] AC 51, HL.

[69] eg *Presentaciones Musicales SA v Secunda* [1994] Ch 271 (unauthorized institution of legal proceedings ratifiable). Such a question can involve consideration of whether the act is void or simply requires cure. *Restatement, Third, Agency,* does not mention such a rule and takes the view that a forgery can be ratified: see §4.03 and Comment.

[70] An old leading case concerns a company not yet formed: *Kelner v Baxter* (1866) LR 2 CP 174. The promoter might be held liable, as happened in the case itself: but the question is quite often dealt with by statute. See 1.112.

[71] As in the Australian case of *Trident General Ins Co Ltd v McNiece Bros Pty Ltd* (1987) 8 NSWLR 270, 276–277, aff'd without reference to the agency points (1988) 165 CLR 107, HCA.

[72] See *Tomlinson (Hauliers) Ltd v Hepburn* [1966] AC 451, HL.

[73] Contracts (Rights of Third Parties) Act 1999, s 1(3).

[74] ie, principals whose name has not been given, but where the third party knows that there is one. See 1.59.

[75] Such a person must be distinguished from an undisclosed principal: see 1.72ff.

[76] cf 1.81.

the contract at a later date. This is not permissible as such, or at least may require a different analysis, but there may also be authority from a number of identified principals and it may be difficult to establish that the agent did not act at the time for the one who later ratified. It may then be asked whether there can be ratification of an unauthorized act purportedly performed for an unidentified principal. If there could, the possibility of later adoption by a principal of an unauthorized contract would be increased. It appears that there can in such a case be ratification:[77] the problem of proof as to the person for whom the contract was made is in fact the same in both situations, and if one is allowed, so should the other be. The question of proof of intent can always be raised.[78] It has however long been clear that where the person acting intended to do so on behalf of a particular person, but gave no indication of this to the third party, the person concerned, called an 'undisclosed principal', cannot ratify, even where the person acting was already an agent of the principal.[79]

(d) Retroactivity of ratification

The whole idea behind ratification is that the later ratifying act supplies the authority not **1.38** originally existent and makes the act concerned retrospectively valid. This retroactivity, if accepted as dogma, can however operate prejudicially to the non-ratifying party, and some element of control is needed. Here difficulties are encountered.

A fairly well-established group of cases concerns situations where property rights are involved. In **1.39** the context of landlord and tenant it has been held that where a notice to quit is served without the authority of the landlord, the landlord cannot ratify it after the time for service has expired;[80] and that a notice to exercise an option (which creates an equitable property right) cannot be ratified after the time for exercise has expired.[81] An ancient leading case applies the same reasoning to the exercise of an unpaid seller's right to stop in transit.[82] Since these cases involve property reasoning it can be said more technically that ratification cannot divest a property right.

A second possible line of reasoning is a wider one, that where a time limit is involved, ratifica- **1.40** tion after the expiry of the limit is inadmissible.[83] There is some overlap between these types of case, since (eg) an accrued defence under the Limitation Act is sometimes spoken of as a property right of which a party ought not to be deprived. But reasoning based on time limits requires that attention be given to the purposes of particular time limits: thus it has been held fairly recently that ratification of the issue of a writ after the expiry of the relevant period of limitation was nevertheless effective.[84]

The most recent authority now suggests a much more general test to cover both these lines **1.41** of reasoning, and perhaps others,[85] that ratification is barred where it would cause unfair prejudice to the party against whom it is invoked.[86]

---

[77] *National Oilwell (UK) Ltd v Davy Offshore Ltd* [1993] 2 Lloyd's Rep 582, 592–597; see FMB Reynolds, 'Some Agency Problems in Insurance Law' in FD Rose (ed), *Consensus ad Idem: Essays in Honour of Guenter Treitel* (1996) 77ff.

[78] See the *National Oilwell* case, n 77.

[79] See 1.81.

[80] *Doe d.Mann v Walters* (1830) 10 B & C 626, 109 ER 583.

[81] *Dibbins v Dibbins* [1896] 2 Ch 348.

[82] *Bird v Brown* (1850) 4 Exch 786, 154 ER 1433.

[83] This would apply to the contractual element in the option in *Dibbins v Dibbins*, n 81.

[84] *Presentaciones Musicales SA v Secunda* [1994] Ch 271, CA.

[85] eg, that ratification must be effected within a reasonable time: see *Metropolitan Asylums Board v Kingham & Sons* (1890) 6 TLR 217. It is suggested by Tan Cheng-Han that this could be the, or a, main control mechanism against unfair operation of the doctrine: see 'The Principle in *Bird v Brown* Revisited' (2002) 117 LQR 626.

[86] See *Smith v Henniker-Major & Co* [2002] EWCA Civ 762, [2003] Ch 182, CA, at [63]ff; *The Borvigilant* [2003] EWCA 935; [2003] 2 Lloyd's Rep 520, CA, at [59]ff. A special rule for insurance law is that policies

1.42 Another well-known difficulty is caused by the application of retroactivity to a situation where the third party purports to withdraw from a contract before ratification. If the contract was made expressly subject to ratification, at common law there is normally no transaction from which withdrawal is needed, and any purported ratification would therefore be ineffective.[87] It is in fact in general difficult to see that at common law the doctrine of ratification can apply at all to a contract made with an agent known to have no authority.[88] Even if the contract is stated as being subject to ratification, on common law reasoning it is difficult to see that an arrangement in which the principal has a choice as to whether to be bound is a conditional contract in the normal sense. Any liability in such a case would require to be based on something like a promise to keep the offer open, if consideration can be found for it; or would be that of the agent.

1.43 But if a contract is made without the agent having authority, and the third party then discovers this, the argument for permitting the third party to withdraw despite subsequent ratification is strong: for a start, the third party is otherwise left in a state of uncertainty. A view that the third party is nevertheless bound by a ratification in such a case is usually derived from the famous, even notorious[89] case of *Bolton Partners v Lambert*.[90] But in that case the third party 'withdrew', not because he had discovered that the agent had not been authorized, but because he alleged that the contract had not reached the binding stage, and also that the contract had been induced by misrepresentations, on both of which points he eventually failed: it would appear that he was not at the time aware of any lack of authority.[91] Hence, however famous, the case is not as clear as is sometimes supposed. The reasoning recently adopted and referred to above would seem helpful for this situation also: the court should similarly ask whether ratification would cause unfair prejudice to the third party.

(e) External and internal effects of ratification

1.44 Obviously, where an act is ratified it ranks as having been valid when done: that is the purpose of the doctrine. But the difficulties discussed above serve as a warning that such a simple unitary description of the availability and effects of ratification cannot be given. It is necessary again to differentiate the internal and external aspects of agency. The discussion above concerns the external consequences of ratification. A further external consequence, which has not been mentioned, is that the ratification protects the agent against the third party. If the act had not been ratified, the agent would have been liable to the third party for loss caused by purporting to have an authority which he did not have, under the contractual doctrine of breach of warranty of authority, which is discussed later.[92] If ratification occurs, there is still a technical breach of contract, but it is likely, though not certain, to cause no loss, as the third party will get what he bargained for. Such loss can occur where, eg, the third party spends money in proceeding against principal or agent before the ratification occurs.

---

of insurance may be ratified after loss, even by one who knows of the loss: *National Oilwell (UK) Ltd v Davy Offshore Ltd* [1993] 2 Lloyd's Rep 582.

[87] See *Watson v Davies* [1931] 1 Ch 455.

[88] See *Bowstead and Reynolds on Agency* (20th edn, 2014) paras 2-050, 2-085. The UNIDROIT *Principles of International Commercial Contracts* (2004), art.2.2.9(3) gives the third party the right to withdraw on giving notice, which would suggest that ratification is envisaged as applying even where the third party knows that the agent was not authorized. See T Krebs, 'Harmonization and How Not to Do it: Agency in the UNIDROIT Principles of International Commercial Contracts' [2009] LMCLQ 57, 68–70.

[89] It ranks for a specific disavowal in *Restatement, Third, Agency*, §4.05(1).

[90] (1889) 41 Ch D 295.

[91] The account given in H Kötz, *European Contract Law* (1998) is incorrect on this point.

[92] See 1.112ff.

The internal situation requires, however, more careful analysis in this context. The obvious result of ratification is that the principal confirms that the agent has acted acceptably in exceeding his authority, and so is liable to the agent for commission, reimbursement of expenses and so forth as if the act had been authorized. The proper explanation of this, where the internal relationship is contractual, is that he has waived the agent's breach of duty (or 'exonerated' the agent), though gratuitous agency may cause more difficulties of analysis. But a principal may ratify reluctantly, to preserve his commercial reputation, or because he has no practical alternative. In such a case he does not necessarily waive the breach of duty on the internal relationship, and in appropriate cases the agent may be liable to him for loss caused by exceeding his authority.[93] In such a case the right to commission would be unlikely to arise, and the right to reimbursement and indemnity would usually be doubtful also.[94]

C. The External Effects of Agency

(1) Express and Implied Actual Authority

Under the central principle of agency law an agent has the authority which he has been given by his principal, which in appropriate cases gives him power to affect his principal's legal position as regards third parties. This sort of authority is called actual authority, to distinguish it from apparent authority, which is discussed separately below.[95] The agent is regarded as having been actually authorized by the principal.

Assuming it exists, the next question is how far this authority extends. It should be remembered however that on the analysis adopted in this chapter there can be agents who have no authority to alter their principal's legal position at all;[96] and to such persons the idea of conferring authority is not really applicable, though they may in some situations have a very limited authority.

(a) Express authority

The conferring of authority may be express: even this may be subject to disputes of interpretation. But disputes more often concern the implied conferring of authority. In both cases the law creates (or extends) the authority, and hence the agent's power: but only, in this context, by objectively interpreting the internal relationship between principal and agent—not, as in the case of apparent authority, by looking to the impression received by the third party.

The authority may be conferred in a formal document. Such a document is usually called a power of attorney, and precedents for these are to be found in the Powers of Attorney Act 1971[97] and books of precedents. Such documents do not need to confer powers of a comprehensive nature, though they sometimes do so.[98] Their wording is on the whole strictly construed against the agent. This may seem a breach of the normal practice of construing contract terms *contra proferentem*: but not all such documents are contractual (eg, a power of

1.45

1.46

1.47

1.48

1.49

---

[93] There may be a difference in the degree of knowledge required of the principal in each situation, since in the first there is no need to protect the reasonable interests of the third party: see *Ing Re (UK) Ltd v R&V Versicherung AG* [2006] EWHC 1544 (Comm), [2006] 2 All ER (Comm) 870, at [38]ff.

[94] *Suncorp Insurance and Finance v Milano Assicurazioni SpA* [1993] 2 Lloyd's Rep 225, 234–235.

[95] See 1.60ff.

[96] See 1.15.

[97] Section 10 and Sch 1. The juristic significance of this is easy to overlook: see 1.07.

[98] Statutory provisions of a detailed nature protect attorneys (agents) who act in good faith, and third parties dealing with them: Powers of Attorney Act 1971, s 5.

attorney would not normally be), and in general in this area it may be appropriate to take the view that the transfer of power is a dangerous exercise and should not be presumed to have occurred beyond what is clear. Such construction may plainly be applied to powers of attorney, precedents for which sometimes employ very wide wording. An ordinary letter might not attract such hostile construction.

(b) Implied authority

1.50 Beyond this there are numerous examples of implied authority. Terminology here is not universally agreed, but implied authority may for convenience be roughly divided as follows:

(i) Incidental authority

1.51 An agent authorized to do a particular thing is impliedly authorized to do all lesser things required to achieve the principal object. An example is a solicitor acting in the sale of a house.

(ii) Usual authority

1.52 This term tends only to be found in textbooks and may be dangerous to use, in that too much significance is sometimes attributed to it as being a possible separate notion, especially in the area of the undisclosed principal.[99] But the general idea which is normally intended to be conveyed is straightforward. Usual authority has two facets. The first is that if one person puts another in a position in which there would usually, in the course of business, be authority to do certain things, that person has implied authority to do those things: eg, a managing director.[100] The second is that if one person uses the services of a person in the course of that person's trade or profession, that person is authorized to do what is normally done in the same context in pursuance of that trade or profession: eg, a solicitor or auctioneer. This is a form of actual authority which is often very relevant in apparent authority situations.[101]

(iii) Customary authority

1.53 An agent authorized to act in a particular market, such as a Stock Exchange or Lloyd's, may be impliedly authorized to do all that is customary in such markets. This category is limited. Legal customs are difficult to prove: they must be certain and notorious, and not unreasonable, in the sense that they may not change the nature of the contract. For example, a custom permitting an agent to assume the role of seller to his principal would not be effective unless known to the principal,[102] in which case he is accepting the change of status of one who might otherwise appear an agent. But where agents customarily or usually do certain things (without a legal custom being proved), these may be impliedly authorized under the categories of incidental authority or usual authority, already referred to.

(iv) Residual category

1.54 It is obvious that an agent may be impliedly authorized by virtue of special features of the fact situation which do not fall into any particular category.

1.55 All the above types of authority may be negatived, as regards actual authority, by a prohibition or exclusion by the principal.

---

[99] See 1.72ff.
[100] See the leading case of *Freeman & Lockyer v Buckhurst Park Properties (Mangal) Ltd* [1964] 2 QB 480, CA.
[101] See 1.62.
[102] *Robinson v Mollett* (1875) LR 7 HL 802, HL.

(c) Other considerations relating to authority

It is sometimes said that the fact that the agent is acting in fraud of his principal does not **1.56** negative his authority.[103] This proposition really concerns apparent authority[104] (or liability in tort); for an agent could not easily be regarded as having actual authority to act in fraud, or contrary to the interests, of his principal, even if the act was one of a type authorized.[105]

It might be appropriate to add another category of authority, under which an agent is impliedly **1.57** authorized in situations of necessity to do things which would not otherwise be authorized.[106] This could be called 'authority of necessity'. However, such authority could equally well be brought within either (i) or (iii) above, or within the residual implied authority referred to in (iv). The present status of such reasoning in English law is unfortunately confused by the fact that there is an ancient set of cases on so-called 'agency of necessity' which has led to a specialized and dogmatic doctrine developed in the area of maritime commerce before modern, more general principles of agency were fully worked out. It is discussed below.[107]

(2) Actual and Apparent Authority

(a) Actual authority

If one asks when persons have power as agents to change the legal positions of their prin- **1.58** cipals, the starting point is that they can do so when they act within the authority actually conferred on them, the actual authority, whether this is express or to be implied from the circumstances (including the interpretation of documents). The paradigm reasoning now to be discussed applies to contract: agency reasoning in connection with property may require different emphasis. Subject to an exception to be mentioned, it only applies to an agent who purports to act as such.

An agent who so acts may do so in one of two ways: first, where he identifies his principal, **1.59** and secondly, where he does not do so but indicates at the time of acting that he is act- ing for a principal—whether expressly (as by writing, in a phrase obviously much used in nineteenth-century commerce 'Bought for our principals'), or impliedly, as where a broker acts in a situation where it is known that, as brokers do, he always, or almost always, acts for others. These situations can be referred to as involving 'named' or 'unnamed' principals, but the words 'identified' and 'unidentified' principal are probably better, as a principal can be clearly identified without his actual name being given. In such a case proof of the agent's intention will be important.[108]

(b) Apparent authority

But an immense addition to this basic principle is provided by the doctrine of apparent **1.60** (sometimes called 'ostensible') authority, to which reference has already been made. Under it, a principal may be liable to a third party though the agent is in fact not authorized at all (eg, because internally, as between him and the agent, the principal has never authorized or even forbidden the particular act), but he nevertheless appears to the third party to be so.

---

[103] See *Hambro v Burnand* [1904] 2 KB 10, CA, sometimes treated, probably wrongly, as a case on actual authority.

[104] As to which see 1.60ff.

[105] See *Hopkins v TL Dallas Group Ltd* [2004] EWHC 1379, [2005] 1 BCLC 543; *Criterion Properties plc v Stratford UK Properties LLC* [2004] UKHL 28, [2004] 1 WLR 1846, HL; *Bowstead and Reynolds on Agency* (20th edn, 2014) Art 23; for the effect of equity see para.8-119.

[106] As in *Gokal Chand-Jagan Nath v Nand Ram Das-Atma Ram* [1939] AC 106, PC.

[107] See 1.94ff.

[108] See 1.37ff.

This doctrine applies even though the agent is acting in fraud of the principal, unless the third party has reason to know this, in which case an assumption that he was misled would be unjustified.[109]

(i) Basis of doctrine

1.61 In virtually all legal systems such a doctrine is normally traced back and attributed at root to the actions of the principal. Guidance for common law is obtained from the US *Restatement, Third, Agency*, which states that apparent authority exists 'when a third party reasonably believes the actor has authority to act on behalf of a principal and that belief is traceable to the principal's manifestations'.[110] A different system addressing itself first to the reliance and reasonable beliefs of the third party rather than the principal's manifestations may be pragmatic[111] but probably lacks sufficient juristic basis to be widely acceptable. The most obvious way of detecting such authority is from specific manifestations by the principal, eg, accepting transactions entered into by the agent, paying accounts submitted and so forth. A power of attorney to which there were reservations communicated to the agent only would create apparent authority in its clearest form.

1.62 In determining whether a third party is reasonable in a belief that the agent is authorized, the categories of implied authority come in again, particularly those of incidental and usual authority. The third party is entitled to assume, unless he has indications to the contrary, that the agent has the authority which someone put in his position would normally have. Indeed, many of the cases on implied authority actually arise in the context of apparent authority, and in older cases the reasoning used is often by modern standards confused, in so far as the clear distinction between the internal and external aspects of agency, and between implied and apparent authority, was not clearly established until the early twentieth century.

1.63 Such reasoning is obviously essential for the fair solution of commercial and other disputes, but its theoretical basis in common law is not absolutely clear. It must, for the reasons as to the paradigm of agency given above,[112] come as a supplement to central agency reasoning. General external reasoning, that certain powers arise from the holding of a particular position whether or not there is internal authorization, is not deployed (though it might have been had the common law, as at one time seemed likely, made more use of the imprecise notion of the 'general agent',[113] and as will be seen there are signs of it in connection with property transfer through agents[114]).

1.64 The doctrine has normally hitherto been regarded as based on estoppel arising from a representation, express or implied, by the principal that the agent is authorized. A famous passage which requires reproduction in full comes from a judgment of Diplock LJ, later Lord Diplock, in the leading case on the topic (which actually concerns company law):

> An 'apparent' or 'ostensible' authority...is a legal relationship between the principal and the contractor created by a representation, made by the principal to the contractor, intended to be and in fact acted upon by the contractor, that the agent has authority to enter on behalf of the principal into a contract of the kind within the scope of the 'apparent' authority, so as to render the principal liable to perform any obligations imposed upon him by such

---

[109] See *Hambro v Burnand* [1904] 2 KB 10, CA.
[110] § 2.03.
[111] It appears that the effect of French law may be represented in such a way: see Busch and McGregor (eds), *The Unauthorised Agent* (2009) ch 2.
[112] See 1.09.
[113] See 1.24.
[114] See 1.117ff.

contract. To the relationship so created the agent is a stranger. He need not be (although he generally is) aware of the existence of the representation but he must not purport to make the agreement as principal himself. The representation, when acted on by the contractor by entering into a contract with the agent, operates as an estoppel, preventing the principal from asserting that he is not bound by the contract. It is irrelevant whether the agent had actual authority to enter into the contract.[115]

This passage clearly bases the doctrine on estoppel. If the classic requirements of estoppel[116] are to apply, such reasoning would require evidence of a clear representation by the principal, intended to be acted on (with, in many commercial situations especially those regarding companies, the possibility of consequent problems as to authorization by one agent to another to make such a representation); and reliance by the third party, with consequent problems as to the extent to which he should inquire into the authority of an agent. Some estoppel reasoning has also limited the effect of the estoppel to what is required to satisfy the equity in the particular case, and perhaps in any case to reliance loss.[117]

None of these requirements is, however, strictly insisted on in the context of apparent authority. In many cases the principal's 'representation'[118] is of a very general nature, eg appointing someone managing director (the subject matter of the case quoted above), and the reliance intended by the principal does not seem to go beyond dealing on the assumption that the agent is authorized. Except where formal documents such as powers of attorney are known to be involved,[119] a duty of inquiry is not imposed, though there are cases where knowledge will be imputed to the third party on an objective basis. And where there is apparent authority, it is clear that the transaction in question is completely valid (as opposed to any form of validation *pro tanto*). **1.65**

The question of what enquiries the third party should have made in order to establish reliance on authority which is otherwise apparent has only recently been specifically addressed. In a case before the Hong Kong Court of Final Appeal[120] the leading judgment[121] adopts a test that, if there was an appearance of authority, the third party is entitled to rely on it unless the third party had actual knowledge that there was no authority, or his belief was 'dishonest or irrational'. Although the decision itself is beyond doubt, it can be said that such an approach confers excessive protection on the third party. It has however been followed in England in a case where it was said that the reasonableness of the third party's belief was 'neither here nor there'.[122] **1.66**

---

[115] *Freeman & Lockyer v Buckhurst Park Properties (Mangal) Ltd* [1964] 2 QB 480, CA (where a person not properly appointed was permitted to act as managing director). A useful exposition is also to be found in the judgment of Lord Denning MR in another company law case, *Hely-Hutchinson v Brayhead Ltd* [1968] 1 QB 549, 583, CA.

[116] See 1.71.

[117] See different views expressed in *Commonwealth of Australia v Verwayen* (1990) 170 CLR 394, HCA.

[118] *Restatement, Third Agency* uses the better word 'manifestation': see §§1.03, 3.03, 9.61. In *PEC Asia Ltd v Golden Rice Co Ltd* [2014] EWHC 1583 (Comm) it was held that repeated transactions would not of themselves create apparent authority; but see criticism by Watts, "Some Wear and Tear on *Armagas v Mundogas*" [2015] LMCLQ 36.

[119] Here there may be a duty to examine the power: see *Jacobs v Morris* [1902] 1 Ch 816.

[120] *Thanakhorn Kasikorn Thai Chamchat v Akai Holdings Ltd* (2010) 13 HKCFAR 479 (Court of Final Appeal, Hong Kong).

[121] Delivered by Lord Neuberger.

[122] *Quinn v CC Automotive Group Ltd* [2010] EWCA Civ 1412, [2011] 2 All ER (Comm) 584, CA, at [27]. See also *Lexi Holdings v Pannone & Partners* [2009] EWHC 2590 (Ch); *Newcastle International Airport v Eversheds LLP* [2012] EWHC 2648 (Ch), [2013] PNLR 5; *Acute Property Developments Ltd v Apostolou* [2013] EWHC 200 (Ch), [2013] Bus LR D22. This does not entirely accord with recent authority on the inquiries to be made in connection with the bona fide purchaser doctrine: see *Credit Agricole Corp v Papadimitriou* [2015] UKPC 13; see also *Gray v Smith* [2013] EWHC 4136 (Comm), [2014] 2 All ER (Comm) 359.

1.67 The result of employing estoppel reasoning is that the doctrine only operates to impose liability on the principal; he cannot sue unless he ratifies (though there would often not be much trouble establishing this). An alternative explanation of the doctrine can however be put forward, that it is based on an extension to contracts made through an agent of the objective interpretation normally applied to contracts in general.[123] This reasoning however makes it difficult to see why the principal cannot sue on such transactions even without ratifying.[124] Indeed, proponents of this view suggest that he can do so, presumably by proving that if sued he would be liable under the doctrine of apparent authority. Such a view is not easy to justify in theory and is in any case certainly contrary to the way in which the doctrine is normally stated in England.[125] It also involves abandoning for such situations the safeguards against unfair ratification.[126] It seems right therefore to accept that apparent authority is based on estoppel, but to accept also that the requirements for estoppel are different in different contexts;[127] and that the requirements in connection with apparent authority require specific formulation.

1.68 Difficult marginal situations can arise where an agent is known not to be authorized to enter into transactions, but is in general authorized to communicate information relevant to them, eg as to whether a particular transaction has been approved, or to act in connection with them, eg to sign letters of contractual offer which imply such approval. An example would be a company secretary communicating decisions of the board.[128] If such reasoning is extensively employed the doctrine of apparent authority could give greater protection to the third party than might be expected. Thus in a fairly recent English case the branch manager of a bank was known not to have authority to approve a loan application but had authority to sign a letter making an offer of a loan and hence to indicate whether it had been approved. The bank was held liable on such a letter for not making the loan.[129] In some cases however a proper analysis might be that the principal should be liable in tort on the agent's false representation.[130] The guiding principle must be that the manifestation of authority cannot emerge entirely from the agent himself.

(ii) Application to companies

1.69 Special problems arise for such reasoning in connection with companies. Its application is complicated by four factors. The first, already mentioned, is that the initial authorization or representation must normally come from another agent of the company.[131] The second is the doctrine, now largely abolished, that certain acts are ultra vires the company's powers as set out

---

[123] This view is taken in *Restatement, Third, Agency*, § 2.03 Comment c. See also Krebs, n 18.

[124] See *Restatement, Third, Agency,* vol 1 at p 136, accepting that he can. Only one decision is given as authority for such an action.

[125] A recent example is *Ing Re (UK) Ltd v Versicherung AG* [2006] EWHC 1544 (Comm), [2006] 2 All ER (Comm) 870.

[126] See 1.38ff.

[127] See Handley, *Estoppel by Conduct and Representation* (2006) ch 1, denying the existence of any 'overarching estoppel'.

[128] An example given in *Kelly v Fraser* [2012] UKPC 25, [2013] 1 AC 450, PC at [13] (the case involved a vice-president of the employee benefits division of a company and the trustees of its pension fund).

[129] *First Energy (UK) Ltd v Hungarian International Bank Ltd* [1993] 2 Lloyd's Rep 194, CA; cf an important earlier case, *Armagas Ltd v Mundogas SA (The Ocean Frost)* [1986] AC 717, HL (chartering manager: principal not bound, because agent did no more than say that he had obtained authorization) and *Hirst v Etherington* [1999] Lloyd's Rep PN 938, CA (assurance by partner to third party that undertaking given by him was in the normal course of business (which alone would confer actual authority), not sufficient to bind his partner).

[130] ie in tort: see 1.131.

[131] An Australian case on this point, *Crabtree-Vickers Pty Ltd v Australian Direct Mail and Advertising & Addressing Pty Ltd* (1975) 133 CLR 72, HCA, seems to go too far in requiring actual authorization.

in its constitution and so ineffective: granted its existence, there was also doubt about the scope of this doctrine, particularly in connection with acts of a type authorized but which were done for improper motives.[132] The third was a notion that persons dealing with companies would be taken to have constructive notice of their public documents, and so be unable to plead reliance when inspection of them would have shown that the act in question was outside the company's powers, or that delegation to the agent in question was not authorized.[133] In contrast, there were rules special to company law protecting third parties where delegation could have been authorized but the third party had no way of knowing whether it had been.[134] The law in England has been much changed by statute, which has abolished most of the doctrine of ultra vires, abolished the constructive notice rule and protects third parties dealing with boards of directors or persons authorized by them.[135] There can however be situations not caught by these protections where some of the previous difficulties of agency law may remain.

(iii) Scope of doctrine

Apparent authority reasoning applies most frequently to persons who are already agents, where some authority that they might normally be expected to have was never conferred, or was initially excluded. It also applies where a person had authority, but it has, unknown to the third party, been withdrawn.[136] It also applies to the comparatively rare situations where a person who has no agency authority whatever is allowed to act as if he had. A straightforward example is a person permitted to act as managing director who has never been properly appointed;[137] but more picturesque situations can also arise.[138] Such authority is often easier to establish than actual authority.

1.70

(iv) Estoppel as to existence of agency relationship

What is referred to above as 'classic' estoppel reasoning[139] has however a role to play where true agency reasoning cannot be deployed, but the requirements of estoppel can: eg, where a person himself makes no manifestation of authority but is at fault in not causing or correcting impressions which another is giving or has given in connection with him.[140] The normal requirements of estoppel, in particular the requirement of reliance, would often be more easily satisfied.

1.71

(3) Doctrine of the Undisclosed Principal

The doctrine of apparent authority stresses the external aspect of an agency situation; and any legal system requires some mechanism to achieve the result which that doctrine achieves. There is however another doctrine which is based initially on the internal aspect of agency and sometimes causes surprise. It is the so-called doctrine of the undisclosed principal. Under

1.72

---

[132] Many of the problems were settled in *Rolled Steel Products (Holdings) Ltd v British Steel Corp* [1986] Ch 246, CA.

[133] *Rama Corp v Proved Tin & General Investments Ltd* [1952] 2 QB 147, 149.

[134] The so-called rule in *Royal British Bank v Turquand* (1856) 6 E & B 327, 119 ER 886.

[135] See especially Companies Act 1985, ss 35, 35A, 35B (superseded by Companies Act 2006, ss 39, 40). See EPL 3.40, EPL 3.56ff.

[136] See 1.103.

[137] As in *Freeman & Lockyer v Buckhurst Park Properties (Mangal) Ltd* [1964] 2 QB 480, CA.

[138] See the remarkable American case of *Hoddesdon v Koos Bros* 135 A 2d 702 (AD NJ 1957), US (impostor 'salesman' in shop: explained however as a possible case of negligence by proprietor). A surprising application of the latter reasoning is *Pacific Carriers Ltd v BNP Paribas* (2004) 218 CLR 451, HCA, concerning an illegible signature by a person entrusted with an official rubber stamp.

[139] See 1.64.

[140] eg *Spiro v Lintern* [1973] 1 WLR 1002, where a person who had neither authorized nor ratified a transaction was held estopped by later conduct from alleging its invalidity. See *Restatement Third, Agency*, §2.05.

this doctrine, where the act of an agent is internally authorized between principal and agent, but the agent in acting does not purport to act for a principal, the principal may, subject to certain limits to be explained, be liable and entitled on the agent's contracts. The agent is also liable and entitled, again subject to certain limits.[141] The application of the doctrine must necessarily rest on proof of intention of the principal to confer authority,[142] and also of the agent as to whether he is acting in pursuance of such authority at the time he acts.[143] This unusual doctrine makes a third party liable to a person whose connection with the transaction was completely unknown to him, though it also allows him to sue that person. Obviously it can be linked with notions of vicarious liability in tort law, and used as a powerful tool by those who seek to unify agency rules between contract and tort.

(a) Comparison with indirect representation in civil law

1.73 Civil lawyers engaged in comparative study not infrequently assume that the situation with which the doctrine deals is that of indirect representation, or the *commissionnaire*, who as between himself and his principal is an agent undertaking only best endeavours and so forth, but deals on his own account with the outside world, though he may be assumed or even known to be acting for a principal.[144] In such cases, the principal is inaccessible to the third party, and the third party inaccessible to the principal. Some civil law systems then take the view that the principal ought to be entitled to intervene in certain circumstances, though perhaps should not so easily be liable: intervention (subject to restrictions) is not unlike assignment, but liability gives the third party a bonus for which he had not bargained.[145] Intervention when permitted in such systems is achieved by various mechanisms, including giving the principal a direct action against the third party in specific circumstances, particularly insolvency of the agent.

1.74 This equation of the doctrine with indirect representation situations seems likely to be too superficial.[146] It is fairly clear that the undisclosed principal doctrine only applies where the principal has authorized the agent to create privity of contract with a third party, but for reasons connected with principal or agent the principal's existence is not disclosed. This is not the same as indirect representation, where such authorization is ex hypothesi not present. It is however true that the undisclosed principal doctrine is said to have originated with property transactions involving the nineteenth-century factor, who, as stated above,[147] held goods for a (usually) overseas principal and sometimes dealt on his own account and sometimes as agent, not always making clear which. It is said that the principal was permitted to intervene in the factor's bankruptcy and claim goods as his; and that somehow this right was developed into a contractual doctrine allowing not only the right to sue in contract but also the liability to be sued.[148] Overall, the doctrine is plainly connected with one of the great factual puzzles of all agency analysis: the person in commerce who sometimes acts on his own account and sometimes for others, and does not make clear in a particular transaction which he is doing. This doctrine makes both liable, though perhaps in the alternative.[149] 'It has often been doubted'

---

[141] See 1.109 and 1.110.

[142] See discussion in *The Jascon 5* [2006] EWCA Civ 889, [2009] 2 Lloyd's Rep 195, at [25], [26]; *VTB Capital plc v Nutritek Intl Corp* [2012] EWCA Civ 808, [2012] 2 Lloyd's Rep 313, at [89]; [2013] UKSC 5, [2013] 2 AC 357, at [140]).

[143] The same point arises in the case of unidentified principals: see 1.37, 1.59.

[144] See 1.18.

[145] See eg Zweigert and Kötz, *Introduction to Comparative Law* (3rd edn, 1998) 436–441.

[146] See eg *Hutton v Bulloch* (1874) LR 9 QB 572.

[147] See 1.24.

[148] See the seminal article of AL Goodhart and CJ Hamson, 'Undisclosed Principals in Contract' (1932) 4 CLJ 320.

[149] See 1.82.

said Blackburn J of it 'whether it was originally right so to hold: but doubts of this sort come now too late'. The result is that when 'the vendor discovers that in reality there is an undisclosed principal behind, he is entitled to take advantage of this unexpected godsend'.[150]

It seems in fact more likely that the *commissionnaire* would have been dealt with by an old **1.75** rule called the 'foreign principal' rule, under which a foreign principal was assumed *not* to authorize his agent to bring him into privity with third parties elsewhere (or the converse). This rule was finally rejected in 1968, but at least so long as it applied, it meant that the foreign principal of the *commissionnaire* could not sue *or* be sued.[151] In other situations it seems that the *commissionnaire*, being a functionary not known to English law, might often be treated by an English court as an agent for an *unidentified* principal, who would then become liable and entitled by virtue of simpler reasoning: this in general seems to have happened with stockbrokers in the nineteenth century.[152]

Despite its original connection with the nineteenth-century factor, who might indeed have **1.76** been something like a *commissionnaire*, the doctrine of the undisclosed principal seems often to apply to persons discharging no named function, who need not be thought by the third party to act in any representative capacity at all: the discovery that they do so then adds a new dimension to the legal scene. The doctrine is by no means fully worked out, and many cases do not make clear whether they are talking of completely undisclosed or merely unidentified principals. Analogies with assignment and with trusts reasoning (which can be deployed to some extent in many agency situations) prove to be analogies only. It does seem however to be accepted that the straight reasoning that the contract is really that of the principal (though this is sometimes said) is inappropriate. The situation is one of controlled intervention on a contract by one not party to it.[153]

(b) Limitation and exclusion of the doctrine

Such a doctrine requires limits. One is obvious: the doctrine does not permit intervention on **1.77** formal written instruments, where the stated name of a party has a special significance. This is true of deeds, on which there is special case law; but also of negotiable instruments, and other documents such as bills of lading and waybills, where the right to sue is controlled by a statute which refers to naming or identification of the person entitled to sue (or requires indorsement to such a person or in blank).[154]

Beyond this, the doctrine is subject to an ill-defined exception to prevent intervention in **1.78** inappropriate cases. This exception has proved extremely difficult to formulate, for if (eg) one person knows that another will not sell to him he can often legitimately avoid this by getting a third person to buy, and then to resell to him,[155] and it is difficult therefore to see why the result should be different if he merely uses an agent.[156]

For a time it was said that the analogy of assignment should be followed, and that a principal **1.79** could not intervene where the benefit of the contract was not assignable or its burden could not be vicariously performed.[157] This was denied, however, in a Hong Kong case concerning

---

[150] *Armstrong v Stokes* (1873) LR 7 QB 598, 604.

[151] See 1.107.

[152] See eg *Hodgkinson v Kelly* (1868) LR 6 Eq 496.

[153] This view was accepted in the Court of Appeal in *Welsh Development Agency v Export Finance Co* [1992] BCLC 148, CA: see 173, 182.

[154] See Carriage of Goods by Sea Act 1992, ss 1(3), 2(1)(b); 3.109ff, 3.113; *East West Corp v DKBS AF 1912 A/S* [2003] EWCA Civ 83, [2003] QB 1509, at [16]–[18].

[155] As in *Nash v Dix* (1898) 78 LT 445.

[156] As in *Dyster v Randall & Sons* [1926] Ch 932.

[157] This was the view of Goodhart and Hamson, n 148.

a contract of insurance: it was held that even if the contract had been expressly made unassignable, intervention was permitted on the ground that the identity of the assured was on the facts a matter of indifference to the third party (the insurer).[158] This shows that non-assignability is not enough; the mere fact that the benefit of a contract cannot be *transferred* does not necessarily mean that at the formation stage the third party was not in a commercial situation willing to accept the involvement of a principal as well as an agent. But it may be in any case that the decision should be regarded as one concerning an unidentified rather than an undisclosed principal.

1.80 The most recent authority, derived from this case, indicates that the exclusion of the undisclosed principal operates only on the basis that such exclusion is implicit in the interpretation of the contract; but no clear indication is given as to when this should be, and the common law as to implied terms in contract, insofar as it is relevant, is fairly strict. It is also clear that the exclusion need not be express, and that naming or even description of the agent as filling some capacity are not necessarily sufficient to exclude intervention. This is one of the comparatively few areas in common law where a principle of good faith might provide reasoning not otherwise available. At present, in the background is what is described in the case in question as a 'beneficial assumption in commercial cases', that in an ordinary commercial contract it may be assumed that a person is 'willing to treat as a party to the contract anyone on whose behalf the agent may have been authorized to contract', 'unless either [he] manifests his unwillingness or there are other circumstances which should lead the agent to realise that [he] was not so willing'.[159] This statement of Diplock LJ is contrary to the spirit of many of the rules on formation of contract *inter partes* but is obviously favourable to a wide undisclosed principal doctrine, as well as to a broad rule concerning unidentified principals.

(c) Other difficulties of the doctrine

1.81 A separate problem concerns the application of the doctrine of ratification. If an *unidentified* principal can ratify when his agent acts without authority,[160] it seems a small step to allow the *undisclosed* principal to ratify; but it was long ago held that this could not be done.[161] Presumably to allow ratification simply on the basis that the unauthorized agent says that he intended at the time of acting to do so for the principal is regarded as one step too far. It would allow too easy intervention by one person on the contract of another.[162] That may be correct if one thinks in terms of an agent who has never been authorized by the principal at all. But if one thinks of the situation (which the case in question in fact concerned) where the agent already has some authority and simply exceeds it, if the undisclosed principal chooses to ratify it is arguable that he should at any rate be liable. The result would certainly be beneficial to the third party.

1.82 A further difficulty is caused by the fact that it was decided in the nineteenth century that the liability is alternative; that is to say, if the third party obtains judgment against the agent he can no longer sue the principal because the cause of action is merged in the judgment, and

---

[158] *Siu Yin Kwan v Eastern Insurance Co Ltd* [1994] 2 AC 199, PC. For a recent example where intervention was not permitted in the insurance context see *The Jascon 5* [2006] EWCA Civ 889, [2006] 2 Lloyd's Rep 195, CA.

[159] *Teheran-Europe Co Ltd v ST Belton (Tractors) Ltd* [1968] 2 QB 545, CA, 555, cited in *Siu Yin Kwan*, n 158, at 209.

[160] See 1.37.

[161] *Keighley, Maxsted & Co v Durant* [1901] AC 240, HL.

[162] H Kötz, *European Contract Law* (1998) 233 states that for this restriction 'there is no good reason'. This is an oversimplified assessment.

vice versa.[163] There is further authority that the third party can also lose his right against one simply by manifesting an election, or choice, to sue the other, though this is more doubtful.[164] There seems no real reason why either should be so[165] and these notions of merger and election have not fared well in this context in the United States.[166]

Finally, all common law treatment of the undisclosed principal doctrine involves discussion **1.83** of a famous nineteenth-century case at first instance, *Watteau v Fenwick*.[167] In this case the proprietor of a hotel sold the hotel to another and continued to run it as the buyer's manager. The buyer (the new owner) forbade the manager to buy cigars on credit, but the manager, who had done so when he owned the hotel, continued to do so. Cigars were supplied on credit by a third party who was not aware that the manager no longer owned the hotel. The new owner was held liable. There was therefore no apparent authority, and no actual authority either. On agency reasoning the decision is virtually impossible to justify,[168] but the interesting nature of the fact situation has ensured that it is regularly discussed in connection with the undisclosed principal doctrine, and various justifications have been offered (some of which, of course, run off into wider principles intended to apply to both contract and tort).[169]

The whole undisclosed principal doctrine, despite simplified explanations, favourable and **1.84** unfavourable, from external observers in works on comparative law, remains therefore highly uncertain. Further problems appear in the following paragraphs.[170] It is nevertheless a tool which, used in an appropriate way, is capable of being a useful one for the resolution of disputes.

(4) Defences to Contract Actions

In general the position here is straightforward: the principal is entitled against the third party **1.85** and the third party against the principal. As already stated,[171] in the case of apparent authority, however, the doctrine only makes the principal liable: he cannot sue without ratifying.

Considerable difficulties, the details of which are beyond the scope of this chapter, arise in **1.86** connection with the pleading of defences in contractual actions. In normal agency situations, that is to say, situations of disclosed principals, whether identified or unidentified, where the principal sues he can be met by contractual defences as if the contract had been made with himself, but not by defences valid against the agent only; and where he is sued he can likewise plead defences arising on the contract, but not defences valid between him and the agent only. The undisclosed principal, however, intervenes on the contract of another. Hence

---

[163] *Priestly v Fernie* (1863) 2 H & C 977, 159 ER 820; *Kendall v Hamilton* (1879) 4 App Cas 504, HL,513–514.

[164] The most recent leading English cases are *Clarkson Booker Ltd v Andjel* [1964] 2 QB 775 and *Chestertons v Barone* [1987] 1 EGLR 15, 17, CA.

[165] See 1.110. For a full discussion see *Bowstead and Reynolds on Agency* (20th edn, 2014) Art 84.

[166] Merger was rejected as regards an undisclosed principal in *Grinder v Bryans Road Building & Supply Co*, 432 A 2d 453 (Md App, 1981), US; see also *Tower Cranes of America Inc v Public Service Co* 702 F Supp 371 (DNH, 1988), US and *Crown Controls Inc v Smiley* 756 P 2d 717 (Wash, 1988), US.

[167] [1893] 1 QB 346.

[168] As was said by Bingham J in *Rhodian River Shipping Co SA v Holla Maritime Corp (The Rhodian River)* [1984] 1 Lloyd's Rep 373, 379. But see *Restatement Third, Agency*, §2.06 (2) and (surprisingly) UNIDROIT *Principles of International Commercial Contracts* (2004), art 2.2.4(2), which adopts such a solution.

[169] An example is AM Tettenborn 'Agents, Business Owners and Estoppel' [1998] CLJ 274. But usual authority, see 1.52, or the doctrine of apparent ownership, see 1.122, are sometimes suggested in this context.

[170] There are also problems as to damages, see 1.109, 1.110.

[171] See 1.67.

if he sues he can be met by defences personal to the agent which had accrued before the third party learned that there was a principal involved; and if he is sued he can probably plead the agent's defences.

1.87 Well-known problems of principle, largely associated with the undisclosed principal doctrine, arise where third party or principal settles with the agent, and the money is not passed on. Must he pay again? In a normal *disclosed* agency situation, again, the third party can only settle with (or, by similar reasoning, set off a debt owed by) the agent if the agent had actual or apparent authority to receive payment. Equally, the principal is only discharged against the third party by paying the agent (or, again by similar reasoning, can only set off a debt owed to him by the agent) if the third party leads him to believe that the agent has paid the third party, or that the third party looks only to the agent for payment.

1.88 Where the principal is *undisclosed*, however, the third party must in principle, until he learns of the principal, be entitled to settle with the agent or exercise a set-off against him; and defences accrued up to the time of such discovery should be available against the principal. This is consistent with the idea of intervention by the principal on another's contract. However, a leading case usually discussed in this connection suggests a basic rule very like that for disclosed principals: that the third party's right to do so is based on the fault of the principal in misleading the third party, as by giving the agent possession of goods, and that if there is no such fault such defences cannot be pleaded. The case in question, *Cooke & Sons v Eshelby*,[172] concerns the perennially difficult situation, to which reference has already been made, of a person (here a broker) who sometimes dealt as principal and sometimes as agent. The third party admitted that at the relevant time he had no particular belief one way or the other, and was held unable to set off against the principal a debt due to him from the agent personally. This is therefore probably a case on a disclosed but unidentified principal, but as has been said, the difficulty in telling such a person from an undisclosed principal is a further problem of the undisclosed principal doctrine.

1.89 Finally comes the case where the undisclosed principal settles with the agent before the third party hears of the principal. Here another famous case, *Armstrong v Stokes*,[173] holds that the principal is no longer liable. The case has been criticized and even doubted.[174] The view put forward in authorities that doubt this conclusion is, reciprocally to that above concerning settlement by third party with agent, that the undisclosed principal should only be discharged if there are acts of the third party that indicate to the principal that the agent has settled the account with the third party, on which the principal relies: ie that the settlement by the principal is attributable to the third party. But as the third party does not know of the principal at the time of the settlement it is difficult to see how his acts *vis-à-vis* the agent can ever be plausibly read in this way. In *Armstrong v Stokes* it was specifically found that the third party had not induced the principal to believe that he (the third party) had settled with the agent,[175] yet the principal was held discharged. The general rule as to the liability of an undisclosed principal was said to be 'subject to an exception, which is not so well established as the rule, and is not very accurately defined, viz, that nothing has occurred to make it unjust that the undisclosed principal should be called upon to make payment to the vendor',[176] and that a 'rigid rule…would produce intolerable hardship'.[177] This approach seems better than that suggested in the decisions disapproving the case.

---

[172] (1887) 12 App Cas 271.
[173] (1872) LR 7 QB 598.
[174] In *Irvine & Co v Watson & Sons* (1880) 5 QBD 414 and *Davison v Donaldson* (1882) 9 QBD 623.
[175] (1872) LR 7 QB 598, 610.
[176] (1872) LR 7 QB 598, 604.
[177] (1872) LR 7 QB 598, 610.

The leading cases appear again actually to concern disclosed but unidentified principals, **1.90** where a rule that the principal is only discharged when he acts in reliance on conduct of the third party is of course not inappropriate. The fact situation in *Armstrong v Stokes*, however, does appear to have concerned a person operating more or less in the manner of a *commissionnaire*,[178] and the issue raised was whether the undisclosed principal doctrine continues the principal's liability when he has settled with his agent before the third party has any knowledge of him. On this two views are possible, and the position in English law has not yet been finally determined. This is another obscurity of the undisclosed principal doctrine.

(5) Delegation of Agency Functions

The confidential nature of his role means that the prima facie rule is that an agent may not **1.91** delegate his function: the principal was relying on his discretion and expertise. The Latin maxim *delegatus non potest delegare* is often cited in this connection. This means that acts done by unauthorized subagents will not be effective, as was held in old cases on service of notice to quit by this means. Mere ministerial acts can however be performed through others, and this principle might save some notices to quit and similar situations.

Delegation may however be expressly or impliedly authorized. An example of implied author- **1.92** ization arises in cases of emergency, without recourse to agency of necessity principles.[179] The principles of apparent authority may also validate an act by an unauthorized subagent; as may those of ratification.[180]

Where delegation is authorized, the acts of the subagent, done on behalf of the agent, will, **1.93** in accordance with the principles of authority already described,[181] bind and entitle the principal as being the agent's acts. A question then arises as to whether the subagent has direct contractual privity (where the agency relationship is contractual) with the principal, or not. Obviously the agent may be authorized to create such privity:[182] in such a case he is doing little more than appoint another agent to the principal. The prima facie rule here is however that this has not been done unless there are other indications.[183] The subagent would normally have contractual privity with the agent only and the agent is regarded as performing through another and liable to his principal accordingly if anything goes wrong. There is however a strong argument for holding the subagent directly liable to the principal in matters not requiring a contractual action, and this argument has been much developed in the United States.[184] For example, there is no requirement that to be a fiduciary a person has to be an agent of the person to whom he owes fiduciary obligations, and in England it has been held that the subagent is a fiduciary in connection with the taking of a bribe.[185] Fairly recent developments of the law in those fields enable it to be argued that he should be liable to the principal in restitution or tort.[186] The field is as yet incompletely developed.

---

[178] See 1.18.
[179] See the leading case of *De Bussche v Alt* (1878) 8 Ch D 286; 1.94ff.
[180] See 1.33ff.
[181] See 1.46ff.
[182] As was the case in *De Bussche v Alt*, n 157, itself.
[183] *Calico Printers Assn Ltd v Barclays Bank Ltd* (1931) 145 LT 51; and see in a modern context *Prentis Donegan & Partners Ltd v Leeds & Leeds Co Inc* [1998] 2 Lloyd's Rep 326.
[184] See Seavey (1955) 68 Harvard L Rev 658.
[185] *Powell & Thomas v Evan Jones & Co* [1905] 1 KB 11.
[186] As in *Henderson v Merrett Syndicates Ltd* [1995] 2 AC 145, HL (managing agent at Lloyd's: but there was a close relationship between the parties). As to the position under the Commercial Agents Regulations (see 1.05) see *Light v Ty Europe Ltd* [2003] EWCA Civ 1238; [2004] 1 Lloyd's Rep 693, CA.

(6) Agency of Necessity

1.94   Reference has already been made to this topic in connection with the notion of authority,[187] but it is so unusual that it deserves brief separate treatment. In English law a long-established and discrete group of decisions confer on an agent the authority in emergency to act in ways which would not otherwise be authorized. The doctrine derives almost entirely from cases about shipmasters, who might have to act in situations of emergency far from home, and, rather quaintly, the acceptor of a bill of exchange for honour of the drawee.[188]

1.95   The first of the examples concerns both the internal and external aspects of agency, but mostly the external, since the principal is bound by the contract or (often) property disposition, as where the master sells or hypothecates the ship or cargo in a distant port; the second exclusively concerns the internal aspect, since it entitles the acceptor to reimbursement and indemnity. The doctrine is however supposed to be a single one, and carries specific rules of a rather ancient and also maritime flavour: there must be impracticability of communication with the principal, the action must be necessary, and the agent must have acted bona fide in the principal's interests. It would seem also that the act must not be prohibited by the principal: this is to be inferred from the fact that communication must be impracticable. The inference must be that if it is practicable, the principal could forbid the act.

1.96   If the internal and external aspects are separated, it can be seen that the external situation requires no more than the normal rules as to actual and apparent authority, with a rider that the actual, and hence apparent, authority of an agent is enlarged in an emergency unless this is forbidden by the principal.[189] Even if the act is forbidden, a third party who has no reason to know of the prohibition should be able to rely on apparent authority,[190] and the same should be the case if he wrongly but reasonably thought that an emergency had arisen or that communication was impracticable. This would not be the case under the ancient rules, which, like the Factors Acts,[191] require specific internal facts, whether or not known to the third party, for their operation. Actual authority would carry with it the normal rights to reimbursement and indemnity as regards authorized acts. This seems to be the position in the United States.[192]

1.97   The pure internal situations covered by the doctrine, exemplified by the acceptor for honour, raise more general questions of restitution for benefits conferred, and sometimes of bailment, and should not in more sophisticated days be connected with agency reasoning at all. Consistently with this, it has been held in *China Pacific SA v Food Corp of India (The Winson)*,[193] concerning the costs of warehousing after salvage, that the strict requirements as to necessity do not apply in purely internal situations involving the right of a bailee to indemnity.[194]

1.98   As to the external situation, however, in a more recent case, *The Choko Star*,[195] involving the making of a salvage contract on behalf of cargo, the Court of Appeal simply applied the

---

[187] See 1.57.
[188] Bills of Exchange Act 1882, ss 65–68.
[189] See 1.57.
[190] As in *The Unique Mariner* [1978] 1 Lloyd's Rep 438.
[191] See 1.125. Other examples of this are *Brocklesby v Temperance BS* [1895] AC 173, HL (see 1.123) and *Hambro v Burnand* [1904] 2 KB 10 (see 1.56).
[192] See *Restatement, Third, Agency* 2.02 comment f.
[193] [1982] AC 939, HL.
[194] See *Petroleo Brasileiro SA v ENE Kos 1 Ltd* [2012] UKSC 17, [2012] 2 AC 164 SC, at [118].
[195] [1990] 1 Lloyd's Rep 516, CA.

old requirements, which are really appropriate to days before the evolution of the present rules as to actual and (especially) apparent authority. It seems undesirable that this special doctrine, largely evolved to meet needs of sailing ships in the nineteenth century, should remain in its ancient and undeveloped form; but the matter awaits a case in which the Supreme Court can resolve it.

(7) Termination of Authority

As regards termination of authority, separate treatment of the internal and external aspects of agency is again required. **1.99**

(a) The authority

As regards the initial authority it is normally accepted that the principal can withdraw it at any time, regardless of whether he promised not to do so. 'The proper conduct of the affairs of life necessitates that this should be so.'[196] This is indeed one of the features which justifies distinguishing the granting or conferring of authority from the accompanying contract.[197] Where the agency is contractual, the withdrawal may be a breach of contract making the principal liable to the agent in damages or give rise to other remedies; but the authority itself is regarded as inherently revocable and the agent ceases to be entitled to reimbursement or indemnity[198] except in respect of acts done before the revocation. So actual authority will cease not only when some agreed time limit elapses, or the parties agree that it should, or its purpose is fulfilled, or its purpose is frustrated, but also whenever the principal terminates it, whatever the contractual position with regard to such termination. Such termination would normally require notice to the agent to prevent actual authority continuing. But if notice was given to the third party but not to the agent it seems that not only apparent but also actual authority no longer exists[199]—subject to the agent's internal rights against the principal in such a case. **1.100**

To this there is one exception. In some situations agency reasoning is used to reinforce a security: a simple example occurs where a person mortgaging chattels confers authority on the lender to sell them if the debt is not repaid.[200] Obviously a revocation of such authority by the borrower would thwart the whole arrangement, so it is not allowed: the arrangement is referred to as an 'authority coupled with an interest', or in the *Restatement, Third* as 'power given as security'.[201] The agency power is of course not a true one at all: an agent by definition has to act in his principal's interests, but in this case the agent is given the authority in order to protect his own interests. **1.101**

The result of this is that it is not possible to create irrevocable authority in a normal agency situation merely by promising not to revoke. This view seems correct in principle, but may cause serious problems in practice: the remedy of an agent acting on such a promise not to revoke lies in contract against the principal only. Various devices have been employed to draw **1.102**

---

[196] *Frith v Frith* [1906] AC 254, HL, 259 *per* Lord Atkinson. For a modern American example see *Government Guarantee Fund v Hyatt Corp* 95 F 3d 291 (3rd Cir, 1996), US (agency to manage hotel).

[197] See 1.07.

[198] See 1.151.

[199] But see a Canadian decision to the contrary, *Robert Simpson Co v Godson* [1937] 1 DLR 354, criticized by Wright (1937) 15 Can Bar Rev 196.

[200] The leading cases are *Walsh v Whitcomb* (1797) 2 Esp 565, 170 ER 456 and *Smart v Sandars* (1848) 5 CB 895, 136 ER 1132. But they go back to times when presuppositions as to assignment and security were quite different from those of the present day and historical work is needed on the evolution of this rule.

[201] §3.12.

the sting of this rule, in particular by extending the 'security' reasoning to the underwriting of share issues.[202] But it is by no means certain that they will be effective.[203] In connection with Lloyd's, it has been held that the right of a broker to commission on future transactions was not such an interest, and the view was expressed that an 'interest of a purely commercial kind' cannot of itself be sufficient to make authority irrevocable. [204]

(b) Apparent authority

1.103 The doctrine of apparent authority will operate to protect the third party in many cases of this type; for a principal's representation that an agent has authority may be continuing or valid unless corrected.[205] There is sometimes statutory protection for the third party in the case of powers of attorney.[206] Estoppel may also operate in some situations. The third party also has the protection of the agent's warranty of authority.[207]

(c) Capacity

1.104 Special considerations arise in situations of loss of capacity. The principal may, unknown to the agent, die or become mentally incapable. In such a case the actual authority is assumed to cease to exist because there is no longer any competent principal; and this reasoning can be argued to prevent apparent authority also. One well-known decision however holds that apparent authority can survive the principal's mental incapacity,[208] though a later decision held the agent liable for breach of warranty of authority in such a case, which is inconsistent.[209] The continuation of apparent authority can be justified in the cases both of death and mental incapacity on the ground that the representation may rank as continuing until withdrawn, which would certainly be more protective of third parties. This is a well-known problem in many jurisdictions. Provision was made for some such situations by the Enduring Powers of Attorney Act 1985, which allows the creation of powers of attorney which survive supervening mental incapacity. This has been superseded by the Mental Capacity Act 2005, which creates a wider 'Lasting Power of Attorney'. Permission of the court is however normally needed to act after that time. There is also statutory protection in the case of powers of attorney.[210] Bankruptcy and insolvency raise specialized questions.

---

[202] *Re Hannan's Empress Gold Mining and Development Co, Carmichael's Case* [1896] 2 Ch 643. But cf *Schindler v Brie* [2003] EWHC 1804, [2003] WTLR 1361 (authority not drafted so as to be irrevocable).

[203] See FMB Reynolds, 'When is an Agent's Authority Irrevocable?' in RF Cranston (ed), *Making Commercial Law: Essays in Honour of Roy Goode* (1997) ch 10. An injunction against revocation may perhaps sometimes be available: see *Lauritzencool AB v Lady Navigation Ltd* [2005] EWCA Civ 579, [2005] 1 WLR 3686, CA and material there cited.

[204] See *Temple Legal Protection Ltd v QBE Insurance (Europe) Ltd* [2009] EWCA Civ 453, [2009] 1 CLC.553, CA, at [52].

[205] *Rockland Industries Ltd v Amerada Minerals Corp of Canada* [1980] 2 SCR 2, (1980) 108 DLR (3d) 513, SC Can; *AMB Generali Holding AG v SEB Trygg Liv Holding AB* [2005] EWCA Civ 1237, [2006] 1 Lloyd's Rep 318, at [28]ff.

[206] See Powers of Attorney Act 1971, s 5.

[207] See 1.112.

[208] *Drew v Nunn* (1879) 4 QBD 661, CA.

[209] *Yonge v Toynbee* [1910] 1 KB 215, usually regarded as a leading case, but arising in the context of the limited context of the warranty given by a solicitor regarding his client in litigation, and connected with the court's jurisdiction over solicitors. The case for termination by reason of mental incapacity is weaker. In connection with death, *Restatement, Third, Agency* §3.07(2) provides that actual authority is not revoked by death till the agent knows of it.

[210] Powers of Attorney Act 1971, s 5.

D. The Agent and Third Parties

(1) Rights and Liabilities on the Main Contract

(a) General principles

Staying in the paradigm field of contract, where an agent who has actual or apparent authority **1.105** makes a contract for his principal, whether he identifies the principal or not, he may create, as has been already stated, a legal relationship between his principal and the third party. If we turn now to the position of the agent, it might then be assumed that he drops out of the transaction. Such a result can be based on the intention of the third party, who intends to deal with the principal and not with the agent.

But although there are cases, especially in the nineteenth century, which seem to assume this **1.106** result by regarding the salient question on a particular set of relevant facts as being one as to whether the contract is with either the agent or the principal, it is now clear that such a rule is too simple. Whatever the position in other legal systems, the breadth of common law agency principles does not require that the agent drop out of the transaction at all. Though he will usually do so, it is perfectly possible that he may be liable and (less commonly) entitled on it together with his principal.

On general principles of concurrent liability, his liability may be joint, or joint and several; **1.107** or be a separate liability as a guarantor of some sort; or arise from a completely separate, probably collateral, contract. The cases indicating liability in the agent come from various contexts. Some relate to situations where the principal is foreign. Here the older view was that the local agent contracted for himself: this was justified, not only on the basis that the local counterparty would expect the liability of someone within his own jurisdiction, but also on the more surprising basis that the foreign principal did not authorize the agent to bring him into contractual privity with persons in another country.[211] There is here plainly some connection with indirect representation, ie with the functions of *commissionnaires* in other countries.[212] This so-called 'foreign principal' doctrine has however now been rejected in England. It has instead been said[213] that the fact that the principal is foreign is an indication that the agent intends to undertake liability *together with* him.

Another case producing such an effect involves a one-man company, holding its effective **1.108** proprietor liable on the facts as a contracting party together with the company.[214] A long line of cases recognize trade usages and practices under which an agent at certain times and in certain places is liable together with his principal.[215] There are special decisions, some of them rather unusual, on the rights and liabilities of two special types of agent: auctioneers, who of course still exist, and factors, who in the sense of the term used in the old cases do not.[216] *Restatement, Agency, Third*[217] even suggests a prima facie rule that agents for

---

[211] See *Armstrong v Stokes* (1872) LR 7 QB 598, 605; *Teheran-Europe Co Ltd v ST Belton (Tractors) Ltd* [1968] 2 QB 545, CA, 557–558.

[212] cf *Hutton v Bulloch* (1874) LR 9 QB 572. See also 1.18ff.

[213] In the *Teheran-Europe* case, n 211.

[214] *The Swan* [1968] 1 Lloyd's Rep 5. This is a specialized example of agency reasoning utilized in connection with problems of the corporate veil. See also *VTB Capital plc v Nutritek Intl Corp* [2012] EWCA Civ 808, [2012] 2 Lloyd's Rep 313, at [90]; on appeal [2013] UKSC 5, [2013] 2 AC 337, SC, at [131]–[143]; 1.25.

[215] A fairly recent example is *Cory Brothers Shipping Ltd v Baldan Ltd* [1997] 2 Lloyd's Rep 58.

[216] For details see Murdoch, *Law of Estate Agency and Auctions* (5th edn, 2009); *Bowstead and Reynolds on Agency* (20th edn, 2014) paras 1-042, 9-023.

[217] §6.02.

unidentified principals are parties to the contract, though the English Court of Appeal has refused to go so far.[218] Such a rule would be more drastic than those sometimes found in civil law countries, which may make the agent liable only if he does not reveal the name of his principal on demand and within a reasonable time. The latter result could in common law only be achieved by proof of a trade usage or practice, as already mentioned;[219] though of course should the matter proceed to litigation discovery could usually be obtained.

(b) Agent of undisclosed principal

1.109 Where the principal is undisclosed, the third party intends to deal with the agent and not with the principal. This then provides a separate situation for the agent's personal liability; and indeed not only is the principal's intervention subject, as already mentioned, to any equities between agent and third party accruing before the third party had notice of the principal's existence, but the third party cannot be prevented from insisting on the agent's liability should he so wish.[220] Where in such situation it is the agent that sues, a major problem of theory can arise as to whether one party can recover loss suffered by another. This is one of the early examples of a problem to which attention is now being more generally addressed.[221]

1.110 As already stated, this liability of the agent of the undisclosed principal is at least in some respects alternative, and the third party may be barred from suing the agent by obtaining judgment against the principal, or even perhaps manifesting an election or choice to hold the principal liable. This is itself unsatisfactory.[222] Further difficulty is however caused by the fact that some cases assume that the doctrines of merger and election apply also to cases where both agent and *disclosed* principal are liable. This seems quite contrary to principle and in any case could not apply where the agent's liability is on a separate contract. As with other problematic situations, the difficulties start with cases where it is not clear whether the principal should be regarded as undisclosed or merely as unidentified. They are also confused by straight disputes on formation of contract, turning on the question with which of two possible parties a contract was originally made, and difficulties are made worse by cases where summary judgment is obtained against one party or the other without the facts being argued and analysed, and it is later argued that there has been merger.[223] Though an attempt has been made in New Zealand to cut through the difficulties,[224] and there is useful authority in the United States, the problems of merger and election are not yet fully resolved in England.

(c) Oral and written contracts

1.111 In the case of an oral contract the question as to the agent's liability and right to sue will be one of interpretation of the parties' intentions in accordance with the above principles. But where the contract is written, these intentions may well have to yield to, or be derived from, the actual wording used. There are many cases on this topic, though they do not raise great questions of principle[225] beyond the normal canons of interpretation.[226] Obviously

---

[218] *N & J Vlassopoulos Ltd v Ney Shipping Co (The Santa Carina)* [1977] 1 Lloyd's Rep 478 (unwritten contract); see also in Canada *Chartwell Shipping Ltd v QNS Paper Co Ltd* [1989] 2 SCR 683; (1989) 62 DLR (4th) 36, SC Can (written contract).

[219] eg *Hutchinson v Tatham* (1873) LR 8 CP 482.

[220] *Montgomerie v UK Mutual SS Assn* [1891] 1 QB 370, 372.

[221] See *Alfred McAlpine Construction Ltd v Panatown Ltd* [2001] 1 AC 518, HL; also *L/M International Construction Ltd v The Circle Ltd Partnership* (1995) 49 Con LR 12, 31–33; Unberath, *Transferred Loss* (2003) ch 7 esp 175ff.

[222] See 1.82.

[223] See discussion in *Bowstead and Reynolds on Agency* (20th edn, 2014) Art 82.

[224] *LC Fowler & Sons Ltd v St Stephens College Board of Governors* [1991] 3 NZLR 304, SCNZ.

reliance is placed on signatures; but the body of a document must be taken into account also. Furthermore, account must be taken of the parol evidence rule, which may not permit oral evidence that contradicts the tenor of a document.[227] Where however it simply adds another party to an existing contract, as will often be the case in this context, it can be accepted.[228] As already mentioned, there are special rules for deeds and other formal documents such as bills of exchange and bills of lading.[229]

(2) Liability of the Unauthorized Agent

Where an agent purports to have authority from a principal and has not, all legal systems seek **1.112** to make the agent (sometimes called in civil law *falsus procurator*) liable on some basis. Some old English cases succeed in treating him as his own principal,[230] but such reasoning is difficult to sustain. Where his principal did not exist, some early cases on prospective companies not yet incorporated succeeded in treating him as undertaking personal liability on the basis that some legal effect to the transaction must have been intended.[231] This particular problem is dealt with by statute.[232] Liability in tort where the profession of authority was wilfully false has been long accepted; and more recently liability in negligence for misrepresentation causing economic loss has been accepted as actionable in appropriate cases. A broader basis for the agent's liability was however discovered as far back as 1857 and remains as the main technique for imposing such liability.[233] Anyone purporting to act as agent is deemed, in the absence of contrary indication, to warrant, ie promise absolutely, that he has authority. This is called warranty of authority, and is a form of implied collateral contract, perhaps the oldest example of this genre in English law. The liability is not based on negligence: it is one of guarantee. It can of course be excluded by an agent who makes it clear that he does not promise that he has authority, or for some other reason is not to be regarded as doing so: such an argument was accepted in a case where an agent signed 'by telegraphic authority'.[234] The strict liability is sometime criticized by lawyers trained in other systems, but the criticism seems to rest largely on an assertion of different values.

The damages for breach of this promise ('breach of warranty of authority') will normally be **1.113** such as to put the third party in the position in which he would have been if the agent had had authority: hence if the principal is insolvent, and damages would not have been effectively recoverable against him, the agent's breach may cause no loss.[235] If the principal ratifies, the better view seems to be that the agent is still in breach of contract but causes no loss.[236] In

---

[225] A well-known starting point is *Universal SN Co v McKelvie* [1923] AC 492, HL. Many examples appear in *Bowstead and Reynolds on Agency* (20th edn, 2014) Art 99.

[226] See *Chitty on Contracts* (31st edn, 2012) paras 12-041ff.

[227] See *Chitty on Contracts* (31st edn, 2012) paras 12-096ff.

[228] *Higgins v Senior* (1841) 8 M & W 834.

[229] See 1.31.

[230] See *Gardiner v Heading* [1928] 2 KB 284; *Rayner v Grote* (1846) 15 M & W 359, 153 ER 888.

[231] eg *Kelner v Baxter* (1866) LR 2 CP 174.

[232] Companies Act 1985, s 36C(1), held to confer a right of action also in *Braymist Ltd v Wise Finance Co Ltd* [2002] EWCA Civ 127, [2002] Ch 273, CA. See now Companies Act 2006, s 51.

[233] The leading case is still *Collen v Wright* (1857) 7 E & B 310, 119 ER 1259, affd (1857) 8 E & B 647, 120 ER 241. See FMB Reynolds, 'Breach of Warranty of Authority in Modern Times' [2012] LMCLQ 189. Some commentators state a preference for a rule that the agent only undertakes a duty of care: but if one rule is well established, it is that of strict liability in this context, despite the fact that professionals, eg solicitors, are normally liable only for negligence.

[234] *Lilly, Wilson & Co v Smales, Eeles & Co* [1892] 1 QB 456. Evidence was given of the commercial understanding of the phrase.

[235] *Firbank's Executors v Humphreys* (1886) 18 QBD 54, CA. For a more complex example in connection with a false bill of lading, see *Heskell v Continental Express Ltd* [1950] 1 All ER 1033.

this sort of case damages often include consequential loss, such as the expense of an abortive action against, or at least negotiations with, the principal.

1.114 Much however turns on the context of the warranty which is detected. In the context of costs in litigation it has been held that solicitors promise (to the court) that they have a principal who exists, has capacity[237] and has authorized proceedings.[238] This reasoning could be used to solve the problem of non-existent principals.[239] But there is no promise that the principal has been correctly named,[240] and use of this specialized reasoning within the general law of contract has led to the assertion of a very narrow warranty, amounting to little more than one of due care by a solicitor acting for a client who has given a false identity.[241] On the other hand, a warranty has been held to be given to someone other than the third party; eg, to a mortgage lender who lent to a purchaser on a representation by the vendor's solicitor.[242]

(3) Agent's Liability in Tort

1.115 An agent is liable for his own torts. 'No one can escape liability for his fraud by saying "I wish to make it clear that I am committing this fraud on behalf of someone else and I am not to be personally liable"'.[243] Fraud is indeed a good example for this: another is defamation. But in the sphere of negligence there may be scope for argument. A solicitor for one side to a dispute who gives a (non-contractual) undertaking to the other may sometimes be held to have undertaken a duty of care;[244] and it may be possible to hold the person operating a one-man company personally liable by this route.[245] On the other hand a solicitor for one party to a conveyance who negligently gives wrong answers to inquiries from the other party has been held not liable to the other party, on the basis that he owed a duty to his principal only; though his principal would have been.[246] Whether or not this latter is correct (it has been said to be based on a rule peculiar to solicitors in conveyancing),[247] there are certainly cases where company directors have been held to undertake no personal duty when acting on behalf of their companies, the assumption being that the company *would* be liable;[248] and it may be that such reasoning, which is still the subject of controversy,[249] could sometimes be extended to others who are not directors. It is said however that an agent may not be liable

---

[236] The matter turns on whether apparent authority should be recognized as authority for this purpose.

[237] *Yonge v Toynbee* [1910] 1 KB 215 (supervening insanity).

[238] *Nelson v Nelson* [1997] 1 WLR 233, CA (no warranty of validity of action by person who was bankrupt).

[239] See 1.112.

[240] *AMB Generali Holding AG v SEB Trygg Holding AB* [2005] EWCA Civ 12337, [2006] 1 Lloyd's Rep 318, at [60]ff, following reasoning in *Nelson v Nelson* [1997] 1 WLR 233, CA; *Knight Frank LLP v Du Haney* [2011] EWCA Civ 404.

[241] *Excel Securities plc v Masood* [2010] 1 Lloyd's Rep PN 165; *Cheshire Mortgage Corp Ltd v Grandison* [2012] CSIH 66, [2013] PNLR 3. This can be regarded as attenuating the warranty too much: see Reynolds, 'Breach of Warranty of Authority in Modern Times' [2012] LMCLQ 189.

[242] *Penn v Bristol & West BS* [1997] 1 WLR 1356, CA.

[243] *Standard Chartered Bank v Pakistan National Shipping Corp (No 4)* [2002] UKHL 43, [2003] 1 AC 959, at [21], *per* Lord Hoffmann. As to fraud by directors see *Jetivia SA v Bilta (UK) Ltd* [2015] UKSC 23, [2015] 1 WLR 1168.

[244] *Al Kandari v JR Brown & Co* [1988] QB 665, CA. An agent cannot be liable under s 2(1) of the Misrepresentation Act 1967 (see EPL 8.169) by reason of its wording.

[245] *Fairline Shipping Corp v Adamson* [1975] QB 180.

[246] *Gran Gelato Ltd v Richcliff (Group) Ltd* [1992] Ch 560.

[247] *McCullagh v Lane Fox & Partners Ltd* [1996] 1 EGLR 35, CA, 43 *per* Hobhouse LJ; Cane (1992) 108 LQR 539.

[248] *Williams v Natural Life Health Foods Ltd* [1998] 1 WLR 830, HL; *Trevor Ivory Ltd v Anderson* [1992] 2 NZLR 517, CANZ. See EPL 17.168ff.

[249] See eg Flannigan (2002) 81 Can Bar Rev 247; Campbell and Armour [2003] CLJ 290; Reynolds (2003) 33 HKLJ 51; Stevens [2005] LMCLQ 101.

for the tort of inducement of breach of contract by his principal, for the true liability is that of the principal for the breach of contract.[250] This may be true if the agent is simply acting for his principal in breaking the contract. But if he acts in a way which breaches his own legal duty to his principal and also induces such a breach, he might be liable.[251] A significant line of cases holds an agent not liable in conversion where he deals with property on the instructions of his principal in a purely ministerial way.[252] These can be used to suggest a similar defence (largely) for banks in connection with the handling of money.

(4) Unjust Enrichment

Difficult questions arise where money is paid to an agent which is prima facie recoverable **1.116** in unjust enrichment, as eg where it is paid to him by mistake. If it is paid in pursuance of a transaction entered into by the agent personally, or in connection with a wrong done by the agent, the agent is clearly liable to repay.[253] Beyond this two competing principles are available. One is that money paid to the agent for the principal is paid to the principal and the principal is the person liable to repay it.[254] This is not unlike the tortious defence of ministerial receipt referred to above. The other is that where money is paid to the agent which is not due, he is himself liable to repay it unless he has, before notice of any claim for its repayment, in good faith paid it to his principal.[255] This latter defence is not unlike the defence of change of position available in unjust enrichment,[256] but is in fact separate and much older.[257] A distinction has been suggested between cases where the duty to repay arises immediately, as in the case of money paid by mistake, where the agent is liable; and those where it arises later, as where the contract on which it is paid later fails for some reason. This distinction has difficulties, and some of the cases cited in this connection do not really concern agents at all, eg where the first receiver is a bank. The matter is one for the law of unjust enrichment.[258]

E. The Use of Agency Reasoning in Non-contractual Situations

(1) Agency Reasoning in Connection with Property Issues

The text so far has largely concerned questions of contract made through agents. The same **1.117** reasoning applies, however, in the law of property: a person may transfer property through an agent, or acquire property through an agent.

(a) Land

(i) Conveyance by agent

In the case of land, one would of course expect special rules. In general, only the owner of **1.118** land can convey it, and unregistered land must be transferred by deed, a formal document signed and witnessed. The procedure for registered land involves a deed also.[259] A deed can

---

[250] *Said v Butt* [1920] 3 KB 497.
[251] See *The Leon* [1991] 2 Lloyd's Rep 611.
[252] eg *National Mercantile Bank v Rymill* (1881) 44 LT 767 (delivery of horses sold by another)
[253] *Snowdon v Davis* (1808) 1 Taunt 359.
[254] *Ellis v Goulton* [1893] 1 QB 350.
[255] *Buller v Harrison* (1777) 2 Cowp 565, 98 ER 1243.
[256] See Goff and Jones, *Unjust Enrichment* (8th edn. 2011), paras 28-14ff.
[257] See *Portman BS v Hamlin Taylor Neck* [1998] 4 All ER 202, CA.
[258] See A Burrows, *Law of Restitution* (3rd edn, 2011) 558ff; Stevens [2005] LMCLQ 101. For a recent decision see *Jones v Churcher* [2009] EWHC 722 (QB), [2009] 2 Lloyd's Rep 94.

be executed by a mere amanuensis, but otherwise an agent executing a deed for his principal would normally require authorization by power of attorney, a formal document conferring the appropriate authority, which must itself be a deed.[260] An agent can enter into a *contract* regarding land on his principal's behalf, and this does not need formal authorization (though the contract itself would be subject to a requirement of writing):[261] it would confer equitable (but not legal) proprietary rights on the principal.

(ii) Conveyance to agent

1.119 If an agent takes a conveyance to himself on his principal's behalf, he holds the land on trust for his principal despite the lack of written evidence required by statute,[262] for to allow insistence on invalidity of the contract would permit the rule (which stems from the Statute of Frauds 1677) to be used as an instrument of fraud.[263]

(b) Chattels

(i) Conveyance by agent

1.120 In the case of chattels there are usually no such formal requirements, and an agent can have actual authority to transfer his principal's property, neither the conferring of authority nor the transfer of the chattel requiring (except in special situations) formality. The doctrine of apparent authority is also applicable here.[264] In that context the latter doctrine causes special difficulties if, as is normally said, it is based on estoppel, for estoppel is a doctrine operating only between two parties and their privies, a notion considerably developed in connection with land; whereas it has been said by Devlin J, a distinguished authority, that in respect of chattels the effect of a transfer by an agent with apparent authority, at least under a sale, is to confer 'a real title and not merely a metaphysical title by estoppel',[265] ie one which is good against the world.

1.121 Current English authority suggests that (though more specific 'classic'[266] estoppel situations are, as in contract, also perfectly possible) the estoppel principle invoked is a general one concerning persons held out to the world as authorized to sell goods, and probably also to transfer them in other ways. It is reinforced in the context of sale of goods by section 21 of the Sale of Goods Act 1979, which refers to cases where the 'owner is by his conduct precluded from denying the seller's authority to sell'. The lack in common law of any general provision protecting bona fide purchasers of chattels means however that the mere holding of the goods of another does not give rise to apparent authority to dispose of them, for if it did 'no one would be safe in parting with possession of anything'.[267] Something additional is required such as some written authority to dispose of them, or the fact that the holder is a person who normally disposes of the goods of others, such as the nineteenth-century factor.

1.122 In this context there are two special variants of the reasoning. The first is the doctrine of apparent ownership, which arises where one person allows another to appear as the owner of goods. Although true estoppel is possible here also, it seems that the general doctrine is no more than a stronger example of that referred to above. However, to trigger it off, it is again

---

[259] See Land Registration Act 2002, s 25; Land Registration Rules 2003, Sch 9.
[260] Powers of Attorney Act 1971 as amended, s 1(1).
[261] Law of Property (Miscellaneous Provisions) Act 1989, s 2.
[262] Law of Property Act 1925, s 53.
[263] *Rochefoucauld v Boustead* [1897] 1 Ch 196, CA.
[264] *Eastern Distributors Ltd v Goldring* [1957] 2 QB 600, CA.
[265] *Eastern Distributors Ltd v Goldring* [1957] 2 QB 600, 611, CA.
[266] See 1.71.
[267] *Weiner v Gill* [1905] 2 KB 172, 182; and see *Farquharson Bros & Co v King & Co* [1902] AC 325, HL.

not sufficient merely to allow someone else to hold one's goods or even documents of title or other documents relating to them, for that person might be a mere bailee: something more is again needed, such as signing a document offering to buy the goods from that person, or permitting registration of the goods in that person's name.[268]

A situation raising greater problems of analysis is the not uncommon one of a person given a **1.123** document, such as part of the indicia of title to property, and authorized to raise money on the security of it, who then borrows more than was authorized. Such a person has no actual authority as regards the sum borrowed, and the mere possession of indicia of title does not confer apparent authority to make a property disposition at all. Nevertheless a well-known but controversial group of cases holds the principal bound on such facts.[269] The principle (if there is one), which has been called the 'arming principle',[270] creates a problem which awaits resolution. The cases seem to involve a confusion with quite different property principles relating to priority of mortgages and it is unlikely that much should be made of them. It is however conceivable that a principal exposing himself to such risks could be regarded as conferring *actual* authority.

Statute here intervenes to protect third parties. The need arose in connection with the **1.124** nineteenth-century factor who, as has been said,[271] was an intermediary holding goods on consignment, often from overseas, who might own them or not and might deal on his own account or on the account of a principal elsewhere. When factors sold goods, the buyer and subsequent buyers were protected by the doctrine of apparent authority as described above, for the factor legitimately held the goods (or the documents of title to them) and his occupation involved the selling of the goods of others. The doctrine of apparent ownership might also sometimes apply. Factors however often raised money on the security of goods by pledging them, or when they were in transit by pledging them by means of the documents representing them (which might arrive long before the goods themselves). It was established that a factor had no apparent authority to *pledge* goods as opposed to selling them. The third party might however have no way of knowing whether the factor owned the goods, or was authorized by the owner, or not.

To deal with the problem a series of statutes were passed during the nineteenth century to **1.125** protect third parties in such cases (including that of sale): they are referred to as the Factors Acts. They contain various specialized provisions for achieving some of the same effects as are achieved in some other countries by more general rules protecting bona fide purchasers. That most relevant to basic agency law is section 2 of the Factors Act 1889, which protects third parties buying in good faith from a 'mercantile agent' who is in possession of goods or documents of title to goods (this phrase being interpreted in a wide sense) with the consent of the owner. In many circumstances this legislation can be relied on without the need for establishing apparent authority. The Act is not however entirely a statutory expression of apparent authority as it contains specific requirements that must exist, yet the existence of which may not be knowable by the third party. This is true in particular of whether the transferor is a 'mercantile agent' (a term defined in a somewhat circular way, but giving rise to considerable case law), whether he holds the goods or documents with the consent of the owner, and in what capacity he holds them, which must be that of a mercantile agent.

---

[268] See *Pickering v Busk* (1812) 15 East 38, 104 ER 758; *Central Newbury Car Auctions Ltd v Unity Finance Ltd* [1957] 1 QB 371, CA; Watts (2002) 2 OU Commonwealth LJ 93.

[269] The leading case is *Brocklesby v Temperance BS* [1895] AC 173, HL.

[270] *Macmillan Inc v Bishopsgate Investment Trust plc (No 2)* [1995] 1 WLR 978, 1012,

[271] See 1.24.

(ii) Conveyance to agent

1.126 Difficulties regarding land apart, property can also be acquired through an agent, though the agent may of course nevertheless retain *possession*. This is made easier by the fact that in the contract of sale of goods property passes by mere intention. Acquisition through *undisclosed* principals raises (as usual) greater problems, since the third party is (often, at least) unaware of the existence of the principal and hence does not intend to transfer property to him. On the basis of pure intention (which controls the transfer of property in sale[272]) property would be transferred to the agent, who then retransfers it (or should) to the principal. On the other hand it is said that the original purpose of the doctrine was to allow intervention by the principal in the agent's bankruptcy, and this would appear to require immediate vesting in the principal. A notoriously obscure, but conceptually significant, provision of the Sale of Goods Act 1979,[273] basing itself on nineteenth-century cases on factors and (perhaps) foreign *commissionnaires*,[274] appears to assume that the property vests first in the agent, as it gives him the rights of an unpaid seller against a buyer in respect of disposal of the goods and stoppage in transit.

(2) Agency Reasoning Used Against the Principal in Tort Cases

1.127 In the United States, traditional agency courses sought to discern general principles of representation applicable in both contract and in tort situations. Such an exercise is, at least for English law, one of major theoretical creativity, in that the approach to questions of liability for the acts of others in tort law is for the most part quite different from that taken in contract and property law. The treatment adopted in this chapter is to treat agency law as relevant to contract (including some restitutionary situations) and property; and hence largely to omit discussion of tort liability.[275] Nevertheless, there is some overlap and brief reference to tort is necessary.

1.128 The normal starting point for liability for torts in English law has been to take a distinction between 'servants' and 'independent contractors'. It is assumed that for both the liability, when it exists, is vicarious: that is to say the employee (formerly referred to as 'servant') or independent contractor commits a wrong for which he is responsible, but for which the employer or principal is also responsible. Such vicarious liability is in common law usually treated as a form of strict liability. As to servants or employees, the liability has traditionally been regarded as covering acts done within the course of their employment, even where they do something which they have been forbidden to do. However, recently the test has been reformulated, in response to a need to create vicarious liability where the employee is guilty of wilful wrongdoing, to require that the tort was 'so closely connected with his employment that it would be fair and just to hold the [employer] vicariously liable'.[276] This has been taken to replace the traditional test, which looked in such cases at whether the employee's actions were an unauthorized mode of performing an authorized act.

---

[272] Sale of Goods Act 1979, s 17.
[273] Sale of Goods Act 1979, s 38(2).
[274] eg *Tetley v Shand* (1871) 25 LT 658; *Cassaboglou v Gibb* (1883) 11 QBD 797. See 9.18.
[275] See 1.26, 1.27.
[276] *Lister v Hesley Hall Ltd* [2001] UKHL 22, [2002] 1 AC 215, HL. The problem has been analysed also in Canada: *Bazley v Currie* [1999] 2 SCR 534, SC Can: and Australia: *New South Wales v Lepore* (2004) 212 CLR 511, HCA. All these cases concern abuse of children by employees of schools. The test now adopted comes from the Canadian case, and was rejected in Australia. But recent decisions appear to be widening the scope further: see *UGE v Trustees of the Portsmouth Roman Catholic Diocesan Trust* [2012] EWCA Civ 938, [2012] 4 All ER 1152; *Various Claimants v Catholic Child Welfare Society* [2012] UKSC 56, [2013] 2 AC 1. See in general EPL 17.367ff.

The wrongs of deceit and misrepresentation are frequently committed in connection with **1.129** a contract, by a person who may or may not have authority to make the statement in question. Hence where these are involved, the terminology of authority, and the word 'agent' for the employee, may seem more natural and appropriate than that of employer and employee. It has furthermore been held in connection with the tort of deceit that where there is no liability on the basis of authority reasoning (which would include apparent authority reasoning) the tort 'course of employment' reasoning (as then used) could not be invoked to make the principal liable on a statement which the agent was known by the third party to have no authority to make;[277] and the reasoning is capable of being extended to other torts of misrepresentation also. However, it has recently been held in the context of bank employees that this deceit reasoning goes no further, and that for negligence causing economic loss the principal is liable on the basis of 'close connection' rather than that of actual or apparent authority.[278]

As to independent contractors, a standard view has been that there was no vicarious liability **1.130** for them except in the case where they were performing a non-delegable duty. It has however proved difficult to identify and provide a rationale for such duties. It is probably better to regard liability for independent contractors as not vicarious, but as occurring in the course of a primary liability of a principal to secure certain sorts of result. Indeed, a result of the recent reformulation of the applicability of liability for employees referred to above, it may be that such an explanation will eventually envelop that also.[279]

The relevance of agency here is that the principal may sometimes be liable for economic loss **1.131** caused by negligent statements by persons who can reasonably be called independent contractors but who are also persons in respect of some of whose activities the notion of authority, and even the term agent, seems relevant and applicable. Thus a principal may be liable for statements by estate agents[280] and solicitors.[281] There is leading authority that in the case of misrepresentation, the tort involves an assumption of responsibility for the truth of the statement.[282] Where the agent personally assumes such responsibility[283] the principal may or may not also be liable for his statements, depending on whether they are actually or apparently authorized. But in some circumstances the agent does not do so at all, yet it is assumed that the principal would still be liable, and this must also be on the basis of the statement being authorized.[284] This indicates a role for authority reasoning in this context even if it is correct that it does not apply in the context of employment. Even if the 'close connection' test for vicarious liability is appropriate in respect of liability for employees, it would here give an even looser rule for situations involving negligent statements.

---

[277] *Armagas Ltd v Mundogas SA (The Ocean Frost)* [1986] AC 717, HL.

[278] So v *HSBC Bank plc* [2009] EWCA Civ 296, [2009] 1 CLC 503, CA; but cf *Kooragang Investments plc v Richardson & Wrench Ltd* [1982] AC 462, PC. See Watts, 'Some Wear and Tear on *Armagas v Mundogas*' [2015] LMCLQ 36.

[279] See *Lister v Hesley Hall Ltd*, n 276, at [55] *per* Lord Hobhouse of Woodborough. This category is addressed and somewhat extended in *Woodland v Essex CC* [2013] UKSC 66, [2014] AC 537.

[280] See *Armstrong v Strain* [1952] 1 QB 232.

[281] *Cemp Properties (UK) Ltd v Dentsply Research and Development Corp* [1989] 2 EGLR 196. See also *Gran Gelato Ltd v Richcliff Group Ltd* [1992] Ch 560.

[282] *Williams v Natural Life Health Foods Ltd* [1998] 1 WLR 830, HL (report by director to third party).

[283] See 1.115.

[284] *Williams v Natural Life Health Foods Ltd* [1998] 1 WLR 830, HL. See also *Gran Gelato Ltd v Richcliff Group Ltd*, n 281. An unusual case is *Colonial Mutual Life Assurance Society Ltd v Producers and Citizens Cooperative Insurance Co of Australia* (1931) 46 CLR 41, HCA, where an insurance company was held liable for defamation of another company by an independent insurance representative.

(3) Notification, Notice and Knowledge Through the Agent

1.132 Agency reasoning is also deployed in situations where it is necessary to determine whether a particular person or organization had been notified of, had notice of or knew (or must be taken to have known) certain information. This is an obvious use for such reasoning, particularly in the case of companies, where any knowledge must necessarily be of a human being connected with it. It is however far from clear when such notice can be attributed to a principal through his agent.

1.133 Where the question concerns formal notification, such as a notice to quit, problems can generally be solved by the normal principles of authority, that is to say, by asking whether the person giving or receiving the notification had actual or apparent authority to give or receive it.[285]

1.134 Where however it concerns actual or constructive notice, as in the doctrine of the bona fide purchaser without notice, or under section 2 of the Factors Act 1889;[286] or knowledge or imputed knowledge, as in the case of accessory liability to a breach of trust or fiduciary duty, the question is more difficult. It is certainly true that the law may impute knowledge to a principal which an agent acquired while acting as agent, and that in some situations knowledge which the agent already had when he became agent, or acquired outside his agency function, may also be so imputed; but a proper analysis of the cases is beyond the scope of this chapter.[287] Sometimes the matter is one of interpreting what a statutory provision was intended to cover. It is in this area that leading examples of 'organ' reasoning are to be found: that is to say, cases where notice or knowledge is sought to be attributed to a company.[288] It is said that for this purpose the knowledge must be of a person within the organization who has management or control—not necessarily in general, but in relation to the activity in question.[289]

F. The Internal Relationship Between Principal and Agent

1.135 This topic covers not only agents who have power to affect their principal's position externally, but also agents who only have the internal relationship with their principals, elsewhere referred to as 'canvassing agents', and, if the category exists at common law, *commissionnaires* or 'indirect agents'.[290] It requires division into two topics: the duties of the agent towards the principal, and the duties of the principal towards the agent. The former topic is far more extensive, because common law has always thought of the principal as being in need of protection against the agent, rather than the reverse. With the former topic it is also necessary to distinguish between common law and equity, as the rules of equity are prominent in this area.

---

[285] eg *Tanham v Nicholson* (1872) LR 5 HL 561.

[286] See 1.125.

[287] See the exposition of Hoffmann LJ in *El Ajou v Dollar Land Holdings Ltd* [1994] 2 All ER 685, CA: but cf *Permanent Trustee Australia Co Ltd v FAI General Insurance Co Ltd* (2001) 50 NSWLR 679, CA NSW, esp at [76]ff (reversed on other grounds (2003) 214 CLR 514, HCA). Such imputation may not necessarily apply where the agent is defrauding the principal: eg *Rolland v Hart* (1871) LR 6 Ch App 678. See *Stone & Rolls v Moore Stephens* [2009] UKHL 39, [2009] 1 AC 1391, HL; *Jetivia SA v Bilta (UK) Ltd* [2015] UKSC 23 [2015] 1 WLR 1168. See in general on this difficult topic *Bowstead and Reynolds on Agency* (20th edn, 2014) Art 95.

[288] See 1.22.

[289] See 1.22.

[290] See 1.15ff.

(1) Duties of the Agent Towards the Principal

(a) Common law

Where a contract between principal and agent is involved, the duties will be based on the **1.136** express or implied terms of that contract. The first question may be whether the agent has promised to act at all: if not, he is only liable if he does so. This can be true, eg, of estate agency arrangements, where the agent need not promise to act in any way,[291] and of some powers of attorney. The common law is fairly strict as regards the implication of terms, but there is no great difficulty in holding a person promising services, which is what a contractual agent does, to be under a duty of care to act in the principal's interest, in accordance with normal standards of reasonableness and also, when an agent in a trade or profession is involved, the normal standards of that trade or profession. An agent may not act outside his authority, however much it may seem prudent to do so, unless perhaps some situation of necessity is involved;[292] and, if he has accepted specific instructions, must carry them out however imprudent he believes them to be.[293] These are rare examples of strict liability of an agent.[294] If he acts in such a way as to make the principal liable under the doctrine of apparent authority he may be liable to his principal, sometimes even if the principal ratifies.[295] If a person who has no contractual relationship with the principal does the same, it would seem that he should be liable to the principal in tort on the same basis.[296]

A contractual agent can also in English law be liable to his principal in tort,[297] and such **1.137** liability may yield slightly different results, eg in connection with operation of the limitation period. It could not however increase the contractual duty.[298] A gratuitous agent, ie one operating under an arrangement where no consideration can be found, cannot of course be liable in contract, and hence his only liability is in tort. This means that he cannot in principle be held liable for pure non-feasance. But someone who can be called a gratuitous agent can fairly easily be regarded as having undertaken a responsibility which generates a duty to go through with it with due care.[299] The duty undertaken in such a case is not different in principle from that applicable to a non-gratuitous agent, as the common law does not accept specific differences of duty for different types of situation. It has been expressed in general terms as 'that which may reasonably be expected of him in all the circumstances'.[300] In practice, of course, there are likely to be differences from contractual agency.

---

[291] ie in common law terms the contract may be unilateral—the agent need not act, but if he does and qualifies for commission he is entitled to it: see *Luxor (Eastbourne) Ltd v Cooper* [1941] AC 108, HL. This is not inevitable: in particular the appointment of an 'exclusive agent' is normally taken to indicate a bilateral contract with obligations on the agent as well as on the principal.

[292] See 1.94.

[293] This has arisen in connection with stockbrokers: eg *RH Deacon & Co v Varga* (1972) 30 DLR (3d) 653, aff'd (1973) 41 DLR (4th) 767n; *Volkers v Midland Doherty* (1985) 17 DLR (4th) 343.

[294] See 1.12.

[295] See 1.45.

[296] See *Bowstead and Reynolds on Agency* (20th edn, 2014) para 6-003.

[297] *Henderson v Merrett Syndicates Ltd* [1995] 2 AC 145, HL.

[298] *Tai Hing Cotton Mill Ltd v Liu Chong Hing Bank Ltd* [1986] AC 80, PC.

[299] See *Henderson v Merrett Syndicates Ltd*, n 297; *London Borough of Bromley v Ellis* [1971] 1 Lloyd's Rep 97; *Norwest Refrigeration Services Pty Ltd v Bain Dawes (WA) Pty Ltd* (1984) 157 CLR 149, HCA. The matter frequently comes up in connection with insurance, especially its renewal: the persons concerned may well be or have been agents in other respects. Sometimes such an agent is in effect 'self-appointed': in such a case he may owe the same sort of duty, and may be liable for going outside it. See *Montrod Ltd v Grundkotter Fleischvertriebs GmbH* [2001] EWCA Civ 1954, [2002] 1 WLR 1975, CA.

[300] *Chaudhry v Prabakhar* [1989] 1 WLR 29, 34, 37, CA (person undertaking to inspect car for another).

(b) Equity: fiduciary duties[301]

1.138 A conspicuous feature of the law of agency, already mentioned, is that all agents are potentially subject to the special controls imposed by equity on fiduciaries generally. It has been said that 'A fiduciary is someone who has undertaken to act for and on behalf of another in a particular matter in circumstances which give rise to a relationship of trust and confidence.'[302] This definition plainly covers persons exercising agency functions.

1.139 The equitable rules relating to fiduciaries fill gaps which might otherwise be created by the comparative reluctance of common law, at any rate in England, to find implied contract terms; and provide a technique for situations where in other systems notions of good faith might be invoked. But they may go further. 'The essence of a fiduciary obligation is that it creates obligations of a different character from those deriving from the contract itself.'[303] The law on fiduciary duties is rich and flexible, though still in a process of development and differing among common law countries. The rules are a variant of the duties originally imposed on express trustees, and stem from the same principles of equity. But they are and always have been of a more moderate nature than those for express trustees: eg, instead of forbidding certain sorts of act altogether, as in the case of trustees purchasing trust property, they normally only regard such acts as wrong if they are done without full disclosure to the beneficiary of the duty. Older cases made more use of the trust analogy than is common nowadays, when there is more attention to the development of general principles of equity.

1.140 The fiduciary duties are not confined to agency situations but stem from those general principles; hence it can be said that such duties are not a defining feature of the internal agency relationship at all, but simply a set of external rules which can often be applicable in agency situations. This question of the extent to which the fiduciary duties should be regarded as a definitional feature of agency is susceptible of sustained argument, and it has already been suggested that the answer to it is to some extent a matter of preference in exposition.[304] In *Kelly v Cooper*, a fairly recent Privy Council decision concerning an estate agent in Bermuda, holding that there was no duty on such an agent to reveal to one client the plans of another even though they affected the first client, there are strong dicta that the relationship between principal and agent turns only on the terms of the contract between them.[305] Assuming the actual decision to be correct, it simply decides that the fiduciary duty does not extend as far as had been argued: any duty lay at common law only.[306] Fiduciary duties can however operate for estate agents in other respects. No one could doubt, eg, that such an agent should not conceal offers made to him for his client. Agency is in fact a paradigm case for the application of fiduciary duties, and though they can be complied with by disclosure, or modified by agreement or by the circumstances, if they are totally excluded, the supposed agency relationship might no longer rank as such. Even a messenger with a specific message to carry could be under limited duties, eg not to take a bribe or make a secret profit in connection with its delivery.

1.141 It is sometimes argued that the basic fiduciary duties are negative, in that they prohibit conduct rather than impose positive duties; and sometimes also that they are confined to two

---

[301] This is part of a wider topic, on which see McGhee (gen ed), *Snell's Equity* (33rd edn, 2015) ch 7; *Bowstead and Reynolds on Agency* (20th edn, 2014) Arts 43 ff. See discussion at EPL 17.328ff.
[302] *Bristol & West BS v Mothew* [1998] Ch 1, 18, *per* Millett LJ.
[303] *Re Goldcorp Exchange Ltd* [1995] 1 AC 74, 98, PC, *per* Lord Mustill.
[304] See 1.17.
[305] *Kelly v Cooper* [1993] AC 205, HL, see esp 213–214, *per* Lord Browne-Wilkinson.
[306] There is useful discussion of the case in *Rossetti Marketing Ltd v Diamond Sofa Co Ltd* [2012] EWCA Civ 1021; [2013] 1 All ER (Comm) 308, CA.

basic prophylactic duties, not to profit from one's position and not to assume a position in which there could be a conflict of interest.[307] These basic duties then manifest themselves in situations where more specific findings are made and more specific remedies employed. On this approach, other duties relevant to agents may also arise: they can be brought within the scope of a looser term such as 'duties of loyalty', but though related, are not all rightly described as fiduciary. They are to be found particularly in connection with company directors, eg a duty to reveal wrongdoing by others,[308] and, according to one case, by the director himself of his own wrongdoing.[309] The question can then arise whether such a duty extends to employees, at any rate senior employees, also.[310] This distinction is not often, if at all, made in the cases, where the term 'fiduciary' is often used in a very wide sense; but it can be a useful guide to their analysis.

(i) Scope of the duties

The applicability of the fiduciary duties and their extent varies very much from one situation to another. There have been numerous warnings in the cases as to the misuse of fiduciary reasoning.[311] It has been said that 'The precise scope of [the obligation] must be moulded according to the nature of the relationship.'[312] The main potentially applicable fiduciary duties may however be listed as follows. The agent must not use his position[313] or his principal's property[314] to secure undisclosed benefits, called 'secret profits', for himself: this rule has been applied very strictly even where the principal would without the agent's intervention have done worse financially, and has sometimes been stated in stern terms which would find a breach of duty because there was no more than a possibility that a conflict of interest *might* arise.[315] He must not without disclosure (which could be satisfied where there was general knowledge and acceptance of a practice) take secret commissions or discounts, often referred to more directly as bribes, from the other party to a transaction, and if he does so is liable whether or not the payment (or promise of it) influenced him.[316] The agent must make full disclosure when he deals with his principal: he must not without disclosure when employed to buy, sell his own property (including where it was acquired for the purpose of such a sale)

1.142

---

[307] See R Nolan, 'A Fuduciary Duty to Disclose?' (1997) 113 LQR 220; R Flannigan, 'Fiduciary Duties of Shareholders and Directors' [2004] JBL 277; R Flannigan, 'The Adulteration of Fiduciary Doctrines in Corporate Law' (2006) 122 LQR 449; M Conaglen, *Fiduciary Loyalty* (2010).

[308] *Bell v Lever Bros* [1932] AC 161.

[309] *Item Software (UK) Ltd v Fassihi* [2004] EWCA Civ 1244, [2005] ICR 450, CA. The fiduciary and other duties of directors are now governed by the Companies Act 2006. See EPL 3.62, EPL 3.77ff.

[310] See *Helmet Integrated Systems Ltd v Tunnard* [2006] EWCA Civ 1735, [2007] IRLR 126 on intention to leave a post and compete.

[311] A famous example is the dictum of Fletcher Moulton LJ in *Re Coomber* [1911] 1 Ch 723, 728–729, CA.

[312] *New Zealand Netherlands Society 'Oranje' Inc v Kuys* [1973] 1 WLR 1126, 1130, PC, *per* Lord Wilberforce.

[313] A possible example is *Phipps v Boardman* [1967] 2 AC 46, though the persons who so profited were not really agents in the technical sense.

[314] See the unusual case of *Reid-Newfoundland Co v Anglo-American Telegraph Co Ltd* [1912] AC 555, PC (profit from unauthorized use of telegraph wire).

[315] eg *Phipps v Boardman*, n 313, at 111; *Aberdeen Rly Co v Blaikie Brothers* (18540 1 Macq 461, 471, *per* Lord Cranworth LC.

[316] *Harrington v Victoria Graving Dock Co* (1878) 3 QBD 549. The rules as regards bribery, though raising conceptual difficulties as to remedies, are fairly well worked out. The principle is however wider and probably applies to participation in any breach of fiduciary duty by the agent. The seminal case, *Panama & South Pacific Telegraph Co v India Rubber, Gutta Percha and Telegraph Works Co* (1878) LR 10 Ch App 515, does not concern actual bribery; but see *Tigris International NV v South China Airlines Co Ltd* [2014] EWCA Civ 1649. See further *Petrotrade Inc v Smith* [2000] 1 Lloyd's Rep 486; *Fyffes Group Ltd v Templeman* [2000] 2 Lloyd's Rep 643. Bribery is partly regulated by the Bribery Act 2010.

to his principal;[317] nor when employed to sell may he without disclosure buy the property himself.[318] He must not use or make a profit from his principal's confidential information; though this goes outside the scope of fiduciary duties and depends largely on the law as to breach of confidence, which applies in many spheres other than that of agency.[319]

1.143 All these situations involve a conflict of interest, or potential conflict, between agent and principal. But the fiduciary duties extend also to situations where there is or may be a conflict of interest between two principals, each of which is entitled to the agent's full loyalty: his loyalty to one may put him in breach of his duty to the other, and he must disclose the position to each,[320] even if the matters in respect of which he acts for them are different.[321] The court in *Kelly v Cooper*, referred to above,[322] found no such duty in the case of an estate agent; but the conflict could arise in other areas of activity. Even if he discloses to each that he is acting for the other, the agent 'must not allow the performance of his obligations to one principal to be influenced by his relationship with the other'; nor must he get into a position where 'he cannot fulfil his obligations to one without failing in his obligations to the other'.[323] Problems more specifically based on the law as to breach of confidence may arise also where he has information in respect of a former client which his duty to a present client arguably may require him to disclose. Questions may arise in both the above contexts within firms (eg, of solicitors or accountants), as to whether protection from such conflicts of interest in which different parts of the firm are involved may be secured by 'Chinese walls'. English courts have not always looked favourably on such devices.[324]

(ii) Exclusion of fiduciary duties

1.144 With the abolition of 'single capacity' rules in financial markets (ie rules that inter alia prevent agents from acting also in other capacities), clauses have been increasingly inserted into intermediaries' contracts which seek to establish that the intermediary may, eg, sell his own shares to the principal and in general act in a way inconsistent with the fiduciary duties. Such clauses should only in principle be valid if they constitute the relevant disclosure, or make clear that the person concerned does not act as agent in the legal sense, at least in the relevant respects.[325] Standards are also sometimes laid down by regulatory bodies, and it is argued or assumed that compliance with these cannot contravene the fiduciary duties. It is not clear that this is always correct: a power to override duties imposed by law would need to be clearly conferred. Current practice is based on public regulation of the financial markets,[326] but the fiduciary principles of private law have not yet been completely superseded.

---

[317] *Regier v Campbell-Stuart* [1939] Ch 766.

[318] *Dunne v English* (1874) LR 18 Eq 524. Even where there is disclosure, there may in both these cases be an additional requirement that he proves the transaction is a fair one.

[319] The different role of confidence principles is well exemplified in the *Prince Jefri Bolkiah* case, n 324.

[320] *Clark Boyce v Mouat* [1994] 1 AC 428, PC; *Imageview Management Ltd v Jack* [2009] EWCA Civ 63, [2009] 2 All ER 666, CA (a striking decision: agent to find employment for footballer accepted fee from employer of footballer for obtaining immigration permit for client).

[321] *Marks & Spencer plc v Freshfields Bruckhaus Deringer* [2004] EWCA Civ 741, [2005] PNLR 4; affirming [2004] EWHC 1337, [2004] 1 WLR 2331.

[322] [1993] AC 205, HL: see 1.140.

[323] *Bristol & West BS v Mothew* [1998] Ch 1, CA, 19, *per* Millett LJ. For examples see *Moody v Cox & Hatt* [1917] 2 Ch 71, CA; *Hilton v Barker Booth & Eastwood* [2005] UKHL 8, [2005] 1 WLR 567, HL, though both largely concerning the position of solicitors.

[324] *Prince Jefri Bolkiah v KPMG* [1999] 2 AC 222, HL (accountants); the *Marks & Spencer* case, n 321 (solicitors); Hollander and Salzedo, *Conflicts of Interest and Chinese Walls* (4th edn, 2011).

[325] A very wide clause was assumed to be valid unless statute intervenes in *Spread Trustee Co Ltd v Hutcheson* [2011] UKPC 13, [2012] 2 AC 194.

[326] Financial Services and Markets Act 2000, as amended, esp by Financial Services and Markets Act 2012.

(iii) Remedies[327]

1.145 The liability of an agent to his principal is often referred to as a duty to account, and this phrase is sometimes loosely used. The words hark back to the traditional remedy against the agent, which was to seek an account in equity. Nowadays the phrase tends to be used in a more general sense to refer to remedies for the principal against the agent, whether *in rem* or *in personam*. The Limitation Act 1980[328] itself recognizes that the claims which give rise to the duty to account may differ. The general remedy of equity is (apart from the decrees of specific performance and injunction) the detection of a trust; and the basic approach to breach of fiduciary duties can be said to be that the law assumes that the agent who makes a secret profit has done so on his principal's account[329] and therefore holds that profit on constructive trust for his principal. For a long time it was assumed that this principle, even if applicable to other benefits obtained, did not extend to bribes, but a well-known Privy Council decision of 1994 held that it did.[330] Although some expressed doubt, this proprietary result has recently been approved by the Supreme Court, with the implication that it applies outside the sphere of bribery.[331] The proprietary remedy raises problems (as do other situations where trusts are found) because of the priority in bankruptcy which it accords. It may also give a more favourable position when limitation of actions is invoked, because the normal rules do not apply to actions to recover trust property from a trustee;[332] and it may give rise to a further right to trace property in equity.[333] Hence there has also been a trend towards regarding the duty to account as one often operating *in personam* only.[334] Where agents buy from or sell to their principals, rescission is available;[335] and in the case of bribery the transaction may even be rescinded against the third party (who is also liable in damages).[336] In the case of conflict between the interests of two principals, one of them may obtain an injunction to restrain the agent from acting as he proposes.[337]

1.146 The jurisdiction of courts of equity to award damages has long been controversial, but there are obviously cases where it can only be said that a breach of duty has caused loss. It is now accepted that there are cases where damages (sometimes referred to as 'equitable compensation') can be awarded in connection with such loss, even though the duty broken only lies in equity.[338] This jurisdiction is currently developing.[339] It may apply, eg, not only

---

[327] See EPL ch 21, esp 21.133–21.137, 21.156–21.158.

[328] Section 23.

[329] See a seminal article by the Hon Sir Peter Millett (later Lord Millett), 'Bribes and Secret Commissions' [1993] Restitution L Rev 7; also 'Bribes and Secret Commissions Again' [2012] CLJ 583.

[330] *A-G for Hong Kong v Reid* [1994] 1 AC 324, PC (but regarded at the time as valid for English law also).

[331] *FHR European Ventures LLP v Cedar Capital Partners LLC* [2014] UKSC 45, [2015] AC 250. See Gummow, (2015) 131 LQR 21.

[332] Limitation Act 1980, s 21(1); and there are differences in respect of other equitable claims also. For a recent decision see *Williams v Central Bank of Nigeria* [2014] UKSC 10, [2014] AC 1189.

[333] See Goff and Jones, *Unjust Enrichment* (8th edn, 2011) ch 7.

[334] See *Warman International Ltd v Dwyer* (1995) 182 CLR 544, HCA.

[335] The question of profits may require different treatment in the case of agents selling property to their principals. If the agent acquires the property and sells it to his principal, there may be a secret profit, but if he sells property which he already holds the right may be to rescission only.

[336] See *Mahesan v Malaysian Government Officers Cooperative Housing Society Ltd* [1979] AC 374, PC. No credit need be given, in the calculation of damages, for a bribe received: *Logicrose v Southend United FC* [1988] 1 WLR 1256. See n 316.

[337] As in the *Prince Jefri Bolkiah* case, n 324 and the *Marks & Spencer* case, n 321. The cases here overlap with protection against breach of confidence, a separate topic.

[338] *Target Holdings Ltd v Redferns* [1996] AC 421, HL. This decision is usually taken as the leading one on the topic for English law; but the true issue can be said to have been the narrower one of restoring the trust estate. See *Youyang Pty Ltd v Minter Ellison Morris Fletcher* (2003) 212 CLR 484, HCA; S Elliott and J Edelman, '*Target Holdings* Considered in Australia' (2003) 119 LQR 545.

[339] Most recently in *AIB Group plc v Mark Redler & Co* [2014] UKSC 58, [2014] 3 WLR 1367 (see Ho, (2015) 131 LQR 213); see also valuable discussion in *Libertarian Investments Ltd v Hall* [2014] HKC 368, HKCFA.

in cases of conflict of duty and interest, but also in cases of conflict of duty and duty: where an injunction is not appropriate, an award of damages for loss caused may be. Often however such awards can be justified on common law principles as based on fraud, or breach of a contractual duty to take care or to place the agent's knowledge at the disposal of the principal. Where this is so the special features of the equitable rules are not to be invoked merely because they might create slightly different results in connection, eg, with damages,[340] or as to limitation periods.[341] Nevertheless, awards made for breach of pure fiduciary duties are not necessarily affected by the same limits as apply to common law damages in respect of remoteness, contributory negligence and so forth, though the courts will be reluctant to compensate for loss which would have occurred in any case.[342] The whole area is one in which decisions from other common law countries, especially Australia, are of considerable significance.[343] In Canada[344] and New Zealand,[345] more extreme views are held to the effect that the question of remedy is secondary and, when arrived at after the question of breach of duty is determined, should be dealt with entirely flexibly. Such flexibility is found in England in breach of confidence cases, but less elsewhere.

1.147 Without any question of breach of duty, an agent may also hold money which emanates from his principal, or which comes in from outside for his principal. In insolvency situations (and other situations such as limitation) it may be important to know whether such money is held on trust, ie whether in respect of this money the agent is a trustee, or whether he is merely a debtor to his principal. This is one of the situations where trust and agency clearly overlap. It might seem that the agent would always be bound to hold such money on trust, for one of his traditional duties is to keep his principal's money separate. However, by definition that duty only applies where the agent has what can be called 'the principal's money'. Thus it is clear that in many circumstances an agent is put in funds by his principal on the understanding that he will account overall only on an *in personam* basis, and/or where it is assumed that the agent will maintain a cash flow with respect to money emanating from external sources without holding any of it on trust.[346] But where the agent is given money by his principal for a specific purpose, or where money is given to him by a third party to hold for his principal, there may be a trust; and a trust is more likely where the agent receives money in connection with a single transaction than when he maintains a general cash flow over several transactions and accounts periodically.[347] The question of how appropriate it is to accord a priority in bankruptcy is one that is or should be taken into account in the determination of such questions as these.

---

[340] *Bristol & West BS v Mothew* [1998] Ch 1, CA.

[341] *Paragon Finance v DB Thakerar & Co* [1999] 1 All ER 400, CA; see also *Coulthard v Disco Mix Club Ltd* [2000] 1 WLR 707.

[342] *Target Holdings Ltd v Redferns*, n 338; *AIB Group plc v Mark Redler & Co*, n 339; see also *Swindle v Harrison* [1997] 4 All ER 705, CA.

[343] Two leading Australian decisions on the nature of fiduciary obligation are *Breen v Williams* (1996) 186 CLR 71, HCA and *Pilmer v Duke Group Ltd* (2001) 207 CLR 165. See also the *Hospital Products* case, n 359 and *Chan v Zacharia* (19840 154 CLR 178, HCA.

[344] *Lac Minerals v International Corona Resources Ltd* [1989] 2 SCR 574, (1989) 61 DLR (4th) 14, SC Can. Canadian courts go further also as regards the incidence of fiduciary duties: eg, *Norberg v Wynrib* [1992] 2 SCR 226, (1992) 92 DLR (4th) 449, SC Can (medical practitioner). But cf *McInerney v MacDonald* [1992] 2 SCR 138; *KLB v British Columbia* [2003] 2 SCR 403, (2003) 230 DLR (4th) 513, SC Can.

[345] *Day v Mead* [1987] 2 NZLR 443, CA NZ; *Aquaculture Corp v New Zealand Green Mussel Co* [1990] 3 NZLR 299, CA NZ. cf *Bank of New Zealand v New Zealand Guardian Trust Co Ltd* [1999] 1 NZLR 664, CA NZ.

[346] eg *Neste Oy v Lloyds Bank plc* [1983] 2 Lloyd's Rep 658. There is relevant discussion at a more complex level in *Lehman Brothers International Ltd v CRC Credit Fund Ltd* [2012] UKSC 6, [2012] 3 All ER 1.

[347] Two leading cases are *Burdick v Garrick* (1870) LR 5 Ch App 233 and *Kirkham v Peel* (1880) 43 LT 171, aff'd (1880) 44 LT 195, CA. There is a valuable discussion in *Walker v Corboy* (1990) 19 NSWLR 382, CANSW; for a more recent relevant decision, see *Triffit Nurseries v Salads Etcetera Ltd* [2000] 1 All ER Comm 737, CA.

(iv) Commercial agents

Similar duties are briefly laid down in the Commercial Agents (Council Directive) Regulations **1.148** 1993. They mostly correspond to the common law duties; but the counterpart to the equitable duties is a broad one to act 'dutifully and in good faith'.[348] It seems likely that courts in common law countries will interpret this duty in a way broadly consistent with the fiduciary duties already existing; but it may be appropriate to go further.

(2) Rights of the Agent Against the Principal

(a) Commission

The main right of the agent against the principal is to remuneration, which is typically **1.149** expressed as commission. A gratuitous agent is not of course so entitled; but in most cases, especially of professional agents, it will be assumed that a normal or reasonable commission was impliedly agreed if nothing was said about this when the agent was engaged.[349]

An enormous number of cases concern the right of the agent to commission. In England, **1.150** many of them concern real estate agents, but their significance is usually general and they can be cited in connection with any commission dispute. The only principle that emerges is that the right depends entirely on the terms of the particular contract. It can be said that in the case of sale of land, the agent is intended to get his commission from the purchase price,[350] and only if he is an (or perhaps sometimes 'the') effective cause of the sale: on the latter point in particular there is much case law.[351] This may be relevant if no terms are specified, or by way of providing criteria for interpretation of contract terms that are obscure, but is not conclusive. Commission may be due in circumstances far short of this. There is no general notion that the principal will not prevent the agent from earning remuneration:[352] in most cases he is free not to deal with persons introduced by the agent, to find customers himself, to revoke the agent's authority or even to close down his business. Understandings as to the meaning of 'sole' or 'exclusive' agency may be relevant. Occasionally a term may be implied that the principal will not behave in certain ways; in one case there is reference to 'a term which prevents the vendor from acting unreasonably to the possible gain of the vendor and the loss of the agent',[353] which is an example of an implied term creating an effect similar to that of a requirement of good faith. Such an implication would however be fairly rare. The assumption is often that the agent earns quite a high commission if he succeeds, and until then takes risks. It is also true that some agency contracts do not place any duty on the agent to do anything.[354] The right to remuneration may of course not be exercisable in respect of illegal and other prohibited transactions. An agent who commits a breach of duty, including fiduciary duty, may forfeit his right to commission and have to return commission paid.[355] The breach will normally justify termination of any contract under which the agent operates.

---

[348] Regulation 4(1).
[349] eg *Way v Latilla* [1937] 3 All ER 759.
[350] See *Midgley Estates Ltd v Hand* [1952] 2 QB 432, 435–436, *per* Jenkins LJ.
[351] For a dramatic example see *Hodges & Sons v Hackbridge Park Residential Hotel Ltd* [1940] 1 KB 404, where the purchaser introduced acquired the property compulsorily. The agent was not entitled to commission. Another recently articulated way of approaching the matter, applicable where commission is earned for an 'introduction' in respect of land, is to say that the introduction must be to the purchaser, not to the property: see *Foxtons Ltd v Bicknell* [2008] EWCA Civ 419, [2008] 2 EGLR 23, CA. But nothing can defeat clear specific terms. For more detail see *Bowstead and Reynolds on Agency* (20th edn, 2014), Arts 56, 57.
[352] See *Luxor (Eastbourne) Ltd v Cooper* [1941] AC 108, HL.
[353] *Alpha Trading Ltd v Dunnshaw-Patten Ltd* [1981] QB 290, CA.
[354] See 1.136.
[355] See *Imageview Management Ltd v Jack* [2009] EWCA Civ 63, [2009] 2 All ER 666, CA and the cases discussed therein; criticized by P Watts, 'Restitution and Conflicted Agency', (2009) 125 LQR 369.

(b) Reimbursement and indemnity

1.151 An agent has the right to be reimbursed expenses and indemnified against liabilities incurred on authorized transactions,[356] including some in respect of which he could not himself be sued, as eg barristers' fees,[357] provided again that these are not illegal or otherwise affected by statute. Where the agency is contractual, the duty may be explicable as based on contract; but where it is not the basis appears to be unjust enrichment.

(c) Lien

1.152 The agent may also have a lien, ie a right to retain his principal's property as security for his claims against his principal. This may be confined to property held in connection with the transaction on which money is owed;[358] but certain types of intermediary have by custom a general lien, ie one applying to debts incurred in connection with other transactions also.

(d) Fiduciary duties

1.153 It is normally assumed that principals owe no fiduciary duties to their agents. In so far as it has arisen, the matter has been considered in connection with franchisors and persons in similar positions. Since they normally sell to their franchisees, or can be said in general to be at arm's length commercially, the view is taken that they owe them no fiduciary duties. This question is not however beyond argument. The fiduciary principles are not confined to agents and are of potential general application. The main obstacle to the franchisor owing fiduciary obligations is that his relationship with the franchisee is usually a commercially adverse one, eg of seller and buyer.[359]

1.154 As already stated, the authority itself may be terminated without notice, but the agent may be entitled to notice or be otherwise protected by a right to damages under an accompanying contract. There is difficult case law on the question whether the principal's promise is subject to an implied term that it only operates so long as he carries on business, and so forth.[360]

(e) Commercial agents

1.155 The Commercial Agents (Council Directive) Regulations 1993 regulate, for those agents to whom they refer, the right to commission, in a manner more specific than the general common law rules,[361] though it is not always clear whether or not they are mandatory and to what extent they can be modified by contract terms.[362] They contain a provision requiring the principal to supply information from which commission may be calculated,[363] though how this is intended to operate is again not clear. They also impose on the agent[364] and on the principal[365] unexcludable duties, which would not necessarily be implied at common law, to act 'dutifully and in good faith', and impose on the principal more specific duties concerning

---

[356] For a recent discussion see *Linklaters v HSBC Bank plc* [2005] EWHC 1113 (Comm), [2003] 2 Lloyd's Rep 545.

[357] *Rhodes v Fielder, Jones & Harrison* (1919) 89 LJKB 15.

[358] See *Withers LLP v Langbar International Ltd* [2011] EWCA Civ 1419, [2011] 1 WLR 1748, CA.

[359] See extensive discussion, and different views, in the leading case of *Hospital Products Ltd v US Surgical Corp* (1984) 156 CLR 41, HCA (held no fiduciary duty on distributor). The imposition of fiduciary duties on a seller was rejected in *Jirna Ltd v Mr Donut of Canada Ltd* (1971) 22 DLR (3d) 639, Can.

[360] See *Bowstead and Reynolds on Agency* (20th edn, 2014) para 10-042.

[361] Commercial Agents (Council Directive) Regulations 1993, SI 1993/3053, regs 6–11. See 1.150.

[362] This is especially true of the remuneration provisions, regs 6–10.

[363] Commercial Agents (Council Directive) Regulations 1993, SI 1993/3053, reg 12.

[364] Commercial Agents (Council Directive) Regulations 1993, SI 1993/3053, reg 3(1).

[365] Commercial Agents (Council Directive) Regulations 1993, SI 1993/3053, reg 4(1).

the provision of information relating to the operation of the contract,[366] and the provision of a written contract.[367] There are no specific provisions in the Regulations as to reimbursement or indemnity of the type described above as available at common law.

The position of a commercial agent is however in this context unique in the United Kingdom, **1.156** in that he is entitled to special payments on termination of the agency contract, and his right to these cannot be excluded. These provisions originate from French and (especially) German law and are based on a perception that the agent should be entitled to some form of recompense for work done in building up a clientèle from which the principal benefits. Thus where his authority ends, whether because terminated or in accordance with its terms, or by death or retirement (but not where it is terminated by the agent or by his breach) he is entitled to be 'indemnified…or compensated for damage'. Member states were bound to make provision for one or the other, and in the United Kingdom indemnity only applies where agreed by the parties, but the right to compensation, which operates by way of default, cannot be excluded[368] (though it would not apply if the contract is terminated by reason of the agent's default).

The *indemnity* applies to the extent that new customers have been introduced or business **1.157** increased, and is calculated on an equitable basis, not to exceed one year's remuneration on a five-year average: the right to damages for breach of contract persists. This is similar to pre-existing German law. The right to damages in addition is specifically preserved.[369] The right to *compensation*, clearly derived from existing French law, seems to be based on the idea of causing patrimonial loss in respect of a quasi-joint enterprise, whether there is a breach of contract by the principal or not. It may often lead to a smaller award than the indemnity. The House of Lords has recently ruled on the appropriate method of assessment, to the effect that 'what is to be valued is the income stream which the agency would have generated'[370] and that 'compensation should be calculated by reference to the value of the agency on the assumption that it continued'.[371] The right to common law damages is not specifically preserved, but nor is it excluded, and there must be some situations to which it is appropriate.[372]

It appears that the cause of action for such awards should be regarded as statutory.[373] The **1.158** only comparison in English law is constituted by the protections against unfair dismissal and redundancy offered by employment law, which have not been thought appropriate for agents in general. Indeed, the assumption of English law, arising once more out of the generality of the notion of agency, has been that by reason of the extensive powers accorded to many agents, it is principals who need protection against abuse of position by their agents rather than the reverse.[374]

---

[366] Commercial Agents (Council Directive) Regulations 1993, SI 1993/3053, reg 4(2),(3).

[367] Commercial Agents (Council Directive) Regulations 1993, SI 1993/3053, reg 13.

[368] Commercial Agents (Council Directive) Regulations 1993, SI 1993/3053, regs 17, 19. For a recent example where an ingenious attempt at exclusion failed see *Shearman v Hunter Boot Ltd* [2013] EWHC 47 (QB), [2014] ECC 12.

[369] Commercial Agents (Council Directive) Regulations 1993, SI 1993/3053, reg 17(5).

[370] *Lonsdale v Howard & Hallam Ltd* [2007] UKHL 32, [2007] 1 WLR 2055, at [12]. The possibility that an agency has no value is considered in *Warren v Drukkerij Plach BV* [2014] EWCA Civ 993, [2015] 1 Lloyd's Rep 111.

[371] *Lonsdale v Howard & Hallam Ltd* [2007] UKHL 32, [2007] 1 WLR 2055, at [21], broadly accepting the judgment in the Court of Appeal in the same case, [2004] EWCA Civ 63, [2006] 1 WLR 1281, and not accepting a different approach employed in the Court of Session in *King v T Tunnock & Co Ltd* 2000 SC 424. Recent examples of calculation are provided by *McQuillan v McCormick* [2010] EWHC 1112 (QB), [2011] ECC 18 and *Invicta UK Ltd v International Brands Ltd* [2013] EWHC 1564 (QB), [2013] ECC 30.

[372] See *Bowstead and Reynolds on Agency* (20th edn, 2014) paras 11-040ff.

[373] *Fern Computer Consultancy Ltd v Intergraph Cadworx & Analysis Solutions Inc* [2014] EWHC 2908 (Ch), [2014] Bus LR 1397, [38]ff.

[374] See 1.138ff.

2

SALE OF GOODS[1]

A. The Statutory Regime

(1) Introduction

For many years the law relating to the sale of goods was governed primarily by the Sale of **2.01** Goods Act 1893. The Act was a codifying statute; the long title stated that it was an 'Act for codifying the Law relating to the Sale of Goods'. After a number of amendments had been made to the 1893 Act it was eventually consolidated in the Sale of Goods Act 1979. The 1979 Act has since been amended on five principal occasions,[2] and most recently in the Consumer Rights Act 2015. A number of interpretative difficulties have been caused by the fact that the original statute was a codifying statute[3] which was then consolidated[4] and subsequently amended.[5] The patchwork of amendments led one judge to state that 'in terms of the proper construction of its provisions, the Act of 1979 is not to be regarded as more than the sum of

---

[1] For more detailed consideration of the rules of law see *Benjamin: Sale of Goods* (9th edn, 2014); M Bridge, *The Sale of Goods* (3rd edn, 2014); J Adams and H MacQueen (eds) *Atiyah's Sale of Goods* (12th edn, 2010); E McKendrick (ed), *Sale of Goods* (2000).

[2] By the Sale of Goods (Amendment) Act 1994, the Sale and Supply of Goods Act 1994, the Sale of Goods (Amendment) Act 1995, the Sale and Supply of Goods to Consumers Regulations 2002, SI 2002/3045, the latter implementing Council Directive (EC) 1999/44 on Certain Aspects of the Sale of Consumer Goods and Associated Guarantees [1999] OJ L171/12) and which has now been revoked, and the Consumer Rights Act 2015.

[3] The proper approach to the interpretation of a codifying statute was set out by Lord Herschell LC in *Bank of England v Vagliano Brothers* [1891] AC 107, 144–145, HL. The essence of this approach was significantly to curtail the ability of the courts to go outside the code to resolve interpretative difficulties. This approach was not, however, literally followed by the courts. Examples can be found of cases in which courts have had regard to pre-1893 case law when interpreting the 1893 Act and, in more recent times, the courts have been more creative or liberal in their interpretation of the legislation and refused to allow it to 'fossilize the law': see, for example, *Ashington Piggeries Ltd v Christopher Hill Ltd* [1972] AC 441, 501, HL.

[4] In the case of consolidating statutes the courts have greater liberty to resort to cases decided under the previous legislation because of the operation of the presumption that a consolidating statute does not alter the previous law.

[5] The question whether the courts should, when seeking to ascertain the meaning of the amended provision, have regard to cases decided under the legislation prior to its amendment has provoked judicial disagreement. In *Rogers v Parish (Scarborough) Ltd* [1987] QB 933, 942, CA Mustill LJ stated that resort should not be had to the old case law, a view which was not shared by Lloyd LJ in *M/S Aswan Engineering Establishment Co v Lupdine Ltd* [1987] 1 WLR 1, 6, CA.

its parts',[6] so that a particular phrase might not have the same meaning throughout the Act if the terms were introduced at different stages in the legislative development of what is now the 1979 Act.

2.02 Statements that the 1893 Act is a 'Code'[7] or that the 1979 Act is a 'single code'[8] are apt to mislead. They give the impression that the legislation is the sole repository of the law relating to the sale of goods, when this is far from being the case. The Act is built upon common law foundations[9] and the common law (here used to include equity) has had and continues to have a significant impact upon the development of the law. Thus the Sale of Goods Act has little to say about matters relating to the formation of a contract and to vitiating factors, such as fraud, misrepresentation, duress and mistake.[10] Developments in the general law of contract relating to breach of contract and the classification of terms in a contract have also had an impact on sale of goods law.[11] The impact of judge-made law can also be seen in relation to documentary sales, such as cif (cost, insurance, freight) and fob (free on board) contracts, where the judge-made rules have had a greater impact on the development of the law than the rules formulated in the Sale of Goods Act 1979.[12] The Sale of Goods Act 1979 may be the first port of call for the lawyer seeking to advise on a sale of goods problem but it is not necessarily the last nor the most important.

(a) Application of the Sale of Goods Act 1979

2.03 The Sale of Goods Act 1979 applies to the commercial sale of goods (that is to say, a sale which takes place between two businesses) and documentary sales. Until recently, there was no separate statute which regulated consumer sales and so the latter had to be accommodated within the 1979 Act. Over the years this accommodation became increasingly uneasy and the enactment of the Consumer Rights Act 2015, which makes separate provision for consumer sales and takes them out of the 1979 Act, has therefore been widely welcomed. The drafting of the 2015 Act differs in many respects from that of the 1979 Act. Many of the provisions of the 1979 Act take the form of 'default' rules, that is to say, the rule contained in the Act applies in the absence of an agreement to the contrary by the parties. It was this flexibility which enabled the legislation to survive for as long as it did and, indeed, it is noticeable that it is at the points at which the Act laid down mandatory rules that it attracted the most criticism.[13] The Consumer Rights Act, by contrast, contains more by way of mandatory rules, thus reflecting the desire to protect the interests of consumers. The 1893 Act has also been praised as 'a superb work of draftsmanship'[14] but the more informal style of the 2015 Act

---

[6] *Stevenson v Rogers* [1999] QB 1028, 1040, CA.

[7] See eg *Re Wait* [1927] 1 Ch 606, CA, where there are a number of references to the Sale of Goods Act 1893 as a Code in the judgments of Lord Hanworth MR (616, 617, 620) and Atkin LJ (630–631, 634–637).

[8] *Stevenson v Rogers* [1999] QB 1028, 1040, CA.

[9] In the sense that the provisions of the 1893 Act reflect, with modifications, the case law on sale of goods as it had developed in the latter part of the nineteenth century.

[10] See eg s 62(2) of the Sale of Goods Act 1979 which specifically preserves the common law rules except in so far as they are inconsistent with the provisions of the Act. 'Common law' here almost certainly includes the rules of equity: *Benjamin*, n 1, at paras 1-008 and 1-009.

[11] Of particular significance in this context is the development of the innominate or intermediate term in *Hong Kong Fir Shipping Co Ltd v Kawasaki Kisen Kaisha Ltd* [1962] 2 QB 26, CA (see further ch 8). The impact of this case on sale of goods law can be seen in *Cehave NV v Bremer Handelsgesellschaft mbH (The Hansa Nord)* [1976] QB 44, CA.

[12] See generally M Bridge, *The International Sale of Goods—Law and Practice* (3rd edn, 2013).

[13] Thus s 16 of the Sale of Goods Act 1979 which laid down a rule of law that property could not pass in the case of the sale of unascertained goods was heavily criticized in its application to the sale of part of a bulk of goods. Reform has now been introduced in the form of ss 20A and 20B of the Act, see 2.22.

[14] E McKendrick (ed) *Goode on Commercial Law* (LexisNexis, 4th edn, 2009) 205.

is unlikely to attract such praise. While the terms treated as included in a contract of sale concluded between a trader and a consumer resemble those to be found in the 1979 Act, the remedial regime is rather more complex[15] and is designed to afford to consumers a wider array of remedies than those to be found in the 1979 Act. This chapter will focus principally on the 1979 Act and will only deal incidentally with the 2015 Act, drawing attention, where appropriate, to those areas where the rights and duties of the parties to a contract governed by the 2015 Act differ from those applicable to contracts governed by the 1979 Act.

(b) International sales

Not only does the Sale of Goods Act 1979 apply to a wide range of domestic contracts, it **2.04** also applies to international sales. English law has not yet followed the path taken by many nations in distinguishing formally between domestic and international sales. In the international realm pressure has grown in recent years for the creation of a uniform set of rules that can be applied to sales contracts and the most influential document which has as its aim the promotion of uniformity is the UN Convention on Contracts for the International Sale of Goods (generally referred to as the 'Vienna Convention' or, more commonly, 'CISG').[16] The Convention has now been ratified by eighty-three states and came into force on 1 January 1988. The United Kingdom is one of the few major trading nations which has not ratified the Convention.[17] When, or if, the Convention is introduced into English law, it will effect a major change to the law relating to the international sale of goods in this country, particularly in remedial terms.[18]

International sales contracts have made a significant contribution to the development of **2.05** English sale of goods law. The reason for this is that many international sales contracts, particularly commodity sales, are governed by English law as a result of the decision of the parties to choose English law as the law that is to govern their contract. The international sale contracts which have been litigated most frequently in the English courts are 'fob' contracts and 'cif' contracts, both of which typically involve arrangements for the carriage of goods by sea as well as their sale. The matters referred to by the initials indicate the extent of the seller's obligations, and hence what the buyer is paying for, in relation to, eg, carriage and insurance of the goods. There is a range of contracts in use in practice. At one end of the spectrum is the 'ex works' contract under which it is for the buyer to collect the goods from the seller's works or factory. At the other end of the spectrum is a 'delivery duty paid' contract under which the seller agrees to deliver the goods to the named place in the country of the buyer and to pay all costs involved in delivering the goods at that place, including import duties and taxes. In between are a range of standard contracts, such as 'fas' contracts (free alongside ship), 'cfr' contracts (cost and freight) together with a range of contracts used for container transportation and multi-modal transportation. Standardization of the content of many of these contracts has been achieved as a result of the formulation by the International Chamber of Commerce of Incoterms (currently Incoterms, 2010), a set of trade terms the primary function of which is to define the obligations of buyers and sellers in relation to matters such as delivery, payment, insurance, export and import licences, and the transfer of risk. Incoterms do not have the force of law in England but they can, and often are, incorporated as contract terms into contracts for the international sale of goods.

---

[15] See further 2.69–2.72.

[16] On which see generally P Schlechtriem and I Schwenzer (ed by I Schwenzer) *Commentary on the UN Convention on the International Sale of Goods (CISG)* (3rd (English) edition, 2010).

[17] A valuable outline of the Convention, explaining its potential significance for English lawyers, is provided by M Bridge, n 12, at chs 10–12.

[18] On which see FMB Reynolds, 'A Note of Caution' in P Birks (ed), *The Frontiers of Liability* (1994) 18–28.

(c) European developments

2.06 A tentative step towards the possible harmonization of European sale of goods law was taken in 2011 with the publication of a proposal for an EU Regulation which would create a Common European Sales Law.[19] The proposed Regulation would permit parties to certain contracts of sale to choose the Common European Sales Law to govern their contract. But the Regulation would only apply to certain categories of sales contract. First, it would apply only to cross-border contracts.[20] Second, the seller of the goods must be a trader and, in the case where both parties to the contract are traders, at least one of them must be a small or medium-sized enterprise.[21] Where it has been validly chosen by the parties, the Common European Sales Law will 'govern the matters addressed in its rules' and it will also govern the compliance with, and remedies for failure to comply with, the pre-contractual information duties.[22] In the event that the Regulation is adopted, it will be interesting to see the extent to which it is chosen by the parties in preference to the sales law of a particular jurisdiction. The proposal has attracted some criticism,[23] and it does depart in some significant respects from the current English law, but it may be that the discernible drift towards the greater harmonization of private law in Europe will lead to its implementation and to the further convergence of sales law across Europe. However, progress remains slow and the determined nature of the resistance to this development may prevent it from achieving the force of law.

(2) *The Scope of the Sale of Goods Act 1979*

2.07 The scope of the Sale of Goods Act 1979 (hereafter 'the Act') is obviously confined to contracts for the sale of goods. It is therefore necessary to define a contract for the sale of goods in order to ascertain the limits of the Act. A contract of sale is defined as a 'contract by which the seller transfers or agrees to transfer the property in the goods to the buyer for a money consideration, called the price'.[24] It can be seen from this definition that sale of goods law is essentially an amalgam of contract law and personal property law. The definition can be broken down into a number of distinct components; there must be (a) a contract, (b) goods, (c) price, and (d) transfer of property. Each of these elements is worthy of further elaboration.

(a) A contract

2.08 The existence and validity of the contract is essentially a matter for the general law of contract[25] as is the capacity of the parties to enter into a contract for the sale of goods.[26] A gift of goods, not being a contract, is outside the scope of the Act.[27] A sale is, however, more than a contract. It is both a contract and a conveyance. In the case where the property is transferred

---

[19] Proposal for a Regulation of the European Parliament and of the Council on a Common European Sales Law Com (2011) 635 final, recital 12. The Law Commission and the Scottish Law Commission have published an Advice to the UK Government on the Proposal. <http://lawcommission.justice.gov.uk/docs/Common_European_Sales_Law_Advice.pdf>

[20] Article 4.

[21] Article 7.

[22] Article 11.

[23] For an example see S Whittaker, 'The Proposed "Common European Sales Law": Legal Framework and the Agreement of the Parties' (2012) 75 MLR 578.

[24] Sale of Goods Act 1979, s 2(1). For the equivalent definition in the Consumer Rights Act 2015, see s 5.

[25] Sale of Goods Act 1979, s 62(2). The rules relating to the existence and validity of a contract are discussed in EPL ch 8.

[26] Sale of Goods Act 1979, s 3(1). Note, however, the obligation to pay a reasonable price for 'necessaries' set out in s 3(2) and (3).

[27] The distinction between a gift and a contract is not always easy to draw: *Esso Petroleum Co Ltd v Commissioners of Customs & Excise* [1976] 1 WLR 1, HL (albeit on the facts it was held that the contract between the parties was not one for the sale of the coins).

to the buyer at the time of entry into the contract, the transaction is described in the Act as a sale.[28] But where the property is to pass at some future time or subject to the later fulfilment of a particular condition, it is defined as an agreement to sell.[29] There are no longer any formal requirements which apply to entry into contracts for the sale of goods.[30]

(b) Goods

(i) Distinguished from services or work and materials

The Act only applies to goods. It has no application to contracts for services or for work and **2.09** materials. This obviously can give rise to difficult questions of demarcation because it is not always easy to distinguish between a contract for the sale of goods and one for services; the different types of contract can, in certain circumstances, shade into each other. The distinction between them has been held to turn essentially on the 'substance' of the contract; if the substance of the contract is the skill and labour then the contract is likely to be one for work and materials but if the substance of the contract is the end product then it is likely that it will be regarded as a contract of sale.[31] The distinction between the two types of contract is not of great practical importance today, largely because the terms implied into contracts for the sale of goods and contracts for work and materials are very similar.[32]

(ii) Definition

Goods is defined in section 61(1) of the Act as including 'all personal chattels other than **2.10** things in action and money' and 'emblements, industrial growing crops, and things attached to or forming part of the land which are agreed to be severed before sale or under the contract of sale' and an 'undivided share in goods'. The scope of the Act is therefore broad. Yet its scope continues to be tested by the infinite variety of transactions entered into in the modern world. Thus, while the sale of computer hardware will constitute a sale of goods, the picture is less clear in relation to the sale of computer software.[33] The status of a contract for the sale of human remains or human tissue, where it is lawful to enter into such a contract, remains uncertain.[34] At the margins it has also proved to be difficult to distinguish between the sale of personal chattels (within the Act) and the sale of land (outwith the Act) and between the sale of tangible property (within the Act) and the sale of intangibles (generally outside the Act). The problems in the former category have been reduced by the extended definition of goods which in general brings the sale of crops and natural products within the scope of the Act.[35]

---

[28] Sale of Goods Act 1979, s 2(4).

[29] Sale of Goods Act 1979, s 2(5).

[30] Formal requirements were repealed by the Law Reform (Enforcement of Contracts) Act 1954.

[31] *Robinson v Graves* [1935] 1 KB 579, CA. The problems associated with this test are explored in more detail in *Benjamin*, n 1, at paras 1-041–1-047.

[32] Implied terms are discussed in more detail at 2.29–2.40A.

[33] In *London Borough of Southwark v IBM UK Ltd* [2011] EWHC 549 (TCC), 135 Con LR 136, at [96] Aikenhead J stated (obiter) that in his view computer software could be 'goods' for the purposes of the Act, But for a more restrictive view see *St Albans City & District Council v International Computers Ltd* [1996] 4 All ER 481, 493, CA where Sir Iain Glidewell stated (obiter) that a computer program was not itself 'goods' within the statutory definition and see also *Your Response Ltd v Datateam Business Media Ltd* [2014] EWCA Civ 281, [2015] QB 41, at [20]. For more detailed consideration of the issues see P Kohler and N Palmer, 'Information as Property' in N Palmer and E McKendrick (eds), *Interests in Goods* (2nd edn, 1998) 1, 17–19.

[34] See generally R Magnusson, 'Proprietary Rights in Human Tissues' in N Palmer and E McKendrick (eds), *Interests in Goods* (2nd edn, 1998) 25, esp 46–48. There is probably no absolute rule today which prevents such contracts being regarded as a sale of goods. Evidence of a more relaxed approach by the courts to rights in human remains can be seen in the decision of the Court of Appeal in *Dobson v North Tyneside Health Authority* [1997] 1 WLR 596, CA.

[35] The courts had previously experienced great difficulty in deciding whether or not a sale of crops or natural products was a sale of goods and the cases were not at all easy to reconcile: see *Benjamin*, n 1, at

In the latter category the exclusion of things or choses in action means that documentary intangibles do not fall within the scope of the Act: for example, shares, debts, bills of lading and negotiable instruments do not constitute goods.

(iii) Categories of goods

2.11 The Act also distinguishes between different types of goods. Reference is made in the Act to 'existing', 'future', 'specific', 'ascertained', and 'unascertained' goods. To an extent these categories intersect; eg existing goods may be either specific or unascertained. The distinctions assume considerable significance in the context of the passing of property in goods. Existing goods are goods which are owned or possessed by the seller,[36] whereas future goods are goods to be manufactured or acquired by the seller after the making of the contract of sale.[37] Specific goods are goods which are identified and agreed upon at the time a contract of sale is made.[38]

2.12 There is no definition of 'ascertained' or 'unascertained'[39] within the Act itself. The meaning of these phrases has therefore been worked out by the courts.[40]

(c) Price

2.13 The price is the money consideration paid by the buyer. Where the consideration provided by the buyer assumes a form other than the payment of money the contract cannot be one of sale. Thus contracts of exchange or barter do not fall within the scope of the Act.[41] The price payable must generally be fixed by the parties because otherwise a court may conclude that no contract has in fact been made.[42] The price may, however, be fixed in one of three ways: it can be fixed by the terms of the contract itself, it may be left to be fixed in a manner agreed by the contract, or it may be determined by the course of dealing between the parties.[43] Where the price has not been determined in one of these three ways the buyer must pay a reasonable price.[44] What constitutes a reasonable price is a question of fact which depends upon all the facts and circumstances of the case.

---

paras 1-093, 1-094. Provided that there is an obligation to sever, the contract is likely to be one for the sale of goods. Indeed, the definition is so wide that it may overlap with the definition of contracts for the sale of land in other statutory contexts.

[36] Sale of Goods Act 1979, s 5(1). Thus goods may actually exist but nevertheless not constitute existing goods for the purposes of the Act because they are not in the ownership or possession of the seller at the relevant time; such goods are classified by the Act as 'future goods'.

[37] Sale of Goods Act 1979, ss 5(1) and 61(1). A sale of future goods can only be an agreement to sell; it cannot be a sale.

[38] Sale of Goods Act 1979, s 61(1). The definition also includes 'an undivided share, specified as a fraction or percentage, of goods identified and agreed on as aforesaid'.

[39] The category of unascertained goods must now be subdivided into wholly unascertained goods and, as it has come to be labelled, quasi-specific goods.

[40] Discussed in more detail at 2.16–2.22.

[41] *Harrison v Luke* (1845) 14 M & W 139, 153 ER 423, Exchequer Division. More difficult is the case where the consideration provided by the buyer consists partly of money and partly of goods (as might be the case where a car is traded in in part-exchange for a new car). Such a transaction is probably a contract of sale (see *Aldridge v Johnson* (1857) 7 E & B 885, 119 ER 1476, Court of Queen's Bench; cf *Flynn v Mackin* [1974] IR 101, Supreme Court). If it is not a sale it will probably fall within the scope of Part I of the Supply of Goods and Services Act 1982. Given the similarity between the two Acts in many cases the classification of the contract will not have practical consequences.

[42] See eg *May and Butcher Ltd v R* [1934] 2 KB 17n, HL.

[43] Sale of Goods Act 1979, s 8(1).

[44] Sale of Goods Act 1979, s 8(2). The correct meaning of 'determined' is not entirely clear. Where the contract is silent as to price it is clear that s 8(2) can be invoked. It is less clear whether it can be invoked where there is a mechanism in the 'contract' but it is too uncertain to be enforced. In such a case s 8(2) may be inapplicable.

(d) Transfer of property

The transfer of property is central to the definition of a sale. Where the contract involves the **2.14** transfer of possession or the use of goods but not the transfer of property it cannot be a sale. Thus a contract of hire, such as a finance lease, does not fall within the scope of the Act, nor does a hire-purchase contract. But the fact that the transfer of property is postponed to a date subsequent to the conclusion of the contract does not in itself take the contract outside the scope of the Act. So a conditional sale[45] falls within its scope.[46] 'Property' is defined in the Act as 'the general property in goods, and not merely a special property'.[47] Thus, the transfer of a limited possessory interest, eg by way of bailment[48] or pledge,[49] does not fall within the scope of the Act. This definition of 'property' provides very limited guidance and much academic ink has been spilt on the meaning to be given to 'property' or 'title' as used in the Act.[50] Although the matter is not entirely free from doubt, it would appear that 'property' does not mean the best possible title but that it means any title provided that it is a title to the absolute legal interest in the goods. Thus there can be a sale of goods where the seller has only possessory title to the goods provided that the seller transfers the entirety of such title as he possesses to the buyer.

B. Transfer of Property and Risk

(1) The Passing of Property

The question whether or not property has passed from the seller to the buyer is obviously **2.15** one of fundamental importance, particularly in the context of the insolvency of one or other party. But the significance of 'property' is not confined to insolvency. It extends to such matters as the passing of risk[51] and the entitlement of the seller to bring an action for the price of the goods.[52] Indeed, the Act has been criticized because of the 'excessive importance'[53] which

---

[45] It can sometimes be difficult to distinguish between a conditional sale agreement and a hire-purchase agreement. eg in *Forthright Finance Ltd v Carlyle Finance Ltd* [1997] 4 All ER 90, CA an agreement which conferred an option to purchase which option was deemed to have been exercised when all the instalments had been paid, unless the hirer elected not to take title to the goods, was held to be a conditional sale and not a hire-purchase.

[46] Of course a conditional sale may also fall within the scope of other legislation, most notably the Consumer Credit Act 1974.

[47] Sale of Goods Act 1979, s 61(1).

[48] Bailment is discussed in greater detail in ch 5. The relationship between bailment and sale has assumed practical significance in the context of retention of title clauses, discussed at 2.23.

[49] Pledge is in any event expressly excluded by s 62(4) of the Sale of Goods Act 1979.

[50] In particular, the heading 'transfer of property as between seller and buyer' immediately prior to s 16 has attracted criticism because, of course, the distinguishing feature of the transfer of property is its binding effect on third parties: see eg *Atiyah's Sale of Goods*, n 1, at 305. For discussion see G Battersby and A Preston, 'The Concepts of "Property", "Title", and "Owner" Used in the Sale of Goods Act 1893' (1972) 35 MLR 268; HL Ho 'Some Reflections on "Property" and "Title" in the Sale of Goods Act' [1997] CLJ 571; G Battersby, 'A reconsideration of "Property" and "Title" in the Sale of Goods Act' [2001] JBL 1; and Tan Yock Lin, 'Does Ownership Matter in the Sale of Goods?' [2011] JBL 749.

[51] Sale of Goods Act 1979, s 20(1) which provides that risk prima facie passes with property, discussed in 2.26.

[52] Sale of Goods Act 1979, s 49(1), discussed in 2.60.

[53] E McKendrick (ed) *Goode on Commercial Law* (4th edn, 2009) 237. Further illustrations of the significance of property in English sale of goods law are provided in *Goode on Commercial Law* at 237–239. These criticisms are very much influenced by the functional approach of Professor K Llewellyn (see 'Through Title to Contract and a Bit Beyond' (1938) 15 New York ULR 159) but the merits of this functional approach are not universally shared: see eg *Atiyah's Sale of Goods*, n 1, at 310, albeit that the editors express in the current edition a view contrary to that taken by Professor Atiyah.

it attaches to the concept of property. When deciding whether or not property in the goods has passed in any given case to the buyer, it is important to distinguish between the different types of goods recognized by the Act.

(a) Specific or ascertained goods

(i) The intention of the parties

2.16 The central rule, embodied in section 17 of the Act is that, in the case of the sale of specific or ascertained goods, property passes at such time as the parties to the contract intend it to pass.[54] The intention of the parties is to be derived from the terms of the contract, the conduct of the parties and all the circumstances of the case.[55] Thus it is not the delivery of the goods, control over the goods or payment of the price which operate to transfer property; it is the intention of the parties. Delivery, control or payment may be relevant in so far as they can be used to demonstrate the intention of the parties; but they are not conclusive in themselves. Contracting parties frequently make provision in the contract for the passing of property[56] and, in some standard form contracts, it is accepted that property generally passes at a particular point in time, eg the delivery of documents.[57] In an effort to provide the commercial world with some guidance, the Act contains a number of 'rules' which the courts are directed to use when seeking to discern the intention of the parties.[58] These rules are no more than presumptions; they are not conclusive in their effect. The strength of the presumption varies from rule to rule.

(ii) Presumption in respect of goods in a deliverable state

2.17 In the case of an unconditional contract[59] for the sale of specific goods[60] in a deliverable state[61] property in the goods passes to the buyer when the contract is made.[62] This presumption is applicable even in the case where the date of payment or the time for delivery has been postponed to some later date. However, the presumption has much less force today than in former times: 'in modern times very little is needed to give rise to the inference that the property in specific goods is to pass only on delivery or payment.'[63] Where the contract is one for the sale of specific goods and the seller[64] is bound to do something to the goods for the purpose of putting them into a deliverable state, property does not pass until the thing is

---

[54] Sale of Goods Act 1979, s 17(1).

[55] Sale of Goods Act 1979, s 17(2). The relevant conduct of the parties can include their conduct subsequent to the making of the contract: *Tanks & Vessels Industries v Devon Cider* [2009] EWHC 1360 (Ch), at [50].

[56] The most common example, perhaps, is the retention of title clause, discussed in 2.23.

[57] In the case of a cif contract property normally passes to the buyer when the buyer pays the price in exchange for the relevant documents. But in such a case property passes because this is the intention of the parties, not because the documents themselves contain some particular properties which enable property to pass irrespective of the intention of the parties.

[58] Sale of Goods Act 1979, s 18.

[59] Although 'unconditional' qualifies 'contract', what is in fact meant is a contract for the unconditional sale of goods.

[60] Defined in 2.11 and n 38: see further *Kursell v Timber Operators and Contractors Ltd* [1927] 1 KB 298, CA (where the rule was held to be inapplicable because the goods were not specific).

[61] 'Deliverable state' is defined in s 61(5) as 'such a state that the buyer would under the contract be bound to take delivery of them'.

[62] Sale of Goods Act 1979, s 18, r 1. An example of the application of the rule is provided by *Dennant v Skinner* [1948] 2 KB 164, KBD.

[63] *RV Ward Ltd v Bignall* [1967] 1 QB 534, 545, CA.

[64] Where it is the buyer or a third party who must do the act the rule is inapplicable and resort must be had instead to the general rule in s 17.

done and the buyer has notice that it has been done.[65] In the case of a contract for the sale of goods in a deliverable state but where the seller[66] is bound to weigh, measure, test or do some other act or thing with reference to the goods for the purpose of ascertaining the price, the property does not pass until the act or thing is done and the buyer has notice that it has been done.[67]

(iii) Delivery 'on approval' or on 'sale or return' terms

Rather more difficulty arises where goods are delivered to the buyer 'on approval or on sale or return or other similar terms'.[68] In such a case property passes to the buyer when he signifies his approval or acceptance to the seller or does any other act adopting the transaction.[69] Such approval or acceptance may be express or implied.[70] If the buyer does not signify his approval or acceptance to the seller but retains the goods without giving notice of rejection, property may nevertheless pass to the buyer when, if a time has been fixed for the return of the goods, that time has expired, or, if no time has been fixed, on the expiry of a reasonable time.[71] A buyer's notice of rejection need not be in writing and it will generally suffice if it identifies the goods to be returned generically so long as the generic description enables the goods to be identified with certainty.[72]   **2.18**

(b) Future or unascertained goods.

In the case of future or unascertained goods the intention of the parties cannot be determinative of the time at which property passes because, until such time as the goods which are the subject matter of the contract have been identified with sufficient precision, it is impossible to conclude that property has passed. However, the extent of the identification of the goods which the law requires before property can pass has proved to be a difficult issue. There are two principal ways in which property may pass. The first is by the 'unconditional appropriation' of the goods to the contract.[73] The second is as a result of the operation of section 20A of the Sale of Goods Act 1979.   **2.19**

(i) 'Unconditional appropriation' of the goods

The idea that property in future or unascertained goods can pass as a result of the 'unconditional appropriation' of the goods to the contract has a long history but it only operates within very narrow confines.[74] There are a number of elements here. The first is that there   **2.20**

---

[65] Sale of Goods Act 1979, s 18, r 2. Examples of the application of the rule are provided by *Underwood Ltd v Burgh Castle Brick and Cement Syndicate* [1922] 1 KB 343, KBD and *Kulkarni v Manor Credit (Davenham) Ltd* [2010] EWCA Civ 69, [2011] 2 Lloyd's Rep 431.

[66] Again, the rule is inapplicable where the act is to be done by the buyer or a third party: see eg *Nanka Bruce v Commonwealth Trust Ltd* [1926] AC 77, PC.

[67] Sale of Goods Act 1979, s 18, r 3. An example of the application of the rule is provided by *Rugg v Minett* (1809) 11 East 210, 103 ER 985, KBD.

[68] Sale of Goods Act 1979, s 18, r 4. It has been argued that a distinction should in fact be drawn between sales on approval and transactions entered into on a 'sale or return' basis: see J Adams, 'Sales "on Approval" and "Sale or Return"' in J Adams (ed), *Essays for Clive Schmitthoff* (1983) 1.

[69] Sale of Goods Act 1979, s 18, r 4(a). Until property passes, the prospective buyer holds the goods as bailee: *Atari Corporation (UK) Ltd v Electronic Boutique Stores (UK) Ltd* [1998] QB 539, 549, CA. The buyer has an option whether or not to buy, although it would appear that the seller is unable to withdraw his 'offer' to sell the goods. The latter rule has been criticized by I Brown, 'The Sale of Goods and Sale or Return Transactions' (1998) 114 LQR 198.

[70] *Kirkham v Attenborough* [1897] 1 QB 291, CA. In effect this rule can operate as an additional exception to the *nemo dat* rule, on which see 2.24 and 2.25.

[71] Sale of Goods Act 1979, s 18, r 4(b).

[72] *Atari Corporation (UK) Ltd v Electronic Boutique Stores (UK) Ltd* [1998] QB 539, CA.

[73] The 'rule' can be found in s 18, r 5(1) and (2).

[74] *Carlos Federspiel SA v Charles Twigg* [1957] 1 Lloyd's Rep 240, QBD. A more liberal approach has been taken in other jurisdictions so that the approach adopted in the *Carlos Federspiel* case may yet be open to

must have been an appropriation of the goods to the contract. The exact meaning of appropriation is difficult to pin down. Essentially, it is an overt act of one party,[75] the purpose of which is to identify the goods to be sold.[76] Where the goods are part of a bulk, identification requires that there has been severance of the portion to be sold from the whole.[77] Secondly, that appropriation must have been unconditional, in the sense that it must irrevocably[78] identify certain goods as the goods which are the subject matter of the contract and it must have been assented to by both parties.[79] This is a difficult requirement to satisfy; usually 'it is the last act to be performed by the seller'.[80] The clearest example of an unconditional appropriation is delivery, actual or constructive,[81] of the goods to the buyer or to a carrier.[82] But unconditional appropriation can take place short of delivery provided that it is irrevocable and assented to by both buyer and seller.[83] Thirdly, the contract must be one for the sale of goods by description[84] and the goods must be of the contract description. Finally the goods must be in a deliverable state.[85]

2.21 Where goods have not been unconditionally appropriated to the contract and therefore remain unascertained, section 16 of the Act provides that property in the goods cannot pass until they have been ascertained. This is a rule of law out of which the parties cannot contract. Furthermore, the original section 16 did not distinguish between cases in which the goods were wholly unascertained and cases in which the goods were 'quasi-specific' (that is to say, the bulk in which the goods were contained could be identified but the buyer's share in the goods could not). In both cases section 16 stated that property could not pass. The application of this rule to cases of quasi-specific goods proved to be very controversial.[86] Although there were certain exceptional cases in which a buyer of part of a bulk of goods was able to establish that property had passed[87] these exceptions operated within a very narrow compass.

---

re-examination in the higher courts (*Re Goldcorp Exchange Ltd* [1995] 1 AC 74, 90, PC). However, while there has been some emphasis on the 'flexibility' of the law, there are no signs of a radical reconsideration by the English courts: *Kulkarni v Manor Credit (Davenham) Ltd* [2010] EWCA Civ 69, [2011] 2 Lloyd's Rep 431, at [28] et seq.

[75] It is usually the seller but it may be the buyer.

[76] eg in the case of a cif contract this is often done by issuing a notice of appropriation.

[77] *Healy v Howlett & Sons* [1917] 1 KB 337, KBD; *Laurie & Morewood v Dudin & Sons* [1926] 1 KB 223, CA.

[78] If the seller remains free to change his mind then there can be no unconditional appropriation of the goods: *Carlos Federspiel SA v Charles Twigg* [1957] 1 Lloyd's Rep 240, QBD.

[79] Problems tend to arise where it is alleged that the assent took place prior to the appropriation. Where the assent is subsequent to the appropriation it is rather easier to show that there has been an unconditional appropriation.

[80] *Carlos Federspiel SA v Charles Twigg* [1957] 1 Lloyd's Rep 240, 255, QBD.

[81] Constructive delivery involves the transfer of control over the goods to the buyer, without the transfer of physical possession of the goods, for example by the transfer of a document of title relating to the goods.

[82] 'Appropriation by delivery' is in fact regulated by s 18, r 5(2). Note that there will be no unconditional appropriation where the seller reserves the right of disposal of the goods.

[83] *Hendy Lennox (Industrial Engines) Ltd v Graham Puttick Ltd* [1984] 1 WLR 485, 495, QBD.

[84] The meaning of which is discussed in 2.33.

[85] As defined in Sale of Goods Act 1979, s 61(5), on which see n 61.

[86] See eg *Re Wait* [1927] 1 Ch 606, CA; *Re London Wine Co (Shippers) Ltd* [1986] Palmer's Company Cases 121, Ch D; *Re Goldcorp Exchange Ltd* [1995] 1 AC 74, PC.

[87] Apart from cases where the buyer was able to show that the goods had been unconditionally appropriated to the contract, buyers could show that property had passed to them where the goods had been ascertained by exhaustion (see eg *Karlshamns Oljefabriker v Eastport Navigation Corporation (The Elafi)* [1981] 2 Lloyd's Rep 679, QBD and s 18, r 5(3) and (4) of the Sale of Goods Act 1979), where the parties intended to create a co-ownership of the bulk (as in *Re Staytlon Fletcher Ltd* [1994] 1 WLR 1181, Ch D) and, in certain limited circumstances, equity provided the purchaser with some proprietary relief. But the intervention of equity is a vexed issue. The dominant judicial attitude seems to be one of hostility to the intervention

(ii) Section 20A of the 1979 Act: purchasers of part of a bulk

Parliament eventually intervened in the form of the Sale of Goods (Amendment) Act 1995 to   **2.22**
provide certain purchasers of part of a bulk with proprietary rather than merely contractual
rights, by declaring them to be owners in common of the bulk. This new right is, however,
rather narrowly drawn. First, a buyer must establish that the goods form part of a bulk of
goods.[88] 'Bulk' is rather restrictively defined[89] as a mass or collection of goods which is contained in a defined space or area and is such that any goods in the bulk are interchangeable
with any other goods therein of the same number or quantity.[90] Secondly, the buyer must
have paid the price for some or all of the goods. A buyer who satisfies these conditions is then
declared to be an owner in common of the bulk. The effect of the new provision is, essentially,
that the buyer is entitled to recover such share as the quantity of goods paid for and due to
him out of the bulk bears to the quantity of the goods in the bulk at that time.[91] In order to
protect a buyer in the security of his receipts, it has been provided that one buyer is deemed
to have consented to another buyer taking delivery of his share of the goods due to him which
form part of the bulk.[92] So, where it is discovered that there is a shortfall in the bulk of the
goods, the buyers who do not receive their full entitlement do not have an action against the
buyers who have obtained their full entitlement but must content themselves with a claim
against the seller for short delivery.[93]

(c) Reservation of right of disposal

A seller of goods is entitled to retain a right of disposal of the goods until certain conditions   **2.23**
are met.[94] Sellers have endeavoured to exploit this potential to the full by inserting into the
contract of sale a clause which seeks to reserve ownership in the goods until payment for
them has been made and so provide a substantial measure of protection in the event of the
insolvency of the buyer.[95] Initially the courts were receptive to such attempts by sellers and
adopted a liberal approach to the interpretation and the validity of these clauses.[96] More
recently the courts have had a change of heart and adopted a much more restrictive approach
both to issues of interpretation[97] and validity. Where the goods the subject of the retention
of title clause have not been mixed by the buyer with any other goods belonging to him, then
effect is likely to be given to the clause by the courts. This is so even where the clause states

---

of equity in commercial matters (see *Re Goldcorp Exchange Ltd* [1995] 1 AC 74, PC), although occasional
examples of the infiltration of equity can be found (see *Hunter v Moss* [1994] 1 WLR 452, CA and *Re
Harvard Securities Ltd (in liq)* [1997] 2 BCLC 369, Ch D and, more generally, S Worthington, 'Sorting Out
Ownership Interests in a Bulk: Gifts, Sales and Trusts' [1999] JBL 1).

[88] If there is no bulk and the goods are wholly unascertained then s 16 of the Sale of Goods Act 1979
continues to apply and property cannot pass.

[89] Sale of Goods Act 1979, s 61(1).

[90] A particular problem is whether a contractual provision which entitles the seller to supply the goods from
outside the defined source prevents there being a bulk. On the facts of both *Re London Wine Co (Shippers) Ltd*
[1986] Palmer's Company Cases 121, Ch D and *Re Goldcorp Exchange Ltd* [1995] 1 AC 74, PC it was held
that there was no bulk and the same answer would appear to follow under s 20A.

[91] Sale of Goods Act 1979, s 20A.

[92] Sale of Goods Act 1979, s 20B. The provision is rather cumbersome. The point does not appear to have
caused practical problems in other jurisdictions.

[93] Although it is open to the buyers collectively to adjust the losses between themselves: see Sale of Goods
Act 1979, s 20B(3).

[94] Sale of Goods Act 1979, s 19(1). See eg *Transpacific Eternity SA v Kanematsu Corporation (The 'Antares
III')* [2002] 1 Lloyd's Rep 233.

[95] Retention of title clauses are discussed in more detail in 8.82–8.86.

[96] *Aluminium Industrie Vaasen BV v Romalpa Aluminium Co Ltd* [1976] 1 WLR 676, CA.

[97] See eg *Chaigley Farms Ltd v Crawford, Kaye & Grayshire Ltd* [1996] BCC 957.

that property[98] in the goods shall not pass until the buyer has discharged all liabilities which are owed to the seller.[99] But where the goods have been mixed with other goods it is unlikely that the reservation of title clause will be effective to prevent property from passing[100] unless the goods can be easily unmixed.[101] Where the goods have been sub-sold by the buyer and the seller seeks to claim the proceeds of the sale, it is unlikely that the retention of title clause will be effective. Although there is authority which supports the validity of such a clause,[102] the weight of authority supports the conclusion that such a clause will be interpreted as a charge which requires to be registered if it is to be effective.[103]

(2) Transfer of Title by a Non-Owner

(a) Nemo dat quod non habet

2.24 The location of property rights also assumes considerable significance in the case of what are alleged to be unauthorized dealings in goods belonging to another. The general rule, enshrined in section 21 of the Act, is that a seller cannot give a buyer a better title than he, the seller, had; this rule is commonly expressed in the maxim *nemo dat quod non habet*.[104] This rule has been subject to some criticism in its application to contracts for the sale of goods on the ground that it is commercially inconvenient in that it fails to protect third parties who buy in all good faith, unaware of the seller's lack of title.[105] Good faith buyers are said to be particularly worthy of protection because of the need to encourage the free-flow of commerce, which can only be done by creating an environment in which buyers can purchase with confidence. The difficulty here is that the law is essentially seeking to strike a balance between competing interests: the claim of the original owner of the goods and the claim of the good faith purchaser.[106] English law, unlike some civil law systems, starts from the position that it is the claim of the original owner which has priority, but the exceptions reflect the desire of the courts and the legislature to protect the third party purchaser.

(b) Exceptions to the *nemo dat* rule

2.25 Broadly speaking,[107] the law prefers the interest of the third party where the original owner took the risk, or is held to have assumed the risk, that the goods would be sold without his

---

[98] It is not enough for the seller to seek to retain the equitable interest in the goods. A court will view an attempt to retain the equitable interest as a charge which is void for want of registration: see *Re Bond Worth* [1980] Ch 228, Ch D, although the case is not without its critics.

[99] *Armour v Thyssen Edelstahlwerke AG* [1991] 2 AC 339, HL.

[100] *Borden (UK) Ltd v Scottish Timber Products Ltd* [1981] Ch 25, CA; *Re Peachdart Ltd* [1984] Ch 131, Ch D; *Clough Mill Ltd v Martin* [1985] 1 WLR 111, CA.

[101] *Hendy Lennox (Industrial Engines) Ltd v Graham Puttick Ltd* [1984] 1 WLR 485, QBD.

[102] *Aluminium Industrie Vaasen BV v Romalpa Aluminium Co Ltd* [1976] 1 WLR 676, CA.

[103] *E Pfeiffer Weinkellerei-Weineinkauf GmbH v Arbuthnot Factors Ltd* [1988] 1 WLR 150, Ch D; *Re Weldtech Equipment Ltd* [1991] BCC 16, Ch D; *Compaq Computer Ltd v Abercorn Group Ltd* [1991] BCC 484, Ch D.

[104] It is obviously necessary to ascertain the title which the seller has at the outset. Where the seller has a voidable title to the goods and that title has not been set aside at the time at which the seller sold the goods to a buyer who was unaware of the defect in the seller's title then the buyer obtains good title (Sale of Goods Act 1979, s 23. As to the mode of rescission, see *Car & Universal Finance Ltd v Caldwell* [1965] 1 QB 525, CA). Where, however, the title which the seller has is void, the seller has no title which he can transfer to the buyer.

[105] Of course, the buyer will ordinarily have a claim against the person who sold the goods to him for breach of s 12 of the Act (discussed in 2.29 and 2.30) but that right of action is of little practical utility when, as is often the case, that party is insolvent.

[106] See the judgment of Denning LJ in *Bishopsgate Motor Finance Corp v Transport Brakes Ltd* [1949] 1 KB 332, 336–337, CA.

[107] The *nemo dat* rule and its exceptions are discussed in a wide context in EPL 4.487ff. The statutory exceptions to *nemo dat* are rather convoluted and are set out here in outline only. For more detailed consideration see *Benjamin*, n 1, at ch 7.

actual authority or was in some way at fault in relation to the sale of goods. Thus a non-owner can pass good title to a buyer if he has actual or apparent authority from the owner to enter into the sale or where, by his conduct, the owner is estopped or prevented from asserting his ownership of the goods.[108] Similarly a mercantile agent[109] who is in possession of the goods or of the documents of title[110] to the goods with the consent[111] of the owner and who sells[112] the goods in the ordinary course of his business as a mercantile agent[113] can pass good title to the buyer provided that the buyer buys in good faith[114] and without notice[115] of the want of authority.[116] A buyer who, having bought the goods from the seller, allows the seller to continue[117] in possession of the goods runs the risk that the seller may sell[118] the goods again and so confer a good title on a subsequent purchaser who buys in good faith and without knowledge of the previous sale.[119] Similarly, a seller who retains title to the goods but nevertheless allows a buyer or person who has agreed to buy[120] them into possession of the goods runs the risk that the buyer may sell[121] the goods to a subsequent buyer and so confer good title on that subsequent purchaser provided that he is in good faith and has no notice of the right of the original seller.[122] Where, however, the goods are stolen from the original owner, he will generally be able to recover them or their value even from a bona fide purchaser for value.[123] In such a case the owner has not entrusted the goods into the custody of another person and so cannot be said to have assumed the risk that they would be sold without his

---

[108] Estoppel operates within very narrow limits here: see eg *Moorgate Mercantile Co v Twitchings* [1977] AC 890, HL; *Lloyds & Scottish Finance Ltd v Williamson* [1965] 1 WLR 404, CA; *Eastern Distributors Ltd v Goldring* [1957] 2 QB 600, CA.

[109] Defined in s 1(1) of the Factors Act 1889.

[110] Defined in s 1(4) of the Factors Act 1889.

[111] The consent must relate to possession of the goods in the capacity of a mercantile agent: *Pearson v Rose & Young Ltd* [1951] 1 KB 275, CA.

[112] Or pledges or otherwise disposes of the goods. A contract to sell the goods does not suffice.

[113] *Oppenheimer v Attenborough & Son* [1908] 1 KB 221, CA; *Pearson v Rose & Young Ltd* [1951] 1 KB 275, CA.

[114] By which is meant honesty in fact; see Sale of Goods Act 1979, s 61(3).

[115] Although constructive notice does not generally apply to commercial transactions (*Manchester Trust v Furness* [1895] 2 QB 539, CA), the test of notice probably contains an objective element so that the buyer cannot turn a blind eye to the obvious (*Feuer Leather Corporation v Frank Johnstone & Sons Ltd* [1981] Commercial LR 251, CA).

[116] Factors Act 1889, s 2(1).

[117] While the seller must continue in possession, he need not do so in his capacity as seller. He can do so as a bailee: *Pacific Motor Auctions Pty Ltd v Motor Credits (Hire Finance) Ltd* [1965] AC 867, PC; *Worcester Works Finance Ltd v Cooden Engineering Co Ltd* [1972] 1 QB 210, CA.

[118] Or pledge or otherwise dispose of the goods. There must be a delivery or transfer of the goods or documents of title to the subsequent buyer. It would appear that the delivery need not be actual but can be constructive: *Michael Gerson (Leasing) Ltd v Wilkinson* [2001] QB 514, CA, noted by Ulph (2001) 64 *MLR* 481.

[119] Sale of Goods Act 1979, s 24.

[120] A person who has obtained goods on hire-purchase terms has not agreed to buy the goods. It is thus vital in this context to distinguish between a conditional sale agreement and a hire-purchase agreement: see *Forthright Finance Ltd v Carlyle Finance Ltd* [1997] 4 All ER 90, CA.

[121] Or pledge or otherwise dispose of the goods. There must be a delivery or transfer of the goods or documents of title to the subsequent buyer. It would appear that the delivery need not be actual but can be constructive: *Forsythe International (UK) Ltd v Silver Shipping Co Ltd* [1994] 1 WLR 1334, QBD.

[122] Sale of Goods Act 1979, s 25(1). 'Good faith' is defined in s 61(3) of the Act and the test which the courts apply in relation to notice is an objective one: *Forsythe International (UK) Ltd v Silver Shipping Co Ltd* [1994] 1 WLR 1334, 1349–1351, QBD (see n 114).

[123] *National Employers Mutual General Insurance Association Ltd v Jones* [1990] 1 AC 24, HL. But the old rule which enabled a buyer in 'market overt' to obtain good title (even against an owner whose goods had been stolen) has been abolished by the Sale of Goods (Amendment) Act 1994. While the 'market overt' rule protected the third party purchaser, and so could be said to have facilitated trade, its abuses, both actual and perceived, led to its abolition.

authority. The law has been criticized for its complexity.[124] Proposals were made to extend the scope of protection for innocent purchasers of goods[125] but they were not implemented.

(3) Risk of Loss or Damage[126]

(a) The prima facie rule and its displacement

2.26 The prima facie rule laid down in section 20(1) of the Act is that risk passes with property. So, if the seller is the owner of the goods at the time of loss or damage, then prima facie he is the one who must bear the loss, even if the goods are in the possession or control of the buyer; conversely if it is the buyer who is the owner of the goods then he must bear the loss. This linkage of property and risk has been criticized as another example of the Act's pre-occupation with the importance of property. Many other legal systems link the passage of risk to possession or control of the goods.[127] However the rule laid down in the Act is only a prima facie one and it can be, and very often is, displaced by the express or implied terms of the contract. The passage of risk and property are most often decoupled in the case of international sales contracts, such as cif and fob contracts.[128] Similarly, a seller may reserve property in the goods until the buyer makes payment, but is unlikely to retain the risk of loss or damage to the goods which will pass to the buyer at an earlier stage.[129] In the case of contracts for the sale of goods from a bulk it is possible for risk to pass to the buyer before property passes provided that there is evidence, such as the transmission to the buyer of a delivery warrant entitling the buyer to take delivery of the goods, from which the court can infer that it was the intention of the parties that risk should pass to the buyer.[130] Where delivery has been delayed through the fault of the seller or the buyer the risk lies with the party at fault as regards any loss which might not have occurred but for such fault.[131]

2.26A The link between risk and the passage of property has also been broken in the context of consumer sale contracts that fall within the scope of the Consumer Rights Act 2015. Thus

---

[124] There are other exceptions to the *nemo dat* rule, notably Part III of the Hire-Purchase Act 1965 (re-enacted in Sch 4 to the Consumer Credit Act 1974), which applies to motor vehicles which are subject to a hire-purchase or conditional sale agreement.

[125] DTI Consultation Document, Transfer of Title: Sections 21–26 of the Sale of Goods Act 1979 (DTI, January 1994). The DTI proposed that the present law should be replaced by a 'broad principle...that where the owner of goods has entrusted those goods to, or acquiesced in their possession by, another person, then an innocent purchaser of those goods should acquire good title'.

[126] See generally L Sealy, 'Risk in the Law of Sale' [1972] CLJ 225.

[127] A tendency which is reflected in Articles 67–69 of the Vienna Convention where the passage of risk is, broadly speaking, linked to control of the goods. Where, under a contract governed by English law, risk passes with possession or control of the goods that will be a product of the intention of the parties and not the default rule enshrined in the Act.

[128] In the case of fob contracts risk generally passes on shipment (although the precise time in the shipment process when risk passes to the buyer remains unclear; see *Pyrene Co Ltd v Scindia Navigation Co Ltd* [1954] 2 QB 402, QBD), while property passes when the goods are loaded on board the ship. However it is not uncommon for sellers to take out the bill of lading in their own name with the intention of reserving property in the goods (see eg *The Ciudad de Pasto and Ciudad de Neiva* [1988] 2 Lloyd's Rep 208, CA); this practice does not affect the passage of risk. In the case of cif contracts risk passes as from the date of shipment, whereas property generally passes when the buyer makes payment in return for receipt of the relevant documents.

[129] A fact which can cause problems for the buyer where the goods are damaged by the negligence of a third party, see *Leigh and Sillivan Ltd v Aliakmon Shipping Ltd* [1986] AC 785, HL. In such a case the buyer is unlikely to have a claim against the third party in tort but may possibly have an action in contract where the contract involves the carriage of goods by sea (see Carriage of Goods by Sea Act 1992, s 2(1)).

[130] *Sterns Ltd v Vickers* [1923] 1 KB 78, CA where, it should be noted, that the warehouseman had attorned to the buyer. The case may have been decided otherwise in the absence of such attornment. *Sterns* should be contrasted with *Healy v Howlett & Sons* [1917] 1 KB 337, KBD.

[131] Sale of Goods Act 1979, s 20(2). The operation of this rule is illustrated by *Demby Hamilton & Co Ltd v Barden* [1949] 1 All ER 435, KBD.

section 29 of the Act provides that goods remain at the trader's risk until they come into the physical possession of the consumer or of a person identified by the consumer to take possession of the goods.[131a] In the case where goods are delivered to a carrier who is commissioned by the consumer to deliver the goods and is not a carrier the trader has named as an option for the consumer, then risk passes to the consumer on and after delivery to the carrier.[131b] Attaching the transfer of risk to physical possession is more appropriate for consumer sale contracts and, as has been noted, is more consistent with the approach taken in a number of legal systems which link the passage of risk to possession or control of the goods.

(b) Goods that have already perished when the contract is made

In the case of a contract for the sale of specific goods,[132] and the goods without the knowledge of the seller have perished[133] at the time when the contract is made, the contract is void.[134] Where the seller has assumed, or is held to have assumed, the risk of the non-existence of the goods, it may be that he can be held liable in damages,[135] although such a proposition does not fit easily with a strict reading of the Act.[136] Where there is an agreement to sell[137] specific goods[138] and subsequently the goods, without any fault[139] on the part of the seller or buyer, perish[140] before the risk passes to the buyer, the agreement is avoided.[141] In the case where only a part of the goods perish the agreement to sell is likely to be avoided in relation to the portion which has perished[142] but the obligation of the seller to deliver the goods which have not perished may still be enforceable.[143]

2.27

C. The Contract

(1) The Terms of the Contract

A contract of sale is likely to consist of a mixture of express and implied terms. Little needs to be said here about express terms. In the event of a dispute a court will interpret them in the usual way.[144] The implied terms are, however, a distinctive feature of the Sale of Goods Act 1979 and, as such, require greater comment. These terms are implied into the contract in

2.28

[131a] Consumer Rights Act 2015, s 29(2).

[131b] Consumer Rights Act 2015, s 29(3) and (4).

[132] As to the meaning of which see 2.11 and n 38.

[133] Which extends to goods which have been stolen (*Barrow, Lane & Ballard Ltd v Phillip Phillips & Co Ltd* [1929] 1 KB 574, KBD) but not to goods which have never existed (*McRae v Commonwealth Disposals Commission* (1951) 84 CLR, 377, High Court of Australia).

[134] Sale of Goods Act 1979, s 6. The section was probably intended to give effect to the decision of the House of Lords in *Couturier v Hastie* (1856) 5 HLC 673, HL, although the word 'mistake' was nowhere used in the judgments of their Lordships.

[135] As was the case in *McRae v Commonwealth Disposals Commission* (1951) 84 CLR 377, High Court of Australia.

[136] The fact that s 6 states that the contract is void and makes no provision for the parties to agree otherwise may suggest that the draftsman intended the rule to be absolute but this view is not supported by *Benjamin*, n 1, at 1–132 or *Atiyah's Sale of Goods*, n 1 at 99–104.

[137] It is otherwise where there is a sale.

[138] As to the meaning of which see para 2.11 and n 38.

[139] Fault is defined in s 61(1) as 'wrongful act or default'.

[140] As to the meaning of which see n 133.

[141] Sale of Goods Act 1979, s 7.

[142] See *Howell v Coupland* (1874) LR 9 QB 462; aff'd (1876) 1 QBD 258, CA. The case is, however, a difficult one, on which see G Treitel, *Frustration and Force Majeure* (3rd edn, 2014) 4–049ff.

[143] *HR and S Sainsbury Ltd v Street* [1972] 1 WLR 834, Assizes. However the buyer is not under an obligation to accept a partial delivery as a result of s 30(1) of the Sale of Goods Act 1979, see 2.44.

[144] The rules of construction adopted by the courts are set out in EPL ch 8.

an attempt to protect the position of a buyer of goods and substantial restrictions are placed upon the ability of a seller to exclude them. Similar terms are 'treated as included'[144a] in consumer contracts that fall within the scope of the Consumer Rights Act 2015 and the ability of a trader to exclude their operation is severely restricted.[144b]

(a) Implied terms about title

(i) Right to sell the goods

2.29 Section 12(1) of the Act provides that there is an implied term that in the case of a sale the seller has 'a right[145] to sell the goods' and, in the case of an agreement to sell, that 'he will have such a right at the time when the property is to pass'.[146] This implied term has a temporal limitation. It applies only at the moment of sale or, in the case of an agreement to sell, at the moment at which property passes to the buyer; it has no future or continuing application.[147] This implied term has the status of a condition[148] so that a breach of it, in principle, gives to the buyer the right to reject the goods and terminate the contract. Section 12 provides evidence of the importance which English law attaches to the concept of property; what the buyer is deemed to have contracted for is title to the goods, not possession of them. Thus a buyer can reject the goods on the ground of the seller's lack of title to sell even where, prior to rejection, he was able to enjoy substantial possession and use of the goods.[149] These decisions have been criticized[150] on the ground that they resulted in the unjust enrichment of the buyers. But it can be argued that any such unjust enrichment was 'at the expense' of the true owner of the goods and not the seller so that there can be no justification for imposing on the buyer an obligation to pay the seller for the use of someone else's goods. A buyer who finds that he is unable to deal in the goods because, eg, he can be restrained by injunction from doing so, may be able to establish a breach of section 12(1).[151]

(ii) Free from undisclosed charge or incumbrance

2.30 Section 12(2) also implies a warranty[152] that the goods are free and will remain free until the time when the property is to pass from any charge or encumbrance not disclosed or known

---

[144a] This is the language used in the Act in preference to the more traditional terminology of the implication of terms. But it would appear that the difference is one of terminology, not substance.

[144b] Consumer Rights Act 2015, s 29.

[145] The fact that the word used is 'right' not 'power' implies that there is a breach of s 12 even where the buyer obtains good title by virtue of an exception to the *nemo dat* rule. The point is not, however, resolved as a matter of authority. Dicta in *R v Wheeler* (1991) 92 Cr App Rep 279, CA support the view that there is a breach of s 12, whereas dicta in *Niblett v Confectioners' Materials Co* [1921] 3 KB 387, 401–402, CA and *Karlshamns Oljefabriker v Eastport Navigation Corporation (The Elafi)* [1981] 2 Lloyd's Rep 679, 685, QBD suggest the contrary. See generally I Brown, 'The Scope of Section 12 of the Sale of Goods Act' (1992) 108 LQR 221.

[146] Thus the seller under a conditional sale contract need only ensure that he has title to transfer at the moment when property passes to the buyer. But such a seller may be required by the express terms of the contract to be the owner of the goods at the moment of entry into the contract: *Barber v NWS Bank plc* [1996] 1 WLR 641, CA.

[147] *Microbeads AG v Vinhurst Road Markings Ltd* [1975] 1 WLR 218, 221–222, CA.

[148] Sale of Goods Act 1979, s 12(5A).

[149] *Rowland v Divall* [1923] 2 KB 500, CA; *Butterworth v Kingsway Motors Ltd* [1954] 1 WLR 1286, Assizes; *Barber v NWS Bank plc* [1996] 1 WLR 641, CA.

[150] See eg M Bridge, 'The Title Obligations of the Seller of Goods' in N Palmer and E McKendrick (eds), *Interests in Goods* (2nd edn, 1998) 303; *Benjamin*, n 1, at 4–006.

[151] *Niblett v Confectioners' Materials Co* [1921] 3 KB 387, CA. The interference must relate to the buyer's ability to sell or to deal in the goods: it does not suffice to show simply that there has been an interference with the possession of the buyer: *Great Elephant Corporation v Trafigura Beheer* [2012] EWHC 1745 (Comm), [2012] 2 Lloyd's Rep 503, at [99].

[152] Sale of Goods Act 1979, s 12(5A).

to the buyer before the contract is made[153] and that the buyer will enjoy quiet possession of the goods except in so far as it may be disturbed by the owner or other person entitled to the benefit of any charge or encumbrance so disclosed or known.[154] The warranty of quiet possession is of a continuing nature and so can encompass future acts which may interrupt the buyer in his quiet possession of the goods.[155]

(iii) Exclusion clauses

While a seller cannot exclude liability to a buyer for breach of section 12,[156] he can agree 'to **2.31** transfer only such title as he or a third person may have'.[157] The line between the sale of a limited title and the attempt to exclude liability is not always an easy one to draw.[158]

(b) Correspondence with description

Section 13(1) of the Act states that 'Where there is a contract for the sale of goods by descrip- **2.32** tion, there is an implied term[159] that the goods will correspond with the description.' This short sentence has proved to be one of the most troublesome in the whole Act. The nub of the problem is that not all descriptive words fall within the scope of the section and the courts have found it extremely difficult to devise a test which can distinguish those descriptive words which fall within its scope from those which do not. Some descriptive words may have no legal force at all.[160] Others may be mere representations which are not incorporated into the contract.[161] Many descriptive words are express, not implied terms of the contract and it cannot be the case that all express terms fall within the scope of section 13.[162]

(i) Requirement of sale 'by description'

The key to delimiting section 13 lies in the requirement that the sale must be one 'by descrip- **2.33** tion'. Some points are tolerably clear. Where the contract is one for the sale of unascertained goods[163] or future goods[164] the sale will generally be by description because the descriptive words will serve to identify the goods. More problematic is the application of section 13 to the sale of specific goods. Where the buyer has not seen the specific goods, the sale will

---

[153] Sale of Goods Act 1979, s 12(2)(a). This subsection is of little if any practical significance. Most cases which fall within its scope also fall within s 12(1).

[154] Sale of Goods Act 1979, s 12(2)(b).

[155] *Microbeads AG v Vinhurst Road Markings Ltd* [1975] 1 WLR 218, CA; *Empresa Exportadora de Azucar v Industria Azucarera Nacional SA (The Playa Larga)* [1983] 2 Lloyd's Rep 171, CA; *Great Elephant Corporation v Trafigura Beheer* [2012] EWHC 1745 (Comm), [2012] 2 Lloyd's Rep 503. The ambit of the warranty, in terms of its duration, is not entirely clear. But it is not limited to disturbance by the seller himself; it can extend, in certain circumstances, to disturbance by a third party (see the *Microbeads* case at 222–223).

[156] Unfair Contract Terms Act 1977, s 6(1)(a).

[157] Sale of Goods Act 1979, s 12(3). A seller in such a case must also comply with the requirements laid down in s 12(4) and (5).

[158] eg, in the context of exclusion clauses there has been a long debate over whether or not such clauses exist to define the obligations of the parties or whether they operate to provide a defence to a breach of an obligation.

[159] The 'term' is stated to be a condition of the contract (s 13(1A)) so that a breach of it, in principle, gives the buyer the right to reject the goods and terminate the contract.

[160] As in *Reardon Smith Lines Ltd v Hansen Tangen* [1976] 1 WLR 989, HL (in relation to the yard at which the ship was to be built).

[161] *Oscar Chess Ltd v Williams* [1957] 1 WLR 370, CA. In such a case the usual remedies for misrepresentation will be available. The practical difficulty here is that it is often difficult to tell whether a statement is a term or a mere representation. On this distinction see EPL ch 8.

[162] If they did, s 13 would amount to a statement that there is an *implied* term that the seller must comply with the *express* terms of the contract.

[163] Defined in n 39.

[164] Defined in 2.11 and n 37. Not all sales of future goods are by description. Where the goods have been requested by the buyer and are in the ownership of a third party, the sale may not be one by description.

generally be one by description.[165] Where the parties have met and the buyer has seen the goods, the simplest approach to take would have been to conclude that such a sale cannot be by description. However, the courts have refused to take this line and instead concluded that such a sale can, in appropriate circumstances, be by description.[166] To constitute a sale by description the buyer must show that the description was 'influential in the sale...so as to become an essential term...of the contract',[167] that he relied upon the descriptive words,[168] and that the words used served to identify the goods rather than their attributes.[169] Once it is concluded that the sale is 'by description' the standard applied by the courts is a very strict one[170] so that even minor deviations from specification in principle[171] give the buyer a right to reject the goods and terminate the contract.

(ii) Exclusion clauses

2.34 Section 13 applies to all contracts of sale; it is not confined to sales which take place in the course of a business.[172] The term can be excluded if it is reasonable to do so.[173]

(c) **Satisfactory quality and fitness for purpose**

2.35 Reflecting the influence which the principle of *caveat emptor* has exerted over the development of sale of goods law, there is no implied term 'about the quality or fitness for any particular purpose of goods supplied under a contract of sale'[174] other than those expressly provided for in sections 14 and 15 of the Act. Section 14 contains two such terms, namely that the goods must be of 'satisfactory quality'[175] and they must be reasonably fit for their purpose.[176] These implied terms only apply where the seller[177] sells 'in the course of a business' but these words are to be given a wide construction[178] and do not require that the seller

---

[165] As in *Varley v Whipp* [1900] 1 KB 513, QBD.

[166] *Grant v Australian Knitting Mills Ltd* [1936] AC 85, 100, HL. Further s 13(3) of the Act states that a sale is not prevented from being a sale by description by reason only that the goods, having been exposed for sale or hire, are selected by the buyer.

[167] *Harlingdon & Leinster Enterprises Ltd v Christopher Hull Fine Art Ltd* [1991] 1 QB 564, 571, CA.

[168] *Harlingdon & Leinster Enterprises Ltd v Christopher Hull Fine Art Ltd* [1991] 1 QB 564, 574, CA. The invocation of reliance here has not gone without criticism.

[169] The line between identity and attributes is a notoriously difficult one to draw but it has been invoked by the courts in this context: see eg *Ashington Piggeries Ltd v Christopher Hill Ltd* [1972] AC 441, 503–504, HL and *Reardon Smith Line Ltd v Yngvar Hansen-Tangen* [1976] 1 WLR 989, 999, HL.

[170] See eg *Arcos Ltd v EA Ronaasen & Son* [1933] AC 470, HL and *Re Moore & Co and Landauer & Co* [1921] 2 KB 519, CA. These cases might now be decided differently as a result of the enactment of s 15A of the Sale of Goods Act 1979.

[171] Subject to the controls enacted in s 15A of the Sale of Goods Act 1979. There had been a suggestion that the courts would themselves reconsider the appropriateness of such a strict approach (*Reardon Smith Line Ltd v Yngvar Hansen-Tangen* [1976] 1 WLR 989, 998, HL) but that reconsideration never took place.

[172] As is the case with the terms implied by s 14 of the Act.

[173] Unfair Contract Terms Act 1977, s 6(3).

[174] Sale of Goods Act 1979, s 14(1). A point that was overlooked by the trial judge but not by the Court of Appeal in *Lowe v W Machell Joinery Ltd* [2011] EWCA Civ 794, [2011] BLR 591, at [39]. See also *KG Bominflot Bunkergesellschaft Für Mineralöle mnH & Co v Petroplus Marketing AG (The 'Mercini Lady')* [2010] EWCA Civ 1145, [2011] 1 Lloyd's Rep 442, at [45].

[175] Sale of Goods Act 1979, s 14(2).

[176] Sale of Goods Act 1979, s 14(3).

[177] Where the sale is effected by an agent acting in the course of a business, the principal is caught by these implied terms unless the principal is not selling in the course of a business and either the buyer knows the fact or reasonable steps are taken to bring it to the notice of the buyer before the contract is made: Sale of Goods Act 1979, s 14(5). This provision applies to undisclosed principals, in which case both the principal and the agent may incur liability (*Boyter v Thomson* [1995] 2 AC 629, HL).

[178] *Stevenson v Rogers* [1999] QB 1028, CA (sale by fisherman of his fishing boat held to take place in the course of his business), followed by the Inner House of the Court of Session in *MacDonald v Pollock* [2011] CSIH 12, [2012] 1 Lloyd's Rep 425 (a case also involving the sale of a fishing vessel); cf *Feldarol Foundry plc*

habitually or regularly deal in goods of the type sold.[179] What is excluded from the Act is a 'purely private sale of goods outside the confines of the business (if any) carried on by the seller'.[180]

(i) Of satisfactory quality

The implied term[181] that the goods supplied under the contract must be of satisfactory qual-   **2.36**
ity is of relatively recent origin, having been first introduced in the Sale and Supply of Goods Act 1994. It replaced the implied term which required that the goods be of 'merchantable quality'. Case law on the meaning of 'satisfactory quality' has taken time to build up.[182] In these circumstances the cases on the meaning of 'merchantable quality' may continue to provide limited assistance,[183] albeit that Parliament did not intend 'satisfactory quality' to be synonymous with 'merchantable quality'. The guidance within the Act itself is very limited. Its central provision is rather vague, if not circular. It states that 'goods are of satisfactory quality if they meet the standard that a reasonable person would regard as satisfactory, taking account of any description of the goods, the price (if relevant) and all the other relevant factors'[184] but does not state what a reasonable person would expect. However the Act does provide an indication of the factors which may be relevant.[185] The quality of the goods includes their state and condition and 'in appropriate cases'[186] the following may be aspects of the quality of goods: (a) fitness for all the purposes for which goods of the kind in question are commonly supplied,[187] (b) appearance and finish, (c) freedom from minor defects, (d) safety,[188] and (e) durability.[189] This indicative list has clearly been drafted principally with consumer contracts in mind and may not apply so well to commercial contracts, although

---

v Hermes Leasing (London) Ltd [2004] EWCA Civ 747, CA and *R & B Customers Brokers Co Ltd v United Dominion Trust Ltd* [1988] 1 WLR 321, CA where a much narrower construction was adopted of the words 'in the course of a business' in the context of the former s 12 of the Unfair Contract Terms Act 1977.

[179] 'Business' is defined in s 61(1) of the Sale of Goods Act 1979 as including 'a profession and the activities of any government department... or local or public authority'.

[180] *Stevenson v Rogers* [1999] QB 1028, 1039, CA. The potential anomalies created by this decision are explored by I Brown, 'Sale of Goods in the Course of a Business' (1999) 115 LQR 384.

[181] The term is declared to be a condition by s 14(6).

[182] The leading cases include *Balmoral Group Ltd v Borealis (UK) Ltd* [2006] EWHC 1900 (Comm), [2006] 2 Lloyd's Rep 629, at [140]–[141]; *Bramhill v Edwards* [2004] EWCA Civ 403, [2004] 2 Lloyd's Rep 653; *Jewson Ltd v Boyhan* [2003] EWCA Civ 1030, [2004] 1 Lloyd's Rep 505; and *Britvic Soft Drinks Ltd v Messer UK Ltd* [2002] 1 Lloyd's Rep 20 (the meaning of 'satisfactory quality' was not considered when the case was appealed to the Court of Appeal).

[183] Some of the leading cases on 'merchantable quality' are briefly summarized in *Benjamin*, n 1, at 11-044. The influence of these cases is likely to become increasingly muted as time goes by.

[184] Sale of Goods Act 1979, s 14(2A). A relevant circumstance may be the fact that the goods were second-hand (see eg *Bartlett v Sidney Marcus Ltd* [1965] 1 WLR 1013, CA; cf *Shine v General Guarantee Corp Ltd* [1988] 1 All ER 911, CA).

[185] Sale of Goods Act 1979, s 14(2B).

[186] What constitutes an 'appropriate case' is a matter of conjecture. It may mean no more than the factors listed are not decisive.

[187] The use of the word 'all' rather than 'some' imposes a higher standard on the seller than was the case under the old 'merchantable quality' standard (where the goods had only to be fit for 'one or more' purposes: *Aswan Engineering Establishment Ltd v Lupdine Ltd* [1987] 1 WLR 1, CA). But note the word 'commonly' which is likely to qualify the seller's obligations.

[188] Where the goods are unsafe a claim may also arise under Part I of the Consumer Protection Act 1987, on which see EPL 17.269–17.273.

[189] While durability is undoubtedly a relevant factor, it remains the case that the time at which the goods must be of satisfactory quality is the time of delivery (*Whitecap Leisure Ltd v John H Rundle Ltd* [2008] EWCA Civ 429, [2008] 2 Lloyd's Rep 216, at [45]). While the courts generally adhere to the rule that it is the condition of the goods at the time of delivery that is crucial (*KG Bominflot Bunkergesellschaft Für Mineralöle mnH & Co v Petroplus Marketing AG (The 'Mercini Lady')* [2010] EWCA Civ 1145, [2011] 1 Lloyd's Rep 442), the appearance of a defect very shortly after delivery may be used in evidence to suggest that the goods were not of satisfactory quality at the time of delivery (*Mash & Murrell Ltd v Joseph I Emmanuel Ltd* [1961] 1 WLR 862).

it must be said that, to some extent, the list has simply made explicit what was implicit in the case law on merchantable quality.[190] The satisfactory quality implied term establishes a 'general standard which goods are required to reach',[191] and it is 'primarily directed towards substandard goods.'[192] Liability is, in principle, strict.[193] Essentially the question whether or not goods are of satisfactory quality is a jury-type issue, involving questions of degree, albeit with the scales weighted in favour of the consumer buyer.

2.37 The implied term does not extend to any matter (a) which is specifically drawn to the buyer's attention before the contract is made, (b) in the case where the buyer examines the goods before the contract is made, which that[194] examination ought to reveal[195] or, (c) in the case of a sale by sample, a matter which would have been apparent on a reasonable examination of the sample.[196]

(ii) Fit for their purpose

2.38 In order to establish a breach of the implied term[197] that the goods must be reasonably fit for their purpose,[198] the buyer must expressly or by implication[199] make known to the seller[200] any particular purpose for which the goods are being bought, whether or not that is a purpose for which such goods are commonly supplied. Thus, where goods are bought for their customary purpose the buyer need not disclose it; the court will imply that that is the purpose for which the goods have been bought.[201] A 'particular purpose' means 'a given purpose, known or communicated' and 'is not necessarily a narrow or closely particularised purpose'.[202] The purpose may therefore be a wide one and extend to the foreseeable range of purposes for which such goods are bought.[203] On the other hand, where goods are required for a special or unusual purpose, the buyer must generally make

---

[190] eg freedom from minor defects and the appearance and finish of the goods were regarded as relevant factors in *Rogers v Parish (Scarborough) Ltd* [1987] QB 933, 944, CA. The relevance of the durability of the goods was much more uncertain under the old law, although there were some dicta which indicated that it was pertinent (see eg *Lambert v Lewis* [1982] AC 225, 276, HL).

[191] *Jewson Ltd v Boyhan* [2003] EWCA Civ 1030, [2004] 1 Lloyd's Rep 505, at [46].

[192] *Balmoral Group Ltd v Borealis (UK) Ltd* [2006] EWHC 1900 (Comm), [2006] 2 Lloyd's Rep 629, at [140]. The goods may be sub-standard even in the case where they comply with the buyer's express requirements: *Lowe v W Machell Joinery Ltd* [2011] EWCA Civ 794, [2011] BLR 591 (staircase not of satisfactory quality because it did not comply with the Building Regulations, even though it did meet the buyers' requirements).

[193] That is to say, there is no requirement that the seller be at fault in any way.

[194] In other words, the examination actually carried out, not one which might have been but was not carried out (*MacDonald v Pollock* [2011] CSIH 12, [2012] 1 Lloyd's Rep 425, at [34]). This point was overlooked by the Court of Appeal in *Bramhill v Edwards* [2004] EWCA Civ 403; [2004] 2 Lloyd's Rep 653, at [51], [54] (on which see C Twigg-Flesner 'Examination prior to purchase: a cautionary note' (2005) 121 LQR 205).

[195] Where the defect is latent it should not be particularly difficult to show that the buyer ought not to have discovered it (see eg *Wren v Holt* [1903] 1 KB 610).

[196] Sale of Goods Act 1979, s 14(2C). The onus would appear to be on the seller to show that the implied term is not applicable.

[197] The term is declared to be a condition by s 14(6).

[198] Sale of Goods Act 1979, s 14(3).

[199] The implication that the purpose has been made known to the seller may be derived from a previous course of dealing between the parties or from a prior order placed by the buyer: *Makers (UK) Ltd v BSS Group plc* [2011] EWCA Civ 809, [2011] TCLR 7.

[200] Or, where the purchase price or part of it is payable by instalments and the goods were previously sold by a credit-broker to the seller, to that credit-broker.

[201] *Priest v Last* [1903] 2 KB 148, CA.

[202] *Henry Kendall & Sons v William Lillico & Sons Ltd* [1969] 2 AC 31, 114, HL.

[203] *Ashington Piggeries Ltd v Christopher Hill Ltd* [1972] AC 441, 477, HL; *Henry Kendall & Sons (a firm) v William Lillico & Sons Ltd* [1969] 2 AC 31, 114–115, HL; cf *Aswan Engineering Establishment Ltd v Lupdine Ltd* [1987] 1 WLR 1, 16–17, CA.

that purpose known to the seller.[204] Where the failure of the goods to meet the intended purpose arises from an idiosyncrasy, either of the buyer himself or in the circumstances of his use of the goods, which has not been made known to the seller the seller is not liable, even in the case where the buyer was unaware of the idiosyncrasy.[205] The buyer need not prove that he has relied upon the skill and judgment of the seller; it is for the seller to prove that he did not so rely[206] or that his reliance was unreasonable.[207] Liability of the seller is, in principle, strict[208] but the extent of the obligation is only to sell goods which are *reasonably* fit for their purpose; they need not be completely or absolutely suitable for their purpose.[209] The absence or inadequacy of instructions or warnings may render goods not reasonably fit for their purpose.[210]

(iii) Exclusion clauses

These two implied terms can be excluded if it is reasonable to do so.[211] **2.39**

(d) Correspondence with sample

Section 15 of the Act implies a term[212] that, in the case of a sale by sample,[213] the bulk will **2.40**
correspond with the sample in quality[214] and that the goods will be free from any defect making their quality unsatisfactory which would not be apparent on a reasonable examination of the sample.[215] This implied term applies to all sales, not only to those which take place in the course of a business and can be excluded if it is reasonable to do so.[216]

(e) Consumer sales

The Consumer Rights Act 2015 'treats as included' in a contract for the sale of goods con- **2.40A**
cluded between a trader and a consumer a term that (i) the quality of the goods is satisfactory;[217] (ii) the goods are reasonably fit for their purpose;[218] (iii) the goods will match

---

[204] *Slater v Finning Ltd* [1997] AC 473, 487, HL. Where the buyer does disclose his purpose in buying, the specifications laid down by the buyer are likely to limit the range of goods which can satisfy the purpose: see, for example, *Bristol Tramways etc Carriage Co Ltd v Fiat Motors Ltd* [1910] 2 KB 731, CA.

[205] *Slater v Finning Ltd* [1997] AC 473, HL; *Griffiths v Peter Conway Ltd* [1939] 1 All ER 685, CA. However a seller may be liable where the goods are likely to cause damage in a wide range of circumstances, but are particularly dangerous in relation to the use to which the claimant put the goods: *Ashington Piggeries Ltd v Christopher Hill Ltd* [1972] AC 441, HL.

[206] As, eg, where the buyer relied on his own skill and judgment (see *Tehran-Europe Co Ltd v ST Belton (Tractors) Ltd* [1968] 2 QB 545, CA). The fact that the buyer has provided specifications for the goods does not exclude the possibility of reliance by the buyer on the seller (*Cammell Laird & Co Ltd v Manganese Bronze and Brass Co Ltd* [1934] AC 402, HL).

[207] *Jewson Ltd v Boyhan* [2003] EWCA Civ 1030; [2004] 1 Lloyd's Rep 505, at [61].

[208] *Frost v Aylesbury Dairy Co Ltd* [1905] 1 KB 608, CA; *Henry Kendall & Sons v William Lillico & Sons Ltd* [1969] 2 AC 31, 84, HL.

[209] *Henry Kendall & Sons v William Lillico & Sons Ltd* [1969] 2 AC 31, 115, HL; *Bartlett v Sidney Marcus Ltd* [1965] 1 WLR 1013, CA.

[210] *Wormell v RHM Agricultural (East) Ltd* [1987] 1 WLR 1091, CA (albeit that on the facts the goods were found to be reasonably fit for their purpose).

[211] Unfair Contract Terms Act 1977, s 6(3).

[212] The term has the status of a condition: Sale of Goods Act 1979, s 15(3).

[213] A contract for sale by sample is made where there is an express or implied term to that effect in the contract: Unfair Contract Terms Act 1977, s 15(1).

[214] The correspondence must be precise (*E & S Ruben v Faire Bros Ltd* [1949] 1 KB 254, QBD) unless the sample is intended for visual examination only, where material differences may not involve a breach by the seller (*FE Hookway & Co Ltd v Alfred Isaacs & Son* [1954] 1 Lloyd's Rep 491, QBD).

[215] *James Drummond and Sons v EH Van Ingen & Co Ltd* (1887) 12 App Cas 284, 297, HL.

[216] Unfair Contract Terms Act 1977, s 6(3).

[217] Consumer Rights Act 2015, s 9.

[218] Consumer Rights Act 2015, s 10.

their description;[219] (iv) the goods will correspond with sample;[220] (v) the goods will match a model seen or examined by the consumer before entering into the contract;[221] (vi) the trader has a right to sell the goods;[222] (vii) the goods are free from any charge or encumbrance which has not been disclosed;[223] (viii) the consumer will enjoy quiet possession of the goods[224] and (ix) the goods will be installed correctly where installation forms part of the contract and they are to be installed by the trader or under his responsibility.[225] Broadly speaking the content of these terms resembles those to be found in the 1979 Act and it can be expected that cases decided under the 1979 Act will have some persuasive value in relation to the interpretation of these terms. But there are factors to be taken into account in consumer sales which are not included in the 1979 Act. So, for example, a factor to be taken into account when deciding whether or not goods are of satisfactory quality under the 2015 Act is any public statement about the specific characteristics of the goods made by the trader, the producer or his representative, particularly in advertising or on labelling.[226] However, a public statement is not to be taken into account if the trader shows that (i) at the time the contract was made, he was not, and could not reasonably have been, aware of the statement; (ii) before the contract was made, the statement had been publicly withdrawn or, to the extent that it contained anything which was incorrect or misleading, it had been publicly corrected, or (iii) the consumer's decision to contract for the goods could not have been influenced by the statement.[227] A term of such a contract is not binding on the consumer to the extent that it would exclude or restrict the trader's liability in respect of a breach of any of these terms.[228]

(2) Performance of the Contract

2.41 Other than compliance with the implied terms, the principal obligation of the seller is to deliver the goods. The buyer in turn must accept and pay for them in accordance with the terms of the contract of sale.[229] Unless otherwise agreed, delivery and payment are concurrent conditions.[230] Both obligations are frequently regulated by the express terms of the contract. In the absence of an express term, the Act lays down some default rules, particularly in the case of delivery.

(a) Delivery

2.42 Delivery is defined in the Act as 'the voluntary transfer of possession from one person to another'.[231] In most domestic sale transactions delivery will take the form of the transfer of physical possession of the goods to the buyer. But it need not do so. Delivery can be

---

219 Consumer Rights Act 2015, s 11.
220 Consumer Rights Act 2015, s 12.
221 Consumer Rights Act 2015, s 13.
222 Consumer Rights Act 2015, s 17(1).
223 Consumer Rights Act 2015, s 17(5).
224 Consumer Rights Act 2015, s 17(3).
225 Consumer Rights Act 2015, s 16.
226 Consumer Rights Act 2015, s 9(5) and (6).
227 Consumer Rights Act 2015, s 9(7).
228 Consumer rights Act 2015, s 31.
229 Sale of Goods Act 1979, s 27.
230 Sale of Goods Act 1979, s 28. Thus the seller must be ready and willing to give possession of the goods to the buyer in exchange for the price and the buyer must be ready and willing to pay the price in exchange for the possession of the goods. In the case of documentary sales, the obligation of the buyer is generally to pay the price in exchange for the relevant documents.
231 Sale of Goods Act 1979, s 61(1). The Consumer Rights Act 2015 contains some particular rules on delivery applicable to contracts of sale concluded between a trader and a consumer: s 28

constructive in the sense that what is transferred to the buyer is control of the goods[232] rather than physical possession. Thus in international sale transactions the seller will often perform his delivery obligation by transferring to the buyer a bill of lading which will give the buyer legal control over the goods.[233] Where the goods are in the possession of a third party at the time of entry into the contract of sale, there is no delivery of the goods until the third party attorns to the buyer.[234] Where the seller is authorized or required to send the goods to the buyer, delivery of the goods to a carrier (whether named by the buyer or not) for the purpose of transmission to the buyer is prima facie deemed to be a delivery of goods to the buyer.[235] The seller must, however, enter into a reasonable contract of carriage with the carrier.[236] Where the seller agrees to deliver the goods at his own risk at a place other than where they are sold, the buyer must nevertheless, unless otherwise agreed, take any risk of deterioration in the goods necessarily incident to the course of transit.[237]

(i) Related conditions

Unless otherwise agreed, the place of delivery is the seller's place of business[238] so that it is the **2.43** duty of the buyer to collect the goods. If no time for delivery is fixed by the contract[239] and the seller is bound to send the goods to the buyer, he must do so within a reasonable time.[240] Delivery must be made or tendered at a reasonable hour.[241] The seller must bear the cost of delivering the goods and of putting the goods into a deliverable state[242] while the buyer must bear the cost of receiving delivery.

(ii) Delivery of incorrect quantity

Where the seller delivers insufficient goods to the buyer, the buyer may reject them or he **2.44** may accept them;[243] the choice is his. If he does accept them he must pay for them at the contract rate. Where the seller delivers more than he contracted to sell the buyer may reject all of the goods delivered, accept the amount for which he contracted and reject the surplus

---

[232] Another example might be the transfer of some object, such as a key, which gives physical control over the goods themselves. This is sometimes regarded as a form of constructive delivery but it might be more accurate to regard it as a species of physical delivery.

[233] In the case of a cif contract the seller's delivery obligation actually relates to the documents rather than the goods: see *Benjamin*, n 1, at 19-073. A cif seller must not prevent delivery of the goods from taking place but he is not under an obligation to ensure that actual delivery of the goods takes place.

[234] Sale of Goods Act 1979, s 29(4). A third party attorns to the buyer when he acknowledges to the buyer that he holds the goods on the buyer's behalf.

[235] Sale of Goods Act 1979, s 32(1). This provision does not apply to contracts of sale that fall within the Consumer Rights Act 2015.

[236] Sale of Goods Act 1979, s 32(2). A failure to do so may entitle the buyer to reject the goods or to claim damages. Where the goods are sent by a route involving sea transit the seller must give the buyer sufficient notice to enable him to insure the goods. A failure to do so has the consequence that the goods remain at the risk of the seller: Sale of Goods Act 1979, s 32(3). This subsection has been held to apply to fob contracts (*Wimble Sons & Co v Rosenberg & Sons* [1913] 3 KB 743, CA).

[237] Sale of Goods Act 1979, s 33. This provision does not apply to fob and cif contracts where the goods are generally at the buyer's risk after shipment nor does it apply to contracts of sale that fall within the Consumer Rights Act 2015.

[238] Sale of Goods Act 1979, s 29(2). However in the case of a contract for the sale of specific goods, which to the knowledge of both parties at the date of entry into the contract are in some other place, the place of delivery is that other place.

[239] Note that contracts may frequently provide that the time of delivery is of the essence of the contract. Breach of such a time stipulation will give the buyer the right to terminate further performance of the contract, on which see 2.47.

[240] Sale of Goods Act 1979, s 29(3).

[241] Sale of Goods Act 1979, s 29(5).

[242] Sale of Goods Act 1979, s 29(6).

[243] Sale of Goods Act 1979, s 30(1). This section does not apply to contracts of sale that fall within the Consumer Rights Act 2015.

or accept the entire delivery and pay for the excess at the contract rate.[244] Once again, the choice belongs to the buyer. The buyer's right to reject is however restricted because the buyer cannot reject the goods where the shortfall or the excess is so slight that it would be unreasonable for him to reject.[245]

(iii) Delivery in instalments

2.45 Instalment deliveries are rather more complex. A buyer is not bound to accept delivery of goods by instalments unless he agrees to do so.[246] Where the buyer does so agree and the seller makes defective deliveries in respect of one or more instalment the buyer is not necessarily entitled to terminate the whole contract;[247] it depends upon the seriousness of the breach in relation to the delivery obligation as a whole and the likelihood of the breach being repeated.[248]

(b) Payment

2.46 The buyer's obligation to pay the price (in terms of method, place and time of payment) will generally be governed by the terms of the contract. The Act does not purport to regulate the payment obligations of the buyer in any detail. It does however provide that time of payment is not of the essence of the contract unless provision is made in the contract to this effect.[249] Sellers frequently insert such a provision in the contract.[250]

D. Remedies

(1) The Importance of Termination

(a) The pursuit of certainty

2.47 In the event of a failure by a seller or a buyer to perform his obligations under the contract of sale, the law could adopt one of three different approaches. It could encourage the parties to stay together and seek to sort out their difficulties, it could encourage them to walk away from the deal and seek satisfaction elsewhere or it could adopt some combination of these two approaches. English law has tended to take the second of the three approaches, while the Vienna Convention inclines rather more in the direction of the first.[251] Thus in English law the right of a seller or a buyer to cure his failure to perform in accordance with the terms of the contract operates within narrow confines[252] and there is little emphasis on abatement or

---

[244] Sale of Goods Act 1979, s 30(2) and (3).

[245] Sale of Goods Act 1979, s 30(2A). This provision is 'subject to any usage of trade, special agreement, or course of dealing between the parties' (s 35(5)). It is equivalent to s 15A of the Act and the points made in relation to that section (in 2.48) are equally applicable here.

[246] Sale of Goods Act 1979, s 31(1). This section does not apply to contracts of sale that fall within the Consumer Rights Act 2015.

[247] Sale of Goods Act 1979, s 31(2). The same principle applies where the buyer fails to pay the price for one or more instalments which has been delivered.

[248] *Maple Flock Co Ltd v Universal Furniture Products (Wembley) Ltd* [1934] 1 KB 148, CA.

[249] Sale of Goods Act 1979, s 10(1).

[250] The consequences to a buyer of a failure to make payment on time when time is declared to be of the essence can be severe: see *Lombard North Central plc v Butterworth* [1987] QB 527, CA (a case which actually involves a contract of hire but the point also holds good for contracts of sale).

[251] For a very helpful discussion of the remedial provisions of the Vienna Convention from the perspective of an English lawyer see FMB Reynolds, 'A Note of Caution' in P Birks (ed), *The Frontiers of Liability* (1994) 18.

[252] A contracting party may be able to cure his defective performance provided that there is still time for him to tender performance in accordance with the terms of the contract: see generally A Apps, 'The Right to Cure Defective Performance' [1994] LMCLQ 525. The right to cure does not, however, extend beyond the contract period, as in s 2-508 of the Uniform Commercial Code and Art 48 of the Vienna Convention.

reduction of the price as a remedy in the event of breach.[253] The focus is very much on termination of the contract and claims for damages. It is for this reason that the implied terms relating to title to sell, correspondence with description and sample, satisfactory quality and fitness for purpose are all declared to be conditions[254] so that, until recently, any breach, no matter how insignificant, in principle entitled the buyer to reject the goods and terminate the contract. Similarly, sellers often make time of payment of the essence of the contract so that in the event of failure by the buyer to pay on time they can simply terminate the contract. The entitlement to terminate is thus based on the nature of the term broken rather than on the consequences of the breach for the party seeking to terminate.[255] The advantage of this approach is that it has the appearance of certainty and clarity.[256] It has been applied strictly by the English courts, particularly in relation to compliance with time stipulations.[257] But the price has been a certain harshness in application, especially in the case where a party relies on a 'technical' breach of a condition in order to escape from what has turned out to be a bad bargain.[258] The pursuit of certainty also proved to be something of a double-edged sword for the party seeking to terminate because the courts insisted that the right to terminate be exercised within a very short time: the seller as well as the buyer was entitled to know where he stood.[259]

(b) Restrictions on the right to reject: section 15A of the 1979 Act

This emphasis on the virtues of certainty has, however, been reduced as a result of the intervention of Parliament which has effected a delicate but important shift in the balance of rights as between seller and buyer. The right of the buyer to reject the goods has been curtailed but, where the right does arise, the buyer may now have a longer period of time in which to exercise it. The restraint on the right of the buyer[260] to reject is to be found in section 15A of the Sale of Goods Act 1979[261] which states that, where the buyer has established the existence of a right to reject by virtue of a breach by the seller of one of the implied terms contained in sections 13–15 of the Act[262] but the consequences of the breach are so 'slight'

2.48

---

[253] While price reduction may be a remedy which is used by parties in practice, it was not, until the enactment in 2003 of s 48C of the Sale of Goods Act 1979 (now to be found in s 24 of the Consumer Rights Act 2015, on which see 2.69–2.72), the subject of much discussion in the books. Contrast, eg, Art 50 of the Vienna Convention.

[254] The meaning and significance of the classification of a term as a 'condition' is discussed in EPL ch 8.

[255] This is subject to an important qualification in the case of innominate terms where the courts do focus on the consequences of the breach when deciding whether or not a party is entitled to terminate. See generally *Hong Kong Fir Shipping Co Ltd v Kawasaki Kisen Kaisha Ltd* [1962] 2 QB 26, CA, discussed in more detail in EPL ch 8 and, for an application of this type of approach to a contract for the sale of goods, see *Cehave NV v Bremer Handelsgesellschaft mbH (The Hansa Nord)* [1976] QB 44, CA. The Vienna Convention, in Art 25, places greater emphasis on the consequences of the breach.

[256] In that, once it has been established that the term broken is a condition, the right to terminate is clear. However, outside the statutory implied terms, the appearance of certainty may be deceptive because of the doubt which can exist as to whether or not the term is a condition in the first place: see eg *Compagnie Commerciale Sucres et Denrées v C Czarnikow Ltd (The Naxos)* [1990] 1 WLR 1337, HL where the judges had great difficulty in deciding whether or not the term broken was a condition.

[257] See eg *Bowes v Shand* (1877) 2 App Cas 455, HL, *Bunge Corporation v Tradax Export SA* [1981] 1 WLR 711, HL and *Compagnie Commerciale Sucres et Denrées v C Czarnikow Ltd (The Naxos)* [1990] 1 WLR 1337, HL.

[258] See eg *Arcos Ltd v EA Ronaasen & Son* [1933] AC 470, HL.

[259] The most notorious example of the speed with which a buyer was required to exercise his right to reject is *Bernstein v Pamson Motors (Golders Green) Ltd* [1987] 2 All ER 220, QBD. However, in the light of the amendment made to s 35 of the 1979 Act in 1994, *Bernstein* no longer represents the law today: see n 278.

[260] There is no equivalent restraint on the right of the seller and, on this basis, the new provision is open to criticism.

[261] Inserted by s 4 of the Sale and Supply of Goods Act 1994.

[262] Thus the restriction on the right to reject does not apply to a breach of s 12(1) of the Sale of Goods Act 1979, nor does it apply to breach of an express term of the contract which has been classified as a condition.

that it would be unreasonable for him to reject the goods, the buyer is confined to a remedy in damages and cannot terminate the contract. There is, as yet, no case law under section 15A and so it is not clear what constitutes a 'slight' breach for this purpose.[263] It is for the seller to show that the breach is so slight that it would be unreasonable for the buyer to reject the goods.[264] The thrust of the legislation is clear; it aims to prevent buyers from getting out of what is no more than a bad bargain. But in doing so it has introduced uncertainty into commercial transactions.[265] For example, it is not clear what impact the reform will have on the strict approach which the courts have taken towards time stipulations.[266] Section 15A applies 'unless a contrary intention appears in, or is to be implied from, the contract'.[267] But will the courts imply a contrary intention from the commercial context so as to preserve the traditional approach to time stipulations? No clear answer can be given to this question. Much is likely to depend upon the facts of the particular case.[268]

(c) Waiver and acceptance

2.49   The prima facie right to terminate the contract may be lost in certain situations, eg, where the buyer or seller is held to have waived the breach in respect of which he now seeks to terminate the contract.[269]

2.50   The Act also places limits upon a buyer's right to reject the goods.[270] A buyer cannot reject the goods once he is deemed to have accepted them. Acceptance may occur in one of three ways. First, where the buyer intimates to the seller that he has accepted the goods.[271] Secondly, a buyer will be held to have accepted the goods when the goods have been delivered to him, and he does any act in relation to them which is inconsistent with the ownership of the seller.[272] But, crucially, where goods are delivered to a buyer, and he has not previously examined them, he is not deemed to have accepted them until he has had a reasonable opportunity of examining them for the purpose of ascertaining whether they are in conformity with the contract and, in the case of a contract for sale by sample, of comparing the bulk with the sample.[273] Unless otherwise agreed, a seller must on request give a buyer

---

[263] It cannot be assumed that the effect of the section is to turn the implied terms in ss 13–15 into innominate terms or that it has brought English law into line with Art 25 of the Vienna Convention. A breach may not substantially deprive the buyer of the benefit of the bargain (and so satisfy the test in order to enable the buyer to terminate on the occurrence of a breach of an innominate term) but not be 'slight' either so that the buyer remains free to reject. The section has brought English law closer to the Vienna Convention but it is not identical.

[264] Sale of Goods Act 1979, s 15A(3).

[265] And so has been criticized on that ground: see eg G Treitel, *The Law of Contract* (13th edn, 2011, by E Peel) para 18-054.

[266] See n 257.

[267] Sale of Goods Act 1979, s 15A(2).

[268] The onus of proof of establishing a contrary intent is likely to be upon the seller. In the case of commodity contracts it might not be difficult to lead evidence of a contrary intent, but in other markets it might not be so easy for the seller to adduce such evidence.

[269] Waiver is discussed in more detail in EPL ch 8. The application of the doctrines of waiver and estoppel to documentary sales has proved to be particularly problematic. The source of the problem is the decision of the Court of Appeal in *Panchaud Frères SA v Etablissements General Grain Co* [1970] 1 Lloyd's Rep 53, CA, although it has now been held that the case is simply an authority for the application of s 35 of the Act to the case where a cif buyer accepts the documents but rejects or purports to reject the goods (*Glencore Grain Rotterdam BV v Lebanese Organization for International Commerce* [1997] 4 All ER 514, 530–531, CA).

[270] These limits do not apply to contracts of sale that fall within the Consumer Rights Act 2015.

[271] Sale of Goods Act 1979, s 35(1)(a). The intimation may be express or implied.

[272] Sale of Goods Act 1979, s 35(1)(b). The exact meaning of this provision is far from clear. It covers the case where the buyer destroys the goods or otherwise deals with them in such a way that they cannot be restored to the seller. See also *Clegg v Andersson* [2003] EWCA Civ 320, [2003] 2 Lloyd's Rep 32, at [57]–[60].

[273] Sale of Goods Act 1979, s 35(2).

'a reasonable opportunity of examining the goods for the purpose of ascertaining whether or not they are in conformity with the contract'.[274] The place of examination is prima facie the place of delivery, although this presumption is frequently displaced in practice.[275] Finally, a buyer will be deemed to have accepted the goods when, after the lapse of a reasonable time, he retains the goods without intimating to the seller that he has rejected them[276] and, in deciding whether or not a reasonable time has elapsed, the court will consider whether the buyer has had a reasonable opportunity of examining the goods.[277] In the interests of finality the courts previously gave buyers a very short period of time in which to examine the goods[278] but, as a consequence of the amendment introduced the courts now adopt a more benevolent approach when determining what constitutes a reasonable time. Whether or not a reasonable time has elapsed is a matter of fact to be considered in the light of all the circumstances of the case.[279]

A buyer is not deemed to have accepted the goods merely because he asks for, or agrees to, their repair by or under an arrangement with the seller [280] or because the goods are delivered to another under a sub-sale or other disposition.[281] A buyer also has a right of partial rejection, so that a buyer who has the right to reject goods by reason of a breach on the part of the seller that affects some or all of them may accept some of the goods, including, where there are any goods unaffected by the breach, all such goods.[282]   **2.51**

(d) No obligation to return rejected goods

A buyer who lawfully rejects the goods is not obliged to return them to the seller; unless otherwise agreed, the buyer need only intimate to the seller that he refuses to accept the goods.[283]   **2.52**

---

[274] Sale of Goods Act 1979, s 34.

[275] Particularly in the case of documentary or overseas sales.

[276] Sale of Goods Act 1979, s 35(4).

[277] Sale of Goods Act 1979, s 35(5).

[278] *Bernstein v Pamson Motors (Golders Green) Ltd* [1987] 2 All ER 220, QBD. However, the Court of Appeal in *Clegg v Andersson* [2003] EWCA Civ 320, [2003] 2 Lloyd's Rep 32, at [63] concluded that *Bernstein v Pamson Motors (Golders Green) Ltd* no longer represents the law, given the amendments made to the original s 35 of the 1979 Act by the Sale and Supply of Goods Act 1994. Hale LJ stated at [76] that 'if a buyer is seeking information which the seller has agreed to supply which will enable the buyer to make a properly informed choice between acceptance, rejection or cure, and if cure in what way, he cannot have lost his right to reject.' (see FMB Reynolds 'Loss of the right to reject' (2003) 119 LQR 544). There is, however, no absolute rule that a buyer cannot have lost the right to reject while a period of repair is in progress or while a complaint by the buyer and a request for information is being processed by the seller (*Jones v Gallagher (trading as Gallery Kitchens and Bathrooms)* [2004] EWCA Civ 10, [2005] 1 Lloyd's Rep 377 (on which see R Bradgate, 'Remedying the unfit fitted kitchen' (2004) 120 LQR 558).

[279] Sale of Goods Act 1979, s 59; *Jones v Gallagher (trading as Gallery Kitchens and Bathrooms)* [2004] EWCA Civ 10, [2005] 1 Lloyd's Rep 377; *Whitecap Leisure Ltd v John H Rundle Ltd* [2008] EWCA Civ 429, [2008] 2 Lloyd's Rep 216.

[280] Sale of Goods Act 1979, s 35(6)(a), on which see *J & H Ritchie Ltd v Lloyd Ltd* [2007] UKHL 9; [2007] 1 WLR 670. In the light of the decision in *Ritchie* it is likely to be necessary to examine the arrangement made between the seller and the buyer in relation to the repair of the goods with some care. A buyer who allows a seller to incur the expense of repairing the goods may be under an implied obligation to accept and pay for the goods once the repair has been completed. But this is not an inevitable inference. In the case where, eg, goods are taken away by the seller for inspection and, if possible, repair, the court may infer that the seller is obliged, upon request, to inform the buyer of the nature of the problem which required to be remedied and a failure by the seller to provide the buyer with such information may entitle the buyer to reject the goods even in the case where the repair has in fact been carried out to a proper standard.

[281] Sale of Goods Act 1979, s 35(6)(b).

[282] Sale of Goods Act 1979, s 35A.

[283] Sale of Goods Act 1979, s 36.

(2) Remedies of the Seller

2.53　The remedies available to the seller in the event of buyer default may be either personal or proprietary.

(a) Proprietary remedies

2.54　When the buyer is insolvent proprietary remedies obviously assume considerable signifi-cance. Contracts for the sale of goods often make their own provision for proprietary rem-edies via the use of retention of title clauses. The limited efficacy of these clauses has already been noted.[284]

2.55　The Act itself makes provision for a number of real remedies which the seller can exercise against the goods themselves and these can give the seller some protection in the event of buyer insolvency. The rights are, however, hedged round by a number of restrictions which limit their practical utility.[285] These rights are available to an 'unpaid seller' and are applica-ble notwithstanding the fact that property in the goods may have passed to the buyer.[286] A seller is unpaid when the whole of the price has not been paid or tendered or when a bill of exchange or other negotiable instrument has been received as conditional payment and the condition on which it was received has not been fulfilled by reason of the dishonour of the instrument or otherwise.[287]

(i) The seller's lien [288]

2.56　A lien is a possessory security so that the goods must remain in the possession of the seller for the lien to be exercisable.[289] The lien may be exercisable notwithstanding the fact that the buyer has been allowed into possession of the goods for limited purposes, eg to pack them, provided the goods remain in the seller's general control.[290] Where the goods are in posses-sion of the seller, the seller can retain possession of them[291] until payment or tender of the price in three situations: namely, where the goods have been sold without any stipulation as to credit, where the goods have been sold on credit but the term of credit has expired,[292] and where the buyer becomes insolvent.[293] The lien is lost when the seller delivers the goods to a carrier or other bailee for the purpose of transmission to the buyer without reserving the right of disposal of the goods, when the buyer or his agent lawfully[294] obtains possession of the goods, by waiver of the lien or right of retention.[295]

---

[284] See 2.23 and, more generally, 8.82–8.86.

[285] They are often unnecessary or unhelpful in international sales because it is the documents relating to the goods which are of greatest practical importance rather than the rights in relation to the goods themselves.

[286] Where property in the goods has not passed to the buyer, the unpaid seller has a right of withholding delivery similar to and co-extensive with his rights of lien or retention and stoppage in transit where the prop-erty has passed to the buyer (Sale of Goods Act 1979, s 39(2)). Section 39(2) does not expressly provide for the existence of a right of resale in such a case but it seems that the seller should not be in any worse position in this respect than under s 39(1) (see *RV Ward Ltd v Bignall* [1967] 1 QB 534, CA).

[287] Sale of Goods Act 1979, s 38(1). Note also the extended definition of 'seller' in s 38(2).

[288] Sale of Goods Act 1979, s 39(1)(a).

[289] The goods need not remain in his possession as seller; they can be in his possession in his capacity as agent, bailee or custodier for the buyer: Sale of Goods Act 1979, s 39(2).

[290] See eg *Goodall v Skelton* (1794) 2 H Bl 316, 126 ER 570, Court of Common Pleas.

[291] Where there has been part delivery of the goods the seller may exercise a lien over the goods yet to be delivered unless the part delivery demonstrates an agreement to waive the lien or right of retention: Sale of Goods Act 1979, s 42.

[292] Thus the lien is deemed to be waived for the period of the credit. The high incidence of credit sales renders the seller's lien of limited practical relevance.

[293] Sale of Goods Act 1979, s 41(1). Insolvency is defined in s 61(4).

[294] Thus the wrongful taking of the goods by the buyer will not suffice.

[295] Sale of Goods Act 1979, s 43.

(ii) Right of stoppage in transit[296]

This right is more extensive than the lien in that it can be invoked by the unpaid seller after **2.57** he has parted with possession of the goods but it is more limited in that it only arises upon the insolvency[297] of the buyer. The right of stoppage entitles the seller to retain possession of the goods as long as they are in course of transit and he may retain them until payment or tender of the price. Upon exercising his right the seller essentially resumes possession of the goods and so can assert a lien over them. The right can only be exercised while the goods are in transit.[298] The essential idea is that goods are in transit while they are in the possession of a 'middleman'[299] who is independent of both buyer and seller so that the buyer has not yet taken delivery of the goods. If the carrier attorns to the buyer the transit is at an end.[300] The right of stoppage is exercised by the seller taking actual possession of the goods or by giving notice[301] of his claim to the carrier or other bailee or custodier in whose possession the goods are. Once notice has been given, the carrier must redeliver the goods to, or according to the directions of, the seller and the seller must bear the expenses of such redelivery.[302] The seller's right of lien or retention or stoppage in transit is not affected by any sale or other disposition of the goods which the buyer may have made, unless the seller has assented[303] to it.[304] The seller's rights may also be defeated where he has lawfully transferred a document of title to the buyer and the buyer in turn has transferred that document of title to a third party who has taken in good faith and for valuable consideration.[305]

(iii) The right of re-sale[306]

The exercise by the seller of his right of lien or stoppage in transit does not, of itself, operate **2.58** to bring the contract to an end nor does it operate to revest property in the seller.[307] A seller who wishes to bring the contract to an end should notify the buyer of his intention to do so. Additionally the seller is given a right[308] to resell the goods. The seller has a right to resell the goods where the original contract gives him the right to do so[309] and where the buyer has repudiated[310] the contract and the seller has accepted that repudiation, thereby bringing the contract to an end. In addition section 48(3) of the Act provides that where the goods are of a perishable nature, or where the unpaid seller gives notice to the buyer of his intention to resell, and the buyer does not within a reasonable time pay or tender the price, the

---

[296] Sale of Goods Act 1979, s 39(1)(b) and s 44.

[297] Defined in Sale of Goods Act 1979, s 61(4).

[298] Rather elaborate rules on the duration of transit are set out in Sale of Goods Act 1979, s 45.

[299] *Schotsmans v Lancs & Yorks Rly* (1867) LR 2 Ch App 332, 338, CA.

[300] Sale of Goods Act 1979, s 45(3).

[301] The requirements as to notice are set out in s 46(2) and (3).

[302] Sale of Goods Act 1979, s 46(4).

[303] Knowledge of the sub-sale is not the same thing as assent to it. See *Mordaunt Brothers v British Oil and Cake Mills Ltd* [1910] 2 KB 502, KBD and contrast *DF Mount Ltd v Jay and Jay (Provisions) Co Ltd* [1960] 1 QB 159, QBD. A seller who attorns to the sub-buyer must also have assented.

[304] Sale of Goods Act 1979, s 47(1).

[305] Sale of Goods Act 1979, s 47(2). See eg *DF Mount Ltd v Jay and Jay (Provisions) Co Ltd* [1960] 1 QB 159, QBD.

[306] Sale of Goods Act 1979, s 39(1)(c).

[307] Sale of Goods Act 1979, s 48(1).

[308] The seller may also have the power to transfer good title to a second buyer, eg under s 24 or s 48(2) of the Act. Where the seller has power to resell but does not have the right to do so he can confer good title on the third party but will be liable to the buyer in damages. Where the seller also has the right to resell he cannot be liable to the original buyer when he exercises his right to resell.

[309] In such a case the original contract is terminated upon the seller reselling the goods but that termination is without prejudice to any claim which the seller may have for damages: Sale of Goods Act 1979, s 48(4).

[310] The circumstances in which a breach will be held to be repudiatory are discussed in EPL ch 8.

unpaid seller may resell the goods and recover from the original buyer damages for any loss occasioned by his breach of contract. A seller who exercises his right to resell under section 48(3) thereby terminates the contract so that he cannot sue the buyer for the price but must content himself with a claim for damages.[311]

(b) Personal remedies

2.59 A number of personal remedies are available to the seller in the event of buyer default.

(i) Action for the price

2.60 This is a claim in debt and so is unaffected by doctrines such as mitigation. Perhaps rather curiously, the action for the price is limited to cases where 'property in the goods has passed to the buyer and he wrongfully neglects or refuses to pay for the goods according to the terms of the contract'.[312] When property has not passed to the buyer, the seller's only claim is one for damages. A seller will not be entitled to recover the price where, prior to it being payable, he breached the contract in such a way as to disentitle him to the price.[313] The requirement that property must have passed to the buyer does not apply where the price is payable on a day certain[314] irrespective of delivery.[323] Section 49 has been held to be exclusive rather than permissive so that it exhaustively defines the right of the seller to maintain an action for the price.[324] The action for the price does not prevent the seller from bringing an action for damages to recover such consequential loss that he has suffered which is recoverable on ordinary principles.[325]

(ii) Damages for non-acceptance

2.61 Where property in the goods has not passed to the buyer then the seller will have to be content with an action for damages for non-acceptance.[326] The general rule[327] which applies to the assessment of damages is that the seller is entitled to recover 'the estimated loss directly and naturally resulting, in the ordinary course of events, from the buyer's breach of contract'.[328] This is likely to consist of the difference between the contract price and the value of the goods to the seller at the time and place of the breach together with any consequential recoverable losses.[329] The Act also lays down a 'prima facie' rule which is applicable where there is an available market[330] for the goods. In such a case the measure of damages is prima facie to be ascertained by the difference between the contract price and the market or current price at the time or times when the goods ought to have been accepted or, if no time was fixed

---

[311] *RV Ward Ltd v Bignall* [1967] 1 QB 534, CA. One consequence of this conclusion is that the seller is not liable to account to the buyer for any profit which he makes on the resale.

[312] Sale of Goods Act 1979, s 49(1). Contrast s 2-709 of the Uniform Commercial Code, which is favoured by some academic commentators (see eg *Atiyah's Sale of Goods*, n 1, at 483).

[313] *Wayne's Merthyr Steam Coal and Iron Co v Morewood* (1877) 46 LJQB 746, QBD.

[314] On which see *Shell-Mex Ltd v Elton Cop Dyeing Co Ltd* (1928) 34 Commercial Cases 39, QBD.

[323] Sale of Goods Act 1979, s 49(2).

[324] *F G Wilson (Engineering) Ltd v John Holt & Co (Liverpool) Ltd* [2013] EWCA Civ 1232; [2014] 1 WLR 2365, at [40]–[52].

[325] Sale of Goods Act 1979, s 54. See also s 37 which enables the seller to recover from a buyer who refuses to take delivery a reasonable charge for the care and custody of the goods.

[326] Where property has passed to the buyer the seller has an option either to sue for the price or to sue for damages.

[327] So held in *Dem Dis A Turk Ticaret S/A TR v International Agri Trade Co Ltd (The Selda)* [1999] 1 Lloyd's Rep 729, CA.

[328] Sale of Goods Act 1979, s 50(2). This provision may be thought to be rather odd in so far as it deals, not so much with the measure of damages, as with the rule for remoteness of damages, classically expressed in *Hadley v Baxendale* (1854) 9 Exch 341, Court of Exchequer Chamber.

[329] Sale of Goods Act 1979, s 54.

[330] The meaning of 'available market' is discussed in more detail by *Benjamin*, n 1, at 16-063–16-070.

for acceptance, at the time of the refusal to accept.[323] The merit of this rule is that it is clear or abstract and it is consistent with the requirement that the seller must take steps to mitigate his loss but it is open to criticism on the ground that it can lead to results which are rather arbitrary.[324] Where the buyer commits an anticipatory breach of contract and that breach is accepted prior to the date of delivery it would appear that damages continue to be assessed at the date fixed for delivery under the contract[325] unless the seller should have mitigated his loss by re-selling at an earlier date.[326]

(3) Remedies of the Buyer

Here we are concerned largely with the personal remedies available to the buyer. In the event **2.62** of seller insolvency the buyer will wish to show that property in the goods has passed to him under the contract of sale so that he can obtain priority over the seller's other creditors. The buyer may also be entitled to bring a claim in conversion[327] against any person who wrongfully interferes with the goods. In many ways the primary remedy of the buyer in the event of breach by the seller is the right to reject the goods.[328]

(a) Specific performance

English law differs from many civil law systems in that it relegates specific performance to **2.63** a secondary role.[329] The Act gives the court power to make a specific performance order in the case of the breach of a contract to deliver specific[330] or ascertained[331] goods.[332] An order is most likely to be made where the goods are unique[333] and uniqueness may here include commercial uniqueness.[334] Where the goods remain unascertained then the court will not order specific performance,[335] although it is possible that it may do so in an exceptional case.[336]

---

[323] Sale of Goods Act 1979, s 50(3). Where the seller agrees to a postponement of the date of delivery, the relevant date will be the substituted date.

[324] eg, it may enable a seller to make a profit when he sells the goods for a profit at a later date as a result of a rise in the market price: *Campbell Mostyn (Provisions) Ltd v Barnett Trading Co* [1954] 1 Lloyd's Rep 65, CA. Equally, the fact that the seller made a loss because he retained the goods and the market price then fell is irrelevant. The position may be otherwise where the seller has only one item and resells it *immediately* at a profit: in such a case the court may take account of any profit made by the seller on the resale (see *Benjamin*, n 1, at 16-075—16-076). The difficulty with any such exception is that it tends to undermine the abstract nature of the rule.

[325] *Millett v Van Heeck* [1921] 2 KB 369, CA.

[326] *Roth & Co v Taysen Townsend & Co* (1895) 73 LT 628, 629–30, QBD.

[327] The principles which govern a claim for conversion are discussed in EPL ch 17.

[328] Discussed in 2.47–2.51. The buyer may also be able to rescind the contract for misrepresentation in an appropriate case.

[329] The difference between the different systems has resulted in the compromise of Article 28 of the Vienna Convention.

[330] The meaning of which is set out at 2.10 and n 38.

[331] Goods are ascertained if they are identified in accordance with the contract after the contract has been formed: *Re Wait* [1927] 1 Ch 606, 630, CA.

[332] Sale of Goods Act 1979, s 52.

[333] *Falcke v Gray* (1859) 4 Drew 651, 62 ER 250, Vice Chancellor's Court.

[334] *Behnke v Bede Shipping Co Ltd* [1927] 1 KB 649, QBD: cf *Société des Industries Métallurgiques SA v The Bronx Engineering Co Ltd* [1975] 1 Lloyd's Rep 465, CA.

[335] *Re Wait* [1927] 1 Ch 606, CA, where the court emphasized the fact that the 1893 Act was a Code so that it was not possible to go outside its terms in order to find a wider power to order specific performance.

[336] On the basis of *Sky Petroleum Ltd v VIP Petroleum Ltd* [1974] 1 WLR 576, Ch D (the case actually concerned the grant of an interlocutory injunction but it may be applied by analogy to the case of specific performance. The case is, however, a controversial one and it is not easy to reconcile with *Re Wait* [1927] 1 Ch 606, CA.

(b) Recovery of the price

2.64 The buyer may be entitled to recover money paid to the seller where the consideration for the payment has failed.[337] The traditional requirement is that this right is only available where there has been a *total* failure of consideration,[338] although this limitation may not survive further judicial scrutiny.[339]

(c) Damages

2.65 A buyer may bring a claim for damages because the seller has failed to deliver the goods, has delivered them late or has delivered defective goods.

(i) Non-delivery

2.66 Where the seller wrongfully neglects or refuses to deliver the goods to the buyer, the buyer's entitlement to damages corresponds with the seller's entitlement to damages in the event of non-acceptance by the buyer; that is to say the 'available market' test is applied[340] so that the buyer is entitled to recover the difference between the market price of the goods[341] at the time fixed for delivery and the contract price. If there is no available market for the goods, the measure of damages to which the buyer is entitled 'is the estimated loss directly and naturally resulting, in the ordinary course of events, from the seller's breach of contract'.[342]

(ii) Loss suffered by non-delivery

2.67 The Act does not expressly deal with the situation where the seller is late in delivering the goods but the buyer nevertheless accepts delivery and sues for damages for the loss suffered by the late delivery. It would appear that the buyer is prima facie entitled to recover the difference between the market price at the time fixed for delivery and the market price at the time at which delivery was actually made.[343]

(iii) Defective goods

2.68 Where the goods delivered are defective in quality the buyer may either set up against the seller the breach of warranty in diminution or extinction of the price or maintain an action against the seller for the breach of warranty.[344] Where the buyer brings a claim for damages the Act provides both that the measure of damages is 'the estimated loss directly and naturally resulting, in the ordinary course of events, from the breach of warranty'[345] and that, in the case of a breach of warranty of quality, the loss is 'prima facie the difference between the value of the goods at the time of delivery to the buyer and the value they would have had if they had fulfilled the warranty'.[346] The relationship between these two provisions is not an easy one. The former has been stated to be the 'starting point'[347] for the court, while the latter is

---

[337] This right is specifically preserved by s 54 of the Sale of Goods Act 1979. This remedy has assumed particular importance in cases where there has been a breach by the seller of s 12, on which see 2.29.

[338] See further EPL ch 18.

[339] Evidence of judicial reluctance to apply the traditional rule can be seen in *Goss v Chilcott* [1996] AC 788, 798, PC.

[340] Sale of Goods Act 1979, s 51(3).

[341] The relevant price is the buying price at which the buyer could obtain the goods: *Williams Bros v Ed T Agius Ltd* [1914] AC 510, HL.

[342] Sale of Goods Act 1979, s 51(2).

[343] Much more difficult is the question of the entitlement of the buyer to recover loss of profits caused by late delivery: see *Victoria Laundry (Windsor) Ltd v Newman Industries Ltd* [1949] 2 KB 528, CA and the discussion of remoteness of damage in EPL ch 21.

[344] Sale of Goods Act 1979, s 53(1).

[345] Sale of Goods Act 1979, s 53(2).

[346] Sale of Goods Act 1979, s 53(3).

[347] *Bence Graphics International Ltd v Fasson UK Ltd* [1998] QB 87, 102, CA.

simply a prima facie rule which may be displaced on the facts of a particular case. The courts have in some cases declined to award a buyer damages assessed on the diminution in value measure where this would have given him more than his actual loss.[348]

(d) Additional remedies for consumer buyers

Consumer buyers have been given a broader range of remedies in the event that their statutory rights under sections 9–18 of the Consumer Rights Act 2015 are not met. Many of these remedies find their origin in the EC Directive on Certain Aspects of the Sale of Consumer Goods and Associated Guarantees.[349] The Directive was initially implemented into English law by the Sale and Supply of Goods to Consumers Regulations 2002[350] which introduced a new Part 5A into the Sale of Goods Act 1979. These new remedies therefore sat rather awkwardly within the existing framework of the 1979 Act. However, the 2002 Regulations were revoked by the Consumer Rights Act 2015[351] and the opportunity has been taken to make a new start and set out the remedies available to consumer buyers in a new statute. The remedial regime that has been introduced is more elaborate than that to be found in the 1979 Act in that it makes provision for remedies such as repair and replacement which find no formal place in the 1979 Act. However, these remedies were widely invoked by consumer buyers in practice and so the extent of the change that has been made is open to question. The remedies given by the 2015 Act to consumer buyers do not prevent them from resorting to other remedies, such as damages, specific performance, relying on the breach in order to defeat the trader's claim for the price or exercising the right to treat the contract as at an end for breach of an express term of the contract.[352] However, there is one sense in which they may be said to take away from the common law rights of the consumer, to the extent that it is provided that a consumer cannot treat the contract as at an end for breach of a term required by the Act to be treated as included in the contract, except in accordance with the terms of the Act which prescribe the availability of these remedies.[353] These remedies are (i) the short-term right to reject, (ii) the right to repair or replacement and (iii) the right to a price reduction or the final right to reject.[354] However, these three rights (or remedies) are not available in the case of a breach of every term 'treated as included' in the contract. Where the term broken is the trader's right to sell the goods, the consumer has the right to reject but

2.69

---

[348] The cases are not entirely easy to reconcile. On the one hand, in cases such as *Slater v Hoyle & Smith Ltd* [1920] 2 KB 11, CA and *Louis Dreyfus Trading Ltd v Reliance Trading Ltd* [2004] EWHC 525 (Comm), [2004] 2 Lloyd's Rep 243, QB the courts took no account of the profit made by the buyer on a sub-sale of the goods. On the other hand, account was taken of the profit made by the buyer in *Bence Graphics International Ltd v Fasson UK Ltd* [1998] QB 87, CA. The majority in *Bence* were clearly reluctant to award the buyers more than what they perceived to be their actual loss. This view is understandable. But there is another side to the story. Assuming that the trial judge was correct to conclude that the goods which the sellers had supplied were 'worthless', why should they be allowed to keep any part of the payment which they had received for delivering worthless goods? The effect of the decision is also to throw upon the buyer the onus of proving that he has in fact suffered a loss where he has sub-sold the defective goods for the price at which he bought the goods and that onus may not be easy to discharge. More importantly, the effect of the majority approach is to replace a rule which is easy to apply with one which requires a careful scrutiny of the facts and which runs contrary to the thrust of sale of goods law which is to favour an abstract approach to the assessment of damages (for criticism of the *Bence* case along these lines see G Treitel, 'Damages for Breach of Warranty of Quality' (1997) 113 LQR 188).

[349] 1999/44/EC; [1999] OJ L171/12, on which see M Bianca and S Grundmann (eds) *EU Sales Directive Commentary* (Intersentia, 2002).

[350] SI 2002/3045.

[351] Consumer Rights Act 2015, sched 1, para 53.

[352] Consumer Rights Act 2015, s 19(9) – (11).

[353] Consumer Rights Act 2015, s 19(12).

[354] Consumer Rights Act 2015, s 19(3).

repair or replacement is inapplicable.[355] But where the goods do not conform to the contract (that is they are not of satisfactory quality, not reasonably fit for their purpose, do not correspond with description or sample or do not match a model seen or examined) then all three remedies are in principle available.

2.70 The most novel of these remedies in terms of the formal structure of English sales law is the right to repair or replacement, although, as has been noted, repair and replacement are commonly used in practice in consumer sales and the change may be one that has implications in the realm of legal theory rather than practice. Where the consumer requires the trader to repair or replace the goods the trader must repair or replace them within a reasonable time but without causing significant inconvenience to the buyer[356] and must bear any necessary costs incurred in doing so.[357] However, the consumer cannot require the trader to repair or replace the goods if it would be impossible for the trader to do so or if it would be 'disproportionate' compared to the other of those remedies to do so.[358] The language of 'proportionality' is a relative newcomer to this area of law in the UK and may be said to introduce a degree of uncertainty into the law.

2.71 The consumer buyer is also given a short-term right to reject which must be exercised within 30 days of the ownership or possession of the goods having been transferred to the buyer, the goods having been delivered and, where the contract requires the trader to install the goods or to take other action to enable the consumer to use them, the trader has notified the consumer that the action has been taken.[359] The exercise of this right entitles the consumer to reject the goods and to treat the contract as at an end[360] and it is exercised by the consumer indicating to the trader that this is what he is doing.[361] Once the right has been exercised the trader is subject to a duty to give the consumer a refund[362] and the consumer is subject to a duty to make the goods available for collection by the trader or to return them as agreed, albeit that the trader must bear the reasonable costs of returning them, other than any costs incurred by the consumer in returning the goods in person to the place where the consumer took physical possession of them.[363] This right to reject is however, lost on the expiry of the 30 day time limit unless the trader and the consumer agree that it may be exercised later.[364] The right thus given to the consumer is a broad one but it must be exercised within the prescribed time limits.

2.72 The final remedy to which attention is drawn is the right to a price reduction or the final right to reject. The appearance is given of introducing a new remedy into English sales law, namely the remedy of price reduction. Once again, however, the consequence may be more apparent at the level of theory than practice given that the remedy of damages frequently reaches results that are very similar to, if not identical with, the result that is reached through reliance

---

[355] Consumer Rights Act 2015, s 19(6).

[356] Consumer Rights Act 2015, s 23(2). 'Reasonable time' and 'significant inconvenience' are further defined in s 23(5). A consumer who requires a trader to repair or replace goods cannot exercise the short-term right to reject the goods until he has given the seller a reasonable time in which to repair or replace the goods: s 23(6) and (7).

[357] Consumer Rights Act 2015, s 23(2)(b).

[358] 'Disproportion' is further defined in s 23(4). The test to be applied is one that relates to the 'cost' to the trader of providing the remedy; it does not focus upon the benefit which the buyer will obtain from the remedy. The comparison is to be conducted, as between repair and replacement (s 23(4)).

[359] Consumer Rights Act 2015, s 22(3). However, if the goods are of a kind that can reasonably be expected to perish after a shorter period, the time limit for exercising the short-term right to reject in relation to these goods is the end of that shorter period: s 22(4).

[360] Consumer Rights Act 2015, s 20(4).

[361] Consumer Rights Act 2015, s 20(5) and (6).

[362] Consumer Rights Act 2015, s 20(7)(a). The details of how that refund is to be calculated is to be found in s 20(9)–(21).

[363] Consumer Rights Act 2015, s 20(7)(b) and (8).

[364] Consumer Rights Act 2015, s 22(1).

on the remedy of price reduction. The right to a price reduction is the right to require the trader to reduce by an appropriate amount the price the consumer is required to pay under the contract, or anything else the consumer is required to transfer under the contract, and to receive a refund from the trader for anything already paid or otherwise transferred by the consumer above the reduced amount.[365] However, the right to a price reduction and the final right to reject cannot be exercised in combination. The consumer must choose between them[366] but he can only exercise the right in one of the following situations: (i) after one repair or one replacement, the goods do not conform to the contract;[367] (ii) repair or replacement of the goods is impossible or disproportionate;[368] or (iii) the consumer has required the trader to repair or replace the goods, but the trader is in breach of the requirement to do so within a reasonable time and without significant inconvenience to the consumer.[369] If the consumer exercises the final right to reject, any refund to the consumer may be reduced to take account of the use the consumer has had of the goods in the period since they were delivered.[370] The restrictions on the final right to reject reveal a civil rather than a common law orientation in so far as they appear to give greater priority to the repair or replacement of the goods than to the consumer's interest in bringing the contract to an end.

---

[365] Consumer Rights Act 2015, s 24(1). For further details see s 24(2) – (4).
[366] Consumer Rights Act 2015, s 24(5).
[367] Consumer Rights Act 2015, s 24(5)(a)
[368] Consumer Rights Act 2015, s 24(5)(b). that is to say it is impossible or disproportionate under s 23(3).
[369] Consumer Rights Act 2015, s 24(5)(c).
[370] Consumer Rights Act 2015, s 24(8). For further details see s 24(10)–(14).

3

CARRIAGE OF GOODS BY SEA

A. Introduction

(1) General

The law of carriage by sea is simply one specialized contract out of many. Its basic structure **3.01**
is very similar in most if not all developed countries, largely because of the fairly uniform
regime for bill of lading contracts secured by the Hague Rules and their subsequent variants.
Valuable short and longer books on it are available.[1] It may then be asked why it is appropriate to have in this work a special chapter, albeit a brief one, on the subject.

The reasons are twofold. First, for historical reasons English commercial law generally, and the **3.02**
English law of carriage by sea in particular, was much used and relied on in international commerce in the later part of the nineteenth and the early part of the twentieth century. This had
the result that the English law itself became particularly well-developed in this area. That fact
led, when traders and carriers became aware of problems of the conflict of laws, to English law
being selected for many maritime contracts which had little or no connection with England or
the United Kingdom. The overall result is that English law is much used in international shipping and commerce, and London is one of the major centres of maritime dispute resolution,

---

[1] See further Sir R Aikens, R Lord and M Bools, *Bills of Lading* (2006); T Coghlin and others, *Time
Charters* (7th edn, 2014); J Cooke and others, *Voyage Charters* (4th edn, 2014); Sir B Eder and others,
Scrutton on Charterparties and Bills of Lading (22nd edn, 2011) ('Scrutton'); N Gaskell and others, *Bills of
Lading: Law and Contracts* (2000); S Girvin, *Carriage of Goods by Sea* (2nd edn, 2011); Sir G Treitel and FMB
Reynolds, *Carver on Bills of Lading* (3rd edn, 2011) ('Carver').

whether by litigation or arbitration,[2] in the world. There are of course several other significant jurisdictions in this context; and within the common law family there are important differences of approach and technique in the United States, another major jurisdiction for the resolution of maritime disputes. But in the result English law is one of the principal systems of private law encountered in the area, and this makes its approach worth setting down.

3.03 The second reason is that much of the general English common law of contract derives in fact from reasoning deployed and developed in shipping cases.[3] In most (but not all) common law countries the law of contract is uncodified and derived from legal decisions. What those legal decisions concern in common law countries depends to some extent on what subject matter happens to be litigated to their highest tribunals, and also on what sort of cases are reported. In England, for the reasons already given, shipping cases have been conspicuous. The result is that a very considerable part of the common law of contract, especially that concerning frustration and discharge of contract by breach, derives from shipping cases, which go well back into the nineteenth century and still continue. For pure common law reasoning, shipping cases have in England at least been a major source of basic contract doctrine, and continue to be so. (Equity has not been prominent in this area.)

3.04 The contract of carriage by sea differs from other contracts of carriage largely in the scale and length of the operation. Ships are large pieces of equipment and have considerable value in themselves; they can also carry cargo of considerable total size and value. The voyages which they undertake can be very long and take many weeks even now, and of course were much longer in former years. During the transit the ship and its cargo are subjected to many and varied risks, both physical and political (eg, by governmental interference). Also maritime adventures are frequently governed not by one contract between only two parties but by a complexity of different, even if interrelated, arrangements between a variety of parties. For these reasons sea transport has required more extensive and complex law than other forms of transport.

3.05 Sea transport has to be seen, however, also against the background of insurance: the risks are so great that all involved are likely to insure, and one of the main objects of shipping contracts is to allocate risks, so that parties know those for which they are responsible and which they should insure.[4] Thus the cargo owner may insure the risks to his *property* with a cargo underwriter (as a shipowner may insure the risks to his property with a hull underwriter); but shipowners commonly insure most of their *liability* to cargo[5] with a mutual insurance association (traditionally called a 'Protection and Indemnity Association', or 'P & I Club'). Separate insurance may also be effected against the risks that the cargo owner has paid, or the shipowner has not earned, freight for a voyage that is not completed.

3.06 The picture is further complicated where a casualty occurs, requiring services to redeem the situation. Liability to pay a 'salvage' reward to a salvor extricating property from danger rests on the owner of the interest salved (whether ship, cargo or freight)—though, eg, a cargo salvee may seek recourse from a shipowner whose fault caused the casualty.[6] But in cases of a

---

[2] English courts have also exercised considerable control over arbitrators, and this has brought in litigation even on arbitrated disputes. The amount of such control has been much reduced by statutes: the most recent is the Arbitration Act 1996.

[3] Lord Goff of Chieveley has said that for an English lawyer the characteristic commercial contract is one for the carriage of goods by sea: 'The Future of the Common Law' (1997), 46 ICLQ 745, 751. See also FMB Reynolds, 'Maritime and Other Influences in the Common Law' [2002] LMCLQ 182.

[4] See further J Gilman and others (eds), *Arnould's Law of Marine Insurance and Average* (18th edn, 2013); H Bennett, *The Law of Marine Insurance* (2nd edn, 2006); FD Rose, *Marine Insurance: Law and Practice* (2nd edn, 2012).

[5] And for other matters, eg personal injury and oil pollution.

[6] See further FD Rose, *Kennedy & Rose: The Law of Salvage* (8th edn, 2013).

common danger a single interest may incur a loss in order to preserve the common adventure. The classical example is where an item of cargo is jettisoned in order to lighten the vessel; the usual modern example is where the shipowner incurs extraordinary expense to complete the adventure. This is a case of 'general average',[7] requiring all who benefit from that loss to contribute to it—albeit both the person incurring the initial loss and the contributories may insure such risks. All this means that much litigation in this area is often technical, designed to clarify points of risk allocation, and supported or brought by insurers on both sides.

The contract of carriage has also to be seen against the background of the contracts to which **3.07** the goods carried in the ship are subject. There are of course in-house shipments and coastal shipments; but most shipments are made in pursuance of an export or import sale, or allocated (or 'appropriated') to such a sale during the carriage, and it may often be desired to sell (and resell) or raise money on the security of the goods while they are afloat. This is done largely by the use of a document called a bill of lading, which in English law, and doubtless (with differences of detail) in most legal systems, represents the goods, with the result that dealings in the document may represent dealings in the goods. It is likely therefore that any dispute about damage to or loss of the cargo (obviously the main type of dispute in carriage by sea) may involve analysis of the dealings with the goods, at least in order to ascertain who is the right claimant. There may also be involvement of banks, who finance such sales by holding the shipping documents as security. Meanwhile contractual arrangements relating to the ship itself may require careful analysis to determine who is the correct claimant and (especially) defendant.

Finally, a warning is needed that the English rules as to carriage by sea were principally **3.08** worked out in the late nineteenth century and in the earlier part of the twentieth century, against the background of less sophisticated techniques of ship operation than are usual now. They have of course been the subject of constant development, but not all modern changes have yet been fully addressed in litigation. In particular, there are as yet comparatively few decisions concerning carriage in containers, which raise problems different from those which arose under older methods of packaging and handling. Equally, electronic methods of dealing are developing, albeit slowly. The principles worked out under the older methods of dealing are requiring and will require adaptation: but the established principles will remain as a guide unless they are found completely inappropriate.

(2) Types of Contract

Traditionally, there are two types of contract available to a person who wishes to make use of **3.09** a ship. The first is the charterparty. The second is the bill of lading contract. In relation to a particular vessel or voyage, charterparties and bill of lading contracts may exist independently of each other or simultaneously. Despite its inclusion of the word 'party', a charterparty is not a person but a contract, the parties to which are the shipowner and the charterer. The unusual (and ancient) word charterparty is a contraction of the Latin *carta partita*, or divided document—in French *charte partie*. This stemmed from a practice of recording the agreed terms on a document in duplicate and then tearing the document into two parts, so that each party received a copy of the agreed terms; the fact that the parts could only match with their true counterparts evidenced that they were the true terms. In general, a charterparty is a contract for the use of a ship, and it need not involve the carriage of goods. The main types of charterparty are discussed below. However, most charterparties are concluded

---

[7] See further J Cooke and R Cornah (eds), *Lowndes & Rudolf: General Average and the York-Antwerp Rules* (14th edn, 2013); FD Rose, *General Average: Law and Practice* (2nd edn, 2005).

contemplating the carriage of one or many more shipments of goods, either by virtue of the charterparty itself or under contracts made consequent upon the charterparty. Thus, a ship may be chartered for a particular voyage to someone who has a complete cargo, usually of a bulk commodity, which will in effect fill the whole carrying capacity of the ship. Many forms of chartering in this context involve use of the 'tramp ship market', a market of vessels which hold themselves available for such arrangements; such an arrangement can be called shipping on 'tramping terms'. Alternatively, a person may charter a ship with a view to making the ship available (in accordance with the terms of the charterparty) for the carriage of separate consignments for many consignors. The arrangements for their carriage will generally utilize the second main type of contract, the bill of lading contract. The phrase 'bill of lading' (regularly shortened to 'B/L') is an ancient form of 'bill of loading'; the document may be given a different name in other languages (eg, *connaissement, conocimiento de embarque*). Bill of lading contracts will also be discussed more fully below. Goods that are consigned in a ship of a regular line running scheduled services are generally said to be shipped on 'liner terms'.

3.10 It is a general rule that parties' relationships are governed by the particular terms upon which they have contracted rather than the apparent form of their agreement. Thus there is no requirement that either of the above paradigms be adhered to. There can be sub-charters, sub-sub-charters and so forth. There are other variants on chartering. Thus there can be charters (or sub-charters) of particular holds of a vessel or of space. There is in the container trade a recently developed institution called 'slot chartering', under which the (so-called) charterer contracts for a certain number of container 'slots', ie contracts to use and/or pay for, and the carrier contracts to provide, the space occupied by so many containers on a particular voyage or on several voyages, or for periods otherwise determined. These only come within the traditional description of charterparties in a very limited sense.[8] Finally, there can be long-term contracts of affreightment, under which an operator contracts to provide ships to lift cargo within certain periods from certain places, without its being initially settled which ships will be used and when. Such contracts contain provisions for narrowing down to specific vessels at appropriate times, and usually provide for the form of charterparty to be used for the actual voyages.

3.11 Conversely, there is no objection in theory to a shipper under a bill of lading contract filling the whole cargo space. And, even where a ship is chartered (or any of the above variants are used), a bill or bills of lading will normally be issued as well, to provide a receipt for the shipper, to facilitate delivery at destination and to enable dealings with the cargo while it is afloat. This important point is dealt with below.[9]

(3) Terminology

3.12 Unless the reader is clear on the terminology used in this area, misunderstandings can occur. Also, some words used are by modern usage surprising or old-fashioned and may need explanation. A short glossary of traditionally used terms is therefore given at this stage. (A more specific list of terms is used by the Rotterdam Rules, which are discussed below.)

- The owner of the ship may be referred to as the *shipowner* or simply *owner*.
- The captain of the ship is in this context more usually referred to by the older term *master*.
- The person (and a person includes a company) who promises by contract to carry the goods is called the *carrier*. As such, the carrier may not be the person who actually carries

---

[8] The charterer has no control over the general use of the ship. However, the Court of Appeal has held a slot charter to be a charterparty for the purposes of Admiralty jurisdiction: *The Tychy* [1999] 2 Lloyd's Rep 11, CA.

[9] See 3.105ff.

the goods but will be the person who is legally obliged to ensure that the carriage contract is performed. The carrier is usually the shipowner. But, if the ship is under a demise (or 'bareboat') charterparty,[10] the carrier will probably be the demise (or bareboat) charterer. And sometimes the voyage charterer or time charterer of a ship is the carrier: ie, he contracts to carry the goods and performs the contract by using the services of the owner (or demise charterer) as, in effect, a subcontractor.

- The person who sends (or consigns) goods by sea is usually called the *shipper* (or *consignor*). If he has chartered the vessel, he is also the *charterer*. It may sometimes be necessary to distinguish between the person who contracts for the carriage and the person who actually ships the goods: the latter might merely be a seller to the person contracting for carriage and delivering the goods into the custody of the ship in performance of the contract of sale.

- While the goods are afloat their ownership and/or possession may change by reason of dealings between the parties, usually by means of dealing with the documents. The person who owns the goods at any one time is at that time the *cargo owner*; he will therefore normally be the *bill of lading holder*; and the carrier is normally entitled to treat the bill of lading holder as having the rights of the cargo owner. But the cargo owner and the bill of lading holder are not necessarily the same person: the holder of the bill may not at a relevant time own the cargo, and likewise the owner of the cargo may not hold the bill.

- The person who receives the goods at destination may do so by virtue of being the initially intended consignee of them, under a bill of lading or some other document, or he may have acquired rights, eg, on transfer (usually indorsement) of the bill of lading. He may be called the *consignee*, or *indorsee* (of the bill of lading), or again, merely the *cargo owner*. But, since there are so many possibilities concerning who he is, it is often simplest to refer to him as the *receiver* or, if there is a claim, *claimant*.

- The sum payable for the carriage of goods is known as *freight*. It may be paid on delivery of the goods at destination, or in advance (*advance freight*). The sum payable for use of a vessel under a demise charterparty is usually referred to as *hire*; and (despite early use of the expression 'time chartered freight') *hire* is also now used to describe the remuneration payable under a time charterparty. Hire is normally payable in regular periodical instalments.

B. Charterparties

(1) Types of Charterparties

A charterparty (often shortened to 'charter') is a contract whereby (subject to the reservations made above) the carrying capacity of a ship is by contract placed by the owner[11] at the disposal of another person, referred to as the 'charterer'. Charterparties are of two basic types, the voyage charter and the time charter.   **3.13**

(a) The voyage charterparty

The voyage charterparty is 'a contract to carry specified goods on a defined voyage or voyages, the remuneration of the shipowner being a freight calculated according to the quantity of cargo loaded or carried, or sometimes a lump sum freight'.[12] This is the older type of   **3.14**

---

[10] See 3.23f.
[11] Or sometimes demise charterer: see 3.23f.
[12] *Scrutton*, para 4.017.

charterparty and dates from times when only the shipowner could take the responsibility for estimating the risks and likely duration of the voyage and what he needed to charge for it. The destination of the voyage is specified, though the charterer may have discretion to determine or change it within limits. Voyage charters are made on standard contract forms, but their long history means that there is considerable scope for the application of general principle.

3.15 In substance the voyage is undertaken for a fixed price. The risk of delay affecting the profitability of the carriage contract is therefore on the shipowner, and within that price he normally allows fixed free time for loading and unloading, called 'laytime' (lying time), 'laydays' or other variants. The calculation of this—its starting point, whether it can be interrupted and for how long it runs—gives rise to disputes which, because of the great significance of delay in maritime operations, involve in their resolution technical questions of interpretation of wording and, in their result, large sums of money. If the charterer delays the ship beyond laytime he is in breach of contract and liable in damages, but it is normal to agree in advance the rate at (and time during) which these are payable, under the title 'demurrage' (French *demeure*, delay money). This is by modern standards normally classified as liquidated (or agreed) damages for breach of contract by detaining the ship beyond laytime: that is to say, the charterer is not *entitled* to keep the ship on demurrage, but is paying damages for doing so.[13] Demurrage disputes—as to what sorts of losses are covered by demurrage, when demurrage starts and finishes, whether on the terms of the contract it can be interrupted and so forth—are likewise technical and involve large sums of money. Once laytime and time on demurrage have ceased, damages for continuing delay are payable on normal common law principles.

3.16 Another way in which the charterer may cause the shipowner unjustifiable loss of anticipated profit is, when the freight is calculated by quantity or size of the cargo carried, by not utilizing all the cargo space or not shipping the cargo contracted for. Damages for failure to do the former are equivalent to the freight which would have been earned, and are called 'dead freight'. Here too, complex disputes can arise as to whether indications of cargo carrying capacity in the charterparty (or sometimes elsewhere) are contractual promises by the charterer to load that quantity or fill that space, or simply a general indication of the sort of capacity involved. (The same problem can arise in reverse, where the ship proves unable to carry the anticipated quantity.)

3.17 A voyage charterparty is a contract for services (*locatio conductio operarum*), to be rendered by the shipowner, his equipment and employees. It is definitely not a hire of the ship (*locatio conductio rei*), for the ship remains under the control of the shipowner and master.

(b) The time charterparty

3.18 Time charterparties are a later invention and date from times when sail was giving way to steam and ship movements were becoming more predictable. 'The shipowner agrees…to render services for a named period by his master and crew to carry goods put on board the ship by or on behalf of the time charterer'[14] in return for payment of 'hire'. The shipowner is said to 'deliver' the ship to the charterer, at the beginning of the period in which its services are to be made available; and, at the end of that period, the ship should be free of commitments and

---

[13] In theory a stipulation for demurrage could be a penalty, and relief granted against it accordingly: as to penalties, see EPL 21.177ff. But the sum involved is more likely to undercompensate than overcompensate, as high demurrage rates could be a weak selling point. Some standard forms also fix 'dispatch money', a bonus for quick loading or unloading, as a fraction of demurrage; this again discourages high demurrage rates. For a dispute turning on such factors see the famous case of *Suisse Atlantique Cie d'Armement Maritime SA v NV Rotterdamsche Kolen Centrale* [1967] 1 AC 361, HL, which additionally stands as a leading English decision on a much more general issue relating to unfair contract terms.

[14] *Scrutton*, para 4.017.

'redelivered' to the shipowner by the charterer. However, such (re)delivery is metaphorical, as the shipowner and his master remain in control of the vessel throughout. The charterer can give commercial (but not navigational)[15] orders to the shipowner within specified geographical limits (which may be anything from very narrow to 'worldwide') during the charter period. The arrangement is essentially one whereby the shipowner makes available the services of his ship on an agreed basis, within which the charterer arranges for the carriage of cargo (normally cargo belonging to third parties). The contract normally provides for circumstances in which the charterer can give the shipowner orders as to the 'employment' of the vessel (in particular, requiring him to sign bill of lading contracts), in return for which he is obliged to indemnify the shipowner for losses resulting from obedience to such orders.[16] Whether third parties contract for the carriage of their goods with the charterer or the shipowner, the freight payable by cargo owners is ultimately the source of both the shipowner's and the charterer's income and profit, so the charterparty will need to provide for how the financial arrangements are made between its parties. Thus, to ensure that the charterer does not collect freight from cargo owners without paying the hire due under the charterparty, the charterparty may provide that the shipowner has a 'lien' on freights payable under bill of lading contracts.[17]

A time charterparty is similar to a voyage charterparty except in the method of calculation **3.19** of payment and hence the allocation of risk of delay during the carriage. The shipowner is paid by time so will usually have no objection to being delayed by the charterer's orders or failure to give them. Hence a counterpart to the laytime and demurrage regime is required. This is normally provided by an 'off-hire clause', under which no hire is payable while the ship is (in whole or in part, depending on the wording of the clause) in effect not working for the charterer. As with laytime and demurrage, disputes can be complicated and involve large sums of money. The clause basically deals with whether or not hire is payable and does not affect liability in damages on either side, which will turn on the contractual allocation of responsibility for the event causing the delay.

The time at which the charter is due to expire often gives rise to disputes. On the one hand, **3.20** the voyages that the charterer can arrange at the end of the charter period may well not fit precisely within it, and the charterer will be reluctant to pay for unused time, but the shipowner will wish to earn the maximum possible under the contract. On the other hand, if a voyage is prone to overrun, there may be dispute as to whether the shipowner must proceed on it and, if he does, whether remuneration is payable at the contract rate or (more likely) as damages for breach of contract, particularly when market rates have increased.[18] In general, the ship must be redelivered either within a reasonable period after the end of the charter period or in accordance with contractually agreed tolerance. If the ship is redelivered early, freight would normally be payable until the end of the charter period, unless a refusal by the shipowner to take it back was totally unreasonable.[19] Here again complicated disputes involving large sums of money are litigated.[20]

---

[15] The difference may prove highly controversial, for instance if the charterer specifies a route: see *The Hill Harmony* [2001] 1 AC 638.

[16] This includes the obligation to pay the shipowner for caring for the cargo after the shipowner has lawfully exercised his right to withdraw the vessel (3.43–3.45): see *ENE Kos 1 Ltd v Petroleo Brasileiro SA (The Kos)* [2012] UKSC 17, [2012] 2 AC 164.

[17] Such liens can be problematic. See *Western Bulk Shipowning III A/S v Carbofer Mariti e Trading APS (The Western Moscow)* [2012] EWHC 1224 (Comm), [2012] 2 Lloyd's Rep 163.

[18] See *Hyundai Merchant Marine Co v Geduri Chartering Co Ltd (The Peonia)* [1991] 1 Lloyd's Rep 100.

[19] See *Isabella Shipowner SA v Shagang Shipping Co Ltd (The Aquafaith)* [2012] EWHC 1077 (Comm), [2012] 2 Lloyd's Rep 61, interpreting the decision in *White & Carter (Councils) Ltd v McGregor* [1962] AC 413, HL as to an innocent party's entitlement to continue performance despite the other party's repudiatory breach of contract.

[20] For an example see *Torvald Klaveness A/S v Arni Maritime Corp (The Gregos)* [1994] 1 WLR 1465, HL.

3.21 The true nature of a time charter is the subject of some disagreement internationally, but in English law at least it seems clear that, although the charterer can in theory give no orders and simply keep the ship waiting, or use it for storage, it is again a contract for carriage. As such it is a contract for services (*locatio conductio operarum*) rather than a hire of the ship (*locatio rei*), and this despite the use of the term 'hire' for the remuneration payable and other infelicities of terminology (such as 'deliver' and 'redeliver'). The right to the ship's services may be protected in appropriate cases by injunction,[21] although not usually against third parties.[22] The main difference from voyage charters lies in the method of payment and the consequent allocation of delay risks.[23] Time charters are largely made on standard forms and disputes turn largely on the wording of the form used: there is less scope for general principle than with voyage charters.

3.22 There can also be mixed time and voyage charterparties, where the ship is contracted to go to a particular port, but paid on a time basis—perhaps, eg, because the shipowner is uncertain as to the time likely to be required at the destination port. These, often called 'trip charters', are time charters as regards payment; within the voyage route the charterer can give orders[24] and there may be special provisions for delivery and redelivery; but the ship cannot be ordered off the normal route for the voyage.[25]

(c) Demise or 'bareboat' charterparty

3.23 This is a totally different arrangement, as the ancient English word 'demise', formerly used in a property context, indicates. It is not a contract for services at all but rather a contract for the hire of the ship itself (*locatio conductio rei*). The charterer has possession of the ship, employs the master and crew, makes contracts of carriage (whether by charterparty or bill of lading) for it, and for most purposes is the equivalent of owner of it during the duration of the charterparty. Such contracts are not contracts for the carriage of goods by sea and are used for different purposes, such as operating ships without capital expenditure, loan financing and various devices connected with the changing of flags. There are nowadays standard forms of demise charter, though there are older cases on the question whether a particular contractual arrangement constituted a demise or a time charter,[26] which would nowadays more usually be clear.

3.24 In common law terms a demise charter should be in effect a lease of the ship and hence create a right *in rem* available against third parties. Since it operates by contract only, it is not clear to what extent it actually does so. If the charterer has possession of the ship he is a bailee, and hence not so reliant on contractual rights. In other situations he may be entitled to an injunction against third parties, but the full legal position is not worked out, and this appears to be true in some other countries also.[27]

(2) *The Regime Under Which the Goods are Carried*

(a) General common law principles as to carrier's duties

3.25 The general principle in this area is that there is complete freedom of contract. Although international conventions concerning charterparty terms have been mooted, they have not

---

[21] See *Lauritzencool AB v Lady Navigation Inc* [2005] EWCA Civ 579, [2005] 1 WLR 3686.
[22] See *Chitty on Contracts* (31st edn, 2012) ('*Chitty*'), paras 18–128ff.
[23] Though the charterer's power to give orders can involve disputes as to damage to the ship.
[24] *Ocean Tramp Tankers Corp v V/O Sovfracht (The Eugenia)* [1964] 2 QB 226, CA.
[25] See *Temple SS Co Ltd v V/O Sovfracht* (1945) 79 Ll L R 1.
[26] eg *Baumwoll Manufactur von Carl Scheibler v Furness* [1893] AC 8, HL.
[27] See N Palmer and E McKendrick (eds), *Interests in Goods* (2nd edn, 1998) ch 20.

yet come to fruition. The perception is that charterers and shipowners are on a more or less equal bargaining footing: indeed, in contrast with the normal situation under bills of lading, some charterers, such as governmental import or export agencies, may be in a stronger position than shipowning companies.

There are however at common law ancient principles which applied at times when carriage by sea (or by other methods of transport) might be undertaken without written terms. These can still be relevant if no written terms are agreed, and sometimes when the terms of the contract are said to be displaced, as eg by a deviation.[28] They are the principles anciently applicable to common carriers, persons who offered themselves to the public to carry any cargo entrusted to them. As a shipowner carrying under charterparty may often carry for one shipper only, it is arguable that such a person may in fact not be a common carrier; but the same principles as those for common carriers are assumed to be applicable.[29] They apply to bill of lading contracts also. The regime is said to be that the carrier promises to deliver the goods at destination in as good condition as that in which they were when entrusted to him, subject to the 'common law' exceptions of act of God, act of Queen's (King's or public) enemies, inherent vice in the goods (which would cover natural and unavoidable deterioration) and defective packing (a refinement of inherent vice).

3.26

This regime was presumably adequate for older navigation conditions, but during the nineteenth century it became inadequate, and shipowners began drafting detailed contracts to protect themselves in respect of various risks (still referred to nowadays by the traditional phrase 'excepted perils'). The basic common law rule then suffered a not very clearly traced metathesis into certain basic common law principles of interpretation of the contract terms used. These remain valid to this day.[30] They are as follows:

3.27

(i) *Duty to furnish a seaworthy vessel.* This duty, as developed, covers not only fitness to lie in port with cargo aboard and to go to sea, but also to receive and hold cargo ('cargoworthiness'): in all cases, fitness for the voyage intended and as regards the particular cargo. The notion of seaworthiness is quite wide: it includes efficiency of the crew[31] and possession of appropriate navigational aids and documentation. The ship must be 'cargoworthy' on loading and seaworthy on sailing. That is all. Anything which goes wrong subsequently in this respect ranks for consideration under the rules relating to the prosecution of the voyage, to which the next heading, (ii), may be relevant.

(ii) *Duty to exercise due care (ie, not to be negligent in respect) of the cargo loaded.* These duties would of course apply even if the ship never moved. They are really warehousing duties, and a ship is in a sense a floating warehouse.

Two further duties apply to the voyage:

(iii) *Duty to proceed with reasonable dispatch.* The meaning of this is obvious.[32]

(iv) *Duty not to deviate from the contract route.* This attracts special considerations, explained below.[33]

---

[28] See 3.46ff.

[29] See *Scrutton*, para 11.001.

[30] See *Paterson SS Ltd v Canadian Wheat Producers Ltd* [1934] AC 538, 544–545.

[31] See the well-known *Hong Kong Fir* case, at n 58; for a recent example see *The Eurasian Dream* [2002] EWHC 118, [2002] 1 Lloyd's Rep 719 (crew inadequately trained and equipped for carriage of motor cars).

[32] Most cases in fact concern delay on the approach voyage, as to which see 3.36. Delay problems are often caused by the need to complete a previous charter: see, eg *Evera SA v North Shipping Co* [1956] 2 Lloyd's Rep 367.

[33] See 3.46ff.

It is often said that there is a further implied duty: to contribute in general average.[34]

3.28   Contract terms in charterparties and bills of lading are interpreted against the background that these principles are assumed not to have been excluded unless clearly, and there are many dramatic examples of this.[35] But, if they are clearly excluded, freedom of contract applies in both types of contract and the exempting term is valid: unlike the position in some countries, there is no rule of law making terms excluding these duties (eg, excluding liability for negligence) ineffective on grounds of public policy. Indeed, this was one of the factors leading to the adoption of the Hague Rules, which regulate the liability of the carrier under bill of lading contracts.[36] The Unfair Terms in Consumer Contracts Directive[37] is obviously not relevant, as these are not consumer contracts; and the only general law in the United Kingdom on unfair contract terms, the Unfair Contract Terms Act 1977,[38] is specifically excluded from the vast majority of maritime contracts,[39] as from international supply contracts.[40]

(b) Duties of charterer

3.29   Implied duties are here less prominent, but in general a charterer must: have cargo ready (a separate duty, but usually subsumed into the laytime and demurrage obligations); load a full[41] cargo of the merchandise specified; and not without agreement of the owner ship dangerous goods (a topic the subject of much case law, in particular on who takes the risk as to goods not known to either side to be dangerous).[42] These duties are strict, in the absence of other indication.

(c) Loading and unloading

3.30   The questions of who pays for and who takes the risks involved in[43] loading or unloading operations turn on the individual contract. The starting point is often said to be that the charterer lifts the goods to the ship's rail and the shipowner takes them from that point, though it is also said that the duty prima facie rests with the owner.[44] In any case, this is, however, virtually always modified by contract terms, usage or custom of the port.[45] The time at which the risk passes from seller to buyer under a contract of sale of the goods need not be the same as the time when the shipowner assumes responsibility for the goods: the former is more likely to be the moment of crossing the ship's rail,[46] which is thought to be a notion still familiar to merchants.[47]

---

[34]   See 3.06. The obligation is generally imposed by law and has in consequence become a contractually implied term: see a book review by Sir Christopher Staughton (1998) 114 LQR 677.

[35]   eg *Tattersall v National SS Co* (1884) 12 QBD 297.

[36]   See 3.56ff.

[37]   Operative under the Consumer Rights Act 2015, Part 2.

[38]   See EPL 8.110ff.

[39]   Unfair Contract Terms Act 1977, Sch 1 excludes from the Act contracts for the carriage of goods by sea except (i) in respect of exclusion or restriction of liability for death or personal injury resulting from negligence or (ii) in favour of a person dealing as consumer.

[40]   Unfair Contract Terms Act 1977, s 26.

[41]   See 3.16.

[42]   See *The Giannis NK* [1998] AC 605 (a case on the Hague Rules, but a leading case on this topic in general).

[43]   These are not necessarily the same: the burdens could lie on different parties. The standard term 'FIO' ('free in and out') indicates that the freight agreed does not cover the cost of loading or unloading. But the question who takes the responsibility for these functions (as opposed to pays for them) requires further study of the contract terms. See *The Jordan II* [2004] UKHL 49; [2005] 1 WLR 1363.

[44]   See *The Jordan II*, n 43, at [11].

[45]   *Pyrene Co Ltd v Scindia Navigation Co Ltd* [1954] 2 QB 402.

[46]   Which seems to have been the case in *Pyrene Co Ltd v Scindia Navigation Co Ltd* [1954] 2 QB 402.

[47]   However, when risk passes is more complex where the International Chamber of Commerce's INCOTERMS 2010 are used.

(3) Remedies for Breach of the Contract Duties

(a) General common law approach

The English law as to the remedies for breach of the duties in a contract for carriage by sea is **3.31** well developed, and forms the origin of much of the general law on the topic, including the general law on damages.[48]

Any term infringed will normally be an express one in the charterparty, for even the implied **3.32** duties referred to above are usually reproduced in some form, even though limited,[49] in the charterparty itself. For breach of such a term, express or implied, an action for damages will lie for loss caused by that breach (but not for loss not so caused).[50]

However, in many cases the person affected (usually the charterer) may wish to terminate **3.33** the contract: in common law terms, treat it as discharged for breach.[51] This right is of great importance in common law, and does not exclude an additional right to damages. It cannot be exercised if it is waived, ie the person entitled to it clearly indicates that he will not exercise it (so-called 'election').[52] If this occurs, the right to damages remains. That can be waived also, but such a waiver is more difficult to establish, since it amounts to giving up all rights under the contract. As such, to be binding it would normally require consideration.[53]

(b) Termination of the contract

To determine when the breach is sufficiently serious to entitle the innocent party to treat the **3.34** contract as discharged, it can be said that three techniques are available, two of them at least stemming from maritime law.

(i) Condition or warranty

The first technique looks to the term (or promise) of the contract broken and asks whether it **3.35** is a term in respect of which the parties are to be regarded as having agreed that there should be exact compliance.[54] If so, where there has been no such compliance the innocent party may terminate the contract, at least unless the other party can put the matter right within any express or implied time limit, and sue for damages also. Such a term is called a 'condition'; a term not giving rise to this right, but only to a right in damages, is called a 'warranty'. This is an established but curious use of the term 'condition': the term is really a promise rather than a condition. What is the condition is in fact the making good of the promise, which is a condition precedent to the other party's duty to proceed.

---

[48] See EPL ch 21, section B. Curiously, it is arguable that some leading judgments have fallen short of fulfilling commercial law's traditional aim for certainty: eg *Koufos v Czarnikow Ltd (The Heron II)* [1969] 1 AC 350; *Golden Strait Corp v Nippon Yusen Kubishka Kaisha (The Golden Victory)* [2007] UKHL 12, [2007] 2 AC 353; *Transfield Shipping Inc v Mercator Shipping Inc (The Achilleas)* [2008] UKHL 48, [2009] 1 AC 61; cf *Sylvia Shipping Co Ltd v Progress Bulk Carriers Ltd (The Sylvia)* [2010] EWHC 542 (Comm), [2010] 2 Lloyd's Rep 81; *Flame SA v Glory Wealth Shipping Pte Ltd (The Glory Wealth)* [2013] EWHC 3153 (Comm), [2014] QB 1080.

[49] If the duty imposed by the contract term is interpreted as more limited than the common law duty, eg as to the time at which the ship must be seaworthy (which could be the time of making the contract), the common law duty will normally apply also, unless the wording of the clause is interpreted as limiting the common law duty.

[50] For an instructive example see *The Europa* [1908] P 84, where part of the loss was caused by unseaworthiness and part by negligence in navigation (an excepted peril).

[51] See *Chitty*, ch 24.

[52] *Chitty*, paras 24–002ff.

[53] See EPL 8.49ff; *Chitty*, paras 3–085ff.

[54] See *Photo Production Ltd v Securicor Transport Ltd* [1980] AC 827, 849, HL *per* Lord Diplock, who was largely responsible for the development of this branch of the law.

3.36 The origin of this use of the term 'condition' actually stems from the law of carriage of goods by sea. A ship when chartered is often not at the place where it is required to load: it must first proceed there (the voyage to the place of loading often being called the 'approach voyage'). The charterer's duty to load the ship is conditional upon its having been in the place at which it was said to be at the time of the charter. Thus, in the context of nineteenth-century slowness of communication, where a ship was described in the charterparty as 'now in the port of Amsterdam' but at that time had not yet even arrived at Amsterdam, the charterer was held entitled to refuse to load it when it arrived in England, and hence to terminate the contract and sue for damages.[55] The position of the ship at the time of chartering was crucial for the charterer's calculations as to the timescale.

3.37 There is no need for the word 'condition' to be used in the contract; and, even if it is, the court may say that the term in question was not a condition in the technical sense. Most of the statements of fact in charterparties relating to the ship, its flag, carrying capacity and expected readiness to load would rank as conditions, depending always on the interpretation of the particular contract. This technique is still extensively used in this area of the law,[56] and in general of 'time clauses in mercantile contracts'.[57] Even so, late payment of hire should probably not be treated as a breach of condition.[57a]

(ii) Innocent party deprived of 'substantially the whole benefit' of the contract

3.38 The second technique looks at the nature and consequences of the breach. Its classic formulation, derived from the judgment of Diplock LJ in *Hong Kong Fir Shipping Co Ltd v Kawasaki Kisen Kaisha Ltd*,[58] a seminal case for the general law, but actually on the seaworthiness term, asks whether the effect of the breach is to deprive the innocent party of 'substantially the whole benefit' of the contract.[59] This is more adverse to termination than the 'condition' technique: 'deprive of substantially the whole benefit' is not the same as 'substantially deprive of the benefit'. Its most common application is to cases of delay, where it is asked whether (eg) to make the charterer load in the circumstances created by the breach would be to hold him to a different contract from that which he had made.[60] Such a delay is often called a 'frustrating delay', and the test is the same as that in the doctrine of frustration, which releases both parties by a change of circumstances attributable to neither.[61] Indeed, the latter doctrine in its modern form originates in maritime law also, and a party is again released on the same basis, that to make him go ahead would be to hold him to an obligation into which he had not entered.[62] In this case however there is no breach by the other party.

3.39 The origin of this doctrine for the whole common law lies in cases where by virtue of breach of contract the ship arrives from the approach voyage very late for loading: the charterer is not

---

[55] *Behn v Burness* (1863) 3 B & S 751, 122 ER 281.

[56] As to expected readiness to load see *Maredelanto Cia Naviera v Bergbau-Handel GmbH (The Mihalis Angelos)* [1971] 1 QB 164, CA (a leading case on the condition technique). An instructive consideration of various terms in an affreightment contract, and which of them were to be regarded as conditions, is to be found in *The Mavro Vetranic* [1985] 1 Lloyds Rep 580.

[57] See an international sale of goods case, *Bunge Corp v Tradax International SA* [1981] 1 WLR 711, 715–716, HL, *per* Lord Wilberforce. *Cf* the Sale of Goods Act 1979, s 10 (time of payment not of the essence).

[57a] *Spar Shipping AS v Grand China Logistics Holding (Group) Co Ltd* [2015] EWHC 718 (Comm); not following *Kuwait Rocks Co v AMN Bulkcarriers Inc (The Astra)* [2013] EWHC 865 (Comm), [2013] 2 Lloyd's Rep 69.

[58] [1962] 2 QB 26.

[59] See [1962] 2 QB 26, 70–71. In the *Photo Production* case, n 54, Lord Diplock called this a 'fundamental breach' (see 849), which invites confusion with older cases using this notion in connection with unfair exclusion clauses: the *Suisse Atlantique* case [1967] 1 AC 361 concerns this usage.

[60] *Freeman v Taylor* (1831) 8 Bing 124, 131 ER 348.

[61] See EPL 18.439ff.

[62] See *Jackson v Union Marine Insurance Co* (1874) LR 10 CP 125.

bound to load it.[63] If the lateness is a breach of contract, the situation is one for discharge by breach (and damages); if it is excused, there may be frustration and both parties are released.[64]

(iii) Repudiation or renunciation

The third technique, quite close to the second, asks whether one party has behaved towards **3.40** the other in such a way as to indicate repudiation or renunciation of his obligations under the contract.[65] Here the breach need not be of condition, nor its consequences in themselves so drastic as are required by the *Hong Kong Fir* test referred to above,[66] but the situation must be sufficient to raise grave doubts in the innocent party as to the likelihood of the contract's being properly performed over a period. Such reasoning is found in maritime cases, but more often in cases of instalment sales.[67] There are some difficulties in applying this to situations of anticipatory breach of contract, ie where no breach has yet occurred but it reasonably appears that it will occur.[68] Orthodox doctrine, derived from this area of the law, indicates that there is no anticipatory breach merely because a reasonable person would think that the contract would not or could not be performed when the time came: it would be necessary to establish an express or implied refusal to perform, or that it will certainly be impossible to perform at that time.[69] Where there is an actual (as opposed to an anticipatory) breach,[70] however, uncertainty as to what may happen may justify termination of the contract under the third technique.[71]

(c) Specific contract clauses

The inevitable uncertainties of invoking the general law on termination (except where there **3.41** is no doubt that the term concerned ranks as a condition), and the serious consequences of making the wrong decision, lead to the presence in charterparties of clauses designed to enable one party to avoid uncertainty and terminate regardless of whether the general law permits this. Of these, two, one in favour of the charterer and one in favour of the shipowner, deserve explanation here, since they impinge on and interact with general contractual principles.

(i) The cancelling clause

This can be found in voyage and in time charterparties, and in general permits the charterer to **3.42** cancel the contract if the ship does not arrive for loading by a certain time. The same objective could be partially achieved by stipulating that the time of sailing on the approach voyage, or of tender for loading, is a condition of the contract.[72] The cancelling clause is however wider in several respects and cannot be regarded simply as a condition expressed in other wording (against which there is no objection in principle). First, it applies even where the late arrival is excused by an excepted peril, ie is not a breach of contract at all: in this sense it may enable the charterer to act without reference to the doctrine of frustration.[73] Secondly, however, it

---

[63] See *Freeman v Taylor*, n 60; *Jackson v Union Marine Insurance Co Ltd*, n 62. Compare *Behn v Burness*, n 55, where there was breach of a term as to position of the ship and 'condition' reasoning could be used.

[64] See *Jackson v Union Marine Insurance Co*, n 62. The monetary consequences are generally regulated by statute (the Law Reform (Frustrated Contracts) Act 1943) but not in this actual context.

[65] See *Withers v Reynolds* (1831) 2 B & Ad 882, 109 ER 1370 (a case on sale of goods).

[66] See 3.38.

[67] See Sale of Goods Act 1979, s 31.

[68] See EPL 8.431ff; *Chitty*, paras 24–018ff.

[69] *Universal Cargo Carriers Corp v Citati* [1957] 2 QB 401, CA, where a chartered ship sailed away because the master formed the view that no cargo would be forthcoming.

[70] ie occurring at the time at which performance was due, as opposed to earlier.

[71] See *Maple Flock Co Ltd v Universal Furniture Products (Wembley) Co Ltd* [1934] 1 KB 148 (instalment sale).

[72] eg *Glaholm v Hays* (1841) 2 Man & G 257, 133 ER 743.

[73] *Smith v Dart & Son* (1884) 14 QBD 105.

does not displace the general law as to discharge by breach[74] and frustration,[75] with the result that, even if the clause is not exercised, a later frustrating delay would entitle the innocent party to terminate the contract if there was a breach, or, if there was not, the contract could be frustrated. Finally, it may only be exercised exactly according to its terms; under many forms of the clause the charterer may and even must wait until the ship arrives, even if it is certain to be late, before deciding whether to cancel. By the same token, however, a cancellation outside the terms of the clause, eg, too soon,[76] may be ineffective, even if late arrival is at that point inevitable. It will be seen therefore that, as elsewhere in English shipping law, the parties are held strictly to the terms of their contract, and in general no argument is possible that the right was exercised from what may be argued to have been inappropriate motives.

(ii) The withdrawal clause

3.43   This is peculiar to the circumstances of time charterparties. It provides (with many variants of detail) that, if the hire is not paid by or before a certain time, the shipowner may withdraw the vessel, ie terminate the charter. This again protects the shipowner from the general law as to discharge by breach, which does not easily apply to late payment.[77] Again, the power can only be exercised in exact accordance with its terms, but again the motive for doing so is not relevant. So it can sometimes, depending on its formulation, be exercised by a shipowner who has already received late payment (unless this constitutes a waiver, which it is unlikely to do since banks, to whom such payment is made, may have no authority to waive contract terms).[78] On the other hand it cannot be exercised before the time stipulated for its exercise, even if it is clear that timely payment can no longer be made.[79]

3.44   Unlike late arrival, late payment will rarely be excused by any contract term, and the withdrawal clause is therefore almost bound to be exercised in respect of such a breach of contract. It is arguable therefore that, unlike the cancelling clause, it is to be treated as a condition of the contract expressed in other words: interpretation is a matter for the court, and there is no objection to a condition not specifically expressed as such. It seems clear however that this is not so, though a small addition to the wording could give it this effect.[80] The difference in practice is this. If the withdrawal clause is a condition, the shipowner who withdraws the vessel is exercising his right to treat the contract as discharged under the general law and can sue, not only for accrued unpaid instalments, but also for loss of the profit contemplated from the rest of the charterparty, as arising from breach of contract, damages being available at common law in addition to termination. If it is not, no such damages are recoverable, the shipowner having himself chosen to cause the ending of the contract: all that is recoverable is the instalments already due but unpaid.[81] It seems clear that the latter represents the present position in English law. The result is that the shipowner can only sue for full damages for loss of the remainder of the contract if the late payment constituted a repudiatory breach on general principles.[82] Some

---

[74] *Hong Kong Fir Shipping Co Ltd v Kawasaki Kisen Kaisha Ltd* [1962] 2 QB 26, CA.
[75] *Bank Line Ltd v Arthur Capel & Co* [1919] AC 435.
[76] *The Madeleine* [1967] 2 Lloyd's Rep 224.
[77] cf however 3.37.
[78] See on both points *Mardorf Peach & Co v Attica Sea Carriers Corp (The Laconia)* [1977] AC 850, HL.
[79] *Afovos Shipping Co SA v Pagnan & Fratelli (The Afovos)* [1983] 1 WLR 195, though the speech of Lord Diplock seeks to solve the case on the wider and more doubtful ground that the clause constitutes a condition, and there can be no anticipatory breach of condition: 'Anticipatory breach is but a species of the genus repudiation and applies only to fundamental breach' (at 203).
[80] As, in the context of hire purchase, in *Lombard North Central plc v Butterworth* [1987] QB 527, CA ('punctual payment [of] which shall be of the essence').
[81] *Financings Ltd v Baldock* [1963] 2 QB 104.
[82] As in *Leslie Shipping Co v Welstead* [1921] 3 KB 420.

doubt has however been cast on this result in Australia in connection with similar clauses in hire-purchase and other financing contracts, which are of course analogous.[83]

Finally, it will be seen again that the right to withdraw the vessel can, depending on the draft- **3.45** ing of the clause, be exercised in a manner onerous to the charterer, who (or whose bank) may have done no more than make a mistake in telex addresses or time zones. In the context of landlord and tenant similar clauses appear in leases in favour of landlords, but the courts have long exercised a jurisdiction to relieve against forfeiture of the lease by granting more time to pay. It might be arguable that a similar jurisdiction should be exercised in connection with charterparties. The principal difference is that in English law a lease creates a property right, protected in appropriate cases by a decree of specific performance, and it is this right that is pro-tected from being forfeited. The right under a time charter is purely contractual, and a decree of specific performance would rarely be appropriate. For such reasons the House of Lords has rejected any such jurisdiction in the case of the withdrawal clause,[84] citing the firm judgment of Robert Goff LJ in the Court of Appeal below.[85] This is consistent with the absence of any doctrine of good faith in English law, at least in this part of it. It is possible that other common law jurisdictions, particularly those inclined to make more use of equitable doctrines in com-mercial law, might take a different view.[86] In practice, however, the problem is ameliorated by the possibility that parties may also include in the charterparty an anti-technicality clause, restraining the exercise of the right conferred by the withdrawal clause.

(4) Deviation[87]

A somewhat unusual doctrine operates in English law in connection with deviation from the **3.46** contract route. It applies both to voyage charterparties and to bills of lading, including bills of lading governed by the Hague Rules.[88] This route must first be ascertained from the terms of the contract and commercial and navigational practice. It need not be a direct geographical route; and especially in bill of lading contracts, which are likely to involve a ship which calls at several ports, it is unlikely to be so. Most contracts will in fact contain a clause purporting to permit what would otherwise be a deviation in very wide terms, frequently ending with wording such as 'and all of the above shall be deemed to be part of the contract voyage'. Even with such wording these clauses, called 'liberty clauses', have been subjected to very extreme techniques of interpretation *contra proferentem*: they have been read to be consistent with the contract voyage and not as justifying a ship departing from the normal route.[89]

The contract route being ascertained, a deliberate[90] going off it is a deviation unless specially **3.47** justified by the requirements of preserving the safety of the adventure, or saving life.[91] The

---

[83] *Esanda Finance Corp Ltd v Plessnig* (1989) 166 CLR 131, esp *per* Brennan J.

[84] *Scandinavian Trading Tanker Co v Flota Petrolera Ecuatoriana (The Scaptrade)* [1983] 2 AC 694, HL; but cf *Lauritzencool AB v Lady Navigation Inc* [2005] EWCA Civ 579, [2005] 1 WLR 3686, n 21.

[85] [1983] QB 529.

[86] See *Esanda Finance Corp Ltd v Plessnig*, n 83.

[87] See in general FMB Reynolds, 'The Implementation of Private Law Conventions in English Law' in *The Butterworth Lectures 1990–91* (1992).

[88] *Stag Line Ltd v Foscolo Mango & Co Ltd* [1932] AC 328, HL. As to the Hague and Hague-Visby Rules see 3.56ff. There seems no reason why the doctrine should not apply under the Hague-Visby Rules also: even though these have by virtue of their enacting statute the 'force of law', they only apply to contracts, and if the contract is displaced they would be displaced also. However, under the Rotterdam rules, deviation does not displace defences, except in the case of deliberate fault. See 3.72.

[89] eg *Glynn v Margetson & Co* [1893] AC 351, HL (starting off in wrong direction).

[90] A negligent departure from the route could be negligence in navigation, an excepted peril in most contracts.

[91] A deviation to save the property of others, eg for the purpose of earning a salvage award, would not be justified unless permitted by the terms of the contract—which it often is, and is in most bill of lading con-tracts by virtue of the Hague Rules and their variants: see Article IV.4.

accepted result of this in English law at present appears to be that the shipowner, from the moment of the deviation,[92] loses the benefit of all excepted perils and is remitted to the common law position of a common carrier,[93] the common law exceptions also being displaced, with the result that he is liable unless he can establish that the loss would necessarily have occurred even though he had not deviated.[94] Further than this, it appears, though from less strong authority, that he is equally unable to rely on other contract terms to his benefit, eg demurrage clauses operative on discharge,[95] the duty to pay general average contribution in respect of an event occurring after the deviation,[96] and the contract provision for the payment of freight[97] (other than advance freight),[98] though in the first case it is assumed that he can have damages at large for delay beyond laytime, and in the third it has been said that though not entitled to the contract freight he is entitled to reasonable freight,[99] presumably on a restitutionary basis.[100]

3.48 The doctrine is said to be a reaction to the insurance position, under which when a ship went off the normal route it and its cargo were uninsured: hence the carrier, by doing this took on the insurer's liability[101] and became absolutely liable—but subject to the exception regarding events which would have occurred anyway. This could explain the displacement of excepted perils, but not of demurrage, general average and freight provisions.

3.49 The doctrine seems historically to be an amalgamation of rules of: proof regarding bailment (a bailee who stores goods in an unauthorized place is liable unless he can establish that the loss must have occurred anyway);[102] interpretation (excepted perils are not intended to apply where the goods are subjected to risks totally different from those contemplated);[103] insurance (an insurance policy is avoided if the ship deviates);[104] and discharge of contract by breach. This last explanation was accepted in the most authoritative case on the doctrine, the decision of the House of Lords in *Hain SS Co Ltd v Tate & Lyle Ltd*.[105] The main issue in this case was however whether a deviation could be waived: on the basis that it was a breach of condition[106] it was held that it could. But the doctrine of discharge by breach has been further developed since that case, and it is now accepted that, where the innocent party chooses to terminate the contract, it comes to an end at that moment only and not *ab initio*, nor from the time of breach.[107] Since few cargo owners are aware of the deviation when it occurred,[108]

---

[92] For a different approach, that the contract is displaced from the beginning, see the authoritative but in this case extremely doubtful view of *Scrutton*, para 12.014, fn 31. (In an authoritative work of this sort, pregnant footnotes such as this can be of great forensic importance.)

[93] See 3.26.

[94] *Davis v Garrett* (1830) 6 Bing 716, 130 ER 1456. This in effect limits the operative perils to inherent vice.

[95] *US Shipping Board v Bunge y Born* (1925) 23 Ll L Rep 257, though the point was assumed, not argued or decided.

[96] *Hain SS Co Ltd v Tate & Lyle Ltd* (1936) 41 Com Cas 350, HL.

[97] See *Hain SS Co Ltd v Tate & Lyle Ltd* in the Court of Appeal, (1934) 39 Com Cas 259.

[98] Liability for which would accrue on loading and so before deviation: see 3.117.

[99] *Hain SS Co Ltd v Tate & Lyle Ltd* in the House of Lords, (1936) 41 Com Cas 350.

[100] See *Goff & Jones: Law of Unjust Enrichment* (8th edn, 2011) para 3.33.

[101] He was even sometimes called an insurer, though this was to use the word in a different sense from its modern meaning.

[102] *Lilley v Doubleday* (1881) 7 QBD 510.

[103] *Gibaud v Great Eastern Rly Co* [1921] 2 KB 426.

[104] The leading case on this point, *Joseph Thorley Ltd v Orchis SS Co Ltd* [1907] 1 KB 660, invokes, however, the rules on displacement of insurance by unseaworthiness, which, since the seaworthiness duty applies at the time of sailing, applies from that point. This has been a source of confusion. In the case itself the difference does not appear to have mattered, since the ship took a wrong route immediately on leaving port.

[105] See n 96.

[106] See 3.35.

[107] See *Photo Production Ltd v Securicor Transport Ltd* [1980] AC 827, HL.

[108] Though it was so in *Hain v Tate & Lyle*: indeed this is what gave rise to the principal issue, which concerned waiver.

this means that the discharge by breach explanation does not account for substantial features of the doctrine, in particular the displacement of the contract from the moment of deviation, which would in most cases have to be retrospective.

The English doctrine is a tight one, based on a small number of leading cases. It may be **3.50** possible to limit it to geographical deviation only, but there are quite strong arguments for extending it to wrongful stowage on deck, since this, like geographical deviation, may subject the goods to different risks from those contemplated. However, in a fairly recent decision (concerning the time bar under the Hague-Visby Rules) the doctrine was not applied in a case where there had been wrongful deck stowage, and Lloyd LJ expressed doubt as to the continued validity of the special doctrine altogether.[109] And it has now been specifically decided that wrongful deck stowage does not displace the package or unit limitation of the Hague Rules.[110] Although the decision is influenced by the wording of the Rules themselves, it may be assumed that the deviation doctrine, even if valid, should not be extended to wrongful carriage on deck. In the United States it would appear that the doctrine is somewhat wider as to what can be a deviation, but narrower in its consequences. Although it has been suggested that the doctrine is to be justified as a special one of maritime law,[111] its insurance justification seems now to be inapplicable[112] and it is not unlikely that, should the question come before the Supreme Court at the present day, the whole doctrine would be at the very least much reduced in effect, even as to geographical deviation. Until it obtains such a review, however, the position remains uncertain.

C. Carriage Under a Bill of Lading

(1) The Nature of the Contract and How it is Made

The nature of a bill of lading contract has already been explained. It is a contract for the car- **3.51** riage of goods by sea under which, normally, the carrier accepts goods for carriage in a ship carrying many such consignments, very often running to a schedule and calling at many ports, and issues a bill or bills of lading. It is again, and here obviously, a contract for services (*locatio conductio operarum*).

It is important to know in a general way how the bill comes to be issued. Plainly practices **3.52** must vary enormously over the world. But one may start with the proposition that a shipper or his agent may make a reservation for goods to be carried. If so, an issue may arise as to whether this is contractual, ie binds the carrier to carry and (though not necessarily) the shipper to ship.[113] It may or may not be. Depending on the facts, the goods may then be sent down, and at the latest a contract of carriage is (normally) formed when they are loaded on the ship. After they have been loaded (and often after the ship has sailed) the carrier issues a bill of lading[114] to the shipper, usually signed by or on behalf of the master, who is

---

[109] *The Antares (Nos 1 & 2)* [1987] 1 Lloyd's Rep 424. But for a different explanation see Kerr LJ in *State Trading Corp of India Ltd v M Golodetz Ltd* [1989] 2 Lloyd's Rep 277, 287, CA; cf however Lloyd LJ at 289.

[110] *The Kapitan Petko Voivoda* [2003] EWCA Civ 451, [2003] 2 Lloyd's Rep 1.

[111] *Photo Production Ltd v Securicor Transport Ltd* [1980] AC 827, 845, HL *per* Lord Wilberforce.

[112] Because it has long been standard practice for marine policies to extend insurance cover after deviation, under traditionally called 'held covered' clauses: for an example see *Vincentelli v Rowlett* (1911) 16 Com Cas 310.

[113] See *Scancarriers A/S v Aotearoa International Ltd (The Barranduna and the Tarago)* [1985] 2 Lloyd's Rep 419, PC.

[114] The bill may have been drafted by the shipper and issued by the carrier after he has confirmed it; and there is usually more than one copy: see 3.76.

an employee of the owner. The bill of lading being issued after the goods are loaded, it is in theory a record of a contract previously made; hence, if it is not in accord with prior contractual arrangements, they and not the bill in theory prevail.[115] But for most practical purposes the bill of lading constitutes the contract; and it certainly does when in the hands of a third party transferee.[116]

(2) The Common Law

3.53 The regime under which the goods are carried is basically the same as that for voyage charters, with appropriate differences arising from the fact that the whole carrying capacity of the vessel is not being used. The basic common law regime is the same: the principles of interpretation are the same and the deviation rules are likewise applicable, though obviously a ship carrying on bill of lading terms is likely to call at more ports than a ship performing a voyage for a charterer. Dangerous goods raise the same problems. The terms of the contract will not contain the sort of statements about the ship, its position and carrying capacity that are found in charterparties; there will be no provisions (other than incidental ones referring to other contracts) for laytime and demurrage; nor will there be a cancelling clause. The principles as to loading and unloading are the same, though in bill of lading contracts the carrier is likely to undertake these functions: this indeed is a meaning of the phrase 'liner terms'.

3.54 The most conspicuous result of this is that excepted perils favouring the carrier are subject in English law to no more than principles of interpretation, that they do not exclude the basic duties of a carrier unless clearly. On some views such terms could be unfair to cargo interests, as being imposed by carrier monopolies on weaker individual shippers. In the United States wide exclusions could be held void as contrary to public policy.[117] By the end of the nineteenth century the American merchant marine had become less strong than previously, and some American shippers and cargo owners regarded themselves as being at a disadvantage as against European carriers, on whom they depended. This was perhaps the beginning of a division within the shipping industry between those who are perceived as viewing matters from the point of view of cargo shippers and those who are perceived as taking the carrier's position. There is much to be said on both sides.

3.55 An important change was effected by the United States Harter Act of 1893, which established (largely in the interests of cargo) certain basic unexcludable duties of the carrier. The carrier was not permitted to exclude his liability in respect of the two basic duties mentioned above: to provide a seaworthy (including 'cargoworthy') ship, and to exercise due care of the cargo. But there was a *quid pro quo* for the carrier: he was not liable for negligence in navigation or management of the ship (the phrase can be made neater in some other languages, eg, *faute nautique*). The reasons for this protection, which may seem odd to someone unfamiliar with this area of law, were perhaps, first, that in early times when sea carriage was genuinely an 'adventure' it might be difficult to establish negligence in a carrier, or even to establish what happened at all; secondly, the fact that once the ship had sailed the master was out of the owner's control; and, thirdly, some element of assumption (not always justified in modern times at least) that carriers would in their own interests take care in navigation, in order to preserve their ship and indeed the lives of those involved.

---

[115] *The Ardennes* [1951] 1 KB 55.
[116] See 3.92ff.
[117] See eg *Re Missouri SS Co* (1888) 42 Ch D 321, referring to *The Brantford City* (1886) 29 F 373. The court held that the contract was governed by English law because the carrier could not have intended that his terms be void under American law.

(3) The Hague Rules

(a) Emergence of the Hague Rules

Further work on control of bill of lading terms went on in various ways in the late nine- **3.56** teenth century, and after the First World War it was resumed in earnest at meetings of the International Law Association at The Hague in 1921, to a considerable extent under American leadership. A new argument for the work then became prominent: the value of uniformity of the documentation which was used in connection with sea carriage—documentation which can be used to transfer the cargo and with it the contract, and which for the same reason passed and passes through banks financing sales. These came to finance many international sales on the security of the goods as represented by the documents, and had an interest in similarity of regime between one bill of lading and another. It was also true that quite a lot of international uniformity could be secured through the great colonial empires of the time. All this gave an impetus to the idea of an agreed international regime.

The meetings produced draft rules which were the result of compromise between cargo and **3.57** shipowning interests. They were drafted in English and translated into French (the main diplomatic language of the time) and adopted at a Diplomatic Conference in Brussels in 1924. They were then translated back into English. This explains some oddities of phraseology; and in some countries the French text prevails, in some the English (or sometimes the text in some other language). The Rules are normally called the Hague Rules, though they were in fact adopted in Brussels in 1924. Information about them is available the world over. They are not of course a feature specific to English law. Hence, only a very brief account is given here for completeness.

They apply to contracts covered by a bill of lading 'or any similar document of title'.[118] **3.58** They may however be incorporated by agreement into other contracts, such as charterparties. Whether they are effectively applied to other contracts and, if applied, their precise effect, may raise difficult problems of interpretation.[119]

(b) Non-excludable duties of the carrier

The key feature of the Hague Rules was a division of the risks which was in effect the same as **3.59** that under the Harter Act (which, though largely superseded, still applies in limited circumstances in the United States). The carrier owes duties:

(i) of due diligence to furnish a seaworthy (including cargoworthy) ship;[120] and
(ii) properly and carefully to discharge his duties in dealing with the cargo.[121]

The duties which a carrier has are non-excludable,[122] though he may agree that a duty that he might normally have (eg to stow) will be discharged by a charterer or cargo-owner,[123] in which case he will only incur liability if he intervenes significantly in its performance.[123a]

---

[118] Article I(b). See 3.95.
[119] See *Adamastos Shipping Co Ltd v Anglo-Saxon Petroleum Co Ltd* [1959] AC 133 and *Trafigura Beheer BV v Mediterranean Shipping Co SA (The MSC Amsterdam)* [2007] EWCA Civ 794, [2007] 2 Lloyd's Rep 622. The wording of the Rules is not always appropriate for charterparties.
[120] Article III.1.
[121] Article III.2. The common law seaworthiness duty was however a strict one, not merely one of due diligence.
[122] Article III.8.
[123] *Jindal Iron & Steel Co Ltd v Islamic Solidarity Shipping Co Jordan Inc (The Jordan II)* [2004] UKHL 49, [2005] 1 WLR 1363, [2005] 1 Lloyd's Rep 57.
[123a] *Yuzhny Zavod Metall Profil LLC v EEMS Beheerder BV (The Eems Solar)* [2013] 2 Lloyd's Rep 487.

(c) The excepted perils

3.60 In return, the carrier:

(iii) is not liable in respect of seventeen listed exclusions, traditionally again called 'excepted perils', of which the most significant are 'act, neglect or default [ie negligence] in the navigation or management of the ship' (which may be more concisely referred to as 'nautical fault'), and 'fire unless caused by the actual fault or privity of the carrier'.[124]

3.61 It will be seen that this compromise between the interests of cargo and ship places some risks on one party, some on the other. To make it work it is necessary first to know the facts, in order to determine into which sphere of risk the event which occurred came. This, at least in the negotiating stages of a dispute, may result in the burden of proof rules becoming of considerable importance. Even where the facts are known, it may be arguable to the highest tribunal into which sphere of risk those facts came: eg, they might arguably constitute negligence in care of cargo, for which the carrier is liable, or negligence in management of the ship, for which he is not.[125] Equally, a ship may be navigated negligently; but the cause of an event may be held to be an inadequate crew making the ship unseaworthy.[126] It is argued that this creates inefficiency, and that a single rule based on fault liability (as can be found, in slightly different forms, in Conventions on road, rail and air transport) would be preferable.[127]

(d) Limitation of liability

3.62 There was however a new feature introduced. Unless a higher value is stated (which is rare), the carrier's liability in respect of the goods was (and is) limited to a specific sum per 'package or unit'.[128] Reasons for this limitation were: first, (perhaps), that carriers had been able previously by wide exclusions effective in many countries to exclude their liability almost completely; and (a more obvious argument) that carriers do not easily know what purpose goods they carry are intended to serve, or even sometimes what they are: like burglar-alarm suppliers, they cannot undertake unlimited liability. But the sum set was at the time quite high: £100 sterling in the English version, and the same or roughly equivalent sums elsewhere.

(e) Insurance

3.63 As stated above, shipping is dominated by insurance. Therefore within this regime the *cargo owner* may, though he need not, carry general insurance in respect of all or particular risks relating to the goods. This will protect him also against matters in respect of which the carrier is not liable (negligence in navigation or management, etc) and loss above the package/unit limitation. This is insurance of goods. The *carrier* usually insures most of his *liabilities* through a mutual insurance association (P & I Club), or on similar terms in the market, by way of liability insurance. Cargo insurers may prosecute claims against carriers by way of subrogation, with the result that, as already stated, litigated disputes in connection with carriage by sea are often really between insurers.

---

[124] Article IV.1, 2.

[125] For an example of this sort of dispute see an early case on the Rules, *Gosse Millerd Ltd v Canadian Government Merchant Marine Ltd* [1929] AC 223, PC (unseaworthiness or negligence in management). For a more recent example see *The Aquacharm* [1982] 1 Lloyds Rep 7 (unseaworthiness or negligent stowage).

[126] The shipper is under a strict duty not to ship dangerous goods. This, where neither shipper knows or should know of the danger, is a rule of risk allocation.

[127] For the proposed Rotterdam Rules approach, see 3.72.

[128] Article IV.5.

(f) Time bar

Another new feature was that actions against (but not by) the carrier were made subject to **3.64**
a one-year time bar. This is a shorter than usual limitation period, and still a trap for claimants advised by non-specialist lawyers. It is justified on the basis that the carrier cannot be
expected to keep records indefinitely and must be able to close his books on particular voyages fairly quickly. Unfortunately in practice it may prove a very short time for a claimant to
prepare a claim.

(4) The Hague-Visby Rules

The Hague-Visby (or Visby) Rules are the same as the Hague Rules, with the addition of **3.65**
certain fairly minor changes, mostly perceived (rightly or wrongly) by cargo interests as being
for the convenience of carriers, originating from a conference of the CMI (Comité Maritime
International) in Stockholm in 1963. A proposed draft was signed at the ancient Baltic City
of Visby, and a modified version was finally adopted at Brussels in 1968 as a Protocol to the
1924 Convention.[129] The most conspicuous changes dealt with:

(i) 'inflation-proofing' the package or unit limitation (which had been adopted in most
countries as a fixed sum thought appropriate in the 1920s or at some other later time,
but in any case had been over the years subjected to the ravages of inflation)[130] by linking it to gold value by the Poincaré franc, a monetary unit defined by reference to gold
value;[131]

(ii) adding a weight limitation (for bulk cargo and heavy packages): a certain sum per kilo of
gross weight, whichever (of this and the package or unit limitation) is higher;[132]

(iii) the application of the package or unit limitation in respect of containers, a point to
which the Rules of 1924 were not of course directed: whether or not the container itself
is a 'package' depends on whether the bill of lading is filled in so as to 'enumerate' its
contents;[133]

(iv) the application of the Rules to tort actions,[134] especially against stevedores, who were
intended by carriers to be entitled to the same protections as themselves. The strong
English rule as to privity of contract prevented this being achieved unless a special clause
was used, the so-called 'Himalaya' clause,[135] which was held to create a separate contract
between claimant and stevedore incorporating the limit.[136] A new Article IV*bis* was
intended to deal with this problem, referred to in the negotiations as the 'Himalaya
problem', but in fact it does not appear on its wording to protect stevedores, because it

---

[129] For an authoritative and comprehensive account of the Hague-Visby Rules, containing much information as to their genesis and as to the Hague Rules also, see AEJ Diamond, 'The Hague-Visby Rules' [1978]
LMCLQ 225.

[130] In *The Rosa S* [1989] QB 419 it was said that the modern equivalent of £100 in 1924 was, converted
by the relative values of gold between one time and the other, at the later time £6,630.50.

[131] Article IV.5(a).

[132] Article IV.5(a).

[133] Article IV.5(c). The interpretation of the 1924 Rules is, at any rate in England, different and more
favourable to the cargo owner: see *The River Gurara* [1998] QB 610. There had meanwhile been a number of
cases on the application of the Rules to containers in the United States, and a smaller number in Canada and
Australia. For a recent Australian case on the limitation containing most elaborate discussion, see *El Greco
(Australia) Pty Ltd v Mediterranean Shipping Co SA* [2004] FCAFC 202, [2004] 2 Lloyd's Rep 537.

[134] Article IV*bis*.

[135] The reason for this is that the possibility of evading contract terms by suing in tort was first exposed
in a case on carriage of passengers involving the P & O liner 'Himalaya': *Adler v Dickson* [1955] 1 QB 158.
A clause to deal with the problem was then drafted for insertion into bills of lading, which was (and is) col-
loquially referred to as the 'Himalaya' clause.

[136] *New Zealand Shipping Co Ltd v AM Satterthwaite & Co Ltd (The Eurymedon)* [1975] AC 154, PC.

specifically excludes independent contractors.[137] Not all countries favour the extension of the carrier's protections to stevedoring companies;[138]

(v) making the Rules more effective internationally under conflict of laws rules (closing the so-called '*Vita Food* gap').[139]

Words were also inserted dealing with the probative effect of statements in bills of lading.[140] These changes have been in effect in the United Kingdom since 1977.[141]

(a) The SDR Protocol

3.66 Problems with the gold standard applied by the Poincaré franc have led to the later adoption of another Protocol, which states the package or unit and per kilo limitation in terms of special drawing rights on the International Monetary Fund. It is now, under this method, approximately at present US $1,000 per package or unit (which, bearing in mind that a container need not, and will not usually, be a package, is said (by some at least) to be adequate in most situations). This Protocol is effective in the United Kingdom.[142]

(b) International variations

3.67 Over the years since 1924 many countries have adhered to the Hague Rules, with the results that bills of lading governed by the laws of those countries are usually compulsorily governed by those Rules, at least in respect of outward shipments and before the courts of a contracting state of shipment.

3.68 Some countries have moved to the Hague-Visby Rules; and, of those that did, some have adopted the SDR Protocol and some not—which gives three types of regime based on the Hague Rules. Others did not adhere to the Convention at all, but enacted something very similar in their local law (eg until comparatively recently, Greece—raising problems in the conflict of laws).[143] Others again did none of these things; but of these most if not all would recognize a specific incorporation of the Rules into a bill of lading, which is a very common type of clause.

3.69 It will be seen that considerable diversity between regimes has developed. It is also undoubtedly true that the Rules have been interpreted differently from one country to another.[144] But

---

[137] Article IV*bis* 2.

[138] This seems particularly so in Australia.

[139] The problem was first exposed in an appeal to the Privy Council in London from Nova Scotia, *Vita Food Products Inc v Unus Shipping Co Ltd* [1939] AC 277, PC. A bill of lading might contain a clause choosing the law of a country which either did not apply the Rules at all or did not apply them to the voyage in question. This is a manifestation of the problem of the international operation of mandatory rules, towards which Art 9 of the Rome I Regulation on the Law Applicable to Contractual Obligations 2008 is now directed. The solution adopted in England was to give the Rules the 'force of law': since they provide that they apply on (in general) shipment out of contracting states, this binds an English court to apply them to shipment out of any other contracting state, whichever law is applicable to the bill of lading in general. The technique was held effective (in respect of a shipment out of Scotland governed by Dutch law and jurisdiction) in *The Hollandia* [1983] AC 565, HL.

[140] Article III.4, second sentence. These had a useful effect in England because of the old case of *Grant v Norway* (1851) 10 CB 665, 138 ER 263, as to which see 3.82.

[141] Carriage of Goods by Sea Act 1971, effective 1977.

[142] Merchant Shipping Act 1981, s 2(4) (the 1981 Act was repealed by the Merchant Shipping Act 1995 but the Protocol remains effective). The amounts are 666.67 units of account per package or unit or 2 units of account per kilogramme weight of the goods lost or damaged.

[143] See *The Komninos S* [1991] 1 Lloyd's Rep 370.

[144] A well-known example is the so-called 'before and after' problem, concerned with which operations of loading and unloading are covered by the Rules. The English view is that the contract can determine the limits of operation of the Rules in this respect: see *Pyrene Co Ltd v Scindia Navigation Ltd* [1954] 2 QB 402, the reasoning of which is affirmed in *The Jordan II* [2004] UKHL 49, [2005] 1 WLR 1363, HL, n 43. In other countries this might be regarded as an exclusion of the Rules: an example appears in *The Saudi Prince (No 2)* [1988] 1 Lloyd's Rep 1. Similar problems occur in connection with the demise clause: see n 233.

on the whole there has been still a reasonable measure of uniformity worldwide, if differences in detail.

(5) *The Hamburg Rules*

A further possible regime for carriage by sea is that of the Hamburg Rules. These originate **3.70** from work by first UNCTAD and then UNCITRAL in the 1970s and were adopted at a Diplomatic Conference at Hamburg in 1978. They constitute a completely different regime. They were intended further to redress an imbalance that was said to exist in favour of the carrier under the existing regimes and to be prejudicial to developing countries. The main criticism related to the split of risks achieved in 1924, the problems of which have already been mentioned: the Hamburg Rules were intended to replace this with a more or less unitary regime (similar to but not the same as those applicable in carriage by air and road), that the carrier is liable unless he proves that he was not at fault.

The Hamburg Rules have so far been ratified by 34 countries, several of which are land-locked **3.71** and few of which are conspicuously involved in maritime commerce; and of these it does not at present appear that many have actually brought the Rules into force.

(6) *The Rotterdam Rules*

A more radical and comprehensive regime than its predecessors has been formulated in the **3.72** United Nations Convention on Contracts for the International Carriage of Goods Wholly or Partly by Sea 2009, known as the Rotterdam Rules. They are longer and more detailed than the prior regimes and therefore, not surprisingly, the subject of debate. It is not known when, or even whether, they will come into force. Their main features will therefore be outlined briefly:[145]

(i)   They are not confined to sea carriage but take account of the fact that much modern carriage is arranged on a composite 'door to door' basis and may therefore involve carriage by other methods.

(ii)   They apply to contracts of carriage generally, and without restriction by the documents used, but not to charterparties.

(iii)   Their provisions as to documents apply to 'functionally equivalent' electronic transport records agreed to by the carrier and shipper.

(iv)   They apply to carriage on deck, which has traditionally been disfavoured but is a standard modern method.

(v)   Liability is imposed on carriers and persons who physically perform their responsibilities ('maritime performing parties').

(vi)   They impose on the carrier a continuing duty of seaworthiness.

(vii)   If the claimant can prove that loss occurred during the carrier's period of responsibility, the defendant will be liable unless he can rely on a list of rebuttable presumptions of absence of fault (which is like the traditional list of excepted perils, though omitting nautical fault).

(viii) They provide for the role of the goods' 'controlling party'.

(ix)   They provide for the transfer of rights to goods subject to negotiable transport documents.

(x)   They provide duties for delivery and receipt of goods (unlike previous Conventions).

(xi)   The 'Himalaya' protection[146] is more extensive: the Convention's defences are generally available to carriers and maritime performing parties.

---

[145] A more detailed summary appears in *Carver*, which also refers to the literature on the Rules.
[146] See 3.65.

(xii) Attempted reduction of Convention liability is void except in the case of 'volume contracts' (those providing for carriage of a specified quantity of goods in a series of shipments during an agreed period of time).

(xiii) Liability is limited, and deviation does not displace defences, except in the case of deliberate fault.

(xiv) They make provision for jurisdiction and arbitration.

(7) The Present Situation

3.73 The Hague Rules and their variants have provided a more or less international regime but, as with all rules, they have been subject to criticism and do not provide a comprehensive scheme for modern transport by sea and its associated stages. Proposed replacement rules have also had a mixed reception, in part because *ex hypothesi* they constitute a break from the established regime. But, inevitably, even if the international community moves towards a generally accepted new regime, such as the Rotterdam Rules, there will be an intermediate period of greater fragmentation than before or after the new regime becomes established. It remains to be seen, therefore, whether commercial parties and governments prefer to remain with what is familiar and imperfect or risk attempting to move to a different system, which will also be imperfect but is intended to cope better with the modern age.

(8) Global Limitation of Carrier's Liability

3.74 It should be remembered that in most countries shipowners operate *also* under a global limitation of all liability in respect of any single incident, usually related to the tonnage of the ship.[147] This is an ancient privilege, not applicable to other forms of transport.[148]

D. The Functions of the Bill of Lading and Other Documents

(1) The Bill of Lading

3.75 The bill of lading has long been a key document in the performance of international sale transactions, though it is now to some extent being superseded by documents which are simpler at least on their face; and present day paper documentation may in due course itself be superseded by electronic methods. For the present however there is no doubt that an understanding of traditional bills of lading is required for a proper comprehension of international transactions involving carriage by sea. As in the case of contracts of carriage, international sale contracts are frequently governed by English law. The United Kingdom has not adopted the Vienna Convention on International Sales, and the majority of sale disputes litigated in superior tribunals in the United Kingdom involve large scale transactions, often concerning bulk commodities, governed by standard terms which exclude the Convention specifically, and as 'international supply contracts' are not subject to the Unfair Contract Terms Act 1977.[149]

3.76 The bill of lading is a document which states that described goods have been shipped by a named party, in 'apparent good order and condition' unless otherwise stated, for carriage to a designated port on a named ship, and delivery there to a named consignee or in accordance

---

[147] The relevant United Kingdom legislation is the Merchant Shipping Act 1995. This implements the Convention on Limitation of Liability for Maritime Claims of 1976, which has been amended by a 1996 Protocol.

[148] See the Rt Hon Lord Mustill, 'Ships Are Different Or Are They?' [1993] LMCLQ 403.

[149] Section 26. The Convention is not well suited to such contracts.

with other instructions. The principal indications are given in boxes on the face of the document. On the reverse of the traditional bill[150] appear terms of the contract, usually in extremely small type, though these are in most situations subject to the Hague Rules or their variants.[151] As previously explained, it is not normally issued till the goods are on board. In principle it ought to be tendered at destination by the person claiming the goods.[152] By ancient custom it is normal in international carriage to have several bills of lading, each of which ranks as 'the bill of lading', originally in order that different bills might be sent to the destination by different routes, on the basis that at least one might arrive in time to enable the goods to be claimed. The carrier is entitled to deliver against one of these only.[153] This practice obviously gives rise to possibilities of fraud,[154] and buyers, and banks financing sales on letters of credit, will normally require all the bills (a 'full set'), as may buyers. It is not clear what beyond tradition maintains this practice of having several bills of lading at the present day.

(2) Functions of the Bill of Lading

A bill of lading is normally said to be evidence of the contract of carriage, a receipt for the goods and a document of title. To this should be added that it constitutes, by statute in United Kingdom law, a transferable contract. **3.77**

(a) Evidence of the Contract of Carriage

The way in which the contract is made means that the bill of lading, which acknowledges shipment, will in the normal course of things only be issued when the goods are on board. Receipt on board is likely to be the latest moment at which the contract of carriage is made: if the booking of space creates on the facts a contractual obligation, it can be made earlier. Hence it can be said that as regards the original contracting party the bill of lading is no more than evidence of a contract made earlier, and that in case of difference the contract made earlier prevails.[155] **3.78**

This point is however a small one: for most practical purposes the terms on the bill constitute the contract terms, whether by course of dealing, because the shipper is regarded as having accepted the carrier's terms whatever they are, or because the oral contract can be said to be reduced to writing by the bill. And, bills of lading being transferable, there is no doubt that in the hands of the third party the bill of lading constitutes the contract, for the third party has (except in unusual circumstances) no knowledge of the original dealings and has a contract based only on what appears on the face and reverse of the document. Thus a permission given by the original shipper to make what would otherwise be a deviation does not affect the transferee.[156] **3.79**

---

[150] There can be 'short form bills' with a blank reverse, where the terms are incorporated by reference.

[151] See 3.56ff.

[152] This was reaffirmed in *The Sormovskiy 3068* [1994] 2 Lloyd's Rep 266 and *The Houda* [1994] 2 Lloyd's Rep 541. It has been held that the carrier does not perform by delivery against a forged bill of lading: *Motis Exports Ltd v Dampskibsselskabet AF 1912* [2000] 1 Lloyd's Rep 211, CA. But, where bills of lading are extensively traded, they may arrive long after the goods. It is common therefore for charterparties to contain contractual provisions obliging the carrier to deliver without a bill of lading, in return for the promise of an indemnity against any liability incurred as a consequence of so doing (eg, because delivery is made to a person not entitled). Since the carrier may not be covered by his P & I insurance, he should obtain a guarantee from a bank.

[153] This is usually secured by traditional wording on the bill such as 'In witness whereof the master has signed three bills of lading, all of this tenor and date, *one of which being accomplished, the others shall stand void*'. Such bills are called 'originals'. There may also be file copies.

[154] As occurred in *Glyn Mills, Currie & Co v East & West India Dock Co* (1882) 7 App Cas 591.

[155] See 3.52.

[156] See *Leduc & Co v Ward* (1888) 20 QBD 475.

3.80 It may be noted that the bill is not conclusive as to who are the parties to the contract of carriage. It is likely that the party named in the 'shipper' box is such a party, but this need not be so: the party named may be an agent (and in common law there can be agency for completely undisclosed principals)[157] or simply a person who delivered the goods to the ship, perhaps as an fob seller to the person contracting for carriage. In the latter situation, the seller may by virtue of the bill of lading have an initial contract, probably of carriage, with the carrier while he holds the bill as a security against payment, even though the fob buyer has chartered the vessel. And as has been explained, the question of who is the carrier may not be clearly answered by the bill and require solution by techniques of contract interpretation.[158]

(b) Receipt for the Goods

3.81 A bill of lading normally contains printed words such as 'Shipped in apparent good order and condition unless otherwise stated' and is signed on behalf of the carrier. This constitutes an acknowledgment by the carrier that the goods have been received as described: if the goods do not arrive as described or at all, the acknowledgement is obviously of great importance in the maintenance of a claim against the carrier, who may otherwise wish to argue that the goods were never shipped, or short shipped, or were in bad condition on shipment. The words concerned are in the form of a statement not a promise, and hence carry the legal consequences of statements. They therefore constitute prima facie evidence against the carrier: but this can be disproved.

3.82 It might be thought further that under the general common law doctrine of estoppel the carrier would be estopped by such a statement from proving the contrary. In accordance with the normal rules, there is a statement of fact which may be relied on by the holder of the bill.[159] There may be difficulty in proving reliance if the claimant is the original shipper, for as such he should be aware, whether directly or through others, of what was shipped and the condition in which it was at the time. A transferee of the bill of lading, however, will not find it difficult to prove such reliance, simply by 'taking up' the bill, ie buying it or lending money on its security.[160] Difficulties have however been encountered where the complaint is of non-delivery or short delivery and the carrier seeks to prove that, contrary to what is on the bill, the goods were never shipped, or that fewer goods were shipped than what is stated. In the famous nineteenth-century case of *Grant v Norway*[161] it was held that the carrier could rely on the argument that the master had and was generally known to have no authority to sign for goods not on board, with the result that a statement as to quantity shipped did not bind the carrier. This is obsolete reasoning by modern standards: the master may have no actual authority to sign in such a case, but he surely has apparent authority to do so, or at least to state whether the goods are on board or not.[162] The case has never come before the House of Lords or Supreme Court, which alone probably could now overrule it.[163] In the absence

---

[157] See 1.72ff.

[158] The 'identity of carrier' problem: see 3.110ff.

[159] On different kinds of estoppel, all of which bind a person to some statement, state of affairs, assumption, or promise, see EPL 8.53ff, 8.202.

[160] See *Silver v Ocean SS Co* [1930] 1 KB 416.

[161] (1851) 10 CB 665, 138 ER 263.

[162] The leading case rejecting such reasoning, but in a tort claim, is *Lloyd v Grace, Smith & Co* [1912] AC 716, HL. As to apparent authority see 1.60ff.

[163] In *The Nea Tyhi* [1982] 1 Lloyd's Rep 606 and *The Saudi Crown* [1986] 1 Lloyds Rep 261, it was found that there was too much related authority for a judge of first instance to reject the reasoning, though the case could be distinguished.

of judicial decision the matter has now been dealt with by statute;[164] but it is important to understand what it was that gave rise to the statutory reform.[165]

Estoppels on the statements as to apparent good order and condition were never subjected to these difficulties, perhaps because the leading decisions came later, and the carrier can be estopped by such statements.[166] There are, however, some statements, usually inserted by the shipper for reasons of his own documentary requirements, to which the carrier is not in any case as a matter of interpretation usually regarded as attesting despite his signature, eg quality indications.[167]

3.83

In this connection two further problems require discussion. The first arises from the fact that carriers frequently print on their bills of lading 'blanket' clauses indicating that they do not in fact attest to the statements made (which are in general inserted by the shipper in a box on the document). An example is 'All particulars as furnished by the shipper but not checked by the carrier on loading'. Plainly such clauses on their face take away the probative effect of the wording inserted in the boxes. This is unobjectionable where the carrier has in fact no way of checking whether the cargo particulars (which are often required by the associated sale and letter of credit arrangements) are correct. This is true for crates, and containers not 'stuffed' by or for the carrier, and such disclaimers are regular in respect of containerized goods. In other situations they are more objectionable. The Hague Rules and their variants[168] provide that carriers must on demand issue bills of lading making certain statements as to what was shipped and its apparent order and condition,[169] which buyers will obviously want and which also assist in the event of cargo claims. It is difficult to see however what remedy is intended where the carrier inserts disclaimers of the sort mentioned. To hold them invalid as inconsistent with the carrier's liability under the Rules[170] would require robust construction, since in part such provisions are undoubtedly unexceptionable. It is their breadth that causes the problem. It has recently been held in England that the only remedy is for the shipper to refuse the bill of lading;[171] but, since the ship has often sailed when the bill is returned to him, this may be impracticable.[172] A gap in the protection of the Rules seems to exist here.

3.84

The second problem concerns specific reservations as to the apparent condition of the goods on loading. Carriers who wish to protect themselves against the evidentiary effect of such statements may insert reservations in the margin of the bill of lading: an example is 'Bags torn and stained'.[173] A master wishing to protect his owner may be zealous to do this,[174] but

3.85

---

[164] Carriage of Goods by Sea Act 1992, s 4; see also Hague-Visby Rules, Art III.2 (3.65), a less clearly effective provision, which in any case was not specifically directed at this problem.

[165] For an example of the complexities generated, see *Heskell v Continental Express Ltd* [1950] 1 All ER 1033, where the claim was by the original shipper, and was also complicated by the fact that no goods had ever been shipped, thus generating the argument that, the contract of carriage being in this case only made by actual taking on board, there was no contract of carriage on which to sue. The case was however decided before an action in negligence for economic loss caused by statements became available, which occurred in 1964: *Hedley Byrne & Co Ltd v Heller & Partners Ltd* [1964] AC 465, HL.

[166] *Compania Naviera Vasconzada v Churchill & Sim* [1906] 1 KB 237.

[167] *Cox, Patterson & Co v Bruce & Co* (1886) 18 QBD 147.

[168] See 3.56ff.

[169] Article III.3.

[170] Article III.8.

[171] *The Mata K* [1998] 2 Lloyd's Rep 614; see also *The Atlas* [1996] 1 Lloyd's Rep 642.

[172] And, presumably, for a buyer to whom such a bill of lading is tendered to refuse it; but this again may be impracticable and conceivably not even justifiable legally, if the bill can be regarded as of a type current in commerce.

[173] There are numerous technical variants, eg, 'FCL' ('Full Container Load').

[174] An unresolved question arises as to whether the carrier, through the master, owes a duty to the shipper not to add reservations unnecessarily: even if he does, it is far from clear how the duty should be formulated.

a bill so marked is called 'claused' and may not be acceptable under the sale contract and/or letter of credit in pursuance of which the goods are being shipped, which usually call for a 'clean' (ie not claused) bill. Hence, shippers may request the issue of a 'clean' bill and promise to indemnify the carrier against any liability he suffers in a cargo claim because it was not appropriately claused to protect him. Such contracts, though in general quite reasonable in their objectives, are often unenforceable as contrary to public policy, for they may constitute a promise to indemnify against the consequences of what is technically a wilful false statement, ie a fraud.[175]

3.86 It should finally be noted that the person signing the bill as agent may be liable in tort for wilful or negligent false statements in it. He may also be liable for breach of warranty of authority, for agents warrant (in the absence of other indications) that they have authority to sign,[176] and if the goods are not as described he has no such authority. If the signature is that of a ship's agent or the like on behalf of the master, any of these remedies may be worth pursuing.[177]

(c) Document of Title

3.87 In addition to the above features, the bill of lading has a third and important characteristic, that by the custom of merchants such documents are transferred from one person to another while the goods are in transit[178] for the purpose of transferring (or pledging) the goods to which they relate.[179] This effect is reinforced by, or even partly based on, the fact that the goods should not be delivered up except against surrender of one bill.[180]

3.88 The descriptive term used for such a document in English law is 'document of title'. The words are somewhat misleading as they could be taken to suggest that by, and only by, this means can title to the goods be transferred and acquired. The transfer of a document of title certainly can have this effect, but in English law property can be transferred in the contract of sale by mere intention[181] and it is therefore not necessary to use such a document at all. The true significance of the phrase for English law appears to be that by its transfer the *constructive possession* of the goods can be transferred,[182] and the principal consequence of this

---

See discussion of the master's duty in *The David Agmashenebeli* [2002] EWHC 104 (Admlty), [2003] 1 Lloyd's Rep, 92, esp at 105.

[175] *Brown Jenkinson & Co Ltd v Percy Dalton (London) Ltd* [1957] 2 QB 621; compare *Malayan Motor & General Underwriters (Pte) Ltd v Abdul Karim* [1982] 1 Malayan LJ 51, where this was not so and the contract of indemnity was enforceable. A good example of how problems arise is the Australian case *Hunter Grain Pty Ltd v Hyundai Merchant Marine Ltd (The Bunga Kenanga)* (1993) 117 ALR 507.

[176] See 1.112ff.

[177] As in *VIO Rasnoimport v Guthrie & Co Ltd* [1966] 1 Lloyds' Rep 1. But as with all such actions there may be complexities as regards damages: the lack of authority may cause no loss as in *Heskell v Continental Express Ltd*, n 165.

[178] At some point the document must cease to be a document of title. The obvious time for this is when the goods have been delivered at destination against surrender of the bill to a person entitled to them. More complex situations can give rise to difficulties: see *The Future Express* [1992] 2 Lloyd's Rep 79, 96–100 (aff'd without reference to this point [1993] 2 Lloyds Rep 542). The Carriage of Goods by Sea Act 1992 (3.94) assumes that a bill of lading may cease to have effect as such, but relies on the (uncertain) general law to determine when this is: see s 2(2), discussed in *The Ythan* [2005] EWHC 2399 (Comm), [2006] 1 Lloyd's Rep 457.

[179] *Lickbarrow v Mason* (1787) 2 TR 63, 100 ER 35.

[180] Otherwise the carrier will be liable for breach of contract and conversion. In such a case, the carrier may consent to delivery on provision of a 'letter of indemnity', the effect of which is a matter of construction: *Great Eastern Shipping Co Ltd v Far East Chartering Ltd (The Jag Ravi)* [2012] EWCA Civ 180, [2012] 2 Lloyd's Rep 637.

[181] Sale of Goods Act 1979, s 17: subject to special difficulties as to bulk goods, as to which see 2.22ff.

[182] See the *locus classicus* for discussion of this topic, *Benjamin's Sale of Goods* (8th edn, 2010) paras 18-006ff.

is that the cargo can be pledged to a bank while it is afloat: the transferee is also entitled to possessory remedies.

It is possible for a legal system to give the bill of lading the status of something like a nego- **3.89** tiable instrument, in the sense that transfer to a third party acting in good faith may override prior proprietary interests in the goods represented. A bill of lading does not have this feature in English law, and hence though it is often said to be 'negotiable' (or, at least, pure copies are described as 'non-negotiable'), the word 'transferable' might be better. The document is in general treated as if it was the goods. But in principle a person with an interest in goods can only transfer such interest as he has; and whether, on receiving a bill of lading on transfer from its holder, the new holder can acquire a better title than the transferor's depends on the general law of personal property, in particular sale.[183]

Moreover, whatever the extent of his capacity to confer an interest on the transferee, the **3.90** interest transferred depends essentially on the transferor's intention, and he may only intend to confer a limited interest. Thus, a bill may be transferred in order to transfer ownership and possession: this is usually true of sellers transferring against payment. But it may be trans- ferred, usually to a bank, to create a pledge only.[184] Or it may be transferred merely to permit the holder to collect the goods, perhaps as agent of the transferor.[185]

Whether or not a bill is transferable (which it needs to be to constitute a bill of lading in **3.91** the true sense) depends on the form of the bill. It may, initially or by indorsement, provide for delivery to bearer, in which case, like a cheque, it only requires delivery.[186] For a bill to be transferable, and hence a bill of lading in the true sense, the 'consignee' box on the face should contain the words 'or order' or 'or assigns' to indicate that transfer is contemplated. The transfer of the bill is effected: where a person is named as consignee, by mere handing over to that person; where the bill is transferred by a shipper who took it to 'order' (ie his own order), by indorsement and delivery; where it is transferred by a consignee or indorsee, by indorsement and delivery. These last two situations may or may not involve indorsement to a named person ('special indorsement'). If on its face the document provides for delivery only to a particular person, and is therefore non-transferable, it is not a true bill of lading but is instead termed a 'straight' bill of lading or a waybill.

(d) Transfer of the contract

The final receiver of the goods may wish to exercise a cargo claim against the carrier. However, **3.92** on principle since he is not a party to the contract of carriage he cannot do so. Early cases were sometimes able to solve this problem by holding that the seller shipped as agent for the distant buyer, but this is obviously an unreliable device. The law in England was there- fore altered by statute a considerable time ago, by the Bills of Lading Act 1855, which in some form is still operative in many common law territories.[187] This used the mechanism

---

[183] The relevant provisions are ss 21, 24 and 25 of the Sale of Goods Act 1979 and s 2 of the Factors Act 1889. See in general M Bools, *The Bill of Lading* (1997) chs 2, 3. There are differences on this point in the law of the United States.

[184] Where a sale is financed by a bank, transfer of the bill to the bank would normally pass possession (pledge interest) to the bank and property to the buyer.

[185] As in the famous case of *Leigh & Sillavan Ltd v Aliakmon Shipping Co Ltd (The Aliakmon)* [1986] AC 785, HL.

[186] However it can be converted by a subsequent special endorsement. A bill that has been specially indorsed must be reindorsed if a transferee is to sue on it: it is not enough merely to hand it over, as by giving it back: *Keppel Tatlee Bank Ltd v Bandung Shipping Pte Ltd* [2003] 1 Singapore LR 295, [2003] 1 Lloyd's Rep 619, CA Sin.

[187] The United States legislation however was, and is, quite different. All common law countries have however found some form of statute to be necessary.

of transferring not only the benefit but also the burden of the contract (eg, as to payment of freight or dangerous goods) on transfer of the property in the goods by means of the bill of lading. This worked well for more than 100 years, but in the 1970s difficulties began to develop because of the greater size of ships, especially bulk carriers. The rule of English law then operative, that property cannot pass in unascertained goods,[188] led to the result that property in goods carried in such ships would often only pass when the cargo was measured out to different buyers at destination. There were also other complications.

3.93 There were (and still are) two other possibilities for cargo claimants. The first is to sue in tort for loss or destruction of the goods: but this has been held to require that the claimant prove that he had a proprietary or a possessory interest in the goods at the time they were lost or damaged, which might not be easy to establish.[189] The second was to sue on a contract which might be implied where a receiver took delivery of goods in return for payment of outstanding charges (or other consideration for the contract): it might be held that the carrier could be interpreted as agreeing to deliver on bill of lading terms. Such a contract is referred to as a '*Brandt v Liverpool* contract'.[190] The value of this device was much reduced when the Court of Appeal interpreted it strictly in 1989,[191] but it remains a weapon in the armoury which it may occasionally be necessary to invoke in irregular situations even after the legislation of 1992 next referred to.

3.94 The law in England was reformed by statute in the Carriage of Goods by Sea Act 1992,[192] which contains separate provisions as regards benefit and burden of the contract. Similar legislation has been enacted in certain other common law territories. Ability to sue depends on being a named consignee or the 'lawful holder' of the bill of lading,[192a] regardless of the incidence of property:[193] there is a provision to permit the lawful holder to recover loss on behalf of the party really at risk, if that is someone different.[194] It was not practicable to make lawful holders liable on the contract also, for banks holding bills of lading as security, thus ranking as lawful holders, would then have become liable, something that was not the case before[195] and not an intended incident of a letter of credit transaction. Instead, the lawful holder is liable if he also takes or seeks delivery or claims on the contract.[196] A bank realizing its security and doing this would expect to incur liability: indeed this is the basis of the *Brandt v Liverpool* contract. The Act is a complex piece of draftsmanship and some of the first cases on it are controversial.[197] Its conflict of laws status (whether procedural or substantive) is not clear.[198]

---

[188] Sale of Goods Act 1979, s 16; now much modified by the Sale of Goods (Amendment) Act 1995, inserting ss 20A and 20B into the 1979 Act.

[189] *Leigh & Sillavan Ltd v Aliakmon Shipping Co Ltd (The Aliakmon)* [1986] AC 785, HL. See also *The Starsin* [2003] UKHL 12, [2004] 1 AC 715, at [87]ff.

[190] An allusion to the leading (but by no means first) decision on it, *Brandt v Liverpool, Brazil and River Plate Steam Navigation Co* [1924] 1 KB 575.

[191] *The Aramis* [1989] 1 Lloyd's Rep 213.

[192] See *Carver*, ch 5.

[192a] By endorsement with the intention of the indorsor and indorsee for an unconditional transfer of possession to the indorsee: *Standard Chartered Bank v Dorchester LNG (2) Ltd (The Erin Schulte)* [2014] EWCA Civ 1382, [2015] 1 Lloyd's Rep 97.

[193] Carriage of Goods by Sea Act 1992, s 2(1)(a). But a shipper who has indorsed the bill to a lawful holder may nevertheless be able in some situations to claim against the carrier in bailment: see *East West Corp v DKBS AF* [2003] EWCA Civ 83, [2005] QB 1509.

[194] Section 2(4).

[195] See *Sewell v Burdick* (1884) 10 App Cas 74.

[196] Section 3(1). But if he then endorses the bill away he may cease to be liable: see *The Berge Sisar* [2001] UKHL 17, [2002] 2 AC 205, HL.

[197] There is a valuable discussion of its history and operation in *The Berge Sisar*, n 196.

[198] See KS Toh, 'Conflict of Laws Implications of the Carriage of 'Goods by Sea Act 1992' [1994] LMCLQ 280. In general the Contract (Rights of Third Parties) Act 1999 is excluded when the 1992 Act applies: s 6(5). But see Sir G Treitel, *Lex Mercatoria* (ed FD Rose) (2000) ch 17.

(3) 'Straight' Bills of Lading

A bill of lading naming a consignee but not containing a reference to 'order' (or 'assigns'), **3.95** or from which these words have been deleted, may be called a 'straight' bill of lading. Such a document is not transferable (though it often nevertheless contains wording appropriate to an ordinary bill of lading)[199] and its status has been doubtful. It has been held that it is a 'bill of lading or any similar document of title' for the purpose of making the Hague-Visby (or Hague) Rules applicable,[200] and the House of Lords, in deciding this, approved a decision of the Court of Appeal of Singapore[201] to the effect that a carrier must only deliver the goods against surrender of such a document (which would not be true of a non-negotiable sea waybill[202]). It can be transferred once, by physical handing over to the named consignee, who can then sue on it, though the reason in English law for the right to sue is that the document, whatever it is called, must rank as a non-negotiable sea waybill for the purposes of the Act of 1992 by reason of the drafting of that Act. It is not clear whether such a document should really be called a document of title in the general common law sense. Only if it is would the consignee with possession of the document rank as having constructive possession of the goods, wherever they are, through the document alone. The law in the United States is not the same as that stated above.

(4) Other Documents Used in Connection with Sea Carriage

Other documents are sometimes used, which may replace the bill of lading or operate together **3.96** with it. The legal analysis of situations arising out of the use of such documents can be very complex, and in general, where disputes may occur, the bill of lading is much preferable.

(a) Non-negotiable sea waybills[203]

These, a fairly recent invention, are used for short or quick sea transit where the parties do not **3.97** need to trade in the goods or use them as security while they are in transit, and the safeguard that the goods should only be surrendered against a bill of lading is not desired.[204] They simply constitute a memorandum of the contract of carriage or, depending on the circumstances, the contract itself, and a receipt for the goods.[205] The goods are claimed by the consignee identifying himself at destination.

Thus retention of such a document is not likely to give the unpaid seller security: the goods **3.98** can be delivered without it. Equally, a buyer who pays on the issue of such a document takes a risk, for the seller may, depending on the terms of the contract of carriage and/or the agreement of the carrier, be able to redirect the goods to another receiver.[206] Waybills (unlike straight bills of lading) are not bills of lading and do not attract the Hague Rules or variants, though these can be specifically incorporated. The receiver formerly had no rights on the contract of carriage, though may have rights under a *Brandt v Liverpool* contract or in tort;[207] but the Carriage of Goods by Sea Act 1992, which altered the law as to actions on bills of lading,

---

[199] Such as a requirement for surrender of a negotiable bill of lading. This is because such documents often contain words such as 'Not negotiable unless consigned to order', which enables them to be used either way.
[200] *The Rafaela S* [2005] UKHL 11, [2005] 2 AC 423.
[201] *APL Co Pte Ltd v Voss Pte Ltd* [2002] 2 Lloyd's Rep 707, [2002] 4 SLR 481, CA Sin.
[202] See 3.97.
[203] See *Carver*, paras 8–001ff.
[204] Bills of lading frequently arrive long after the goods, especially in certain trades.
[205] See the definition in s 1(3) of the Carriage of Goods by Sea Act 1992.
[206] An attempt is made to deal with this in the CMI Uniform Rules for Sea Waybills.
[207] See 3.93.

now gives rights and (in accordance with its terms) liabilities under the contract of carriage to the person to whom delivery is to be made in accordance with the contract.[208]

(b) Ship's delivery orders[209]

3.99   These are used for splitting bulk cargoes. When large bulk carriers set off, it may not be clear in what proportions the cargo is to be sold, and hence for what quantities bills of lading (even should so many be obtainable) are required. At a later stage therefore a bill of lading holder may obtain delivery orders for specified quantities against surrender of the bill or bills of lading. A ship's delivery order ('ship's D/O') contains an acknowledgement by the carrier, usually against surrender of the bill of lading, that he holds a specific quantity of goods in or from a certain ship, to the order of a certain person.[210] These documents tend to be transferred and indorsed just like bills of lading.

3.100   The main difference with bills of lading is that, like waybills, they are not documents of title, and hence transfer of them does not transfer constructive possession of the goods. For a transferee from the original person to whom the document is issued to gain constructive possession, the order must be returned to the carrier, who must attorn to the new holder. Since these documents are used in connections with parts of a bulk, they also attract the complexities of recent legislation on ownership of part of a bulk.[211] They can also raise many other complexities. As with waybills, the holder formerly had no rights on the contract of carriage, save possibly under a *Brandt v Liverpool* contract[212] or in tort. But now the person to whom delivery of the goods is to be made can sue on the underlying contract of carriage by virtue of the 1992 Act.[213]

3.101   Ship's delivery orders must be carefully distinguished from similar documents issued not by ships but by land-based warehouse operators, sometimes called 'merchant's delivery orders'. These raise similar problems, but they operate after the contract of carriage has ended, are not connected with the contract of carriage by sea and are not affected by the Act of 1992.

(c) Freight forwarder's documents

3.102   Freight forwarders sometimes act as carriers, and as such may issue bills of lading in the normal way, even if they perform the contract of carriage entirely by means of subcontractors. More often however they act as agents and make contracts of carriage on behalf of shippers, who may be disclosed or undisclosed principals to the contracts in question. In some cases of this sort they may issue a document indicating receipt of the goods for carriage, which may on a superficial glance look in its format quite like a bill of lading. They themselves may then obtain a bill of lading. Complex questions may arise as to the effect of the first document and the interrelation between the two, and the documentation used is likely to require careful analysis.[214]

(d) Mate's receipts

3.103   Mate's receipts are preliminary documents used in some circumstances as a preliminary to the issue of a bill of lading. The shipper obtains one on loading, and later exchanges it for a

---

[208] Section 2(1)(b).
[209] See *Carver*, paras 8–028ff.
[210] See the definition in s 1(4) of the Carriage of Goods by Sea Act 1992.
[211] Sale of Goods Act 1979, ss 20A and 20B, inserted by Sale of Goods (Amendment) Act 1995.
[212] As in *Cremer v General Carriers SA* [1974] 1 WLR 341.
[213] Section 2(1)(c).
[214] For examples see *Carrington Slipways Pty Ltd v Patrick Operations Pty Ltd (The Cape Comorin)* (1991) 24 NSWLR 745; *Norfolk Southern Rly Co v James Kirby Pty Ltd* (2004) 125 S Ct 385, US Sup Ct.

signed bill of lading. In theory a mate's receipt is signed by or for the mate (first officer) but such documents are sometimes signed by masters. As would be expected, they are inferior to bills of lading. They are evidence that *some* contract has been made, and there seems in principle no reason why some forms of estoppel should not arise on them; but they are not documents of title (unless so proved) and their effectiveness when retained by way of security is very limited.[215] In one case however the usage of merchants that mate's receipts were used instead of bills of lading was accepted in respect of a local trade,[216] but finally it was rejected on the ground that the document itself was marked 'non-negotiable'.[217]

(e) Combined transport documents

Combined, or multimodal, transport documents are issued by operators of such transport undertaking to carry goods, usually containerized, from one destination to another: neither place need be a port, and different means of transportation may be used. Such documents are to be distinguished from ordinary bills of lading containing provisions under which the carrier agrees to forward the goods on after the principal voyage, usually as agent only (sometimes called 'through bills of lading'). Some combined transport documents purport only to be waybills, and have legal consequences as such. Others are headed as, and are intended to be, bills of lading. They are plainly different from the bills of lading which the main authorities concern, for they envisage carriage in various modes of transport and do not indicate that the goods are on a ship, but merely that they have been received: a purported bill of lading to that effect would only doubtfully be a bill of lading at all.[218] The regime or regimes under which such goods are carried may be uncertain, since, despite the overall undertaking by the operator, the goods may, as they pass through different countries, be subject to various mandatory regimes for the type of transport involved (eg the Hague Rules); and, if the goods do not arrive, or arrive short or damaged, it may also be difficult to know on which leg of the carriage the damage occurred. Although some bills of lading and waybills contain extensive provision to meet such problems, the present status of such documents is therefore in doubt—as to whether they rank as bills of lading and all that that entails, particularly as to whether they constitute documents of title. They are accepted by banks under letters of credit, and it seems likely that they would be accepted as documents of title if the question arises before new electronic methods take over; but at present the situation is uncertain and there is much to be worked out. **3.104**

E. Bill of Lading for Goods in a Chartered Ship

It was stated early in this chapter that, even though a shipper had a full cargo and hence was chartering a vessel, a bill or bills of lading would normally be issued to provide evidence of shipment and facilitate transfer of the cargo during transit. This point now needs further elaboration. **3.105**

Bills of lading for goods in a chartered ship are in fact issued in two different types of situation. They may first be issued to a charterer who requires a receipt, wishes thereby to facilitate delivery, and may wish to be able to transfer the goods after shipment. That is the situation **3.106**

---

[215] See *Nippon Yusen Kaisha v Ramjiban Serowgee* [1938] AC 429, PC.

[216] That between Sarawak and Singapore.

[217] *Chan Cheng Kum v Wah Tat Bank Ltd* [1971] 1 Lloyd's Rep 439, PC. But the bank was held to have security by way of possession without the aid of the document.

[218] See *Diamond Alkali Export Corp v Fl Bourgeois* [1921] 3 KB 443. This fact alone would not prevent it being a bill of lading for the purposes of the Carriage of Goods by Sea Act 1992, which transfers the contract: s 1(2)(b).

referred to at the beginning of this chapter. But there is a second situation, that arising where the ship is under charter, but is used to carry shipments under bills of lading exactly as an owner carrying on liner terms might use it. An obvious background to this situation is that where the charterer is in fact a line operator who has chartered extra tonnage,[219] but there are many other possibilities. For example, a ship operator may enter into contracts of carriage with shippers without owning any ships, but simply chartering them.[220]

(1) Bill of Lading Given to Charterer

3.107   Here there are potentially two contracts of carriage, and they are likely to have different terms: apart from anything else, the Hague Rules or a variant are likely to apply to the bill of lading but not to the charterparty.[221] In this case, as a matter of interpretation, the contract with the charterer is in English law the charterparty, and the bill of lading is merely a receipt: in case of a clash of terms the charterparty prevails.[222] This is so even if, as is common in fob sales, the bill of lading is first issued to a shipper other than the charterer (who may, eg, need it as security against his purchaser) and then indorsed to the charterer.[223] In such a case the bill has already had a contractual operation as such, but loses it.

3.108   When however such a bill of lading is then indorsed to a third party, a contract springs up between that party and the carrier on the bill of lading terms,[224] normally including the Hague Rules. The charterer remains liable and entitled on the charterparty,[225] though particular forms of contract clause can be used to seek to limit this effect.[226] Potentially, however, the carrier has contracts with two parties on different terms, though the problem may be met in part, and some consistency achieved, by incorporation of charterparty terms into the bill of lading.[227]

(2) Bills of Lading Given to Other Shippers

3.109   This occurs where a ship which is chartered is made available for the carriage of goods on bill of lading terms. There are here two main problems: the 'identity of carrier' problem and the 'actual carrier' problem.

(a) The 'identity of carrier' problem

3.110   The difficulty here is to ascertain who is the carrier, ie the party who contracts to carry the goods: the shipowner or the charterer (or even someone else). It is unfortunately true that the bill of lading often does not make this clear; and, unless a requirement that the name of the carrier be stated in a certain way can be identified by international convention, which is some-times suggested, the problem will remain. A particular difficulty for a cargo claimant is that the

---

[219] As in the famous case of *Elder Dempster & Co Ltd v Paterson, Zochonis & Co Ltd* [1924] AC 522, HL.

[220] In some contexts the acronym 'NVOCC' ('Non-vessel owning contracting carrier') or something similar may be used.

[221] Though see 3.58.

[222] *Rodocanachi Sons & Co v Milburn Brothers* (1886) 17 QBD 316.

[223] *President of India v Metcalfe Shipping Co Ltd (The Dunelmia)* [1970] 1 QB 289.

[224] *Hain SS Co v Tate & Lyle Ltd* (1936) 41 Com Cas 350, 357, 364, HL.

[225] See *The Albazero* [1977] AC 774.

[226] Notably the 'cesser' clause, which removes the charterer's liability for matters covered by the carrier's lien. It gives rise to complex problems of interpretation.

[227] From a receiver's point of view the most dangerous clauses which might be incorporated are probably dispute resolution clauses and liens; Traditionally, attempted incorporation has been limited to clauses in charterparties that are directly germane to bill of lading contracts; but a modern approach to construction may allow a "Law and Arbitration" clause to function as a jurisdiction provision: *Caresse Navigation Ltd v Zurich Assurances MAROC (The Channel Ranger)* [2014] EWCA Civ 1366, "[2015] QB 366, [2015] 1 Lloyd's Rep 256.

correct defendant must be established within the Hague Rules limitation period.[228] There are two main indications on the face of the bill: the logo or heading at the top, and the attesting signature at the bottom. The former may well indicate the name of the commercial operator of the vessel—in a simple situation, that of the charterer. The latter is often preceded by printed wording such as 'for the master'. Since the master is normally employed by the shipowner,[229] that would indicate a contract with the shipowner. On the whole English courts tend to give preference to the signature and in the absence of other indications hold the shipowner to be the carrier.[230] This may have the advantage of facilitating arrest of the ship on a cargo claim; but courts from one country to another may differ on the resolution of this question.[231]

If the issue arises in connection with the original shipper, there is the further complication **3.111** that the form of the bill of lading is not conclusive, since in theory at least it only evidences a contract made earlier,[232] and the initial dealings between the relevant parties may have to be taken into account.

Finally, clauses may appear on the reverse of a bill of lading which purport to create the result **3.112** that the contract is with the owner, notwithstanding anything that appears (on the face or elsewhere) to the contrary. They appear in various forms and are often called 'demise' or 'identity of carrier' clauses.[233] If effective, they are, again, in some respects advantageous to a cargo claimant. They raise considerable problems if the court seeks, as it often does in other parts of law, to interpret the document as a whole. It has recently been held however that, where the front is absolutely clear as to who is the carrier, this may prevail over such clauses on the reverse.[234]

(b) The 'actual carrier' problem

Where the contract of carriage is established as made with a *charterer* (which, as has been **3.113** said above, is in English law the minority rather than the majority interpretation) a further difficulty arises. If there is a cargo claim, it may be sought to sue the shipowner who actually carried the goods, who can be called the 'actual carrier' in distinction to the charterer, who may be called the 'contracting carrier'.

The reasons for seeking to do this may vary. It is the shipowner whose operations actually **3.114** caused the loss or damage. The ship may be in port and amenable to arrest. It may not be clear who is legally the carrier until a late stage, when proceedings against the shipowner are under way. Finally, it may be to a claimant's advantage to use the argument that the shipowner, not being a party to the contract of carriage, cannot rely on the exclusions and limitations in it, and in particular the package or unit limitation and time bar of the Hague Rules or a variant.[235]

---

[228] See 3.64.

[229] Or, as always, the demise charterer.

[230] The leading case is *The Rewia* [1991] 2 Lloyd's Rep 325.

[231] This was so in *The Rewia* [1991] 2 Lloyd's Rep 325 itself, where German law was apparently different.

[232] See 3.78.

[233] For the origin of such clauses, which is not what might have been expected, see Lord Roskill (1990) 106 LQR 403. The clause can be said to have a beneficial effect in facilitating arrest of the ship on a cargo claim; but a problem is that such a clause often appears only in very small print on the reverse of the document, and hence can be overlooked until it is (by virtue of the time bar) too late. It is sometimes argued that these clauses are contrary to the Hague Rules in removing the liability of the party who is in truth the carrier. The English view is, rather, that they identify the carrier: see *The Berkshire* [1974] 1 Lloyd's Rep 185.

[234] *The Starsin* [2003] UKHL 12, [2004] 1 AC 715. Some reliance is placed on the Uniform Customs and Practice on Documentary Credits, under which banks do not accept responsibility to look on the reverse of bills of lading: see [126].

[235] See 3.62 and 3.64.

3.115 The action against the shipowner would be in tort, and in general could only be brought by a party who owned, or had a possessory interest in,[236] the goods at the time they were lost or damaged.[237] A claim on any other basis would be a claim for pure economic loss and in general could not be easily brought in English law.[238] This restriction would in practice make claims much more difficult to establish where (as is common) the ownership of the goods had changed several times while they were in transit. Beyond this however the doctrine of privity of contract in English law has made it difficult to avoid the conclusion that the shipowner is unprotected by the Rules. He may be protected if the problem has been foreseen and a 'Himalaya' clause[239] is present in the contract, though the wording of these clauses is not always appropriate to this situation because they were originally designed to protect stevedores and employees rather than actual carriers. A standard form starts by giving the subcontractor (or other relevant party) complete immunity, but in a second paragraph simply purports to confer the benefits of the contract defences (which usually means the Hague or Hague-Visby Rules). The first is appropriate to stevedores, but not to actual carriers, who might, however, justifiably rely on the second part. An important recent decision of the House of Lords[240] holds the first part of the clause void as contrary to Article III.8 of the Hague and Hague-Visby Rules, which in effect prohibit the carrier from contracting out of his responsibilities thereunder,[241] though the reasoning is not completely unanimous. This leaves the second part of the clause to apply to actual carriers. Another clause that may be used is a 'circular indemnity' clause.[242] There is a mysterious provision inserted in the Hague-Visby Rules, Article IV*bis*.1, which might cover this situation, but it is far from clear that it does, and the Court of Appeal has held[243] that it does not.[244] Where these devices are not effective, English courts have experimented with reasoning arising out of the common law concept of bailment (which could assist here, though not in the stevedore situation since stevedores as such are not bailees).[245] The reasoning is that the actual carrier, as bailee or sub-bailee, takes the goods on the terms which he agreed with the contracting carrier, to which the latter has been authorized to subject them.[246] This has not yet been fully worked out, though as in other areas discussion in maritime law may yield reasoning applicable elsewhere, eg in warehousing. The Supreme Court of Canada has in the context of warehousing suggested even wider, largely tort-based reasoning, the application of which has been commended by Lord Goff of Chieveley.[247] In any case it seems now that statutory reform of the law of privity of contract in England may solve the problem, at least where the bill of lading is clear as to such beneficiaries.[248]

---

[236] Such as a bank holding the documents as pledgee.

[237] *Leigh & Sillavan Ltd v Aliakmon Shipping Co Ltd (The Aliakmon)* [1986] AC 785, HL.

[238] *Candlewood Navigation Corp Ltd v Mitsui OSK Lines Ltd (The Mineral Transporter)* [1986] AC 1, HL.

[239] See 3.65.

[240] *The Starsin* [2003] UKHL 12, [2004] 1 AC 715.

[241] See 3.59.

[242] ie a clause under which the shipper promises not to sue the carrier's employees and subcontractors, and to indemnify the carrier for any loss it may cause the carrier in doing so. These clauses are much in use by freight forwarders.

[243] *The Captain Gregos* [1990] 1 Lloyd's Rep 310, though not after very full argument.

[244] The Hamburg Rules (3.70ff) contain provisions intended to deal with the problem, but they are not at all clear: see Arts 10, 11. See now the Rotterdam Rules, 3.72.

[245] *The Pioneer Container* [1994] 2 AC 324, PC; *The Mahkutai* [1996] AC 650, PC. The facts in the first case are particularly instructive as to the complexities which can arise in practice.

[246] This is a possible solution to *The Starsin*, n 240: see at [132]ff. The case was resolved in the basis of the Himalaya clause.

[247] See *London Drugs v Kuehne & Nagel International Ltd* [1992] 3 SCR 299, (1992) 97 DLR (4th) 261, referred to in *The Mahkutai*, n 245, at 665. The *London Drugs* case actually offers three different lines of reasoning, and in respect of a clause that did not even refer to third parties.

[248] See Contracts (Rights of Third Parties) Act 1999, ss 1(5), 6(2)(a).

F. Freight

The rules regarding accrual of freight liability can appear very technical, and, as elsewhere in **3.116** this part of the law, turn very specifically on the contract wording used. All that can be done here is to draw attention to certain salient points. Freight (and hire) is essentially a sum of money payable in return for a service and in accordance with the terms of the contract. Four issues generally arise: (i) when it is payable; (ii) how it is calculated; (iii) whether the circumstances in which it is payable have occurred; and (iv) the consequences if those circumstances have not occurred.

As to (i), the normal understanding, as with many contracts for services, is that it is payable **3.117** on completion of the carriage contract, ie on delivery of the goods at destination (as 'freight collect').[249] This is like paying for a taxi ride. Alternatively (as with buying a ticket for public transport), it may be payable in advance. Advance freight is nowadays commonplace but began as an unusual arrangement, perhaps unique to common law, the origin of which lies in methods of financing and insuring the long voyages between Europe and the Far East in the nineteenth century.[250] Where freight is payable collect, the risk (of not earning it) is prima facie on the carrier; where it is paid in advance, the risk (of having paid it but not having the goods delivered to destination) is prima facie on the payor.

(ii) Freight is generally calculated according to the dimensions, weight or number of pieces of **3.118** the cargo. Thus, if not all of the contract cargo is delivered, it is payable on the amount delivered but not on the amount not delivered. Where cargo is delivered in a damaged condition, it may be queried whether the damaged cargo is in such a state that the contract cargo has not in fact been delivered: in such a case cargo that is delivered in such a condition that it is 'merchantable' as cargo of the contract description is treated as delivered under the contract; otherwise it is not.[251] However, freight may be agreed as a 'lump sum', not conditioned to the dimensions or weight of the cargo. This is like hiring a coach at a fee that is set regardless of the number of passengers that may use it. However, in the case of freight it is more usual that it will not be due unless at least some cargo is shipped. In such a case, provided there is sufficient cargo delivered to rank as a delivery, the full freight is payable.[252]

(iii) Whether or not freight is payable depends on whether the carrier has essentially per- **3.119** formed the service contemplated by the contract. This is normally delivery of cargo at the contract destination in 'merchantable' condition. But in the case of advance freight it is receiving cargo on board and being ready and willing to deliver it to the contract destination.[253]

(iv) The carrier is, like any contracting party, liable for damages for breach of contract, **3.120** whether for failure to perform the contract at all or for performing it defectively, eg, for causing damage to the cargo. But this is a separate issue from whether freight is earned. Thus, if the goods do not arrive at all, no freight is earned and the carrier is liable to pay damages for the cargo owner's loss. If the cause is an excepted peril, the carrier is excused liability for

---

[249] But not at a different place, unless the goods were voluntarily accepted there: *Hopper v Burness* (1876) 1 CPD 137.

[250] See *Allison v Bristol Marine Insurance Co* (1876) 1 App Cas 209, 223, 225.

[251] *Asfar & Co v Blundell* [1896] 1 QB 123, CA (dates saturated by sewage). It appears not yet to have been considered precisely whether the carrier's need under a contract of carriage to deliver in merchantable condition in order to claim freight is affected by the statutory reformulation of a seller's implied duty under a contract of sale to supply to a buyer goods of 'satisfactory' rather than (formerly) of 'merchantable' quality (see 2.36). cf *The Aegean Sea* [1998] 2 Lloyd's Rep 39, 63.

[252] *William Thomas & Sons v Harrowing SS Co* [1915] AC 58, HL.

[253] And, perhaps, the ship sails.

damages; but he has still not delivered the cargo, so he still cannot claim freight. Where some but not all of the goods arrive, or where goods arrive damaged, then the carrier will be entitled to such freight as is earned, and the cargo owner will be entitled to damages for his loss. But the two claims need to be assessed separately. Thus, if the carrier were obliged to deliver 100 packages at £1 per package and only delivers 80, he is entitled not to the anticipated contract freight (£100) but to only the freight he has actually earned (£80). The cargo owner must pay that;[254] but he is also entitled to claim damages for the loss of the other 20 packages (and those damages are at large, to be calculated by the court on all the facts).

3.121   The claim against the carrier must be maintained separately. It cannot be enforced by a simple deduction from freight.[255] This rule is particularly justified on the basis that it should be fairly straightforward to calculate a liquidated claim for the debt to pay freight, but not an unliquidated claim to damages (upon which the parties may well disagree); and the carrier has a lien for unpaid freight that is due,[256] so needs to be able to tell easily when that lien is discharged and he should release the goods.

---

[254] The mere fact that the cargo delivered is damaged does not prevent liability for freight from accruing: *Dakin v Oxley* (1864) 15 CB (NS) 646, 143 ER 938.

[255] *Aries Tanker Corp v Total Transport Ltd (The Aries)* [1977] 1 WLR 185, HL; *Bank of Boston v European Grain and Shipping Ltd (The Dominique)* [1989] AC 1056, HL.

[256] The carrier's lien may cover other matters as well, such as advance freight and demurrage, even sometimes at the port of loading. The law is complex and often involves incorporation of charterparty terms in the bill of lading. See *Scrutton*, ch 18.

4

CARRIAGE OF GOODS BY AIR AND LAND[1]

A. Internal Carriage

(1) The Contract

(a) Applicable law

Contracts to carry goods by rail or road within the United Kingdom are governed by common law. Carriage by air is governed by statutory instrument[2] closely based on the rules for international carriage. However, if there are gaps in the regime, common law usually applies. Otherwise common law is distinct from the law governing international carriage which, therefore, is discussed separately in this chapter: 12.49ff. In practice all the contracts are supplemented importantly by standard terms. Absent any contract, unusual today, internal carriers may have the duties of common carriers at common law. **4.01**

(b) Contract formation

Carriage contracts are concluded like other types of contract.[3] Commonly customers, either consignors or consignees of goods, obtain a copy of the carrier's consignment note or air waybill, and send it with details of the service required to the carrier. Sending the note usually amounts to an offer to contract, an offer which the carrier may accept or reject. Carriers may accept customers' offers expressly or by conduct,[4] such as loading the goods on a trailer going to destination. **4.02**

---

[1] Books referred to in this chapter: Clarke, Air: MA Clarke, *Contracts of Carriage by Air* (2nd edn, 2010); Clarke, CMR: MA Clarke, *International Carriage of Goods by Road: CMR* (5th edn, 2009); Kahn-Freund, O Kahn-Freund, *The Law of Carriage by Inland Transport* (1965). See also MA Clarke and D Yates, *Contracts of Carriage by Land and Air* (2004).

[2] SI 1999/1737.

[3] EPL 8.01ff.

[4] *Brogden v Metropolitan Ry Co* (1877) 2 App Cas 666.

4.03 Parties must agree essential terms such as the destination. Certain terms may be settled implicitly, eg, freight by reference to standard rates.[5] Parties may also refer to carriers' standard terms, such as the Road Haulage Association Conditions of Carriage, 2009; and for rail the Freightliner Conditions 2010. Moreover, carriers advertise their services and, expressly or implicitly, offers by customers may incorporate some of the statements in advertisements.

4.04 Whether terms are indeed part of the contract depends, as with other kinds of contract, on whether customers have signed them[6] or been given sufficient notice that they are to be part of the contract.[7] Even then terms are not binding if they are not accessible to customers (available on request or perhaps on the Internet) as well as being comprehensible.[8] Nor will they bind customers, if they are onerous and unusual, unless specifically drawn to their attention.[9]

4.05 If advertisements by carriers contain actionable misrepresentations, a carriage contract may be rescinded. Apart from misrepresentation, equitable relief, including rescission, may be granted for economic duress amounting to illegitimate commercial pressure. In one case,[10] a carrier, knowing that the commercial survival of the customer depended on delivery, informed it that there would be no more deliveries unless it paid twice the agreed freight rate. Being unable to find another carrier in time, the customer agreed 'unwillingly and under compulsion'.[11] The carrier's enforcement action failed. The customer's consent had been induced by illegitimate pressure.

(2) Transit

(a) Duration

4.06 Transit begins not when the aircraft or motor vehicle moves off but earlier when carriers get (custody and control of) the goods.[12] That is when, as insurers see it, the carriage risk really begins,[13] a matter often regulated by a 'transit clause'.[14] Storage by a carrier in the wrong place would be a serious contract breach, a 'quasi-deviation'.[15] Moreover, to send goods to the wrong destination[16] or on the wrong kind of vehicle[17] is fundamentally different from what has been promised and the contract transit as such has not commenced. Transit ends on delivery, when custody and control pass from the carrier: 4.12.

---

[5] *Foley v Classique Coaches Ltd* [1934] 2 KB 1, CA.

[6] *Harris v GWR Co* (1876) 1 QBD 515.

[7] *Circle Freight International Ltd v Medeast Gulf Exports Ltd* [1988] 2 Lloyd's Rep 427, CA; EPL 8.84, 8.96.

[8] Generally carriers are entitled to assume that customers understand English: *Geier v Kujawa* [1970] 1 Lloyd's Rep 364.

[9] *Lacey's Footwear (Wholesale) Ltd. v Bowler Int. Freight Ltd.* [1997] 2 Lloyd's Rep 369, 384–385, CA.

[10] *Atlas Express Ltd v Kafco (Importers and Distributors) Ltd* [1989] QB 833, 839. Generally: EPL 8.203.

[11] *Atlas Express Ltd v Kafco (Importers and Distributors) Ltd* [1989] QB 833, 838.

[12] *Crow's Transport Ltd v Phoenix Assurance Co Ltd* [1965] 1 Lloyd's Rep 139, 143, CA; *S.CA (Freight) Ltd v Gibson* [1974] 2 Lloyd's Rep 533, 534.

[13] *Re Traders & General Ins Assoc Ltd* (1924) 18 Ll LRep 450, 451.

[14] *Symington & Co v Union Ins Sy of Canton Ltd* (1928) 30 Ll L Rep 280, 283; (1928) 31 Ll L Rep 179, 181, CA. Also storage pending delivery to the consignee: *Crow's Transport Ltd v Phoenix Assurance Co Ltd* [1965] 1 Lloyd's Rep 139, 144, CA.

[15] *Gibaud v GE Ry* [1921] 2 KB 426.

[16] *Israel & Co v Sedgwick* [1893] 1 QB 303, CA; *Nima v Deves* [2002] EWCA Civ 1132, [2003] 2 Lloyd's Rep 327, at [54].

[17] *Kallis (Manufacturers) Ltd v Success Ins Ltd* [1985] 2 Lloyd's Rep 8, PC.

(b) Means

Although contracts may require consignors to provide equipment for loading and unloading, **4.07**
prima facie it is for carriers to choose the appropriate wagon,[18] vehicle or aircraft. The choice
is influenced, however, by the needs of the particular goods, something usually better known
to consignors than carriers, although rarely to a degree that relieves carriers of all responsibility. Sensible parties get together beforehand and agree what is required.

Absent agreement, courts ask whether there is any express or implied[19] term of the contract **4.08**
of carriage governing the type of vehicle or special equipment to be used. The implied warranty, that ships be fit to receive and carry the cargo,[20] is also applied to road vehicles except
that the duty is not absolute but one of reasonable care.[21] Hence courts take account of
what a carrier knew and should have known about the transit and, in particular, the goods.
Arguably the same is true of carriage by rail and by air.

Sub-contracting is usually permitted, expressly or by implication, and is common in carriage **4.09**
by road and by air. Exceptions arise when the personal care, skill or integrity of the contracting carrier is particularly important, eg, in the case of valuables.[22] The Supply of Goods and
Services Act 1982, section 13, requires reasonable care in the selection of competent and
trustworthy sub-contractors.[23] Moreover, arguably, it requires care in the work itself so that,
if sub-contractors are negligent, carriers are liable: carriers can delegate performance but not
responsibility.[24]

(c) Route

If not agreed expressly, it is implied that carriers will take the usual route, if there is one. This **4.10**
is assumed to be the shortest route or that which, to customers' knowledge, carriers normally
take.[25] Courts imply a duty of 'reasonable dispatch'.[26] Nonetheless, road transit includes
ordinary incidents of transit such as convenience breaks for drivers,[27] and minor detours to
avoid obstacles.[28] Moreover, transit may 'be interrupted for efficient and economical loading,
transhipment, discharge and storage to await the most convenient carrier...but not merely
for the commercial convenience of one of the parties'.[29] The degree of interruption allowed
depends on the circumstances.[30]

Unjustified departure from the route is 'quasi-deviation'.[31] If carriage becomes more difficult **4.11**
or more expensive than expected, carriers are obliged nonetheless to perform the contract

---

[18] eg *Gunyan v SE and Chatham Ry* [1915] 2 KB 370.
[19] *Liverpool CC v Irwin* [1977] AC 239; *Scally v Southern Health and Social Security Board* [1992] 1 AC
294.
[20] *Trickett v Queensland Insurance Co* [1936] AC 159, 165.
[21] *John Carter (Fine Worsteds) v Hanson Haulage (Leeds)* [1965] 2 QB 495, 517, 528–529, and 534–535,
CA. Kahn-Freund, 268–269.
[22] *Garnham, Harris & Elton v Alfred Ellis (Transport)* [1967] 2 All ER 940. See also *Edwards v Newland &
Co* [1950] 2 KB 534, CA.
[23] *John Carter (Fine Worsteds) v Hanson Haulage (Leeds)* [1965] 2 QB 495, CA; see also *Gillette Industries
Ltd v W.H. Martin Ltd* [1966] 1 Lloyd's Rep 57, CA; and *Metaalhandel JA Magnus BV v Ardfields Transport
Ltd* [1988] 1 Lloyd's Rep 197.
[24] *Metaalhandel JA Magnus BV v Ardfields Transport Ltd* [1988] 1 Lloyd's Rep 197.
[25] *Hales v LNW Ry Co* (1863) 4 B & S 66, 72.
[26] Clarke, CMR, 210b.
[27] *Sadler Bros Co v Meredith* [1963] 2 Lloyd's Rep 293, 307.
[28] Or similar obstructions: *Taylor v GNR Ry* (1866) LR 1 CP 385, 388.
[29] *Verna Trading Pty Ltd v New India Assurance Co Ltd* [1991] 1 VLR 129, 168 (Vict Sup Ct), a case of
carriage by sea.
[30] *Commercial Union Assurance Co v Niger Co Ltd* (1922) 13 Ll L Rep 75, 81–82, HL.
[31] *LNW Ry Co v Neilson* [1922] AC 263; 'fundamental breach' in carriage by sea: *The Berkshire* [1974] 1
Lloyd's Rep 185, 191.

and to bear the cost: difficulties en route are at carriers' risk.[32] If, however, the only route is blocked, subject to contract terms, the agreed performance has become impossible and the contract is discharged.[33]

(3) Delivery

4.12 Carriers are obliged to deliver goods at the destination agreed. If the precise point of delivery there has not been agreed, a duty is implied to deliver at consignees' place of business,[34] and to notify them.[35] If, however, carriers receive a reasonable request to deliver at a point en route short of destination, they are not only entitled[36] but also obliged to comply, at consignee's expense.

4.13 If carriers have agreed to reach a place and wait until contacted, they hold goods as carriers until the consignee takes them over or until a reasonable time has elapsed, whereafter they hold as bailees for reward,[37] subject commonly to contract terms.[38] If, however, goods reach destination but carriers find that access or unloading facilities there are inadequate or unsafe, carriers are justified in declining to make actual delivery. Transit ends[39] nonetheless when goods have been properly tendered to the consignee;[40] subject commonly to contract terms,[41] which may provide for eventual sale of the goods by the carrier.[42]

4.14 Consignees of goods usually lack transport documents, like bills of lading, which demonstrate their right to the goods; but it suffices that they can identify themselves in other ways as entitled to receive the goods. Carriers, for their part, are obliged to exercise reasonable care[43] to deliver to persons with apparent authority to receive the goods. If goods are delivered in circumstances, which should arouse suspicion, and it turns out that the recipient had no right to the goods, the carrier is liable.[44] Moreover, if a carrier is aware that it was the wrong person, delivery is a fundamental breach of contract, which deprives the carrier of contractual defences.[45]

4.15 Delivery, legally distinct from unloading,[46] is the point when custody and control of the goods pass from carrier to consignee or third party.[47] On the one hand, goods on consignees' premises but still on the carrier's vehicle have not been delivered, even if the premises are locked and the vehicle is not.[48] On the other hand, goods handed over to customs authorities,

---

[32] eg *Tsaskiroglou & Co v Noblee & Thorl GmbH* [1962] AC 93 (carriage by sea).

[33] *Fibrosa SA v Fairburn Lawson Combe Barbour* [1942] 1 KB 12, CA, reversed on different grounds: [1943] AC 32.

[34] Kahn-Freund, 301.

[35] Kahn-Freund, 303, with some support from *Mitchell v Lancashire & Yorkshire Ry Co* (1875) LR 10 QB 256, 260.

[36] *L & NW Ry v Bartlett* (1861) 7 H & N 400, 408; *Cork Distilleries Ltd v GS & W Ry* (1874) LR 7 HL 269.

[37] See *Chapman v GW Ry Co* (1880) 5 QBD 278, 281–282.

[38] See eg RHA Condition 6(2) and Condition 9(3) and *Mitchell v Lancashire & Yorkshire Ry Co* (1875) LR 10 QB 256.

[39] *SCA (Freight) Ltd v Gibson* [1974] 2 Lloyd's Rep 533, 535.

[40] *Heugh v LNW Ry* (1870) LR 5 Ex 51; *Startup v Macdonald* (1843) 6 Man & G 593.

[41] See eg RHA Condition 6.

[42] eg RHA Condition 7.

[43] *M'Kean v M'Ivor* (1870) LR 6 Ex 30, 41.

[44] *Stephenson v Hart* (1828) 4 Bing 576.

[45] *Sze Hai Tong Bank v Rambler Cycle Co* [1959] AC 576, PC. Clarke, CMR, para 240.

[46] Standard contracts regulate loading and unloading without identifying who must do it. Parties must agree that.

[47] *Bartlett & Partners Ltd v Meller* [1961] 1 Lloyd's Rep 487, 489.

[48] *A Tomlinson (Hauliers) Ltd v Hepburn* [1964] 1 Lloyd's Rep 416 appeals on other grounds dismissed: [1966] 1 QB 21, CA, [1966] AC 451.

port authorities or warehousemen, have been delivered, unless the latter are agents of the carrier.[49] Moreover, handing goods over to a third party in mistake for the consignee is also delivery, if done in the reasonable belief that it was the proper consignee.[50] Transit has ended.

(4) Claims: Title to Sue

(a) Agency

Claimants in tort, most likely negligence, must be persons to whom carriers owe a duty of care, usually goods owners. Prima facie consignees are owners, because in sales of goods ex warehouse, ex factory, and free on board (FOB), ownership passes from consignor to consignee when 'the seller delivers the goods…to a carrier…for the purpose of transmission to the buyer, and does not reserve the right of disposal'.[51] **4.16**

Claimants in contract must be party to a contract with the carrier concerned. Early cases support a presumption that the carrier's contract is with the consignee.[52] Prima facie consignees are third parties to carriage contracts negotiated by consignors, but courts have presumed that consignors act as agents of consignees. Hence consignees are bound by contract terms agreed by consignors with carriers,[53] unless they differ from those that a consignee was led reasonably to expect;[54] and can enforce the contract against the carrier concerned. Otherwise contractual rights are enforceable by whoever owns the goods at the time of LDD (loss, damage and delay).[55] **4.17**

(b) Statute

The Contracts (Rights of Third Parties) Act 1999 confers a right of enforcement on third parties, if they are 'expressly identified in the contract by name, as a member of a class or as answering to a particular description': section 1(3). The right of enforcement is conferred by section 1(1) where (a) 'the contract expressly provides' that a person may enforce it; and (b) when a contract term 'purports to confer a benefit on him'. That establishes a presumption, rebuttable, however, 'if on a proper construction of the contract it appears that the parties did not intend the term to be enforceable by the third party': section 1(2).[56] **4.18**

The Law Commission Report which led to the Act gave illustrations, which included the right under the Sale of Goods Act of donees, to whom goods were delivered, against suppliers of the goods.[57] Another concerned the rights of a performing sub-carrier of goods to benefit from defences in the contract concluded by the principal carrier.[58] A similar presumption appears to arise in favour of designated consignees of goods. **4.19**

---

[49] See *Marten v Nippon Sea & Land Ins Co Ltd* (1898) 3 Com Cas 164; and *A Gagniere & Co v The Eastern Co Ltd* (1921) 7 Ll LRep 188, CA.

[50] *Scothorn v South Staffordshire Ry Co* (1853) 8 Exch 341, 344.

[51] Sale of Goods Act 1979, s 18, rules 5(1) and (2).

[52] *Stephenson v Hart* (1828) 4 Bing 476, 487; *Heugh v LNW Ry* (1870) LR 5 Ex 51, 57–58; *The Albazero* [1977] AC 774, 785–786, and cases cited, a review approved in the House of Lords: [1977] AC 774, 842; *Texas Instruments Ltd v Nasan (Europe) Ltd* [1991] 1 Lloyd's Rep 146, 148–149. Kahn-Freund, 210.

[53] *Morris v Martin & Sons* [1966] 1 QB 716, 729–730, CA; *The Pioneer Container* [1994] 2 AC 324; *The Mahkutai* [1996] AC 650; *Spectra Int plc v Hayesoak Ltd* [1997] 1 Lloyd's Rep 153: appeal allowed on a different point: [1998] 1 Lloyd's Rep 162, CA.

[54] eg an unexpected contract route: *Leduc v Ward* (1888) 20 QBD 475, CA, approved by Lord Wright in *Tate & Lyle v Hain SS Co* (1936) 55 Ll L Rep 159, 178, HL.

[55] *The Albazero* [1977] AC 774, 847; *The Kapetan Markos NL (No 2)* [1987] 2 Lloyd's Rep 321, 329, CA.

[56] See *The Laemthong Glory (No 2)* [2005] EWCA Civ 519, [2004] 1 Lloyd's Rep 688, at [49].

[57] Law Com No 242 (1996, Cm 3329), para 7.41.

[58] Law Com No 242 (1996, Cm 3329), para 7.44.

4.20 The right of enforcement is given directly to the third party but by section 1(4), enforcement is 'subject to and in accordance with any other relevant terms of the contract',[59] such as notice of the route agreed between consignor and carrier. Moreover, under section 2(1) the contracting parties are free to vary or cancel a term conferring a right of enforcement, unless inter alia[60] the carrier is aware that the consignee has relied on the term, or the carrier can reasonably be expected to have foreseen that the consignee would rely on the term and the consignee has in fact relied on it. Reliance might well include the case in which the consignee has agreed to sell the goods to another person.

(5) Carriers' Liability

4.21 Carriers are strictly liable to claimants for loss of or damage to goods, as well as delay (LDD), while goods are in their charge (custody and control).[61] Failure to deliver goods in the state in which they were received, or at all, is a breach of the contract of carriage.[62] Concurrent liability in tort, usually negligence, might be established too, but claimants must prove negligence in addition to LDD, and the extent of a carrier's liability in tort is unlikely to be greater than in contract.[63] The advantage of tort actions lies in section 14A of the Limitation Act 1980.[64] In practice most contracts seek to modify the basic liability just described.

4.22 Carriers' first line of defence is proof that LDD was due to some cause for which the carrier is excused by contract. Failing this, a second line of defence is that the action is out of time[65] or that the monetary amount of liability is limited. These defences can be defeated, however, if claimants can establish that the relevant term is unreasonable under the Unfair Contract Terms Act 1977.

(6) Breach of Contract

(a) Loss, damage and delay (LDD)

4.23 Loss, partial or total, occurs when goods become less in volume or quantity than they were before transit. Loss also includes misdelivery,[66] whether to the wrong person[67] or in the wrong place, because the goods are unavailable to the consignee. One should distinguish financial loss which is caused by breach and must be established as such, if claimants are to recover compensation.

4.24 Damage means 'mischief done to property',[68] a change in the physical condition of goods which impairs their value.[69] The precise definition depends on context.[70] For example, fish which is perfectly fit for immediate consumption on delivery, but which has a shortened shelf life because the vehicle was too warm, is damaged goods to consignees who want it not for immediate consumption but for sale later.

---

[59] See also s 1(5).
[60] Other cases of restriction are found in s 2(3).
[61] *Peek v North Staffs Ry* (1863) 10 HL Cas 472, 560.
[62] Common law liability as 'common carrier' is superseded by the contract. In the author's view the same is true of their liability as bailee: Clarke, CMR, para 222.
[63] See 4.31.
[64] See EPL 22.17.
[65] Clarke, CMR, para 218.
[66] *Shipworth v GW Ry* (1888) 59 LT 520.
[67] *Hearn v LSW Ry Co* (1855) 10 Ex 801. See also *Skipworth v GW Ry Co* (1888) 59 LT 520.
[68] *Smith v Brown* (1871) 40 LJQB 214, 218.
[69] *Promet Engineering (Singapore) Pte Ltd v Sturge* [1997] CLC 966, 971, CA.
[70] *Swansea Corp v Harpur* [1912] 3 KB 493, 505, CA.

Carriers are liable for delay, if they deliver later than promised. If not express, 'there is an implied **4.25** contract to deliver within a reasonable time ... using all reasonable exertions'[71] in the circumstances, breach of which implies negligence.[72] Early cases support the implication,[73]although generally in contract law time promises are strictly construed. In practice the point is regulated by contract terms and, eg, carriers may be excused by *force majeure*.[74]

(b) Proof

Delay is proved by reference to the contract and the time of actual delivery. Loss or damage is **4.26** proved by documentation of two kinds. One proves the state or quantity of goods on delivery. The other proves that goods were greater in volume or quantity or in better condition when first taken over. Carriers are obliged not to deliver goods in a state of perfection but in the same state, whatever that was, in which they were taken over.

As to their state on delivery, commonly claimants obtain the report of reliable third parties— **4.27** as soon as possible, to avoid the riposte that the damage or loss (eg vandalism or pilfering) occurred between the time of delivery and report. As to their state on being taken over, proof depends on the efficacy of the consignment note or air waybill, in its role as receipt. Unless carriers have no reasonable means of checking the accuracy of what is stated, such documents are prima facie evidence of statements therein. In practice, however, their evidentiary value is commonly reduced by contract terms. Thus claimants may have to resort to proof of events en route, such as an accident which appears to explain the loss or damage established later. If claimants allege non-delivery of the entire consignment, *ex hypothesi*, there are no goods at destination to be checked, and attention focuses more closely then ever on the transport document and what, if anything, can be proved to have occurred during transit.

(c) Causation[75]

To recover compensation claimants must establish that they have suffered financial loss, of **4.28** which the carrier's breach of contract was the 'effective or dominant' cause.[76] Causation was once regarded largely as an aspect of remoteness of loss or damage[77] but today courts tend to treat it as a separate issue. In most cases claimants must simply establish that *but for* the breach the loss would not have occurred.[78] The main limit on recovery lies in the rule of remoteness together, in some cases, with a limit on the scope of the carrier's duty.[79] Even so, as regards causation, some cases are not simple.

First, if a breach is the first of two or more consecutive causes, the breach remains the effective **4.29** and dominant cause if the intervention of a later cause consisted of 'the very kind of events the terms of engagement were designed to forestall'.[80] These would be events which a carrier had assumed responsibility to guard against, such as theft. Careless carriers are liable for theft, whether the intervention of a thief was probable or not.[81] Second, Devlin J once stated that,

---

[71] *Taylor v GN Ry Co* (1866) LR 1 CP 385, 387. See also *Raphael v Pickford* (1843) 5 Man & G 551; *Postlethwaite v Freeland* (1880) 5 App Cas. 599. Kahn-Freund, 277 et seq.

[72] See the Supply of Goods and Services Act 1982, s 4(1).

[73] eg *Taylor v GN Ry* (1866) LR 1 CP 385.

[74] See N Andrews, M Clarke, A Tettenborn and G Virgo, *Contractual Duties* (2011) 18-006 and references cited.

[75] See EPL 21.40–21.42.

[76] *Heskell v Continental Express Ltd* [1950] 1 All ER 1033.

[77] eg *Monarch SS Co v Karlhmans Oljefabriker* [1949] AC 196, 227–228. As regards remoteness, see 4.39.

[78] *Monarch SS Co v Karlhmans Oljefabriker* [1949] AC 196, 227–228.

[79] See 4.39.

[80] *County Ltd v Girozentrale Securities* [1996] 3 All ER 834, 847, CA.

[81] *Stansbie v Troman* [1948] 2 KB 48; *Lambert v Lewis* [1982] AC 225, 276–277.

if the carrier's breach is one of two concurrent causes, 'both co-operating and both of equal efficacy', the breach is nonetheless 'sufficient to carry a judgment for damages',[82] but not necessarily a judgment for the full amount. If one of those causes is the claimant's fault, the court may apportion liability.[83] In any event, in all cases general contract law imposes a 'duty' to mitigate loss or damage. Thus, eg, claimant consignees whose goods have been damaged must seek alternative goods.[84]

(7) Liability in Tort

(a) Duty of care

4.30 To establish the tort of negligence, claimants must prove breach of a duty of care. In *Customs and Excise Commissioners v Barclays Bank plc*[85] the House of Lords reconsidered the tests for such a duty. It preferred that which asked, 'whether the defendant assumed responsibility for what he said and did', but warned that this test should be applied objectively 'as a sufficient but not a necessary condition of liability', which, 'if answered positively, may obviate the need for further inquiry'.[86] If further inquiry be needed, consideration should be given to 'the particular relationship between the parties in the context of their legal and factual situation as a whole'.[87] In the carriage context one should ask whether carriers were or should have been in control of the operation (affirmative); and whether carriers rather than goods interests are best placed to cover the loss in question by insurance (also affirmative). Indeed, the liability of carriers as such is a traditional 'duty situation', and this is unlikely to be contested.

(b) The context of contract

4.31 The emphasis on assumption of responsibility complements the current approach to the extent of liability in contract.[88] Moreover, when parties to an alleged tort 'have come together against a contractual structure which provides for compensation in the event of a failure of one of the parties involved, the court will be slow to superimpose an added duty of care beyond that which was in the contemplation of the parties at the time that they came together'.[89] So, even when claimant consignees do not contract with a carrier, the contract of carriage between carrier and consignor is the 'contractual structure' in which the court assesses the existence and extent of any duty of care owed by a carrier to claimant consignees. The latter are taken to know that the carriage contract is subject to terms,[90] notably terms limiting carriers' liability; and carriers' duty of care to consignees is modified accordingly. Thus, except that in certain cases where the limitation period may be longer,[91] claimants have little to gain by proving negligence for a claim in tort rather than claiming in contract.

---

[82] *Heskell v Continental Express Ltd* [1950] 1 All ER 1033, 1048, *per* Devlin J.

[83] *Caledonian Ry v Hunter* (1858) 20 Sess Cas 2nd Ser 1097; Law Reform (Contributory Negligence) Act 1945.

[84] *Stroms Bruks A/B v Hutchison* [1905] AC 515.

[85] [2006] UKHL 28, [2007] 1 AC 181.

[86] [2006] UKHL 28, [2007] 1 AC 181, at [4].

[87] [2006] UKHL 28, [2007] 1 AC 181, at [8]. See also at [35] and [53].

[88] See 4.28. See also *Transfield Shipping v Mercator Shipping (The Achilleas)* [2008] UKHL 48, [2009] 1 AC 61, at [10]ff, *per* Lord Hoffmann.

[89] *Pacific Associates Inc v Baxter* [1989] 2 All ER 159, 170, CA; see also *The Nicholas H* [1996] 1 AC 211, 239–240. As regards land carriage similar decisions have been reached, albeit on different reasoning: *Hall v North Eastern Ry Co* (1875) LR 10 QB 437, 442; *Mayfair Photographic Supplies (London) v Baxter Hoare & Co* [1972] 1 Lloyd's Rep 410.

[90] *Circle Freight International Ltd v Medeast Gulf Exports Ltd* [1988] 2 Lloyd's Rep 427, CA.

[91] See the Limitation Act 1980, s 14A.

(8) Counterclaim and Set-off

4.32 In 1995 a road carrier brought a claim for freight charges, and the customer cross-claimed for breach of contract.[92] Cross-claims are usually admitted, but this time the carrier argued for the application of a maritime exception regarding cross-claims.[93] This, said the court, has 'little if any intrinsic justification but applies to carriage of goods by sea because it is a rule of considerable antiquity'.[94] Nonetheless, finding that the exception had been consistently applied to international carriage by road, it held with 'unconcealed reluctance' that the exception also applied to road carriage in the United Kingdom.[95]

4.33 An enduring point in favour of the maritime exception is the desirability of 'speedy settlement of freight and other liquidated demands'.[96] To allow cross-claims or set-off 'would enable unscrupulous persons to make all sorts of unfounded allegations—so as to avoid payment', and that 'even with the most scrupulous, it would lead to undesirable delay'.[97] That is no less true of carriage by road, in which (unlike carriage by rail) carriers are often in the weaker bargaining position.[98] Moreover, in *Overland Shoes Ltd. v Schenkers Ltd.*,[99] a challenge to a 'no set-off' clause in a road contract, on the ground that it was unreasonable and without effect under the Unfair Contract Terms Act 1977, failed.

(9) Contract Defences

(a) Causation

4.34 With one reservation, carriers that establish contract defences are exonerated, provided that the exonerating event caused the LDD. Such clauses are strictly construed. Indeed, arguably the event must be the proximate cause:[100] it must have led more or less inevitably to the LDD.[101] The reservation is that claimants can counter defences by establishing that the real cause, or one of them, was breach of carriers' residual and 'overriding' duty of care. If a carrier's 'negligence has brought on the peril, the damage is attributable to his breach of duty, and the exception does not aid him'.[102] For example, a carrier does nothing about patently inadequate packing but nonetheless pleads the packing as a defence to a damage claim.[103] The defence fails.

(b) External events

4.35 (i) Act of God, a common law defence found in older standard contracts,[104] means some elemental force of nature which could not have been foreseen or, if foreseen, could

---

[92] *United Carriers Ltd v Heritage Food Group (UK) Ltd* [1995] 4 All ER 95.

[93] *Aries Tanker Corp v Total Transport* [1977] 1 All ER 398, HL. The former rationale, the liquidity needed to finance carriage by sea, was rejected altogether in *Gilbert-Ash (Northern) v Modern Engineering (Bristol)* [1974] AC 689, 707 (building contracts).

[94] [1995] 4 All ER 95, 102.

[95] [1995] 4 All ER 95, 102. *Aries* followed in, eg, *Rohlig (UK) Ltd v Rock Unique Ltd* [2011] EWCA Civ 18, [2011] 2 All ER (Comm) 1161; cf *Geldorf Metaal NV v Simon Carves Ltd* [2010] EWCA Civ 667, [2011] 1 Lloyd's Rep 517.

[96] *Dakin v Oxley* (1864) 15 CB NS 646, 667.

[97] *The Brede* [1974] QB 233, 249–250, 254.

[98] No such case on rail carriage has been reported.

[99] [1998] 1 Lloyd's Rep 498, CA.

[100] See *Reardon Smith Line v Ministry of Agriculture, Fisheries and Food* [1960] 1 QB 439, 492; aff'd [1962] 1 QB 42, CA; aff'd on other grounds [1963] AC 691.

[101] The *causa proxima* of insurance law: see 5.90.

[102] *Gill v Manchester, Sheffield & Lincolnshire Ry Co* (1873) LR 8 QB 186, 196; *LNW Ry Co v Hudson* [1920] AC 324, 340.

[103] *LNW Ry Co v Hudson.*

[104] eg RHA Condition 9(2)(b)(i).

not have been guarded against by any ordinary or reasonable precaution.[105] Examples include injury to animals in transit when snow blocked the road.

(ii) 'Strikes' are sometime specifically excluded,[106] as are 'seizure or forfeiture under legal process',[107] which includes events such as detention of debtors' goods.[108]

(iii) Public violence is commonly excluded, notably the 'consequences of war',[109] and 'civil war': war internal to states[110] rather than war between states. Also excluded are 'rebellion' and 'insurrection', which are closely related.[111] Each connotes an organised attempt to overthrow government,[112] whereas another exclusion, 'civil commotion', does not.[113] Lower on the scale of disorder is 'riot', which requires only twelve people,[114] as long as they have a common purpose and use or threaten to use unlawful violence. Controversially, the definition lacks any element of tumult.[115]

(iv) An important defence relating to external events is wording such as 'any cause or event which the Company is unable to avoid and the consequences whereof the Company is unable to prevent by the exercise of reasonable diligence'. This can replace many of the specific defences listed above and reflects the overriding duty of care.[116] The same is largely true of 'force majeure'. However, if carriers are unable to perform the contract through causes entirely beyond their control they can rely on the common law defence of 'frustration'.[117]

(c) State of the goods

4.36   (i) 'Inherent vice' is a defect in goods which, through internal development, tends to their injury or destruction, so that they are unfit for their normal commercial use or purpose for a reasonable time after delivery.[118] Goods are expected to be fit to withstand the ordinary incidents of the transit,[119] assuming they receive the degree of care required either by current practice or by the contract of carriage. 'Insufficient packing', may be excluded expressly but, anyway, is an instance of inherent vice.[120] Sufficiency turns in part on the handling to be expected of the carrier[121] which, in turn, depends on what the carrier can be taken to know about the contents and what it has promised.[122]

---

[105] *Nugent v Smith* (1876) 1 CPD 423, 437 (carriage by sea).

[106] eg *Seeburg v Russian Wood Agency Ltd* (1934) 50 Ll LRep 146.

[107] eg RHA Condition 9(2)(b)(iii).

[108] cf *The Wondrous* [1991] 1 Lloyd's Rep 400, aff'd [1992] 2 Lloyd's Rep 566, CA.

[109] *Kawasaki Kisen Kabushiki Kaisha v Bantham SS Co (No. 2)* [1939] 2 KB 544, CA; *Pesquerias y Secaderos de Bacalao de Espana SA v Beer* (1949) 82 Ll L Rep 501, HL.

[110] *Spinney's (1948) Ltd v Royal Ins Co Ltd* [1980] 1 Lloyd's Rep 406, 429.

[111] *National Oil Co of Zimbabwe (Pte) v Sturge* [1991] 2 Lloyd's Rep 281.

[112] *Spinney's*, n 110, at 437.

[113] See *London & Manchester Plate Glass Co Ltd v Heath* [1913] 3 KB 411, 416, CA; *Levy v Assicurazioni Generali* [1940] AC 791, 800, PC; and *Spinney's*, n 110, at 438.

[114] Public Order Act 1986, s 1(1).

[115] See *The Andreas Lemos* [1982] 2 Lloyd's Rep 483, 492.

[116] See 4.34.

[117] See 8.439ff.

[118] *Blower v GW Ry* (1872) LR 7 CP 655, 662. See also the leading maritime cases: *Albacora SRL v Westtcott & Laurance Line Ltd* [1966] 2 Lloyd's Rep 53, HL; *Noten BV v Harding* [1990] 2 Lloyd's Rep 283, CA; and *Global Process Systems v Syarikat Takaful Malaysia* [2011] UKSC 5, [2011] 1 Lloyd's Rep 560.

[119] *Albacora SRL v Westtcott & Laurance Line Ltd* [1966] 2 Lloyd's Rep 53, 59 and 62, HL.

[120] *LNW Ry Co v Hudson* [1920] AC 324, 333.

[121] *Decca Radar Ltd v Caserite* [1961] 2 Lloyd's Rep 301, 308.

[122] *Hudson*, n 123, at 340; *Lister v Lancs & Yorks Ry Co* [1903] 1 KB 878, 880.

(ii) 'Latent defect' in goods is one not discoverable by the exercise of reasonable care and attention at the time of consignment.[123] Distinguish 'inherent vice' (above), which does not have to be latent. However, carriers' general duty of care[124] is such that 'inherent vice' is unlikely to be an effective defence, unless the vice is 'latent' and thus unknown to the carrier or, if not, there was nothing that the carrier could reasonably be expected to do anyway.

(iii) 'Dangerous goods' are commonly the subject of special contract terms, the effect of which is qualified exclusion of liability. For example, carriers exclude liability in respect of such goods, unless, prior to loading, the carrier has 'received in writing precise and correct identification of the Goods and has further agreed in writing to accept the same for carriage'.[125] If so, carriers are liable in the normal way. If unbeknown to either party the goods are dangerous, this is an instance of 'inherent vice' (above).

(10) Interpretation Contra Proferentem

Ambiguous exoneration clauses are construed *contra proferentem*, ie, restrictively against carriers,[126] albeit less strictly between commercial entities of roughly equal bargaining strength than between carriers and consumers;[127] and less strictly as regards clauses limiting the amount of liability rather than excluding liability altogether.[128] Ambiguity is assessed objectively by the court, ie[129] as understood by lawyers rather than lay persons. Today, however, there is some evidence of a 'softer' approach.[130]   **4.37**

An important application of this rule concerns clauses, whereby carriers seek to exclude liability for negligent breach.[131] If, first, the clause expressly exempts carriers from the consequences of negligence, the clause must be literally applied.[132] Second, if not, courts ask whether the words used are wide enough, in their ordinary meaning, to cover negligence. Third, if so,[133] courts restrict the clause to the underlying strict liability of carriers at common law and construe it restrictively as inapplicable to negligence.[134]   **4.38**

(11) Remedies

(a) **Compensation**

Compensation is recoverable from carriers in accordance with general principles of law.[135] The loss claimed must not be too remote. Claimants may recover loss of profit (expectation   **4.39**

---

[123] *The Amstelslot* [1963] 2 Lloyd's Rep 223, HL (sea).

[124] See 4.34.

[125] EWS, General Conditions of Carriage 2004, Condition 5.

[126] eg *Alexander v Railway Executive* [1951] 2 KB 882. English courts have construed clauses narrowly also when perfectly clear but contrary to commercial common sense, ie, when 'drawn in extravagantly wide terms, which would produce absurd results if applied literally': *UGS Finance Ltd v National Mortgage Bank of Greece* [1964] 1 Lloyd's Rep 446, 453, CA. However, domestic carriage disputes are subject to the Unfair Contract Terms Act 1977: 4.43. It is hard to imagine that, having found a clause reasonable under the Act, the court would then find that it 'would produce absurd results'.

[127] *Photo Production Ltd v Securicor Transport Ltd* [1980] AC 827.

[128] *Ailsa Craig Fishing Co v Malvern Fishing Co* [1983] 1 All ER 101, HL; *George Mitchell (Chesterhall) v Finney Lock Seeds* [1983] 2 AC 803, 814.

[129] *Higgins v Dawson* [1902] AC 1.

[130] eg *Lancashire County Council v Municipal Mutual Ins Co Ltd* [1997] QB 897, 904, CA.

[131] *Canada SS Lines Ltd v R* [1952] AC 192, 208, PC; *The Raphael* [1982] 2 Lloyd's Rep 42, CA.

[132] *Smith v South Wales Switchgear Ltd* [1978] 1 All ER 18, 26, HL.

[133] eg 'any act or omission': *The Raphael*, n 131, at 45.

[134] *Mitchell v Lancs & Yorks Ry Co* (1875) LR10 QB 256; *Alderslade v Hendon Laundry Ltd* [1945] 1 KB 189, 192, CA.

[135] *Ruxley Electronics and Construction Ltd v Forsyth* [1996] AC 344, 365.

loss) only if, at the time of contracting, loss of that kind should have been within the reasonable contemplation of the carrier as not unlikely to result from the breach.[136] This rule will be applied subject, however, to any issues of assumption of responsibility, sometimes raised by what has been called a 'tort' approach.[137] For example, courts ask not only whether the loss was within the contemplation of the carrier as a likely consequence of the delay (remoteness) but also whether and to what extent the carrier has agreed to bear all the consequences.[138] A carrier may be well aware that, if the computer is not delivered on time, the consignee's business will grind to a halt with great loss; but it does not follow that the carrier has undertaken such a degree of responsibility that it must compensate the consignee in full.[139] Generally, however, if late delivery causes goods to miss a market,[140] carriers are liable for customers' loss of profit there.

(b) Other remedies

4.40 In the event of a serious breach of a contract of carriage, the innocent party may terminate the contract in accordance with general principle.[141] Carriers in possession of goods, but facing customer refusal to pay charges, may be entitled to perform the contract in order to retain a lien on the goods as security for payment.[142] A lien 'consists of the right to retain possession of goods of another until his claims are satisfied'.[143] Goods susceptible to possession include documents, however, possession of documents does not give a lien on goods to which the documents relate. Moreover, liens are effective only as long as the lienor retains possession.[144] However, carriers that hand the goods over to sub-carriers nonetheless retain possession of the goods for the purposes of a lien.[145] Rights are lost not only by loss of possession but also by the assertion of entitlement to the goods on grounds incompatible with the exercise of a lien,[146] as well as use of the goods in a manner inconsistent with proper exercise of a lien.[147]

4.41 Liens 'may be particular or general'.[148] Carriers have a particular lien for freight and charges payable on delivery of the goods in question. The lien also extends to the recovery of expenses reasonably incurred to protect and preserve the goods en route[149] unless, of course, the necessity was brought about by the carrier in breach of duty. In contrast, at common law carriers

---

[136] *Hadley v Baxendale* (1859) 9 Ex 341, as interpreted in *The Heron II* [1969] 1 AC 350. See also *The Golden Victory* [2007] UKHL 12, [2007] 2 AC 353 and *The Achilleas* [2008] UKHL 48, [2009] 1 AC 61.

[137] See *South Australia Asset Management Corp v York Montagu Ltd* [1997] AC 191, 214.

[138] R Halson, 'Indemnity Clauses: Remoteness and Causation' [1996] LMCLQ 438–441, 441. *Aneco Reinsurance Underwriting Ltd v Johnson & Higgins Ltd* [2001] UKHL 51, [2002] 1 Lloyd's Rep 157, at [2], [17] and [40].

[139] cf *Hadley v Baxendale* (1859) 9 Ex 341.

[140] Christmas market: *Panalpina Int Transport Ltd v Densil Underwear Ltd* [1981] 1 Lloyd's Rep 187; *The Heron II*, n 136. Regular cattle market: *Simpson v LNW Ry Co* (1876) 1 QBD 274; cf *Horne v Midland Ry Co* (1873) LR 8 CP 131.

[141] *Vitol SA Ltd v Norelf Ltd* [1996] AC 800. See EPL 8.420–8.430.

[142] *White & Carter (Councils) Ltd v McGregor* [1962] AC 413, as applied in *George Barker (Transport) Ltd v Eynon* [1974] 1 Lloyd's Rep 65.

[143] *Hewitt v Court* (1982) 149 CLR 639, 653. Generally see Jackson: DC Jackson, *Enforcement of Maritime Claims* (2nd edn, 1996) ch 20.

[144] Jackson, 443.

[145] Scrutton: SC Boyd, AS Burrows and D Foxton, *Scrutton on Charterparties and Bills of Lading* (22nd edn, 2011).

[146] *Weeks v Goode* (1859) 6 CB (NS) 367.

[147] *Gurr v Cuthbert* (1843) 12 LJ Ex 309. While exercising the lien, quite apart from their duties as carriers, carriers are bound to treat the goods with reasonable care: *Crouch v GW Ry* (1858) 27 LJ Ex 345, 349, *per* Willes J.

[148] *Hewitt v Court* (1982) 149 CLR 639, 653.

[149] Scrutton, 266ff. The lien does not, however, extend to expenses incurred in retaining and maintaining goods in possesion in order to exercise the lien: see Jackson, 440 and cases cited.

have no general lien on goods in their possession, ie no lien on the goods in respect of debts due by the particular customer in respect of other goods and other contracts of carriage. However, carriers have no right to sell the goods,[150] unless there is a commercial necessity to sell, eg, perishable goods,[151] or the goods have been abandoned by the person otherwise entitled to the goods.[152] Today in practice such details are clarified by the widespread use of contractual liens.[153]

Carriers have an action in debt for carriage charges but only for charges due. Thus for charges **4.42** due on delivery, carriers must have properly delivered the goods or, at least, been ready and willing to deliver them. Unless the contract stipulates for advance freight or freight pro rata itineris,[154] freight is presumed to be payable by the consignee on delivery.[155]

(12) Public Policy

(a) Unfair terms

The Unfair Contract Terms Act 1977,[156] nullifies terms altering or reducing business liability **4.43** when their effect is unreasonable. It applies to internal carriage contracts,[157] the terms of which are contained in written standard terms of business such as consignment notes.[158] Reasonableness is a matter of impression formed by reference to certain factors[159] listed here. Contracts of carriage are most affected by factors (i) to (v) and (ix).

(i)   The relative bargaining strength of the parties[160] by reference to whether customers
  (a) knew or should have known that it was possible to enter such a contract with another carrier without having to agree to a such clauses;[161]
  (b) were experienced in transactions of that kind; or
  (c) had relied on the advice of the carrier.
(ii) The party best able to insure against the risk.[162] In the risks associated with carriage indemnity insurance is regarded as more efficient than liability insurance.[163] In practice carriers usually obtain for first party insurance on goods for the benefit of goods owners.[164]

---

[150] *Mulliner v Florence* (1878) 3 QBD 484.

[151] *Prager v Blatspiel Stamp and Heacock Ltd* [1924] 1 KB 566, 573, *per* McCardie J; *Sachs v Miklos* [1948] 2 K.B. 23, 35–36, *per* Lord Goddard CJ, CA.

[152] Scrutton, 382.

[153] eg *K Chellaram & Sons (London) v Butlers Warehousing and Distribution Ltd* [1978] 2 Lloyd's Rep 412, CA, in which it was held that a contractual lien might be effective even against non-contracting goods owners provided that they were aware that such terms might apply. Also *Young (W) & Son (Wholesale Fish Merchants) v BTC* [1955] 2 QB 177. See further Kahn-Freund, 402 et seq.

[154] *Appleby v Myers* (1867) LR 2 CP 651, 661, *per* Blackburn J.

[155] *Dickenson v Lano* (1860) 2 F & F 188, 190, *per* Blackburn J. See also *Barnes v Marshall* (1852) 21 LJQB 388, 118 ER 296; *Metcalfe v Britannia Ironworks* (1877) 2 QBD 423. cf *Christy v Row* (1808) 1 Taunt 300, where there was subsequent agreement for delivery short of destination.

[156] Generally, see EPL 8.110–8.118. Exemption clauses and unfair terms in consumer contracts fall within the Consumer Rights Act 2015 and outside the Unfair Contract Terms Act 1977.

[157] The Act is inapplicable to 'international supply contracts': s 26.

[158] *The Flamar Pride* [1990] 1 Lloyd's Rep 434, 438.

[159] *Smith v Bush* [1990] 1 AC 831, 858. However, the court should 'take care to consider the clause as a whole in the light of the circumstances when the contract was made, in order to judge in the round whether it satisfies the requirement of reasonableness. The court should not be too ready to focus on remote possibilities or to accept arguments that a clause fails the test by reference to relatively uncommon or unlikely situations': *Regus (UK) Ltd v Epcot Solutions Ltd* [2008] EWCA Civ 361, [2009] 1 All ER (Comm) 586, at [36], *per* Rix LJ.

[160] This factor, like the others, is applied by analogy with those listed in Sch 2(a), the direct application of which is restricted to contracts other than contracts of carriage.

[161] *Overseas Medical Supplies Ltd v Orient Transport Services Ltd* [1999] 2 Lloyd's Rep 273, at [21], CA.

[162] Section 11(4). *Monarch Airlines Ltd v London Luton Airport Ltd* [1998] 1 Lloyd's Rep 403, 413.

[163] *Rutter v Palmer* [1922] 2 KB 87, 90, CA.

(iii) The party best able to avoid LDD[165]—usually the carrier.

(iv) Any inducement offered by carriers, such as reduced charges, in return for the reduced liability sought by the exclusion.[166]

(v) Whether the term is in established and widespread use in the trade context.[167] Standard terms of the Road Haulage Association (RHA) or the English Welsh & Scottish Railway Ltd (EWS) are likely to be respected.[168]

(vi) Whether and to what extent customers had actual notice of terms.[169]

(vii) Proportionality:[170] if the loss claimed is large in relation to the carriage charges the term will receive favourable consideration.

(viii) Any special difficulty or danger in performing the work in respect of which liability is excluded or limited.[171]

(ix) In the case of limits on the amount of liability, courts consider '(a) the resources he could expect to be available to him for the purpose of meeting the liability that should arise and (b) how far it was open to him to cover himself by insurance': section 11(4).[172]

(b) Unlawful carriage: non-enforcement

4.44 Contracts of carriage may be void or unenforceable[173] because of how they are formed or performed, or in their purpose. Usually it is because they are contrary to statute containing an express prohibition of some aspect of carriage, which may also prescribe non-enforcement of the contract of carriage. Absent any such prescription, courts have sometimes implied the same consequence.[174] This may be controversial because public policy 'may at times be better served by refusing to nullify a bargain save on serious and sufficient grounds'.[175]

4.45 In one case[176] carriers defended on the ground that the contract was unenforceable because the vehicle was not properly licensed, as required by statute. Pearce LJ pointed out[177] that the contract was not expressly forbidden by the statute, and asked if it was forbidden by implication. The object of the statute, he said, was not 'to interfere with the owner of goods or his facilities for transport, but to control those who provided the transport, with a view to promoting its efficiency'. The carriers' argument failed. In another contrasting case[178] carriers used a vehicle loaded in excess of the permitted statutory weight, which overturned en route. The goods were damaged. The carriers' plea that the contract was illegal and unenforceable was upheld.

---

[164] *Tomlinson (Hauliers) Ltd v Hepburn* [1966] AC 451. Insurance is enforceable by goods owners under the Contracts (Rights of Third Parties) Act 1999.

[165] *Phillips Products Ltd v Hyland* [1987] 2 All ER 620, 629–630, CA.

[166] Schedule 2(b).

[167] Schedule 2(c). *Monarch*, n 162.

[168] *Schenkers Ltd v Overland Shoes Ltd* [1998] 1 Lloyd's Rep 498, CA, unless inconsistent with contract terms agreed by the parties: *DRL Ltd* v *Wincanton Group Ltd* [2011] EWCA Civ 839. cf *Overseas Medical*, n 161.

[169] Schedule 2(c).

[170] *Smith v Bush* [1990] 1 AC 831, 859.

[171] *Smith v Bush* [1990] 1 AC 831, 859.

[172] *Smith v Bush* [1990] 1 AC 831, 859.

[173] A point of doctrinal disagreement but of no immediate importance.

[174] eg *Phoenix General Insurance Co of Greece SA v ADAS* [1988] QB 216, 271–272, CA, citing *Archbolds (Freightage) Ltd v S Spanglett Ltd* [1961] 1 QB 374, CA. cf *St John Shipping Corp v Joseph Rank Ltd* [1957] 1 QB 267, CA.; and *Howard v Shirlstar Container Transport* [1990] 3 All ER 366, CA. See generally EPL 8.211–8.218.

[175] *Vita Food Products Inc v Unus Shipping Co Ltd* [1939] AC 277, 293, PC. The imposition of a fine may suffice; see *St John Shipping*, n 174.

[176] *Archbolds (Freightage)*, n 174.

[177] [1961] 1 QB 374, 385–386.

[178] *Ashmore, Benson, Pease & Co v AV Dawson* [1973] 1 WLR 828, CA.

The difference is that in the second case, not only was there a concern about public safety, but **4.46** the consignors knew or should have known about the overloading, and failed to protest; use of a more suitable vehicle would have cost more. A different decision in the first case would have permitted culpable carriers to defend an action simply by pointing to their own breach of regulation.[179]

When contracts of carriage are unlawful in their purpose, eg, smuggling or the distribu- **4.47** tion of illegal substances, enforcement has also been refused on grounds of public policy. If the smuggling is by the carrier or its employees, a breach of contract remains actionable by customers. If by customers, they cannot enforce the contract of carriage against the carrier,[180] and carriers, if implicated in the illegal venture, will be unable to enforce the contract against customers. Carriers are implicated if they knew or should have known about customers smuggling.[181]

The main consequence in these situations is non-enforcement of the contract, wholly or in **4.48** part.[182] Carriers cannot recover carriage charges. Customers cannot recover damages from carriers for LDD. Moreover, they cannot recover the goods or damages for their detention, if they have to rely on the terms of the contract or on the fact that it is illegal. Although the contract is illegal, carriers can still defend by reference to contract terms or the fact that the contract is unenforceable,[183] or assert property rights obtained under the illegal contract.[184]

B. International Carriage

(1) International Conventions

International contracts of carriage are based largely, albeit not entirely, on international agree- **4.49** ment found in diplomatic conventions, supplemented where necessary by rules of common law.

The oldest convention is CIM for carriage by rail,[185] appended to a framework convention **4.50** called COTIF.[186] The current version of CIM came into force in the UK in June 2006.[187] For carriage by road, CMR[188] was signed at Geneva in 1956 and came into force in the UK in October 1967.[189] Carriage by air in recent times has been subject mainly to the Warsaw Convention 1929 (WSC), as amended by the Hague Protocol 1955 and supplemented by the Guadalajara Convention 1961.[190] However, in 2006 an updated and consolidated version came into force: the Montreal Convention 1999 (MC). In addition, if there is a

---

[179] [1961] 1 QB 374, 385–386.

[180] *Foster v Driscoll* [1929] 1 KB 470, CA; *Regazzoni v KC Sethia* (1944) Ltd [1958] AC 301; *Mackender v Feldia AG* [1967] 2 QB 590, CA.

[181] *Pearce v Brooks* (1866) LR 1 Exch 213.

[182] *Holman v Johnson* (1775) 1 Cowp 341, 343; *Tinsley v Milligan* [1994] 1 AC 340, 355. Occasionally the unlawfulness concerns just part of the contract, and the rest may be enforced: *Fielding & Platt Ltd v Najjar* [1969] 1 WLR 357, 362, CA.

[183] *Bowmakers Ltd v Barnet Instruments Ltd* [1945] KB 65, CA.

[184] *Taylor v Chester* (1869) LR 4 QB 309.

[185] *Règles uniformes concernant le transport international ferroviaire des merchandises*, referred to in France as RUCIM but elsewhere more commonly as CIM. Annexes to CIM deal with, eg, the carriage of dangerous goods.

[186] *Convention relative aux transports internationaux ferroviaires.* See <http://www.otif.org>.

[187] SI 1996/2092.

[188] *La Convention relative au Contrat de Transport International de Marchandises par Route.*

[189] Schedule to the Carriage of Goods by Road Act 1965 (amended by the Carriage by Road and Air Act 1979) and came into force in the UK on 19 October 1967.

sufficient connection with the European Union, compensation of passengers may be affected by EC Regulation.[190]

(2) Scope of Application

(a) Conflicts of law

4.51 Courts characterize a case not as 'contract' but 'international contract of carriage' and apply a unilateral conflicts rule in favour of the appropriate convention as *lex fori*.[192] What makes a case international is not the nationality of the parties but movement of goods from one country to another.[193] Were it nationality, a large cargo aircraft, stopping at different airports in different countries with goods belonging to persons of different nationalities, might well contain goods subject to different air regimes. The territorial factor makes this less likely, and goods can be grouped according to the order of loading and unloading and hence according to the relevant legal regime.

4.52 For CMR it suffices that just one of the states is a Contracting State: Article 1.1. Thus, in practice, CMR extends to Eastern Europe and the Middle East. However, the air regimes are more restricted: both place of departure and place of destination must be in Contracting States: Article 1.2. Many States own airlines and, whether they own and operate airlines or not, take a more than merely regulatory interest in their airspace. All the regimes can be extended by national legislation to internal movements—that is the case in the UK—and be voluntarily adopted by contracting parties.

4.53 None of the regimes cover all matters relating to the contracts in question but, in the case of carriage by air, they are exclusive on what they do cover.[194] CIM and CMR do not prohibit alternative suit in tort but such actions do not extend carrier liability.[195] It should be noted, however, that courts may seek the meaning of concepts in the substratum of national law, eg, even key concepts such as inherent vice and causation.

(b) Factual delimitation

4.54 Each regime defines the activity concerned: the carriage of goods. CIM is for carriage 'by rail' (title). CMR applies to carriage 'by road in vehicles': Art. 1.1. WSC and MC apply to carriage 'performed by aircraft': Article 1.1.[196] Although the regimes apply to contracts of carriage, the liability rules are confined to the period of transit. If carriers fail to take over goods at all, the case is governed by national law.[197] The key feature of transit is not movement but custody and control.[198]

4.55 Goods comprise every transportable object, unless the regime is considered inappropriate. Thus 'funeral consignments' and household goods are excluded from carriage by road: CMR

---

[190] See the Carriage by Air Act 1961 and Carriage by Air (Convention) Order 1967, SI 1967/479.

[191] Such as Regulation (EC) No 261/2004: *Wallentin-Herman v Alitalia*, ECJ Case C-549/07; see Clarke, Air, 2.2.1ff and *Jet2.com Ltd v Huzar* [2014] EWCA Civ 791, [2014] 2 Lloyd's Rep 368.

[192] MA Clarke, *Aspects of the Hague Rules* (1976) 11ff.

[193] As the destination might be changed post contract, what counts is the destination originally agreed: *Grein v Imperial Airways Ltd* [1937] 1 KB 50, 77.

[194] *Sidhu v BA* [1997] AC 430, 453; also *Fellowes v Clyde Helicopters* [1997] 1 All ER 775, HL. As regards the (concurrent) application of the Disability Regulations, see *Hook v British Airways* [2012] EWCA Civ 66, [2012] 1 Lloyd's Rep 386.

[195] CIM Art 41; CMR Art 28.

[196] Concerning the meaning of 'aircraft' see *Laroche v Spirit of Adventure (UK) Ltd* [2009] EWCA Civ 12, [2009] 1 Lloyd's Rep 316.

[197] Clarke, CMR, para 65.

[198] *Westminster Bank v Imperial Airways Ltd* [1936] 2 All ER 890.

Article 1.4, although corpses are commonly repatriated by air subject to WSC or, more commonly, MC. Also a more specific regime may be preferred, eg for postal packets by road: CMR Article 1.4.

Documents, consignment note or waybill, were once a condition of the application of **4.56** regimes such as WSC. Today, however, a transport document is required in all cases but, if none is issued, the relevant regime applies nonetheless.

(3) Claims

(a) Forum

Jurisdiction is in the usual places: carriers' domicile, habitual residence or principal place of **4.57** business, as well as the place of destination and the 'court or tribunal of a contracting country designated by agreement between the parties'.[199] A further possibility, an important reflection of worldwide air freight and electronic trading, is the branch or agency through which the contract of carriage was made.[200] The *lex fori* regulates questions of procedure.[201]

(b) Time

A limitation period of one year is prescribed by CIM Article 47 and CMR Article 32,[202] **4.58** extended in cases of serious breach to two years in CIM and three years in CMR. The air regimes speak not of 'prescription' but of 'extinction',[203] whereby rights of action cease to exist,[204] after two years from when aircraft arrives or should have arrived. The absence of extension for serious breach reflects considerations concerning actions for death and injury to passengers, which are also regulated. Residual aspects such as suspension are governed by the *lex fori*.

(c) Proof of loss

Partial loss or damage to goods is established, first, by proof of the quantity or state of the **4.59** goods on delivery; and, second, by way of contrast, proof of the (greater) quantity or (better) state of the goods when they were taken over, as evidenced by the transport document. As to the first, under CIM Article 42 claimants have only to allege partial loss or damage for carriers to be obliged to arrange an examination of the goods and draw up a report. If its findings are not accepted by claimants, they are entitled to further investigation by an expert appointed by the parties or by the court. CIM reflects the public service role of railways. Compare CMR, Article 30.2, whereby, if consignees check the goods with the carrier, whatever they agree is conclusive, except as regards matters not then apparent.[205] Compare too the air regimes, in many ways the most modern, which do not regulate the process but leave it to the *lex fori*.

As for total loss, if the allegation is non-delivery of the entire consignment, ex hypothesi there **4.60** are no goods to be examined. However, if goods can be proved to have been taken over and not delivered within the stated number of days after the expiry of the transit period, total loss is presumed: eg, CMR Article 20. Much turns on the evidential role of transport documents,

---

[199] CIM Art 46 and CMR Art 31.
[200] *Rothman's of Pall Mall v Saudi Arabian Airlines Corp* [1981] QB 368, CA.
[201] Issues of *lis pendens* are resolved principally by reference to the Brussels Convention 1968: eg *Andrea Merzario Ltd v Spedition Leitner GmbH* [2001] EWCA Civ 61, [2001] 1 Lloyd's Rep 490. Note also Part II of the Civil Jurisdiction and Judgments Act 1982 (Amendment) Order 2000.
[202] Resulting in litigation: *ICI Fibres v MAT Transport* [1987] 1 Lloyd's Rep 354.
[203] WSC Art 29.1; MC Art 35.
[204] eg *Proctor v Jetway* [1982] 2 NSWLR 264, 271.
[205] This shadows the French *constatation aimable*.

which are prima facie evidence of what should have been apparent to carriers when goods are taken over.[206]

4.61 The issue of transport documents containing specified information is required by each regime. The information varies, the main items being the nature and quantity of goods, the number of packages, the consignment weight, marks and (WSC only) dimensions. What is stated about the apparent order and condition of the goods carries with it an implication about the state or sufficiency of packing. Under CIM and CMR carriers may enter reservations on matters which they have no reasonable means of checking, the same being true[207] of the condition of goods or the contents of a package, if it has been actually checked.

(4) Liability

4.62 The regimes apply as terms of the contracts of carriage.[208] This format provides a perspective from which the underlying liability regime is best interpreted. Claimants must prove breach of contract, breach of the strict obligation to deliver goods at destination in the same quantity and condition received, and without delay. Carriers are strictly liable for loss of or damage to the goods occurring while the goods are in their charge qua carrier. Carriers are presumed to have performed as promised until the contrary is proved.[209]

4.63 On proof of breach carriers' first line of defence is to dispute the evidence of loss, damage or delay (LDD) brought by the claimant. The second is that the LDD was caused by claimant fault, inherent vice in the goods or by some other cause which, to a degree that may vary according to the regime, was beyond the carrier's control and for which the carrier has not assumed responsibility. Failing this, the third line of defence is that the claim is out of time, has been brought in the wrong court, or that the monetary amount of liability is limited. Under the land regimes defences in the third line are defeated, if the claimant can establish serious fault on the part of the carrier.

(5) Defences

(a) Patterns

4.64 Carriers' second line of defence lies in one or more of the grounds of exoneration stated in the relevant regime. The long list in CIM compares with the short list of five in MC. Categories of defence are (1) matters in the risk sphere of cargo (eg, inherent vice in goods and insufficient packing), (2) third party intervention (eg, war), and (3) the impact of nature. The last of these are not specified in the regimes but in more venerable standard contracts and are referred to as Act of God. However, category (3) survives in the regimes as an instance of the wider defence of 'unavoidable circumstances'. In addition, in the land regimes carriers may defend by reference to 'special risks': defences by reference to the risk sphere of cargo but with a different and, from the common law perspective, unusual allocation of the onus of proof.[210]

---

[206] Rail: apparent condition of goods and packaging, number of packages, marks, gross mass or quantity otherwise expressed, when loading is performed by carriers: CIM 1999 Art 12.2. Road: apparent condition of goods and packaging, number of packages, marks: Art 9.2. Air: weight, dimensions, packing, number of packages: WSC Art 11 (2); and MC Art 11.2. cf CIM 1980 Art. 21.

[207] Likewise MC Art 11.2.

[208] However, as regards liability, the regimes are presumed to be complete and 'self-contained', eg *Rosewood Trucking Ltd v Balaam* [2005] EWCA Civ 1461, [2006] 1 Lloyd's Rep 429.

[209] CMR Art 30.1; WSC Art 26.1, MC Art 31.1. cf. however, CIM 1999 Art 42.

[210] See 4.72ff.

Note that the Unfair Contract Terms Act 1977 does not apply to contracts governed by CIM, CMR or the corresponding air conventions.[211]

(b) Inherent vice

Inherent vice in the goods, for which the carrier is not responsible, is one of the defences: CIM Article 23.2, CMR Article 17.2, WSC Article 18.3(a), and MC Article 17.2(a). It has the same meaning in each.[212] In *Ulster-Swift v Taunton Meat Haulage*,[213] a typical CMR case, pig carcasses in a refrigerated trailer were decaying on arrival in Basle. The carriers pleaded inherent vice because the carcasses were at too high a temperature, when taken over. The defence would have succeeded, if the trailer itself had been as cool as it should have been; but it was not and the defence failed. At common law goods inadequately packed also suffer from inherent vice, however, in the regimes this is a specific defence. The defence is well known to English shipping and insurance law, to which courts refer.   **4.65**

Inherent vice may also be an instance of 'unavoidable circumstances'[214] or, under the land regimes, a case of 'sensitivity of goods'.[215] However, sensitivity differs, being a permanent feature of all goods of that kind, whereas inherent vice, eg, in *Ulster-Swift*, is found only in some.   **4.66**

(c) Claimant fault

Under the land regimes defences include contributory negligence and claimants' fault, whether consignors or consignees. Indeed carriers can plead the fault of consignors even to claims by consignees. Commonly they allege defective loading or defective packing. The point is controversial but English courts would probably prefer the Austrian view,[216] that the defence is effective only if the claimant was literally at fault. Delay where consignees refuse to accept goods, eg, is not necessarily their fault. Anyway, LDD caused by 'the instructions of the claimant given otherwise than as the result of a wrongful act or neglect on the part of the carrier' is also a specific defence.[217] Fault is not required. An example is instructions about care of goods during transit[218] from a source normally reliable but erroneous on that occasion. However, the defence fails when the instructions were given 'as the result of a wrongful act or neglect on the part of the carrier'. If goods are damaged in transit, carriers at fault and obliged to seek instructions cannot plead the instructions to excuse any extra damage that results.   **4.67**

(d) Third party intervention

An 'act of war or an armed conflict' and 'an act of public authority carried out in connection with the entry, exist or transit of the cargo'[219] are specified defences in MC but not CIM, CMR or WSC, where, however, they may well be instances of 'unavoidable circumstances'.[220]   **4.68**

---

[211] Section 6(5)(b). Also most non-domestic carriage contracts are 'international supply contacts' and thus excluded from the Act: s 26.

[212] *Soya v White* [1983] 1 Lloyd's Rep 122, 126, HL; as it does in carriage by sea: *Global Process Systems v Syarikat Takaful Malaysia* [2011] UKSC 5, [2011] 1 Lloyd's Rep 560.

[213] [1975] 2 Lloyd's Rep 502, aff'd [1977] 1 Lloyd's Rep 346.

[214] eg *Centrocoop Export-Import SA v Brit European Transport* [1984] 2 Lloyd's Rep 618, 625.

[215] See 4.74.

[216] *Loewe* (1976) 11 ETL 311, at [151].

[217] eg CMR Art. 17.2.

[218] eg temperature for fruit: *Cass. 23.2.82* (1983) 18 ETL 13 (France).

[219] Article 18.2 (c) and (d) respectively.

[220] For likely interpretation see 4.35(iv).

(e) Unavoidable circumstances

4.69 An important defence is 'circumstances which the carrier could not avoid'.[221] Air carriers are not liable under WSC if they took 'all necessary measures to avoid the damage or...it was impossible...to take such measures', MC likewise but only for delay.

4.70 This defence is the key to carriers' general duty[222] because the corollary is the benchmark of the degree of care and skill required of them. With one exception, circumstances are unavoidable only if carriers have exercised the 'utmost care'. That is a standard 'somewhere between, on the one hand, a requirement to take every conceivable precaution, however extreme, within the limits of the law and, on the other hand, a duty to do no more than act reasonably in accordance with current practice'.[223] This view was reached by distinguishing *force majeure*, 'due diligence' and 'reasonable care': if such had been intended those well known words would have been used.[224] Nonetheless to apply the defence courts consider the knowledge and information available to carriers and drivers at the time (eg of security measures available), the likelihood of LDD (certain goods are more attractive to thieves than others), and legal regulations (notably permitted driving hours).[225] The duty extends not only to avoiding incidents which cause of LDD but also to mitigating effects of LDD.

4.71 The exception concerns circumstances in the claimant's area of risk. When responding to a threat to the goods arising from defective packing, eg, by consignors, the standard is merely that of reasonable care in the light of current haulage practice.[226] However, a further and tougher CMR exception concerns vehicle defects, carriers' area of risk. The unavoidable circumstances must be *external* to the vehicle.[227] Thus, unless caused by something like vandalism rather than defective manufacture or mounting, carriers are strictly liable for bursting tyres.

4.72 In WSC the words 'all necessary measures' were initially construed to mean 'all reasonable measures', while still imposing a somewhat higher duty on carriers than an ordinary duty of care.[228] Over time, however, the words have been construed more strictly to mean something close to the 'utmost care' of CIM and CMR.[229] This can be seen in the second of two lines of approach to what carriers must prove. The first is an *a priori* approach, whereby, without regard to what actually occurred, carriers must show that all the general measures that could be expected were taken, notably providing airworthy aircraft and competent personnel. The second approach, more likely in the UK, is an *a posteriori* approach whereby courts focus on what actually occurred and ask what could or should have been done about that. This is stricter in that, when causes are unknown carriers are unlikely to be excused.[230] Subject to that, courts reach decisions by consideration of factors similar to those considered in CMR cases.[231]

(6) Special Risks

4.73 When land carriers prove special risks, it is presumed in cases of loss or damage (but not delay), that they were not in breach of contract. When goods are loaded by consignors, eg, carriers prove, not that the loading did cause the loss or damage, but that it *could* have caused

---

[221] See Clarke, CMR, para 74.
[222] See Haenni, *International Encyclopedia of Comparative Law*, vol XII, ch 2, para 243.
[223] *Silber v Islander Trucking* [1985] 2 Lloyd's Rep 243, 247. Also *Cicatiello v Anglo-European Ltd* [1994] 1 Lloyd's Rep 678. Clarke, CMR, para 74e.
[224] Kahn-Freund, 433; also *Silber v Islander Trucking* [1985] 2 Lloyd's Rep 243, 247.
[225] *Silber*, n 223.
[226] See 4.76.
[227] Article 17.3. cf *Walek v Chapman & Ball* [1980] 2 Lloyd's Rep 279.
[228] *Swiss Bank Corp v Brinks-MAT Ltd* [1986] 2 Lloyd's Rep 79, 96–97.
[229] Clarke, Air, 135.
[230] *Panalpina International Transport v Densil Underwear* [1981] 1 Lloyd's Rep 187.
[231] See *Thomas Cook Group Ltd v Air Malta Co Ltd* [1997] 2 Lloyd's Rep 399.

it: no more than a plausible hypothesis.[232] The presumption resembles one in the common law of bailment.[233]

The special risks, listed in CIM Article 23.3 and CMR Article 17.4, are (a) uncovered vehicles; (b) lack of or defective packing of goods which, for the kind of transit agreed, usually need packing;[234] (c) loading or unloading by consignors or consignees; and (d) carriage of sensitive goods, such as fruit or meat.[235] However, if the vehicle 'is specially equipped to protect goods', notably refrigerated vehicles, road carriers must also prove that the equipment was appropriate and in good order.[236] The other special risks are (e) insufficiency of marks or description; (f) carriage of livestock; and (g) under CIM only, risks against which the contract requires an attendant to accompany the goods. **4.74**

Where carriers establish a special risk, it is for claimants to prove that 'the loss or damage was not, in fact, attributable either wholly or partly to one of these risks'.[237] Usually they try to prove the actual cause but they are not obliged to: it suffices to provide evidence of another hypothesis sufficiently plausible to suggest that the cause of loss or damage may not have been the special risk after all. Other issues of proof are for the *lex fori*.[238] **4.75**

Attribution may be partial and responsibility apportioned. For example, rolls of lead worked loose and were damaged during road carriage, due partly to improper loading by the consignor and partly carrier negligence in response to the danger.[239] Carriers' employees cannot simply ignore the fate of goods, especially when third parties are at risk. They have a residual duty of care, firstly, as the corollary of the defence of unavoidable circumstances and the duty to exercise the 'utmost care'.[240] However, secondly, when dealing with special risks, especially defective packing or loading by consignors,[241] their residual duty to respond is pitched at the lower level of reasonable care. Case law across Europe is copious, but uncertainty remains. The concept of special risks is not found in other transport regimes. **4.76**

(7) Remedies

Termination of contract, liens on goods, and recovery of carriage charges are matters for national law; compensation too under WSC and MC but CIM and CMR have rules, including unusual provisions for the possibility that, if lost goods are recovered, claimants may repay the compensation and recover the goods.[242] **4.77**

For damaged goods carriers under CIM and CMR are liable not for cost of repair but for diminution in value[243] by reference to the value of goods not at destination but 'at the place and time at which they were accepted for carriage'.[244] The reason for the latter lies in the intention not to allow compensation for consequential loss, unless there is a declaration of **4.78**

---

[232] See *Ulster-Swift v Taunton Meat Haulage* [1975] 2 Lloyd's Rep 502; affd [1977] 1 Lloyd's Rep 346, CA.

[233] *Levison v Patent Steam Carpet Cleaning Co Ltd* [1978] QB 69, CA; apparently overlooked in *Datec Electronic Holdings Ltd v UPS Ltd* [2005] EWCA Civ 1418, [2006] 1 Lloyd's Rep 279.

[234] *Tetroc v Cross-Con (International)* [1981] 1 Lloyd's Rep 192.

[235] *Donald & Son (Wholesale Meat Contractors) Ltd v Continental Freeze Ltd* 1984 SLT 182. cf inherent vice: 4.65.

[236] CMR Art 18.4; *Ulster-Swift*, n 232.

[237] CMR Art 18.2. Likewise CIM Art 25.2.

[238] *Ulster-Swift*, n 232, at 352.

[239] *OLG Saarbrucken 21.11.74* (1976) 11 ETL 261.

[240] See 4.70.

[241] Clarke, CMR, paras 84 and 87ff.

[242] CMR Art 20; CIM Art 29.

[243] CMR Art 25.1; CIM Art 32.1.

[244] CMR Art 23.1 Idem: CIM Art 30.1. *Buchanan & Co v Babco Forwarding & Shipping (UK)* [1978] AC 141, 151.

special interest[245] or an especially serious breach of contract. The amount must not exceed that payable on a total loss,[246] to which with partial loss the same measure applies.[247]

4.79 In addition to compensation, in case of loss of goods under CMR and CIM 'the carriage charges, Customs duties and other charges incurred in respect of the carriage of the goods shall be refunded'.[248] Narrowly interpreted these are charges, such as the cost of packing and insurance, incurred *for the purpose* of carriage.[249] The broad interpretation preferred by the House of Lords in *Buchanan & Co v Babco Forwarding & Shipping (UK)*[250] extends to expenses *consequential* on how the carriage was actually carried out in breach of contract, such as the cost of surveying damaged goods,[251] or of extra duty payable,[252] as well as return carriage charges.[253] In 2003, however, the Court of Appeal distinguished *Buchanan*,[254] acknowledging 'the need to restrict the scope of *Buchanan*', because it inappropriately imports English rules of remoteness to the scheme of the CMR which 'contemplates an identical liability imposed on a succession of carriers'.[255] The narrow interpretation is also that of most courts in other CMR States.[256]

(8) Maximum Liability

4.80 Carriers should have a viable limit on their exposure. First, the amount must be ascertainable so that carriers can estimate their exposure without having to open packages. So, the limit is usually an amount per unit of weight, including packing. Secondly, the limit must be not so high that liability is uninsurable but not so low that carriers have insufficient incentive to take care.

4.81 The limit varies. CMR has lower limits than CIM. Moves on environmental grounds to reverse the position and make railways more competitive have yet to be realized. The limit for carriage by air, the highest, reflects the value of goods carried by air and high freight charges. A significant feature of MC is a provision for reviewing the limits every five years without resort to the full diplomatic process.[257]

(9) Serious Breach

(a) Wilful misconduct

4.82 Carriers lose their liability limits[258] when they are guilty of serious breach of contract. This is the 'wilful misconduct' of CMR, Article 29.1, taken from the 1929 text of WSC, Article 25, even though the conference knew that in WSC Article 25 the rule had produced an

---

[245] CMR Art 26; CIM Art 35.
[246] CMR Art 25.2; CIM Art 32.2.
[247] CMR Art 23.1; CIM Art 30.1.
[248] CMR Art 23.4; CIM Art 30.4.
[249] The minority view in *Buchanan & Co v Babco Forwarding & Shipping (UK)* [1978] AC 141.
[250] *Buchanan & Co v Babco Forwarding & Shipping (UK)* [1978] AC 141.
[251] *ICI Fibres v MAT Transport* [1987] 1 Lloyd's Rep 354.
[252] *Buchanan*, n 250.
[253] *Thermo Engineers Ltd v Ferrymasters Ltd* [1981] 1 All ER 1142, 1150.
[254] *Sandeman Coprimar SA v Transitos y Transportes Integrales SL* [2003] EWCA Civ 113; [2003] QB 1270.
[255] [42].
[256] Notably Austria, Germany and Holland although not France. It is also the inference from the *travaux préparatoires*: Clarke, CMR, para 98.
[257] Article 24.
[258] Under CMR Art 32.1 the time limit also.

unacceptable divergence between the decisions in civil law countries and decisions in countries of common law,[259] and that it was likely to be changed.[260]

In England the 'starting point' for enquiry about wilful misconduct 'is an enquiry about the conduct ordinarily to be expected in the particular circumstances,' and next to ask whether the acts of omissions 'were so far outside the range of such conduct as to be properly regarded as "misconduct"'.[261]Only then will the court consider 'whether the misconduct is wilful',[262] a search to establish the actor's state of mind. Typically, in *Jones v Bencher*,[263] a CMR case of 1984, the court turned back to nineteenth century railway cases[264] and cases on the unamended WSC, which put a subjective interpretation on 'wilful misconduct'. Nonetheless the CMR rule is said to be substantially the same as the amended WSC and CIM,[265] in which the key elements of the wording are intent to cause damage, recklessness, and knowledge that damage would probably result.   **4.83**

(b) Intent and recklessness

Intent to cause damage is obvious and rarely an issue in litigation. Motive is irrelevant. A pilot who allows perishable cargo to perish while deviating to get a passenger to hospital, has the best of motives but the damage is intentional nonetheless.   **4.84**

A continuum 'runs from simple negligence through gross negligence to intentional misconduct', and recklessness 'lies between gross negligence and intentional harm'.[266] Recklessness is a concept well known at common law. In carriage regimes, however, recklessness must be read in context and in close collocation with the phrase 'with knowledge that damage would probably result'.[267] So English courts require evidence of actual awareness on the part of the actor.   **4.85**

(c) Knowledge and awareness

A person 'must appreciate that he is acting wrongfully, or is wrongfully omitting to act, and yet persists in so acting or omitting to act regardless of the consequences'.[268] This is not easily established when driver or pilot is dead. Thus a more objective approach is found in other countries, notably in air cases in the USA, where the misconduct is 'the wilful performance of an act that is likely to result in damage or wilful action with a reckless disregard of the *probable consequences*'.[269] Courts there have been more ready than courts in England to infer a state of mind from the evidence. Otherwise, they say, claimants would be 'at the mercy of those capable of the most invincible self-deception'.[270] The point is perhaps less compelling   **4.86**

---

[259] R Rodiere, 'La faute inexcusable du transporteur aerien' (1978) 13 ETL 24, 25.

[260] See the travaux preparatoires: TRANS/WP/9/35 No 73, 19–20.

[261] *Air Malta*, n 231, at 407, with reference to *Lacey's Footwear (Wholesale) Ltd v Bowler International Freight Ltd* [1997] 2 Lloyd's Rep 369, CA, on CMR.

[262] *Air Malta*, n 231, at 407.

[263] [1986] 1 Lloyd's Rep 54. See also *Texas Instruments Ltd v Nasan (Europe) Ltd* [1991] 1 Lloyd's Rep 146, 154; and *Lacey's Footwear (Wholesale) Ltd v Bowler International Freight Ltd* [1997] 2 Lloyd's Rep 369, 374, CA.

[264] Notably *Lewis v GWR* (1877) 3 QBD 195, 206, CA, and *Forder v GWR* [1905] 2 KB 532, 535.

[265] Respectively Art 25 and Art 36.

[266] *Saba v Air France*, 78 F 3d 664, 667 (DC Cir, 1996).

[267] *Cortes v American*, 177 F.3d 1272, 1284ff. (11 Cir, 1999).

[268] *Horobin v BOAC* [1952] 2 All ER 1016, 1022. See also *Rustenburg Platinum Mines v SAA* [1977] 1 Lloyd's Rep 564, 569; aff'd [1979] 1 Lloyd's Rep 19 (CA); *Goldman v Thai Airways International* [1983] 1 WLR 1186, CA; and *Lacey's Footwear*, n 263.

[269] *Wing Hang Bk Ltd v JAL Co* (1973) 357 F. Supp. 94, 96–97 (SD NY), with emphasis added. See also *Republic National Bank v Eastern Airlines* (1987) 815 F. 2d 232, 239 (2 Cir.).

[270] *In Re Air Crash near Cali, Columbia*, 985 F Supp 1106, 1129 (SD Fla, 1997). Also *Saba v Air France*, 78 F 3d 664, 667 (DC Cir, 1996).

in England, where there is no jury in such cases and where states of mind, associated eg with fraud, are regularly assessed by the court.

4.87 Wilful misconduct may lie in series of acts or a single act and what 'may amount on one occasion to mere negligence' may amount 'on another to wilful misconduct'.[271] A driver may cross a red light absentmindedly, or quite deliberately because he reckons that the roads are deserted and nothing will cross his path—that is wilful misconduct.[272] The difference is between a risk and a calculated risk.

4.88 The rule now found in MC and CIM but not CMR requires conduct 'with intent to cause damage or recklessly and with knowledge that damage would *probably* result'.[273] However, in *Nugent v Goss Aviation Ltd* the Court of Appeal rejected the argument that such knowledge could be imputed.[274] There must still be 'actual knowledge, in the sense of appreciation or awareness at the time of the conduct in question, that it will probably result in the type of damage caused. Nothing less will do'.[275] It is 'not sufficient to show that, by reason of his training and experience, the pilot ought to have known that damage would probably result from his act or omission. The test is subjective'.[276]

4.89 Nonetheless, as to evidence of awareness, English courts today are moving towards the more objective approach taken in the USA. In particular, in *Nugent* Auld LJ conceded that the 'greater the obviousness of the risk the more likely the tribunal is to infer recklessness and that, the defendant, in so doing, knew that he would probably cause damage'.[277] He also referred to an air cargo case, in which vulnerable goods were left out on the tarmac in a thunderstorm,[278] and where the combination of 'deplorably bad handling' and a failure to call evidence that might excuse it enabled the court to infer recklessness.[279]

(d) Probable results

4.90 Probable results are results that are likely to happen,[280] and thus more than merely foreseeable. Hence, if carriers have an unsafe system for handling cargo, without more, damage to cargo is (reasonably) foreseeable but it is not probable; there may be breach but not serious breach.[281] If, however, some loss or damage is probable, claimants do not have to establish the degree of loss or that is probable.[282] Compensation is recoverable for the entire damage.

---

[271] *Horabin v BOAC* [1952] 2 All ER 1016, 1020.

[272] The illustration is based on a much quoted passage in *Horabin*, eg *Rustenburg Platinum Mines v SAA* [1977] 1 Lloyd's Rep 564, 569.

[273] Emphasis added but the point was underlined by Auld LJ in *Nugent v Goss Aviation Ltd* [2000] 2 Lloyd's Rep 222, 223, CA.

[274] *Nugent v Goss Aviation Ltd* [2000] 2 Lloyd's Rep 222, 223, CA. The argument of Pill LJ at 231, that the probability of damage was 'within his knowledge' even if not present in his mind at the material time; and that, eg, a 'pilot does not escape liability merely because, by reason of, for example, drink or tiredness, he forgets for a moment his training and the general knowledge his experience of flying brings him' was rejected by the other members of the Court.

[275] *Nugent v Goss Aviation Ltd* [2000] 2 Lloyd's Rep 222, 228, CA.

[276] *Nugent v Goss Aviation Ltd* [2000] 2 Lloyd's Rep 222, 232, CA.

[277] *Nugent v Goss Aviation Ltd* [2000] 2 Lloyd's Rep 222, 227, CA.

[278] *SS Pharmaceutical Co Ltd v Quantas Airways Ltd* [1991] 1 Lloyd's Rep 288, CA NSW.

[279] Similar inferences have been drawn by French *Cour de Cassation* when valuable cargo was exposed to theft: *British Airways v UAP* (1992) 27 ETL 141.

[280] *Goldman v Thai Airways International* [1983] 1 WLR 1186, CA.

[281] *Rolls Royce Plc v Heavylift-Volga DNEPR Ltd* [2000] 1 Lloyd's Rep 653.

[282] The inference from *Husain v Olympic*, 116 F Supp 2s 1121, 1140 (ND Cal, 2000).

Allegedly courts must consider whether 'the wilful misconduct (if established) *caused* the loss **4.91** or damage to the goods'.[283] Certainly carrier misconduct must be a 'but for' cause of the deleterious results, but that alone is not sufficient. In the USA it is not required to be the sole cause.[284] English courts are likely to agree. However, for the rest American courts have turned to domestic law, in particular, to tort law.[285] The trouble is that 'tort law' or equivalent differs from country to country, especially on causation. Moreover, the American courts were mostly applying the Warsaw text of 1929 and not the amended text of 1955, in which, it is submitted, there is guidance enough. What matters is simply that the results were *probable* results.

---

283 *Air Malta*, n 231, at 408 (emphasis added).
284 *Korean Air Lines v Alaska*, 22 Avi 17, 388 (Alaska, 1989).
285 *In Re Air Crash near Cali, Columbia*, 985 F Supp 1106, 1146 (SD Fla, 1997).

5

INSURANCE[1]

A. Introduction

(1) Insurance and the Law

Generally, contracts of insurance are governed by the same rules of law and interpretation as **5.01** other kinds of contract.[2] For that reason this chapter starts by presenting the law in a way familiar to readers of general works on contract law. It looks first at the formation of insurance contracts

---

[1] Books referred to in this chapter: Clarke 2009: Clarke, *The Law of Insurance Contracts* (6th edn, 2009); Clarke 2007: *Policies and Perceptions of Insurance in the Twenty-first Century* (revised edn, 2007); MacGillivray: J Birds (ed), *MacGillivray on Insurance Law* (11th edn, 2008); Rose: FD Rose, *Marine Insurance: Law and Practice* (2nd edn, 2012); Summer: J Summer, *Insurance Law and the Financial Ombudsman Service* (2010). For the purposes of this chapter, it has been assumed that the Insurance Act 2015 is not yet in force (it comes into force on 12 August 2016). As regards non-consumer insurance contracts, the Act replaces the present law of disclosure by what is termed a 'duty of fair presentation'. Changes are also made to aspects of the remedy of rescission (and consequent restitution) for non-disclosure. The Act also amends the law on eg warranties (s 10) and fraudulent claims (s 12) in relation to insurance contracts.

[2] See EPL ch 8.

on the basis of mutual consent, next the effect of flaws in consent brought about by mistake, misrepresentation and, a possibility that distinguishes insurance contracts from other contracts, non-disclosure. Once a contract has been validly formed, next comes its content, preceded by an outline of the relevant rules of interpretation—necessary because of the overriding importance of insurance policies. After that the law presented is particular to insurance: insuring clauses, which express cover in positive terms, exclusions delimiting cover in negative terms and giving cover its final shape, and warranties which underlie the contract of insurance as conditions precedent to cover. Finally, the chapter deals with policyholder claims against insurers for the sum insured. The rules apply to both marine and non-marine contracts, unless otherwise indicated.

(2) Insurance Contracts

5.02 All-embracing 'definitions' of insurance, found in some common law countries, are regarded in England as too bland to be useful.[3] There is an element of insurance in any binding promise by one person to another in which the law recognizes as an assumption of risk. Clearly, not all such arrangements can be regarded as insurance contracts.[4] The attitude of English courts remains that of Templeman J: 'no difficulty has ever arisen in practice, and therefore there has been no all-embracing definition'. He went on to explain that definition is undesirable because they 'tend sometimes to obscure and occasionally to exclude that which ought to be included'.[5] Mostly it is clear whether there is insurance or not, but there is a marginal penumbra of obscurity where traditional insurance products meet the ingenuity of innovative financial markets. From this perspective the Financial Services Authority (FSA) observed that there are nonetheless some 'generally accepted' features of archetypical insurance,[6] as described by Channell J in the *Prudential case*,[7] and that contracts lacking those elements are unlikely to be classified as insurance.

5.03 First, the business must be insurance business.[8] The insurer may be a charity and insurance may be just one part of its business, but that is insurance business nonetheless. Second, there must be a legally binding promise[9] to pay—in money or in kind.[10] Usually it is money, but sometimes insurers provide something other than or in addition to money: services such as reinstatement of damaged buildings in property insurance and, in travel insurance, transport home and medical treatment.[11] Third, the promise to pay must be contingent on the occurrence of a specified event, such as fire or death. Fourth, at the time of contract the event must be uncertain,[12] uncertain as to whether it will occur (eg fire), as to when it will occur

---

[3] Clarke, 2009, 1-1.

[4] Assumption of risk is insufficient to draw the (difficult) distinction between insurance and any other 'normal' contract, in which there is a secondary promise by a contractor to pay damages for its breach of primary promises. One answer in the USA is the 'principal object' test, eg, a product guarantee is ancillary to the sale of the product which is what characterizes the transaction and distinguishes it from insurance: Williams, 'Distinguishing "Insurance" from Investment Products under the McCarran-Ferguson Act' 98 Col L Rev 1996, 2019ff (1998). However, this test was rejected in *Fuji Finance Inc v Aetna Life Ins Co Ltd* [1997] Ch 173, CA.

[5] *DTI v St Christopher Motorists Assn* [1974] 1 Lloyd's Rep 17, 18ff. As regards the definition of reinsurance see *Wasa Int Ins Co v Lexington Ins Co* [2009] UKHL 40, [2010] 1 AC 180.

[6] <http://www.fsa.gov.uk/pubs/policy/ps04_19.pdf>, para 6.3.4. Patten LJ in *Digital Satellite Warranty Cover Ltd v FSA* [2011] EWCA Civ 1413, [2012] Lloyd's Rep IR 112, at [6] confirmed that on the issue of definition one is 'left to apply the general law'.

[7] *Prudential Ins Co v IRC* [1904] 2 KB 658, 663.

[8] *Hall d'Ath v British Provident Assn* (1932) 48 TLR 240.

[9] *Medical Defence Union Ltd v Dept of Trade* [1980] Ch 82.

[10] *Hampton v Toxteth Co-operative Provident Sy Ltd* [1915] 1 Ch 721, CA.

[11] Thus a promise, an 'extended warranty', to repair domestic satellite equipment might be insurance: *Re Digital Satellite Warranty Cover Ltd and Others* [2011] EWHC 122 (Ch); appeal dismissed [2011] EWCA Civ 1413, [2012] Lloyd's Rep IR 112. An appeal to the Supreme Court was dismissed: [2013] UKSC 7.

[12] *Medical Defence*, n 9, at 89.

(eg death), or as to how often it will occur (eg damage to taxis). Moreover, fifth, the event must be one that is adverse to policyholders.

Adversity is obvious in cases such as fire or burglary. Doubt has been expressed about finan- **5.04**
cial vehicles such as life polices maturing at a stated age, such as 65.[13] In England this is valid insurance. As was said in Australia, a whole life policy is an insurance against dying too soon, an endowment policy maturing before death is insurance against living too long.[14] For some people the passage of the years is unkind and uncomfortable. Money may be spent to ease the discomfort. Courts approach issues of this kind with a mixture of principle and pragmatism.

B. Contracting

(1) The Process

Contracts of insurance like other contracts are made when the offer of one party is accepted **5.05**
by the other party, the insurer. Insurance applicants, especially applicants for standard con-sumer cover, may deal directly with insurers. In other cases they deal through insurance inter-mediaries, such as brokers. Relations with intermediaries are governed by the law of agency, as well as regulations made under the Financial Services and Markets Act 2000 (FSMA).[15]

Whether through intermediaries or not, applicants commonly obtain a quotation from an **5.06**
insurer. In the language of contract law the quotation is an 'invitation to treat'. Applicants who 'accept' the quotation by completing the insurer's proposal form, submit what the law sees as an offer—to be accepted (or not) by the insurer. If insurers are not willing to accept offers, they may respond with a counter-offer,[16] which may (or may not) be accepted by the applicant. Applicants may respond with a further (counter) offer of their own for acceptance (or rejection) by the insurer. This process continues until a final counter-offer from one of them is accepted or rejected. The template of offer and acceptance, although useful,[17] is not a rigid or exclusive format for concluding insurance contracts; it is just a guide.[18]

Contracts are concluded when offers are accepted unless, important in this context, parties **5.07**
agree otherwise. Acceptance of an offer, provided that the offeror accepts a new term, is not acceptance at all: no contract results.[19] Agreement on terms, however, *may* still be no contract if subject to satisfaction of specified conditions. Such 'conditions precedent' are found in life or health insurance, where insurers commonly require payment of premium or satisfactory medical reports before becoming bound.

Here the first possibility is that there is not a binding contract of insurance at the time of **5.08**
agreement until the condition is satisfied.[20] The second is that there is a contract from the time of agreement (acceptance) but no cover until the condition is satisfied.[21] Alternatively, the same situation may be seen as a contract of insurance with cover from the time of

---

[13] *Medical Defence*, n 9, at 93, *per* Megarry V-C: a 'feat of survival can hardly be called an event that is adverse to his interests'.
[14] *National Mutual Life Assn v FCT* [1959] HCA 6, (1959) 102 CLR 29, 45.
[15] See 5.50.
[16] eg *Canning v Farquhar* (1886) 16 QBD 727, CA.
[17] *The Zephyr* [1984] 1 Lloyd's Rep 58, 72.
[18] *CTI Inc v Oceanus Mutual Underwriting Assn (Bermuda) Ltd* [1984] 1 Lloyd's Rep 476, 505, CA. cf *Tekdata Interconnections Ltd v Amphenol Ltd* [2009] EWCA Civ 1209, at [10]ff, [2010] 1 Lloyd's Rep 357, 359ff, *per* Longmore LJ; Morgan, 'Battle of the Forms: Restating the Orthodox' [2010] CLJ 230.
[19] *Canning*, n 16.
[20] *Canning*, n 16, at 731.
[21] *Canning*, n 16, at 731.

agreement but cover that may be defeated later by, eg, an unfavourable medical report; the contract is subject to a 'condition subsequent'.[22] A further alternative is that there is not one contract but two: a preliminary contract with interim cover and, if the condition is satisfied (the report is favourable) a main contract for the full period of cover.[23]

(2) Certainty of Terms

5.09   Unless contracting parties appear to be certain about the essentials of what they are binding themselves to, courts are slow to infer intention to contract. Uncertainty may appear both in what parties have said (ambiguity), and in what parties have not said (incompleteness). Terms essential to insurance contracts are terms which identify the parties, the kind of risk covered (eg fire), the subject-matter (eg St. John's College), the duration of cover (commonly one year), and the premium to be paid by the policyholder. In some instances, notably life insurance, parties must agree the amount of money payable under the policy: they alone can put a value on the life insured. In other instances, such as property insurance, the amount payable is the amount of actual loss but insurers often stipulate a ceiling on this amount. Such terms have to be expressed but other terms (eg duration and premium)[24] can be implied.

5.10   Implied terms are categorised according to their source. First, terms may be implied by law, ie from statute[25] or, when necessary to give business efficacy to the contract,[26] from precedent. Second, terms may be implied from previous dealings between the particular parties.[27] Third, terms may be implied from customs of the insurance market. An important instance is the presumption that applications for insurance are on the basis of insurers' standard terms (if any) for the kind of risk in question.[28]

5.11   Marine insurance merits special mention. The law differs in certain respects mentioned in this chapter. Marine cover is identified by subject-matter: ships (hull), cargo, and freight which can be separately insured.[29] Reinsurance of such subject-matter is also regarded as marine.[30] Further, whereas, unless otherwise specified, the insurance period for non-marine insurance is customarily one year, marine insurance differs in two respects that should be noted. First, cargo may be insured for the transit in question. Alternatively, regular exporters insured all cargo of the type they deal with for a period (often one year) under 'floating' or 'open covers.[31] Second, ships are under voyage policies or time policies.[32]

---

[22]   The Canadian view: *Zurich Life Ins Co v Davies* (1981) 130 DLR (3d) 748, 751, Can SC.

[23]   The Scots view in *Sickness & Accident Assurance Assn Ltd v General Accident Assurance Corp Ltd* (1892) 19 R 977, 985.

[24]   *American Airlines Inc v Hope* [1973] 1 Lloyd's Rep 233, CA, aff'd on other points [1974] 2 Lloyd's Rep 301; *Baker v Black Sea & Baltic General Ins Co* [1998] 1 WLR 974, 983, HL.

[25]   None at all in the case of non-marine insurance; cf Marine Insurance Act 1906, ss 36ff.

[26]   *Scally v Southern Health & Services Board* [1992] 1 AC 294.

[27]   *Hope*, n 24, at 253.

[28]   *General Accident Ins Corp v Cronk* (1901) 17 TLR 233; *Rust v Abbey Life Assurance Co Ltd* [1979] 2 Lloyd's Rep 334, 339, CA. Marine insurance is commonly contracted on one of the standard Institute Clauses developed by the London Underwriters, such as the Institute Cargo Clauses (A) (1/1/09): Rose, Appendix 10.

[29]   Marine Insurance Act, s 90.

[30]   *WASA Int Ins Co v Lexington Ins Co* [2009] UKHL 40, [2010] 1 AC 180; noted critically by Gurses, '*Wasa v Lexington*: the Exception or the Rule?' (2010) 73 MLR 119.

[31]   Marine Insurance Act, s 29. Rose, 6.65ff.

[32]   Marine Insurance Act, s 25. Rose, ch 10.

(3) Certainty of Intention

Offers must indicate a definite willingness to be bound on the part of the offeror. This is a   **5.12**
matter of construction of the offer. Documents that appear to contain firm offers, such as
insurance application forms, are presumed to do so. No such presumption arises, if there is
reason to infer otherwise from context. That is usually the case of documents issued by insurers inviting applications; it makes little sense for insurers to be bound without first assessing
the particular risk.

Definite offers may come to an end before being accepted. First, unaccepted offers end   **5.13**
after any period of time stipulated for acceptance or, in the absence of stipulation, a
reasonable time.[33] Second, offers end on the failure of a condition subject to which an
offer was made.[34] Offers by insurers are implicitly conditional on there being no material
change in the risk proposed between offer and acceptance.[35] Third, offers end on rejection.
Counter-offers are regarded as rejections;[36] but a response by the offeree is a counter-offer
only if it is inconsistent with the offer.[37] Fourth, offers end by revocation[38] communicated
to the offeree.[39]

(4) Unequivocal Acceptance

Acceptance of an offer must be unequivocal, unconditional, and communicated to the offeror,   **5.14**
whether by speech or conduct.[40] Payment or premium, and policy delivery are examples of
such conduct, although not essential to conclude contracts unless required by the terms of
the offer.[41] Silence is equivocal and not normally sufficient evidence of acceptance,[42] or that
can be inferred from the circumstances of the case.[43]

If the terms purportedly accepted differ from the terms of the offer, there is no acceptance.   **5.15**
However, the difference must be definitive. Sometimes insurers respond to applications with
a policy in general terms which are not tailored to the application but can be reconciled with
it; that may well be valid acceptance. Sometimes a response with different terms is a tentative
move to see if the other will agree to them. Such moves are not acceptance but nor are they
rejection of the other's position, which remains on the table to be taken up. If, however, a
response with different terms is not tentative but firm, it is a counter-offer which rejects and
extinguishes the last offer.[44] The legal nature of all such moves depends on the interpretation
of reasonable persons in receipt of such.[45]

In addition, however clear the apparent intention of parties, their consent must be genuine.   **5.16**
If either or both are sufficiently mistaken about the terms of the contract or the nature of
the subject-matter, what appears to be a contract of insurance may have been vitiated by the

---

[33] *Ramsgate Victoria Hotel Co v Montefiore* (1866) LR 1 Ex 109.
[34] *Financings Ltd v Stimson* [1962] 1 WLR 1184, CA.
[35] *Canning v Farquhar* (1886) 16 QBD 727, 733, CA.
[36] *Lark v Outhwaite* [1991] 2 Lloyd's Rep 132,139.
[37] *Jones v Daniel* [1894] 2 Ch 332, 335.
[38] *Canning*, n 35, at 731.
[39] *Byrne & Co v Van Tienhoven & Co* (1880) 5 CPD 344; *General Re Corp v Forsak Fennia Patria* [1982]
QB 1022; reversed on other grounds [1983] QB 856, CA.
[40] See EPL 8.07ff.
[41] *Xenos v Wickham* (1866) LR 2 HL 296; *Wooding v Monmouthshire Mutual Indemnity Sy Ltd* [1939] 4
All ER 570, HL.
[42] *The Anticlizo* [1987] 2 Lloyd's Rep 130, CA.
[43] *New Hampshire Ins Co v MGN Ltd* [1997] LRLR 24, 54, CA.
[44] *Allis-Chalmers Co v Maryland Fidelity Co* (1916) 114 LT 433, HL.
[45] *Lark v Outhwaite* [1991] 2 Lloyd's Rep 132, 139.

mistake. Cases of this kind concerning insurance contracts have rarely been reported.[46] In the unlikely event of a mistake about the identity of one of the parties, the issue will be resolved by reference to the policy.[47]

(5) Communicated Acceptance

5.17 Acceptance does not conclude a contract until the fact of acceptance has been communicated to the offeror.[48] Buyers of insurance through intermediaries may think they have obtained cover simply by communicating with the intermediary. However, in the case of brokers eg, acceptance is generally ineffective until the broker communicates it to the chosen insurer.[49]

5.18 Acceptance has been communicated when received but, in a world of global business and communication, when is that? To answer that courts today proceed 'by reference to the intentions of the parties, by sound business practice, and in some cases by a judgment where the risks should lie'.[50] Generally the answer is the point of receipt. First, anyone who gives out a telephone[51] or telex number,[52] or an email or postal address,[53] represents that any message properly sent there during business hours will be dealt with.[54] Second, people who publish their email addresses, phone or telex numbers are usually the better risk avoider, as regards what happens to information that has reached the address or number, especially in large firms like insurance companies.[55] Third, a receipt rule of this kind best meets the need for certainty. In the case of email, however, those who give out their address have chosen the server but do not control it. Hence messages are deemed to be received when the addressee is able to access them.[56]

5.19 Receipt of acceptance is a requirement that may be waived by the offeror.[57] Offerors who send offers by post impliedly authorize the offeree to use the same medium to accept the offer, although in law postal acceptance is effective to conclude the contract when sent. Offerors assume the risks of the authorised medium, unless acceptance is lost or delayed by the fault of the offeree: that is not a risk they are taken to have assumed. People keen to accept an offer of cover can cut the corner and the risk by sending their acceptance by any other mode which satisfies the apparent concerns of the sender as to speed, proof or confidentiality. Only if a mode of acceptance is exclusive, must it be followed in any event.

5.20 Finally, offerors may waive the requirement of communication altogether: in that case, once there is evidence that an offeree's intention is to accept, there is a contract, whether the offeror is aware of it or not. Waiver may be inferred from the practice of the insurance market.[58] An established instance is that, if insurers sign and seal a policy of the kind applied for, acceptance is effective at that time, whether the applicant is aware of it or not.[59]

---

[46] See Clarke, 2009, ch 21.
[47] *Shogun Finance Ltd v Hudson* [2003] UKHL 62, [2004] 1 AC 919.
[48] *Brinkibon Ltd v Stahag Stahl mbH* [1982] 1 All ER 293, HL.
[49] *Manufacturers' Mutual Ins Ltd v John Boardman Ins Brokers Pty Ltd* [1994] HCA 16, (1993–1994) 179 CLR 650.
[50] *Brinkibon*, n 48, at 296.
[51] *Hadenfayre Ltd v British National Ins Sy Ltd* [1984] 2 Lloyd's Rep 393.
[52] *The Brimnes* [1975] QB 929, 945, CA.
[53] *Holwell Securities Ltd v Hughes* [1974] 1 All ER 161, 164, CA.
[54] *The Brimnes*, n 52.
[55] *Hadenfayre*, n 51; *Nissho Iwai Petroleum Co Inc v Cargill International SA* [1993] 1 Lloyd's Rep 80, 84.
[56] See the Electronic Commerce (EC Directive) Regulations 2002, SI 2002/2013, which also provide that where orders are placed using electronic means, the insurer must acknowledge receipt of the order without undue delay.
[57] See EPL 8.09ff.
[58] eg interim motor cover: *Taylor v Allon* [1966] 1 QB 304.
[59] *Xenos v Wickham* (1866) LR 2 HL 296.

(6) Lloyd's[60]

Applicants instruct a Lloyd's broker,[61] who prepares a standard 'MR slip' stating the essen-   **5.21**
tials of the risk proposed and takes it around the Lloyd's market seeking subscriptions to the
risk.[62] Subscription by initialling the slip ('scratching') signifies acceptance of (usually a small
part of) the risk offered. The broker continues around the market until the amount sought
has been fully subscribed.[63] In the case of more specialized risks, underwriters may subscribe
as 'following' underwriters through the agency of a 'leading' underwriter, the contracts of all
underwriters concerned being nonetheless separate. Full disclosure is made by brokers only
to the leader and by market practice that is sufficient for all of them.[64] The followers trust the
judgement of the leaders.

Market practice at Lloyd's creates difficulties in law. First, if the broker fails to obtain sub-   **5.22**
scriptions the broker's client, who is seeking cover may well look elsewhere for insurance. Can
the contracts of insurance already concluded, the subscriptions, be cancelled? Second, the
broker can obtain contracts for all of the risk but only by agreeing different terms with different underwriters. However, 'market practice abhors a slip on different terms; it is possible but
daft',[65] from the point of view of administering the cover and the associated transaction costs.
These difficulties have been solved by market practice—to the satisfaction of the market but
not their legal advisers.[66]

Except in practice for reinsurance, a policy on the terms of the slip is issued later although,   **5.23**
apart from marine insurance, insurance policies are not required by law.[67] Lloyd's policies,
once issued, are evidence of the series of separate contracts between the insured and each
member of each syndicate whose underwriter has scratched the slip.[68] Since 1992 all this
could be done electronically.[69]

(7) Renewal

Renewal of cover for a further period and on broadly the same terms as before but, perhaps,   **5.24**
with slight changes such as the amount of premium, is regarded as the conclusion of a new

---

[60] Generally: Clarke, 2009, 11-3; MacGillivray, 35–38ff.

[61] Since January 2009, Lloyd's byelaws specify the conditions under which syndicates' managing agents
can accept business from persons other than Lloyd's brokers or transact business otherwise than through
or with (other) intermediaries. Such persons include intermediaries who meet regulatory requirements or
professional standards equivalent to those required by the EU Insurance Mediation Directive; have adequate
arrangements for the conduct of business in the London market; have suitable procedures in place to ensure
that 'insurance monies' are properly safeguarded; have adequate professional indemnity insurance; and can
demonstrate their ability to meet other criteria from time to time prescribed: Legislative Reform (Lloyd's)
Order (Market Provisions) Byelaw (No 1 of 2009).
    Moreover, at Lloyds, claims too are regulated. The 'Combined' Lloyd's Claims Scheme took effect from 1
January 2012 for certain categories of claim.

[62] *American Airlines Inc v Hope* [1974] 2 Lloyd's Rep 301, 304, HL.

[63] Concerning over-subscription and the practice of signing-down, see *The Zephyr* [1984] 1 Lloyd's Rep
58, 72.

[64] *Aneco Re Underwriting Ltd v Johnson & Higgins* [1998] 1 Lloyd's Rep 565. Also *International
Management Group v Simmonds* [2003] EWHC 177 (Comm), [2004] Lloyd's Rep IR 247; and *Dunlop
Haywards v Erinaceous* [2009] EWCA Civ 354, [2009] Lloyd's Rep IR 464.

[65] *General Reinsurance Corp. v Forsak. Fennia Patria* [1982] 2 QB 1022, 1039.

[66] See this case on appeal: [1983] 1 QB 856 (CA).

[67] *Thompson v Adams* (1889) 23 QBD 361.

[68] *General Reinsurance*, n 65, at 864.

[69] eg, since October 2010, certain endorsements have been agreed electronically over the Lloyd's electronic
exchange system, using ACORD standards.

contract.[70] When insurers send renewal notices to policyholders, these are an offer of cover for the further period for acceptance (or rejection) by policyholders. However, insurers are not obliged to renew and, therefore, are not obliged to send out renewal notices.[71]

5.25 As renewal of insurance is a new contract, some of the terms may be new and terms, therefore, of which the policyholder may be unaware. However, although policyholders are expected to read the policy when they first contract, they are entitled to presume that, apart from the level of premium and the dates, renewal is on broadly the same terms as before. If the insurer intends otherwise, it must give clear notice of the new terms.[72] Moreover, insurers have had statutory duties about 'product disclosure' which lead to the same result.[73]

C. Validity

(1) Contracts Enforced

5.26 A duly concluded contract will be enforced. Exceptions occur when a 'contract' is void for mistake, which is very rare in insurance, or void (or unenforceable) because it is unlawful.[74] If the insurance contracted for is unlawful in a sense which is or should be obvious to the party who seeks to enforce the contract, it will not be enforced.[75] If the unlawfulness is not obvious, the position is the same[76] but the unlawfulness must be established by the insurer as if it were an express exception to cover. The unlawfulness may be that the 'insured' lacks insurable interest and, therefore, that the insurance is contrary to public policy. Alternatively, it may be that the insurance is the vehicle for promotion of an unlawful object or because, although that was not the intention, enforcement in the particular case would have that effect. Liability insurance, eg, is unlawful if it would relieve policyholders of the burden of penalties for crime or awards of damages that public policy requires them to bear themselves.

(2) Insurable Interest: Property[77]

5.27 Contracts of insurance are unlawful, if policyholders lack insurable interest. For it to be lawful, policyholders must have, first, a relation in fact to the subject-matter insured giving rise

---

[70] cf variation or extension of cover during the current period which is not an entirely new contract: *Jones Construction Co v Alliance Assurance Co Ltd* [1961] 1 Lloyd's Rep 121, CA. The difference is a matter of intention and degree.

[71] *Windus v Lord Tredegar* (1866) 15 LT 108, HL. Exceptionally (eg *Palomar v Guthrie*, 583 So 2d 1304 (Ala, 1991)) a contract term requiring notice has been implied from previous dealings in the USA and, in principle, the same could be held in the UK.

[72] *Burnett v Westminster Bank* [1966] 1 QB 742, CA.

[73] See Insurance Conduct of Business Rules 5 http://fsahandbook.info/FSA/handbook.jsp?doc=/handbook/ICOB/. In 2008 ICOB was replaced by ICOBS; arguably failure to give notice is contrary to the spirit of the rules of disclosure found in ICOBS Rule 6.

[74] Generally, see Clarke, 2009, ch 24. In particular, a current issue is the possibility of 'discrimination based on any ground such as sex, race', contrary to the EU Charter of Fundamental Rights, Art 21, binding on parties to the Treaty of Lisbon 2007. In this connection see *Association Belge de Consommateurs Test-Achats*, Case C–236/09, [2011] 2 CMLR 38, [2011] Lloyd's Rep IR 296, in which the ECJ accepted the Opinion of the Advocate General that in Art 5(2) of the Gender Directive (2004/113/EC) sex is a 'determining factor' in the assessment of risk by insurers, that that was incompatible with the principle of equal treatment under EU law and hence was unlawful.

[75] In such a case a defence rests on the maxim *ex turpi causa: Stone & Rolls Ltd v Moore & Stephens* [2009] UKHL 39, [2009] 1 AC 1391; see also *Safeway Stores Ltd v Twigger* [2010] EWCA Civ 1472, [2011] 1 Lloyd's Rep 462.

[76] *Harse v Pearl Life Assurance Co* [1904] 1 KB 558, CA.

[77] See Clarke, 2009, ch 3 (life insurance) and ch 4 (property insurance).

to an economic interest such that, if it is lost or damaged they will be worse off. Second, they must have a 'legal or equitable relation' to the subject-matter.[78]

In most common law countries the second requirement has been abandoned as pointless in modern society;[79] and unnecessary. Nonetheless English law persists with a rule which Waller LJ demonstrated is difficult to define in words applicable to all situations.[80] Much depends on the context and the terms of the policy. In particular, he pointed out that there is 'no hard and fast rule that because the nature of an insurable interest relates to a liability to compensate for loss, that insurable interest could only be covered by a liability policy rather than a policy insuring property or life or indeed properties or lives. [It] is a question of construction'.[81] **5.28**

In the case of liability insurance, it is sometimes said that the subject-matter is the insured's liability. However, it makes more sense to say that what is covered is the assets of the insured against loss in the event of his or her liability to third parties. It also chimes with the classic description of insurable interest by Lord Eldon as 'a right in the *property*, or a right derivable out of some contract about the *property*, which in either case may be lost upon some contingency affecting the possession or enjoyment of the party'.[82] **5.29**

Reinsurance was once thought to be liability insurance: that reinsurers cover the liability of primary insurers to meet their obligations to pay policyholders. Reinsurers are not liable to pay 'until the amount of the reinsured's liability has been ascertained by judgment, award or settlement',[83] and this remains true. Today, however, the established view is that reinsurance is not insurance of 'the primary insurer's potential liability or disbursement' but 'an independent contract between reinsured and reinsurer in which the subject-matter of the insurance is the same as that of the primary insurance, that is to say, the risk to the ship or goods or whatever might be insured'.[84] Reinsurance claimants prove not what they paid to primary policyholders but the loss suffered by the latter. **5.30**

Other instances are less problematic. Section 1 of the Life Assurance Act 1774 prohibits life insurance without interest. Section 2 requires the life to be named in policy: the policyholder or in a limited range of cases, a third person; see para 5.34. In the case of indemnity insurance, such as fire insurance, the subject-matter is the property insured against loss by fire. Section 4 of the Marine Insurance Act 1906 (MIA) expresses the common law rule by prohibiting 'wager' policies. In all apparently bona fide cases, however, courts lean in favour of finding an insurable interest in commercial transactions.[85] **5.31**

The marine market, in particular, has dealt with difficult cases by 'honour' policies: unenforceable in law but rarely challenged in practice. Otherwise known as PPI (policy proof of interest) insurances, they include, eg, insurance of anticipated profits and policies on goods in transit, insured on shipment, but which later increase in value to an extent that is hard to pre-estimate.[86] In view of the personal character of most risks (the 'moral hazard'), most **5.32**

---

[78] *Macaura v Northern Assurance Co* [1925] AC 619.
[79] See eg *Kosmopoulos v Constitution Ins Co* [1987] 1 SCR 2, Can SC.
[80] *Feasey v Sun Life Assurance Co of Canada* [2003] EWCA Civ 885, [2003] Lloyd's Rep IR 637, CA.
[81] *Feasey v Sun Life Assurance Co of Canada* [2003] EWCA Civ 885, [2003] Lloyd's Rep IR 637, CA, at [97]. See also [119]–[120] and [123]. *Ramco (UK) Ltd v International Insurance Co of Hannover Ltd* [2004] EWCA Civ 675, [2004] 2 Lloyd's Rep 595, CA.
[82] *Lucena v Craufurd* (1806) 2 Bos & Pul 269, 321.
[83] *CGU Int Ins plc v Astrazeneca Ins Co Ltd* [2005] EWHC 2755 (Comm); [2006] Lloyd's Rep IR 409, at [126].
[84] *Charter Reinsurance Co Ltd v Fagan* [1997] AC 313, 392, and 387; *WASA v Lexington* [2009] UKHL 40, [2010] 1 AC 180.
[85] *CGU*, n 83, at [71].
[86] MIA, s 4(2)(b). Rose, 3.1ff.

insurances cannot be assigned.[87] However, marine insurance, notably cargo insurance would be largely ineffective, if assignment were not possible and, indeed, facilitated.[88]

5.33   English law requires that the insured have an insurable interest at the time of loss: MIA, section 6(1) states the common law rule for all indemnity insurance. Although they often do, the law does not require policyholders to have an insurable interest at the time of contract, except in the case of life insurance,[89] which differs in this,[90] and other respects.

(3) Insurable Interest: Life

5.34   People's affection for themselves is presumed to be such that they will not kill themselves, and that gives them an insurable interest in their own life.[91] Similarly people are allowed to insure those who traditionally are their very nearest and dearest. Thus in England husbands may insure their wives[92] and wives their husbands[93] but, curiously, not their children.[94] Nor is insurance allowed between co-habitees—in theory, however, practice stretches theory. An important instance is 'keyman' insurance, whereby firms insure personnel whose continued life and health is crucial to the prosperity of the firm. Firms cannot insure the life of the monarch, but they can contract 'business interruption' or 'consequential loss' insurances, ie insurance against loss of profits, against the impact of national mourning. However, these are indemnity insurances, so firms face the difficulty of proving actual loss. That is why nobody has disputed keyman life insurance of 'star' racing drivers, footballers or fashion models, as well as less prominent back room boffins. Nobody doubts that the death of a star may cause loss but the amount is likely to be hard to prove. Keyman life insurance is non-indemnity (contingency) insurance; and the policy pays the amount insured, without proof of loss.

5.35   The 'keyman' case shows that, although theoretically grounded originally on affection,[95] the real basis of life insurance is financial dependence. Wives, eg, need financial support when husbands die, no less today when the income of both is needed to discharge a mortgage. But the law still lacks consistency.[96] One of the earliest instances of enforceable life insurance was that of creditors on the life of their debtors,[97] but children cannot contract insurance on the life of the parents that support them, eg, through college, unless they make parents their legal debtors. Employers can insure the lives of key employees but the right of employees to insure the life of their employer, even in the case of the 'one man' company, is severely circumscribed.[98]

(4) Unlawful Insurance

5.36   Insurance purporting to cover property (such as contraband) in the course of committing a crime (an unlawful voyage) will not be enforced.[99] Moreover, courts will not enforce an

---

[87] See Clarke, 2009, ch 6; M Smith, *The Law of Assignment* (2007) ch 17; and R Surridge, B Murphy and N John (eds), *Houseman's Law of Life Assurance* (13th edn, 2007) ch 2, section 1.

[88] See Rose, ch 7.

[89] There 'is no real legal difference in the meanings of "insurance" and "assurance" and the two terms may be (and often have been) treated as synonyms in the life insurance context. Usually, "insurance" is preferred today to avoid confusion': AA Tarr and J-A R Tarr, 'Insurance' in *The Laws of Australia*, (1999) 22.1.307.

[90] *Barnes v London, Edinburgh & Glasgow Life Assurance Co* [1891] 1 QB 864, CA.

[91] *Griffiths v Fleming* [1909] 1 KB 805, CA.

[92] *Griffiths v Fleming* [1909] 1 KB 805, CA.

[93] *Griffiths v Fleming* [1909] 1 KB 805, CA.

[94] *Harse v Pearl Life Assurance Co* [1904] 1 KB 558, CA.

[95] *Griffiths*, n 92, at 821.

[96] The law in other common law countries is more accommodating: Clarke, 2009, 3-7.

[97] *Godsall v Boldero* (1807) 9 East 72.

[98] To the pecuniary of rights of continued employment: *Hebdon v West* (1863) 3 B & S 579.

[99] *Lubbock v Potts* (1806) 7 East 449.

indemnity in respect of a penalty imposed by a court on a policyholder in respect of offences involving intent[100] or culpable negligence.[101] The court must have regard 'to the necessity of deterring him and others from doing the same thing again'.[102] However, distinguish punitive damages: punishment and deterrence are not the only purposes of such damages, which also serve, eg, to appease victims. So, prevailing public policy allows insurance against payment,[103] although in practice many liability policies exclude such cover.

Liability to a passer-by for injury caused by dangerous driving getting away from the scene of **5.37** the crime will be covered[104] but, curiously, liability for a similar injury inflicted with firearms will not.[105] In *Gardner v Moore*[106] the House of Lords accepted the view of Diplock LJ that the 'court has to weigh the gravity of the anti-social act and the extent to which it will be encouraged by enforcing the right sought to be enforced against the social harm which will be caused if the right is not enforced' and that social policy favoured compensation for road victims.[107] From such statements it seems that enforcement is less likely when there is no third party in need of compensation.[108] They might also suggest that similar 'balancing up' should be applied to all other kinds of liability insurance, however, it now seems not.

More recently courts have declined the task of 'balancing', partly because they consider that **5.38** social engineering is not their job, in the absence of clear instructions from Parliament;[109] and partly because the requisite information may be lacking.[110] The position now is that victims of crime will get liability insurance money compensation only when the liability insurance is compulsory.[111] This position would be easier to understand and thus to support, if a principled line were apparent between where liability insurance is compulsory and where it is not.[112]

D. Misrepresentation

(1) Flawed Consent

Contracts are void or voidable if the consent of either party is sufficiently flawed. Consent **5.39** is flawed if one party is mistaken about a fundamental feature of the contract (mistake), or is induced to contract on the basis of wrong information (misrepresentation) or insufficient information (non-disclosure).[113] Operative mistake affecting insurance is rare.[114]

---

[100] *Smith (WH) & Sons v Clinton* (1909) 99 LT 840: a promise to indemnify a publisher against criminal libel damages.

[101] *Askey v Golden Wine Co Ltd* (1948) 64 TLR 379.

[102] *Askey v Golden Wine Co Ltd* (1948) 64 TLR 379, 380: there was 'culpable negligence': selling liquor unfit for consumption. In *Osman v Moss* [1970] 1 Lloyd's Rep 313, CA, however, a convicted motorist had reason to believe that his insurance was valid, and the indemnity was enforced.

[103] *Lancashire CC v Municipal Mutual Ins Ltd* [1995] LRLR 293; aff'd [1996] 3 All ER 545, CA.

[104] *Gardner v Moore* [1984] AC 548.

[105] *Gray v Barr* [1971] 2 QB 554, 587, CA.

[106] [1984] AC 548. The motorist drove his van at a pedestrian in anger and severely injured him.

[107] *Hardy v MIB* [1964] 2 QB 745, 767–768, CA.

[108] *Haseldine v Hosken* [1933] 1 KB 822, 833, CA.

[109] eg Devlin, *The Enforcement of Morals* (1965) 56.

[110] Clarke, 2009, 275ff.

[111] *Charlton v Fisher* [2001] EWCA Civ 112, [2001] Lloyd's Rep IR 287, at [83]. Notably under the Road Traffic Act 1988, s 151.

[112] RK Lewis, 'When you must insure' (2004) 154 NLJ 1474.

[113] Clarke, 2009, chs 21–23; MacGillivray, chs 15–18.

[114] *Pritchard v Merchants' & Tradesmen's Mutual Life Assurance Sy* (1858) 3 CB (NS) 622: parties contracting life reinsurance, were unaware that the life had dropped (died).

5.40   Either party's consent may be flawed but, in practice, the question usually arises, when claims are brought: insurers defend on the ground that their consent was flawed by the way the risk was presented at the time of contract, be it by misrepresentation, non-disclosure or both. Often clear lines cannot be drawn between them. If an applicant states that in the past five years one burglary has occurred at the premises whereas in truth there were two, is that misrepresentation of the number of burglaries or non-disclosure of the second? Legally the defences are distinct but the law has important features in common and developments in the law in the last decade of the twentieth century have been in the direction of convergence. Moreover, for 'retail' customers of insurers,[115] there have been significant changes in the law made under section 138 of the Financial Services and Markets Act 2000 (FSMA), in the form of 'rules' and 'guidance', by the FSA;[116] and for consumers an important change was made by the Consumer Insurance (Disclosure and Representations) Act 2012.[117]

(2) Truth

5.41   An operative misrepresentation is an untrue statement of fact (or law) by an applicant which induces[118] the insurer to make the contract of insurance. A statement is untrue if it is substantially untrue in the context in which it was made, objectively viewed,[119] ie if the degree of inaccuracy would be material to prudent insurers of that kind.[120] Such a misrepresentation is nonetheless a misrepresentation, and actionable as such, if it is made innocently and in good faith. Truth does not mean true to the best of the knowledge and belief of the applicant unless, as is common for consumers, that is what is stated in the form which insurance applicants must complete.[121]

(3) Fact and Opinion

5.42   To be factual, statements must be statements about the present or past. Distinguish, first, statements about the future. Statements about security precautions the applicant plans to take next month against theft are not present facts.[122] However, if the applicant has no intention to carry out those plans, the statement is an untrue statement of fact about current management intention.[123] Second, to be fact statements must be statements that the applicant appears (to the insurers) to have the knowledge, information or experience to make. Otherwise they are mere statements of opinion which the law does not regard as actionable representations of fact,[124] and which reasonable insurers should realize cannot be relied on. That is the key to the distinction. Thus, eg, confident assertions by overweight applicants of 60 that they are in the best of health are opinions; but medical 'opinion', that their blood pressure is too high,[125] is fact.

---

[115] These are natural persons acting for purposes outside their trade, business or profession.

[116] See http://fsahandbook.info/FSA/handbook.jsp?doc=/handbook/ICOBS/. The FSA (<http://www.fscs.org.uk>) is also required to make rules in respect of the protection of policyholders in the event of insurer insolvency; see McVea, 'The Financial Services Compensation Scheme and deposit insurance reform' [2008] LMCLQ 389.

[117] See Law Com No 319; Scots Law Com No 219; Summer, 13.24ff.

[118] Generally, see EPL 8.159ff and 5.53; also Clarke 2009, 23–27ff.

[119] *McInerny v Lloyds Bank Ltd* [1974] 1 Lloyd's Rep 246, 254, CA.

[120] *Yorke v Yorkshire Ins Co* [1918] 1 KB 662, 669. Concerning what is material, see 5.45.

[121] *Economides v Commercial Union Assurance Co plc* [1998] QB 587, CA; Clarke 2009, 23–28C1ff.

[122] *Benham v United Guarantie and Life Assurance Co* (1852) 7 Exch 744.

[123] *Hill v Citadel Ins Co Ltd* [1995] LRLR 218, 227, aff'd [1997] LRLR 167, CA. See also promissory warranties: 5.71 and Clarke 2009, 20–25.

[124] *Bisset v Wilkinson* [1927] AC 177, PC.

[125] *British Equitable Ins Co v Great Western Ry* (1869) 20 LT 422.

Controversy continues over opinions of probity, and associated moral hazard. If the appli- **5.43**
cant's CEO has been charged with fraudulent accounting, that, it might be said, states no
more than the prosecutor's opinion, which has yet to be established as fact by a court of
law. However, imminent prosecution is a fact that must be disclosed.[126] What counts is less
whether prosecution is factual than whether it is material. Indeed applicants must disclose
any 'rumours which materially affect the risk, even when these subsequently turn out to have
been unfounded',[127] including rumours circulating in the press. Insurance law backs insurers and their suspicion that there may be no smoke without fire in the face of the righteous
indignation of applicants.[128] However, the law is subject to two qualifications.

First, the materiality of a rumour must be judged subject to the possibility raised by Lord **5.44**
Mance that, if there had been full disclosure, 'it would have embraced *all* aspects of the
insured's knowledge, including his own statement of his innocence and such independent
evidence as he had to support that by the time of placing'.[129] This might well 'throw a different light' on whether rumours are material. Materiality must be judged by reference to all
of the evidence available at the time of placing, whether disclosed or not. Subsequently this
view was accepted, with a second qualification. The test is 'an objective test, and the characteristics to be imputed to a prudent insurer are in substance a matter for the courts to decide'.
A robust court thus has room to manoeuvre, including 'room for a test of proportionality,
having regard to the nature of the risk and the moral hazard under consideration'. On that
basis there may be disclosable matters which, in the view of the court, are 'too old, or insuf-
ficiently serious to require disclosure'.[130]

(4) Materiality and Inducement

To be material, misrepresentation does not have to be one likely to influence the judgement of **5.45**
insurers decisively; it is enough, it has been said, that the representation was 'actively present'
in the mind of the person assessing the risk.[131] That was said in the context of fraud. Be that
as it may,[132] the law also requires inducement in the sense of causation: that the actual underwriter was decisively influenced by the misrepresentation. The same requirement is found in
respect of the hypothetical influence of material facts undisclosed: see 5.52 and 5.53.

In general contract law received doctrine is that it is irrelevant that the representee was care- **5.46**
less in not discovering that the representation was untrue. The usual citation in support is
Redgrave v Hurd. That decision can be explained, however, on the basis that the representor
should himself have been much better informed than the misrepresentee (about relevant documents in his own possession).[133] A review of precedent today indicates that courts 'balance
the equities',[134] case by case; and that each time they ask whether the risk should be allocated

---

[126] *March Cabaret & Casino Club Ltd v London Assurance* [1975] 1 Lloyd's Rep 169, 177; *The Dora* [1989]
1 Lloyd's Rep 69, 93.
[127] *CTI Inc v Oceanus Mutual Underwriting Assn (Bermuda) Ltd* [1984] 1 Lloyd's Rep 475, 506, CA;
Brotherton v Aseguradora Colseguros (No 2) [2003] EWCA Civ 705, [2003] Lloyd's Rep IR 746; *North Star
Shipping Ltd v Sphere Drake Ins plc* [2006] EWCA Civ 378, [2006] 2 Lloyd's Rep 183.
[128] *North Star Shipping Ltd v Sphere Drake Ins plc* [2006] EWCA Civ 378, [2006] 2 Lloyd's Rep 183, at
[17]ff.
[129] *Brotherton (No 2)*, n 127, at [22], *per* Mance LJ.
[130] *Norwich Union Ins Ltd v Meisels* [2006] EWHC 2811, [2007] Lloyd's Rep IR 69, at [25].
[131] *Edgington v Fitzmaurice* (1885) 29 Ch D 459, 483, CA.
[132] In actions for damages for deceit, however, the general law requires causation: *Smith v Chadwick*
(1884) 9 App Cas 187, 195–196.
[133] (1881) 20 Ch D 1 (CA).
[134] See eg *Peekay v ANZ Banking Group Ltd* [2006] EWCA Civ 386, [2006] 2 Lloyd's Rep 511; and *Kyle
Bay Ltd (t/a Astons Night Club) v Underwriters* [2007] EWCA Civ 57, [2007] Lloyd's Rep IR 460. Furmston
(ed), *Butterworth's The Law of Contract* (4th edn, 2010) 4.42.

to the representor or the representee, as appropriate, applicant or insurer. In particular, they ask which party was better informed or best placed to be better informed. In the insurance world today that person will often be the representee, the insurer.[135]

E. Non-disclosure

(1) Disclosure

5.47 The duty of disclosure is sometimes described as a duty of insurance good faith,[136] or utmost good faith; but it is an information duty quite distinct from general duties of good faith recognised in civil law countries such as France and Germany. In the insurance context the issue of disclosure usually arises as a defence to a claim, so it is insurers who seek to prove breach of the duty, to prove *non*-disclosure. Note also that, if an insurer proves a prima facie breach, the defence will still fail, if the insured proves that the undisclosed fact was already known to the insurer[137] or that its disclosure was waived by the insurer.[138]

5.48 Disclosure means communication of material facts to the right persons,[139] persons in the company underwriting such risks. This may be done directly, eg, at Lloyd's,[140] or, in the case of mass risks, through an agent of the insurer who can be expected to pass the information to the underwriters. The information comprises all facts known to the applicant at the time of contracting that are material to the risk.

(2) Facts Material to the Risk

5.49 Material facts comprise every 'circumstance which would influence the judgement of a prudent insurer in fixing the premium, or determining whether he will take the risk': MIA, section 18(2), which states the common law rule applicable to both marine and non-marine insurance. The 'prudent insurer' is not the particular insurer[141] but a stereotype in the relevant sector of the market[142] at the time of the contract.[143] The stereotype is controversial. In Scotland and many other common law countries the point of reference is the 'reasonable insured'.[144]

5.50 For natural persons acting for purposes outside their trade, business or profession ('retail customers') the law changed with effect from 14 January 2005 on the entry into force of rules made under section 138 of the Financial Services and Markets Act 2000 (FSMA).[145] These included rules for general insurance, the Insurance Conduct of Business Rules (ICOBS),[146] which apply to all 'non-investment insurance contracts' other than reinsurance contracts and

---

[135] With careless insurers, courts may reach a similar result by finding that the insurer has waived the matter.

[136] Clarke, 2009, chs 23 and 27; MacGillivray, ch 17; P MacDonald Eggers, S Picken and P Foss, *Good Faith and Insurance Contracts* (3rd edn, 2010) ch 7ff.

[137] See 5.57.

[138] See 5.58.

[139] *Hadenfayre Ltd v British National Ins Sy Ltd* [1984] 2 Lloyd's Rep 393.

[140] Concerning Lloyd's see Clarke, 2009, 11-3; and J Burling and K Lazarus (eds), *Research Handbook on International Insuramce Law and Regulation* (2011) chs 17 and 18.

[141] cf the requirement of inducement: 5.53.

[142] *Zurich General Accident & Liability Ins Co Ltd v Morrison* [1942] 2 KB 53, 58, CA; *CTI Inc v Oceanus Mutual Underwriting Assn (Bermuda) Ltd* [1984] 1 Lloyd's Rep 476, 511.

[143] *Associated Oil Carriers Ltd v Union Ins Sy of Canton Ltd* [1917] 2 KB 184.

[144] *Cuthbertson v Friends' Provident Life Office* 2006 SLT 597.

[145] Clarke 2009, 7–1.

[146] <http://fsahandbook.info/FSA/handbook.jsp?doc=/handbook/ICOBS>.

'contracts of large risks' (marine, aviation and transport, credit and surety and other commercial risks) where the risk is situated outside the EEA.[147]

ICOBS (Rules 8.1.1 and 2) provide that 'except where there is evidence of fraud', insurers **5.51** must 'not unreasonably reject a claim' on the grounds of non-disclosure of a fact material to the risk that the retail customer *could not reasonably be expected to have disclosed*, thus basing the test of materiality not on the perspective of prudent insurers but on the view of reasonable applicants. However, insurers prohibited from rejecting a claim by this Rule are still free to decide that they want a claimant off their books and rescind the contract on the basis of the common law and the stricter prudent's insurer test.

(3) Influence

As with actionable misrepresentation,[148] material facts must be such as would 'influence' the **5.52** judgement of prudent insurers: MIA, section 18(2)—applicable to both marine and non-marine insurance. Influence does not have to be decisive in the sense that, if a fact had been disclosed, the insurer would have declined the risk or offered different terms. It is enough that prudent insurers would have considered it relevant;[149] there are nonetheless degrees of relevance. 'The difference is whether the relevance of the hypothetical facts, assuming that they had been disclosed, is judged at the moment the underwriter is deciding whether or not to accept the risk or at the moment when he undertakes an investigation of the risk'.[150] The former is the Australian view and probably the UK position also.[151] Exception is made for information which evidently diminishes rather than increases the risk: that might well influence judgement but does not have to be disclosed.[152] Note also that, except in cases of fraud, when materiality is not required,[153] there is a similar 'influence' rule for operative misrepresentation.[154]

(4) Inducement

The mildness of the requirement of influence on prudent insurers[155] matters little because, **5.53** whether misrepresented or undisclosed, the facts must also have induced the *actual* insurer to contract the insurance—decisively. The facts must have been such that, if they had been disclosed, the insurer would have declined the risk or offered less favourable terms.[156] However, this stricter requirement is easily met: where there 'is a material representation *calculated to induce* him to enter into the contract, it is an inference of fact that he *was* induced by the representation to enter into it'.[157] This is a presumption of general contract law applicable to misrepresentations that applies also to insurance contracts for both misrepresentation and non-disclosure.[158] Examples in property insurance are past fires or theft at the premises insured.

---

[147] ICOBS 1 Annex 1.
[148] Section D.5.
[149] *Pan Atlantic Ins Co Ltd v Pine Top Ins Co Ltd* [1995] 1 AC 501.
[150] *Barclay Holdings (Australia) Pty Ltd v British National Ins Co Ltd* (1987) 8 NSWLR 514, 523.
[151] *CTI*, n 143.
[152] See *The Dora* [1989] 1 Lloyd's Rep 69, 90.
[153] *Smith v Kay* (1859) 4 HLC 750.
[154] See 5.45.
[155] See 5.45.
[156] *Pan Atlantic Ins Co Ltd v Pine Top Ins Co Ltd* [1995] 1 AC 501.
[157] *Redgrave v Hurd* (1881) 20 Ch D 1, 21, CA, emphasis supplied. See also in this sense: *Smith v Chadwick* (1884) 9 App Cas 187, 196; and *Halsbury's Laws of England* (4th edn), Vol 31, para 1067, which was applied to a case of non-disclosure in *St Paul Fire & Marine Ins Co (UK) v McConnell Dowell Constructors* [1995] 2 Lloyd's Rep 116, 127, CA.
[158] *Assicurazioni Generali SpA v ARIG* [2002] EWCA Civ 1642, [2003] 1 WLR 577, at [61], CA. That is what Lord Mustill referred to as a 'presumption of inducement': *Pan Atlantic*, n 156, at 551. The presumption was applied, eg, in *Aneco Reinsurance Underwriting Ltd v Johnson & Higgins Ltd* [1998] 1 Lloyd's Rep 565.

5.54 Except in such cases of presumed inducement, inducement must be proved by insurers.[159] Proof might take the form of evidence from the practice of the actual underwriter, if available.[160] If not, insurers might show that the market (of prudent underwriters) would have been induced thereby and therefore, it probably had that effect on the actual underwriter.[161] A plea of misrepresentation is open to the objection that it was not relied upon by the insurer in question and thus did not induce the particular contract.[162] Likewise, claimants may argue that undisclosed information would have had no effect if disclosed because the insurer relied on its own sources or investigation; insurers often send assessors to survey the risk, eg, of fire and burglary. The insurer's reply may well be, of course, that reliance was placed on the application as well as the assessors' report. However, if the claimant's objection succeeds, the insurer's plea fails for want of inducement.

(5) Facts Known to Applicants

5.55 A misrepresentation is actionable nonetheless because what made it untrue was some fact quite unknown to the applicant. Non-disclosure, however, is not actionable at all if the information is not something that applicants knew or could reasonably be expected to know.[163] Applicants are expected to know, first, information they can be expected to acquire 'in the ordinary course of business'.[164] Second, they are treated as knowing what is known or should be known to their agents.[165] The agents include not only agents they employ to contract the insurance[166] but also those employed for some other purpose but whose work includes the receipt or collation of relevant information.[167] Applicants should check with such persons before contracting insurance. Third, the knowledge of a firm may be composite. A chief executive officer, who may well be the person contracting the insurance, may be taken to know something known only to the chairman,[168] including knowledge acquired by the latter before becoming chairman.[169]

5.56 Composite knowledge has become problematic as firms, not least partnerships, have become larger. Prima facie professionals in partnership are insured against partnership liability jointly. In England the received rule is that when two or more persons 'are jointly insured and their interests are inseparably connected so that loss or gain necessarily affects them [all] the misconduct of one is sufficient to contaminate the whole insurance'.[170] The skeleton in the cupboard may bring the whole house down. The past peculations of one partner may leave the rest without cover. Although the 'contamination' rule does not apply to insurance that is not joint but composite,[171] it still applies to joint insurance. In Canada, which received the

---

[159] *Assicurazioni Generali v ARIG* [2003] 1 WLR 577, at [61], CA, *per* Clarke LJ.

[160] See eg *GE Capital Corporate Finance Group v Bankers Trust Co* [1995] 1 WLR 172, CA, concerning the disclosure of past transactions that might bear on investment strategy.

[161] See eg *St Paul Fire*, n 157.

[162] *Smith v Land & House Property Corp* (1884) 28 Ch D 7, 15, CA.

[163] *Joel v Law Union & Crown Ins Co* [1908] 2 KB 863, CA. This rule was not changed by the Consumer Insurance (Disclosure and Representations) Act 2012, however, the more focussed questions that must now be asked by insurers (s 2) may well 'jog' memories.

[164] *Proudfoot v Montefiore* (1867) LR 2 QB 511, 521–522. cf *PCW Syndicates v PCW Reinsurers* [1996] 1 All ER 774, CA.

[165] *Blackburn v Vigors* (1887) 12 App Cas 531, 536–537. MIA, s 19.

[166] *ANZ Ltd v Colonial & Eagle Wharves Ltd* [1960] 2 Lloyd's Rep 241; *Group Josi Re v Walbrook Ins Co Ltd* [1996] 1 WLR 1152, CA. It matters not that the material information was acquired while working for another client: *PCW*, n 164, at 149 and 157.

[167] *Blackburn v Vigors* (1887) 12 App Cas 531, 541.

[168] *Regina Fur Co v Bossom* [1957] 2 Lloyd's Rep 466.

[169] *ERC Frankona Re v American Nat Ins* Co [2005] EWHC 1381, [2006] Lloyd's Rep IR 157.

[170] *Samuel v Dumas* [1924] AC 431, 445.

[171] *New Hampshire Ins Co v MGN Ltd* [1997] LRLR 24, CA.

same rule from England, the Supreme Court has based the 'contamination' rule on contract interpretation rather than public policy,[172] and has thus enabled lower courts to leave the liability cover of large firms of lawyers intact.[173] Courts in England may well follow that line today.[174] Meanwhile groups contracting insurance can contract out of the 'contamination' rule with clauses, described as 'anti-avoidance clauses' or 'incontestable clauses'.[175]

(6) Facts Known to Insurers

Applicants are not obliged to disclose material facts already known to the insurer.[176] For example, every insurer 'is presumed to be acquainted with the practice of the trade he insures.'[177] Moreover, insurers are expected to keep up with current affairs and to make a connection between reported events and the kind of risks they cover. However, insurers are not expected to recall facts peculiar to a particular applicant, unless referred to the relevant sources by the applicant, even if the facts have been widely reported in the media. This is especially true of past events, however prominently reported at the time, and which appeared then to have no bearing on the insurer's business but which turn out to be relevant to a risk written later.[178] Moreover, even where relevant information is on file, English precedent does not expect insurers to retrieve it and check it before writing new risks. However, the precedents concerned paper records[179] and, in the light of decisions in other common law countries,[180] it may well be that the use of computers and the availability of powerful search engines will lead to different decisions in future.

5.57

(7) Waiver

Insurers cannot plead non-disclosure of information, the disclosure of which they have waived. The possibility of waiver arises at three points in the relationship. First, insurers may waive disclosure altogether from the beginning. Marine cargo insurers commonly contract 'seaworthiness admitted': consignors are not expected to know material information about the suitability of the vessel in question.[181] Second, where material information has been disclosed but not in sufficient detail to enable prudent insurers to assess its full significance, insurers may press for further particulars. If they do not, the result is that they have waived (further) performance of the duty, as regards those particulars. This type of waiver sometimes shades into the first type. Third, sometimes when a claim comes in, insurers discover non-disclosure, but nonetheless wish to affirm the contract and keep the customer. Strictly

5.58

---

[172] *Scott v Wawanesa Mutual Ins Co* (1989) 59 DLR (4th) 660, 667, SCC; apparently the view taken in *Samuel v Dumas*, n 170. cf the more recent *State of The Netherlands v Youell* [1998] 1 Lloyd's Rep 236, CA.

[173] See *Fisher v Guardian Ins Co Ltd* (1995) 123 DLR (4th) 336, 350.

[174] If they have not already done so.

[175] *Anstey v British Natural Premium Life Assn Ltd* (1908) 24 TLR 871, CA; and *Toomey v Eagle Star Ins Co Ltd (No 2)* [1995] 2 Lloyd's Rep 88. The clauses are also referred to as 'severability' clauses and (eg, in Australia) as 'non-imputation' and 'truth of statement' clauses.

[176] *Carter v Boehm* (1766) 3 Burr 1905, 1911. MIA, s 18(3)(b). cf *HIH Casualty & General Ins Ltd v Chase Manhattan Bank* [2003] Lloyd's Rep IR 230, at [86]–[87], HL.

[177] *Noble v Kennaway* (1780) 2 Doug 511, 513.

[178] *Bates v Hewitt* (1867) LR 2 QB 595; *Greenhill v Federal Ins Co* [1927] 1 KB 65, CA; *Malhi v Abbey Life Assurance Co Ltd* [1996] LRLR 237, CA. The point is controversial; cf *Carter v Boehm* (1766) 3 Burr 1905; *Glencore Int v Alpina Ins Co Ltd* [2003] EWHC 2792 (Comm), [2004] 1 Lloyd's Rep 111. Clarke, 2006, 23-9B.

[179] *Malhi v Abbey Life Assurance Co Ltd* [1996] LRLR 237, CA. cf *Columbia National Life Ins Co v Rodgers*, 116 F 2d 705 (10 Cir, 1940), cert den 313 US 561.

[180] eg *Coronation Ins Co v Taku Air Transport Ltd* (1991) 85 DLR (4th) 609, SCC.

[181] Concerning non-marine insurance, see *HIH Casualty & General Ins Ltd v Chase Manhattan Bank* [2001] 1 Lloyd's Rep 30, at [23].

speaking that is waiver not of disclosure but of the right of rescission. In the third instance, in particular, the waiver argument is sometimes framed as estoppel.[182]

5.59 Omission to answer any questions at all about the risk at the beginning and failure of the insurer to object is not waiver.[183] That is not the positive conduct required by the law for waiver. However, if insurers ask questions about some things but not about other related things, that may amount to waiver of disclosure of the latter.[184] For example, to ask about burglaries on the premises over the last five years is waiver (of the second kind) about information about any burglaries before that. An instance of a similar kind arises where applicants have disclosed information which puts insurers on enquiry but insurers do not pursue the matter. That is waiver of what enquiry would have disclosed.[185] In the landmark case of *Carter v Boehm*,[186] insurance was taken out in 1760 on 'Fort Marlborough', which was located, as the insurer knew, in a potential theatre of war. Lord Mansfield held that, given the insurer's knowledge, it was for the insurer to enquire about the defences and the likelihood of successful attack. For many years, however, a relatively mundane instance of this kind of waiver has been where applicants give the insurer the opportunity to consult documents,[187] such as the proposer's records. The applicant is considered to have disclosed the contents of all the documents concerned.

(8) Consumers

5.60 With effect from 2013, if an applicant is a consumer, the common law duty of disclosure to *volunteer* material information to insurers was 'replaced' by a duty to answer questions raised by the insurer.[188]

F. Remedies

(1) Rescission[189]

5.61 The effect of operative misrepresentation or non-disclosure is that the insurer's consent to the insurance contract is flawed. Accordingly, the purpose of any remedy at law is to negate the effect. To achieve this an award of damages would be neither inappropriate nor without precedent.[190] However, no award of such damages in favour of insurers has been reported. Moreover, a right to damages for breach of the insurance duty of good faith, as such, has been rejected.[191] In practice the insurer's remedy lies in avoidance of the contract,

---

[182] There are differences between waiver and estoppel but the differences are usually of no consequence in context: Clarke, 2009, 23-11 and 26-4; MacGillivray, 17–83ff.

[183] *McCormick v National Motor & Accident Ins Union* (1934) 49 Ll L Rep 361, 363; *Schoolman v Hall* [1951] 1 Lloyd's Rep 139, CA.

[184] *Schoolman v Hall* [1951] 1 Lloyd's Rep 139, 143, CA; *Roberts v Plaisted* [1989] 2 Lloyd's Rep 341, CA; *Wise (Underwriting Agency) Ltd v Grupo Nacional Provincial SA* [2004] EWCA Civ 962, [2004] 2 Lloyd's Rep 483, at [118] CA.

[185] *Asfar & Co v Blundell* [1896] 1 QB 123, 129, CA.

[186] (1766) 3 Burr 1905. cf *Greenhill* v *Federal Ins Co* [1927] 1 KB 65, CA.

[187] *Pan Atlantic Ins Co Ltd v Pine Top Ins Co Ltd* [1993] 1 Lloyd's Rep 496, CA, aff'd on other grounds: [1995] 1 AC 501.

[188] The Consumer Insurance (Disclosure and Representations) Act 2012, s 2(4). However, if they are an unusually bad risk, it appears that under residual common law consumers must disclose this to the insurer, whether asked about it or not.

[189] See EPL 8.175ff.

[190] eg. under the Misrepresentation Act 1967, s 2(1) or, in the case of fraud, for the tort of deceit: *London Assurance Co v Clare* (1937) 57 Ll L Rep 254, 270.

[191] *Banque Financière de la Cite SA v Westgate Ins Co Ltd* [1990] QB 665, CA, aff'd on different grounds: [1991] 2 AC 249. cf *HIH Casualty & General Ins Ltd v Chase Manhattan Bank* [2001] EWCA Civ 1250, [2001] 2 Lloyd's Rep 483, at [163] and [169].

rescission.[192] Rescission is not automatic. Insurers have a right of election: they can either rescind the contract or affirm the contract,[193] and if the choice is rescission, that requires not court intervention but simply notice to the insured. Rescission dates from the time of notice.[194] The effect is that it 'terminates the contract, puts the parties *in statu quo ante* and restores things, as between them, to the position in which they stood before the contract was entered into'.[195] Rescission, therefore, is retroactive and must be total.[196] Thus, insurers are not liable for claims arising prior to the date of rescission. Moreover, as a matter of general principle of restitution, insurers must return premium,[197] unless the contract provides otherwise.[198]

As regards retroactivity, exception is made, first, for extensions of cover, which are treated as **5.62** severable parts of the main contract so that what happens to the extension does not necessarily affect the rest of the contract.[199] Second, exception is made for arbitration clauses,[200] which are regarded as distinct from or collateral to the main contract. When that is rescinded the clauses survive. Third, by analogy, the same applies to jurisdiction clauses.[201] Fourth, if a single policy covers two distinct classes of property, each being a distinct subject of insurance, rescission as regards one class may not affect the other.[202] Similarly, in the case of a single policy covering jointly the liability of a number of members of a firm, the current tendency is to see the policy as one recording as many contracts as there are members insured, so that avoidance of one does not affect the others.[203] Finally, when ICOBS came into force in January 2005,[204] insurers entitled to rescind insurance on account of non-disclosure or misrepresentation might nonetheless be bound to pay the claim, as long as the claimant was not in business or fraudulent.[205] This rule applies, it seems, whether in a particular case insurers elect to rescind the contract or not.

(2) Limits on Rescission

In the case of misrepresentations made 'otherwise than fraudulently', ie those made negli- **5.63** gently or innocently, section 2(2) of the Misrepresentation Act 1967 gives courts a discretion to refuse rescission and to award damages instead. Section 2(2) affects any person who 'has entered into a contract after a misrepresentation has been *made* to him'.[206] Hence, it seems,

---

[192] The words are used 'more or less interchangeably': *HIH Casualty & General Ins Ltd v Chase Manhattan Bank* [2001] EWCA Civ 1250, [2001] 2 Lloyd's Rep 483, at [174].

[193] *Mackender v Feldia AG* [1966] 2 Lloyd's Rep 449, 455, CA.

[194] *Reese River Silver Mining Co Ltd v Smith* (1869) LR 4 HL 64.

[195] *Abram Steamship Co Ltd v Westville Shipping Co Ltd* [1923] AC 773, 781; see also *Johnson v Agnew* [1980] AC 367.

[196] *Urquhart v Macpherson* (1878) 3 App Cas 831, PC; *West v National Motor & Accident Union* [1955] 1 Lloyd's Rep 207, CA. For exceptions, see Clarke, 2009, 23-17C.

[197] *Cornhill Ins Co Ltd v L & B Assenheim* (1937) 58 Ll L Rep 27, 31.

[198] *Sun Fire Office v Hart* (1889) 14 App Cas 98, PC.

[199] *The Star Sea* [1997] 1 Lloyd's Rep 360, 370, CA.

[200] *Harbour Ins Co (UK) Ltd v Kansa General Inteernational Ins Co Ltd* [1992] 1 Lloyd's Rep 81, 91.

[201] *Pan Atlantic Ins Co Ltd v Pine Top Ins Co Ltd* [1993] 1 Lloyd's Rep 496, 502, CA.

[202] By analogy with breach of insurance warranty, and *Printpak v AGF Ins Ltd* [1999] Lloyd's Rep IR 542, CA.

[203] See 5.56.

[204] See 5.50.

[205] Rule 7.3.6 (2). cf ICOBS, Rule 8.1.2(1), in force since 6 January 2008 which replaced ICOB Rule 7.3.6(2) with a similar rule.

[206] Emphasis added.

[207] See 5.61 and *Highlands Ins Co v Continental Ins Co* [1987] 1 Lloyd's Rep 109, 118.

whereas it applies to half truths—statements literally true but rendered false by related omission, it does not apply to 'pure' non-disclosure. Insurance cases are likely to be few and far between.[207]

5.64 A second limit is affirmation of the contract, sometimes called waiver of the right to rescind, by misrepresentee insurers. This must 'be an informed choice made with knowledge of the facts giving rise to the right'.[208] If insurers know the true facts about the risk, knowledge of the right to rescind will be presumed;[209] and if then they affirm the cover unequivocally, they lose the right to rescind on this occasion and the cover continues. That is the rule, whether policyholders rely on the affirmation or not.[210] However, reliance has the lesser function that, if present, it will clinch the matter, eg, in cases in which insurers remain silent and the insurer's intention, to affirm or not, is unclear. In *Clough*,[211] Mellor J said that 'as long as he has made no election, he retains the right to determine it either way, subject to this, that if, in the interval whilst he is deliberating,…in consequence of his delay, the position even of the wrongdoer is affected, it will preclude him from exercising his right to rescind'. Delay in reaching a decision is sometimes stated to be a distinct bar to rescission. The better view of the insurance cases, however, is probably that it is not a distinct bar but a kind of affirmation.[212]

5.65 A third limit may be unconscionability: that to allow rescission would be unfair to the policyholder. The issue arises in cases where, by the time the insurer purports to rescind, it has become clear that the misrepresentation or non-disclosure was such that, had the insurer been aware of the true or full picture at the time of contracting, the insurer would have issued exactly the same policy anyway. The short answer originally given obiter in *Brotherton*[213] appears to be that insurers can rescind nonetheless; the alleged limit does not exist. Insurers can rescind simply by notice[214] and thus without court control or supervision. Further, issues of materiality and inducement should be judged at the time of contract only and not later when the contract is rescinded.[215] The question was more directly in point subsequently in *Drake*[216] in which the Court of Appeal majority confirmed that insurers' rights to rescind depend not on what was disclosed at the time of contract but on the true facts at that time, as they appeared later. On the broader question whether, if an insurer had a right to avoid for non disclosure, that right was constrained by the doctrine of good faith, Rix LJ, in particular, gave a cautious and qualified but affirmative answer.[217] His answer appears to be in accord with general contract law,[218] as well as judicial statements about rescission. Lord Lloyd once reminded us that, as 'Lord Mansfield warned in *Carter v Boehm*,…, there may be circumstances in which an insurer, by asserting a right to avoid for non-disclosure, would himself be

---

[208] *The Kanchenjunga* [1990] 1 Lloyd's Rep 391, 399, HL; *Eagle Star Ins Co Ltd v National Westminster Finance Australia Ltd* (1985) 58 ALR 165, 174, PC; *Hill v Citadel Ins Co Ltd* [1997] LRLR 167, CA.

[209] *Eagle Star Ins Co Ltd v National Westminster Finance Australia Ltd* (1985) 58 ALR 165, 174, PC.

[210] *The Kanchenjunga*, n 208.

[211] *Clough v LNWR* (1871) LR 7 Ex 26, 35; see also *Morrison v Universal Marine Ins Co* (1873) LR 8 Ex 197, Ex Ch; *Simon Haynes, Barlas & Ireland v Beer* (1945) 78 Ll L Rep 337, 369.

[212] See eg *Allen v Robles*, [1969] 2 Lloyd's Rep 61, 64, CA.

[213] *Brotherton v Asegurado Colseguros SA (No 2)* [2003] EWCA Civ 704, [2003] Lloyd's Rep IR 746.

[214] See 5.61.

[215] *Brotherton*, n 213, at [27]ff, *per* Mance LJ.

[216] *Drake Ins plc v Provident Ins plc* [2003] EWCA Civ 1834, [2004] QB 601.

[217] *Drake Ins plc v Provident Ins plc* [2003] EWCA Civ 1834, [2004] QB 601, at [88]ff.

[218] Clarke, 2009, 23-181.

[219] *Pan Atlantic Ins Co Ltd v Pine Top Ins Co Ltd* [1995] 1 AC 501, 555; *Carter v Boehm* (1766) 3 Burr 1906, 1918.

[220] At [85]–[86], together with a similar statement by Lord Hobhouse in the *Star Sea, Manifest Shipping Co Ltd v Uni-Polaris Shipping Co Ltd* [2001] UKHL 1, [2003] 1 AC 469, at [57]. See also *Spence v Crawford* [1939] 3 All ER 271, 278.

guilty of want of utmost good faith.'[219] This reminder was accepted by Rix LJ in *Drake*,[220] who concluded inter alia that 'the doctrine of good faith should be capable of limiting the insurer's right to avoid in circumstances where that remedy, which has been described in recent years as draconian, would operate unfairly'.[221]

(3) Clauses Affecting Rescission

The right to rescind for non-disclosure is commonly modified by policy terms, whereby, eg, the insurer undertakes not to 'exercise its rights to avoid this Policy where it is alleged that there has been non-disclosure or misrepresentation of facts' by the insured, provided that the insured shall establish to the satisfaction of the insurer that the insured in this regard was 'free of any fraudulent conduct or intent to deceive'. **5.66**

(a) Validity

One issue arising out of these clauses is the 'bootstrap' point. In *Toomey (No 2)*,[222] a reinsurer pleaded misrepresentation and the claimant insurer countered by reliance on a clause, which stated that the reinsurance was 'neither cancellable nor avoidable by either party'. However, the reinsurer argued that the defences was circular: the clause could only be effective if contained in a valid contract not subject to avoidance; but contracts like that *in casu* were valid only if the clause was effective. The logic of this objection appealed to Colman J, but he felt bound by precedent[223] and analogy with jurisdiction and arbitration clauses, which survive avoidance or termination of the contract. However, the analogy is rough. A clause about forum or dispute procedure is more easily detached from the core of the contract than one concerning the very validity of the contract itself. **5.67**

Could the same result be achieved without resorting to the dubious logic of bootstraps? Colman J started from the premise that the clause was an exclusion of liability in favour of a party in breach of duty imposed by the contract or by the law. Subsequently Aikens J started from a different premise.[224] Given that the scope of the duty of disclosure can be limited by what is (or is not) required of applicants when they complete the application, 'it is conceptually possible to draft a clause in a contract of insurance whereby the parties agree that the *duty of disclosure* of the assured (or his agent) is excluded'. In other words, if applicants are not obliged to disclose something, the contract cannot be breached on that account, the contract is valid and the clause also.[225] For misrepresentation the Aikens approach is more difficult. English law does not normally speak of a 'duty' not to misrepresent facts, a duty to be excluded by contract, as the judge suggested. Given, however, the context—utmost good faith, the law might well countenance waiver on certain points of duty to make an accurate presentation of the risk. Courts are likely to be receptive to argument for enforcing clauses modifying the sometimes exorbitant effects of misrepresentation and non-disclosure, if that is what parties have intended. **5.68**

---

[221] *Drake*, n 216, at [87]. On the facts of *Drake*, however, he concluded at [90] that it was not 'open to this court to go behind the finding of the judge that Provident acted in perfectly good faith in avoiding the contract'. Further see M Clarke, 'Rescission: a bridge too far for insurance good faith?' [2012] LMCLQ 611.

[222] *Toomey v Eagle Star Ins Co Ltd (No 2)* [1995] 2 Lloyd's Rep 88.

[223] See *Pan Atlantic Ins Co Ltd v Pine Top Ins Co Ltd* [1993] 1 Lloyd's Rep 496, 502, CA.

[224] *HIH Casualty & General Ins Ltd v Chase Manhattan Bank* [2001] 1 Lloyd's Rep 30.

[225] [2001] 1 Lloyd's Rep 30, at [24]; see also [64]. This point, not central to the appeal, was apparently accepted: [2001] 2 Lloyd's Rep 483, at [128] and [141]. Likewise: [2003] UKHL 6, [2003] 2 Lloyd's Rep 61, HL, at [6] and [59].

(b) The satisfied insurer

5.69 Another issue is the meaning of 'the satisfaction of the insurer'. How demanding are insurers entitled to be? In other insurance contexts the meaning has been limited to particulars 'with which reasonable men would be satisfied'.[226] More recently, in such a case,[227] insurers argued that it was sufficient that their decision (not to pay) was made in (subjective) good faith. The effect of the argument would have been that insurers would be judge in their own cause, unless claimants could successfully challenge their good faith in court. Against that argument, the claimant contended that the insurers were under an implied obligation to act reasonably. Tuckey J drew a distinction between the evidence insurers can call for ('vouching'), and their evaluation of that evidence; and held that the 'proof satisfactory' clause was confined to 'vouching' and, moreover, that their evidential demands must be reasonable. As to evaluation, in the absence of precedent, the judge was less sure. To reach a result that 'the insurer's decision to reject an adequately vouched claim cannot be disputed in the courts on grounds other than lack of good faith', as contended by the insurers, 'very clear words would be required'. However, to say that the insurers evaluation must always be reasonable, as contended by the claimant, was not 'necessary'. Moreover, if so 'the Court's role is restricted. I feel instinctively unhappy about such a restriction'.[228] *Quaere* whether in practice insurers' evidential demands ('vouching') and evaluation of the evidence can be easily separated.

G. Cover

(1) Insuring Clauses

5.70 Insurance buyers pay for cover: usually the right to a sum of money on the occurrence of the insured event. In the case of contingency (non-indemnity) insurance, notably life insurance, the sum is fixed, and the amount depends mainly on how much (premium) is paid for the cover. In the case of indemnity insurance, the insurance money payable depends principally on the amount of loss suffered. Consequential loss is not covered unless specifically insured.[229] Constructive total loss is recoverable in marine insurance only.[230] Cover, notably the insured event, is defined in the insuring clauses of the policy.

(i) In property insurance, the event is usually damage to identified property caused by stated perils. Damage to tangible property usually means a change in the physical state of the property.[231] Damage has also been described as 'mischief done to property',[232] but the precise meaning depends on the context.[233]

---

[226] *Moore v Woolsey* (1854) 4 El & Bl 243, 256. See also in his sense: *London Guarantie Co v Fearnley* (1880) 5 App Cas 911, 916, *per* Lord Blackburn. Idem re party discretion in other commercial contexts; eg, *Niarchos (London) Ltd v Shell Tankers Ltd* [1961] 2 Lloyd's Rep 496; Clarke [2012] LMCLQ 611.

[227] *Napier v UNUM* [1996] 2 Lloyd's Rep 550.

[228] *Napier v UNUM* [1996] 2 Lloyd's Rep 550, 553–554.

[229] *Theobald v Railway Passengers Assurance Co* (1854) 10 Exch 45.

[230] *Moore v Evans* [1918] AC 185; MIA, s 60. Rose, 21.2ff.

[231] *Bolton MBC v Municipal Mutual Ins Ltd* [2006] EWCA Civ 50, [2006] 1 WLR 1492. See also *Pilkington (UK) Ltd v CGU Ins plc* [2004] EWCA Civ 23, [2004] Lloyd's Rep IR 891.

[232] *Smith v Brown* (1871) 40 LJQB 214, 218.

[233] *Swansea Corp v Harpur* [1912] 3 KB 493, CA.

[234] eg *Dhak v INA (UK) Ltd* [1996] 1 Lloyd's Rep 632, CA.

[235] *De Souza v Home & Overseas Ins Co Ltd* [1995] LRLR 453, CA. *Hawley v Luminar Leisure* [2006] EWCA Civ 18, [2006] Lloyd's Rep IR 307.

(ii) Personal accident insurance covers accidental 'bodily injury', ie, any localized abnormal condition of the living body, trauma both outside and inside the body,[234] but not disease.[235]

(iii) All risks insurance covers any loss or damage to property which was not a certainty at the time of contract.[236] Excluded, therefore, are the effects of inherent vice,[237] and ordinary wear and tear.[238] Also excluded, as it is in all kinds of insurance, is that caused by policyholders' 'wilful misconduct'.[239]

(iv) People sometimes say that there is no smoke without fire, but for fire insurance, there must be ignition.[240] If so, there is fire regardless of cause, be it lightning,[241] spontaneous ignition[242] or arson by a third party.[243] Explosions caused by fire are covered[244] but not fires caused by explosion,[245] although they are often included expressly in fire insurance policies. Fire caused by policyholder negligence is covered[246] but not fire started deliberately (wilful misconduct) unless for some greater good, eg, lest shipping fall into enemy hands.[247] Fire cover includes the immediate consequences of fire: damage by water to extinguish fire,[248] by smoke[249] and by falling masonry,[250] but not loss caused by theft or looting.[251]

(v) Liability insurance covers the monetary impact of legal claims[252] against policyholders and, crucially, sometimes the cost of defending claims.[253] 'Claims made' insurance covers claims made against policyholders during the period of cover. However, policies often cover claims brought after the period, provided that the insurer has been notified during the insurance period of circumstances suggesting that such a claim might be brought.[254] As insurance generally does not cover loss deliberately or wilfully caused by the insured, liability does not cover deliberate breach of contract, lest policyholders be tempted to transfer to their insurer their liability loss on a bad deal.

---

[236] *British & Foreign Marine Ins Co Ltd v Gaunt* [1921] 2 AC 41.

[237] Inherent vice means the risk of deterioration of the goods shipped as a result of their natural behaviour in the ordinary course of events without the intervention of any fortuitous external accident or casualty: *The Cendor Mopu, Global Process Systems* v *Syarikat Takaful Malaysia* [2011] UKSC 5, [2011] 1 Lloyd's Rep 560; see, in particular, Lord Clarke at [110]–[111].

[238] *Gaunt*, n 236, at 46.

[239] *Gaunt*, n 236, at 57. The current definition of 'wilful misconduct' has been developed largely in the context of the carriage of goods, for which see, eg, M Clarke, *Contracts of Carriage by Air* (2nd edn, 2010) 142ff.

[240] *Everett v London Assurance Co* (1865) 19 CB (NS) 126.

[241] *Gordon v Rimmington* (1807) 1 Camp 123.

[242] *Tempus Shipping Co Ltd v Dreyfus & Co Ltd* [1930] 1 KB 699, 708.

[243] *Upjohn v Hitchens* [1918] 2 KB 48, CA.

[244] *Curtis & Harvey (Canada) Ltd v North British & Mercantile Ins Co Ltd* [1921] 1 AC 303, PC.

[245] *Boiler Inspection & Ins Co of Canada v Sherman-Williams Co of Canada Ltd* [1951] AC 319, PC.

[246] *Shaw v Robberds* (1837) 6 Ad & E 75; *Harris v Poland* [1941] 1 KB 462.

[247] *Gordon v Rimmington* (1807) 1 Camp 123.

[248] *Symington & Co v Union Ins Sy of Canton Ltd* (1928) 34 Com Cas 23, CA.

[249] *The Diamond* [1906] P 282.

[250] *Re Hooley Hill Rubber & Chemical Co Ltd v Royal Insurance Co Ltd* [1920] 1 KB 257, 271–272, CA.

[251] *Marsden v City & County Assurance Co* (1865) LR 1 CP 232.

[252] *Thorman v NHIC (UK) Ltd* [1988] 1 Lloyd's Rep 7, CA. Usually claims based in tort but not those based in contract; see eg *Tesco Stores Ltd v Constable* [2008] EWCA Civ 362, [2008] Lloyd's Rep IR 636, unless there is a 'Contractual Liability Extension'.

[253] eg *Callery v Gray (No 1)* [2002] UKHL 28, [2002] 1 WLR 2000; but not automatically: *Brice v JH Wackerbarth (Australasia) Pty ltd* [1974] 2 Lloyd's Rep 274, CA; and *Palmer v Palmer* [2008] EWCA Civ 46, [2008] Lloyd's Rep IR 535. Excluded is the cost of mitigating the state of property to avoid liability: *Yorkshire Water Services Ltd v Sun Alliance & London Ins Plc (No 1)* [1997] 2 Lloyd's Rep 21, CA.

[254] *J Rothschild Ins Plc v Collyear* [1999] Lloyd's Rep IR 6; *Layher Ltd v Lowe* [2000] Lloyd's Rep IR 510, CA.

[255] *Figre Ltd v Mander* [1999] Lloyd's Rep IR 193. Clarke, 2006, ch 13.

Insurance cover comes at a cost: premium, essentially monetary payment like any other. Time is not of the essence.[255] However, there are some harsh rules. In life insurance, if payment is later than the 'days of grace' allowed by the policy, cover ends and many years of 'investment' are lost. No property interest is involved so, even for aged and forgetful policyholders, there can be no relief against forfeiture.[256] Moreover, if indemnity cover 'has once commenced, there shall be no apportionment or return of premium afterwards'.[257]

(2) Interpretation

5.71 When reading contracts, the overriding aim has sometimes been said to be to find the intention of the parties.[258] However, today the trend is to the 'objective theory' of interpretation; although the aim is still 'to give effect to the intention of the parties', the methodology 'is not to probe the real intentions of the parties but to ascertain the contextual meaning of the relevant contractual language. Intention is determined by reference to expressed rather than actual intention'.[259]

5.72 Insurance contracts have been described in the USA as the archetype of 'contracts of adhesion', tantamount to private or delegated legislation.[260] Legislation they are not: unlike that of some countries, English law does not prescribe the standard forms, these products are the proud work of insurers; there are many forms vying with each other in the market place. They are subject nonetheless to the same rules of interpretation as other commercial contracts,[261] an outline of which follows.

(i) Words are to be understood in their ordinary sense as they would be understood by ordinary people.[262] Ordinary people use a dictionary and are assumed to know what is going on in the world immediately around them.[263] Moreover, the ordinary person is a useful ally who can be summoned to the aid of a court that might have reason to eschew the pursuit of precision and construe words as a matter of impression.[264] Be that as it may, words are to be understood not in isolation but in context. The immediate context is a series of circles: the phrase, then the sentence, the paragraph and the policy section. In that context words are read with the aid of certain traditional canons of interpretation. The chief canons of interpretation are, first, that, if particular words have a generic character, more general following words are construed as having the same character (*eiusdem generis*). Thus 'flood' in 'storm, tempest or flood' means a sudden flood on a large scale.[265] Second, the express mention of one thing may imply the exclusion of another related thing (*expressio unius est exclusio alterius*). Thus if policy term A is expressed to be a 'condition precedent' to cover but policy term B is not, the inference is that indeed term B is not.[266]

---

[256] *The Scaptrade* [1983] 2 AC 694.
[257] *Tyrie v Fletcher* (1777) 2 Cowp 666, 668.
[258] Clarke, 2009, ch 15; MacGillivray, ch 11; and Summer, ch 5.
[259] *Deutsche Genossenschaftsbank v Burnhope* [1996] 1 Lloyd's Rep 113, 122, HL. See EPL 8.05ff.
[260] VP Goldberg, 'Institutional Change and the Quasi-Invisible Hand' (1974) 17 J L & Econ 461, 484.
[261] *Cementation Piling & Foundations Ltd v Aegon Ins Ltd* [1995] 1 Lloyd's Rep 97, 101, CA.
[262] eg, 'actually paid' means 'really paid' and not 'notionally paid' or 'prospectively paid': *Charter Re Co Ltd v Fagan* [1996] 2 Lloyd's Rep 113, 116, HL. The ordinary meaning will be ignored, however, if it is obvious that there has been an error: *Dumford Trading AG v OAO Atlantrybflot* [2005] EWCA Civ 24, [2005] 1 Lloyd's Rep 289, at [27], *per* Rix LJ.
[263] *Investors Compensation Scheme Ltd v West Bromwich BS* [1998] 1 WLR 896, 912, (HL).
[264] *Lewis Emanuel & Son Ltd v Hepburn* [1960] 1 Lloyd's Rep 304, 308.
[265] *Young v Sun Alliance & London Ins. Ltd* [1976] 2 Lloyds Rep 189, 191, (CA).
[266] *Home Ins Co v Victoria-Montreal Fire Ins Co* [1907] AC 59, 64.
[267] *Woolfall & Rimmer Ltd v Moyle* [1942] 1 KB 66, 73ff, (CA).

(ii) In the event of inconsistency in the ordinary meaning of words in different parts of the contract, courts adopt the meaning that best reflects the intention of the parties.[267] In particular, preference is given to non-standard parts of a policy, such as the Schedule, to which the parties gave actual attention[268] or which appear to better reflect their final intention.[269] In the important instance of inconsistency between a master policy and a certificate issued to a beneficiary of the policy, priority is accorded to the certificate.[270]

(iii) If it appears that the words have been used in a special sense, either, first, as previously defined by the courts, eg 'theft',[271] or, second, the sense used in a particular commercial context, such as 'motor racing',[272] the words will be interpreted in that special sense. The same is true of the sense used in a particular commercial context with which both parties are familiar.[273] This rule is justified as promoting the interests of certainty in commercial transactions.

(iv) If, after the application of rules (i) and (ii), the meaning remains unclear and rule (iii) does not assist, courts are faced with ambiguity. In this situation the words will be read with reference to any evidence of the immediate purpose of the wording;[274] and the words will be construed *contra proferentem*, ie against the insurer and liberally in favour of policyholders.[275] Ambiguity is a relative matter. At common law words are not ambiguous or unclear just because they are complex; if lawyers can find the meaning of words, the words are not ambiguous.[276] Consumers,[277] however, benefit from the Consumer Rights Act 2015, Part 2 (replacing the Unfair Terms in Consumer Contracts Regulations 1999).[278] Written contract terms must be 'expressed in plain and intelligible language',[279] plain and intelligible not only to lawyers but to non-lawyers.[280] To pronounce on particular wordings has been the responsibility of the Office of Fair Trading (OFT). The OFT has condemned 'legal jargon' such as 'indemnify', 'consequential loss', and 'events beyond your control'.[281]

(v) Rule (v) is the rule against absurdity.[282] The meaning of words must be intelligible but it does not have to be reasonable, however much courts dislike it, unless the result can be described as absurd. So, if application of the other rules produces a result that is so very unreasonable or inconvenient as to be absurd, that result will be ignored.[283] For example, the contention of an insurer that literal effect should be given to an exclusion of injury caused by degenerative conditions was rejected, because that would include the

---

[268] *Farmers Coop Ltd v National Benefit Assurance Co Ltd* (1922) 13 Ll L Rep 417, 530, 533, CA.

[269] *Izzard v Universal Ins Co Ltd* [1937] AC 773.

[270] *D & J Koskas v Standard Marine Ins Co Ltd* (1927) 32 Com Cas 160, CA; *De Monchy v Phoenix Ins Co of Hartford* (1928) 33 Com Cas 197, CA.

[271] *Deutsche Genossenschaftsbank v Burnhope* [1996] 1 Lloyd's Rep 113, HL. See also *The Starsin* [2004] 1 AC 75, [7]. cf policies for cover in other jurisdictions: *Canelhas Comercio Importacao e Exportacao Ltd v Wooldridge* [2004] EWCA Civ 984, [2004] Lloyd's Rep IR 914.

[272] *Scragg v UK Temperance & General Provident Institution* [1976] 2 Lloyd's Rep 227, 233.

[273] *The Kleovoulos of Rhodes* [2003] EWCA Civ 12, [2003] 1 Lloyd's Rep 138, [26].

[274] *Cornish v Accident Ins Co* (1889) 23 QBD 452, 456, (CA).

[275] eg *English v Western Ins Co* (1940) 67 Ll L Rep 45, CA.

[276] *Higgins v Dawson* [1902] AC 1.

[277] An individual contracting insurance wholly or mainly outside that individual's trade, business, craft, or profession: Consumer Rights Act 2015, s 2(3).

[278] SI 1999/2083.

[279] Consumer Rights Act 2015, s 64(3). See also s 69.

[280] *Unfair Contract Terms*, OFT Bulletin No 4, December 1997, 16.

[281] Respectively OFT Bulletin No 25 (8), No 5 (72) and No 25 (8). Bulletins can be read at <http://www.oft.gov.uk>. The OFT's role is now performed by the Competition and Markets Authority.

[282] *Smit Tak Offshore Services Ltd v Youell* [1992] 1 Lloyds Rep 154, 159, CA.

[283] *Prenn v Simmonds* [1971] 1 WLR 1381, 1385, HL.

[284] *Blackburn Rovers Football & Athletic Club plc v Avon* [2006] EWHC 840, [2005] Lloyd's Rep IR 239, reversed on different grounds: [2005] EWCA Civ 423, [2005] Lloyd's Rep IR 239. See also *Charter Reinsurance Ltd v Fagan* [1996] 2 Lloyds Rep 113, 118, HL.

normal ageing process and the effect would be substantially to deprive the policyholder of the protection that the insurance was designed to provide.[284] To find a sensible meaning, courts looks to the external context,[285] in particular the commercial purpose of the policy broadly conceived.

5.73 Contracts generally are interpreted in a broader context than in the past. In the past interpretation was conducted largely within the boundaries of the policy itself, in accordance with the parol evidence rule. Exceptions were confined to rule (iii) (ambiguity) and rule (v) (absurdity) where courts look beyond the policy to ascertain, eg, the purpose of the insurance. But in the *ICS* case[286] Lord Hoffmann said that the meaning of a document, 'is what the parties using those words against the relevant background would reasonably have been understood to mean'; and the background is 'absolutely anything which would have affected the way in which the language of the document would have been understood by a reasonable man', and which a reasonable man would have regarded as relevant,[287] except evidence of previous negotiations.[288] This statement opened the stable door once formed by the parol evidence rule.

5.74 Decisions reported since 1998 suggest that the impact of Lord Hoffmann's statement on insurance cases has been limited. In *MDIS Ltd v Swinbank*, eg, the Court of Appeal followed his approach but the background it looked at was something 'well known amongst insurance lawyers and indeed brokers for many years'.[289] Certain judges with experience of the Commercial court have been critical. It is 'hard to imagine a ruling more calculated to perpetuate the vast cost of commercial litigation'.[290] That was also the view of Saville LJ,[291] who raised the further objection that third parties 'are unlikely in the nature of things to be aware of the surrounding circumstances' in which the contract was concluded and are entitled to take the wording at face value. This point affects cargo and transit insurance, where buyers usually get an insurance document from their seller who contracted the cover, as well as employees insured under a group scheme arranged for them by their employer. Indeed, Lord Hoffmann did qualify his statement with the requirement that the background information must have been 'reasonably available to the parties'; and accessibility, surely, must take account of the parties' resources, both financial and otherwise. Lord Bingham approved the Hoffmann statement but continued: 'the court reads the terms of the contract as a whole, giving the words used their natural and ordinary meaning in the context of the agreement, the parties' relationship and all the relevant facts surrounding the transaction *so far as known to the parties*'.[292] Lord Hoffmann's statement, thus qualified, is now widely accepted but applied with caution.[293]

---

[285] *Toomey v Eagle Star Ins Co Ltd (No 1)* [1994] 1 Lloyd's Rep 516, 519–520, CA.

[286] *Investors Compensation Scheme Ltd v West Bromwich BS* [1998] 1 WLR 896, 912–913, HL.

[287] *BCCI SA v Ali (No 1)* [2002] UKHL 8, [2002] 1 AC 251, at [39].

[288] *Prenn v Simmonds* [1971] 1 WLR 1381, 1384, HL; and *Chartbrook v Persimmon Homes* [2009] UKHL 38, [2009] AC 1101, at [33] and [42], *per* Lord Hoffmann.

[289] *MDIS Ltd v Swinbank* [1999] Lloyd's Rep IR 516, 522, CA. Idem *King v Brandywine Reinsurance Co (UK) Ltd* [2005] EWCA Civ 235, [2005] 1 Lloyd's Rep 655, in which insurers were taken to be aware of what was available to them in the reinsurance market.

[290] C Staughton, 'Interpretation of Contracts' [1999] CLJ 303, 307. The Civil Procedure Rules, whereby judges assume responsibility for case management, state in Part 1.1 (2) (C) that the handling of a case is to be proportionate to the financial position of the parties.

[291] *Nat Bank of Sharjah v Dellborg*, CA, 9 July 1997; Thorpe and Judge LJJ concurred. Note also the observation of Lord Mance in *Durham v BAI* [2012] UKSC 14, [2012] 1 WLR 867, at [19].

[292] *BCCI v Ali* [2001] UKHL 8, [2001] 1 AC 251, at [8], emphasis added.

[293] eg *Estafnous v Leeds & London Business Centres* [2011] EWCA Civ 1157, [2011] 42 EG 121.

(3) Conditions

Policy terms can be grouped according to their function. Suppose motor insurance covering **5.75** (a) private saloon car SI23 JEB against inter alia theft, provided that (b) it is locked, and that (c) reasonable steps are taken to maintain the vehicle in efficient condition; and requiring also (d) that any theft be notified to the police and to the insurer within 48 hours.

(i) Term (a) defines cover in positive terms of the subject-matter of the insurance, the car, and the perils covered.[294] Term (b) is called an exception (but also sometimes an exclusion, restriction, or limit); this too defines cover but in negative terms, qualifying term (a). Term (c) also qualifies cover, but in a different way, and is called a warranty. Term (d) has nothing to do with the scope of cover, but is designed, in part at least, to make the contract less burdensome to the insurer; these are called procedural conditions and are considered later[295]

(ii) Term (a) is case-specific as regards the car. If the registration number is changed, the subject-matter remains the same and cover continues. If, however, the vehicle is modified, eg for rallying, or the policyholder replaces it, for the purpose of insurance the car originally insured no longer exists—just as if it had been destroyed. Cover ends.

(iii) Term (b) in common with term (c) may be called a condition and operates to defeat a claim. However, they differ importantly in that breach of (b) must be a cause of the loss claimed, whereas breach of (c) defeats a claim regardless. Moreover, if the policyholder is in breach of (b), the effect on cover is not permanent but only suspensive. However, if the brakes are out of order, unless repaired as soon as reasonably possible, their condition is a breach of warranty, term (c), and the effect is that the cover ends immediately and automatically. Breach of term (d), unlike the others, gives insurers a right, albeit one they never exercise, to damages, but generally does not defeat claims or end cover.

(4) Conditions Precedent: Warranties

Warranties are 'conditions precedent' to cover, and breach of warranty terminates cover,[296] **5.76** even though there may be no causal connection at all between the breach and either the loss that occurred or the risk of such loss.[297]

In marine insurance two important warranties, seaworthiness and legality, are implied by **5.77** statute.[298] However, to identify warranties generally, the first step is to see whether the contract itself classifies terms as such. What policies describe as 'conditions' are not necessarily warranties. On the one hand, the consequences of breach of warranty are so severe for policyholders that if 'there is any ambiguity, it must be construed most strongly against' the insurer[299] and, therefore, as something less draconian than a warranty. On the other hand, it is not necessary that the word 'warranty' be used.[300] In the past one way of creating warranties was to write a 'basis' clause, that the proposal 'shall be the basis of this contract', in the proposal. Courts, which regard them as a trap for most policyholders, are hostile to these

---

[294] Such as theft, a peril defined by law.

[295] See 5.86ff.

[296] *The Good Luck* [1992] 1 AC 233. However, insurers must not 'unreasonably reject a claim (including by terminating or avoiding a *policy*)' (Insurance Conduct of Business Rules (ICOBS) Rule 8.1.1(3)).

[297] *Dawsons Ltd v Bonnin* [1922] 2 AC 413. However, they are restrictively construed; see eg *Pratt v Aigaion Ins Co SA (The Resolute)* [2008] EWCA Civ 1314, [2009] 1 Lloyd's Rep 225, at [9]ff, *per* Sir Anthony Clarke, MR.

[298] Respectively MIA, s 39 and s 40. See Rose, 9.40ff.

[299] *Thomson v Weems* (1884) 9 App Cas 671, 682.

[300] *Dawsons*, n 297.

clauses,[301] and they have been legislatively nullified in consumer contracts.[302] Where policies do not settle the issue, courts seek the essential nature of the term by asking whether it is aimed at circumstances which give rise to an increase of risk that is more than *temporary*: if temporary, terms are likely to be construed not as warranties but as exceptions.

5.78 Increase in the risk may be addressed more directly by clauses requiring policyholders to notify the insurers of any risk. More draconian clauses purport to suspend cover until the insurer has agreed to continue it. Courts have refused to apply these literally.[303] However, to counter judicial construction like that insurers may include cancellation clauses on, eg, 30 days' notice, so that they can escape bad risks. These clauses have been enforced regardless of the motives of the insurer.[304]

(5) Exceptions

5.79 Exceptions define the scope of the cover in negative terms. Exceptions qualify insuring clauses, and limit the extent of the cover provided by the latter. Some policies, such as professional indemnity (PI) policies, contain a separate section headed 'Exclusions'. This is usually sufficient to distinguish them from the warranties[305] which are found in the policies' 'Conditions'. In case of doubt courts seek the essential nature of the term. If the circumstances envisaged by a condition give rise to an increase of risk that is no more than *temporary*, terms are likely to be construed not as warranties but as exceptions.

5.80 Exceptions can be classified as follows. First, descriptive exceptions concern subject-matter, eg, in PI policies claims for bodily injury are commonly excluded. Regions of the world may be excluded from travel policies unless an additional premium (AP) is paid. Second, circumstantial exceptions state situations in which loss tends to occur but which insurers do not cover in standard policies. Thus travel policies may exclude loss caused by disease; or medical expenses incurred in the USA. Third, 'temporal' exceptions, found eg in travel or accident policies, exclude injury sustained 'while intoxicated'. To establish a descriptive exception, usually insurers must prove no more than the circumstance envisaged, eg, that the claim against the policyholder is based on bodily injury. To establish circumstantial exceptions, insurers must also establish causation,[306] eg, that the hospital expense was incurred as a result of disease rather than accident, eg, sunstroke rather than breaking a leg. To establish temporal exceptions, insurers must establish only that the circumstance prevailed at the time, in the example given, that the policyholder was intoxicated at the time of the injury.[307]

5.81 The Unfair Contract Terms Act 1977 does not apply to insurance contracts,[308] although the spirit of the Act has been applied by the Insurance Ombudsman, in particular, to policy provisions producing an unexpected loss of cover.[309] Insurance contracts are not excluded from the Consumer Rights Act 2015 (replacing the Unfair Terms in Consumer Contracts

---

[301] *Zurich General Accident & Liability Insurance Co Ltd v Morrison* [1942] 2 KB 53, CA.

[302] By the Consumer Insurance (Disclosure and Representations) Act 2012, s 6(2).

[303] *Kausar v Eagle Star Ins Co Ltd* [2000] Lloyd's Rep IR 52, CA. See also *Hussain v Brown* [1996] 1 Lloyd's Rep 627, CA.

[304] *Sun Fire Office v Hart* (1889) 14 App Cas 98, PC. cf *Kazakhstan Wool Processors (Europe) Ltd v NCM* [2000] Lloyd's Rep IR 371, CA.

[305] See 13.77.

[306] *Munro Brice v War Risk Association* [1918] 2 KB 78; *Fraser v Furman (Productions) Ltd* [1967] 1 WLR 898, 905, CA.

[307] *Kennedy v Smith* 1976 SLT 110.

[308] Schedule 1, para 1(a).

[309] *Annual Report 1990*, para 2.4. Summer, 1.22.

Regulations 1999)[310] which has two main thrusts. One requires that terms are transparent and prominent and, in case of doubt, 'the interpretation which is most favourable to the consumer shall prevail'.[311] The other, that certain terms must not be unfair, does not apply to core provisions.[312] Section 64(1) of the 2015 Act provides that a term of a consumer contract may not be assessed for fairness to the extent that '(a) it specifies the main subject matter of the contract, or (b) the assessment is of the appropriateness of the price payable under the contract by comparison with the goods, digital content or services supplied under it.' Thus, insofar as insurance exceptions define the scope of cover, they are core terms outside the 2015 Act protection.[313]

(6) Procedural Conditions

Many policy conditions are merely procedural, ie designed to make the policy 'work' in a way **5.82** which is least costly to the insurer. A leading example is the condition requiring notice of loss to the insurer.[314] Others concern jurisdiction and arbitration. An associated underlying rule of law is that which establishes policyholders' duty of co-operation.[315] An instance of that is the duty of policyholders to assist the insurer to exercise rights in subrogation against any other person responsible for the loss insured.[316]

H. Claims

(1) Claimants

Persons primarily entitled to claim under insurance contracts are the policyholders, who con- **5.83** tract the insurance, and sometimes others who are insured under the policy in question. The latter, however, are barred from enforcing claims by the common law rule of privity of contract, unless entitled by statute.[317] The earliest surviving statute of this kind is the Married Women's Property Act 1882. Section 11 provides that a 'policy of assurance effected by any man on his own life, and expressed to be for the benefit of his wife, or of his children, or of his wife and children, any of them, or by any woman on her own life, and expressed to be for the benefit of her husband, or of her children, or of her husband and children, or any of them, shall create a trust in favour of the objects therein named' and be enforceable as such.

More recently and more importantly, the Contracts (Rights of Third Parties) Act 1999, sec- **5.84** tion 1(1), confers a right of enforcement on third parties in general, provided that the intention of the contracting parties to that effect is clear and the third parties are sufficiently identified. By section 1(3), third parties must be 'expressly identified in the contract by name, as a member of a class or as answering to a particular description'. This means, notably, that liability insurance can be extended to persons such as subcontractors, that the benefit of life

---

[310] SI 1999/2083. eg, in a property claim arising out of a fire, a requirement that on demand the claimant's evidence include his or her bank statements is not unreasonable under the Regulations: *Parker v NFU Mutual* [2012] EWHC 2156 (Comm). Nor is it unreasonable under ICOBS r 8.1.10; concerning which see 5.51.

[311] Consumer Rights Act 2015, s 69.

[312] See *Office of Fair Trading v Abbey National plc* [2009] UKSC 6, [2010] 1 AC 696.

[313] Generally see *Director General of Fair Trading v First National Bank* [2001] UKHL 52, [2002] 1 AC 481; applied in eg *Du Plessis v Fontgary Leisure Parks* [2012] EWCA Civ 409.

[314] See 5.86.

[315] *Mackay v Dick* (1881) 6 App Cas 251.

[316] In this regard see *Bee v Jenson (No 2)* [2007] EWCA Civ 923, at [8], [2008] Lloyd's Rep IR 221, *per* Morison J.

[317] Clarke, 2009, ch 5.

insurance can be extended beyond spouses, and that employers can contract accident and medical insurance for employees, which the latter can enforce themselves.

5.85 Important in the area of liability insurance is the Third Parties (Rights Against Insurers) Act 1930: claimants have a direct right of action against liability insurers of debtors who are bankrupt. The conception behind the Act led to direct actions against debtors, whether bankrupt or not, in the case of motor insurance: Road Traffic Act 1988, section 151. For cases that elude section 151, there are the Uninsured Drivers Agreement 1999 and the Untraced Drivers Agreement 2003. The Agreements are between the Motor Insurers' Bureau (MIB) and the government. Arguably victims can enforce the Agreements under the Contracts (Rights of Third Parties) Act 1999. Problems with the Third Parties (Rights Against Insurers) Act 1930 have led to the Third Parties (Rights against Insurers) Act 2010 but this has yet to come into force.

(2) Notice of Loss

5.86 A common 'procedural' policy condition requires notice of loss to the insurer within a certain time. If not, as a matter of common sense as well as common law, there will be implied a term requiring reasonable notice of loss. Express terms requiring 'immediate' notice are not construed literally but as meaning the same. What is reasonable depends on striking a balance between the interests of the parties. Claimants may need time to discover that the loss has occurred at all, or that relevant insurance is in place.[318] Insurers want notice as soon as possible to test claims before the evidence disappears, and to mitigate the extent of loss. If notice is required within a period specified in the policy, eg 14 days, courts' hands are tied, however, subject to the effect of legislation.[319]

5.87 Notice is not effective until received by the right person,[320] usually the person apparently authorised to handle claims. Insurers' local agents, but not brokers,[321] are usually authorized channels of communication to that person, and notice to brokers is effective, provided it is in time to reach the handler in the normal course of business within the time required. Insurers bear the risk of flaws in their information channels.[322] Notice in time is commonly expressed to be and enforced as a condition precedent to the claim. Otherwise the effect of late notice on claims is controversial.[323]

(3) Proof of Loss

5.88 Claimants must not only give notice of loss but also, sooner or later, prove what is alleged in the notice. In the case of indemnity insurance, claimants must prove loss in respect of the property insured—loss in the sense of financial loss, or deprivation of the property

---

[318] *Verelst's Administratrix v Motor Union Ins. Co.* [1925] 2 KB 137.

[319] See 5.72(iv). *Bankers Ins. Co. Ltd v South* [2003] EWHC 380 (QB), [2004] Lloyd's Rep IR 1.

[320] *Holwell Securities Ltd v Hughes* [1974] 1 All ER 161, CA; *HLB Kidsons v Lloyd's Underwriters* [2008] EWCA 1206, [2009] Lloyd's Rep IR 178.

[321] *Roche v Roberts* (1921) 9 Ll L Rep 59.

[322] *A/S Rendal v Arcos Ltd* (1937) 58 Ll L Rep 287, HL.

[323] See Clarke, 2009, 26-2G.

[324] Clarke, 2009, 16-1 and 16-2; instances of what, arguably, may be deprivation loss are: *Masefield v Amlin* [2011] EWCA Civ 24, [2011] 1 Lloyd's Rep 630 ('piratical seizure'); and *The Bunga Melati Dua, Masefield v Amlin* [2011] EWCA Civ 24, [2011] 1 Lloyd's Rep 630 (ransom paid to kidnappers). Liability insurance may give rise to difficult issues of policy interpretation (cover) and causation; see for instance *Durham v BAI (Run Off) Ltd*; 5 [2012] UKSC 14, [2012] 1 WLR 867.

[325] *British & Foreign Marine Ins Co Ltd v Gaunt* [1921] 2 AC 43.

[326] *Munro Brice & Co v War Risk Association* [1918] 2 KB 78; and *Fraser v BN Furman (Productions) Ltd* [1967] 1 WLR 898, 905, CA.

[327] *The Galatia* [1979] 2 All ER 726.

concerned;[324] and in that regard the amount of the loss suffered; and in all cases that the loss was caused by an event (peril) covered by the policy.[325] As to the distribution of the onus of proof,[326] if, eg, a claimant shows that cargo was damaged by fire, it is for the insurer to show that the fire was caused by an exception, such as inherent vice.[327] The scope of the exception (fire caused by inherent vice) is narrower than the scope of the cover (fire from whatever cause). Compare general exceptions, such as an excess of £100 in a motor policy; these operate in all cases, the claimants must show damage in excess of £100 to establish a claim in the first place.[328]

Proof is on the balance of probabilities, unless the defence alleges fraud or wilful misconduct, **5.89** such as arson, by the policyholder. Then the onus will be heavier: on a sliding scale in the direction of the criminal law rule, that requires proof beyond reasonable doubt, according to the gravity of the allegation.[329] Policies sometimes require 'proof satisfactory to the insurer', but this has been held to mean such proof as the insurer might *reasonably* require.[330]

(4) Causation

Claimants must show that the loss was caused by an insured peril. The law sees causation as **5.90** a matter of policy construction; and that only perils (or excepted causes) actually mentioned as such in the policy are to be considered as possible causes.[331] However, given the purpose of most insurance, there is strong presumption that policyholder negligence is covered.[332] Effective risk assessment requires prediction on the basis of a close connection between the peril and the loss, and thus the intention of insurers is that the cause, whether peril or exception, must be a 'proximate' cause of the loss claimed. Accordingly, of the possible causes mentioned, the proximate cause is that which led (more or less) inevitably to the *kind* of loss in question.[333] Further, however, if the proximate cause is a peril insured, insurers are liable for the entire loss, even though its extent was not inevitable, as long as its extent was not too remote.[334]

If, as may be,[335] there is more than one proximate cause, and an insured peril leads (more or **5.91** less inevitably) to an excepted and proximate cause of loss, the loss is covered.[336] If, however, an excepted cause leads to an insured peril, and to loss, the loss is not covered.[337] If two such causes, one covered and one excepted, are construed to be not consecutive but to operate concurrently, the loss is not covered.[338]

---

[328] *Munro Brice*, n 328.
[329] *Hornal v Neuberger Products* [1957] 1 QB 247, CA; *Re H* [1996] AC 563.
[330] See 5.69.
[331] *The Miss Jay Jay* [1987] 1 Lloyds Rep 32, CA.
[332] *Canada Rice Mills Ltd v Union Marine & General Ins Co Ltd* [1941] AC 55, PC.
[333] *Leyland Shipping* Co Ltd v Norwich Union Fire Ins Society Ltd [1918] AC 350; *The Cendor Mopu, Global Process Systems v Syarikat Takaful Malaysia* [2011] UKSC 5, [2011] 1 Lloyd's Rep 560; and Lord Mance in *Ene Kos 1 Ltd v Petroleo Brasileiro SA* [2012] UKSC 17, [2012] 2 Lloyd's Rep 292, at [48].
[334] *Reischer v Borwick* [1894] 2 QB 548, CA.
[335] *Midland Mainline Ltd v Eagle Star Ins Co Ltd* [2004] EWCA Civ 1042, [2004] 2 Lloyd's Rep 604, CA.
[336] *Re Etherington and Lancashire & Yorkshire Accident Insurance Co's Arbitration* [1909] 1 KB 591, CA.
[337] *The Salem* [1983] 1 Lloyd's Rep 342, HL.
[338] *Wayne Tank & Pump Co Ltd v Employers' Liability Corp* [1973] 2 Lloyd's Rep 237, CA. cf, however, *The Aliza Glacial* [2002] EWCA Civ 577, [2002] 2 Lloyd's Rep 421.
[339] *Oei v Foster* [1982] 2 Lloyd's Rep 170, 174–175.
[340] *Oei v Foster* [1982] 2 Lloyd's Rep 170, 174–175.
[341] *Wayne Tank*, n 338, at 240. See also *Global Process v Syarikat Takaful Malaysia Berhad* [2011] UKSC 5, [2011] 1 Lloyd's Rep 560, at [46], *per* Lord Saville.

5.92   'Rules' of interpretation like these may be changed by clear policy language. However, 'originating from', 'in consequence of', 'arising from', 'effectively caused by', and 'directly caused by' have all been construed as meaning 'proximate cause'.[339] On the other hand, phrases like 'directly or indirectly' indicate a looser connection.[340] Alternatively, some judges, led at one time by Lord Denning,[341] dismiss 'rules' of causation as an intellectual abstraction, and argue that proximate causes can be identified simply and solely by common sense. This position is attractive in its simplicity; however, as Lord Mustill once observed: 'Common sense for one person may be uncommon sense for another.'[342] Arguably this approach is a fiat for judicial intuition and, consequently, policyholder suspicion.

(5) Good Faith

5.93   Whenever policyholders supply information to enable insurers to make a decision about cover, they must observe a legal duty of good faith, a duty which continues throughout the insurance period at a level appropriate to the decision in question. The duty ends as regards a particular claim when the claim has been paid, or rejected; in the event of rejection the policyholder must accept the rejection or commence proceedings.[343] Evidently a fraudulent claim is not one made in good faith.

(a) The meaning of fraud

5.94   To defeat claims on grounds of fraud, insurers must show them to be 'wilfully false' in a 'substantial respect'.[344] Claims are wilfully false if the claimant knows that it is false, does not believe it to be true or makes it recklessly, not caring whether it is true or false,[345] ie a case of common law fraud.[346] Prima facie deliberate exaggeration is fraud; some cases suggest that exaggeration is not fraud but merely a bargaining position,[347] however, the balance of precedent confirms that it is fraud.[348] Nonetheless, claimants usually get the benefit of any reasonable doubt. After all, claimants are human, 'different views of values are common; memory is faulty'.[349]

5.95   Whether a falsehood is substantial depends on the *de minimis* rule. More significant is the associated requirement that the falsehood be material. Until 2002 falsehood was not material unless it had a decisive effect on the readiness of the insurer to pay—whether to pay and to whom, or the amount to be paid;[350] thus, false evidence submitted to bolster a claim otherwise valid was not material.[351] However, in *The Aegeon*[352] fraud was extended to 'fraudulent devices' employed by claimants, who believe that that they have indeed suffered the loss claimed, but seek to improve or embellish the facts by telling lies. Such claimants nonetheless seek to gain by the device, albeit not from insurers. Fraud, said Roche J, includes deceit used to secure 'quicker payment of the money than would have been obtained if the truth had been told'.[353] Indeed, if 'time is money' a claimant is significantly better off, and it is

---

[342] 'Humpty Dumpty and Risk Management' [1997] LMCLQ 488–501, 500. See also Clarke, 2009, 25-1.
[343]   *The Star Sea* [2003] 1 AC 469.
[344]   *Britton v Royal Ins Co* (1866) 4 F & F 905.
[345]   *Lek v Mathews* (1927) 29 Ll L Rep 141, 145, HL.
[346]   *Twinsectra Ltd v Yardley* [2002] UKHL 12, [2002] 2 AC 164.
[347]   *Nsubuga v Commercial Union Assurance Co plc* [1998] 2 Lloyd's Rep 682.
[348]   *Orakpo v Barclays Insurance Services* [1995] LRLR 443, CA.
[349]   *Soler v United Firemen's Ins Co*, 299 US 45, 50 (1936).
[350]   cf material misrepresentations: 5.45.
[351]   *The Mercandian Continent* [2001] EWCA Civ 1275; [2001] 2 Lloyd's Rep 563, [35].
[352]   *Agapitos v Agnew (No 1)*[2002] EWCA Civ 247, [2003] QB 556.
[353]   *Wisenthal v World Auxiliary Ins Corp Ltd* (1930) 38 Ll L Rep 54, 61.

not a lie which necessarily damages the insurer—the fraud may save insurers the cost of prolonged investigation of a claim. Only irrelevant falsehood such as concealment to avoid embarrassment, will be excluded from this broad notion of fraud. Morally, the device rule can be supported, but doubts stem from the severe consequences that follow a finding of fraud.

(b) The consequences of fraud

If fraud is discovered after a claim has been paid, insurers may recover the money as money **5.96** paid by mistake. If fraud is established before any or all of the insurance money has been paid, insurers are not obliged to pay any of the amount claimed, even a genuine but exaggerated claim: courts apply the maxim *fraus omnia corrumpit* to discourage dishonesty.[354] Further, insurers are usually entitled to terminate insurance contracts under a policy provision. Anyway, fraud being a breach of the duty of good faith, insurers are entitled to terminate by law.[355] Some feel that, as with contracts under the general law,[356] termination should be allowed only if policyholder breach is 'substantial'. However, the contrary view, also in harmony with contract law at large, is that fraud is a factor that pumps up the perceived gravity of breach. Certain contractual relationships, among them the insurance relationship, can only work properly if trust and confidence are maintained.[357] Any fraud puts a new and darker light on a policyholder and, therefore, insurers are entitled to reconsider and, if so minded, terminate their contract.[358] Precedent[359] exists for the more drastic consequence of 'forfeiture', which would be retroactive and require claimants to reimburse any insurance money received during the insurance period. However, in the words of Lord Hobhouse, termination 'only applies prospectively and does not affect accrued rights'. The idea of forfeiture, that a failure of good faith at the end of the insurance period should entitle the insurer to recover the amount of a good faith claim paid earlier in the period 'cannot be reconciled with principle'.[360]

I. Indemnity

(1) Amount

Under life or other non-indemnity (contingency) policies successful claimants recover the **5.97** amount stipulated in the policy. Under indemnity policies the object of payment is to put claimants in the position they would have been in, if the insured loss had not occurred. Claimants recover their actual provable loss subject, however, to certain limits. One is that the amount recoverable is reduced by any indemnity for the same loss already obtained from a third party. Commonly other limits on the amount recoverable are expressed in or implied from the policy.

(i) Limits are implied from the nature of the cover. A fire policy covers loss or damage caused by fire but not cost incurred, however reasonably, to prevent fire.[361]

---

[354] *Galloway v Guardian Royal Exchange (UK) Ltd* [1999] Lloyd's Rep IR 209, CA.
[355] *Orakpo*, n 348.
[356] *Hongkong Fir Shipping Co Ltd v Kawasaki Kisen Kaisha Ltd* [1962] 2 QB 26, CA.
[357] Generally: *Malik v Bank of Credit and Commerce International SA* [1998] AC 20.
[358] Concerning the fraud problems posed by joint insurance contracted by associations, see 5.56.
[359] Surveyed by Rix J in *Royal Boskalis Westminster NV v Mountain* [1997] LRLR 523, 593.
[360] *The Star Sea* [2003] 1 AC 469, at [50].
[361] *Yorkshire Water Services Ltd v Sun Alliance & London Ins plc* [1997] 2 Lloyd's Rep 21, CA. cf Clarke, 2009, 28-8G.
[362] See M Simpson (ed), *Professional Negligence and Liability* (2013) 5–162ff.

(ii) Policies commonly limit the amount of recoverable loss to specified sums. Unless otherwise stipulated, insurers are liable for any number of successive losses caused by insured perils during the insurance period, whether individually subject to such limits or not, even though the aggregate of amounts payable exceeds the ceiling; there is a presumption in favour of full indemnity. Commonly, however, the overall amount recoverable is limited by means of aggregation clauses.[362]

(iii) If property has been insured but undervalued, the amount of any insurance money payable on a claim is 'subject to average': the amount is limited to the proportion of actual loss, which the sum insured bears to the actual value of the property insured at the time of the loss. If, eg, property insured for 10x is actually worth 12x, actual loss of 6x is subject to average (10:12) and the amount payable is limited to 5x (10 x 6/12).

(iv) Policies usually contain an 'excess clause' (deductible), whereby the insured bear the first part of any loss, expressed as an amount of money or as a percentage of loss. The purpose is to encourage policyholders to be risk averse, and to reduce the transaction costs incurred by insurers by ruling out small claims.

(v) Policies may exclude, eg, any loss 'in respect of which the insured is entitled to indemnity under any other insurance except in respect of any excess beyond the amount which would have been payable under such insurance, if this policy had not been effected'. Such clauses are troublesome. The effect is to convert the insurance into 'excess of loss' insurance: a contract on a different layer of risk from any other covering the same risk and, therefore, one designed to exclude contribution between insurers. If two policies on the same risk contain such clauses, prima facie neither insurance pays, a result described as absurd and unjust.[363] In England that has been avoided by a robust rule of construction that looks 'at each policy independently and if each would be liable but for the existence of the other, then the exclusions would be treated as cancelling each other out, both insurers are then liable', and the one who pays can claim contribution from the other.[364]

5.98 In contrast, claimants may recover more (or less) than their actual loss in the case of 'valued policies'.[365] A valued policy is one which stipulates that, in the event of a claim, the property insured shall be assumed to have the value stated therein, without more.

(2) The Measure of Indemnity

5.99 Recoverable loss is assessed at the time it occurred.[366] Insurers undertake to hold their policyholders harmless—as if the loss had not occurred at all, and the measure of loss is analogous to that found in the law of tort. It involves 'two quite different measures of damage, or, occasionally a combination of the two. The first is to take the capital value of the property in an undamaged state and to compare it with its value in a damaged state. The second is to take the cost of repair or reinstatement. Which is appropriate will depend on a number of factors, such as the plaintiff's future intentions as to the use of the property and the reasonableness of those intentions'.[367]

---

362 *National Employers' Mutual General Ins Assn Ltd v Haydon* [1980] 2 Lloyd's Rep 149, 152.
363 *National Employers' Mutual General Ins Assn Ltd v Haydon* [1980] 2 Lloyd's Rep 149, 152.
364 *National Employers' Mutual General Ins Assn Ltd v Haydon* [1980] 2 Lloyd's Rep 149, 152.
365 See 5.32 concerning 'honour' policies.
366 *Castellain v Preston* (1883) 11 QBD 380, CA.
367 *Dodd Properties (Kent) Ltd v Canterbury CC* [1980] 1 All ER 928, 938, CA.
368 *Leppard v Excess Insurance Co Ltd* [1979] 2 Lloyd's Rep 91, 96, CA.
369 *Dominion Mosaics & Tile Co Ltd v Trafalgar Trucking Co Ltd* [1990] 2 All ER 246, CA.
370 *Keystone Properties Ltd v Sun Alliance & London Ins*, 1993 SC 494.
371 *Westminster Fire Office v Glasgow Provident Investment Sy* (1888) 13 App Cas 699.

In the case of real property, if policyholders intended to sell the property, the basis of assess- **5.100**
ment is the market value of the property.[368] If that was not their intention but becomes their
intention as an immediate consequence of the loss, the measure is likely to be the cost of finding alternative property.[369] If their intention was to retain and use the property, the measure
of indemnity is the cost of reinstatement, whether they intend to use the insurance money
to reinstate the property or not.[370] As regards claimants under the insurance with a security
interest in property, their loss is the amount of their debt outstanding.[371]

What is true of real property is broadly true also of other kinds of corporeal property. If the prop- **5.101**
erty was for sale at the time of loss, reference is made to the market. If the thing is such that there
is a second-hand market, that is the relevant market; but, if there is no such market, the only way
to indemnify the claimant may be to repair it (even at unreasonable cost) or to replace it with a
new one.[372] When the property is fine art, and there are two markets (the auction market and
the private dealers' market) it is the market where it is likely to fetch the higher price.[373] When
the property is commercial, the measure of value is the value of the property as part of a going
concern and not that obtainable upon a 'break-up sale' of the insured's business. Similarly, the
value of components may be their value as part of a greater manufactured product.

When property is replaced or reinstated, the amount recoverable, it has been said,[374] should **5.102**
be subject to a discount for depreciation—an allowance or deduction for the 'betterment' of
the thing reinstated. On the other hand, deduction 'would be the equivalent of forcing the
plaintiffs to invest money in the modernizing of their plant which might be highly inconvenient for them'.[375] Whether the doctrine of betterment still applies to insurance cases is not
entirely clear, but the safer view is that it does.[376] In practice the issue is often settled by the
policy, eg, 'replacement cost basis' cover, or cover 'new for old'.

(3) Reinstatement

Insurers are entitled to reinstate property rather than pay insurance money under a policy **5.103**
term to that effect, if any, or, if they suspect fraud or arson, under the Fires Prevention
(Metropolis) Act 1774, section 83. Section 83 also obliges insurers to reinstate, if requested
to reinstate by persons other than the insured but with an interest in premises damaged by
fire, such as tenants[377] and mortgagees.[378] If insurers elect for reinstatement, the effect is that
the insurer 'is in the same position as if he had originally contracted to do the act which he
has elected to do'.[379] If, however, reinstatement becomes physically or legally impossible, the
better view is that the insurer is not discharged but that the obligation to pay the loss as insurance money revives.[380] If reinstatement work is undertaken, like builders or repairers, insurers are liable, if the work is poor under legislation such as the Supply of Goods and Services
Act 1982, and the Sale of Goods Act 1979. To appoint competent contractors to reinstate is

---

[372] *Dominion Mosaics*, n 369, at 255.
[373] *Quorum A/S v Schramm* [2002] 1 Lloyd's Rep 249.
[374] *Reynolds v Phoenix Assurance Co Ltd* [1978] 2 Lloyd's Rep 440, 450ff.
[375] *Harbutts Plasticine Ltd v Wayne Tank & Pump Co Ltd* [1970] 1 QB 447, CA.
[376] See *Dominion Mosaics*, n 369.
[377] *Wimbledon Golf Club v Imperial Ins Co* (1902) 18 TLR 815.
[378] *Sinnott v Bowden* [1912] 2 Ch 414.
[379] *Brown v Royal Ins Co* (1859) 1 El & El 853, 858–859.
[380] Clarke, 2009, 29-2C.
[381] *Anderson v Commercial Union Assurance Co* (1885) 55 LJQB 146; *Argy Trading Development Co Ltd v Lapid Developments Ltd* [1977] 1 Lloyd's Rep 67.
[382] *Davidson v Guardian Royal Exchange Assurance* [1979] 1 Lloyd's Rep 406.
[383] *General Accident Fire & Life Assurance Corp Ltd v Midland Bk Ltd* [1940] 2 KB 388, CA. cf composite insurance: *New Hampshire Ins Co v MGN Ltd* [1997] LRLR 24, CA.

not enough: insurers are responsible for the quality of the work.[381] Moreover, reinstatement must be completed within a reasonable time, otherwise the insurer is liable to pay damages to the insured for loss of use.[382]

(4) Payment

5.104 Payment must be to the policyholder, or in joint insurance, to any one of them,[383] or to any other designated persons (loss payees) such as mortgagees. If payment is made by mistake as to amount or entitlement, recovery is governed by the law of restitution.[384] Dispute settlements are stand alone contracts subject to the usual rules of contract validity and, in particular, subject to certain assumptions of risk. On the one hand, courts are 'very slow to infer that a party intended to surrender rights and claims of which he was unaware and could not have been aware'.[385] On the other, courts readily infer that insurers might well accept short-term losses for long-term gains from continued contractual relations with a particular customer or to maintain market reputation for prompt settlement. The inference is reinforced by the principle of finality and public policy to avoid unnecessary litigation.[386]

(5) Recovery by Insurers from Third Parties

5.105 Having paid claimants, insurers may wish to seek recovery from third parties responsible for the loss. In the case of accident policies, eg, they may seek recovery in the shoes of the claimant against persons liable to the claimant for the accident: an action in subrogation. If there is more than one insurer on risk, the one who has paid may seek contribution any of the others.

(6) Non-Payment

5.106 Express terms apart, insurance is an agreement to pay a sum on the occurrence of the insured event. In the case of contingency (non-indemnity) insurance, actions against insurers are regarded as actions for debt. Although the court has a discretion to award interest against debtors who pay late, potentially two kinds of loss are left uncompensated. First, the court has no power to award interest if the debtor pays late but before proceedings for recovery have been begun; and, secondly, interest as such does not compensate special damage over and beyond loss of the normal use of the money. However, the better view is that usual rules of remoteness of damage apply.[387]

5.107 In the case of indemnity insurance, insurance contract law differs from general contract law. The insurers' obligation to pay is regarded as an obligation to pay damages[388] for breach of contract for failure to prevent the insured suffering loss,[389] although the duty actually to pay the policyholder may be postponed, both in reality and in law, until loss has been quantified.[390] It 'is not a condition precedent...that the plaintiff has quantified the amount of his claim'; and 'the insurer may technically be in breach of his contract before any demand is made on him'.[391] This is not what most people might expect. If a roof is damaged by fire and the insurer elects to have it repaired but the work is done badly, that insurer, like any repairer,

---

[384] *Kelly v Solari* (1841) 9 M & W 54; *Lipkin Gorman v Karpnale Ltd* [1991] 2 AC 548.
[385] *Bank of Credit and Commerce International SA v Ali (No 1)* [2001] UKHL 8, [2002] 1 AC 251, at [10].
[386] eg *Barclays plc v Villers* [2001] Lloyd's Rep IR 162.
[387] See EPL 21.27–21.39, 21.59–21.61.
[388] *Sprung v Royal Ins. Co* [1997] CLC 70, CA.
[389] *The Italia Express* [1992] 2 Lloyd's Rep 281.
[390] *Virk v Gan Life Holdings plc* [2000] Lloyd's Rep IR 159, CA.
[391] *Chandris v Argo Ins Co Ltd* [1963] 2 Lloyd's Rep 65, 74. cf *Jabbour v The Custodian of Absentee Israeli Property* [1954] 1 WLR 139, 144.

is liable for consequent rain damage to contents to the policyholder. If insurers elect to pay insurance money instead, but pay late with the same result, because the policyholder cannot afford to have the roof repaired, people might reasonably expect insurers to be liable for the damage. That is the law in other common law jurisdictions,[392] as well as Scotland.[393] In England that is the view of the Financial Ombudsman Service (FOS)[394]—but not the courts. A more sensible view of indemnity insurance can be based on policy terms, as well as the nature of contracts of insurance: simply that payment is not due at all until after the procedural conditions, such as notice and proof, have been satisfied. On that basis late payment puts insurers in breach of contract like any other. However, good sense has not prevailed. Although criticized,[395] the reasoning and the rule stand for the time being.

In general contract law damages are now recoverable for distress in cases of breach of promise **5.108** to ensure peace of mind or freedom from distress,[396] benefits often promised by advertisements on television promoting the sale of insurance. Such damages in insurance cases have been awarded by the FOS[397] and by courts in other countries of common law, but the limited precedent to date in England is to the contrary.[398]

In the relatively rare case of an insolvent insurer, claimants once obtained recovery from the **5.109** Policyholders Protection Board under the Policyholders Protection Act 1975, as amended in 1997. With effect from 30 November 2001 that scheme was replaced by the Financial Services Compensation Scheme (FSCS), established under Part XV of the Financial Services and Markets Act 2000. The amount recoverable varies according to the kind of policy in question.[399]

---

[392] Clarke, 2009, 30-9B1.
[393] *Scott Lithgow Ltd v Sec of State for Defence* (1989) 45 BLR 1, HL.
[394] Summer, 3.6 and 3.25.
[395] See Clarke, 'Compensation for failure to pay money due' [2008] JBL 291 with reference to *Sempra Metals v Inland Revenue* [2007] UKHL 34, [2008] 1 AC 561; Law Commission, Joint Consultation Paper, 'Insurance Contract Law: Post Contract Duties and Other Issues' (LCCP 201/ SLCDP 152) 2011 Ch 1.
[396] See EPL 21.51–21.52.
[397] *Ombudsman News*, January 2002.
[398] Clarke, 2009, 30-9C.
[399] See Clarke, 2009, 30-11.

6

BANKING

A. Overview

(1) Global Financial Crisis

The global financial crisis that lasted from 2007 to 2009 continues to have a profound effect **6.01** on the way that banks are regulated and on the relationship between banks and their customers. The run on Northern Rock in September 2007 undermined depositor confidence in the solvency of banks and required the government to step in to take Northern Rock into temporary public ownership, as well as provide financial guarantees to ease the fears of depositors in general.[1] The collapse of Lehman Brothers in September 2008 raised fundamental concerns about retail banking and (inherently riskier) investment banking being conducted within the same banking group.[2]

The crisis, which began in August 2007 with a liquidity freeze resulting from the collapse of **6.02** the mortgage-backed securities market, soon raised widespread fears about significant undercapitalization of the banking sector and concern over counterparty credit risk. Governments and central banks scrambled to address the problem. The economic downturn that resulted from the global financial crisis has itself contributed to a European sovereign debt crisis which the governments of Greece and Spain, in particular, continue to battle with at the time of writing. Due to the fact that modern banking is multifunctional and multijurisdictional, the response of those charged with the regulation of banking and financial services has had to be international, regional and national in outlook.[3] Within the European Union, this has led to

---

[1] The Banking (Special Provisions) Act 2008 allowed Northern Rock to be nationalized. It has since been replaced by the Banking Act 2009.

[2] The UK Government endorsed the recommendations of the Independent Commission on Banking (September 2011) that retail banking activities of UK banks be 'ring-fenced' from activities of its broader group, especially investment banking activities. The Financial Services (Banking Reform) Act 2013 introduces a retail ring-fence for banks.

[3] See E Ferran, N Moloney, JG Hill and JC Coffee, *The Regulatory Aftermath of the Global Financial Crisis* (2012).

the establishment of a European Banking Union, which is designed to safeguard the financial sector by ensuring that banks in the euro zone are stronger and more suitably supervised.[3a]

(2) *UK Regulatory Reform*

6.03   The global financial crisis led to widespread criticism of the UK's banking and financial services regulator, the Financial Services Authority (FSA), whose functions, responsibilities and powers were set out in the Financial Services and Markets Act 2000 (FSMA 2000). This resulted in the Government proposing reform of the regulatory system and the enactment of the Financial Services Act 2012, which introduces key structural changes to the structure of financial regulation in the UK, mainly through amendment of the FSMA 2000. The FSA has been dismantled and replaced by two new regulatory bodies: the Prudential Regulation Authority (PRA) and the Financial Conduct Authority (FCA). The PRA, a subsidiary of the Bank of England, has been tasked with the prudential regulation of deposit takers, insurers and a small number of significant investment firms. The FCA regulates conduct of business in retail and wholesale markets, and supervises the trading infrastructure that supports those markets. The FCA is also responsible for the prudential regulation of firms that are not regulated by the PRA and, since April 2014, for the regulation of consumer credit business. The 2012 Act also gave the Bank of England, acting through a new Financial Policy Committee, macro-prudential responsibility for oversight of the financial system.

(3) *Banking and Payment Services Conduct Regime*

6.04   The UK banking sector tried to ward off the threat of increased regulatory control of banking activities, especially in the retail sector, through a series of Banking Codes and Business Banking Codes based on voluntary self-regulation. However, the global financial crisis made regulatory intervention inevitable. The need to implement the conduct of business aspects of the Payment Services Directive in November 2009 provided the opportunity to abandon self-regulation and replace it with a new Banking and Payment Services conduct regime. This regime comprises the FCA's Banking Conduct of Business Sourcebook[4] and the Payment Services Regulations 2009.[5]

(a)   **Banking Conduct of Business Sourcebook**

6.05   The Banking Conduct of Business Sourcebook (BCOBS) applies to firms[6] with respect to the regulated activity of accepting deposits from banking customers carried on from an establishment in the UK and activities connected with that activity (eg processing cheque transactions and the provision of foreign exchange services).[7] Banking customers are defined as consumers, micro-enterprises[8] and charities with an annual income of less that £1 million. BCOBS

[3a] The European Banking Union applies to all Member States in the euro zone and those non-euro area Member States who have opted to participate in the Banking Union. The UK government has confirmed that the UK will not participate in the European Banking Union.

[4] Located in the FCA's Handbook at www.fshandbook.info/FS/html/FCA/BCOBS. Since 1 April 2014, a bank's consumer credit related activities (eg overdrafts and credit cards) have been regulated by the FCA according to the conduct of business standards set out in the FCA's Consumer Credit Sourcebook (CONC).

[5] SI 2009/209 as amended, implementing the Payment Services Directive 2007/64/EC (a revised and recast Payment Services Directive is due soon). The Banking Code and the Business Banking Code were withdrawn in November 2009. Those aspects of the Codes dealing with lending are now to be found in the Lending Code (March 2011, revised October 2014), itself a voluntary code of practice.

[6] ie UK authorized banks, building societies and e-money issuers (but not small e-money issuers), credit unions and incoming EEA branches of credit institutions.

[7] BCOBS, 1.1.1R.

[8] A micro-enterprise is defined in the FCA's *Handbook* glossary as 'an enterprise which (a) employs fewer than 10 persons; and (b) has a turnover or annual balance sheet that does not exceed €2 million', and includes the self-employed, family businesses, partnerships and associations regularly engaged in economic activity.

provides rules and guidance on the following areas of activity to the extent that this would not be contrary to the provisions of the Payment Services Directive:[9] communications with banking customers and financial promotions;[10] distance communications;[11] information to be communicated to banking customers, including appropriate information and statements of account;[12] post-sale requirements on prompt, efficient and fair service, moving accounts, and lost and dormant accounts;[13] and cancellation, including the right to cancel and the effects of cancellation.[14] Under section 138D(2) of the FSMA 2000, a 'private person' who has suffered loss as the result of a breach of the BCOBS rules has a right of action for breach of statutory duty.[15]

(b) Payment Services Regulations 2009

The Payment Services Regulations 2009 (PSRs) introduced a new regulatory regime for payment services from 1 November 2009.[16] Payment services include the execution of payment transactions, card issuing, merchant acquiring, money remittance, certain services based on mobile phones or other electronic devices, and the operation of 'payment accounts'. Regulation 2 defines a 'payment account' as 'an account held in the name of one or more payment service users which is used for the execution of payment transactions', and a 'payment transaction' as 'an act, initiated by the payer or payee, of placing, transferring or withdrawing funds, irrespective of any underlying obligations between the payer and the payee'. Thus, payment accounts include current accounts and easy access savings accounts. The PSRs focus only on electronic means of payment; they do not apply to cash-only transactions directly between payer and payee[17] or payments based on paper instruments such as cheques.[18]

6.06

In the context of retail banking, the PSRs impose conduct of business requirements on payment services that fall within the scope of the Regulations. For the PSRs to apply (a) the payment services must be provided from an establishment maintained by a payment service provider or its agent in the UK, (b) the payment service providers of both the payer and the payee must be located within the EEA, and (c) the transaction or payment account must be in either euro or sterling, or another member state currency.[19] The PSRs conduct of business rules specify the information to be provided to the payment service user (Part 5)[20] and set out the rights and obligations of payment service users and providers (Part 6). Except where the payment service user is a consumer, a micro-enterprise or

6.07

---

[9] BCOBS, 1.1.4R(3). Except as provided for in BCOBS 1.1.4R, BCOBS does not apply to payment services where Parts 5 and 6 of the Payment Services Regulations 2009 apply.

[10] BCOBS, ch 2.

[11] BCOBS, ch 3.

[12] BCOBS, ch 4.

[13] BCOBS, ch 5.

[14] BCOBS, ch 6.

[15] The definition of a 'private person' (which corresponds to that in the PSRs, reg 120(3): n 23) is to be found in FSMA 2000 (Rights of Action) Regulations 2001, SI 2001/2256, as amended. See also *Titan Steel Wheels Ltd v Royal Bank of Scotland plc* [2010] EWHC 211 (Comm), [2010] 2 Lloyd's Rep 92 at [68]–[70]; *Camerata Property Inc v Credit Suisse Securities (Europe) Ltd* [2010] EWHC 7 (Comm) at [89]–[98]; *Bailey v Barclays Bank plc* [2014] EWHC 2882 (QB) at [44].

[16] Parts 2–4 of the PSRs deal with the regulation of non-bank payment service providers, such as money remitters and non-bank credit card issuers.

[17] But the placement and withdrawal of cash to and from a payment account is within the scope of the PSRs.

[18] Schedule 1, Part 2(f), (g).

[19] Regulations 33(1), 51(1). Rules relating to value date and availability of funds in reg 73 apply regardless of whether the payment service providers of both payer and payee are located within the EEA (reg 51(2)).

[20] Which differ according to whether the payment transaction takes place under a 'single payment service contract' or a 'framework contract'.

a charity as defined in the Regulations,[21] payment service providers may contract out of most conduct of business requirements.[22] Any breach of the requirements of Parts 5 or 6 is actionable as a breach of statutory duty by a private person who suffers loss as a result of the contravention.[23]

B. The Bank-Customer Relationship

(1) Definition of a Bank

6.08 The terms 'bank', 'banker' and 'banking' cannot be uniformly defined for all purposes. It is now common for most statutes, especially those dealing with regulatory matters, to define a bank in terms of a domestic institution granted permission by the PRA to accept deposits or an 'EEA firm' authorized in another European Economic Area state to accept deposits and, relying on its 'single European passport', doing so in the UK.[24] Relatively few statutes use the terms 'bank', 'banker' and 'banking' without further or proper definition. The most important statutes that fall into this category are the Bills of Exchange Act 1882 and the Cheques Act 1957, where a 'banker' is defined to include 'a body of persons whether incorporated or not who carry on the business of banking'.[25] In such cases, it is necessary to turn to the common law for a definition of the 'business of banking'. The common law definition is also important because under the general law certain rights and duties are only conferred on a 'bank' or 'banker', eg the banker's lien,[26] the banker's right to combine accounts,[27] and the banker's duty of confidentiality.[28] The common law definition of a 'bank' is based on treating it as an institution engaged in banking business. The leading case is *United Dominion Trust v Kirkwood*,[29] where Lord Denning MR described the main facets of banking business as the conduct of current accounts, the payment of cheques and the collection of cheques for customers.[30] Diplock and Harman LJJ agreed.[31] However, their Lordships took different views to as to the importance of reputation for determining whether or not a given institution was a bank. Lord Denning was prepared to hold an institution to be a bank merely because it was so regarded in the business community,[32] Diplock LJ considered the question of reputation to be of marginal importance,[33] and Harman LJ, dissenting in the actual decision in the case, thought it irrelevant.[34] It is submitted that, in the interests of certainty, the test of whether an institution is or is not a bank should be entirely objective and should not based on subjective criteria such as reputation.

---

[21] ie annual income of less than £1 million.

[22] Regulations 33(4), 51(3) (the 'corporate opt-out').

[23] Regulation 120(1). In this regulation, a 'private person' means (a) any individual, except where the individual suffers the loss in question in the course of providing payment services; and (b) any person who is not an individual, except where that person suffers the loss in question in the course of carrying on business of any kind (reg 120(3)). A fiduciary or representative may also, generally, bring the action on behalf of a private person (reg 120(2)). See also the cases cited in n 15 above.

[24] See FSMA 2000, s 31(1)(a) and Part 4A (PRA permission); s 31(1)(b) and Sch 3 (EEA firm).

[25] Bills of Exchange Act 1882, s 2; Cheques Act 1957, s 6(1).

[26] See EP Ellinger, E Lomnicka & CVM Hare, *Ellinger's Modern Banking Law* (5th edn, 2011), at 864–867.

[27] 6.52–6.53.

[28] 6.46–6.51. It should be noted that a duty of confidentiality can also arise between a bank and someone who is not its customer.

[29] [1966] 2 QB 431, CA.

[30] At 447.

[31] Diplock LJ, at 466, held them to be 'essential' characteristics.

[32] At 454.

[33] At 475–476.

[34] At 460–461.

The courts have consistently held that banking business may change over time.[35] In recent **6.09** years the use of cheques has declined and money is frequently transferred into and out of bank accounts using electronic means. In the light of this modern practice, it is submitted that the common law definition of the terms 'bank', 'banking' and 'banking business' should not turn on the precise mechanism by which money is paid into and out of bank accounts.[36]

An institution may be held to be a bank even though its activities are not confined to the carrying **6.10** on of banking business.[37] The issue turns on whether the institution's banking business is real in terms of its entire business. It is immaterial that the size of the institution's banking business is negligible in comparison with that of a clearing bank. It is also irrelevant that the institution does not carry on all facets of banking business and that its main activities are in different fields.

(2) Definition of a Customer

There are occasions when it is important to ascertain whether a person is or is not a customer **6.11** of a bank. First, there are particular incidents that attach to the bank-*customer* relationship, eg the bank's duty to obey its customer's mandate,[38] to exercise reasonable care and skill,[39] and the duty of confidentiality.[40] Secondly, some statutes use the term 'customer' without further definition, as is the case with section 4 of the Cheques Act 1957.[41]

A person becomes a customer of a bank either when the bank opens an account in his **6.12** name[42] or when the bank agrees to open the account in question.[43] Where a bank performs a casual service for a person, such as, eg, cashing a cheque for someone introduced by one of its customers, that person does not become a customer even if the service is performed on a regular basis.[44] The bank-customer relationship turns on the flow of funds into and out of the customer's account and the mechanisms that bring about those movements. But modern banks also offer a wide variety of other services to account and non-account holders alike, eg, financial advice, fund management, bank finance. In the broadest sense, those who receive these other services are also 'customers' of the bank. However, for the purposes of the bank-customer relationship it is the holding of an account which is critical.

A person does not become a customer of a bank just because an account is opened in that **6.13** person's name.[45] The account must be opened with the customer's authority or, if not, he must have subsequently ratified the opening of the account.[46] A person may open an account in the name of a nominee and remain the bank's customer.[47] In all cases it is important for a bank to follow 'customer due diligence measures' as required by the Money Laundering

---

[35] *Woods v Martins Bank Ltd* [1959] 1 QB 55, 70; *United Dominion Trust Ltd v Kirkwood*, n 29, at 446.
[36] See *Commissioners of the State Savings Bank of Victoria v Permewan, Wright & Co Ltd* (1915) 19 CLR 457, 470–471, Aust HC.
[37] *Re Roe's Legal Charge* [1982] 2 Lloyd's Rep 370, CA.
[38] 6.19–6.39.
[39] 6.40–6.42.
[40] 6.46–6.51.
[41] 6.71.
[42] *Lacave & Co v Crédit Lyonnais* [1887] 1 QB 148.
[43] *Ladbroke & Co v Todd* (1914) 30 TLR 433; *Woods v Martins Bank Ltd* [1959] 1 QB 55.
[44] *Great Western Railway Co v London and County Banking Co Ltd* [1901] AC 414, HL; *Taxation Comrs v English, Scottish and Australian Bank Ltd* [1920] AC 683, PC.
[45] *Stoney Stanton Supplies (Coventry) Ltd v Midland Bank Ltd* [1966] 2 Lloyd's Rep 373, CA.
[46] *Rowlandson v National Westminster Bank Ltd* [1978] 1 WLR 798.
[47] *Thavorn v Bank of Credit and Commerce International SA* [1985] 1 Lloyd's Rep 259. But where an account is opened in the name of a company, it is the company and not its sole owner that is the bank's customer: *Diamantides v JP Morgan Chase Bank* [2005] EWHC 263 (Comm), upheld on different grounds [2005] EWCA Civ 1612.

Regulations 2007.[48] Such measures consist of identifying and verifying the identity of the customer and any 'beneficial owner' of the customer,[49] and obtaining information on the purpose and intended nature of the business relationship.[50]

(3) Nature of the Bank-Customer Relationship

6.14 The relationship between bank and customer is contractual and includes the relationship of creditor and debtor with regard to the balance in the customer's bank account. The classic formulation comes from Lord Cottenham in *Foley v Hill*:[51]

> Money, when paid into a bank account, ceases altogether to be the money of the principal... it is then the money of the banker, who is bound to return an equivalent by paying a similar sum to that deposited with him when he is asked for it... The money placed in the custody of a banker is, to all intents and purposes, the money of the banker, to do with as he pleases...

When the account is in credit, the customer is the creditor and the bank the debtor; when the account is overdrawn, the roles are reversed.[52]

6.15 The nature of the bank-customer relationship was further analysed by the Court of Appeal in *Joachimson v Swiss Bank Corporation*.[53] Atkin LJ, giving the leading judgment,[54] stated that there was only one contract between a bank and its customer, the implied terms of which included the following: the bank undertakes to receive money and to collect cheques for its customer's account; the proceeds so received are not held in trust by the bank but represent a loan from the customer which the bank undertakes to repay; the bank undertakes to repay on the customer's demand at the branch where the account is kept during banking hours;[55] the customer undertakes to exercise reasonable care in executing his written orders so as not to mislead the bank or to facilitate forgery. His Lordship concluded that the bank was not liable to pay its customer until he had demanded payment.

6.16 The requirement that the customer must make a demand for payment before the bank is liable to repay sums deposited to the credit of the account is central to the operation of a current account or of a savings account which provides for payment at call.[56] The limitation period will only start to run from the day on which the amount is payable, which means that

---

[48] SI 2007/2157, as amended, reg 7.

[49] A 'beneficial owner' of a customer includes, eg, anyone who ultimately owns or controls 25% of the shares or voting rights in a non-listed company, or who exercises control over the management of a company (reg 6).

[50] Regulation 5.

[51] (1848) 2 HLC 28, 36.

[52] The bank is entitled to repayment of an overdraft on demand unless otherwise agreed (*Williams and Glyn's Bank v Barnes* [1981] Com LR 205). It is important to construe the terms of the facility letter under which the overdraft is granted. Facility letters are usually expressed in such a way that the bank will be held to have reserved the right to call for repayment on demand even though a fixed time period for the facility may have been indicated (*Lloyds Bank plc v Lampert* [1999] 1 All ER (Comm) 161, CA; *Bank of Ireland v AMCD (Property Holdings) Ltd* [2001] 2 All ER (Comm) 894). In exceptional circumstances, a reservation of the right to repayment on demand may be held repugnant to the agreement as a whole and be read subject to the overriding provision that the debt should be repayable at a fixed future date (*Titford Property Co Ltd v Cannon Street Acceptances Ltd*, unreported, 22 May 1975).

[53] [1921] 3 KB 110, CA.

[54] At 127.

[55] Atkin LJ left open the question whether the customer's demand for repayment must be in writing. But even a customer's irrevocable authority to a bank to accept the written demand of a particular person may be overridden by the oral instructions of the customer himself: *Morrell v Workers Savings & Loan Bank* [2007] UKPC 3, at [10]. See also *Earles v Barclays Bank plc* [2009] EWHC 2500 (QB), at [17].

[56] In the case of a fixed deposit, maturing at a predetermined time, the amount involved becomes payable on a designated day.

it commences on the day on which the demand is made and refused.[57] The fact that modern banks allow their customers to access their accounts at distance, eg, through the use of telephone and Internet banking services, or through the use of debit cards, illustrates that the requirement to make demand at the branch where the account is keep is frequently waived.[58]

Modern practice is for banks to require their customers to sign an account mandate when opening an account. The mandate contains detailed express terms relating to the operation of the account. Similarly, other account services, such as telephone or Internet banking or account-linked credit and debit cards, will usually be provided by banks under separate written contracts. These contracts are inevitably based on the bank's own written standard terms and conditions. Depending on the type of account, or other service provided, the bank's standard terms and conditions must take account of the requirements of the Banking Conduct of Business Sourcebook (BCOBS), the Payment Services Regulations 2009 and/ or the Lending Code.[59] Terms of the contract may also be controlled by common law rules, such as the *contra proferentem* rule or the rule against penalty clauses, and also by general contract law statutes, namely Part 2 of the Consumer Rights Act 2015 (controlling unfair terms in 'consumer contracts') and the Unfair Contract Terms Act 1977 (controlling, principally, exemption clauses in other contracts).[60]   **6.17**

The general rule is that the bank-customer contract and the account contract are governed by the law of the place of the branch where the account is kept, unless there is an agreement to the contrary.[61] In the absence of contrary agreement, where the customer has accounts held at branches of the same bank located in different countries, each account will be governed by law of the country where the account-holding branch is located.[62]   **6.18**

(4) Bank's Duty to Honour the Customer's Mandate

(a) The duty

The bank is under an obligation to honour cheques drawn by the customer provided there are sufficient funds in the customer's account to meet the cheque or the bank has agreed to provide   **6.19**

---

[57] *National Bank of Commerce v National Westminster Bank* [1990] 2 Lloyd's Rep 514; *Bank of Baroda v ASAA Mahomed* [1999] Lloyd's Rep (Bank) 14, CA. At common law, where an account has lain dormant for many years the court *may* infer that the sum due has been repaid: *Douglas v Lloyd's Bank Ltd* (1924) 34 Com Cas 263. Under the Dormant Bank and Building Society Accounts Act 2008, s 1, a bank or building society that transfers the credit balance of an account that has remained dormant for 15 years or more to an authorized reclaim fund is protected from the customer's claim for repayment of the balance. Regulation 59 of the Payment Services Regulations 2009 contains a separate time-bar for exercising rights of redress under regs 61, 75, 76 or 77 (see nn 312, 316 and 332 below).

[58] In Singapore it has even been tentatively suggested that, in the light of modern technological and business developments, the requirement for a demand to be made at the branch where the account is kept may no longer represent good law: *Damayanti Kantilal Doshi v Indian Bank* [1999] 4 SLR 1, 11, Sing CA.

[59] 6.04–6.07. For a general review of the statutory requirements placed on banks when opening current accounts and certain types of savings accounts, see *Ellinger's Modern Banking Law*, n 26, at 226–233, 262–263. BCOBS gives a customer a period of 14 calendar days in which to cancel an account contract (subject to limited exceptions) without incurring any penalty and without having to give any reason: BCOBS 6.1.1, 6.3.1.

[60] There are also controls in the Consumer Credit Act 1974.

[61] This is the position under the common law and also applied under the Contracts Applicable Law Act 1990 (*Sierra Leone Telecommunications Co Ltd v Barclays Bank plc* [1998] 2 All ER 821, 827). The same principle continues to apply under EC Regulations 593/2008 on the Law Applicable to Contractual Obligations (in force 17 December 2009), arts 4(1)(b), 19(2), although the applicable law may be that of the jurisdiction where the bank has its head office when two or more accounts are held in different jurisdictions (art 4(2)). See *Ellinger's Modern Banking Law*, n 26, at 380–381.

[62] *Libyan Arab Foreign Bank v Bankers Trust Co* [1989] QB 728, 747; *Libyan Arab Foreign Bank v Manufacturers Hanover Trust Co* [1989] 1 Lloyd's Rep 608, 616–617.

the customer with overdraft facilities sufficient to meet the cheque.[63] Where the bank honours its customer's cheque it acts within its mandate and is entitled to debit the customer's account with the amount of the cheque.[64] The bank may also agree to honour payment instructions delivered by other means, eg, by use of a debit card or by use of a password communicated to the bank over a telephone or Internet link. The bank is probably not obliged to provide these services to its customer without special agreement.[65] Banks have standard terms and conditions that govern the operation of a customer's current account and which provide for access to the account through electronic means. These terms and conditions usually reflect the statutory rights and duties that apply through the provisions of the Payment Services Regulations 2009 ('PSRs'),[65a] and also the FCA's Banking Conduct of Business Sourcebook, which provide mandatory rules for those residual cases where the PSRs do not apply.[65b] Regulation 66(5) of the PSRs provides that '[w]here all the conditions of the payer's framework contract[65c] have been satisfied, the payment service provider may not refuse to execute an authorised payment order irrespective of whether the payment order is initiated by the payer or by or through a payee, unless such execution is otherwise unlawful.'[65d] The PSRs do not apply to cheques.[65e]

(b) Limits on the duty

6.20 There are several limitations to the bank's duty to honour its customer's payment instructions.

(i) Lack of funds

6.21 The bank is obliged to honour its customer's payment instruction only if there are sufficient cleared funds in the customer account or available by way of an agreed overdraft facility.[66] Where there are insufficient funds available to cover the full amount of the customer's payment instruction, the bank may ignore it completely. The customer's payment instruction then stands as an offer to the bank to extend credit to him on the bank's standard terms as to interest and other charges, unless other terms have been agreed between them.[67] The bank may accept or reject this offer.[68]

---

[63] *Joachimson v Swiss Bank Corp*, n 53 above; *Bank of New South Wales v Laing* [1954] AC 135, 154.

[64] *Sierra Leone Telecommunication Co Ltd v Barclays Bank plc*, n 61, at 827.

[65] *Libyan Arab Foreign Bank v Bankers Trust Co*, n 62, at 749.

[65a] SI 2009/209, as amended. See generally, 6.06–6.07 and 6.100–6.106. The PSRs may be disapplied in favour of the Consumer Credit Act 1974, ss 83–84.

[65b] BCOBS, Ch. 5, in particular BCOBS, 5.1.11R (bank's liability for unauthorized payments) and 5.1.12R (banking customer's liability for unauthorized payments). BCOBS 5.1.11R–5.1.19R are similar to Part 6 of the PSRs (as to which, see 6.100–6.106).

[65c] For the definition of a 'framework contract', see n 192 below.

[65d] But note the 'force majeure' provision set out in reg 79.

[65e] PSRs, Sch 1, Part 2(g).

[66] See n 63.

[67] *Emerald Meats (London) Ltd v AIB Group (UK) Ltd* [2002] EWCA Civ 460, at [12], CA; *Lloyds Bank plc v Voller* [2000] 2 All ER (Comm) 978, 982, CA; *Barclays Bank Ltd v WJ Sims, Son & Cooke (Southern) Ltd* [1980] QB 677, 699. In *Office of Fair Trading v Abbey National plc* [2009] UKSC 6, [2009] 3 WLR 1215, the Supreme Court, when considering the scope of the Unfair Terms in Consumer Contracts Regulations 1999, held that bank charges levied on personal account customers in respect of unauthorized overdrafts constitute part of the price or remuneration for the banking services provided and that, insofar as the terms giving rise to the charges are in plain intelligible language, no assessment of the fairness of those terms may relate to their adequacy as against the services provided. Part 2 of the Consumer Rights Act 2015 has revoked and replaced the 1999 Regulations. Section 64(2) of the 2015 Act introduces an additional requirement for the application of the exclusion from the test of unfairness of terms relating to the main subject-matter of the contract or the price/quality ratio: the term must be both transparent (expressed in plain and intelligible language and, in the case of a written term, legible: sub-s (3)) and (which is new) prominent (brought to the consumer's attention in such a way that an average consumer would be aware of the term: sub-ss (4)–(5)).

[68] See cases cited in n 67.

(ii) Unclear or irregular instructions

The customer's payment instructions must be unambiguous in form otherwise the bank **6.22** may refuse payment.[69] Where the instructions are given by cheque, the bank may refuse to pay if the cheque is not properly drawn.[70] In the absence of special instructions to the contrary from their customers, it is the practice of banks not to pay a 'stale' cheque, ie one presented for payment six months or more after the date written on it. The practice is so widespread that there is probably a term implied into the bank-customer contract that the bank may refuse to honour a cheque if not presented until an unreasonable time after its date.

(iii) Unauthorized instructions

Where a bank has reasonable grounds for believing that there is a serious or real possibility **6.23** that a payment instruction has been given without the proper authority of its customer, although it is regular and in accordance with the mandate, the bank is justified in refusing to honour the instruction—the bank would be in breach of duty to its customer if, without inquiry, it did otherwise.[71] Similarly, where a bank has serious grounds for doubting the continuing authority of those operating the account on behalf of the customer, the bank is entitled, and indeed bound, to refuse to honour their payment instructions, at least until the court determines the identity of the authorized signatories or the signatories are able to provide the bank with adequate evidence of continuing authority.[72]

(iv) Renders the bank liable to a third party

A bank is entitled, and indeed bound, to refuse to pay a payment instruction where to do so **6.24** would render it liable as an accessory to misfeasance or breach of trust.[73] The bank must have positive evidence of misfeasance or breach of trust: mere suspicion is not enough to refuse its customer's instructions.[74]

(v) Renders the bank criminally liable

A bank must freeze an account where it knows or suspects that the account contains the **6.25** proceeds of crime.[75] The bank does not act in breach of contract by refusing to honour its customer's payment instructions where it is suspicious that the money in the account is criminal property.[76]

(vi) Third party debt orders

A third party debt order, formerly called a 'garnishee order', is an order of the court granted **6.26** to a judgment creditor, which attaches to funds held by a third party (eg a bank) who owes

---

[69] *London Joint Stock Bank Ltd v Macmillan* [1918] AC 777, 815, HL.
[70] *Cunliffe Brooks & Co v Blackburn and District Benefit Building Society* (1884) 9 App Cas 857, 864, HL.
[71] *Barclays Bank plc v Quincecare Ltd* [1992] 4 All ER 363, 375–376; *Lipkin Gorman (a firm) v Karpnale Ltd* [1989] 1 WLR 1340, 1376, 1378. See 6.42.
[72] *Sierra Leone Telecommunications Co Ltd v Barclays Bank plc*, n 61.
[73] *Royal Brunei Airlines Sdn Bhd v Tan* [1995] 2 AC 378, PC.
[74] *TTS International v Cantrade Private Bank* (1995), unreported decision of the Royal Court of Jersey.
[75] *Squirrell Ltd v National Westminster Bank plc* [2005] EWHC 664 (Ch), [2006] 1 WLR 637, considering s 328 of the Proceeds of Crime Act 2002 (facilitation offence).
[76] *K Ltd v National Westminster Bank plc* [2006] EWCA Civ 1039, [2007] 1 WLR 311, where it was held that the bank does not have to adduce evidence to support any such suspicion or show that there were reasonable grounds for the suspicion. But the bank may have to prove it held the relevant suspicion: *Shah v HSBC Private Bank (UK) Ltd* [2010] EWCA Civ 31, [2011] 1 All ER 67 and [2012] EWHC 1283 (QB) (Supperstone J held, at [45] and [236], that there was an implied term in the banking contract that permitted the bank, because it suspected money laundering, to delay the execution of its customer's payment instruction until it received consent from the relevant authorities under the Proceeds of Crime Act 2002).

money to the judgment debtor (eg the bank's customer).[77] Once an interim order is served on the bank, it must not make any payment from its customer's account that reduces the balance below the amount specified in the order. Should the court make the order final,[78] the bank will be ordered to pay over the amount specified in the order to the judgment creditor. Compliance with the final order discharges the bank's indebtedness to its own customer.[79]

(vii) Freezing injunctions

6.27 Where a bank has notice of a freezing injunction directed to its customer, the bank's duty to honour the customer's mandate is suspended.[80] However, the terms of the injunction may allow payment of trade creditors in the ordinary course of business.[81] Freezing injunctions have been held not to affect a bank's duty to make payment under letters of credit, negotiable instruments and documentary collections, save in very exceptional circumstances.[82] The courts are most reluctant to grant a freezing injunction against a bank itself as this would affect the bank's ability to pay its creditors their due debts.[83]

(viii) Customer's death or insanity

6.28 Under section 75(2) of the Bills of Exchange Act 1882, the bank's duty and authority to pay cheques is terminated when it obtains notice of the customer's death. This section overrides the general rule that an agent's authority is automatically determined by the principal's death. As the bank-customer relationship is not purely one of principal and agent, it is submitted that notice of the customer's insanity, and not merely the insanity itself, terminates the bank's authority to pay.[84]

(ix) Winding up or bankruptcy of customer

6.29 By section 127 of the Insolvency Act 1986, in a winding up of a company by the court, any disposition of the company's property made after the commencement of the winding-up is, unless the court otherwise orders, void. Payments into an account in credit have been held not to constitute dispositions of the company's property as the amount standing to the credit

---

[77] Part 72 of the Civil Procedure Rules 1998. The debt must be 'due or accruing due to the judgment debtor from the [bank]', which means that the debt must be owed solely to the judgment debtor (*Taurus Petroleum Ltd v State Oil Marketing Company of the Ministry of Oil, Republic of Iraq* [2013] EWHC 3494 (Comm), [2014] 1 Lloyd's Rep 432) and be repayable to the judgment debtor on demand and not to someone else (*Merchant International Co Ltd v Natsionalna Aktsionerma Kompaniia Naftogaz Ukrainy* [2014] EWCA Civ 1603).

[78] A court will not make the order final where there is a prior equitable charge or flawed asset arrangement over the account: *Fraser v Oystertec plc* [2004] EWHC 1582 (Ch), [2005] BPIR 381; nor will it do so where the account in question is held at an overseas branch or bank: *Société Eram Shipping Co Ltd v Compagnie Internationale de Navigation* [2003] UKHL 30, [2004] 1 AC 260; *Kuwait Oil Tanker Co SAK v Qabazard* [2003] UKHL 31, [2004] 1 AC 300 (but see also *Masri v Consolidated Contractors International Co SAL* [2008] EWCA Civ 303, [2009] QB 450, at [41]–[42], [47]).

[79] But there is no discharge if the bank pays in reliance on only an interim order: *Crantrave Ltd v Lloyds TSB Bank plc* [2000] QB 917, CA.

[80] *Z Ltd v A-Z and AA-LL* [1982] QB 558, CA. But a bank given notice of the grant of a freezing injunction does not owe the successful applicant a duty to take reasonable care to comply with its terms: *Customs and Excise Commissioners v Barclays Bank plc* [2006] UKHL 28, [2007] 1 AC 181.

[81] *Iraqi Ministry of Defence v Arcepey Shipping Co SA* [1981] QB 65. Cheques supported by cheque guarantee cards used to fall outside the ambit of the injunction, but such cards are no longer in use in the UK (6.73).

[82] *Z Ltd v A-Z and AA-LL*, n 80, at 592–593; *Lewis & Peat (Produce) Ltd v Almatu Properties Ltd* [1993] 2 Bank LR 45, CA.

[83] *Polly Peck International plc v Nadir (No 2)* [1992] 4 All ER 769, CA; *Camdex International Ltd v Bank of Zambia (No 2)* [1997] 1 All ER 728, CA.

[84] But the position may be different were an order has been made under the Mental Capacity Act 2005: see AG Guest, *Chalmers and Guest on Bills of Exchange and Cheques* (17th edn, 2009) para 13–047.

of the customer's account is increased.[85] Payments into an overdrawn account do constitute dispositions of the company's property and are void under section 127 unless validated by the court.[86] Payments made out of a company's bank account, whether the account is in credit or overdrawn, have been held not to constitute a disposition of the company's property to the bank, which merely acts as the company's agent in making a disposition in favour of the third party.[87] In any event, a bank is well advised to ask the company for a validation order under section 127 before allowing it to continue to operate the account as notice of the winding-up petition terminates the bank's authority to honour its customer's cheques.[88] If a disposition is made in good faith in the ordinary course of business when the parties are unaware of the presentation of the petition, and it is completed before the winding up order is made, the court is likely to validate it.[89] Similar principles apply in the case of the bankruptcy of a customer.[90]

(x) Countermand

Under section 75(1) of the Bills of Exchange Act 1882, the bank's authority or mandate to pay a cheque drawn on it by its customer is determined by countermand of payment. Notice of countermand must be clear and unambiguous,[91] and it must be brought to the actual (not merely constructive) notice of the bank.[92] Unless otherwise agreed, notice of countermand must be given to the branch of the bank were the account is kept.[93] Where a customer is given access to his account by electronic means, eg, by debit card or through telephone or Internet banking services, the specific contract allowing such access will usually contain express provision dealing with countermand. In any event, the Payment Services Regulations 2009 restrict the ability of the payer to revoke a payment order given by electronic means by providing, as a general rule, that the payer cannot revoke his order once it has been received by his bank.[94]

6.30

(c) Remedies for wrongful dishonour of customer's mandate

Wrongful dishonour of the customer's cheque or other payment instruction will render the bank liable in damages for breach of contract.[95] For many years the amount of damages recoverable by the customer differed according to whether he was a trader or a non-trader. Where the customer was a trader he could recover substantial damages for injury to his credit and reputation without proof of actual loss,[96] but where he was a non-trader he could only recover nominal damages for breach of contract, unless he proved actual loss.[97] However, the distinction between traders and non-traders was swept away in *Kpohraror v Woolwich*

6.31

---

[85] *Re Barn Crown Ltd* [1994] 4 All ER 42.

[86] *Re Gray's Inn Construction Ltd* [1980] 1 WLR 711, CA.

[87] *Hollicourt (Contracts) Ltd v Bank of Ireland* [2001] Ch 555, CA, endorsing the ruling of Lightman J in *Coutts & Co v Stock* [2000] 1 WLR 906.

[88] *Pettit v Novakovic* [2007] BPIR 1643, at [7]. Presentation of the petition does not *automatically* terminate the bank's mandate: *Hollicourt (Contracts) Ltd v Bank of Ireland*, n 87.

[89] Unless it can be challenged as a preference: *Re Tain Construction Ltd* [2003] BPIR 1188.

[90] Insolvency Act 1986, s 284. But there are differences between the two regimes and differences between s 127 and s 284: *Pettit v Novakovic*, n 88.

[91] *Westminster Bank v Hilton* (1926) 43 TLR 124, HL.

[92] *Curtice v London City and Midland Bank Ltd* [1908] 1 KB 293, CA.

[93] *London, Provincial and South Western Bank Ltd v Buszard* (1918) 35 TLR 142.

[94] SI 2009/209, reg 67(1) (for time of receipt, see reg 65). See reg 67(2) for revocation of orders initiated by or through the payee, and reg 67(3) for revocation of a direct debit. For further provisions relating to revocation: see reg 67(4)–(6).

[95] But there remains uncertainty as to whether the Payment Services Regulations 2009, SI 2009/209, establish an exclusive remedial regime for (electronic) payments that fall within their scope: see 6.100.

[96] *Wilson v United Counties Bank Ltd* [1920] AC 102, 112, HL.

[97] *Gibbons v Westminster Bank* [1939] 2 KB 882; *Rae v Yorkshire Bank plc* [1988] FLR 1, CA.

Building Society,[98] where the Court of Appeal held that in every case—trader and non-trader alike—there is a presumption of fact that the customer suffers some injury to his credit and reputation when his cheque is wrongfully dishonoured.

6.32   A bank which wrongfully dishonours its customer's cheque may also be liable to its customer, the drawer, in defamation. It is standard banking practice for the drawer's bank to note the reason for dishonour on the cheque, and this statement will be passed back to the collecting bank and the holder of the cheque. Where the drawer's bank implies that the cheque was dishonoured for supposed lack of funds (eg, by using the now notorious phrase 'refer to drawer'—held to be potentially defamatory by the jury in *Jayson v Midland Bank Ltd*),[99] the drawer will have an action for defamation against his bank should it turn out that the cheque was wrongfully dishonoured. Dishonour of a cheque without stating a reason is probably not defamatory.[100]

(d) Defences

6.33   Common law and equity confer certain defences on a bank charged with having breached its duty to honour its customer's mandate.[100a] Those statutory defences available to a bank upon which a cheque is drawn are considered later in this chapter.[101]

(i) Breach of duty

6.34   The customer owes a duty to his bank to exercise reasonably care when drawing a cheque (or other payment order) so as not to facilitate fraud or forgery.[102] The customer will be held responsible for any loss sustained by the bank as a result of his breach of duty. The test is whether the customer was careless, and this must be assessed in the light of all the circumstances.[103] The duty is of narrow scope. Negligence which is not connected with the actual drawing of the cheque or other payment order does not usually afford a defence to the bank.[104]

(ii) Estoppel

6.35   The customer may be precluded (estopped) by his conduct from denying that a payment was authorized. The customer may have made an explicit representation to the bank to that effect.[105] Alternatively, the customer may have failed to inform the bank of forgeries or other fraudulent use of his account as soon as he became aware of it.[106] The customer must have actual knowledge of the fraud or forgery, constructive knowledge, in the sense of merely having the means of knowledge, is not enough.[107]

---

[98] [1996] 4 All ER 119, CA.

[99] [1968] 1 Lloyd's Rep 409.

[100] *Frost v London Joint Stock Bank Ltd* (1906) 22 TLR 760, CA.

[100a] This section of the chapter reflects the general common law and equity as it emerged before the enactment of the PSRs (see 6.06–6.07). The pre-2009 law remains applicable to cheques (as cheques fall outside the scope of the PSRs) and to other payment transactions that do not fall within the scope of the PSRs. (For the scope of the PSRs, see 6.06–6.07. The contractual terms and conditions upon which the bank supplies its services would also require consideration in such cases.) In respect of payment transactions that fall within their scope, the PSRs do not expressly preserve the common law and equitable position in general (see 6.100).

[101] 6.66–6.67.

[102] *London Joint Stock Bank Ltd v Macmillan* [1918] AC 777, HL.

[103] *Slingsby v District Bank Ltd* [1931] 2 KB 588, aff'd [1932] 1 KB 544; cf *Lumsden & Co v London Trustee Savings Bank* [1971] 1 Lloyd's Rep 114, 121.

[104] *Bank of Ireland v Evans' Trustees* (1855) 5 HLC 389.

[105] *Brown v Westminster Bank Ltd* [1964] 2 Lloyd's Rep 187.

[106] *Greenwood v Martins Bank Ltd* [1933] AC 51, HL.

[107] *Price Meats Ltd v Barclays Bank plc* [2002] 2 All ER (Comm) 346; *Patel v Standard Chartered Bank* [2001] 1 Lloyd's Rep 229.

(iii) Wider duty?

In *Tai Hing Cotton Mill Ltd v Liu Chong Hing Bank Ltd*,[108] a case involving cheque fraud, **6.36** the Privy Council rejected the idea that a customer owes his bank a wider duty to run his business in such a way as to make it difficult for fraud to occur,[109] or that he owes a duty to check his periodic bank statements to identify the fraudulent use of his account at an early stage and thereby prevent further fraud.[110] These duties were not to be implied into the bank-customer contract and did not arise in tort. Lord Scarman, delivering the advice of the Privy Council, said that the solution was for banks to increase the severity of their terms of business,[111] eg, through the use of 'verification clauses' which require the customer to notify the bank within a specific time of any errors in his bank statement, which would otherwise be deemed correct.[112] *Tai Hing* has been much criticized but still remains good law for cheques.[113] However, the obligations, and potential liability, of customers accessing their accounts by electronic means must now be assessed in the light of the Payment Services Regulations 2009, which require the customer using a payment card or device for making electronic funds transfers to 'take all reasonable steps to keep its personalised safety features safe'.[114]

(iv) Ratification

Ratification may occur where a bank pays a cheque drawn in breach of mandate but the **6.37** customer nevertheless approves the transaction or the breach of mandate, or elects to treat the transaction as valid.[115]

(v) Liggett defence

A bank may be able to raise a defence to the customer's claim that his account was wrongly **6.38** debited by pleading that the payment was made for the benefit of the customer in payment of his debts. This is known as the *Liggett* defence, taking its name from *Liggett (Liverpool) Ltd v Barclays Bank Ltd*.[116] In that case the bank was in breach of mandate because it honoured cheques signed by only one director of its corporate customer when signatures of two directors were required. The cheques were drawn in favour of the customer's creditors. Wright J held that the bank was entitled to debit the customer's account because the payments discharged the customer's debts and the bank was entitled to take over (ie to be subrogated to)

---

[108] [1986] AC 80. See also *Lewes Sanitary Steam Co Ltd v Barclay & Co Ltd* (1906) 95 LT 444; *Kepitigalla Rubber Estates Ltd v National Bank of India Ltd* [1909] 2 KB 1010.

[109] The extent to which a bank could claim that the customer is to be held vicariously liable for his employee's fraud remains uncertain: the defence was pleaded but not pursued in *Tai Hing* (see further, *Ellinger's Modern Banking Law*, n 26, at 497–498).

[110] See also *Wealdon Woodlands (Kent) Ltd v National Westminster Bank Ltd* (1983) 133 NLJ 719.

[111] At 106.

[112] But note that the verification clauses in *Tai Hing* were held to be ineffective on grounds of construction (see also *Financial Institutions Services Ltd v Negril Negril Holdings Ltd* [2004] UKPC 40, at [43]; *Morrell v Workers Savings & Loan Bank* [2007] UKPC 3, at [33]). There could also be problems with the Unfair Contract Terms Act 1977, s 13(1)(c), and the Consumer Rights Act 2015, s 63(1) and Sch 2, Part 1, para 20.

[113] See, eg, the penetrating criticism of C Hare 'The duties of bank customers: Whither Tai Hing?' (2012) 23 JBFLP 182.

[114] SI 2009/209, regs 57(2), 62(2), See further, 6.06–6.07.

[115] *London Intercontinental Trust Ltd v Barclays Bank Ltd* [1980] 1 Lloyd's Rep 241; *HJ Symons & Co v Barclays Bank plc* [2003] EWHC 1249 (Comm); *Senex Holdings Ltd v National Westminster Bank plc* [2012] EWHC 131 (Comm), [2012] 1 All ER (Comm) 1130; cf *Limpgrange Ltd v BCCI SA* [1986] Fin LR 36, distinguished in *Swotbook.com Ltd v Royal Bank of Scotland plc* [2011] EWHC 2025 (QB), at [43]–[48] (but still held no ratification). A forged signature cannot be ratified (*Brook v Hook* (1871) LR 6 Ex 89), but it may be 'adopted' by the customer (*Greenwood v Martins Bank Ltd* [1932] 1 KB 371, 379, *per* Scrutton LJ).

[116] [1928] 1 KB 48.

the creditors' remedies against the customer. *Liggett* can be explained as reversing the unjust enrichment of the customer at the expense of the bank, the unjust factor being the bank's mistake.[117]

6.39 The *Liggett* defence rarely succeeds. It is a well established rule that the payment of another's debt does not discharge that debt unless the payment is authorized, ratified or made under legal compulsion or by necessity.[118] In *Re Cleadon Trust Ltd*,[119] a majority of the Court of Appeal considered that the decision in *Liggett* could be upheld only on the basis that the bank had been expressly authorized to pay by one of the company's directors, and that the director himself had the company's authority to do this, even though the director was not authorized to draw a cheque on the company's account for that purpose on his signature alone.[120] The majority's reasoning has since been applied by the Court of Appeal in *Crantrave Ltd v Lloyds TSB Bank plc*,[121] where it was held that the *Liggett* defence arises only where the payment from the account is applied to reduce the customer's debt with the customer's authority, or if the customer has ratified the payment.[122] This means that the *Liggett* defence would not be available where the bank ignored the customer's earlier, effective countermand of a payment instruction, there being no authority to discharge the customer's debt.[123]

(5) Bank's Duty of Care

6.40 It is an implied term of the bank-customer contract that the bank will exercise reasonable care and skill when carrying out operations that fall within that contract.[124] The standard of reasonable care and skill is an objective standard applicable to banks.[125] The duty may also arise concurrently in tort.[126] But where the bank provides specialist banking services to financially sophisticated customers under the terms of contractual documentation drafted by specialist lawyers, the court will be slow to find a duty of care in tort going beyond the rights and obligations carefully set out in the documents.[127] In those exceptional cases where a bank

---

[117] See generally EPL 18.56ff.

[118] See C Mitchell, P Mitchell and S Watterson (eds), *Goff & Jones' The Law of Unjust Enrichment* (8th edn, 2011) paras 5–38 et seq.

[119] [1939] Ch 286.

[120] Reasoning which is itself open to challenge: see C Mitchell, *The Law of Subrogation* (1994) 128–129.

[121] [2000] QB 917, followed in *Swotbook.com Ltd v Royal Bank of Scotland plc*, n 115, at [49]–[56].

[122] It should be noted, however, that Pill and May LJJ also considered that the bank might have a defence to a claim for breach of mandate where it could be established on the evidence that the customer had been 'unjustly enriched' by the unauthorized payment ([2000] QB 917, 924 and 925). See further, *Goff & Jones*, n 118, at para 5-45.

[123] *Liggett* can be distinguished from *Barclays Bank Ltd v WJ Simms Son & Cooke (Southern) Ltd* [1980] QB 677, 700, on this reasoning.

[124] Supply of Goods and Services Act 1982, s 13.

[125] *Selangor United Rubber Estates Ltd v Cradock (a bankrupt) (No 3)* [1968] 1 WLR 1555. In determining whether a bank has acted negligently, regard must be had to all relevant circumstances as well as to standard banking practices: see, eg, *Schioler v Westminster Bank Ltd* [1970] 2 QB 719. The bank is normally under no duty to advise or warn its customer as to the risks attendant on following his instructions: *Redmond v Allied British Banks plc* [1987] FLR 307, 311; *Winnetka Trading Corp v Julius Baer International Ltd* [2011] EWHC 2030 (Ch), [2012] 1 BCLC 588, at [94].

[126] *Henderson v Merrett Syndicates Ltd* [1995] 2 AC 145, HL.

[127] *IFE Fund SA v Goldman Sachs International* [2006] EWHC 2887 (Comm), [2007] 1 Lloyd's Rep 264, at [63], affd [2007] EWCA Civ 811, [2007] 2 Lloyd's Rep 449; applied in *Maple Leaf Macro Volatility Master Fund v Rouvroy* [2009] EWHC 257 (Comm), [2009] 1 Lloyd's Rep 475, at [369]; *Barclays Bank Plc v Svizera Holdings BV* [2014] EWHC 1020 (Comm) at [68]–[70] (applying the opinion of Lord Hodge in *Grant Estates Ltd v Royal Bank of Scotland Plc* [2012] CSOH 133 at [73] as to when a tortious duty of care to advise would arise in the case of a bank or other financial institution); cf *Sumitomo Bank Ltd v Banque Bruxelles Lambert SA* [1997] 1 Lloyd's Rep 487, 513. Recent cases on the mis-selling of financial products have stressed

and its customer are in a fiduciary relationship, a duty of care may be imposed as a matter of fiduciary law.[128]

The bank's duty to exercise reasonable care and skill may also arise when services are provided **6.41** outside a contractual relationship. Thus, a bank may be held liable in tort for negligent advice/misstatements made to customers,[129] and to non-customers, under the *Hedley Byrne* principle.[130] The House of Lords has held that the *Hedley Byrne* principle extends beyond negligent advice/misstatements so that it can apply to economic loss caused by negligent provision of services, and that the basis of a *Hedley Byrne* claim is an assumption of responsibility by the defendant to the claimant.[131] The fact that the bank accepts a request for advice is strong evidence of an assumption of responsibility, although an antecedent request for advice is not necessary where the advice is given within the scope of the bank's business.[132] Where a bank assumes a duty to exercise reasonable care in giving advice and complies with that duty, it does not normally assume a further continuing obligation to keep the advice under review and, if necessary, correct it in the light of supervening events.[133] Furthermore, a bank will not be liable where information or advice supplied by it to a customer is passed on without the bank's knowledge to third parties who rely on it.[134]

---

that contract terms can negative the existence of a duty of care and/or give rise to a contractual estoppel: the leading authority is *Springwell Navigation Corp v JP Morgan Chase Bank* [2010] EWCA Civ 1221, [2010] 2 CLC 705, applying *Peekay Intermark Ltd v ANZ Banking Group* [2006] EWCA Civ 386, [2006] 2 Lloyd's Rep 511. See also, eg, *Barclays Bank Plc v Svizera Holdings BV*, above, at [58]–[63], [71]; *Crestsign Ltd v National Westminster Bank plc* [2014] EWHC 3043 (Ch) at [113]–[114], [119]; *Credit Suisse International v Stichting Vestia Groep* [2014] EWHC 3103 (Comm) at [307]–[308] (contractual estoppel applied to agreement about a state of affairs in the future) and [309]–[310] (questioning whether contractual estoppel is really a form of estoppel at all). A 'disclaimer' cannot create a contractual estoppel when not part of the contract (*Taberna Europe CDO II plc v Selskabet AF1.September 2008 (In Bankruptcy)* [2015] EWHC 971 (Comm) at [120]). See further G McMeel, 'Documentary Fundamentalism in the Senior Courts: the myth of contractual estoppel' [2011] LMCLQ 185. There is also a regulatory regime that controls the way banks provide investment advice and sell investment products contained within the FSMA 2000, and the FCA's conduct of business rules made thereunder. Breach of FCA rules is actionable as a breach of statutory duty by a 'private person' suffering loss (FSMA 2000, s 138D). There is no common law duty of care to comply with the FSMA 2000 regulatory regime: *Brown v InnovatorOne plc* [2012] EWHC 1321 (Comm), at [1276]. See also *Green & Rowley v Royal Bank of Scotland plc* [2013] EWCA Civ 1197, [2013] 2 CLC 634 where the Court of Appeal held that the existence of a statutory means of enforcement of the (now FCA's) conduct of business rules, under (what is now) the FSMA 2000, s 138D, meant that no separate co-extensive common law duty of care arose and there could be no claim for breach of those rules other than under s 138D. The bank did not undertake an advisory duty in *Green & Rowley* and so the case was distinguished in *Crestsign Ltd v National Westminster Bank plc*, above, where advice was given and a duty of care would have arisen if it had not been for the bank's express disclaimer of responsibility.

[128] See 6.44.

[129] *Box v Midland Bank Ltd* [1979] 2 Lloyd's Rep 391.

[130] *Hedley Byrne & Co Ltd v Heller & Partners Ltd* [1964] AC 465, HL, where a bank only avoided liability for negligent advice given about a customer's credit-worthiness in a bank reference provided to a third party because of its disclaimer. See also *Playboy Club London Ltd v Banca Nazionale Del Lavoro SpA* [2014] EWHC 2613 (QB) on the existence and scope of a duty of care when the request for a bank reference came from an associate company of the casino that relied upon it.

[131] *Henderson v Merrett Syndicates Ltd*, n 126; *Williams v Natural Life Health Foods Ltd* [1998] 1 WLR 830, HL. But in *Customs & Excise Commissioners v Barclays Bank plc* [2006] UKHL 28, [2007] 1 AC 181, the House of Lords held that, in cases of pure economic loss, an 'assumption of responsibility' was a sufficient, but not a necessary, condition for the imposition of a duty of care: whether there was a duty of care could also turn on the threefold test of foreseeability, proximity and whether it was fair, just and reasonable to impose the duty.

[132] *Morgan v Lloyds Bank plc* [1998] Lloyd's Rep (Bank) 73, 80, CA.

[133] *Fennoscandia Ltd v Clarke* [1999] 1 All ER (Comm) 365, CA.

[134] *Mann v Coutts & Co* [2003] EWHC 2138 (Comm), [2004] 1 All ER (Comm) 1, applying *Caparo Industries plc v Dickman* [1990] 2 AC 605, HL; cf *Riyad Bank v Ahli United Bank (UK) plc* [2006] EWCA Civ 780, [2006] 2 Lloyd's Rep 292.

6.42   The bank's duty to honour its customer's mandate and its duty to exercise reasonable care and skill in the execution of its customer's order to transfer money may sometimes conflict. The problem could arise, eg, where the director of a company is authorized to draw cheques on the company's account, but does so to defraud the company. Where the account is in credit, the bank's primary obligation is to honour cheques drawn within the bank's mandate, but the bank would act in breach of its duty of care owed to its customer if it honoured a cheque knowing the authorized signatory was defrauding that customer, or if it turned a blind eye to the obvious.[135] In other cases, the bank would be in breach of its duty of care, and so should refrain from executing an order, where it has reasonable grounds (although not necessarily proof) for believing that the order was an attempt to misappropriate funds.[136] Whether the bank has such reasonable grounds for belief is to be assessed on an objective basis according to the standards of the ordinary prudent banker.[137] It has been held that where the signatory of a cheque is not necessarily the account holder,[138] or the signatory of the cheque is not the only person who is liable on it,[139] then 'the possibility of fraud is always more likely to be present'.[140] By contrast, where the apparent signatory of the cheque is himself the account holder, then 'if the bank has no reason not to believe the signatory to be genuine, no question on the face of it can arise of some fraud being committed on the signatory'.[141] Similarly, if one joint account holder was entitled under the mandate to draw on the account in his name alone, and he did so in breach of a private agreement with the other account holders, it is unlikely that the bank would be held to be in breach of a duty of care owed to the other account holders unless the bank had some reason for supposing that the mandate was being abused by the joint account holder.[142]

(6) Bank's Fiduciary Duties

6.43   The core banking activities of deposit-taking and lending are not fiduciary in character.[143] It is well-established that 'on the face of it the relationship between a bank and its customer is not a fiduciary relationship'.[144] A fiduciary is expected to act selflessly, whereas a bank can usually be expected to further its own commercial interests ahead of those of its customer.[145] Some other activities that modern multifunctional banks engage in are more obviously fiduciary in character, eg, where a bank acts as a trustee of an investment fund, or where a bank has power to manage its customer's investments under the terms of a discretionary management

---

[135] *Lipkin Gorman (a firm) v Karpnale Ltd* [1989] 1 WLR 1340, 1356, 1372, 1377, CA; *Barclays Bank plc v Quincecare* [1992] 4 All ER 363, 376.

[136] N 135.

[137] N 135.

[138] As in *Barclays Bank plc v Quincecare*, n 135.

[139] As in *Lipkin Gorman (a firm) v Karpnale Ltd*, n 135.

[140] *Verjee v CIBC Bank & Trust Co (Channel Islands) Ltd* [2001] Lloyd's Rep (Bank) 279, 282. But full weight must also be given to the principle 'that trust, not distrust, is . . . the basis of a bank's dealings with its customers': *Quincecare*, n 135, at 376).

[141] *Verjee v CIBC Bank & Trust Co (Channel Islands) Ltd*, n 140, at 282.

[142] *Royal Bank of Scotland plc v Fielding* [2004] EWCA Civ 64, at [107]–[108].

[143] *Foley v Hill*, n 51.

[144] *Governor and Company of the Bank of Scotland v A Ltd* [2001] EWCA Civ 52, [2001] Lloyd's Rep (Bank) 73, at [25]. But some activities of a multifunctional bank may give rise to fiduciary duties, eg acting as custodian of its customer's securities (*JP Morgan Chase Bank v Springwell Navigation Corp* [2008] EWHC 1186 (Comm) at [573], affirmed [2010] EWCA Civ 1221, [2010] 2 CLC 705; *Forsta Ap-Fonden v Bank of New York Mellon SA* [2013] EWHC 3127 (Comm) at [173]). Even then, the fact the bank is a fiduciary in some respects does not mean that it is a fiduciary in all respects (*Forsta Ap-Fonden v Bank of New York Mellon SA*, above, at [174]; *Saltri III v MD Mezzanine SA SICAR* [2012] EWHC 3025 (Comm), [2013] 1 All ER (Comm) 661 at [123]).

[145] In *National Westminster Bank plc v Morgan* [1983] 3 All ER 85, 91, Dunn LJ famously observed that banks 'are not charitable institutions'.

agreement. But even then, it always remains open to the bank to exclude or modify the fiduciary obligations that it would otherwise owe through the terms of the underlying contract under which the services are provided.[146]

In an exceptional case a bank might be held to owe fiduciary obligations to its customer,[147] as where it knows that the customer is placing his trust and confidence in the bank and is relying on it. This was the explanation given by Salmon J in *Woods v Martins Bank Ltd*[148] when holding that the defendant bank was liable for advice given to the financially naïve claimant to invest in a company that had a substantial overdraft with the bank. Liability would be much more likely to be imposed today under the *Hedley Byrne* principle[149] without reference to fiduciary concepts.[150] Nevertheless, the possibility remains that a fiduciary relationship might arise in those rare cases where the customer has placed trust and confidence in the bank so as to give it influence over him.[151] **6.44**

It is important to distinguish between those situations where a bank is held liable for breach of fiduciary duty and where a bank becomes liable 'as a constructive trustee'. The bank can be held liable as a constructive trustee either because it has beneficially received misapplied trust property,[152] or because it has assisted or otherwise been an accessory to another's breach of trust, when it might not have received any property at all.[153] The bank is liable for receipt only if the state of its knowledge is such as to make it unconscionable for the bank to retain the benefit of the receipt;[154] it is liable as an accessory only where it has acted dishonestly.[155] **6.45**

---

[146] *Kelly v Cooper* [1993] AC 205, 214–215, PC; *Henderson v Merrett Syndicates Ltd* [1995] 2 AC 145, 206, HL But subject to the usual statutory controls on exemption clauses, unless the clause is in a trust deed when the Unfair Contract Terms Act 1977 has been held not to apply (*Baker v JE Baker & Co (Transport) Ltd* [2006] EWCA Civ 464).

[147] *Fahad Al Tamimi v Mohamad Khodari* [2009] EWCA Civ 1109, at [42].

[148] [1959] 1 QB 55. *Woods* pre-dates *Hedley Byrne*.

[149] *Hedley Byrne & Co Ltd v Heller & Partners Ltd*, n 130.

[150] As it was in *Verity & Spindler v Lloyds Bank plc* [1995] CLC 1557, in many ways a similar case to *Woods*.

[151] See *Lloyds Bank Ltd v Bundy* [1975] QB 326, CA, where the unusual circumstances of the case were expressly recognized by the court itself (at 340 and 347). Contrast, *National Westminster Bank plc v Morgan* [1985] AC 686, HL, reversing [1983] 3 All ER 85.

[152] See *Agip (Africa) Ltd v Jackson* [1990] Ch 265, 292, where Millett J (obiter) stressed that paying and collecting banks would not normally be brought within the receipt category because they do not generally receive money for their own benefit, acting only as their customer's agent, but that the position would be otherwise if the collecting bank used the money to reduce or discharge the customer's overdraft (and there must also be a conscious appropriation of the sum paid into the account in reduction of the overdraft: PJ Millett, 'Tracing the Proceeds of Fraud' (1991) 107 LQR 71, 83, fn 46). See generally EPL 18.167–18.171.

[153] Hence why it is misleading to describe the bank as a 'constructive trustee': see, eg, *Dubai Aluminium Co Ltd v Salaam* [2002] UKHL 48, [2003] 2 AC 366, at [141], *per* Lord Millett. Both are cases of 'ancillary liability' where the intervention of equity is 'purely remedial': *Williams v Central Bank of Nigeria* [2014] UKSC 10, [2014] AC 1189 at [9], per Lord Sumption JSC.

[154] *Bank of Credit and Commerce International (Overseas) Ltd v Akindele* [2001] Ch 437, 455, CA; endorsed by the Court of Appeal in *Criterion Properties plc v Stratford UK Properties LLC* [2003] EWCA Civ 1883, [2003] 1 WLR 2108, at [20]–[39] (aff'd on different grounds [2004] UKHL 28, [2004] 1 WLR 1846); *Charter plc v City Index Ltd* [2007] EWCA Civ 1382, [2008] Ch 313, at [8]; *Uzinterimpex JSC v Standard Bank plc* [2008] EWCA Civ 819, [2008] 2 Lloyd's Rep 456, at [37]–[46]. But doubts have been expressed as to the utility of a test based on unconscionability as opposed to one based on knowledge: see, eg, *Relfo Ltd (In Liquidation) v Varsani* [2012] EWHC 2168 (Ch) at [79]–[80], affirmed [2014] EWCA Civ 360.

[155] *Royal Brunei Airlines v Tan* [1995] 2 AC 378, 389, 392, PC. Dishonesty in this context means that the defendant knew of the elements of the transaction which made it dishonest according to normally accepted standards of behaviour even though he may not himself have been conscious that the transaction was dishonest: *Twinsectra Ltd v Yardley* [2002] UKHL 12, [2002] 2 AC 164, HL, as explained in *Barlow Clowes International Ltd v Eurotrust International Ltd* [2005] UKPC 27, [2006] 1 All ER (Comm) 478, at [10]–[18]; *Abou-Rahmah v Abacha* [2006] EWCA Civ 1492, [2007] 1 Lloyd's Rep 115, at [66], [94]; *Starglade Properties Ltd v Nash* [2010] EWCA Civ 134, at [32]. See EPL 17.363–17.366.

(7) Bank's Duty of Confidentiality

(a) The duty

6.46 It was established in *Tournier v National Provincial and Union Bank of England* that a bank is under a common law duty of confidentiality, arising out of an implied term of the bank-customer contract, in relation to information concerning its customer and his affairs which it acquired in the character of his banker.[156] The duty extends to all information gained by virtue of the banking relationship and is not limited to information from or about the account itself.[157] The bank remains subject to the duty even after the termination of the bank-customer relationship in respect of information acquired by the bank during the currency of that relationship. The courts take a common sense approach when deciding which information is caught by the duty. It has been held, eg, that a bank did not breach the duty by revealing information to someone who had already obtained it from another source, in this case, under the statutory scheme for the registration and cancellations of cautions over land.[158]

(b) Qualifications

6.47 The bank's duty of confidentiality is not absolute but is a qualified one. It does not exist in the four exceptional circumstances identified by Bankes LJ in *Tournier*.[159]

(i) Where disclosure is under compulsion of law

6.48 There is an increasing amount of legislation under which disclosure can be compelled, including the Banker's Book Evidence Act 1879,[160] the Police and Criminal Evidence Act 1984[161] the Companies Act 1985,[162] and the Insolvency Act 1986.[163] Legislation to combat money laundering and the financing of terrorist activities is particularly draconian. A bank commits an offence if it fails to disclose to the police its knowledge or suspicion, or that it has reasonable grounds for knowledge or suspicion, that a customer is engaged in money laundering or terrorist offences.[164] Such disclosure is a 'protected disclosure', ie it 'is not to be taken to

---

[156] [1924] 1 KB 461, CA. The Lending Code, n 5, states that '[p]ersonal information will be treated as private and confidential' (para 15). cf R Cranston, *Principles of Banking Law* (2nd edn, 2002) 171–174, where the bank's duty of confidentiality is located within the general principles governing breach of confidence rather than treated as a discrete area of law. In any event, those general principles, set out by Lord Goff in *A-G v Guardian Newspapers Ltd (No 2)* [1990] 1 AC 109, 281–282, can be used to protect confidential information revealed to a bank by a customer in a non-banking context (eg when the bank provides investment advice or asset management services) or by a non-customer (eg when presenting a business plan to secure bank finance). See also *Douglas v Hello! Ltd (No 3)* [2007] UKHL 21, [2008] 1 AC 1, [272]–[275], [292], [307], HL. The bank may also give an express undertaking to keep such information confidential (see, eg, *Primary Group (UK) Ltd v Royal Bank of Scotland Plc* [2014] EWHC 1082 (Ch), where *Wrotham Park/* negotiation damages awarded for breach). Personal data relating to customers who are natural persons is held by a bank subject to the Data Protection Act 1998.
[157] The judgments of Bankes LJ (at 473) and Atkin LJ (at 485) being preferred to that of Scrutton LJ (at 481) on this point. See also Lord Donaldson MR in *Barclays Bank plc v Taylor* [1989] 3 All ER 563, 565.
[158] *Christofi v Barclays Bank plc* [1999] 2 All ER (Comm) 417, CA: the Court of Appeal added that the situation would be otherwise where the bank had expressly undertaken not to reveal the information.
[159] See n 156, at 472–473.
[160] Section 7.
[161] Section 9. See *Barclays Bank plc v Taylor*, n 157, CA: bank owes no duty to customer to oppose application for disclosure or to inform him that application has been made. cf *Robertson v Canadian Imperial Bank of Commerce* [1994] 1 WLR 1493, PC: bank might be under a duty to use best endeavours to inform customer of service of witness summons.
[162] Sections 434(2), 452(1A).
[163] Sections 236, 366.
[164] Proceeds of Crime Act 2002, s 330; Terrorism Act 2000, s 21A. The threshold for suspicion is low: *K Ltd v National Westminster Bank plc*, n 76, at [16]; applied in *Shah v HSBC Private Bank plc* [2010] EWCA Civ 31, [2010] 3 All ER 477, at [21] and [2012] EWHC 1283 (QB), at [67]–[69]).

breach any restriction on the disclosure of information (however arising)'.[165] Banks may also be the subject of *Norwich Pharmacal* orders,[166] *Bankers Trust* orders[167] and disclosure orders made in aid of a tracing claim.[168]

(ii) Where there is a duty to the public to disclose

Whereas the first qualification *requires* information to be disclosed by the bank, this qualification *permits* disclosure by the bank. However, given the amount of legislation which requires or permits disclosure by a bank, this second qualification is of only limited value. There are few cases where the courts have had to adjudicate on the propriety of disclosure by a bank under this qualification.[169] **6.49**

(iii) Where the interests of the bank require disclosure

In *Tournier*,[170] Bankes LJ said the qualification would apply, eg, when, in order to claim repayment of an overdraft, the bank disclosed that the customer's account was overdrawn. But the self-serving nature of this qualification makes it the most controversial.[171] In *Sutherland v Barclays Bank Ltd*[172] it was held that the qualification justified disclosure of information by the bank to the customer's husband when the bank's reputation was questioned by him. This qualification cannot be used to justify the transfer of customer information to other companies for marketing purposes.[173] **6.50**

(iv) Where the disclosure is made by the express or implied consent of the customer

For many years banks have provided each other with credit references relating to their customers. In *Turner v Royal Bank of Scotland plc*,[174] the bank tried to justify the practice on the ground that their customers gave their implied consent to it when they opened their accounts. The Court of Appeal held that the bank had breached its duty of confidentiality as the practice was not sufficiently well known to the bank's customers to make it an implied term of the bank-customer contract. **6.51**

(8) Bank's Right of Combination

In certain circumstances a bank may combine a customer's bank accounts by setting the credit balance on one account off against the debit balance on another to determine the total **6.52**

---

[165] Proceeds of Crime Act 2002, 337(1); Terrorism Act 2000, s 21B(1).

[166] See, eg, *Santander UK Plc v National Westminster Bank Plc* [2014] EWHC 2626 (Ch); *Credit Suisse Trust Ltd v Intesa Sanpaolo SpA* [2014] EWHC 1447 (Ch).

[167] *Bankers Trust Co v Shapira* [1980] 1 WLR 1277, CA.

[168] See *AJ Bekhor & Co Ltd v Bilton* [1981] QB 923, 953–955, CA.

[169] See, eg, *Libyan Arab Foreign Bank v Bankers Trust Co*, n 62; *Pharaon v Bank of Credit and Commerce International SA (in liquidation)* [1998] 4 All ER 455.

[170] See n 156, at 473.

[171] See Cranston, n 156, at 174–176; R Spearman, 'Disclosure of confidential information: *Tournier* and "disclosure in the interests of the bank" reappraised' [2012] JIBFL 78.

[172] (1938) 5 LDAB 163, CA, where it was also said that the disclosure was justified on grounds of implied consent (wife allowed husband to join telephone conversation with bank). See also *Kaupthing Singer & Friedlander Ltd v Coomber* [2011] EWHC 3589 (Ch), [2012] BPIR 774 at [52], [56]; *Deutsche Bank (Suisse) SA v Khan* [2013] EWHC 482 (Comm) at [384]–[393]; *Primary Group (UK) Ltd v Royal Bank of Scotland Plc* [2014] EWHC 1082 (Ch) at [192], where disclosure was held not to be 'reasonably necessary' for the bank's own protection.

[173] The Lending Code, n 5, at paras 23–35. See also the Data Protection Act 1998, s 11(1) and the Privacy Electronic Communications (EC Directive) Regulations 2003, SI 2003/2426.

[174] [1999] 2 All ER (Comm) 64 (*quaere* whether *Turner* applies to business customers: *Ellinger's Modern Banking Law*, n 26, at 195–197). The Banking and Business Banking Codes, n 14.04, later made bankers' references subject to the customer's express consent, but the Lending Code, n 5, makes no direct reference to them (although it does cover disclosure to credit reference agencies and to debt collection agencies).

state of indebtedness between that customer and the bank. This is known as the banker's right of combination. It may allow the bank to refuse to honour a payment instruction received from the customer unless the overall credit balance on the customer's accounts taken together is sufficient to meet the payment. Of course, the bank would only seek to do this where it was doubtful about the customer's solvency. A customer has no right to insist that the bank excise its right of combination so that a cheque is honoured when there are insufficient funds in the particular account on which it is drawn.[175] However, in practice, the bank will usually honour the customer's cheque and hold the credit balances on other accounts as security for the overdraft, combining the accounts if necessary.

6.53 The banker's right of combination should not be confused with the exercise of a banker's lien.[176] A lien is a right to retain possession of property that belongs to someone else, and the bank has no lien over funds which, when deposited by the customer, becomes its own property.[177] The right of combination is a particular form of contractual set-off.[178] It may be excluded by express or implied agreement of the bank and customer, however, it is more common for the bank to reinforce or even increase the ambit of its right of combination through express provision in the bank-customer contract. The bank may exercise its right of combination without notice to its customer, unless the bank has previously agreed not to combine accounts; if it were otherwise the bank would run the risk that a customer placed on notice of combination would empty the account in credit and render the right of combination useless.[179] The banker's right of combination is lost if the bank and customer have agreed to keep accounts separate.[180] Such an agreement may be implied, as is usually the case when a customer opens a loan account,[181] or where a deposit account has a fixed maturity date as opposed to being repayable on demand. Combination is also inapplicable where a fund is deposited with the bank for a special purpose of which it has knowledge.[182] There is some controversy as to whether the mere fact of maintaining accounts in different currencies or different jurisdictions should itself give rise to an implied agreement not to combine.[183] Further, an account opened by a customer as trustee, agent or nominee of another person, may not be combined with the customer's private account.[184] However, unless the bank-customer

---

[175] *Garnett v McKewan* (1872) LR 8 Exch 10, 14.

[176] For the banker's lien, see *Ellinger's Modern Banking Law*, n 26, at 864–867.

[177] *In re Spectrum Plus Ltd* [2005] UKHL 41, [2005] 2 AC 680, at [60], *per* Lord Hope. See also *Halesowen Presswork and Assemblies Ltd v National Westminster Bank Ltd* [1971] 1 QB 1, 46, *per* Buckley LJ. But a credit balance on the account can be charged to the bank: *Re Bank of Credit and Commerce International SA (No 8)* [1998] AC 214.

[178] PR Wood, *English and International Set-Off* (1989) 92–94; L Gullifer, *Goode's Legal Problems of Credit and Security* (5th edn, 2013) paras [7.31] et seq; cf S McCracken, *The Banker's Remedy of Set-Off* (3rd edn, 2010) ch 1; R Derham, *The Law of Set-Off* (4th edn, 2010) ch 15.

[179] But the question of notice remains open: see *Ellinger's Modern Banking Law*, n 26, at 261–263 considering, inter alia, the Lending Code, n 5, at para 195. For retail customers, the bank's right of combination is now regulated by the FCA's *Banking Conduct of Business Sourcebook* (BCOBS), which imposes certain information requirements pre-contract (BCOBS 4.1.4AG(2)(a)(i),(ii)), pre-use of set-off rights (BCOBS 4.1.4AG(2)(b)(i),(ii)) and post-use of set-off rights (BCOBS 4.1.4AG(2)(c)). BCOBS also imposes limits on the use of set-off rights against retail customers: see BCOBS 5.1.3AG(1), (2)(a) (customer must be left with a 'subsistence balance'); BCOBS 5.1.3AG(2)(b)(i),(ii) (no set-off of personal debts against ring-fenced or earmarked funds) and BCOBS 5.1.3BG(1), (2) (refund is usual remedy unless not fair to do so).

[180] *Barclays Bank Ltd v Okenarhe* [1966] 2 Lloyd's Rep 87, 95; cf the statutory right of set-off on insolvency under s 323 of the Insolvency Act 1986, applies to companies under r 4.90 of the Insolvency Rules 1986, which cannot be overridden by contract: *Halesowen Presswork and Assemblies Ltd v National Westminster Bank Ltd* [1972] AC 785 at 805, 809, 824, HL. In the context of administration, see Insolvency Rules 1986, r 2.85.

[181] *Bradford Old Bank Ltd v Sutcliffe* [1918] 2 KB 833.

[182] *Barclays Bank Ltd v Quistclose Investments Ltd* [1970] AC 567, HL.

[183] McCracken, n 178, at 33.

[184] *Union Bank of Australia v Murray-Aynsley* [1898] AC 693.

contract provides otherwise, the bank may be able to exercise an equitable right of set-off between a personal account and a 'nominee' account, if there is clear and undisputed evidence that the customer entitled to the funds in both accounts is one and the same person.[185] There is some uncertainty as to the availability of combination between a customer's personal account and a joint account. Dicta in some cases suggests that combination can only occur when the customer is entitled to the entire interest in the joint account,[186] however, it is submitted that combination should be allowed where it can be clearly established that the debtor is solely entitled to a discrete part of the joint account.[187]

(9) Termination of the Bank-Customer Relationship

Usually the courts deal with termination of the bank-customer relationship in the context of closure of the customer's account, although it is important to note that some aspects of the relationship may continue beyond then, eg, the bank's duty of confidentiality in respect of the customer's account extends beyond the point when the account is closed,[188] and the customer's claims in respect of unauthorized transactions will, in the absence of an agreement to the contrary, continue to be valid.[189] **6.54**

Fixed term deposit accounts will mature at the agreed time so that neither bank nor customer may unilaterally terminate their relationship before then, although in practice the bank will usually allow the customer to close the account prematurely on sufferance of an interest penalty. Under the common law, customers with current accounts or easy access savings accounts may unilaterally terminate the relationship at any time by drawing out the remaining funds *and* asking for the account to be closed.[190] For accounts that fall within the scope of the Payment Services Regulations 2009 (PSRs),[191] the contract may be terminated by the customer at any time, unless a period of notice (not exceeding one month) has been agreed.[192] **6.55**

Termination by the bank is treated differently. At common law, 'in the absence of express contrary agreement or statutory impediment, a contract by a bank to provide banking services to a customer is terminable upon reasonable notice'.[193] Under the PSRs, for 'framework contracts', such as current accounts and easy access savings accounts, a bank may only close an account opened for an indefinite period by giving at least two months' notice, if the contract so provides.[194] **6.56**

---

[185] *SAMA v Dresdner Bank AG* [2004] EWCA Civ 1074, [2005] 1 Lloyd's Rep 12, CA; *Uttamchandami v Central Bank of India* (1989) 133 Sol Jo 262, CA; *Bhogal v Punjab National Bank* [1988] 2 All ER 296, CA.
[186] *Ex p Morier* (1879) 12 Ch D 491, 496, CA; *Bhogal v Punjab National Bank* [1988] 2 All ER 296, 301, CA.
[187] See *Abbey National plc v McCann* [1997] NIJB 158, 172, NICA.
[188] *Tournier v National Provincial and Union Bank of England*, n 156, at 473, CA.
[189] *Limpgrange Ltd v Bank of Credit and Commerce International SA*, n 115.
[190] *Bank of Baroda v ASAA Mahomed* [1999] Bank LR 14, CA.
[191] SI 2009/209, as amended (6.06–6.07).
[192] Termination of a 'framework contract', such as one for a current account or easy access savings account, is covered in reg 43. A framework contract is defined in reg 2 to mean 'a contract for payment services which govern the future execution of individual and successive payment transactions and which may contain the obligation and conditions for setting up a payment account.' Where the framework contract is also a regulated agreement under the Consumer Credit Act 1974, reg 43 does not apply (reg 34).
[193] *National Commercial Bank of Jamaica Ltd v Olint Corporation Ltd* [2009] UKPC 16, at [1], *per* Lord Hoffmann. As to what constitutes a reasonable period of notice, see *Prosperity Ltd v Lloyds Bank Ltd* (1923) 39 TLR 372. See also *Olint* at [16]–[21] (application for injunction refused on grounds that, where customer disputes closure of his account, damages will usually be an adequate remedy).
[194] Regulation 43(4).

C. Payment Methods

(1) Cheques

(a) Definition

6.57 Section 73 of the Bills of Exchange Act 1882 (BEA) defines a cheque as a bill of exchange drawn on a banker payable on demand, and, except as otherwise provided in Part III of the BEA, the provisions of that Act applicable to a bill of exchange payable on demand apply to cheques. A bill of exchange is an unconditional order in writing, addressed by one person to another, signed by the person giving it, requiring the person to whom it is addressed to pay a sum certain in money on demand or at a fixed or determinable future time to or to the order of a specified person, or to bearer.[195]

(b) Functions

6.58 A cheque is capable of performing two different functions. The first is a payment function enabling the drawer of the cheque to instruct his bank to make payment to himself or a third party, and the holder to obtain payment from the drawer. The second is a transfer and negotiation function enabling title to the cheque to be passed by transfer from person to person and for the transferee to enforce his rights under the cheque free from any defects in title of the transferor.

6.59 The payment function is the most important function of a cheque.[196] Modern banking law and practice means that virtually all cheques issued in the UK since 1992 are crossed cheques marked 'account payee' or 'account payee only' which makes the cheque non-transferable and, therefore, non-negotiable.[197] Most of the law relating to negotiability and indorsement is irrelevant to the typical modern cheque and is not considered in this chapter.[198]

(c) Cheques as payment instructions

(i) Basic rules

6.60 A cheque constitutes the customer's mandate to his bank to make payment from his account. The rules relating to honouring the customer's mandate are considered in 6.19 to 6.39 above and are relevant in this context. Three rules merit repetition. First, the bank is only obliged to honour a cheque drawn on its customer's account where there are sufficient funds in the account to meet the whole of the amount of the cheque or where the cheque is within an agreed overdraft facility.[199] Secondly, the cheque must be signed by the customer or other

---

[195] BEA, s 3. A cheque is not invalid by reason of the fact it is ante-dated or post-dated (BEA, s 13(2)) or even not dated at all (BEA, s 3(4); *Aspinall's Club Ltd v Fouad Al-Zayat* [2007] EWCA Civ 1001, at [27]).

[196] Unless the facts indicate otherwise, payment by cheque operates as conditional payment only (*Re Charge Card Services* [1989] Ch 497, 511, CA; *Crockfords Club Ltd v Mehta* [1992] 1 WLR 355, 366, CA; *Homes v Smith* [2000] Lloyd's Rep (Bank) 139, at [35], CA). It is likely that the use of a cheque guarantee card to support the cheque did not alter this presumption (*Re Charge Card Services* [1987] Ch 150, 166, *per* Millett J, obiter; the Court of Appeal left the issue open: cheque guarantee cards are no longer in use in the UK). Cross claims for unliquidated damages cannot be set up in answer to a claim on a cheque (*Nova (Jersey) Knit Ltd v Kammgarn Spinnerei GmbH* [1977] 1 WLR 713, HL) but one for total (or quantified partial) failure of consideration can offer a defence against the payee, as can a defence which calls the validity of the cheque into question, eg that its issue was induced by fraud or conspiracy (*Solo Industries UK Ltd v Canara Bank* [2001] EWCA Civ 1059, [2001] 2 All ER (Comm) 217).

[197] BEA, s 81A(1), inserted by the Cheques Act 1992.

[198] The law can be found in AG Guest, *Chalmers and Guest on Bills of Exchange and Cheques* (17th edn, 2009); N Elliott, J Odgers and JM Phillips, *Byles on Bills of Exchange and Cheques* (29th edn, 2013).

[199] 6.21.

mandated signatory. A forged or unauthorized signature is 'wholly inoperative',[200] which means that where the drawer's signature is forged or unauthorized the bank cannot debit the account. In some cases the customer may be estopped from raising the fraud against the bank,[201] in other cases the bank may be able to rely on the fact that the customer's negligence allowed the fraud to take place.[202] Thirdly, a cheque can be countermanded under section 75 of the BEA.[203] The bank must receive the countermand in time for it to refuse payment of the cheque.[204]

(ii) Crossed cheques

A cheque is crossed when two parallel transverse lines are drawn across its face. This is a **6.61** general crossing and means that the cheque must be presented for payment through a bank account.[205] The holder of the cheque cannot present it in person for cash. Sometimes the name of a bank will be written on the face of the cheque. This is a special crossing and means that the cheque must be presented for payment through the named bank.[206] A transferee of a crossed cheque which is also marked 'not negotiable' cannot acquire a better title than his transferor had, although the cheque remains transferable.[207] An uncrossed cheque marked 'not negotiable' is probably non-transferable.[208] Crossed cheques marked 'not negotiable' and uncrossed cheques are hardly ever seen today.

In 1992, following the enactment of the Cheques Act 1992, which introduced section 81A(1) **6.62** into the BEA, where a cheque is crossed and bears across its face the words 'account payee' or 'a/c payee', either with or without the word 'only', the cheque is non-transferable and is only valid as between the parties to it, ie the drawer and the payee. Today virtually all cheque forms supplied by UK banks to their customers are crossed and pre-printed 'account payee'. Only the named payee can be the holder of such a cheque.

In general, only the drawer and holder may cross a cheque.[209] Where a cheque is crossed **6.63** specially, the bank to whom it is crossed may again cross it specially to another bank for collection.[210] The bank on whom the cheque is drawn (the drawer's bank) must be careful to pay in accordance with the crossing. The crossing is part of the mandate and failure to adhere to it prevents the bank from debiting the drawer's account.[211] Moreover, section 79(2) of the BEA provides that the bank will be liable to the 'true owner' of the cheque for any loss incurred owing to the cheque having been paid contrary to the crossing, eg, where a thief steals a crossed cheque from the payee and the bank allows the thief to present it for payment over the counter. If the true owner is the drawer he will have no claim since he can require the bank to reinstate his account.[212] Section 79(2) goes on to protect the drawer's bank against a claim by the true owner, and allows the bank to debit the drawer's account, where the cheque

---

[200] BEA, s 24.
[201] 6.35.
[202] 6.34.
[203] 6.30. The terms of issue of a cheque guarantee card usually prohibited countermand of a cheque supported by the card (such cards are no longer in use in the UK: see 6.73).
[204] See further *Chalmers and Guest*, n 198, at para 13-039.
[205] BEA, s 76(1), sometimes the words 'and company' are inserted between the parallel lines but this adds nothing.
[206] BEA, s 76(2).
[207] BEA, s 81.
[208] *Hibernian Bank Ltd v Gysin and Hanson* [1939] 1 KB 483, CA.
[209] BEA, s 77(1)–(4).
[210] BEA, s 77(5). Where a bank receives an uncrossed cheque, or a cheque crossed generally, for collection, it may cross it specially to itself (s 77(6)). This sub-section adds little.
[211] *Bellamy v Majoribanks* (1852) 7 Exch 389, 404; *Bobbett v Pinkett* (1876) 1 Ex D 368, 372.
[212] *Channon v English, Scottish & Australian Bank* (1918) 18 SR (NSW) 30, 38.

does not appear (i) to be crossed, or (ii) to have had a crossing which has been obliterated, or (iii) to have a crossing which has been added to or amended in an unauthorized manner, provided that the bank acted in good faith and without negligence.

(iii) Collection of cheques

6.64 A cheque is a debit instrument. On receipt of a cheque, the payee will give it to his bank (the collecting bank) which will then present it for payment to the drawer's bank (the paying bank). This process is known as collecting the cheque. The cheque clearing system facilitates the process by enabling the bulk presentation of cheques from collecting banks to paying banks in order that they may be paid or dishonoured.[213] Not all cheques are presented for payment through the clearing system. Sometimes the payee will request his bank to make a special presentation of the cheque directly to the branch of the paying bank upon which it is drawn thereby speeding up the process. Cheques drawn on the same or different branches of the payee's bank do not go through the clearing.

6.65 It used to be the case that a cheque had to be physically presented for payment at the branch of the bank on which it was drawn.[214] This is no longer required. In 1996 the Bills of Exchange Act 1882 was amended to allow for 'cheque truncation', ie the presentation of a cheque by electronic transmission of essential 'code-line' information about the cheque. The process did not take off and most of those amendments have now been repealed by s 13 of the Small Business, Enterprise and Employment Act 2015. Section 13 of the 2015 Act introduces fresh amendments to the 1882 Act that allow for cheques to be cleared through presentation of an electronic image of the cheque in place of presentation of the cheque itself.[214a] This would, for example, enable a customer to take a photograph of her cheque on her smartphone and pay it in to her bank electronically via the bank's mobile banking app.

(d) The paying bank

6.66 We have already considered the common law defences that may be available to the drawer's (paying) bank when it pays a cheque in breach of mandate.[215] There are also a number of statutory defences available to the paying bank. Section 60 of the BEA protects a bank that pays a cheque payable to order that bears an indorsement that is forged or which was made without authority. Section 1 of the Cheques Act 1957 protects a bank that pays a cheque that lacks a proper indorsement. In both cases the bank must show that it acted in good faith and in the ordinary course of business.[216] However, the modern practice of banks providing their customers with pre-printed 'account payee' (non-transferable) cheque forms has rendered both defences of marginal relevance as such cheques are not payable to order and do not require indorsement.

6.67 Section 80 of the BEA protects a bank that pays a crossed cheque to a bank that collects the cheque on behalf of someone who is not the true owner.[217] The bank must show that it

---

[213] For details of how the cheque clearing system works, see *Ellinger's Modern Banking Law*, n 26, at 390–398. On 12 July 2011, the Payments Council announced that it was reversing its earlier decision to close the cheque clearing system in 2018.

[214] *Barclays Bank plc v Bank of England* [1985] 1 All ER 385, 386.

[214a] See Part 4A of the Bills of Exchange Act 1882 (as inserted by s 13). Section 13 came into force on 26 March 2015 for the purposes of enabling the making of regulations under Part 4A of the 1882 Act, and it will come into force on 31 July 2016 for all other purposes: Small Business, Enterprise and Employment Act 2015, s 164(4).

[215] 6.33–6.39.

[216] *Carpenters' Co v British Mutual Banking Co Ltd* [1938] 1 KB 511, CA.

[217] The true owner is the person with an immediate right to possession of the cheque: *Marquess of Bute v Barclays Bank Ltd* [1955] 1 QB 202. In cases of misappropriation, the identity of the true owner depends

made the payment in good faith and without negligence. Where the bank falls within the protection of the section it may debit its customer's account and it is given a defence against any action in conversion brought against it by the true owner. Section 80 affords protection where the cheque bears a forged or unauthorized indorsement, but it will not protect the paying bank where the drawer's signature has been forged or made without his authority as the instrument is not then a cheque at all, for the signature is wholly inoperative.[218] Neither will the section protect the paying bank where the cheque has been materially altered so as to be caught by section 64(1) of the BEA. The effect of the material alteration is to render the instrument void with the result that it is no longer a cheque but a 'worthless piece of paper'.[219] However, the paying bank can normally ignore any purported indorsement on an 'account payee' cheque, as it is the responsibility of the collecting bank to ensure that a non-transferable cheque is collected only for the account of the named payee.[220]

(e) The collecting bank

The collecting bank owes its customer a duty to collect a cheque promptly and, once collected, to credit the customer's account with the amount. In the absence of an express provision in the bank-customer contract, it is likely that a term will be implied to the effect that cheques are to be collected within a reasonable time, which will be fixed according to the custom and practice of bankers.[221] The fact that the vast majority of cheques drawn on one bank and collected by another are presented for payment through the cheque clearing system means that a court would have regard to all reasonable rules of practice of the clearing system when deciding what is a reasonable time. **6.68**

The collecting bank receives the cheque as agent for its customer for the purposes of collecting it on the customer's behalf.[222] For these purposes, the collecting bank's customer may be another domestic or foreign bank using the collecting bank as its agent to gain access to the cheque clearing system.[223] In theory, the collecting bank could give the customer value for the cheque and collect the cheque, to the extent that value was given, on its own behalf as a holder for value, but the fact that banks now invariably issue cheque forms to their customers crossed 'account payee', thereby making the cheque non-transferable, means that this is very rare indeed, for a collecting bank cannot become the holder of a non-transferable cheque.[224] **6.69**

Where the collecting bank collects a cheque for anyone other than the true owner,[225] the bank may be liable to the true owner for conversion of the cheque. For the purposes of an action in conversion, the cheque is deemed to have a value equal to the amount for which it is drawn.[226] **6.70**

---

on whether the cheque has been delivered by the drawer to the payee. If it is uncertain whether a cheque was misappropriated whilst in the hands of the drawer or the payee, by s 21(3) of the BEA the payee will be deemed to have received a valid and unconditional delivery of the cheque, and hence be the true owner, until the contrary is proved: *Surrey Asset Finance Ltd v National Westminster Bank plc* (2000) Times, 30 November; permission to appeal refused [2001] EWCA Civ 60.

[218] BEA, s 24.

[219] *Smith v Lloyds TSB Bank plc* [2000] 2 All ER 693, 703, CA. BEA, s 64(1), is said to be an application of the rule in *Pigot's Case* (1614) 11 Co Rep 26b (*Habibsons Bank Ltd v Standard Chartered Bank (Hong Kong) Ltd* [2010] EWCA Civ 1335, [2011] QB 943, at [28]).

[220] BEA, s 81A(2). But additional circumstances might reveal negligence on the part of the paying bank (see *Chalmers and Guest*, n 198, at para 14-028).

[221] BEA, s 45(2) and s 74(2).

[222] But the proceeds of the cheque are not held on trust for the customer: *Emerald Meats (London) Ltd v AIB Group (UK) Ltd*, n 67.

[223] *Hon Soc of the Middle Temple v Lloyds Bank plc* [1999] 1 All ER (Comm) 193; *Linklaters (a firm) v HSBC Bank plc* [2003] EWHC 1113 (Comm), [2003] 2 Lloyd's Rep 545.

[224] Hence why the collecting bank's defence of holder in due course is not considered in this chapter.

[225] See n 217.

[226] *Morison v London County and Westminster Bank Ltd* [1914] 3 KB 356, 365, CA.

The rule does not apply where the cheque has been materially altered by an unauthorized person for then it is deemed to be a 'worthless piece of paper'.[227] Alternatively, the amount received for the cheque may be recovered from the bank by the true owner as money had and received. In theory, the collecting bank may have a right of indemnity or recourse against its customer, but in practice this may prove worthless.[228] As the collecting bank will have a defence to the restitutionary claim for money had and received if it has already paid the proceeds of the cheque over to its customer in good faith and in ignorance of the claim, the most common form of action brought by the true owner against the bank is an action in conversion.

6.71 The main statutory defence that a collecting bank can raise to a claim in conversion is to be found in section 4(1) of the Cheques Act 1957.[229] The section provides as follows:

Where a banker, in good faith and without negligence—
(a) receives payment for a customer of an instrument to which this section applies; or
(b) having credited a customer's account with the amount of such an instrument, receives payment thereof for himself;
and the customer has no title, or a defective title, to the instrument, the banker does not incur any liability to the true owner of the instrument by reason only of having received payment thereof.

The section applies to a cheque and protects the collecting bank from claims for conversion and also for money had and received.[230]

6.72 To avail itself of the protection afforded by section 4, the collecting bank must be able to prove that it acted in good faith and without negligence. Often good faith is presumed and negligence is in issue. Negligence is judged against the objective standard of the reasonable banker.[231] A failure by the bank properly to identify its customer when opening the account is likely to be held to be negligent.[232] Similarly, there may be negligence in the collecting of the cheque itself, eg, in the absence of special circumstances, it would generally be negligent to collect payment of an 'account payee' cheque for someone other than the named payee without further inquiry.[233] But in each case the enquiry is fact sensitive and current banking practice is highly relevant to the issue of negligence.[234] There are differing views as to whether the bank's negligence should be disregarded where it can be shown that it had no causative effect on the true owner's loss.[235]

---

[227] *Smith v Lloyds TSB Group plc*, n 219, applying BEA, s 64(1).

[228] Unless the customer is a bank itself: *Hon Soc of the Middle Temple v Lloyds Bank plc*, n 223; *Linklaters (a firm) v HSBC Bank plc*, n 223.

[229] There is also a statutory defence of contributory negligence in s 47 of the Banking Act 1979. Common law defences of ratification, illegality and even the *Liggett* defence (6.38) may also apply.

[230] *Capital and Counties Bank Ltd v Gordon* [1903] AC 240, HL.

[231] *Marfani & Co Ltd v Midland Bank Ltd* [1968] 1 WLR 956, 973, CA; *Linklaters (a firm) v HSBC Bank plc*, n 232, at [106].

[232] *Marfani & Co Ltd v Midland Bank Ltd* [1968] 1 WLR 956, 973, CA. Banks must also have proper procedures for identifying their customers so as to comply with the Money Laundering Regulations 2007, n 48.

[233] When acting as agent for a domestic collecting bank it would generally be reasonable for the collecting agent to assume its principal was aware of its responsibilities under the Cheques Act 1992 and that the principal would ensure that the cheque was collected for the named payee: *Hon Soc of the Middle Temple v Lloyds Bank plc*, n 223 (held collecting agent not entitled to assume foreign bank aware of responsibilities under the 1992 Act).

[234] *Architects of Wine Ltd v Barclays Bank plc* [2007] EWCA Civ 239, [2007] 2 All ER (Comm) 285, at [12], *per* Rix LJ, who added that '[a] bank's evidence about its practice is, especially if unchallenged, relevant evidence of the current practice of bankers'.

[235] Contrast A Malik & J Odgers (eds) *Paget's Law of Banking* (14th edn, 2014) para 27.23, citing, inter alia, *Marfani & Co Ltd v Midland Bank Ltd*, n 209, at 976, CA, *Hon Soc of the Middle Temple v Lloyds Bank plc*, n 223, at 226, with M Brindle & R Cox (eds), *Law of Bank Payments* (4th edn, 2010) para 7–160, citing, inter alia, *Thackwell v Barclays Bank plc* [1986] 1 All ER 676, 684.

Recent legislative reforms allowing for the collection of a cheque through transmission of a **6.72A** digital image of the cheque seek to place liability for fraud or error on the shoulders of the collecting bank. The government considered that the collecting bank, which collects the digital image and introduces it into the clearing system, was best placed to implement measures to make the system secure, detect security risks at the earliest stage and reduce fraud in the system. We have seen that s 13 of the Small Business, Enterprise and Employment Act 2015 inserts a new Part 4A into the Bills of Exchange Act 1882 to allow for the electronic presentation of cheques by the collecting bank to the drawee bank for payment.[235a] Under new s 89E(1), the Treasury may by regulations make provision for the 'responsible banker' to compensate any person for any loss of a kind specified by the regulations which that person incurs in connection with electronic presentation or purported electronic presentation of a cheque or other relevant instrument.[235b] The Explanatory Notes to the Small Business, Enterprise and Employment Act 2015 explain that such regulations could, for example, provide for a claim by the drawer of the cheque or the bank that paid the cheque where the payment was made to the wrong account because of a defect in the image, or where the image had been created fraudulently.[235c] The term 'responsible banker' is defined in sub-s.(3) to mean (a) the banker who is authorized to collect payment of the instrument on a customer's behalf, or (b) if the holder of the instrument is a banker, that banker. It should be noted that, under sub-s (5), the regulations may make provision for (a) the responsible banker to be required to pay compensation irrespective of fault (ie strict liability); and (b) the amount of compensation to be reduced by virtue of anything done, or any failure to act, by the person to whom compensation is payable (ie contributory negligence). Sub-s (6) makes it clear that if a bank has to pay compensation under the regulations, it is not prevented from making a claim against another party for a contribution towards compensation.

(2) Payment Cards

(a) Cheque cards

Cheque cards are no longer in use in the UK.[236] In the past, a cheque card was issued by a **6.73** bank for use with its customer's cheques. Through the card the bank undertook to the payee of the cheque that payment would be made (up to the limit indicated on the card itself) regardless of the state of the customer's account, provided that certain conditions were met. In *Re Charge Card Services*,[237] Millett J described the obligation undertaken by the bank to the payee as being not to dishonour the cheque on presentation for lack of funds in the account, so that the bank was obliged, if necessary, to advance moneys to the customer to meet it. The description 'cheque guarantee card', as this type of card was sometimes described, was strictly a misnomer because the obligation assumed by the bank was not a secondary obligation dependent on default by the card-holder, but a separate independent obligation.[238]

(b) Credit cards and charge cards

A credit card gives the card-holder a revolving credit facility with a monthly credit limit. The **6.74** card-holder does not have to settle his account in full at the end of the each month but has the option to take extended credit, subject to an obligation to make a specified minimum payment each month. Amounts outstanding at the end of a set period commencing with the

---

[235a] See 6.55 and, in particular, see n 214a above for commencement dates.
[235b] At the time of writing, regulations are still awaited.
[235c] Explanatory Notes, para 160.
[236] The UK's Domestic Cheque Card Scheme was closed on 30 June 2011.
[237] [1987] Ch 150, 166 (aff'd [1989] Ch 497).
[238] *First Sport Ltd v Barclays Bank plc* [1993] 1 WLR 1229, 1236, CA.

date of the monthly statement attract interest charged on a daily basis. Unlike a credit card, the main function of a charge card is to facilitate payment, rather than to provide a credit facility. The holder of a charge card must normally settle his account in full within a specified period after the date of a monthly statement. Overdue accounts may be charged a sum equal to interest but this is described by the card-issuer as 'liquidated damages'. In the case of both credit cards and charge cards, a separate card account is usually maintained for the card-holder and payments are made into the account from a current account with a bank by cheque, by direct debit or sometimes even by standing order. In fact, there are more similarities than differences between credit cards and charge cards. Charge card agreements are generally treated as being the same as credit card agreements for the purposes of the Consumer Credit Act 1974, although they remain exempt from 'connected lender liability' under section 75.[239]

6.75 The contractual relations involved in credit or charge card transactions were identified by the Court of Appeal in *Re Charge Card Services Ltd* as follows:[240] (i) between card-holder and supplier, ie contract of sale or supply; (ii) between card-issuing bank and card-holder; and (iii) between card-issuing bank and supplier. *Re Charge Card Services Ltd* involved a simplified 'three-party' card scheme, ie a single card-issuer, a card-holder and a supplier. In fact there are often four parties involved in any particular transaction.[241] The fourth party is known as a 'merchant acquirer'. The merchant acquirer (often the supplier's own bank) gives the supplier admission to the scheme.[242] The merchant acquirer arranges to receive credit card and transaction details from the supplier and makes the appropriate payments to the supplier less a handling charge. Under the terms of a master agreement between the banks, the merchant acquirer obtains reimbursement from the card-issuer.

6.76 Payment by credit card or charge card is presumed to be intended by the parties to constitute absolute payment, as the supplier accepts the card-issuer's payment undertaking, or that of the merchant acquirer who admitted him to the scheme, in place of the card-holder's liability.[243]

(c) Debit cards

6.77 A debit card can be used to obtain cash or make a payment at point of sale or at distance, eg, over the telephone or Internet. The card-holder's current account is debited for such a transaction without deferment of payment. Debit card transactions are electronic and use EFTPOS systems.[244] EFTPOS allows payment to be made for goods and services by the electronic transfer of funds from the customer's account to the supplier's account. Where the system is entirely on-line, this could be virtually instantaneous.

6.78 Debit card transactions involve four discrete contractual relationships: (i) between card-holder and supplier, ie the contract of sale or supply;[245] (ii) between card-issuing bank and card-holder, giving the card-holder authority to use the card and the card-issuing bank authority to debit the card-holder's account with the amount of any transaction entered into; (iii) between supplier and merchant acquirer, obliging the supplier to accept all cards

---

[239] 6.89–6.90.

[240] [1989] Ch 497, 509.

[241] Alternatively, the arrangement may be only 'two-party' as where the card is issued by a shop or store for purchase of their own goods or services.

[242] On the merchant acquirer's own terms and conditions: see *Lancore Services Ltd v Barclays Bank plc* [2009] EWCA Civ 752, [2010] 1 All ER 763 (and summarizing the process of credit card payments at [4]–[10]).

[243] *Re Charge Card Services Ltd* [1989] Ch 497, CA.

[244] EFTPOS stands for Electronic Funds Transfer at Point of Sale.

[245] *Debenhams Retail plc v Customs & Excise Commissioners* [2005] EWCA Civ 892, [2005] STC 1155.

issued under the scheme in payment for goods or services and containing the merchant acquirer's undertaking to pay the supplier for the value of goods and services supplied;[246] and (iv) between the participating banks and financial institutions, covering various matters including the means of transfer of funds from one institution to another. By analogy with payment by credit card,[247] payment by debit card probably constitutes absolute payment.

(d) ATM cards

Automated teller machines (ATMs) are not a method of payment but a means of providing **6.79** customers with cash, so as to pay for goods and services. The ATM or cash card can be used only in the ATMs of the card-issuing bank and those of other banks with whom the issuing bank has reached an agreement.[248] There is some dispute as to whether these other banks act as agents of the card-issuing bank when dispensing cash to the card-holder, or whether they act as principals. An ATM function is usually incorporated into credit cards and debit cards.

(e) Digital cash cards

Digital cash (or 'electronic money') systems are either smart card systems, where electronic **6.80** value is stored in a microchip on a smart card, or software based systems where tokens or coins are stored in the memory of a computer. The 'value', 'tokens' or 'coins' take the form of digital information. Digital cash allows payment to be made simply by transferring digital information directly between debtor and creditor so that value is transferred immediately upon delivery. In some systems the recipient of digital cash can immediately use it to pay for other goods or services. Other systems require the token to be deposited in a bank account or with the issuer who will then issue a token of equivalent value or credit the value to an account.

Digital cash systems depend on various contractual relationships for legal effect. Digital cash **6.81** is issued by an 'originator' (a private company) to banks participating in the scheme that pay for it in real funds. Participating banks re-issue digital cash to customers by charging their digital cash card, or the memory of their computer in a software system, with digital information representing the value purchased from the bank by the customer (usually through a debit to their account). There is a clear contractual relationship between the originator and the participating banks and between those banks and their own customers. However, for a digital cash scheme to operate, holders of digital cash must have confidence that the originator will ultimately be liable to redeem the digital cash for real value. This can be achieved by treating digital cash systems as giving rise to a series of standing offers of unilateral contracts,[249] or through reliance on the Contracts (Rights of Third Parties) Act 1999, so long as the originator and participating banks have not contracted out of that Act.[250]

Digital cash does not constitute legal tender.[251] By analogy with payment by credit card,[252] **6.82** payment by digital cash card probably constitutes absolute payment.

---

[246] The merchant acquirer was held entitled to withhold payment in *Do-Buy 925 Ltd v National Westminster Bank plc* [2010] EWHC 2862 (QB) (and summarizing the process of debit card payments at [7]–[13]).
[247] See n 243.
[248] See *Royal Bank of Scotland Group plc v Commissioner of Customs and Excise* [2002] STC 575.
[249] See R Hooley, 'Payment in a Cashless Society' in BAK Rider (ed), *The Realm of Company Law—A Collection of Papers in Honour of Professor Leonard Sealy* (1998) 245.
[250] Section 1(2).
[251] Hooley, n 249, 250–256.
[252] See n 243.

(f) Liability for unauthorized transactions

(i) Terms of the contract

6.83 Resolution of any dispute between card-holder and card-issuer, card-holder and supplier, supplier and card-issuer (or other financial institution that admitted the supplier to the scheme), and between the financial institutions that are members of the particular payment card scheme, will normally depend on the terms of the contract governing the relevant contractual relationship in issue.[253] The card-issuing contract and the merchant agreement by which a supplier becomes a member of a particular scheme will generally be on the bank's or other financial institution's written standard terms of business and be caught by the Unfair Contract Terms Act 1977.[254] But the 1977 Act only catches terms which can broadly be described as 'exclusion' or 'limitation' clauses.[255] Part 2 of the Consumer Rights Act 2015 is much broader in scope catching virtually all terms in a consumer contract.[256] Part 2 applies to the card-issuing contract where the contracting card-holder is a consumer (defined in such as way as to exclude companies), but not where the card-holder is acting in a business capacity. Part 2 does not apply to a merchant agreement between a supplier and the bank or other financial institution that admitted the supplier to the scheme.

(ii) Consumer Credit Act 1974

6.84 In certain circumstances the card-holder may be able to argue that his payment card is a 'credit-token',[257] issued to him under a 'credit-token agreement',[258] and that his liability for unauthorized use should be limited under sections 83 and 84 of the Consumer Credit Act 1974 (CCA), in effect, to a maximum of £50 prior to notification to the bank that the card is lost, stolen or otherwise liable to misuse.[259] On the other hand, the card-holder can be held liable for all loss occasioned through use of the card by a person who acquired possession of it with his consent.[260] However, after the card-issuer has been so notified in accordance with the provisions of section 84, the card-holder will not be liable for further loss arising from use of the card.[261] Moreover, where the Act applies and the card-holder claims that the use of his card was unauthorized, then under section 171(4)(b) of the CCA it is for the bank to prove either that the use was authorized, or that the use occurred before the bank had been given notice as stated above.

6.85 The protection offered by sections 83 and 84 of the CCA only applies to payment cards issued under credit-token agreements. Credit cards and charge cards are issued under

---

[253] It is likely that many card-issuers will have drafted their standard terms and conditions of use to reflect the protection offered to consumer, micro-enterprise and small charity credit card-holders in the Lending Code, n 6, section 6.

[254] Although the Consumer Rights Act 2015 amends the Unfair Contract Terms Act 1977 so as no longer to apply to 'consumer contracts' or 'consumer notices' as defined by the 2015 Act.

[255] EPL 8.110–8.118.

[256] Part 2 of the 2015 Act revokes and replaces the Unfair Terms in Consumer Contract Regulations 1999, SI 1999/2083. But s 64 of the 2015 Act provides that there is to be no test of unfairness of terms relating to the main subject-matter of the contract or the price/quality ratio so long as those terms are both transparent (expressed in plain and intelligible language and, in the case of a written term, legible) and prominent (brought to the consumer's attention in such a way that an average consumer would be aware of the term), and not a term listed in Part 1 of Sch 2 to the 2015 Act.

[257] CCA, s 14(1).

[258] CCA, s 14(2).

[259] The card-holder will also not be liable for misuse of a card that is lost or stolen before being 'accepted' by him (CCA, s 66).

[260] CCA, s 84(2).

[261] CCA, s 84(3).

credit-token agreements when issued to an individual (including a sole trader or small part-nership).[262] But there is some controversy as to whether debit cards and ATM cards are protected by these provisions.[263] It seems reasonably certain that digital cash cards are not covered by the protection offered by sections 83–84.

(iii) Payment Services Regulations 2009

The PSRs[264] provide card-holders with protection against unauthorized use of a wider range **6.86** of payment cards than is offered by the CCA, which may well only extend to credit cards and charge cards. Where the CCA applies to the unauthorized use of a payment card issued under the terms of a regulated consumer credit agreement, certain regulations within the PSRs are disapplied and sections 66, 83 and 84 of the Act apply instead.[265] However, the protection afforded by the PSRs is significant because they extend to payment cards that are probably not caught by the CCA, eg, debit cards, ATM cards and digital cash cards.[266]

Except in relation to agreements that are regulated by the CCA, where an executed payment **6.87** transaction is not properly authorized, the card-issuer must immediately refund the amount of the unauthorized payment transaction to the card-holder and, where applicable, restore the debited payment account to the state it would have been in had the unauthorized payment transaction not taken place.[267] In order to claim a refund or restoration of his account, the card-holder must notify the card-issuer without delay on becoming aware of the unauthor-ized nature of the transaction and, in any event, this must be done not later than 13 months after the debit date.[268] The onus is on the card-issuer to prove that the transaction was 'authenticated',[269] accurately recorded, and not affected by a technical breakdown or some other deficiency.[270] The mere use of the card is not of itself necessarily sufficient to prove either that the transaction was authorized by the card-holder or that he acted fraudulently or failed with intent or gross negligence to keep his personal security features safe.[271] These card-issuer obligations apply in relation to regulated agreements covered by the CCA.[272]

Regulation 57 places the card-holder under several express obligations, including that he **6.88** must 'take all reasonable steps' to keep his personalized security features (eg his PIN) safe[273] and notify the issuer 'in the agreed manner and without undue delay' once he has become aware of the loss, theft, misappropriation, or unauthorized use of the card.[274] Again, these obligations also apply even with regard to credit tokens covered by the CCA.[275] Except in

---

[262] 'Individual' is defined in s 189(1) of the CCA 1974.

[263] *Ellinger's Modern Banking Law*, n 26, at 664–668.

[264] SI 2009/209 as amended. See 6.06–6.07, especially for the scope of the PSRs.

[265] 6.84–6.85.

[266] There are some exceptions, eg, store cards issued by a retailer for use in store or digital cash cards that can only be used in a limited number of outlets (see Sch 1, para 2(k)). Note there are special provisions deal-ing with liability for misuse of 'low value' payment instruments (reg 53).

[267] Regulation 61.

[268] Regulation 59(1) (but not if the bank has failed to comply with various information requirements in Part 5 of the PSRs: reg 59(2)). Regulated agreements under the CCA fall outside reg 59 of the PSRs and ss 66, 83 and 84 of the Act apply instead (reg 52).

[269] 'Authenticated' means the use of any procedure by which the issuer is able to verify the use of the card, including its personalized security features (reg 60(2)).

[270] Regulation 60(1). The corporate opt-out applies to s 60, see n 22.

[271] Regulation 60(3).

[272] *Ellinger's Modern Banking Law*, n 26, at 676.

[273] Regulation 57(2).

[274] Regulation 57(1)(b).

[275] *Ellinger's Modern Banking Law*, n 26, at 675. There is no corporate opt-out, but as regards 'low value instruments' contracting out of reg 57(1)(b) is permitted.

the case of agreements that are regulated by the CCA, the card-holder is liable for all losses incurred in respect of an unauthorized payment transaction where he has (a) acted fraudulently, or (b) has with intent or gross negligence failed to comply with regulation 57,[276] otherwise the card-holder's liability is limited to £50 at most.[277] In certain circumstances,[278] the non-fraudulent card-holder will not be liable for any losses incurred in respect of an unauthorized payment transaction, namely where the losses arose after notification to the issuer of the loss, theft, misappropriation or unauthorized use of the card, where the issuer failed to provide him with the appropriate means for notification and where the card was used in connection with a 'distance contract' (other than an excepted contract).[279]

(g) Connected lender liability

6.89 Section 75(1) of the CCA provides that 'if a debtor under a debtor-credit-supplier agreement falling within section 12(b) or (c) of the Act has, in relation to a transaction financed by the agreement, any claim against the supplier in respect of a misrepresentation or breach of contract, he shall have a like claim against the creditor,[280] who, with the supplier, shall accordingly be jointly and severally liable to the debtor'.[281] In the context of payment cards, this important provision only applies to purchases made using 'three-party' credit cards (being debtor-creditor-supplier agreements), although it has been held that 'four-party' credit card transactions (supplier recruited by merchant acquirer who is not the card issuer) also fall within section 75(1).[282] It does not apply to purchases made using a 'two-party' credit card (which fall under section 12(a), not section 12(b) or (c), of the CCA), or a charge card (which are exempted by section 75(3)(c) of the CCA), or an EFTPOS debit card (which is expressly excluded from the operation of section 75 by section 187(3A) of the CCA), or a cheque card (which are not debtor-creditor-supplier agreements), or an ATM card (again, not debtor-creditor-supplier agreements), or a digital cash card (again, not debtor-creditor-supplier agreements). Where section 75 applies, so as to make the credit card-issuer liable to the card-holder who has contracted with the issuer (where an additional non-contracting card-holder uses the card section 75 does not apply), then the card-issuer is entitled to be indemnified by the supplier, subject to any agreement between them.[283] The card-holder has a claim against the issuer even if, in entering the transaction with the supplier, he has exceeded his credit limit or otherwise contravened the credit agreement.[284]

---

[276] Regulation 62(2).

[277] Regulation 62(1).

[278] See reg 62(3).

[279] 'Distance contract' and 'excepted contract' have the meanings given in the Consumer Protection (Distance Selling) Regulations 2000, SI 2000/2334, regs 3, 5. Note that reg 21 of SI 2000/2334 and reg 14 of the Financial Services (Distance Marketing) Regulations 2004, SI 2004/2095 (both protecting consumers where 'fraudulent use' was made of their 'payment cards' in connection with 'distance contracts') were revoked by the PSRs, Sch 6, Part 2.

[280] A 'like claim' does not include a right to rescind the credit agreement on the ground that the debtor is entitled to rescind the underlying supply contract, but the debtor can still rescind the credit agreement on the ground that it includes an implied term that it is conditional upon the survival of the supply agreement: *Durkin v DSG Retail Ltd* [2014] UKSC 21, [2014] 1 WLR 1148.

[281] See also CCA, s 56(1)(c), (2), which provides that negotiations by the supplier with the debtor are deemed to be conducted by him as agent of the creditor. This means that a card-issuer may be held liable for any misrepresentations made by the supplier. See also *Scotland v British Credit Trust Ltd* [2014] EWCA Civ 790.

[282] *Office of Fair Trading v Lloyds TSB Bank plc* [2006] EWCA Civ 268, [2007] QB 1 (no appeal on this issue before the House of Lords). See also *Governor and Company of the Bank of Scotland v Alfred Truman* [2005] EWHC 583 (QB) (five parties involved).

[283] CCA, s 75(2).

[284] CCA, s 75(4).

There is an important limitation to the availability of a section 75 claim against a card-issuer. **6.90** By virtue of section 75(3), section 75(1) does not apply to a claim 'so far as the claim relates to any single item to which the supplier has attached a cash price not exceeding £100 or more than £30,000'.[285] However, it should be noted that a claim may be made where a credit card is used to make part payment of less than £100 in respect of an item priced over £100. In *Office of Fair Trading v Lloyds TSB Bank plc*,[286] the House of Lords held that section 75 applies where a UK issued card is used to finance a transaction with a foreign supplier.

(3) Funds Transfers

(a) Nature of a funds transfer

Funds transfers involve the movement of credit balances from one bank account to another. **6.91** A funds transfer system can be paper-based, eg, as currently with bank giro credit transfers, but modern banking relies much more heavily on electronic funds transfer (EFT) systems where the messages that pass between the banks involved in the funds transfer process are in electronic form. In all funds transfer operations, whether paper-based or electronic, the movement of a credit balance from one account to another is brought about through adjustment of the balances of the payer's and the payee's accounts. There is no transfer of property by this process, simply the adjustment of separate property rights of the payer and the payee against their own banks.[287]

(b) Payment by funds transfer

Payment through the use of a funds transfer system is not payment by legal tender. Unless he **6.92** has expressly or impliedly agreed to accept payment by some other means, a creditor is entitled to demand, and is only obliged to accept, payment in legal tender.[288] The mere fact that the creditor has a bank account is not in itself to be construed as evidencing implied consent to accept payment into that account.[289] But the courts have been willing to construe the terms of commercial contracts to allow for payment through the transfer of funds between bank accounts.[290]

(c) Credit and debit transfers

A credit transfer involves the payer giving instructions to his own bank to cause the account **6.93** of the payee, at the same or another bank, to be credited. The payer's instructions can be for an individual credit transfer, eg, through a CHAPS payment, or for a recurring transfer of

---

[285] Where the cash value of goods or services is over £30,000 there may be creditor liability under s 75A of the CCA 1974 ('linked credit agreements') where there is a claim for breach of contract (only) against the supplier and the debtor has taken steps to exhaust his remedies against the supplier. There are a number of other qualifying conditions set out in s 75A.

[286] [2007] UKHL 48, [2008] 1 AC 316. For unresolved issues, see C Hare, 'Credit cards and connected lender liability' [2008] LMCLQ 333, 338.

[287] *R v Preddy* [1996] AC 815, 834, HL. The debt owed to the payer by his bank, assuming his account is in credit, is not assigned to the payee: *Libyan Arab Foreign Bank v Bankers Trust Co* [1989] QB 728, 750; *Customs & Excise Comrs v FDR Ltd* [2000] STC 672, at [36]–[37], CA; *Foskett v McKeown* [2001] 1 AC 102, 128, HL.

[288] See, eg, *Libyan Arab Foreign Bank v Bankers Trust Co*, n 287.

[289] *Customs & Excise Comrs v National Westminster Bank plc* [2002] EWHC 2204 (Ch); [2003] 1 All ER (Comm) 327, applying *TSB Bank of Scotland plc v Welwyn Hatfield DC* [1993] 2 Bank LR 267.

[290] See, eg, *Tenax Steamship Co Ltd v The Brimnes (Owners), The Brimnes* [1975] QB 929, CA. But transfer of funds to an account other than the one stipulated in the underlying contract will not constitute payment or even a valid tender of payment: *PT Berlian Laju Tanker TBK v Nuse Shipping Ltd* [2008] EWHC 1330 (Comm), [2008] 1 CLC 967, at [67].

funds under a standing order.[291] In the case of a debit transfer, it is the payee who conveys instructions to his own bank to collect funds from the payer's bank. These instructions may be initiated by the payer himself and passed on to the payee, eg, as happens with the collection of cheques; alternatively, they may be initiated by the payee himself pursuant to the originator's authority, as happens with direct debits.[292]

6.94 A payer's order to his bank to make a credit transfer to the payee is not a negotiable instrument.[293] The same applies in the case of debit transfer orders, save where the debit transfer is effected by cheque, which may be a negotiable instrument.[294] However, it has been held that payment arrangements of the parties by direct debit are to be treated as assimilated to those of payment by cheque so that there can be no set-off or counterclaim arising from the underlying contract unless there is fraud or failure of consideration.[295]

(d) Clearing and settlement

6.95 Where the payer and the payee have accounts at the same bank, the transfer of funds between the two accounts will usually involve a simple internal accounting exercise at the bank (known as an 'in-house' transfer). The payer's account is debited and the payee's account is credited. Where they hold accounts at different banks (known as an 'inter-bank' transfer), payment instructions will pass from bank to bank, sometimes via intermediary banks. The process of exchanging payment instructions between participating banks is known as clearing. Each inter-bank payment instruction must be paid by the bank sending the instruction to the bank receiving it. It is this process, whereby payment is made between the banks themselves of their obligations *inter se*, which is known as settlement.

6.96 Settlement can occur either on a bilateral or a multilateral basis. Bilateral settlement occurs where the bank sending the payment instruction and the bank receiving it are correspondents, meaning that each holds an account with the other. Multilateral settlement involves the settlement of accounts of the sending bank and the receiving bank held at a third bank. The banks that participate in the main paper-based and electronic funds transfer systems that operate in the UK settle across accounts held at the Bank of England.

6.97 Settlement can also be either gross or net. With gross settlement, the sending and receiving banks settle each payment order separately without regard to any other payment obligations arising between them. This is usually done on a real-time basis, with settlement across the accounts of participating banks held at the Bank of England as each payment is processed. With net settlement, the mutual payment obligations of the parties are set off against each other and only the net balances paid. Net balances are usually settled either at the end of the day or the next day.[296]

---

[291] But a bank is under no duty to make a standing order payment if there are insufficient funds to the credit of the account, or overdraft facility available, when the payment is to be made, and is under no duty subsequently to monitor the account to establish whether sufficient funds have been paid into the account to meet the payment: *Whitehead v National Westminster Bank Ltd*, The Times, 9 June 1982.

[292] The payee's failure properly to implement a correctly completed direct debit mandate might constitute a breach of an implied term of the underlying contract between them, or even a breach of a duty of care in tort owed by the payee to the payer: *Weldon v GRE Linked Life Assurance Ltd* [2000] All ER (Comm) 914.

[293] *The Brimnes*, n 290, at 949, 969. There are good reasons for distinguishing cheques from funds transfer systems: see Brindle & Cox, n 235, at para 3–005.

[294] But not if it is crossed 'account payee': see 6.59.

[295] *Esso Petroleum Co Ltd v Milton* [1997] 1 WLR 938, CA (criticized by R Hooley [1997] CLJ 500 and A Tettenborn (1997) 113 LQR 374).

[296] Or several times each day for the Faster Payment Service (6.98).

(e) Clearing systems

There are five major clearing systems in the United Kingdom:[297] **6.98**

(i)   the cheque clearing system, which is used for the physical exchange of cheques (cheque truncation has only been partially adopted in the UK);[298]

(ii) the credit clearing system, which is a paper-based credit transfer system used for the physical exchange of high-volume, low-value, credit collections such as bank giro credits;[299]

(iii) BACS, which provides high-volume, low-value, bulk electronic clearing services for credit and debit transfers, including standing orders, direct debits, wages and salaries, pensions and other government benefits;

(iv) CHAPS, which is an electronic real-time gross settlement credit transfer system for sterling, normally used for high-value transfers;[300]

(v)   Faster Payment Service, which offers a near real-time facility for Internet and telephone transfers between bank accounts, with standing orders processed on a same day basis.

Each clearing system has its own rules. These rules are binding on the members of the system *inter se*. A customer of a member bank may be bound by, and able to rely on, the system rules against his own bank through an implied term of the bank-customer contract.[301] The customer is taken to have contracted with reference to the reasonable usage of bankers, including those system rules which represent such reasonable usage.[302] However, where system rules derogate from the customer's existing rights, the usage codified in the rules will be deemed unreasonable and will not bind the customer without his full knowledge and consent.[303] **6.99**

(f) Duties of the banks involved in a funds transfer

(i) *Payment Services Regulations 2009*

The PSRs impose conduct of business requirements on payment services (incorporating both payment transactions and the operation of payment accounts) that are within their scope.[304] For a funds transfers falling within their scope, the PSRs do not expressly preserve the remedies that the parties might otherwise have had at common law.[305] Whether this means that the PSRs establish an exclusive remedial regime when applicable must await determination **6.100**

---

[297] Part 5 of the Banking Act 2009 provides the statutory framework for oversight by the Bank of England of interbank payment systems that are systemically important. The Financial Services (Banking Reform) Act 2013 creates a new competition-focused, economic regulator of retail payment systems in the UK: the new Payment Systems Regulator became fully operational on 1 April 2015.

[298] See 6.65 for the introduction of cheque imaging under new Part 4A of the Bills of Exchange Act 1882, inserted by s 13 of the Small Business, Enterprise and Employment Act 2015, which will eliminate the need for the physical exchange of cheques through clearing.

[299] New legislation allowing for cheque imaging (see 6.65) also extends to other paper instruments such as bank giro credits (see s 89B of the Bills of Exchange Act 1882, inserted by s 13 of the Small Business, Enterprise and Employment Act 2015).

[300] A euro credit transfer system operated by CHAPS closed in May 2008. Domestic and cross-border payments in euro can be made throughout the EU using a system called Target2 (and other euro payment mechanisms).

[301] System rules usually expressly exclude the operation of the Contract (Rights of Third Parties) Act 1999.

[302] *Hare v Henty* (1861) 10 CBNS 65; *Tayeb v HSBC Bank plc* [2004] EWHC 1529, [2004] 4 All ER 1024, at [57]; *Tidal Energy Ltd v Bank of Scotland plc* [2014] EWCA Civ 1107, [2014] 2 Lloyd's Rep 549 at [48]–[49], [59].

[303] *Barclays Bank plc v Bank of England* [1985] 1 All ER 385, 394; *Turner v Royal Bank of Scotland plc* [1999] 2 All ER (Comm) 664, CA.

[304] SI 2009/209 as amended. See 6.06–6.07 for scope.

[305] But note, e.g., the express preservation of general common law rights in the context of termination of a framework contract, see reg 43(7).

by the courts.[306] For a funds transfer falling outside the scope of the PSRs, it would be necessary to consider the position at common law.

(ii) Payer's bank

6.101   Under the PSRs the payer's bank is subjected to a regime of strict liability for non-execution or defective execution of the payer's instructions, whereas the bank's liability at common law turns on its failure to exercise reasonable care and skill in and about the execution of the payer's payment instructions.[307] In the case of a payment order initiated by the payer, as with a CHAPS transfer or a standing order, the payer's bank is liable to the payer for the correct execution of the payment transaction unless it can prove to the payer that the correct amount was received by the payee's bank on time.[308] If the payer's bank is liable, it must refund the amount of the defective or non-executed transaction to the payer without undue delay, and, where applicable, restore the debited payment account to the state it would have been in had the transaction not occurred at all.[309] Where the payment transaction is initiated by the payee, as with direct debits, the payer's bank will be liable to refund the payer the amount of the direct debit payment, and if necessary re-credit the payer's account, if the payee's bank has been able to prove that it carried out its end of the payment transaction properly, ie it has sent the payment instruction (in the correct amount and within the correct timescale), and the correct payee's details, to the payer's bank, so that failure to receive the correct amount of funds within the correct timescale lies with the payer's bank rather than with the payee's bank.[310] The payer can also claim for any charges and any interest incurred as a result of the non-execution or defective execution

---

[306] *Ellinger's Modern Banking Law*, n 26, at 618–619. Arguably, the common law continues to apply in those cases where the payment service provider has exercised the 'corporate opt-out' and contracted out of the PSRs conduct of business requirements (see n 22).

[307] *Royal Products Ltd v Midland Bank Ltd* [1981] 2 Lloyd's Rep 194, 198 (payer's bank would also be vicariously liable for negligence of its employees and agents). In the normal course of events, the payer's bank will not owe the payee a duty of care in tort: *Wells v First National Commercial Bank* [1998] PNLR 552, CA. It is unlikely that the payer and his bank intend to confer an enforceable benefit on the payee so as to allow him to take advantage of the Contracts (Rights of Third Parties) Act 1999, ss 1(1)(b), 1(2), and, in any event, it is common practice for banks to exclude the operation of the Act in this context. Under the common law, the payer's bank will usually be precluded from debiting the payer's account when acting outside its mandate (see 6.19). But in *Tidal Energy Ltd v Bank of Scotland Plc* [2014] EWCA Civ 1107, [2014] EWCA Civ 2780 (QB), the Court of Appeal, by a majority, construed a CHAPS transfer order in accordance with banking practice and held that a CHAPS transfer was within mandate when the payment was made to an account matching the sort code and account number—but not the name of the payee/beneficiary customer—provided by the payer.

[308] Regulation 75(2). The general rule is that the payer's bank must ensure that the amount of the payment transaction is credited to the account of the payee's bank by the end of the business day following receipt of the payment order: reg 70(1); but subject to exceptions in the case of payment instructions initiated by way of a paper payment order, and certain payment transactions (eg not in euro or sterling) executed wholly within the EEA: reg 70(3), (4). See also *Tidal Energy Ltd v Bank of Scotland plc* [2013] EWHC 2780 (QB), [2013] 2 Lloyd's Rep 605 at [22] (affirmed [2014] EWCA Civ 1107 without reference to this point), where HHJ Havelock-Allan QC said (obiter) that if reg 75 had applied to the transfer (it did not because the PSRs had been expressly excluded by the bank's terms and conditions), the unique identifier given by the payer would have been incorrect because there was a mismatch between the payee's name, on the one hand, and the account number and sort code, on the other, in which case reg 74(2) would have applied. Regulation 74(2) states that '[w]here the unique identifier provided by the payment service user is incorrect, the payment service provider is not liable under regulation 75 or 76 for non-execution or defective execution of the payment transaction, but the payment service provider–(a) must make reasonable efforts to recover the funds involved in the payment transaction; and (b) may, if agreed in the framework contract, charge the payment service user for any such recovery'.

[309] Regulation 75(4). Liability under reg 75 does not apply if reg 79 (force majeure) applies. The 'corporate opt-out' (n 22) applies to reg 75 (reg 51(3)).

[310] Regulation 76(2), (5). Liability under reg 76 does not apply if reg 79 (force majeure) applies. The 'corporate opt-out' (n 22) applies to reg 76 (see reg 51(3)).

of the payment transaction.[311] However, in order to obtain the redress stated above, the payer must notify the payer's bank without delay, and in any event no later than 13 months after the debit date, on becoming aware of any unauthorized or incorrectly executed payment transactions.[312] The payer's bank is given a right of recourse, which applies where the non-execution or defective execution of a payment transaction is 'attributable' to the payee's bank or an intermediary bank.[313]

For a payment transaction to be authorised, the payer must have given his consent to the execution of the payment transaction or to the execution of a series of payment transactions of which the payment transaction forms part.[313a] The payer may have given his consent before or, if agreed, after the execution of the payment transaction, and it must be in the form, and in accordance with the procedure, agreed between the payer and the payer's bank.[313b] The payer's bank is liable to the payer for execution of an unauthorized payment transaction and it must refund the amount of the unauthorized payment to him.[314] If the unauthorized payment has been debited from the payer's account, the payer's bank must restore the debit to that account.[315] In order to claim a refund or restoration of his account following an unauthorized payment transaction, the payer must notify his bank without delay on becoming aware of the unauthorized nature of the transaction and, in any event, this must be done no later than 13 months after the debit date.[316] The payer may also be entitled to a refund from the payer's bank where an authorized payment transaction is initiated by or through the payee, as with a direct debit, where the payer did not specify the exact amount of the payment when initially authorizing the direct debit and the amount of the payment 'exceeded the amount that the payer could reasonably have expected taking into account the payer's previous spending pattern, the conditions of the framework contract and the circumstances of the case'.[317] **6.102**

(iii) Payee's bank

Part 6 of the PSRs contains provisions relating to the rights and obligations of the payee's bank in the provision of payment services that are within scope.[318] First, in the case of a direct debit, the payee's bank must transmit the payment order to the payer's bank within the time limits it has agreed with the payee.[319] The payee's bank must then credit the amount of the payment to the payee's account following its receipt of the funds.[320] The payee's bank must ensure that the amount of the payment is at the payee's disposal immediately after that amount has been credited to the payee bank's account.[321] The transferred funds must **6.103**

---

[311] Regulation 77.
[312] Regulation 59(1), which makes the payment service user's reporting obligation a condition for redress under regs 61, 75, 76 or 77. Regulation 59(2) relieves the payment service user of this obligation if his bank has failed to comply with various information requirements in Part 5 of the PSRs.
[313] Regulation 78.
[313a] Regulation 55(1).
[313b] Regulation 55(2). For withdrawal of consent, see reg 55(3)–(4). A framework contract may give the payment service provider the right to stop the use of the payment instrument on reasonable grounds relating to (a) security of the payment instrument; and (b) the suspected unauthorized or fraudulent use of the payment instrument (reg 56(2)).
[314] Regulation 61(a).
[315] Regulation 61(b).
[316] See n 312. For onus of proof and circumstances when the payer may be held liable for an unauthorized payment transaction, see 6.87–6.88.
[317] Regulation 63(2).
[318] See 6.06–6.07.
[319] Regulation 70(6).
[320] Regulation 70(5).
[321] Regulation 73(2).

start to earn interest by the end of the business day upon which the payee's bank received those funds.[322] Secondly, the payee's bank must ensure that the full amount of the payment is transferred to the payee and that no charges are deducted from that amount.[323] In the case of a direct debit, the payee's bank is liable to reimburse the payee for any unauthorized charges deducted from the amount transferred.[324] Thirdly, in the case of the incorrect execution of a payment order initiated by the payer, if the payer's bank can prove that the funds were transferred to the payee's bank within the relevant time limits,[325] responsibility for the non-execution or defective execution of the payment transaction shifts to the payee's bank, which must then immediately make available to the payee a sum equivalent to the amount of the transfer and, where applicable, credit the corresponding amount to the payee's account.[326] Where the payment transaction is initiated by the payee, the payee's bank is liable to the payee for the correct transmission of the payment order to the payer's bank within the relevant time limits.[327] Where the payee's bank is so liable, it must immediately re-transmit the payment order to the payer's bank,[328] and it must, on request, make immediate efforts to trace the payment transaction and notify the payee of the outcome.[329] It remains open to the payee's bank to prove that it correctly transmitted the payment order to the payer's bank in time, and in such a case liability for the non-execution or defective execution of the payment transaction shifts to the payer's bank, which must refund the amount of the payment to the payer and, where necessary, re-credit his account.[330] The payee can also claim for any charges and any interest incurred as a result of the non-execution or defective execution of the payment transaction.[331] However, in order to obtain the redress stated above, the payee must notify the payee's bank without delay, and in any event no later than 13 months after the debit date, on becoming aware of any incorrectly executed payment transactions.[332] The payee's bank will not be liable for an incorrectly executed transfer where the unique identifier (eg the payer's account number, sort code or bank details) provided by the payee is incorrect, although the bank must make reasonable efforts to recover the funds involved in the transaction.[333] The payee's bank is given a right of recourse where the non-execution or defective execution of a payment transaction is 'attributable' to the payer's bank or an intermediary bank.[334]

6.104 In the case of a credit transfer, where the payee has supplied the payer with details of his bank account, the payee's bank is deemed to have his authority to accept funds into the account.[335]

---

[322] Regulation 73(1).

[323] Regulation 68(1). Subject to agreed charges being levied: reg 68(2). For controls on the level of charges, see reg 54.

[324] Regulation 68(3)(b). The payer's bank is responsible for reimbursing the payee for unauthorized deductions where the payer initiates the payment transaction (reg 68(3)(a)).

[325] For relevant time limits, see reg 70(1), (3), (4).

[326] Regulation 75(5).

[327] Regulation 76(2). The payee's bank must transmit the relevant payment order within the time-limits agreed between the payee and his bank: reg 70(6).

[328] Regulation 76(3).

[329] Regulation 76(4).

[330] Regulation 76(5).

[331] Regulation 77.

[332] Regulation 59(1), which makes the payment service user's reporting obligation a condition for redress under regs 61, 75, 76 or 77. Regulation 59(2) relieves the payment service user of this obligation if his bank has failed to comply with various information requirements in Part 5 of the PSRs.

[333] Regulation 74(2) (and see n 308). The payee's bank can also avoid liability in cases of force majeure (reg 79).

[334] Regulation 78.

[335] *Royal Products Ltd v Midland Bank Ltd*, n 307, at 198; *Dovey v Bank of New Zealand* [2000] 2 NZLR 641, 649–650, NZCA. cf *Customs & Excise Comrs v National Westminster Bank plc*, n 289; *PT Berlian Laju Tanker TBK v Nuse Shipping Ltd*, n 290.

In direct debits the bank nominated by the payee to accept payment from the payer's bank does so as the payee's agent. In some cases, however, where the payer makes payment contrary to the terms of his underlying contract with the payee, eg, late payment of hire under a charterparty, the payee's bank will be deemed to receive the payment purely in a ministerial capacity and not to have accepted it on the payee's behalf.[336] The payee may then accept or reject the payment, so long as he has not waived his right of rejection, eg, by representing to the payer that the payee's bank has his authority to accept the payment.

(iv) Intermediary banks

Intermediary banks may be employed in domestic transfers, eg, to give the payer's bank, the payee's bank or both banks, access to a funds transfer system when not members of that system. Intermediary banks are more commonly used in international funds transfers. It has been held that the payer's bank is deemed to have the payer's authority to employ the services of an intermediary bank to effect the transfer where it would be normal banking practice to use an intermediary.[337] The intermediary bank will act as the payer's sub-agent, but there will usually be no privity of contract between them.[338]   **6.105**

The position under the PSRs appears to differ from that at common law in two ways.[339] First, whereas at common law the intermediary bank's liability turns on its negligence, under the PSRs the bank's liability appears to be strict.[340] Secondly, the common law appears to limit the payer's bank or payee's bank to recoupment of losses from the intermediary bank that it actually instructed, whereas the PSRs appear to offer the payer's bank or payee's bank a right of action against the intermediary bank responsible for the loss (or to which the loss is 'attributable'), even though there is no direct contractual link between the two banks.   **6.106**

(4) Documentary Credits

(a) Function

A documentary credit represents a bank's assurance of payment against presentation of specified documents.[341] It is a common method of payment in international sales.[341a] The seller stipulates in the contract of sale that payment is to be by documentary credit. The buyer (the 'applicant' for the credit) then gets his bank (the 'issuing bank') to issue a credit in favour of   **6.107**

---

[336] *Mardorf Peach & Co Ltd v Attica Sea Carriers Corpn of Liberia, The Laconia* [1977] AC 850, 871–872, HL. cf R King, 'The Receiving Bank's Role in Credit Transfer Transactions' (1982) 45 MLR 369.

[337] *Royal Products Ltd v Midland Bank Ltd*, n 307, at 197–198. It is submitted the same principle applies where the payee's bank employs an intermediary bank.

[338] *Calico Printers' Association Ltd v Barclays Bank Ltd* (1931) 145 LT 51, aff'd at 58; *Royal Products*, n 307, at 198. See also *Grosvenor Casinos Ltd v National Bank of Abu Dhabi* [2008] EWHC 511 (Comm), [2008] 2 All ER (Comm) 112, at [157], distinguishing *Bastone & Firminger Ltd v Nasima Enterprises (Nigeria) Ltd* [1996] CLC 1902, 1908.

[339] *Ellinger's Modern Banking Law*, n 26, at 618–619.

[340] Regulation 78. Subject to certain defences, including force majeure (reg 79).

[341] The terms 'documentary credit', 'banker's commercial credit' and 'commercial letter of credit' are synonymous. Standby credits, performance bonds and demand guarantees have a different function to that of documentary credits. Whereas the function of documentary credits is to provide payment for goods and services against documents, the function of standby credits, performance bonds and demand guarantees is to provide security against default in performance of the underlying contract. See generally, M Bridge (ed). *Benjamin's Sale of Goods* (9th edn, 2014) ch 24; and also 8.163.

[341a] There has been a decrease in the use of documentary credits as 'open account' trading has become more popular. The decline in use is likely to continue with the development of the Bank Payment Obligation, which is an irrevocable conditional undertaking to pay given from one bank to another (but different from a documentary credit as, eg, there is no checking and transmission of physical documents by banks). In April 2013, the International Chamber of Commerce adopted Uniform Rules for Bank Payment Obligations (ICC Publication No 750E).

the seller (the 'beneficiary' of the credit), so that the seller has the bank's independent payment undertaking. The issuing bank may get another bank (the 'confirming bank') in the buyer's country to add its own payment undertaking to the credit if this is required under the terms of the underlying contract of sale. Sometimes the bank (the 'advising bank') in the buyer's country will merely advise the buyer that the credit has been opened without adding its own payment undertaking. Subject to the solvency of the bank,[342] the seller is certain of payment under the credit provided he can present conforming documents to the 'nominated bank' (often the confirming bank) and comply with the other terms of the credit.

(b) Uniform Customs and Practice

6.108 The Uniform Customs and Practice for Documentary Credits (UCP) is a set of rules governing the use of documentary credits. It was first published by the International Chamber of Commerce (ICC) in 1933 and has been revised six times since then. UCP 600, the most recent revision, came into effect on 1 July 2007.[343] A supplement to the UCP, called the eUCP, deals with the electronic presentation of documents.

6.109 The UCP applies to any documentary credit 'when the text of the credit expressly indicates that it is subject to these rules'.[344] It has been argued that, even in the absence of express incorporation, the UCP may be incorporated as a matter of business practice because it is so widely used by banks all over the world.[345] However, given the wording of UCP 600, express incorporation is advised. The eUCP must be expressly incorporated into the credit if it is to apply.[346] Incorporation of the eUCP has the effect of incorporating the UCP into the credit without express incorporation of the UCP.[347]

6.110 The UCP may be expressly excluded by the terms of the credit.[348] Unless there has been express exclusion of the UCP, the courts will endeavour to construe the express terms of the credit so as to avoid conflict with the rules of the UCP.[349] If there is conflict, then the express terms of the credit prevail over the UCP.[350] The courts interpret the UCP 'in accordance with its underlying aims and purposes reflecting international practice and the expectations of international bankers and international traders so that it underpins the operation of letters of credit in international trade'.[351]

(c) Types of credit

6.111 UCP 600 defines a documentary credit as 'any arrangement, however named or described, that is irrevocable and thereby constitutes a definite undertaking of the issuing bank to honour a complying presentation'.[352] The bank may undertake to pay on sight of the specified

---

[342] Unless otherwise agreed, payment by documentary credit constitutes conditional payment of the price so that if it is not honoured, the debt is not discharged and the seller has a remedy in damages against both bank and buyer: *WJ Alan & Co Ltd v El Nasr Export and Import Co* [1972] 2 QB 189, 212, CA.

[343] Unless otherwise stated, all references in this chapter are to this revision.

[344] UCP 600, art 1.

[345] E McKendrick, *Goode on Commercial Law* (4th edn, 2009) 1077, relying on analogous case of *Harlow and Jones Ltd v American Express Bank Ltd* [1990] 2 Lloyd's Rep 343.

[346] eUCP, art e1(b).

[347] eUCP, art e2(a).

[348] UCP 600, art 1.

[349] *Forestal Mimosa Ltd v Oriental Credit Ltd* [1986] 1 WLR 631, 639, CA.

[350] *Royal Bank of Scotland plc v Cassa di Risparmio Delle Provincie Lombard* [1992] 1 Bank LR 251, 256, CA.

[351] *Fortis Bank SA/NV v Indian Overseas Bank* [2011] EWCA Civ 58, [2011] 2 Lloyd's Rep 33, at [29], *per* Thomas LJ (who added '[a] literalistic and national approach must be avoided'); *Glencore International AG v Bank of China* [1996] 1 Lloyd's Rep 135, 148, CA.

[352] UCP 600, art 2.

documents, or to incur a deferred payment undertaking and pay at maturity,[353] or to accept a bill of exchange drawn by the beneficiary and pay at maturity.[354] A complying presentation is one which is in accordance with the terms and conditions of the credit, the UCP and international standard banking practice.[355]

A credit may be either *revocable* or *irrevocable*. But UCP 600 does not apply to revocable **6.112** credits, ie where the issuing bank is free to modify or cancel the credit at any time without notice to the beneficiary.[356] Except as otherwise provided by UCP 600, article 38 (transferable credits), an irrevocable credit cannot be modified or cancelled after it has been communicated to the beneficiary without the consent of the issuing bank, confirming bank, if any, and the beneficiary.[357] A credit which does not indicate whether it is revocable or irrevocable will be deemed irrevocable.[358]

A credit may be either *confirmed* or *unconfirmed*. A confirmed credit is one to which the **6.113** advising bank has added its own definite undertaking to honour or negotiate the credit, provided there is a complying presentation.[359] This is done in response to a request from the issuing bank. The credit is unconfirmed when the advising bank has not provided such an undertaking. In practice, an advising bank will only confirm an irrevocable credit.[359a] Sometimes the advising bank will confirm the credit at the request of the beneficiary. This is called a 'silent confirmation'.[360]

A credit may be either a *straight* credit or a *negotiation* credit. With a straight credit the issuing **6.114** bank's payment undertaking is directed solely to the beneficiary. With a negotiation credit, the issuing bank's payment undertaking is not confined to the beneficiary but extends to the nominated bank authorized to negotiate (ie purchase) bills of exchange ('drafts') drawn by the beneficiary on another party (often, but not always, the issuing bank) and/or documents which strictly comply with the terms and conditions of the credit.[361] By UCP 600, article 7(c), an issuing bank undertakes to reimburse a nominated bank that has honoured or negotiated a complying presentation and forwarded the documents to the issuing bank.[362]

---

[353] Where there is an assignment of the beneficiary's rights under a deferred payment credit to the nominated bank before maturity, equities available against the beneficiary are also available against the bank: *Banco Santander SA v Bayfern Ltd* [2000] 1 All ER (Comm) 776, CA. But see now UCP 600, arts 7(c), 8(c) and 12(b). Article 12(b) was intended to shift the risk of fraud back to the issuing bank and reverse the outcome in *Santander*, but there is doubt as to whether it has achieved that end (see D Horowitz, 'Banco Santander and the UCP 600' [2008] JBL 508).

[354] UCP 600, art 2.

[355] UCP 600, art 2.

[356] Revocable credits are rare, but if the parties to the underlying contract want to use one, they should make the credit subject to UCP 500, an earlier version of the UCP, which extends to revocable credits.

[357] UCP 600, art 10.

[358] UCP 600, art 3.

[359] UCP 600, art 2.

[359a] And so an advising bank must be careful not to use language in its communications with the beneficiary that would lead a court to find that the bank had accepted direct liability for payment of the credit: see *Den Danske Bank A/S v Surinam Shipping Ltd* [2014] UKPC 10.

[360] Where an issuing bank permits the advising bank to confirm a letter of credit at the beneficiary's request and expense, the advising bank is treated as a 'confirming bank' for the purposes of UCP 600: *Fortis Bank SA/NV v Indian Overseas Bank* [2009] EWHC 2303 (Comm), [2010] 1 Lloyd's Rep. 227 at [59]–[60], Hamblen J.

[361] UCP 600, art 2.

[362] See *Société Générale SA v Saad Trading* [2011] EWHC 2424 (Comm), [2011] 2 CLC 629, at [45]–[46], where Teare J held that art 7(c) requires the nominated bank to forward to the issuing bank all the documents presented to it under the terms of the credit without exception.

(d) Fundamental principles

(i) Strict compliance

6.115 The principle of strict compliance requires that tendered documents must strictly comply with the terms of the credit. In the words of Viscount Sumner in *Equitable Trust Co of New York v Dawson Partners Ltd*: '[t]here is no room for documents which are almost the same, or which will do just as well'.[363] The principle applies to all contracts arising out of a documentary credit transaction.[364]

6.116 The wording of the credit is of paramount importance when determining whether there has been compliance with its terms. Even an apparently trivial discrepancy will justify rejection of the documents if the credit is specific as to that requirement.[365] On the other hand, the courts are willing to overlook a trivial defect in the tendered documents where there is a patent typographical error or other obvious slip or omission.[366] But where it is not clear whether the departure from the detail set out in the credit was a draftsman's error or not, the discrepancy justifies the rejection of the documents.[367] It is sometimes difficult to draw a clear line between the two types of cases.[368]

6.117 A 'mirror image' interpretation of the strict compliance rule is unworkable in practice. Rejection of tendered documents becomes the norm. Bankers have recognized this for some time. This has led the ICC to promote a more flexible approach to documentary compliance. Article 14(a) of UCP 600 calls on the banks 'to examine a presentation to determine, on the basis of the documents alone, whether or not the documents appear on their face to constitute a complying presentation'. It will be recalled that a complying presentation is one in accordance with, *inter alia*, international standard banking practices.[369] The ICC has detailed relevant practices in a publication called *International Standard Banking Practices for the Examination of Documents under Documentary Letters of Credit*.[370] In addition, the latest revision of the UCP contains a number of new provisions which are designed to ensure that tendered documents are not rejected for overly technical reasons, eg, that documents need not be mirror images of each other, merely that they must not be inconsistent,[371] that non-documentary conditions are to be ignored unless they can be clearly linked to a document stipulated in the credit.[372]

---

[363] (1927) 27 Ll L Rep 49, 52 (a bank v applicant case). See also *Swotbook.com Ltd v Royal Bank of Scotland plc* [2011] EWHC 2025 (QB), at [24] (a bank v applicant case): but note (at [7] and [55]) that the issuing bank's application form contained a deemed compliance clause which was challenged by the applicant in its pleadings as unreasonable under s 3 of the Unfair Contract Terms Act 1977 (the clause was not relied on at trial and so the issue was not considered further).

[364] *JH Rayner & Co Ltd v Hambro's Bank Ltd* [1943] KB 37, CA (a beneficiary v bank case); *Bank Meli Iran v Barclays Bank DCO* [1951] 2 Lloyd's Rep 367 (a bank v bank case); cf *Bunge Corpn v Vegetable Vitamin Foods (Pte) Ltd* [1985] 1 Lloyd's Rep 613 (where 'substantial compliance' test used in underlying contract).

[365] *Seaconsar Far East Ltd v Bank Markasi Jomhouri Islami Iran* [1993] 1 Lloyd's Rep 236, CA (reversed on other grounds, [1994] 1 AC 438) and [1999] 1 Lloyd's Rep 36, 38, CA.

[366] See, eg, *Hing Yip Hing Fat Co Ltd v Daiwa Bank Ltd* [1991] 2 HKLR 35, HKSC.

[367] See, eg, *Bulgrains & Co Ltd v Shinhan Bank* [2013] EWHC 2498 (QB) at [24], where the claimant beneficiary was identified in the credit as 'Bulgrains Co Ltd' but in the tendered commercial invoice as 'Bulgrains & Co Ltd'.

[368] *Kredietbank Antwerp v Midland Bank plc* [1999] 1 All ER (Comm) 801, 806, CA. But UCP 600, art 14(j) does clarify the position where the addresses and contact details (phone, fax, e-mail etc) of the beneficiary and the applicant do not correspond.

[369] 6.111.

[370] 2013 revision, ICC Publication No 745.

[371] UCP 600, art 14(d).

[372] UCP 600, art 14(h). Note also the following provisions of UCP 600, which also appeared in UCP 500, namely, art 14(e) (for documents other than the commercial invoice) and art 30 (tolerances).

The basic rule is that original documents must be tendered to the bank, unless the credit calls **6.118** for copy documents. But, in a world dominated by the word-processor and the photocopier, there has been uncertainty as to what constitutes an original document, uncertainty that has been reflected in the case law.[373] Article 17 of UCP 600 clears up the uncertainty. It states that at least one original of each stipulated document must be tendered,[374] and provides that a bank must treat as original any document bearing an apparently original signature, mark, stamp or label of the issuer of the document, unless the document itself indicates that it is not original.[375] Unless a document indicates otherwise, a bank is also to accept a document as original (i) if it appears to be written, typed, perforated or stamped by the document issuer's hand; or (ii) appears to be on the document issuer's original stationery; or (iii) states that it is an original, unless the statement appears not to apply to the document presented.[376]

(ii) Autonomy of the credit

A documentary credit is separate from, and independent of, the underlying contract between **6.119** the applicant and the beneficiary, and from the relationship between the issuing bank and the applicant or between the banks themselves. In general, therefore, the beneficiary's breach of the underlying contract is no defence to the issuing bank or to the confirming bank. By the same token, the issuing bank cannot refuse to honour its undertaking just because of the applicant's failure to put it in funds.

The principle of autonomy of the credit is enshrined in the UCP. Article 4 of UCP 600 pro- **6.120** vides that 'a credit by its nature is a separate transaction from the sale or other contract on which it may be based. Banks are in no way concerned with or bound by such contract, even if any reference whatsoever to it is included in the credit'. The autonomy rule is also linked to the principle, to be found in article 5, that in credit operations '[b]anks deal with documents and not with goods, services or performance to which the documents may relate'. Similarly, article 34 makes clear that in credit operations banks have no responsibility for anything other than conformity of the documents to the credit. The English courts have applied the principle of autonomy of the credit on numerous occasions.[377]

(iii) Autonomy and the fraud exception

The autonomy principle is not absolute. The most important exception to the rule is where **6.121** there is a fraud on the part of the beneficiary or his agent in relation to the presentation of documents to the bank.[378] The classic formulation of the fraud exception to the autonomy

---

[373] See *Glencore International AG v Bank of China*, n 351; *Kredietbank Antwerp v Midland Bank plc*, n 368, *Crédit Industriel et Commercial v China Merchants Bank* [2002] EWHC 973 (Comm), [2002] 2 All ER (Comm) 427.

[374] UCP 600, art 17(a).

[375] UCP 600, art 17(b).

[376] UCP 600, art 17(c).

[377] See, eg, *United City Merchants (Investments) Ltd v Royal Bank of Canada, The American Accord* [1983] 1 AC 168, 182–183, HL; *Tukan Timber Ltd v Barclays Bank plc* [1987] 1 Lloyd's Rep 171, 174; *Themehelp Ltd v West* [1996] QB 84, 89, CA; *Petrologic Capital SA v Banque Cantonale de Genève* [2012] EWHC 453 (Comm), at [56]; *Taurus Petroleum Ltd v State Oil Marketing Company of the Ministry of Oil, Republic of Iraq* [2013] EWHC 3494 (Comm), [2014] 1 Lloyd's Rep 432 at [43]; *Mauri Garments Trading & Marketing Ltd v Mauritius Commercial Bank Ltd* [2015] UKPC 14 at [16] (decided under law of Mauritius). But the autonomy principle does not preclude looking at the terms of the credit to see what it is that the bank is paying: *Ibrahim v Barclays Bank plc* [2012] EWCA Civ 640, [2012] 2 BCLC 1, at [61], CA.

[378] One other exception is where illegality taints the credit itself; but it is uncertain whether the English courts will enforce a credit, not itself tainted with illegality, where the credit has been entered into pursuant to an underlying contract that is itself illegal: see *Mahonia v JP Morgan Chase Bank* [2003] 2 Lloyd's Rep 911, at [68]; *Group Josi Re v Walbrook Insurance* [1996] 1 WLR 1152, 1164, CA. A further exception is where a bank exercises a right of set-off against the sum due to the beneficiary under the credit: *Hong Kong and Shanghai Banking Corporation v Kloeckner & Co AG* [1990] 2 QB 514; *Safa v Banque du Caire* [2000] 2 Lloyd's Rep

principle is to be found in the speech of Lord Diplock in *United City Merchants (Investments) Ltd v Royal Bank of Canada*.[379] Lord Diplock began by affirming the principle that with credits the parties deal in documents, and not in goods, and continued:[380]

> To this general statement of principle as to the contractual obligations of the confirming bank to the seller, there is one established exception: that is where the seller, for the purposes of drawing on the credit, fraudulently presents to the confirming bank documents that contain, expressly or by implication, material representations of fact that to his knowledge are untrue.

If the fraud is a fraud by an independent third party, as it was in *United City Merchants*, where the fraud was that of loading brokers, who were the carrier's agents, then the beneficiary can still enforce the credit. Moreover, there is no separate exception to the autonomy principle that applies simply because the tendered document is a 'nullity' in the sense that it is a forgery or executed without the authority of the person by whom it purports to be issued.[381]

6.122 A bank is not justified in refusing to honour the credit unless fraud is clearly established.[382] Mere suspicion is not enough.[383] By contrast, if the bank is unaware of the fraud, and accepts the documents and pays the beneficiary, it may claim reimbursement from the applicant or the issuing bank, as the case may be, despite the fact that evidence of fraud has since come to light.[384] The applicant for the credit who alleges fraud on the part of the beneficiary may apply to the court for an interim injunction to restrain the bank from honouring the credit. In practice, such injunctions are rarely granted. There are three hurdles that face the applicant. First, there may be difficulty in establishing a cause of action against a bank other than the issuing bank.[385] If the applicant is enjoining the issuing bank it can rely on an implied term of the contract between them to the effect that the bank must not pay out on a fraudulent claim.[386] In cases where the beneficiary has agreed not to draw on the credit unless certain conditions are fulfilled, the applicant may find it easier to enjoin the beneficiary.[387] Secondly, the burden of proof is high. At the interim stage it must be clearly established that the only realistic inference is (a) that the beneficiary could not honestly have believed in the validity of its demands under the credit and (b) that the bank was aware of the fraud.[388] Thirdly, the balance of convenience will almost always be against the grant of an injunction.[389] The

---

600; *Lehman Brothers Commodity Services Inc v Credit Agricole Corporate and Investment Bank* [2011] EWHC 1390 (Comm), [2012] 1 All ER (Comm) 254.

[379] See n 377.

[380] See n 377 , at 183.

[381] *Montrod Ltd v Grundkotter Fleischvertriebs GmbH* [2001] EWCA Civ 1954, [2002] 1 All ER (Comm) 257, CA; cf *Beam Technology (MFG) PTE Ltd v Standard Chartered Bank* [2003] 1 SLR 597, Sing CA.

[382] *Edward Owen (Engineering) Ltd v Barclays Bank International Ltd* [1978] QB 159, 169, 173, 175, CA.

[383] *Society of Lloyd's v Canadian Imperial Bank of Commerce* [1993] 2 Lloyd's Rep 579.

[384] *Gian Singh & Co Ltd v Banque de l'Indochine* [1974] 2 All ER 754, PC.

[385] cf *Group Josi Re v Walbrook Insurance*, n 378, at 1160.

[386] *Czarnikow-Rionda Sugar Trading Inc v Standard Bank London Ltd* [1999] 2 Lloyd's Rep 187. cf *Petrologic Capital SA v Banque Cantonale de Genève*, n 377, at [52]–[56] (held applicant unable to rely on the Contract (Rights of Third Parties) Act 1999 so as to enforce an English law and jurisdiction clause contained in the credit in an action to prevent the issuing bank from paying the beneficiary).

[387] *Sirius International Insurance Corp (Publ) v FAI General Insurance Co Ltd* [2003] EWCA Civ 470, [2003] 1 WLR 2214 (reversed on other grounds, [2004] 1 WLR 3251); *Simon Carves Ltd v Ensus UK Ltd* [2011] EWHC 657 (TCC), [2011] BLR 340, at [33]–[34]; *Doosan Babcock Ltd v Comercializadora de Equipos y Materiales Mabe Limitada* [2013] EWHC 3201 (TCC), [2014] BLR 33 at [36]; *MW High Tech Projects UK Ltd v Biffa Waste Services Ltd* [2015] EWHC 949 (TCC) at [34].

[388] *Alternative Power Solution Ltd v Central Electricity Board* [2014] UKPC 31, [2015] 1 WLR 697 at [59], applying *United Trading Corp v Allied Arab Bank Ltd* [1985] 2 Lloyd's Rep. 554, 561 (Ackner LJ).

[389] *Czarnikow-Rionda*, n 386; *Alternative Power Solution Ltd v Central Electricity Board*, n 388, at [79].

applicant may do better to seek a freezing order against the beneficiary, freezing the proceeds of the credit in his hands.

(e) Examination and rejection of documents

UCP 600 states that a bank must examine tendered documents to determine whether they appear on their face to constitute a complying presentation. Unlike UCP 500,[390] the version of the UCP that immediately preceded it, UCP 600 does not expressly state that the bank must conduct its examination with reasonable care. It was felt that the general reference to reasonable care was unnecessary as UCP 600, supplemented by ISBP, adopted a significantly more detailed approach to compliance.[391] Each bank has a maximum of five banking days following the day of presentation to determine if the presentation is complying.[392] **6.123**

UCP 600 provides that where a bank decides to refuse to honour or negotiate the credit, it must give a single notice to that effect to the presenter.[393] The notice must state each discrepancy in respect of which the bank refuses to honour or negotiate,[394] and also specify what the bank intends to do with the documents.[395] The notice must be given by telecommunication or, if that is not possible, by other expeditious means no later than the close of the fifth banking day following the day of presentation.[396] If an issuing bank or a confirming bank fails to act in accordance with these rules, the bank is precluded from claiming that the documents do not constitute a complying presentation.[397] **6.124**

---

[390] UCP 500, art 13(a).

[391] G. Collyer, *Commentary on UCP 600* (2007, ICC Publication No. 680), p 62. See also *Benjamin's Sale of Goods* (9th edn, 2014), para 23-094.

[392] UCP 600, art 14(b) (a 'banking day' is defined in art 2). cf UCP 500, art 13(b), which gave the bank a reasonable time, not to exceed seven banking days, to examine the documents and make the determination.

[393] UCP 600, art 16(c).

[394] UCP 600, art 16(c). cf *Kydon Compania Naviera SA v National Westminster Bank Ltd, The Lena* [1981] 1 Lloyd's Rep 68, 79, for the position at common law.

[395] The bank must act in accordance with the statement contained in the notice with reasonable promptness: see *Fortis Bank SA/NV v Indian Overseas Bank* , n 351, at [41]–[45]; and, in related proceedings, [2011] EWHC 538 (Comm), [2011] 2 Lloyd's Rep 190, at [35] as to what constitutes 'reasonable promptness'.

[396] UCP 600, art 16(d).

[397] UCP 600, art 16(f).

7

BAILMENT

A. Definition and General Character

(1) Introduction

(a) Bailment as voluntary possession

Bailment is a legal relationship distinct from both contract and tort.[1] It exists whenever one **7.01** person (the bailee) is voluntarily in possession of goods which belong to another (the bailor).[2] The bailee gets a special property while the bailor retains the general property.[3] Common forms of bailment are carriage of goods, delivery for custody or repair, hire, pledge and loan.

---

[1] *Building and Civil Engineering Holidays Scheme Management Ltd v Post Office* [1966] 1 QB 247, 261, CA, *per* Lord Denning MR; *The Pioneer Container* [1994] 2 AC 324, 341–342, PC, *per* Lord Goff of Chieveley; *Sutcliffe v Chief Constable of West Yorkshire* [1996] RTR 86, 90, CA, *per* Otton LJ.

[2] *The Pioneer Container* [1994] 2 AC 324, PC; *East West Corp v DKBS 1912* [2003] EWCA Civ 83, [2003] QB 1509; *Sandeman Coprimar SA v Transitos y Transportes Integrales SL* [2003] EWCA Civ 113, [2003] QB 1270; *Marcq v Christie Manson & Woods Ltd (t/a Christie's)* [2003] EWCA Civ 731, [2004] QB 286. In *East West Corp v DKBS 1912* at 1530 Mance LJ approved the statement in NE Palmer, *Bailment* (2nd edn, 1991) para 1285, and see now *Palmer on Bailment* (3rd edn, 2009) para 1-016, that: 'The important question is not the literal meaning of bailment but the circle of relationships within which its characteristic duties will apply. For most practical purposes, any person who comes knowingly into the possession of another's goods is, prima facie, a bailee.'

[3] Thus, 'it is of the essence of a bailment that the general property in the goods concerned remains in the bailor, while only a special property passes to the bailee': *Re Bond Worth Ltd* [1980] Ch 228, 247, *per* Slade LJ.

The concept of bailment underlies many modern commercial transactions such as title retention,[4] marine salvage[5] and finance leasing.[6]

(b) Basic obligations common to all bailments

7.02 Bailment imposes certain basic obligations on every bailee. The bailee must take reasonable care of the goods and abstain from converting them.[7] He must not deviate from the terms of the bailment and becomes an insurer of the goods if he does so.[8] In most cases he must also refrain from denying the bailor's title.[9] These obligations can normally be varied by special agreement,[10] and in some cases they are superseded by statute.[11] Where goods are lost or damaged while in the bailee's possession the bailee is liable unless he can show that the misadventure occurred independently of his fault.[12] In this and other respects[13] bailment is an independent legal relation[14] having qualities not complemented by the normal law of contract or tort.[15] It is a relationship *sui generis*.[16]

(c) Bailment and delivery, contract, agreement

7.03 A bailment can arise without any physical delivery of goods from the bailor to the bailee.[17] A seller of goods who remains in possession after property has passed to the buyer holds as a bailee.[18] A bailee of goods whose bailor sells them during the bailment becomes the bailee of the new owner once he attorns to the new owner.[19] Bailment can also arise without any contract or agreement between the parties and without the bailor's consent.[20] A gratuitous

---

[4] *Clough Mill Ltd v Martin* [1985] 1 WLR 111, CA; *Whitecap Leisure Ltd v John H Rundle Ltd* [2008] EWCA Civ 429.

[5] *China Pacific SA v Food Corp of India, (The Winson)* [1982] AC 939, HL, and see *ENE Kos I Ltd v Petroleo Brasiliero SA (No 2)* [2012] UKSC 17, [2012] 2 WLR 976.

[6] *On-Demand Information plc v Michael Gerson (Finance) plc* [2002] UKHL 12, [2003] 1 AC 368. For a discussion of the use of bailment principles in claims relating to historic and artistic chattels see Palmer, 'The Role of Bailment in Cultural Property Claims' (2014) 19 Art Antiquity and Law 197.

[7] *Morris v CW Martin & Sons Ltd* [1966] 1 QB 716, 738, CA, *per* Salmon LJ. See now also *East West Corp v DKBS 1912* [2003] EWCA Civ 83, [2003] QB 1509.

[8] *Lilley v Doubleday* (1881) 7 QBD 510; *Shaw & Co v Symmons & Sons Ltd* [1917] 1 KB 799; *Mitchell v Ealing London Borough Council* [1979] QB 1.

[9] *Biddle v Bond* (1865) 6 B & S 225, 122 ER 1179; *Ross v Edwards & Co* (1895) 73 LT 100. The prohibition on denying title can be avoided by procedural machinery established under statute; see Torts (Interference with Goods) Act 1977, s 8; 7.24.

[10] Subject to the Unfair Contract Terms Act 1977, and the Consumer Protection Act 2015.

[11] The most notable examples are bailments by way of international carriage of goods: see chs 3, 4.

[12] *Travers & Sons v Cooper* [1915] 1 KB 73; *Port Swettenham Authority v TW Wu & Co (M) Sdn Bhd* [1979] AC 580, PC; *Frans Maas (UK) Ltd v Samsung Electronics* [2004] EWHC 1502, [2004] 2 Lloyd's Rep 251; *Coopers Payen Ltd v Southampton Container Terminal Ltd* [2003] EWCA Civ 1223, [2003] 1 Lloyd's Rep 331.

[13] eg, the binding effect of a promise given by an unrewarded bailee in relation to the goods, and the liability of such a bailee for a deviation from the terms of the bailment, despite in each case the absence of any underlying contractual relationship: see 7.38.

[14] *Sutcliffe v Chief Constable of West Yorkshire* [1996] RTR 86, 90, CA, *per* Otton LJ.

[15] See generally *Palmer on Bailment* (3rd edn, 2009) ch 1.

[16] *Yearworth v North Bristol NH Trust* [2009] EWCA Civ 37, [2010] QB 1, at [48h], *per* Lord Judge CJ (a valuable summary of general bailment principle); *Deakin and Wolf v Card Rax Ltd* [2011] EWPCC 3, at [112], *per* His Honour Judge Fysh QC (Patents County Court).

[17] *Palmer on Bailment* (3rd edn, 2009) paras 1-023–1-024.

[18] *Union Transport Finance v Ballardie* [1937] 1 KB 510; *Worcester Works Finance Ltd v Cooden Engineering Co Ltd* [1972] 1 QB 210.

[19] F Pollock and RS Wright, *An Essay on Possession in the Common Law* (1888) 134; 7.78 et seq. See now also *East West Corp v DKBS 1912* [2003] EWCA Civ 83, [2003] QB 1509.

[20] *The Pioneer Container* [1994] 2 AC 324, PC; *Palmer on Bailment* (3rd edn, 2009) paras 1012–1046; *East West Corp v DKBS 1912* [2003] EWCA Civ 83, [2003] QB 1509.

loan of goods is not a contract[21] but is still a bailment.[22] Where a bailee sub-bails,[23] three bailments are likely to arise: between bailor and head bailee,[24] between head bailee and sub-bailee,[25] and between bailor and sub-bailee.[26] A finder of goods is treated as a bailee,[27] as is a person who assumes possession without the owner's express or implied consent.[28] But an involuntary bailee (ie, someone in possession without his consent)[29] is not strictly a bailee because he is not voluntarily in possession.[30] The same can be said of an 'unconscious bailee' who is unaware of his possession of goods, or of the fact that goods in his possession belong to another.[31]

(d) Bailment and prior possession and ownership

A bailment can arise without any previous possession on the part of the bailor.[32] A bailment exists where goods are sold to one person but delivered directly on his instructions to another, who has agreed to hold them as his bailee.[33] From the moment that he receives possession the recipient is the bailee of the new owner.[34]   **7.04**

Bailments can arise where the bailor is not the owner.[35] All that is necessary is that the bailor should have some superior right to the possession of the goods.[36] Subject to that requirement,   **7.05**

---

[21] *Walker v Watson* [1974] 2 NZLR 175; cf *Blakemore v Bristol & Exeter Rly* (1858) 8 E & B 1035, 1051–1052, 120 ER 385, 391, *per* Coleridge J.

[22] See further 7.45.

[23] *The Pioneer Container* [1994] 2 AC 324, PC (the leading modern authority). See now also *East West Corp v DKBS 1912* [2003] EWCA Civ 83, [2003] QB 1509; *Sandeman Coprimar SA v Transitos y Transportes Integrales SL* [2003] QB 1270.

[24] *Morris v CW Martin & Sons Ltd* [1966] 1 QB 716, CA; cf *Metaalhandel JA Magnus BV v Ardfields Transport Ltd* [1988] 1 Lloyd's Rep 197 (quasi-bailment).

[25] *The Hamburg Star* [1994] 1 Lloyd's Rep 399.

[26] *The Pioneer Container* [1994] 2 AC 324, PC; and see for earlier authority *Morris v CW Martin & Sons Ltd* [1966] 1 QB 716, CA; *Gilchrist, Watt and Sanderson Pty Ltd v York Products Pty Ltd* [1970] 1 WLR 1262, PC; *James Buchanan & Co Ltd v Hay's Transport Services Ltd* [1972] 2 Lloyd's Rep 535.

[27] *The Pioneer Container* [1994] 2 AC 324, 336–338, PC, *per* Lord Goff; *Southland Hospital Board v Perkins Estate* [1986] 1 NZLR 373, 375–376, *per* Cook J; cf *Parker v British Airways Board* [1982] QB 1004, 1017, CA, *per* Donaldson LJ; and see generally *Palmer on Bailment* (3rd edn, 2009) ch 26.

[28] *Burns v Roffey* (HC, 16 March 1982); *Ngan v The Queen* [2007] NZSC 105 (police lawfully took possession, as 'bailees of necessity', of banknotes left unattended and unprotected in aftermath of car crash).

[29] See generally 7.86 et seq.

[30] *Lethbridge v Phillips* (1819) 2 Stark 544, 171 ER 731; *Howard v Harris* (1884) Cab & Ellis 253; *Neuwith v Over Darwen Co-operative Society Ltd* (1894) 63 LJQB 290 (possessor owes no general duty of care); and see *Robot Arenas Ltd v Waterfield* [2010] EWHC 115 (QB).

[31] *AVX Ltd v EGM Solders Ltd The Times*, 7 July 1982; *Consentino v Dominion Express Co* (1906) 4 WLR 48; 7.91 et seq; *Marcq v Christie Manson & Woods Ltd (t/a Christie's)* [2003] EWCA Civ 731; [2004] QB 286; *Robot Arenas Ltd v Waterfield* [2010] EWHC 115 (QB),

[32] See *Palmer on Bailment* (3rd edn, 2009) para 1-024..

[33] *Belvoir Finance Co Ltd v Stapleton* [1971] 1 QB 210, CA; *Johnson Matthey & Co Ltd v Constantine Terminals Ltd* [1976] 2 Lloyd's Rep 215 (not followed in *The Pioneer Container* [1994] 2 AC 324, PC, but not on this point).

[34] For cases where liability akin to that of a bailee can arise even before the reception of possession, see 7.85 et seq.

[35] *Palmer on Bailment* (3rd edn, 2009) ch 2; N Palmer, 'Possessory Title' in N Palmer and E McKendrick, *Interests in Goods* (2nd edn, 1998).

[36] *Leigh and Sillivan Ltd v Aliakmon Shipping Co Ltd (The Aliakmon)* [1986] 1 AC 785, 809, HL, *per* Lord Brandon; *Green v Stevens* (1857) 2 H & N 146; *The Hamburg Star* [1994] 1 Lloyd's Rep 399; *Mayflower Foods Ltd v Barnard Bros Ltd* (HC, 9 August 1996); *MCC Proceeds Inc v Lehmann Bros International (Europe)* [1998] 4 All ER 675, CA; *East West Corp v DKBS 1912* [2003] EWCA Civ 83; [2003] QB 1509; *The Homburg Houtimport BV v Agrosin Private Ltd (The Starsin)* [2003] UKHL 12, [2004] 1 AC 705; cf *China Pacific SA v Food Corp of India (The Winson)* [1982] AC 939, HL. And see *Rdfe v Investec Bank (Australia) Ltd* [2014] VSCA 38 at para 56: "A right to immediate possession is sufficient to found an action is bailment as against all except the true owner." A contractual right of possession will suffice: *Government of the Islamic Republic of Iran v Barakat Galleries Ltd* [2007] EWCA Civ 1374, [2009] QB 22.

a bailment can arise between a head bailee and a sub-bailee,[37] or between an original bailor and bailee where the bailee bails the goods back to the bailor for a period shorter than the original bailment.[38] A bailor is a person who has a reversionary interest in goods.[39] But bailment is a common law relation[40] and the bailor must have a legal interest in the goods;[41] a mere equitable interest (such as that of a beneficiary under a trust)[42] will not suffice,[43] unless that interest draws with it a right to the immediate possession of the subject goods.[44]

(2) The Essential Role of Possession

(a) Bailment obligations and possession

7.06   Possession is central to bailment.[45] Unless one person is in possession of goods to which another has a superior right of possession there can be no bailment.[46] Obligations akin to those on a bailment can arise, however, without possession of another's goods. A person who agrees to take possession of goods at a particular time and fails to do so may owe duties similar to those of a normal bailee,[47] as may a person who, having the option of taking possession of goods or delegating the task to another, chooses to delegate; that person may then

---

[37] *Morris v CW Martin & Sons Ltd* [1966] 1 QB 716, 729, CA, *per* Lord Denning MR; *The Hamburg Star* [1994] 1 Lloyd's Rep 399; *The Pioneer Container* [1994] 2 AC 324, PC.

[38] *Roberts v Wyatt* (1810) 2 Taunt 268, 127 ER 1080; *Brierly v Kendall* (1852) 17 QB 937, 117 ER 1540.

[39] For cases using the word 'reversion' in this context, see *Kwei Tek Chao (t/a Zung Fu Co) v British Traders & Shippers Ltd* [1954] 2 QB 459, 487, *per* Devlin J; *Empressa Exportadora De Azucar v Industria Azucarera Nacional SA (The Playa Larga and Marble Islands)* [1983] 2 Lloyd's Rep 171, 179, CA *per* Ackner LJ; *Candlewood Navigation Corp Ltd v Mitsui OSK Lines Ltd (The Mineral Transporter)* [1986] AC 1, 18, PC *per* Lord Fraser; and see *HSBC Rail (UK) Ltd v Network Rail Infrastructure Ltd* [2005] EWCA Civ 1437, [2006] 1 WLR 643. Counsel have occasionally come to grief by failing to distinguish between the residual ownership of an alleged bailor and the alleged bailor's immediate right of possession, which may not necessarily accompany ownership: see eg *Indian Herbs (UK) Ltd v Hadley & Ottoway Ltd and others* (21 January 1999, CA). In claims for conversion by a party out of possession it is the immediate right of possession that must be shown: *Government of the Islamic Republic of Iran v Barakat Galleries Ltd* [2009] EWCA Civ 1374, [2009] QB 22. In a title retention case this may depend on whether payment for the goods has fallen due: *Whitecap Leisure Ltd v John H Rundle Ltd* [2008] EWCA Civ 429, [2008] 2 Lloyd's Rep 216.

[40] *MCC Proceeds Inc v Lehmann Bros International (Europe)* [1998] 4 All ER 675, 702, CA, *per* Hobhouse LJ.

[41] *MCC Proceeds Inc v Lehmann Bros International (Europe)* [1998] 4 All ER 675, CA; and see *Leigh and Sillivan Ltd v Aliakmon Shipping Co Ltd (The Aliakmon)* [1986] 1 AC 785, HL.

[42] See generally *Halsbury's Laws of England* (4th edn Re-issue) Trusts.

[43] *MCC Proceeds Inc v Lehmann Bros International (Europe)* [1998] 4 All ER 675, CA, explaining *Healey v Healey* [1915] 1 KB 938 and *International Factors Ltd v Rodriguez* [1979] 1 QB 351, CA.

[44] As in *International Factors Ltd v Rodriguez* [1979] 1 QB 351, CA, as explained by *MCC Proceeds Inc v Lehmann Bros International (Europe)* [1998] 4 All ER 675. As to the sufficiency of a right of possession to cast the party thus entitled in the position of a bailor of the possessor, and so to ground a bailment between those parties, see *East West Corp v DKBS 1912* [2003] EWCA Civ 83, [2003] 1 Lloyd's Rep 239; and see further *Government of the Islamic Republic of Iran v Barakat Galleries* Ltd [2007] EWCA 1374, [2009] QB 22 (holder of immediate right to possession may sue in conversion).

[45] See generally *Palmer on Bailment* (3rd edn, 2009) paras 1-131–1-139, chs 5, 6 and 7. The question of possession recurs frequently; the court will ordinarily take account of all the circumstances. For a modern case where a claim in bailment failed on the facts because the particular defendant was not in possession of the goods at the material time see *Hardy v Washington Green Fine Art Publishing Co Ltd* [2010] EWCA Civ 198 noted (2011) 16 Art Antiquity and Law 85. For a modern bailment claim where the defence that the alleged bailee was not in possession failed on the facts see *Mainline Private Hire Ltd v Nolan* [2011] EWCA Civ 189 noted (2011) 16 Art Antiquity and Law 161.

[46] Hence at common law a person cannot bail goods to himself: *Harding v Comr of Inland Revenue* [1977] 1 NZLR 337 (decided under New Zealand property legislation).

[47] *Quiggin v Duff* (1836) 1 M & W 174, 150 ER 394; *Edwards v Newland & Co* [1950] 2 KB 534, CA.

be liable for the defaults of the delegate,[48] as he would if he were bailing the goods under a conventional sub-bailment, having first got possession in person.[49] It is said that a bailment by way of hire[50] can arise though the hirer gets no possession because the chattel is supplied with an operator who continues to be employed by the lessor and to retain possession on his behalf,[51] but that is doubtful.[52]

(b) Bailment and employment

The requirement of possession may mean that no bailment arises between employer and employee.[53] Traditionally, employees who have charge of their employer's property in the course of employment have mere custody and no independent possession.[54] They cannot therefore sue third parties in trespass or conversion[55] and they cannot be liable as bailees.[56] The rule is antiquated and may in any event not apply where there is a substantial distance and lack of control between the employer and the employee,[57] or where the employee receives from a third party goods intended for the employer; in that case, the employee may get an independent possession (and may therefore be a bailee) until he appropriates the goods to the employer.[58] An employee who loses or damages the employer's goods during the course of employment can be sued in tort for negligence[59] and for breach of an implied term of the contract of employment.[60] An employee to whom a chattel is loaned by the employer for a purpose unconnected with employment can of course be a bailee.[61]

7.07

Employers can be bailees of their employees' chattels, as where employees' work tools are left on the employer's premises overnight,[62] or coats are deposited during working hours.[63] A statutory obligation of care[64] may also apply in respect of clothing.[65] In the absence of bailment or statutory obligation, an employer does not normally owe a duty to protect his

7.08

---

[48] *Metaalhandel JA Magnus BV v Ardfields Transport Ltd* [1988] 1 Lloyd's Rep 197; and see *The Pioneer Container* [1994] 2 AC 324, 345, PC, *per* Lord Goff; *Palmer on Bailment* (3rd edn, 2009) paras 23-055–23-064.

[49] See *Morris v CW Martin & Sons Ltd* [1966] 1 QB 716, CA; and *Palmer on Bailment* (3rd edn, 2009) paras 1298–1301.

[50] See generally as to hire 7.61 et seq.

[51] *Fowler v Lock* (1872) LR 7 CP 272, 282, *per* Byles J.

[52] *Palmer on Bailment* (3rd edn, 2009) para 1-131.

[53] *Palmer on Bailment* (3rd edn, 2009) ch 7. For an imaginative but tentative application of the 'no possession' principle in the context of an art bailment and the potential liability of a 'guest curator' see *Kamidian v Holt and others* [2008] EWHC 1483 (Comm).

[54] *Lotus Cars Ltd v Southampton Cargo Handling plc (The Rigoletto); Southampton Cargo Handling plc v Associated British Ports* [2000] 2 Lloyd's Rep 532, 539; *Alexander v Southey* (1821) 5 B & Ald 247, 106 ER 1183; *Associated Portland Cement Manufacturers (1910) Ltd v Ashton* [1915] 2 KB 1, CA; *R v Harding* (1929) 46 TLR 105. The non-possession rule does not apply to agents and independent contractors, who may get possession and be answerable as bailees: *Lotus Cars Ltd v Southampton Cargo Handling plc (The Rigoletto); Southampton Cargo Handling plc v Associated British Ports*. And see 7.20.

[55] *Hopkinson v Gibson* (1805) 2 Smith 2021 (trover).

[56] *Wiebe v Lepp* (1974) 46 DLR (3d) 441. But a general duty of care may be owed, unaccompanied by the peculiar bailee's burden of proof: see 7.33.

[57] *The Jupiter III* [1927] P 122, 131, *per* Hill J, aff'd [1927] P 250; *Boson v Sandford* (1690) 1 Shower 101, 89 ER 477; *Moore v Robinson* (1831) 2 B & Ad 817, 109 ER 1346.

[58] *Marshall v Dibble* [1920] NZLR 497; F Pollock and RS Wright, *An Essay on Possession in the Common Law* (1888) 60.

[59] *Superlux v Plaisted* [1958] Current Law Year Book 195.

[60] *Rowell v Alexander Mackie CAE* (1988) Aust Torts Rep 67, 727, NSWCA.

[61] *Haira v Attorney-General* [1962] NZLR 549.

[62] *MacDonald v Whittaker Textiles (Marysville) Ltd* (1976) 64 DLR (3d) 317.

[63] *Tremear v Park Town Motor Hotels Ltd* [1982] 4 Western Weekly Reports 444.

employees from theft.[66] No such duty arises under the law of occupier's liability,[67] or any implied term of the contract of employment,[68] or the general law of tort.[69]

(c) Machines supplied with operators

7.09 Where a machine is supplied along with an operator, the existence of a bailment between the owner and the client depends on such factors as the identity of the employer for the period of use, the location and nature of the work, the arrangements for safekeeping while the machine is not in use and the degree of control exercised by the party for whose use the machine is engaged.[70] The fact that the operator continues throughout in the general employment of the owner[71] does not count decisively against the creation of a bailment but it is a strong factor in favour of that conclusion.[72] The charterer under a time or voyage charterparty is not a bailee of the vessel but the charterer under a bareboat charter is.[73] Most cases turn on their facts.[74]

(d) Bailments and licences

7.10 The requirement of possession may also prevent a bailment from arising where goods are left on land or premises with the occupier's permission.[75] This question commonly arises under car-parking arrangements,[76] or where patrons deposit garments in cloakrooms at restaurants or other places of public resort.[77] If there is no transfer of possession to the occupier, the relationship is that of licensor and licensee, and the occupier owes no duty to protect the goods against theft.[78] Factors relevant to this distinction include the physical layout of the land,[79] the procedures for reclaiming goods,[80] the presence and function of attendants,[81] the distance between the owner and the goods,[82] the value of the goods,[83] the scale and means of exaction of any fee for the facility,[84] the terms of any documentation issued by the occupier,[85] the

---

[64] Offices, Shops and Railway Premises Act 1963, s 12(1)(9); Factories Act 1961, s 59. Preceding legislation was held to render employers responsible for taking reasonable steps to ensure that the accommodation provided was reasonably secure against the risk of theft: *McCarthy v Daily Mirror Newspapers Ltd* [1949] 1 All ER 801.

[65] *McCarthy v Daily Mirror Newspapers Ltd* [1949] 1 All ER 801.

[66] *Deyong v Shenburn* [1946] 1 KB 227, CA.

[67] *Edwards v West Herts Group Hospital Management Committee* [1957] 1 WLR 415, CA.

[68] *Edwards v West Herts Group Hospital Management Committee* [1957] 1 WLR 415, CA.

[69] *Deyong v Shenburn* [1946] 1 KB 227, CA.

[70] These factors are discussed at length in *Palmer on Bailment* (3rd edn, 2009) ch 7.

[71] See generally as to the test for establishing this: *Mersey Docks and Harbour Board v Coggins and Griffiths (Liverpool) Ltd* [1947] 1 AC 1, HL.

[72] See, eg, *British Crane Hire Corp Ltd v Ipswich Plant Hire Ltd* [1975] 1 QB 303, CA; cf *Deane v Hogg* (1834) 10 Bing 345, 131 ER 937.

[73] *Deane v Hogg* (1834) 10 Bing 345, 131 ER 937; *The Lancaster* [1980] 2 Lloyd's Rep 497.

[74] *Palmer on Bailment* (3rd edn, 2009) paras 7-013–7-037.

[75] *Palmer on Bailment* (3rd edn, 2009) ch 5. The leading authority is *Lotus Cars Ltd v Southampton Cargo Handling plc (The Rigoletto); Southampton Cargo Handling plc v Associated British Ports* [2000] 2 Lloyd's Rep 532.

[76] *Ashby v Tolhurst* [1937] 2 KB 242, CA; *Tinsley v Dudley* [1951] 2 KB 18, CA.

[77] *Samuel v Westminster Wine Co* The Times, 16 May 1959; *Davis v Educated Fish Parlours Ltd* [1966] Current Law Yearbook 539.

[78] *Ashby v Tolhurst* [1937] 2 KB 242, CA.

[79] *Ashby v Tolhurst* [1937] 2 KB 242, CA; *Tinsley v Dudley* [1951] 2 KB 18, CA; *BRS (Contracts) Ltd v Colney Motor Engineering Co Ltd* The Times, 27 November 1958, CA; *BG Transport Service Ltd v Marston Motor Co Ltd* [1970] 1 Lloyd's Rep 371; *Fred Chappell Ltd v National Car Parks Ltd* The Times, 22 May 1987; *Halbauer v Brighton Corp* [1954] 1 WLR 1161, CA; *Hinks v Fleet* The Times, 7 October 1986, CA.

[80] *Ashby v Tolhurst* [1937] 2 KB 242, CA; *Sydney City Council v West* (1965) 114 CLR 481; *Walton's Stores v Sydney City Council* [1968] 2 NSWR 109.

[81] *Ashby v Tolhurst* [1937] 2 KB 242, CA.

commercial expectations of the parties[86] and any other circumstances which indicate whether a duty of care was being assumed.[87]

(3) Consent to Possession

(a) Burden of proof

Just as it is for the person asserting a bailment to prove the necessary possession,[88] so that **7.11** person must also prove that the putative bailee consented to possession.[89]

(b) Implying consent to possession

Consent may be express or implied.[90] It may be inferred from the nature of a containing **7.12** chattel,[91] or from a warning given at the time of deposit,[92] or from the location in which the goods are bailed,[93] or from the character of bailor or bailee.[94] The mere fact that the bailee is unaware of the presence or specific nature of goods in his possession does not preclude a bailment of them.[95] Such a person may still be a bailee where the goods are of a class that could reasonably be expected to be in his possession.[96]

---

[82] *Halbauer v Brighton Corp* [1954] 1 WLR 1161, CA; *Ultzen v Nichols* [1894] 1 QB 92.

[83] *James Buchanan Ltd v Hay's Transport Services Ltd* [1972] 2 Lloyd's Rep 535.

[84] *Ashby v Tolhurst* [1937] 2 KB 242, CA; *Fred Chappell Ltd v National Car Parks Ltd* The Times, 22 May 1987.

[85] *Ashby v Tolhurst* [1937] 2 KB 242, CA; *Fred Chappell Ltd v National Car Parks Ltd* The Times, 22 May 1987; *Sydney City Council v West* (1965) 114 CLR 481; *Walton's Stores v Sydney City Council* [1968] 2 NSWR 109.

[86] *Lotus Cars Ltd v Southampton Cargo Handling plc (The Rigoletto); Southampton Cargo Handling plc v Associated British Ports* [2000] 2 Lloyd's Rep 532.

[87] See further *WD & HO Wills (Australia) Ltd v State Rail Authority of New South Wales* (1998) 43 NSWLR 338; Rdfe v Investec Bank (Australia) Ltd [2014] VSCA 38; *Lotus Cars Ltd v Southampton Cargo Handling plc (The Rigoletto); Southampton Cargo Handling plc v Associated British Ports* [2000] 2 Lloyd's Rep 532, which involved a substantial number of the above-mentioned factors.

[88] *WD & HO Wills (Australia) Ltd v State Rail Authority of New South Wales* (1998) 43 NSWLR 338; *Lotus Cars Ltd v Southampton Cargo Handling plc (The Rigoletto); Southampton Cargo Handling plc v Associated British Ports* [2000] 2 Lloyd's Rep 532; *G Merel & Co Ltd v Chessher* [1961] 1 Lloyd's Rep 534.

[89] *WD & HO Wills (Australia) Ltd v State Rail Authority of New South Wales* (1998) 43 NSWLR 338. In general terms, the alleged bailee must also consent to hold as bailee of the particular party interested in the goods, though such consent can be implied: See *KH Enterprise v Pioneer Container, The Pioneer Container* [1994] AC 324, PC; *Marcq v Christie Manson & Woods Ltd (t/a Christie's)* [2003] EWCA Civ 731, [2004] QB 286, and see 7.82, 7.83.

[90] *Martin v London County Council* [1947] KB 628.

[91] *Moukataff v BOAC* [1967] 1 Lloyd's Rep 396.

[92] *Mendelssohn v Normand Ltd* [1970] 1 QB 177, CA; *Minichiello v Devonshire Hotel (1967) Ltd* (1977) 79 DLR (3d) 619.

[93] *Brown v Toronto Autoparks Ltd* [1955] 2 DLR 525; *Heffron v Imperial Parking Co Ltd* (1976) 46 DLR (3d) 642.

[94] There is no decision exactly in point, but the character of the bailee (and the nature of the bailee's operations) is generally taken to be a factor in gauging the quality of service to which the bailor can reasonably believe himself to be entitled.

[95] See generally *Palmer on Bailment* (3rd edn, 2009) ch 6; cf *AVX Ltd v EGM Solders Ltd* The Times, 7 July 1982.

[96] eg *Mendelssohn v Normand Ltd* [1970] 1 QB 177, CA (suitcase of silver left in Rolls-Royce parked in underground car park by diner at expensive hotel; but here a warning about the presence of valuables was given to an attendant).

(4) Redelivery

(a) In general

7.13 A bailment can arise though the possessor is not obliged to return the goods to the person from whom he received them.[97] Such a bailment may occur where the possessor is instructed to deliver the goods to a third party after an agreed period of possession,[98] or to sell them on the owner's behalf.[99] The delivery of goods to a lessee on hire-purchase[100] or to a buyer on title retention terms[101] is a bailment though the parties contemplate the ultimate transmission of property to the bailee.[102] The sub-bailment is a common example of a bailment where the bailee delivers the goods to a third party yet retains the character of bailee during the subsidiary possession.[103] Similarly, a bailment can arise though it is contemplated by the terms of delivery that the goods will eventually be consumed by the bailee or that their identity will change by reason of amalgamation or other treatment on the part of the bailee.[104] None of these considerations prevents the recipient from becoming a bailee during the interval between his receiving possession and the occurrence of the obliterating event. In this context, however, the bailor must retain some realistic right of possession over the goods for the period before consumption or transformation if the relation during that period is to be classed as a bailment.[105]

(b) Mixtures and fungible goods

7.14 Where fungible goods are delivered by several depositors to a common depository, and are commingled so that the original deposits are unidentifiable, the inability of each depositor to demand redelivery of the specific goods which he has delivered will normally inhibit the creation of a bailment.[106] Such depositors, being unable to identify the subject matter of the alleged bailment, cannot be bailors, cannot enforce the obligations of a bailee against the recipient, and cannot assert a proprietary interest against third parties.[107] That conclusion was reached in several cases where wheat was deposited by numerous depositors in a 'wheat bank' on terms that equivalent quantities could be withdrawn on demand; the court held that no bailment arose.[108] Similar reasoning will normally preclude a bailment where money is delivered on terms that it shall be repaid.[109] It makes no difference in such cases that the

---

[97] *Gamer's Motor Centre (Newcastle) Pty Ltd v Natwest Wholesale Australia Pty Ltd* (1987) 163 CLR 236, (1987) 61 ALJR 415, 426, *per* Dawson J.

[98] *Brambles Security Services Ltd v Bi-Lo Pty Ltd* (1992) Aust Torts Reps 81–161; cf *Wincanton Ltd v P & O Trans European Ltd* [2001] EWCA Civ 227.

[99] eg *Gutter v Tait* (1947) 177 LT 1.

[100] *Motor Mart Ltd v Webb* [1958] NZLR 773.

[101] *Aluminium Industrie Vaassen BV v Romalpa Aluminium Ltd* [1976] 1 WLR 676, CA.

[102] Otherwise where the circumstances indicate no intention to retain any residual property in the deliveror following delivery to the alleged bailee: *Wincanton Ltd v P & O Trans European Ltd* [2001] EWCA Civ 227.

[103] *The Pioneer Container* [1994] 2 AC 324, PC.

[104] *Clough Mill Ltd v Martin* [1985] 1 WLR 111, 116, CA, *per* Robert Goff LJ.

[105] *Borden (UK) Ltd v Scottish Timber Products Ltd* [1981] Ch 25, 35, CA, *per* Bridge LJ; *Wincanton Ltd v P & O Trans European Ltd* [2001] EWCA Civ 227.

[106] *South Australian Insurance Co Ltd v Randell* (1869) LR 3 PC 101, PC; *Chapman Bros Ltd v Verco Bros Ltd* (1933) 49 CLR 306; cf *Mercer v Craven Grain Storage Ltd* [1994] CLC 328, HL; see also *Coleman v Harvey* [1989] 1 NZLR 723.

[107] *Re Goldcorp Exchange Ltd* [1995] 1 AC 74, PC.

[108] *South Australian Insurance Co Ltd v Randell* (1869) LR 3 PC 101, PC; *Chapman Bros Ltd v Verco Bros Ltd* (1933) 49 CLR 306; *Mercer v Craven Grain Storage Ltd* [1994] CLC 328, HL; *Coleman v Harvey* [1989] 1 NZLR 723.

[109] *Walker v British Guarantee Assoc* (1852) 18 QB 277, 118 ER 104; *R v Hassall* (1861) Le & Ca 58, 169 ER 1302; *Brambles Security Services Ltd v Bi-Lo Pty Ltd* (1992) Aust Torts Reps 81–161; *Ferguson v Eakin*

recipient undertakes to deliver up equivalent goods or cash on demand, because the line of heredity between what is deposited and what is returned is broken. Similar disabilities affect at common law the buyer of generic goods who is falsely assured by the seller that the seller will segregate goods answering the contract description and retain possession of them as the buyer's bailee.[110] Such a buyer cannot assert a bailment (or any proprietary interest akin to that of bailor and sustainable against third parties) because he cannot point to any specific goods which are the subject of that bailment;[111] and neither the doctrine of the bailee's estoppel,[112] nor that of attornment,[113] will fortify his rights against a third party creditor of the seller. But a tenancy in common may arise by agreement among individual contributors to a communal pool where an intention to that effect is clearly evinced by the underlying contract,[114] or by statute under certain sales of goods.[115] Such tenancy in common, which confers a legal interest in goods,[116] can extend to the recipient or seller of the goods where he has contributed to the mixed pool upon which the tenancy in common fastens. Its existence enables the depositor or buyer to sue the recipient or seller as a bailee of the recipient or buyer,[117] and to assert a proprietary interest against third parties.[118] That entitlement is, of course, especially important where the recipient or seller is insolvent.

(5) Subject Matter of Bailment

Bailment is limited to tangible chattels. It does not apply to intangible property such as **7.15** a debt or copyright.[119] Obligations akin to those on a bailment may arise, however, from an entrustment of confidential information.[120] It is argued that principles akin to those of

---

(NSWCA, 27 August 1997). And see *Parastatidis v Kotarides* [1978] Victoria Reports 449 (*mutuum*, or loan of money, is not a true bailment). See further as to *mutuum*, *Wincanton Ltd v P & O Trans European Ltd* [2001] EWCA Civ 227; [2001] CLC 962.

[110] *Re Goldcorp Exchange Ltd* [1995] 1 AC 74, PC; *Re London Wine Co (Shippers) Ltd* [1986] Palmer's Company Cases 121.

[111] *Re Goldcorp Exchange Ltd* [1995] 1 AC 74, PC; and see *Re London Wine Co (Shippers) Ltd* [1986] Palmer's Company Cases 121; cf *Re Stapylton Fletcher Ltd* [1994] 1 WLR 1181.

[112] See 7.21 et seq.

[113] See 7.78 et seq.

[114] *Mercer v Craven Grain Storage Ltd* [1994] CLC 328, HL (deposits of grain); *Re Stapylton Fletcher Ltd* [1994] 1 WLR 1181 (sale of wine); cf *Gill and Duffus (Liverpool) Ltd v Scruttons Ltd* [1953] 1 WLR 1407 (where bags of chestnuts consigned to different consignees burst and intermingled in the hold of the vessel, and the master porter rebagged them proportionally to the amounts in the bills of lading, it was held that a tenancy in common arose among the original consignees). See also *Glencore International AG v Metro Trading International Inc* [2001] 1 Lloyd's Rep 2000.

[115] Sale of Goods Act 1979, s 20A, added by the Sale of Goods (Amendment) Act 1995; see 2.21; L Gullifer in *Palmer on Bailment* (3rd edn, 2009) ch 8.

[116] cf *MCC Proceeds Inc v Lehman Bros International (Europe)* [1998] 4 All ER 675, CA (bailment requires legal interest in bailor).

[117] See *Mercer v Craven Grain Storage Ltd* [1994] CLC 328, HL, per Lord Templeman (defendant farmers' co-operative, as recipient of deposits of grain from claimant growers, committed conversion 'if it allowed the mix to be so depleted by withdrawals that the balance remaining was not sufficient to satisfy the demands of the [claimants]'). cf *Wincanton Ltd v P & O Trans European Ltd* [2001] EWCA Civ 227 (no bailment where pallets mixed with others of indistinguishable nature supplied from other sources).

[118] *Mercer v Craven Grain Storage Ltd* [1994] CLC 328, HL; *Re Stapylton Fletcher Ltd* [1994] 1 WLR 1181.

[119] *OBG Ltd v Allan* [2007] UKHL 21, [2007] 2 WLR 920; *Your Response Ltd v Datateam Business Media Ltd* [2014] EWCA Civ 281, [2015] QB 41 (there can be no possessory lien over intangible property, in this case an electronic database).

[120] See *Hospital Products Ltd v United States Surgical Corporation* (1984) 156 CLR 41, 105–106, per Mason J; *Watson v Dolmark Industries Ltd* [1992] 3 NZLR 311, 315, per Cooke J; *Reading v R* [1949] 2 KB 232, 236, per Asquith J. As to whether information can count as property in English private law, see generally *Palmer on Bailment* (3rd edn, 2009) ch 30; N Palmer and P Kohler, 'Information as Property' in N Palmer and E McKendrick (eds), *Interests in Goods* (2nd edn, 1998); 8(1) *Halsbury's Laws of England* (4th edn Re-issue) paras 407, 408.

bailment should govern the 'global custody' of electronically stored securities which have no material existence.[121] Bailment does not apply to live human beings such as children entrusted for custody.[122] Human remains, and human body parts and products , have traditionally boen regarded as incapable of being the subject of proprietary or possessory rights and from this it has been inferred that they cannot be bailed.[123] But even on traditional principles bodily material might become property where it is subjected to treatment rendering it something different from a mere corpse awaiting burial.[124] The Court of Appeal has recognized a bailment of human sperm;[125] and modern law is now likely to recognise other bailments of human material.[126] Money can be bailed, but a bailment of money will arise only where the specific coins or notes are to be returned to the deliveror or applied in accordance with his instructions, as where a bank note is pledged,[127] or shop takings are to be collected by a security company and delivered to the proprietor's bank.[128] Where cash is loaned or deposited in a bank, and the recipient's obligation is merely to repay to the lender or depositor an equivalent amount, the relationship between lender and borrower is one of debtor and creditor not bailor and bailee.[129]

(6) Bailment Distinguished from Other Transactions

(a) Bailment and trust

7.16   Bailment and trust are distinct and, for the most part, mutually exclusive.[130] Their main difference lies in the identity of the person who has the legal property and can confer it on others. In bailments, it is the bailor who has the legal property and can transmit it to third parties, while in trusts it is the trustee who has the legal property and can transmit it to third parties, the beneficiary having only an equitable title.[131] Since bailment is a legal relationship capable of generating legal remedies, only a person with a legal interest can be a bailor.[132] Because there is no bailment between trustee and beneficiary, a beneficiary cannot invoke that line of authority[133] which gives the bailor an immediate right of possession when the bailee commits an act repugnant to the bailment.[134] Certain bailees do, however, occupy a fiduciary position toward their bailors. For example, a pledgee who exercises his power of sale on default by the pledgor holds the surplus proceeds on trust for the pledgor,[135] and a custodian for reward who charges his bailors for the cost of insurance may hold the policy monies on a fiduciary obligation for them.[136] According to circumstances, obligations owed

---

[121] See AW Beaves, 'Global Custody—A Tentative Analysis of Property and Contract' in N Palmer and E McKendrick (eds), *Interests in Goods* (2nd edn, 1998).

[122] cf *ST v North Yorkshire County Council* [1999] IRLR 98; *Lister v Hesley Hall Ltd* [2002] 1 AC 22.

[123] *Dobson v North Tyneside Health Authority and Newcastle Health Authority* [1997] 1 WLR 596, CA; *R v Kelly* [1998] 3 All ER 741, CA.

[124] *Doodeward v Spence* (1908) 6 CLR 406, 414, *per* Griffith CJ; *Dobson v North Tyneside Health Authority and Newcastle Health Authority* [1997] 1 WLR 596, CA; *R v Kelly* [1998] 3 All ER 741, CA.

[125] *Yearworth v North Bristol NH Trust* [2009] EWCA Civ 37, [2010] QB 1; *Palmer on Bailment* (3rd edn, 2009) ch 29.

[126] *R v Kelly* [1998] 3 All ER 741, 750, CA, *per* Rose LJ.

[127] cf *Taylor v Chester* (1869) LR 4 QB 309.

[128] *Brambles Security Services Ltd v Bi-Lo Pty Ltd* (1992) Aust Torts Reps 81–161; cf *Lipkin Gorman v Karpnale Ltd* [1991] 2 AC 548, HL.

[129] *Ferguson v Eakins* (unreported, NSWCA, 27 August 1997).

[130] *MCC Proceeds Inc v Lehmann Bros International (Europe)* [1998] 4 All ER 675, CA.

[131] *MCC Proceeds Inc v Lehmann Bros International (Europe)* [1998] 4 All ER 675, CA.

[132] *MCC Proceeds Inc v Lehmann Bros International (Europe)* [1998] 4 All ER 675, 701–703, CA, *per* Hobhouse LJ.

[133] *Union Transport Finance Ltd v British Car Auctions Ltd* [1978] 2 All ER 385, CA.

[134] *MCC Proceeds Inc v Lehmann Bros International (Europe)* [1998] 4 All ER 675, CA.

[135] *Mathew v TM Sutton Ltd* [1994] 4 All ER 793.

[136] *Re E Dibbens & Sons Ltd* [1990] BCLC 577.

by a holder of goods toward another person who has a reversionary interest in them might alternatively be rationalized in terms of bailment or trust.[137]

(b) Bailment and sale of goods

A bailment, unlike a sale, passes no general property to the recipient party, but merely a special property in the form of possession.[138] Bailment involves the retention of general property by the bailor and does not attract the special legislation applicable to sale.[139] But sale and bailment can co-exist in relation to a single chattel, as where goods are supplied to a person who has agreed to buy them subject to a title retention clause,[140] or on hire-purchase,[141] or where containers are supplied on refundable deposit along with their contents.[142] A bailment of goods on a finance lease closely resembles a sale and has been held in New Zealand[143] to attract at least one of the legal incidents of hire-purchase, namely the special measure of damages applicable in a claim between bailor and bailee, or bailor and third party, respectively.

7.17

Although some judges appear to treat bailment and sale as mutually exclusive in the context of title retention,[144] the mere fact that a person who has voluntary possession of another's goods is given extensive liberties in relation to them (such as the right to consume or alter them, or to dispose of them as a third party) does not confute the existence of a bailment so long as the goods exist and the possessor has possession.[145] If, however, the terms of the agreement give the supplier no realistic prospect of resuming possession of the identical goods before their consumption or disposal, there is probably no bailment.[146] Similarly, a bailment is unlikely to arise where an owner of fungible commodities (such as wheat,[147] flour,[148]

7.18

---

[137] *Re Swan, Witham v Swan* [1915] 1 Ch 829.

[138] *Re Bond Worth Ltd* [1980] Ch 228, 247, *per* Slade J.

[139] Differentiating the two transactions may require detailed examination of the contract: see, eg, *Stellar Chartering & Brokerage Inc v Efibanca-Ente Finanziario Interbancario SpA (The Span Terza) (No 2)* [1984] 1 WLR 27, HL.

[140] See eg *Aluminium Industrie Vaassen BV v Romalpa Aluminium Ltd* [1976] 1 WLR 676, CA; *Armour v Thyssen Edelstahlwerke AG* [1991] 2 AC 339, HL; *Clough Mill v Martin* [1985] 1 WLR 111, CA; *Hendy Lennox (Industrial Engines) Ltd v Grahame Puttick Ltd* [1984] 1 WLR 485; *Re Andrabell Ltd (in liq); Airborne Accessories Ltd v Goodman* [1984] 3 All ER 407; *Re Peachdart Ltd* [1984] Ch 131; *Borden (UK) Ltd v Scottish Timber Products Ltd* [1981] Ch 25, CA; *Re Bond Worth Ltd* [1980] Ch 228; *E Pfeiffer Weinkellerei-Weineinkauf GmbH & Co v Arbuthnot Factors Ltd* [1988] 1 WLR 150; *Compaq Computer Ltd v Abercorn Group Ltd* [1991] BCC 484; *Tatung (UK) Ltd v Galex Telesure Ltd* (1989) 5 BCC 325; *Forsythe International (UK) Ltd v Silver Shipping Co Ltd (The Saetta)* [1993] 2 Lloyd's Rep 268.

[141] See eg *Shogun Finance Ltd v Hudson* [2004] 1 AC 919, [2004] 1 All ER 215, [2004] 1 Lloyd's Rep. 532; *Motor Mart Ltd v Webb* [1958] NZLR 773; *Gamer's Motor Centre (Newcastle) Pty Ltd v Natwest Wholesale Australia Pty Ltd* (1987) 163 CLR 236.

[142] See eg *Geddling v Marsh* [1920] 1 KB 66; *Leitch & Co Ltd v Leydon* 1930 SC 41, 52–53, *per* Lord Clyde; *Doble v David Greig Ltd* [1972] 1 WLR 703; cf *Beecham Foods Ltd v North Supplies (Edmonton) Ltd* [1959] 1 WLR 643. These authorities are discussed in *Palmer on Bailment* (3rd edn, 2009) paras 3-035– 3-039.

[143] *NZ Securities & Finance Ltd v Wrightcars Ltd* [1976] 1 NZLR 77.

[144] See eg *Re Peachdart Ltd* [1984] Ch 131, 142, *per* Vinelott J; *Hendy-Lennox (Industrial Engines) Ltd v Grahame Puttick Ltd* [1984] 1 WLR 485, 499, *per* Staughton J; *Re Andrabell Ltd (in liq); Airborne Accessories Ltd v Goodman* [1984] 3 All ER 407, 414, *per* Peter Gibson J; *E Pfeiffer Weinkellerei-Weineinkauf GmbH & Co v Arbuthnot Factors Ltd* [1988] 1 WLR 150, 159, *per* Phillips J.

[145] *Clough Mill Ltd v Martin* [1985] 1 WLR 111, 116, *per* Robert Goff J.

[146] *Borden (UK) Ltd v Scottish Timber Products Ltd* [1981] Ch 25, 35, CA, *per* Bridge LJ (cf 45, *per* Buckley LJ); *Wincanton Ltd v P & O Trans European Ltd* [2001] EWCA Civ 227.

[147] *South Australian Insurance Co Ltd v Randell* (1869) LR 3 PC 101, PC; *Chapman Bros v Verco Bros & Co Ltd* (1933) 49 CLR 306; *Mercer v Craven Grain Storage Ltd* [1994] CLC 328, HL.

[148] *South Australian Insurance Co Ltd v Randell* (1869) LR 3 PC 101, PC.

fuel[149] or money)[150] deposits them in a general store operated by the recipient, agreeing that they are to be mingled with similar goods belonging to the recipient or to other depositors, and that an equivalent quantity will be redelivered to the depositor. Such an arrangement will normally be construed as a relinquishment of property in the deposited commodities in return for a substituted property in the redelivered commodities, and not as a bailment.[151] But a bailment may arise by agreement (as where all the depositors and the recipient agree that the depositors shall be tenants in common of the overall quantity deposited)[152] or by custom or statute,[153] and may even be imposed by the court in the interests of justice.[154]

(c) Bailment and work and labour

7.19 Occasionally it is unclear whether the delivery of one person's chattel to another, to enable the other to perform work on the chattel and redeliver it to the original owner, is a bailment of the chattel or a contract by which property passes to the recipient and is transferred back to the original deliveror. In each case the solution depends on the intention of the parties as objectively inferred from the terms and circumstances of the contract.[155] According to circumstances, the answer may turn on the terms of the agreement,[156] or trade practice,[157] or the requirements of justice.[158]

(d) Bailment and agency

7.20 Bailment and agency often coincide. A bailee may be the agent of the bailor,[159] and an agent may be the bailee of the principal.[160] Both are transactions where one person may be in the service of the other.[161] But agency and bailment are distinct relations and each can exist without the other. There are parallels however, between the liability of agents and bailees,[162] and the coincidence of the two relations has been seen as justifying convergent results in particular cases.[163]

---

[149] *Stellar Chartering & Brokerage Inc v Efibanca-Ente Finanziario Interbancario SpA (The Span Terza) (No 2)* [1984] 1 WLR 27, HL (coal); *Indian Oil Corp Ltd v Greenstone Shipping SA (Panama) (The Ypatianna)* [1988] QB 345 (oil).

[150] *R v Hassall* (1861) Le & Ca 58, 169 ER 1302; *Coleman v Harvey* [1989] 1 NZLR 723.

[151] *Wincanton Ltd v P & O Trans European Ltd* [2001] EWCA Civ 227; cf *Mercer v Craven Grain Storage Ltd* [1994] CLC 328, HL; *South Australian Insurance Co Ltd v Randell* (1869) LR 3 PC 101, PC.

[152] *Mercer v Craven Grain Storage Ltd* [1994] CLC 328, HL.

[153] Sale of Goods (Amendment) Act 1995, amending Sale of Goods Act 1979.

[154] *Gill and Duffus (Liverpool) Ltd v Scruttons Ltd* [1953] 1 WLR 1407; cf *Coleman v Harvey* [1989] 1 NZLR 723.

[155] *Dixon v London Small Arms Co Ltd* (1876) 1 App Cas 632.

[156] *Moorhouse v Angus and Robertson (No 1) Pty Ltd* [1981] 1 NSWLR 700.

[157] *Best Plastics Ltd v Burnett Jones Ltd* (1984) 10 NZ Recent Law 3.

[158] *Coleman v Harvey* [1989] 1 NZLR 723.

[159] eg a bailee to whom goods are entrusted for sale (*Gutter v Tait* (1947) 177 LT 1) or the bailee of goods under a title retention clause (*Aluminium Industrie Vaassen BV v Romalpa Aluminium Ltd* [1976] 1 WLR 676, CA).

[160] The agent gets a possession independent of the principal: *Lotus Cars Ltd v Southampton Cargo Handling plc (The Rigoletto); Southampton Cargo Handling plc v Associated British Ports* [2000] 2 Lloyd's Rep 532, 539, per Rix LJ, CA; *Transcontainer Express Ltd v Custodian Security Ltd* [1988] 1 Lloyd's Rep 128, 135, CA, per Slade LJ.

[161] This observation, while universally true of agents, is not necessarily true of bailees; eg, the bailee by way of hire is in the relation of bailee for his own advantage, and the same may be said of the bailee under a title retention clause: *Hendy Lennox (Industrial Engines) Ltd v Grahame Puttick Ltd* [1984] 1 WLR 485; *Re Andrabell Ltd (in liq); Airborne Accessories Ltd v Goodman* [1984] 3 All ER 407.

[162] eg, both may generate fiduciary obligations.

[163] eg, those on title retention; see 8.82–8.86 and 2.23.

B. Principles Common to All Bailments

(1) The Bailee's Estoppel

(a) General

At common law, a bailee is estopped from denying his bailor's title.[164] He cannot invoke the **7.21** bailor's lack of title to the goods as a ground for resisting liability to him.[165] The prohibition applies both where the lack of title is relied on as showing a lack of qualification to sue in the bailor, and where it is invoked to show that the bailor has suffered no loss.[166] Martin B said that it would be impossible to transact business on any other basis.[167]

(b) Basis of estoppel

In cases of consensual bailment the prohibition can be analysed as one of the bailee's implied **7.22** undertakings, in return for which possession is conferred.[168] But the estoppel may also apply between a head bailor and a sub-bailee, who have no direct communication.[169] The estoppel appears to apply to all bailments, with the exception of those which arise by finding[170] or wrongful taking,[171] and of those purporting to confer either an ultimate title, or the present use and enjoyment of goods on the bailee: eg, hire-purchase, hire, and the delivery of goods under a conditional sale,[172] where, statute grants the possessor specific rights of security of title and/or possession enabling him to challenge any lack of ownership or right to bail the goods on the part of the bailor.[173] It is highly unlikely that a similar right would operate in favour of the borrower of goods.

(c) Exceptions to the estoppel: common law

There are two sets of exceptions to the general rule, common law and statutory. At common **7.23** law, the bailee's estoppel is displaced where he defends the bailor's claim with the authority of the true owner,[174] or where he is evicted from the goods by title paramount;[175] the latter

---

[164] *Cheesman v Exall* (1851) 6 Exch 341, 155 ER 574; *Biddle v Bond* (1865) 6 B & S 225, 122 ER 1179; *Rogers Sons & Co v Lambert & Co* [1891] 1 QB 318; *Ross v Edwards & Co* (1895) 73 LT 100, PC; *The Albazero* [1977] AC 774, HL; *China Pacific SA v Food Corp of India (The Winson)* [1982] AC 939, HL; *Mayflower Foods Ltd v Barnard Bros Ltd* (HC, 9 August 1996); *East West Corp v DKBS 1912* [2003] EWCA Civ 83, [2003] 1 Lloyd's Rep 239; cf *Sandeman Coprimar SA v Transitos y Transportes Integrales SL* [2003] EWCA Civ 113, [2003] QB 1270. And see Rolfe v Investec Bank (Australia) Ltd [2014] VSCA 38 at para 56.

[165] It appears however that the estoppel does not prevent a bailee who becomes subject to conflicting claims, one from his bailor and one from a third party, from exercising a right to take a reasonable time to investigate title, provided he carries out this inquiry with reasonable thoroughness and speed: *Spencer v S Franses Ltd* [2011] EWHC 1269 (QB). On the question of the necessary pertinacity and despatch of inquiry see also *Atapattu, R. (On the Application of) v Secretary of State for the Home Department* [2011] EWHC 1388 (Admin).

[166] *The Albazero* [1977] AC 774, 841, 846, HL, *per* Lord Diplock; *China Pacific SA v Food Corp of India (The Winson)* [1982] AC 939, 958–960, HL.

[167] *Cheesman v Exall* (1851) 6 Ex 341, 155 ER 574, 346.

[168] *Ross v Edwards & Co* (1895) 73 LT 100, PC.

[169] *The Hamburg Star* [1994] 1 Lloyd's Rep 399 (point arguable).

[170] *Palmer on Bailment* (3rd edn, 2009) ch 26.

[171] *Palmer on Bailment* (3rd edn, 2009) 282.

[172] *Palmer on Bailment* (3rd edn, 2009) 276.

[173] See Supply of Goods and Services Act 1982, s 7 (hire of goods); Supply of Goods (Implied Terms) Act 1973, s 8(1)(a), as amended by the Consumer Credit Act 1974, Sch 4, para 35 (hire purchase).

[174] *Biddle v Bond* (1865) 6 B & S 225, 122 ER 1179; *Rogers Sons & Co v Lambert & Co* [1891] 1 QB 318. cf *Shell UK Ltd v Total UK Ltd* [2010] EWCA Civ 180, [2011] QB 86 (beneficial owner suing tortfeasor and joining legal owner).

[175] *Biddle v Bond* (1865) 6 B & S 225, 122 ER 1179.

exception does not require physical eviction, but merely the making of an adverse demand by the true owner against the bailee.[176] In cases of doubt as to the true location of title the bailee should interplead,[177] though this resource is not available unless there are two or more adverse claims; mere suspicion of a third party claim is not enough.[178] A bailee who elects to deliver the goods to someone other than the party entitled to them is liable to that other party in conversion.[179] A bailee who refuses to deliver the goods to the person entitled may be liable to that person in conversion.[180]

(d) Exceptions to the estoppel: statute

7.24 By statute, a person sued for wrongful interference with goods is entitled to show in accordance with rules of court[181] that someone other than the claimant has a better right to the goods or in right of which he sues, and any rule of law to the contrary (sometimes called *jus tertii*) is abolished.[182] It is unclear whether this provision has abolished the common law grounds on which the bailee might plead the better right of a third party; the only case to consider the point left it open.[183] It is arguable that the statutory exception can be averted by a bailor in one of two ways: either by casting the claim in bailment or contract rather than in tort,[184] or by arguing that the estoppel between bailor and bailee is not a 'rule of law' imposed externally on the parties but an implied term of the bailment, and as such beyond the statute.[185] The defendant in an action for wrongful interference with goods can plead the right of a third party where, at the date of the application or hearing, the third party no longer has that right, provided the right existed at the time of the wrong.[186]

(2) *Possession as Title*

(a) Common law; possession counts as title

7.25 At common law, as against a wrongdoer, the possession of goods counts as title.[187] In the absence of the true owner, the possessor of goods can sue any third person who inflicts a wrong on those goods, and can recover damages calculated as if the possessor were the owner.[188] If the goods are lost or destroyed and the owner brings no claim, the possessor can, in a claim for conversion, trespass, negligence or other tort, recover their full value. If the goods are damaged the possessor can recover, according to circumstances, the diminution in value or the cost of reinstatement.[189] The bailee's right to claim does not depend on

---

[176] *Biddle v Bond* (1865) 6 B & S 225, 122 ER 1179.

[177] CPR Part 50; Sch 1, modifying in part RSC Ord 17, Interpleader.

[178] *Redler Grain Silos Ltd v BICC Ltd* [1982] 1 Lloyd's Rep 435, 438–439, *per* Kerr LJ, 440, *per* Stephenson LJ, CA.

[179] cf *Palmer on Bailment* (3rd edn, 2009) paras 6-015– 6-018.

[180] *Batuit v Hartley* (1872) 26 LT 968.

[181] CPR 19.5A. See *Indian Herbs (UK) Ltd v Hadley & Ottoway Ltd and others* (21 January 1999, CA).

[182] Torts (Interference with Goods) Act 1977, s 8(1).

[183] *De Franco v Comr of Police of the Metropolis The Times*, 8 May 1987, CA.

[184] cf *Sutcliffe v Chief Constable of West Yorkshire* [1996] RTR 86, 90, CA, *per* Otton LJ; *Yearworth v North Bristol NH Trust* [2009] EWCA Civ 37, [2010] QB 1; *Palmer on Bailment* (3rd edn, 2009) para A5-001.

[185] *Palmer on Bailment* (3rd edn, 2009) para 4-057 et seq. These points have never been tested.

[186] *De Franco v Comr of Police of the Metropolis* The Times, 8 May 1987, CA.

[187] *The Winkfield* [1902] P 42; *The Jag Shakti* [1986] AC 337, PC; *O'Sullivan v Williams* [1992] 3 All ER 385, CA; *HSBC Rail (UK) Ltd v Network Rail Infrastucture Ltd* [2005] EWCA Civ 1437, [2006] 1 WLR 643. For a full discussion see *Palmer on Bailment* (3rd edn, 2009) ch 4; N Palmer, 'Possessory Title' in N Palmer and E McKendrick (eds), *Interests in Goods* (2nd edn, 1998) 66–71.

[188] As to the categories of loss recoverable, see *Palmer on Bailment* (3rd edn, 2009) para 4-099 et seq.

[189] cf *HL Motorworks (Willesden) Ltd v Alwahbi* [1977] RTR 276; see *Palmer on Bailment* (3rd edn, 2009) para 4-112.

being personally liable to the bailor for the wrong[190] or on his having the bailor's authority to sue the wrongdoer,[191] or on his having suffered personal loss equivalent to the value of the goods.[192] This principle has been described[193] as an exception to the normal rule that damages are compensatory,[194] for the bailee recovers more than his personal loss.[195]

(b) Destination of damages

The bailee who recovers full damages under this principle must account for them to the **7.26** bailor, though he may subtract the value of his own interest and any other personal losses suffered in consequence of the wrong.[196] Shares are abated rateably where the bailee recovers less than full value in a claim which relieves the wrongdoer of further liability.[197] It is uncertain whether the relationship in regard to these surplus proceeds is one of trust but that analysis seems likely.[198]

The recovery by either bailor[199] or bailee[200] of full damages from the wrongdoer precludes **7.27** any further claim against that wrongdoer by the other party to the bailment. The third party wrongdoer is not relieved of further liability, however, where the person to whom he pays full damages was himself a wrongdoer in possession at the time of the wrong.[201]

(c) Mere right of possession

The general principle applies not only to persons who are in possession of goods at the time **7.28** of a wrong but also to those who have an immediate right to possession, unaccompanied by possession itself, at that time.[202]

(d) Exceptions: common law[203]

The general principle does not apply where the wrongdoer has, since the time of the wrong, **7.29** become the owner of the goods,[204] or where the wrongdoer defends the claim with the

---

[190] *The Winkfield* [1902] P 42, CA.
[191] *The Winkfield* [1902] P 42, CA; *The Albazero* [1977] AC 774, HL; *Glenwood Lumber Co Ltd v Phillips* [1904] AC 405, PC; *Eastern Construction Co Ltd v National Trust Co Ltd* [1914] AC 197, PC; *China Pacific SA v Food Corp of India (The Winson)* [1982] AC 939, HL; and see G McMeel, 'Complex entitlements: the *Albazero* principle and restitution' [1999] Restitution L Rev 22.
[192] *The Winkfield* [1902] P 42, CA.
[193] *The Albazero* [1977] AC 774, 841, HL, *per* Lord Diplock.
[194] See 21.14ff.
[195] cf *The Sanix Ace* [1987] 1 Lloyd's Rep 465, *The Aramis* [1989] 1 Lloyd's Rep 213, CA.
[196] *The Winkfield* [1902] P 42, CA. See further *Palmer on Bailment* (3rd edn, 2009) para 4-077 et seq.
[197] *The Johannis Vatis* [1922] P 92, CA.
[198] No such terminology is employed in *The Winkfield* [1902] P 42, CA or in *O'Sullivan v Williams* [1992] 3 All ER 385, CA; cf *Re E Dibbens & Sons Ltd* [1980] BCLC 577; *Mathew v TM Sutton Ltd* [1994] 4 All ER 793.
[199] *O'Sullivan v Williams* [1992] 3 All ER 385, CA.
[200] *The Winkfield* [1902] P 42, CA.
[201] *Attenborough v London and St Katharine's Dock Co* (1878) 3 CPD 450; cf Torts (Interference with Goods) Act 1977, ss 7, 8.
[202] *The Jag Shakti* [1986] AC 337, PC; *East West Corp v DKBS 1912* [2003] EWCA Civ 83, [2003] 1 Lloyd's Rep 239; *HSBC Rail (UK) Ltd v Network Rail Infrastructure Ltd* [2005] EWCA Civ 1437, [2006] 1 WLR 643 (obiter); and see *Government of the Islamic Republic of Iran v Barakat Galleries Ltd* [2007] EWCA Civ 1374, [2009] QB 22 (immediate right of possession may be contractual and need not derive from a proprietary right); *Shell UK Ltd v Total UK Ltd* [2010] EWCA Civ 180, [2011] QB 86 (beneficial owner without possession or immediate right of possession at the time of wrong may recover damages for foreseeable depreciation or foreseeable cost of reinstatement and consequential losses by joining legal owner).
[203] See generally *Chartered Trust v King* [2001] All ER (D) 310, CA, approving Palmer, *Bailment* (2nd edn, 1991) 316; and see now *Palmer on Bailment* (3rd edn, 2009) paras 4-096–4-098.
[204] *Eastern Construction Co Ltd v National Trust Co and Schmidt* [1914] AC 197, PC; *Webb v Ireland and A-G* [1988] Irish R 353.

owner's authority,[205] or where the act itself was performed under the owner's authority,[206] or where the wrongdoer has an enforceable cross-claim or right of set-off against the bailee,[207] or where an award of full damages would lead to circuity of actions.[208] Nor does it apply where the wrongdoer is the owner or bailor or some other person having an interest in the goods,[209] or where the owner has already recovered full damages from the wrongdoer before the bailee makes a claim against the same person.[210] Of course these exceptions overlap. In all such cases the bailee can recover at most for his personal loss.

(e) Exceptions: statute

7.30 By statute, a defendant in an action for wrongful interference with goods is entitled to show, in accordance with rules of court,[211] that a third person has a better right than the claimant as respects all or any part of the interest claimed by the claimant, or in right of which the claimant claims.[212] The restriction of these provisions to cases of wrongful interference with goods (which are exclusively wrongs in tort)[213] appears to debar their application to claims by bailees against third parties for breach of contract.[214] The provisions apply where the third party had an interest in the goods at the time of the wrong but has since ceased to have that or any other interest.[215] It is uncertain whether the provisions have extinguished the former common law exceptions to the general prohibition on a wrongdoer's pleading the right of a third party in response to claims by a possessor,[216] but it is submitted that they have not.[217]

(3) Insurance

7.31 Under a normal custodial bailment the bailee owes no obligation to the bailor to insure the goods.[218] But a bailee has an insurable interest in the goods[219] and can, under a suitably worded policy,[220] insure them for their full value, even though this may exceed the value of

---

[205] *The Winkfield* [1902] P 42, CA.

[206] *The Winkfield* [1902] P 42, CA.

[207] *The Jag Shakti* [1986] AC 337, 345–346, 348, PC, *per* Lord Brandon, who described this as 'the only exception' to the rule in *The Winkfield* [1902] P 42, CA.

[208] *Maynegrain Pty Ltd v Compafina Bank* [1982] 2 NSWLR 141, 156–157, *per* Hutley JA; reversed without reference to this point [1984] 1 NSWLR 258, PC.

[209] *Brierley v Kendall* (1852) 17 QB 937, 117 ER 1540; and see further *Standard Electronic Apparatus Laboratories Pty Ltd v Stenner* [1960] NSWLR 447; *Maynegrain Pty Ltd v Compafina Bank* [1982] 2 NSWLR 141, 156–157, *per* Hutley JA; reversed without reference to this point [1984] 1 NSWLR 258, PC.

[210] *O'Sullivan v Williams* [1992] 3 All ER 385, CA.

[211] Power to make rules of court is conferred by the Torts (Interference with Goods) Act 1977, s 8(2), without prejudice to any other power of making rules of court: Torts (Interference with Goods) Act 1977, s 8(3). See CPR 19.5A.

[212] Torts (Interference with Goods) Act 1977, s 8(1), which also states that any rule of law to the contrary (sometimes called *jus tertii*) is abolished.

[213] Torts (Interference with Goods) Act 1977, s 1.

[214] See *Palmer on Bailment* (3rd edn, 2009) para 4-144.

[215] *De Franco v Comr of Police of the Metropolis* The Times, 8 May 1987, CA.

[216] *Palmer on Bailment* (3rd edn, 2009) para 4-060.

[217] *Palmer on Bailment* (3rd edn, 2009) para 4-061; *De Franco v Comr of Police of the Metropolis* The Times, 8 May 1987, CA.

[218] See 7.51, n 329. For more detailed discussion, see *Palmer on Bailment* (3rd edn, 2009) paras 14-013–14-018.

[219] *Hepburn v A Tomlinson (Hauliers) Ltd* [1966] AC 451, HL; *Waters and Steel v Monarch Fire and Life Assurance Co* (1856) 5 E & B 870, 119 ER 705; *Castellain v Preston* (1883) 11 QBD 380; *The Albazero* [1977] AC 774, HL; *Feasy v Sun Life Assurance Co of Canada* [2003] EWCA Civ 885; *Ramco (UK) Ltd & Ors v International Insurance Company of Hannover Ltd & Anor* [2003] EWHC 2360 (Comm) (which holds that whether an insurance policy taken out by a bailee covers property or the bailee's liability for it depends on the wording of the particular transaction).

[220] The usual reference is to goods held in trust or on commission. cf *Ramco (UK) Ltd & Ors v International Insurance Company of Hannover Ltd & Anor* [2003] EWHC 2360 (Comm).

his personal interest in them, or the amount of his likely loss in the event of misadventure.[221] Having recovered the insurance proceeds the bailee must account for the excess to the bailor, and he may hold those excess proceeds subject to an equitable proprietary interest in the bailor, at least where the bailor has paid him separately to insure the goods.[222] The bailor also has an insurable interest and where the bailee is a co-insured the bailee may resist a subrogation claim by the bailor's insurer by reference to the principle that an insurer cannot sue one co-insured in the name of another.[223]

C. Gratuitous Bailments and Bailments for Reciprocal Advantage

(a) Reasons for making the distinction

Older authorities drew a distinction between those bailments under which one party receives no benefit (such as gratuitous deposit or loan) and those that benefit both parties (such as custody for reward, or pledge, or hire). Such a distinction was justifiable when the obligations of a bailor and bailee varied along a sliding scale[224] according to the location of benefit. Nowadays, the conceptual differences among different bailments are slight and there is little need to determine whether a bailment is gratuitous or reciprocally beneficial. Our adoption of the distinction is purely for purposes of exposition.   **7.32**

The duty of care required of any bailee, eg, is that of reasonable care in all the circumstances; modern cases reject the older standard of gross negligence as determining the liability of the unrewarded bailee.[225] At least one senior judge has said that the line separating the standards of care demanded of each class of bailee is a very fine one, difficult to discern and impossible to define.[226] While older authority indicates that the ability of a bailee to bind himself by promises greater than the duty which he would owe at common law requires that the bailment be contractual,[227] modern authority has opted squarely for the contrary view.[228] There is some authority for the view that an unrewarded bailee's liability for the unauthorized wrongs of his employees is confined to cases where the bailor is personally negligent in employing or supervising the malefactor.[229]   **7.33**

---

[221] *Hepburn v A Tomlinson (Hauliers) Ltd* [1966] AC 451, HL; *Waters and Steel v Monarch Fire and Life Assurance Co* (1856) 5 E & B 870, 119 ER 705; *Castellain v Preston* (1883) 11 QBD 380.

[222] *Re E Dibbens & Sons Ltd* [1990] BCLC 577; *DG Finance Ltd v Andrew Scott and Eagle Star Insurance Co Ltd* (CA, 15 June 1995). As to the obligation of the bailee to account to the bailor for an excess of any insurance proceeds see *Ramco (UK) Ltd & Ors v International Insurance Company of Hannover Ltd & Anor* [2003] EWHC 2360 (Comm) (15 October 2003).

[223] *Petrofina (UK) Ltd v Magnaload Ltd* [1984] 1 QB 127, 137, *per* Lloyd J, following *Simpson v Thomson* (1877) 3 App Cas 279.

[224] Ranging from gross negligence, through ordinary negligence, to slight neglect: see generally *Coggs v Bernard* (1703) 2 Ld Raym 909, 92 ER 107.

[225] *Houghland v RR Low (Luxury Coaches) Ltd* [1962] 1 QB 694, CA; *Griffiths v Arch Engineering Co (Newport) Ltd* [1968] 3 All ER 217; and see *AVX Ltd v EGM Solders Ltd* The Times, 7 July 1982.

[226] *Port Swettenham Authority v TW Wu & Co (M) Sdn Bhd* [1979] AC 580, 589, PC, *per* Lord Salmon, and see *Sutcliffe v Chief Constable of West Yorkshire* [1996] RTR 86, 90, CA, *per* Otton LJ. See now also *G Bosman (Transport) Ltd v LKW Walter International Transportorganisation AG* [2002] All ER (D) 13 (May), CA; cf *Khan v Grocutt* [2002] All ER (D) 154 (Dec), CA.

[227] *Parastatidis v Kotarides* [1978] Victoria Reports 449 and see 7.38.

[228] *Yearworth and others v North Bristol NHS Trust* [2009] EWCA Civ 37, [2010] QB 10.

[229] *Morris v CW Martin & Sons Ltd* [1966] 1 QB 716, 725, CA, *per* Lord Denning MR (obiter); but this is believed to be wrong. The point was left open by Mance LJ in *East West Corp v DKBS 1912* [2003] EWCA Civ 83 see also *Lister v Hesley Hall* and cf 7.36.

(b) Making the distinction[230]

7.34   A bailment for reward (or mutual advantage) is one which either confers or can reasonably be expected to confer a benefit on both parties. Normally in a bailment for reward one party gets a monetary payment while the other gets the benefit of some service to the goods. The service is usually provided by the bailee to the bailor, as where a bailor bails goods for storage[231] or to be worked on for payment,[232] but it may be provided by the bailor to the bailee, as where the goods are bailed on hire.[233] A bailee who takes custody without specific reward, but expecting remuneration if the owner later engages his services, takes from the beginning as a bailee for reward.[234] But a decision of the House of Lords appears to hold that an original bailee for reward (in this case, a salvor) who retains possession when the contract ceases to exist becomes a gratuitous bailee.[235] A bailment for mutual advantage may arise though reward does not pass directly between the bailor and bailee.[236]

D. Gratuitous Bailments

(1) Gratuitous Custody

(a) Identity and character

7.35   Where one person agrees to take possession of and care for goods belonging to another on terms that the custody is to be unrewarded, the bailment which arises is the type classified by Holt CJ as *depositum*, or gratuitous safekeeping.[237] A bailment of this character can arise as an independent service in itself or incidentally to some other relationship between bailor and bailee.[238] It is not a contract because the bailor supplies no consideration, but the bailee appears to be bound by promises he makes in relation to the goods, from the moment he takes possession.[239]

---

[230] See generally *Palmer on Bailment* (3rd edn, 2009) ch 9; *Wincanton Ltd v P & O Trans European Ltd* [2001] EWCA Civ 227, [2001] CLC 962; *Kamidian v Holt* [2008] EWHC 1483 (Comm), noted (2008) 13 Art Antiquity and Law 327.

[231] See 7.48.

[232] See 7.55 et seq.

[233] See 7.61 et seq.

[234] *Port Swettenham Authority v TW Wu & Co (M) Sdn Bhd* [1979] AC 580, PC; *G Bosman (Transport) Ltd v LKW Walter International Transportorganisation AG* [2002] All ER (D) 13 (May), CA.

[235] *China Pacific SA v Food Corp of India (The Winson)* [1982] AC 939, HL; and see *ENE Kos I Ltd v Petroleo Brasileiro SA (No 2)* [2012] UKSC 17, [2012] 2 WLR 976 (the continuing bailment that occurred when a ship-owner was left in possession of cargo following the ship-owner's termination of a charterparty in Shelltime 3 form was a non-contractual bailment, but one that nonetheless imposed a continuing duty of care; according to Lord Sumption JSC at [20] it was consensual but no longer contractual); cf *City Television v Conference and Training Office Ltd* (CA, 29 November 2001) (the recipient of goods that had been ordered by a third party pursuant to a deception practised on both owner and recipient-possessor was treated, apparently without argument, as a gratuitous bailee).

[236] *Andrews v Home Flats Ltd* [1945] 2 All ER 698; *The Pioneer Container* [1994] 2 AC 324, 338, PC, *per* Lord Goff, citing *Morris v CW Martin & Sons Ltd* [1966] 1 QB 716, CA.

[237] *Coggs v Bernard* (1703) 2 Ld Raym 909, 912–913, 92 ER 107, 110.

[238] See eg *Phipps v New Claridges Hotel* (1905) 22 TLR 49 (hotel and guest); *China Pacific SA v Food Corp of India (The Winson)* [1982] AC 939, HL (salvor and cargo owner).

[239] *Yearworth and others v North Bristol NHS Trust* [2009] EWCA Civ 37, [2010] QB 10; *Kettle v Bromsall* (1738) Willes 118, 125 ER 1087; *Chapman v Morley* (1891) 7 TLR 257; *The Oriental Bank Corporation v The Queen* (1867) 6 SCR (NSW) 122; *Roufos v Brewster* [1971] 2 South Australian State Reports 218, 223–224, *per* Bray CJ (obiter); *Mitchell v Ealing London Borough Council* [1978] 2 WLR 999.

(b) Obligations of gratuitous custodian

The bailee must take reasonable care of the goods, this standard being gauged according to **7.36** all the circumstances of the deposit.[240] Those circumstances will include the value, portability, sensitivity and disposability of the goods, their attractiveness to thieves or vandals, their general vulnerability to crime, the environment where they are kept and in special cases the bailor's knowledge of defects in the bailee's facilities.[241] A further relevant circumstance may be the gratuitous nature of the service,[242] though in cases of gratuitous custody by professional custodians this factor may be subordinate to others, such as the expectation generated in the bailor as to level of service.[243] The duty of care extends to the taking of reasonable measures to protect the goods against the foreseeable acts of vandals.[244] The burden of showing that he has taken reasonable care rests on the bailee.[245] If this burden cannot be discharged, the bailee has the alternative possibility of showing that any lack of reasonable care on his part did not cause or contribute to the loss,[246] but courts are reluctant to allow this defence to succeed where bailees, whose premises are burgled via a security flaw attributable to them, contend that, even without the flaw, the burglars would have succeeded in penetrating the building.[247] Though contrary statements can be cited,[248] the better view is that the depositary is answerable for any theft or collusion in theft on the part of any employee or independent contractor to whom he has delegated any part of his duty of care in relation to the goods, regardless of whether the bailee has been negligent in his employment, training or supervision of the malefactor.[249] A similar principle should apply to acts of deliberate damage. If that is correct, the bailee should also carry the burden of showing, in the event of loss or damage while the goods are in his custody, that the loss or damage was not inflicted by any employee or independent contractor to whom he entrusted the goods.

(c) Bailee's duty to return goods

The bailee must return the goods at the end of the bailment[250] unless he has undertaken to **7.37** deal with them in some other way, in which case that undertaking must be kept.[251] The bailee

---

[240] *Port Swettenham Authority v TW Wu & Co (M) Sdn Bhd* [1979] AC 580, 589, PC, *per* Lord Salmon; *China Pacific SA v Food Corp of India (The Winson)* [1982] AC 939, 960, HL, *per* Lord Diplock; *Yearworth and others v North Bristol NHS Trust* [2009] EWCA Civ 37, [2010] QB 1, CA; *Mitchell v Ealing London Borough Council* [1979] QB 1; *James Buchanan Ltd v Hay's Transport Services Ltd* [1972] 2 Lloyd's Rep 535; *Garlick v W & H Rycroft Ltd* [1982] CAT 277, CA; *Houghland v RR Low (Luxury Coaches) Ltd* [1962] 1 QB 694, CA; *Blount v The War Office* [1953] 1 WLR 736; *City Television v Conference and Training Office* (CA, 29 November 2001); *Khan v Grocutt* [2002] All ER (D) 154 (Dec), CA (bailment of insurance documents); cf *G Bosman (Transport) Ltd v LKW Walter International Transportorganisation AG* [2002] All ER (D) 13 (May), CA.

[241] *Houghland v RR Low (Luxury Coaches) Ltd* [1962] 1 QB 694, CA. See 7.49.

[242] *Garlick v W & H Rycroft Ltd* [1982] CAT 277, CA.

[243] *James Buchanan Ltd v Hay's Transport Services Ltd* [1972] 2 Lloyd's Rep 535; *Port Swettenham Authority v TW Wu & Co (M) Sdn Bhd* [1979] AC 580, PC.

[244] *Mitchell v Ealing London Borough Council* [1979] QB 1; *Garlick v W & H Rycroft Ltd* [1982] CAT 277, CA.

[245] *Port Swettenham Authority v TW Wu & Co (M) Sdn Bhd* [1979] AC 580, PC; *Mitchell v Ealing London Borough Council* [1979] QB 1; *Houghland v RR Low (Luxury Coaches) Ltd* [1962] 1 QB 694, CA.

[246] This proposition is based on analogy with the burden of proof applicable to bailees for reward: see 7.50.

[247] *Fletcher Construction Co Ltd v Webster* [1948] NZLR 514, 519, *per* Callan J.

[248] eg *Morris v CW Martin & Sons Ltd* [1966] 1 QB 716, 725, CA, *per* Lord Denning MR.

[249] *Palmer on Bailment* (3rd edn, 2009) paras 10-026–10-029; 16.50.

[250] *Cranch v White* (1835) 1 Bing NC 414, 420, 131 ER 1176, 1179; *Wetherman v London and Liverpool Bank of Commerce Ltd* (1914) 31 TLR 20; *United States of America and Republic of France v Dollfus Mieg et Cie SA and Bank of England* [1952] AC 582, 611, HL; *Jones v Dowle* (1841) 9 M&W 19, 152 ER 9; *Houghland v RR Low (Luxury Coaches) Ltd* [1962] 1 QB 694; *Capital Finance Co Ltd v Bray* [1964] 1 WLR 323.

[251] *Anon* (1642) March 202, 82 ER 475; *Wilkinson v Verity* (1871) LR 6 CP 206.

need not, however, take the goods to the bailor's premises; it is sufficient if he makes them available for the bailor to collect, unless some other arrangement has been made.[252]

(d) Promises on gratuitous bailments; deviation

7.38 If the bailee promises a greater responsibility than that imposed by common law (eg, to be strictly liable for the safety of the goods,[253] or to return them in the same condition as bailed not excepting reasonable wear and tear,[254] or to keep them in a particular place[255] or at a particular temperature,[256] or return them at a particular time)[257] he appears to be bound by that promise once possession is assumed.[258] That is so notwithstanding the absence of contract through want of consideration from the bailor. Moreover, a gratuitous bailee can be liable for a deviation, in much the same way as a rewarded bailee, so that if he departs from one of the fundamental terms of the bailment he forfeits his status as a bailee and becomes strictly liable for the goods as an insurer.[259] This may occur where the bailee delegates custody to a third person without the bailor's consent,[260] for it is a normal obligation of gratuitous custody that the bailee will exercise the custodial function personally and not vicariously.[261] A deviation may also occur where the bailee retains possession of the goods after the bailor has lawfully demanded their return.[262] When deviation occurs, the bailee is answerable for all ensuing damage or loss, whether caused by his negligence or not, unless the misadventure would have occurred in any event, or can be attributed to the conduct of the bailor.[263] The burden of proving these exonerating events is on the bailee.[264] If the bailee deviates and it later emerges that the goods have been damaged or lost at some unidentified point while in his possession, it is for the bailee to prove that the damage or loss occurred outside the deviation period, at a time when his duty was one of reasonable care.[265]

(e) Duties of bailor

7.39 The bailor owes a duty of reasonable care towards the bailee.[266] He is therefore answerable if the bailee is injured or suffers damage to his real or personal property by reason of some

---

[252] *Capital Finance Co Ltd v Bray* [1964] 1 WLR 323, CA; *Palmer on Bailment* (3rd edn, 2009) para 10-052.
[253] *Kettle v Bromsall* (1728) Willes 118, 125 ER 1087.
[254] *Coggs v Bernard* (1703) 2 Ld Raym 909, 92 ER 107, 109, *per* Powell J.
[255] *Edwards v Newland* [1950] 2 KB 534, CA.
[256] cf *Yearworth and others v North Bristol NHS Trust* [2009] EWCA Civ 37, [2010] QB 10 (involving a bailment of sperm) where Lord Judge CJ observed that the breach of such a promise could be actionable both on the promise itself (despite the gratuitous nature of the bailment) and as a breach of the bailee's duty of care. Liability for deviation was not expressly mentioned.
[257] *Mitchell v Ealing London Borough Council* [1979] QB 1.
[258] 7.35 and *Trefitz & Sons Ltd v Canelli* (1872) LR 4 PC 277.
[259] *Mitchell v Ealing London Borough Council* [1979] QB 1; *Toor v Bassi* (1999) unreported, 20 January, CA; cf *Yearworth and others v North Bristol NHS Trust* [2009] EWCA Civ 37, [2010] QB 10.
[260] *Bringloe v Morrice* (1676) 1 Mod Rep 210, 86 ER 834; see also *Chapman v Robinson* (1969) 71 Western Weekly Reports 515 (obiter) (case of loan).
[261] *Edwards v Newland & Co* [1950] 2 KB 534, CA; *Mitchell v Ealing London Borough Council* [1979] QB 1.
[262] *Mitchell v Ealing London Borough Council* [1979] QB 1.
[263] *Mitchell v Ealing London Borough Council* [1979] QB 1.
[264] *Port Swettenham Authority v TW Wu & Co (M) Sdn Bhd* [1979] AC 580, PC; *Palmer on Bailment* (3rd edn, 2009) para 10-030.
[265] *Mitchell v Ealing London Borough Council* [1979] QB 1; and see *Scheps v Fine Art Logistic Ltd* [2007] EWHC 541 (QB), at [34], *per* Teare J (where the precise fate of a bailed sculpture remained undetermined, and the bailee was for reasons of damages contending that a member of the bailee's staff had unlawfully jettisoned the sculpture from their premises in September 2004, before a significant rise in its value, Teare J held that the evidential burden lay on the defendant bailee to prove that on the balance of probabilities the sculpture was no longer in its custody). cf *JJD SA (a company) v Avon Tyres Ltd* (HC, 19 January 1999), reversed on other grounds (CA, 23 January 2000).
[266] *Palmer on Bailment* (3rd edn, 2009) para 10-046. The point is not covered by authority.

defect in the goods, where the bailor should reasonably have identified and corrected the defect or have warned of it.[267] Since the bailment is not a contract, the bailor is probably not bound by any agreement to leave the goods in the bailee's custody for a fixed period, though symmetry with decisions on the liability of the bailee for superadded promises might suggest otherwise.[268]

Where the bailee is put to expense in safeguarding the goods against some extraordinary **7.40** hazard, and the acts which he performs are compelled by his duty of care, he is entitled to recover his expense from the bailor, at least where the bailor knew that it was being incurred and raised no objection.[269] This follows as a necessary incident of bailment, though recovery might also be allowed on other grounds, such as unjust enrichment.[270] While it is an open question whether the bailee can alternatively rely on the doctrine of agency of necessity as a means of recovering such outlay,[271] modern authority favours restricting that doctrine to cases where the bailee, under the pressure of some exigency, contracts on the bailor's behalf with a third party.[272]

(2) Gratuitous Work and Labour

(a) Comparison with gratuitous deposit

Bailment for gratuitous work and labour (traditionally known as *mandatum*) resembles **7.41** gratuitous deposit, but with two main differences. First, the mandatary's custody of the goods is incidental to his performance of some personal service in relation to them, in relation to which separate obligations are owed. Secondly, the burden of proof in an action for breach of the bailee's promise to perform the gratuitous service differs from that applicable to claims for breach of the bailee's duty of care. In common with the case of contractual promises, it is for the bailor to establish not only the promise itself but three further matters: breach of the

---

[267] There is no authority favouring a strict warranty of safety or fitness to be bailed, either in this context or in that of general bailments for reward: *Palmer on Bailment* (3rd edn, 2009) para 10-046.

[268] See 7.38.

[269] *China Pacific SA v Food Corp of India (The Winson)* [1982] AC 939, HL; *ENE Kos I Ltd v Petroleo Brasileiro SA (No 2)* [2012] UKSC 17, [2012] 2 WLR 976 where at [28] Lord Sumption JSC observed that the present decision and that in *China Pacific* shared three common elements justifying recovery: the cargo was originally bailed to the ship owners under a contract which came to an end while the cargo was still in their possession; as a matters of law the ship owners' obligation to look after the cargo continued despite the termination of the charterparty; and the only reasonable or practical option open to the ship owners once the charterparty came to an end was to retain the cargo until it could be discharged at the port where the vessel was now located. See also *Metall Market 000 v Vitorio Shipping Co Ltd* [2012] EWHC 844 (Comm), at [64], *per* Popplewell J (on appeal [2013] EWCA Civ 650) holding that where a bailee 'incurs expenses in carrying out his duties in preserving and caring for the goods, he has a correlative right to recover such expenses from the owner of the goods, provided that he is not denying possession of the goods to the owner solely on the grounds that he is exercising a lien'. Cf however note 376 below, on the apped from Popplewell J: [2013] EWCA Civ, [2014] QB 760 *Quaere* as to the bailee's right to recover his normal remuneration for storing the goods or his 'opportunity cost' in being obliged to retain cargo in his own vessel or warehouse: the point was left open in *ENE Kos I*, because it was common ground that no distinction was to be made for present purposes between expenses and remuneration: see at [29], *per* Lord Sumption JSC. cf *Garside v Black Horse Ltd* [2010] EWHC 90, at [122], *per* King J: 'In principle I accept that the [bailee] would be entitled to recover against the appropriate party such *expenses* it is able to prove which it has incurred in fulfilling its duty of care under the gratuitous bailment imposed upon it through the failure to collect, by one or other of the other parties... However there can on this line of authority be no claim to storage charges as such.'

[270] See EPL ch 18. This basis was left open in *ENE Kos I Ltd v Petroleo Brasiliero SA (No 2)* [2012] UKSC 17, [2012] 2 WLR 976.

[271] *China Pacific SA v Food Corp of India (The Winson)* [1982] AC 939, HL, 958, *per* Lord Diplock and 965, *per* Lord Simon of Glaisdale. See *Palmer on Bailment* (3rd edn, 2009) paras 10-047–10-051.

[272] *ENE Kos I Ltd v Petroleo Brasileiro SA (No 2)* [2012] UKSC 17, [2012] 2 WLR 976, at [23]–[27], *per* Lord Sumption JSC.

promise, the occurrence of the loss for which the bailor claims, and the causal relation of the breach to the loss.[273]

(b) Duties of the bailee[274]

7.42 Beyond that, the incidents of *mandatum* correspond largely with those of *depositum*: the bailee gets possession which at common law counts as title and enables him to sue third party wrongdoers, his duty is one of reasonable care unless varied by agreement, the duty of care includes a duty to answer for the deliberate wrongdoing of those to whom he lawfully entrusts the goods, he carries the burden of proving either reasonable care or its irrelevance to any loss, and of negativing deliberate misdeeds by employees, the bailee must perform the service and retain custody in person, becoming strictly liable if he departs from this or any other essential term of the bailment, and the mandatary is bound by promises which he has made in relation to the goods (including performance of the personal service for purposes of which possession is given to him) once he takes possession.[275]

(c) Duties of the bailor[276]

7.43 Since *mandatum* is by definition a gratuitous transaction, the mandatary cannot charge for the services once they have been performed and has no lien on the goods. As in the case of *depositum*, however, a mandatary who in discharge of his duty of care and to the knowledge of the mandator expends money to safeguard the goods against extraordinary hazards may recover that cost from the mandator under principles of bailment, and perhaps on the alternative ground of unjust enrichment.[277] Even in that event, however, it seems that he has no lien.

7.44 The mandator owes a duty of reasonable care to ensure that the mandatary is not injured, or his property damaged, by the unsafe condition of the chattel.[278] It is uncertain whether this liability extends to economic loss suffered by the mandatary through the unsuitable nature of the chattel for the task entrusted to him.

(3) Loan for Use

(a) Definition and character

7.45 Gratuitous loan is a form of bailment under which the bailee is allowed the use and enjoyment of the goods without any advantage to the bailor.[279] It is not a contract because the borrower provides no consideration in return for the use of the goods.[280] The borrower gets possession and can exercise the normal possessory remedies against third parties who invade that possession.[281]

---

[273] *Lenkeit v Ebert* [1947] St R Qd 126 (semble); cf *Houghland v RR Low (Luxury Coaches) Ltd* [1962] 1 QB 694, CA.

[274] *Palmer on Bailment* (3rd edn, 2009) para 11-030.

[275] *Yearworth v North Bristol NHS Trust* [2009] EWCA Civ 37, [2010] QB 1; *Oriental Bank Corp v R* (1867) 6 SCR (NSW) 122, 155, *per* Faucett J.

[276] *Palmer on Bailment* (3rd edn, 2009) para 11-030.

[277] See 7.40.

[278] There is no common law authority on this point: *Palmer on Bailment* (3rd edn, 2009) para 11-030. cf *Flack v Hudson* [2001] 2 WLR 982, CA, a decision under the Animals Act 1970.

[279] *Coggs v Bernard* (1703) 2 Ld Raym 909, 918, 92 ER 107, 113, *per* Holt CJ. See also *Wincanton Ltd v P & O Trans European Ltd* [2001] EWCA Civ 227, [2001] CLC 962 (reciprocally beneficial bailment of pallets not a gratuitous loan); *Kamidian v Holt* [2008] EWHC 1483 (Comm).

[280] *Walker v Watson* [1974] 2 NZLR 175; *National Bank of New Zealand Ltd v Waitaki International Processing (NI) Ltd* [1997] 1 NZLR 724; cf *Cottee v Franklin Self-Serve Pty Ltd* (1995) Aust Contract Reports 90–060.

[281] See 7.25 et seq.

(b) Duties of the borrower

The borrower must take reasonable care of the goods.[282] He must return the goods in a con-   **7.46**
dition no worse than that in which they were delivered to him (fair wear and tear excepted)
and compensate the bailor for any damage caused by his negligence or misuse.[283] The borrower is bound, in the event of any loss or impairment of the goods, to show either that he
took due care or that his failure to do so played no part in the misadventure; in the absence
of such proof he is liable to the lender[284] though the true cause of the loss or impairment
remains unknown. His liability extends to any misappropriation or complicity in misappropriation on the part of any employee or independent contractor to whom he has entrusted
the goods for the purpose of discharging any part of his duty of care.[285] The burden of proof
conforms to that applying where the lender alleges a want of due care. If the borrower deviates from the essential or fundamental terms on which his possession was granted he becomes
strictly liable for the goods and must answer for them regardless of whether he is negligent.[286]
Deviation may occur by keeping the goods beyond an agreed return date, or moving them to
a place other than that agreed, or allowing someone other than the borrower or his authorized
personnel to use them.[287] The borrower must return the goods to the bailor, or otherwise
deal with them as he instructs, at the end of the bailment.[288] The borrower is not generally
bound to deliver the goods to the lender's residence or place of business at the end of the
bailment,[289] but must make them available for collection by the lender at the place where
the goods are situated.[290] Where borrowed goods have been dismantled, the borrower must
normally reassemble them before redelivery.[291] Subject to statutory procedures which enable
the joining of third parties in claims for wrongful interference with goods, the borrower is
normally estopped from denying the bailor's title.[292]

(c) Duties of the lender

The lender must exercise reasonable care in ensuring that the goods are safe and fit for their   **7.47**
purpose.[293] It is uncertain whether the negligent lender is liable for pure economic loss
caused by the failure of a loaned chattel to fulfil its intended function:[294] much may depend
on whether the claim is characterized as contractual, tortious or in bailment.[295] Similar

---

[282] *Swann v Seal* (CA, 19 March 1999); *Walker v Watson* [1974] 2 NZLR 175; *Fairley and Stevens (1966) Ltd
v Goldsworthy* (1973) 34 DLR (3d) 554. cf *Wincanton Ltd v P & O Trans European Ltd* [2001] EWCA Civ 227,
[2001] CLC 962 (question whether borrower liable for even 'slight neglect' left open as not material to decision).
[283] *Swann v Seal* (CA, 19 March 1999), *per* Chadwick LJ.
[284] *Houghland v RR Low (Luxury Coaches) Ltd* [1962] 1 QB 694, CA; *Port Swettenham Authority v TW Wu
& Co (M) Sdn Bhd* [1979] AC 580, PC (burden of proof on gratuitous bailee generally).
[285] The rules here are precisely analogous to those which govern the depositary: see 7.36.
[286] *Bringloe v Morrice* (1676) 1 Mod Rep 210, 86 ER 834; *Chapman v Robinson and Ferguson* (1969) 71
Western Weekly Reports 515. The rules here are precisely analogous to those which govern the depositary:
see 16.38.
[287] *Palmer on Bailment* (3rd edn, 2009) paras 12-027–12-029.
[288] *Palmer on Bailment* (3rd edn, 2009) paras 12-027–12-029; *Swann v Seal* (CA, 19 March 1999).
[289] *Capital Finance Co Ltd v Bray* [1964] 1 WLR 323, CA.
[290] *Mitchell v Ealing London Borough Council* [1979] QB 1.
[291] *Palmer on Bailment* (3rd edn, 2009) para 12-031. But the borrower will not normally be liable for
ordinary wear and tear: *Swann v Seal* (CA, 19 March 1999); cf *Moorhouse v Angus and Robertson (No 1) Pty
Ltd* [1981] NSWLR 700, 708 (apparently a case of bailment for mutual advantage).
[292] See 7.21 et seq.
[293] *Griffiths v Arch Engineering Ltd* [1968] 3 All ER 217; *Wheeler v Copas* [1981] 3 All ER 405 (semble); cf
Flack v Hudson [2001] 2 WLR 982, CA; *Blakemore v Bristol and Exeter Rly Co* (1858) 8 E & B 1035, 120 ER
385; *Coughlin v Gillison* [1899] 1 QB 145, CA. *Palmer on Bailment* (3rd edn, 2009) paras 12-002–12-018.
[294] cf *Blakemore v Bristol and Exeter Rly Co* (1858) 8 E & B 1035, 1050–1051, 120 ER 385, 391, *per*
Coleridge J.
[295] *Palmer on Bailment* (3rd edn, 2009) paras 12-019–12-021.

uncertainty surrounds the bailor's ability to withdraw the goods from the bailee before the expiry of an agreed period of use. A contractual analysis suggests that the lender can do this with impunity because the borrower has given no consideration for the promise.[296] But some authorities, relying on the peculiar nature of bailment, argue that he should be bound by his promise.[297] The doctrine of promissory estoppel may also safeguard the borrower's position.

E. Bailments for Reward or Reciprocal Advantage

(1) Custody for Reward

(a) Definition and character

7.48   Bailment by way of custody for reward arises where one person has possession of another's goods on terms that he will store or safeguard those goods in return for an advantage. This form of bailment ranges from direct custody (the entrustment of goods to a warehouse or luggage office)[298] to the many types of incidental custody which arise from the provision of other services; eg, the safekeeping of a client's coat in a restaurant cloakroom,[299] or the custody of an animal by a vet to whom it is bailed for treatment. Most direct forms of custody for reward (and many indirect forms) are governed by special contract terms, beyond the scope of this title. What follows is a short account of the underlying rules of bailment that apply where no special terms obtain.

(b) Duties of the custodian for reward

7.49   Like most bailees the custodian for reward must take reasonable care of the goods.[300] He must exercise the precautions that can reasonably be expected of a reasonably conscientious and competent member of his trade[301] to guard the goods against foreseeable hazards.[302]

---

[296] *Palmer on Bailment* (3rd edn, 2009) para 10-035; cf *Parastatidis v Kotaridis* [1978] Victoria Reports 449 (*mutuum*).

[297] *Palmer on Bailment* (3rd edn, 2009) para 12-021. See the cases on *depositum* and *mandatum*, 7.42–7.43.

[298] *Stallard v GW Rly Co* (1862) 2 B & S 419, 121 ER 1129; *Alexander v Railway Executive* [1951] 2 KB 882. For the purpose of assessing damages, the provision of peace of mind and freedom from anxiety is a major component in the benefits that a reasonable party to the bailment to a bank of a trunk containing valuables would expect to derive from the bank's due performance of its custodial obligations under the bailment: *Andre v Clydesdale Bank plc* [2013] EWHC 169 (Ch), [328].

[299] *Ultzen v Nichols* (1894) 1 QB 92; *Murphy v Hart* (1919) 46 DLR 36.

[300] *Port Swettenham Authority v TW Wu & Co (M) Sdn Bhd* [1979] AC 580, PC; *Coldman v Hill* [1919] 1 KB 443, CA; *Brook's Wharf and Bull Wharf Ltd v Goodman Bros* [1937] 1 KB 534, CA; *Glebe Island Transport Pty Ltd v Continental Seagram Pty Ltd (The Antwerpen)* [1994] 1 Lloyd's Rep 213 (NSWSC). Where a bailee lawfully and with the express or implied consent of the bailor entrusts to a third party the discharge of any part of his duty of care in respect of the goods (as, eg, where he engages a firm of security contractors to patrol the place where the goods are kept, or to install protective devices) he remains responsible for the manner in which the delegated task is performed, and is accordingly liable for the delegate's defaults: *G Bosman (Transport) Ltd v LKW Walter International Transportorganisation AG* [2002] All ER (D) 13 (May), CA, following *British Road Services v Arthur V Crutchley* [1968] 1 All ER 811, CA; cf *East West Corp v DKBS 1912* [2003] EWCA Civ 83, [2003] 1 Lloyd's Rep 239 discussed above. And see further 7.52 (bailee committing deviation where delegation of possession unlawful), 7.83 (sub-bailment).

[301] *Port Swettenham Authority v TW Wu & Co (M) Sdn Bhd* [1979] AC 580, PC; *Houghland v RR Low (Luxury Coaches) Ltd* [1962] 1 QB 694, CA.

[302] *Pitt, Son & Badgery v Proulefco SA* (1984) 52 ALR 389.

These include theft,[303] fire,[304] vandalism,[305] weather,[306] flood,[307] natural deterioration[308] and legal challenges to the bailor's title.[309] The bailee is also liable for any deliberate wrongdoing (or complicity in such wrongdoing) on the part of any employee or independent contractor to whom he has entrusted any part of his duty of care.[310]

(c) Burdens of proof

In any claim for breach of the custodian's duty of care, the bailor must prove both the fact and the breach of the bailment. He must show that the defendant was voluntarily in possession of the goods[311] and that during his possession they were lost, stolen, destroyed, damaged or otherwise impaired.[312] The bailor who alleges damage will therefore fail if he cannot show that the condition of the goods on their return to him was worse than their condition when the bailee got possession. If such matters are proved, the burden shifts to the bailee to show either that he took reasonable care of the goods[313] or that any failure on his part to exercise such care did not cause or contribute to the misadventure.[314] He must also show that the misadventure did not result from the misconduct of any employee or independent contractor to whom he entrusted any part of his duty towards the goods.[315] A bailee who shows that an original threat to the goods occurred without his fault may nevertheless be liable if he failed to take reasonable steps to counter that threat.[316]

7.50

(d) Specific instances of bailee's duty of care

The exercise of reasonable care depends on all the circumstances. It can take many forms. It may require the bailee to exercise care in the appointment,[317] training,[318] and supervision

7.51

---

[303] *Coldman v Hill* [1919] 1 KB 443, CA.

[304] *Smith v Taylor* [1966] 2 Lloyd's Rep 231; *Pitt, Son & Badgery v Proulefco SA* (1984) 52 ALR 389.

[305] *Pitt, Son & Badgery v Proulefco SA* (1984) 52 ALR 389; *Garlick v W & H Rycroft Ltd* [1982] CAT 277, CA.

[306] *Edwards v Newland & Co* [1950] 2 KB 534, CA.

[307] *Harper v Jones* (1879) 4 VLR (L) 536.

[308] *Sharp v Batt* (1930) 25 Tasmanian LR 33 (protection of apples from deterioration).

[309] *Ranson v Platt* [1911] 2 KB 291, CA.

[310] *Morris v CW Martin & Sons Ltd* [1966] 1 QB 716, CA; *Port Swettenham Authority v TW Wu & Co (M) Sdn Bhd* [1979] AC 580, PC; *Frans Maas (UK) Ltd v Samsung Electronics (UK) Ltd* [2004] 2 Lloyd's Rep 282 (bailee's liability extended to defaults of employees entrusted with security of buildings where goods kept). The burden of rebutting theft or complicity in theft by an entrusted employee or independent contractor is on the bailee: *Transmotors Ltd v Robertson, Buckley & Co* [1970] 1 Lloyd's Rep 224. And see generally *Lister v Hesley Hall Ltd* [2002] 1 AC 22, HL; *Brink's Global Services Inc v Igrox Ltd* [2010] EWCA Civ 1207, [2011] IRLR 343 (where the bailee's liability for theft from containers by an employee sent to fumigate them was imposed on general principles of vicarious liability rather than any special principle peculiar to bailees).

[311] *The Ruapehu* (1925) 21 Ll L Rep 310, CA; *Andre v Clydesdale Bank plc* [2013] EWHC 169 (Ch).

[312] *G Merel & Co Ltd v Chessher* [1961] 1 Lloyd's Rep 534; *WD & HO Wills (Australia) Ltd v State Rail Authority of New South Wales* (1998) 43 NSWLR 338, 353–354, *per* Mason P.

[313] *Port Swettenham Authority v TW Wu & Co (M) Sdn Bhd* [1979] AC 580, PC; *The Antwerpen* [1994] 1 Lloyd's Rep 213, 238, NSWCA, *per* Sheller JA.

[314] *Joseph Travers and Sons Ltd v Cooper* [1913] 1 KB 73, CA. See now also *AP(2)T v PS* [2004] EWHC 32, QB.

[315] *Port Swettenham Authority v TW Wu & Co (M) Sdn Bhd* [1979] AC 580, PC; *Morris v CW Martin & Sons Ltd* [1966] 1 QB 716, CA; *G Bosman (Transport) Ltd v LKW Walter International Transportorganisation AG* [2002] All ER (D) 13 (May), CA.

[316] eg *Coldman v Hill* [1919] 1 KB 443, CA (cows; disappearance from bailee's field; failure to tell police or bailor); *Ranson v Platt* [1950] 2 KB 534, CA (third party title claim; inadequate response by bailee who failed to notify bailor); *Edwards v Newland & Co* [1911] 2 KB 291, CA (bomb damage and exposure to weather).

[317] *Mintz v Silverton* (1920) 36 TLR 399; *Nahhas v Pier House (Cheyne Walk) Management* (1984) 270 EG 328.

[318] *Global Dress Co Ltd v WH Boase & Co Ltd* [1966] 2 Lloyd's Rep 72, CA.

of staff,[319] to check or move goods periodically,[320] to monitor the proximity of other potentially noxious goods,[321] to notify the bailor of adverse events,[322] to install alarms[323] or engage security staff,[324] or to develop satisfactory warning routines in general. The bailee must take into account the size, value, rarity, mobility, marketability anonymity, fragility, sensitivity and liquidity of the goods,[325] the human and physical environment within which they are kept,[326] the standards of other reasonable members of his occupation,[327] and any expectations which the bailor can reasonably be expected to hold as to the quality of safekeeping.[328] There is no general obligation to insure[329] but such a duty may arise from agreement,[330] trade custom,[331] or other special circumstance.[332] In many cases the question of insurance can be decided by reference to the normal test for implying terms into contracts, and it is submitted that a similar test should apply within gratuitous bailments or sub-bailments. Small goods of exceptional value are more likely to attract an exceptional duty to insure than bulky or everyday goods.[333] The bailor's knowledge of the circumstances in which the goods are kept, or of the character of the bailee, does not generally relieve the bailee from precautions which it would otherwise have been reasonable to exact from him,[334] but it may relieve him where it affords evidence that the bailor agreed to accept a lower standard of care.[335] It is insufficient for the bailee to show that he had a sophisticated system of safekeeping if he cannot show that he administered that system diligently on the particular occasion.[336]

(e) Deviation

7.52 Even without negligence, the custodian is liable if he departs from one or more of the essential terms of the bailment and the goods are then lost or damaged.[337] In the event of such deviation, and subject to the terms of the agreement, the bailee loses any right to the continued

---

[319] *Morris v CW Martin & Sons Ltd* [1966] 1 QB 716, 726, CA, *per* Lord Denning MR.

[320] *Cowper and Cowper v J & G Goldner Pty Ltd* (1986) 40 South Australian State R 457 (failure to carry out regular checks of animals in transit).

[321] *Pipicella v Stagg* (1983) 32 South Australian State R 464.

[322] *Ranson v Platt* [1911] 2 KB 291, CA; *Coldman v Hill* [1919] 1 KB 443, CA.

[323] *Johnson Matthey & Co Ltd v Constantine Terminals Ltd* [1976] 2 Lloyd's Rep 215, 218 (bailees negligent in omitting to install alarm on roller shuttered doors).

[324] *British Road Services Ltd v Arthur V Crutchley & Co Ltd* [1968] 1 All ER 811, CA.

[325] *Spriggs v Sotheby Parke Bernet & Co* [1986] 1 Lloyd's Rep 487, CA; *Garnham, Harris and Elton Ltd v Alfred W Ellis (Transport) Ltd* [1967] 1 WLR 940.

[326] *British Road Services Ltd v Arthur V Crutchley & Co Ltd* [1968] 1 All ER 811, CA; cf *Brabant & Co v R* [1895] AC 632, PC.

[327] *British Road Services Ltd v Arthur V Crutchley & Co Ltd* [1968] 1 All ER 811, CA.

[328] cf *James Buchanan Ltd v Hay's Transport Services (London) Ltd* [1972] 2 Lloyd's Rep 535.

[329] *Lockspeiser Aircraft Ltd v Brooklands Aircraft Ltd The Times*, 7 March 1990; *Mason v Morrow's Moving & Storage Ltd* [1978] 4 Western Weekly R 534; *Palmer on Bailment* (3rd edn, 2009) paras 14-013–14-018. See also *All Covers and Accessories pty Ltd v Sidawi* [2012] VSC 48 (no general duty to warn of lack of inoccurance).

[330] *Lockspeiser Aircraft Ltd v Brooklands Aircraft Ltd The Times*, 7 March 1990.

[331] *Kay v Shuman The Times*, 22 June 1954.

[332] *Eastman Chemical International AG v NMT Trading and Eagle Transport Ltd* [1972] 2 Lloyd's Rep 25; *Punch v Savoy's Jewellers Ltd* (1986) 26 DLR (4th) 546. cf *Von Traubenberg v Davies, Turner & Co Ltd* [1951] 2 Lloyd's Rep 152, CA (forwarding agent).

[333] *Punch v Savoy's Jewellers Ltd* (1986) 26 DLR (4th) 546.

[334] *Brabant & Co v R* [1895] AC 632, PC; *Edwards v Newland & Co* [1950] 2 KB 534, CA; see generally *Palmer on Bailment* (3rd edn, 2009) paras 14-047–14-050.

[335] *Skyway Service Station Ltd v McDonald* [1986] 1 NZLR 366.

[336] *Port Swettenham Authority v TW Wu & Co (M) Sdn Bhd* [1979] AC 580, 591, PC, *per* Lord Salmon; *Spriggs v Sotheby Parke Bernet & Co* [1986] 1 Lloyd's Rep 487, 492, CA, *per* Neill LJ.

[337] *Lilley v Doubleday* (1881) 7 QBD 510; *Edwards v Newland & Co* [1950] 2 KB 534, CA.

possession of the goods[338] and becomes an insurer of the goods,[339] being liable regardless of any want of reasonable care for all later misadventures except those which he can show would have occurred irrespective of the deviation, or were attributable to the conduct of the bailor.[340] He may also forfeit the protection of any exclusion or limitation clause in the bailment agreement.[341]

(f) Lien and rights against third parties

The custodian has no common law particular lien because he does not improve the goods.[342] **7.53**
Any lien must be stipulated in the contract. A general lien may arise in relation to a particular location or occupation, but such liens are rare and courts do not generally favour them.[343] Being in possession, the custodian can exercise the normal rights of action against third parties who take or injure the goods.[344]

(g) Duties of the bailor

The bailor must pay the agreed charge or, where none is agreed, a reasonable charge.[345] No **7.54**
charge is payable where it is clear from the circumstances that none was intended, eg where the bailment arises incidentally to the bailee's performance of some other service, in respect of which he receives payment or some other advantage. The bailor is liable for injury or damage if he fails to take reasonable care to ensure that the goods are safe and suitable for storage or to warn the custodian that they are not,[346] but, subject to the particular contract, he does not strictly warrant that they are safe or suitable.[347]

(2) Work and Labour for Reward

(a) Comparison with custody for reward

This form of bailment resembles custody for reward, but with the further ingredient that the **7.55**
bailee undertakes to perform some service (other than mere storage or safekeeping) in relation to the goods.[348] Examples are the delivery of an animal to a veterinary surgeon for treatment, or of a garment to a dry cleaner, or of a picture to a restorer, or of shoes to a repairer, or of a car to a garage for servicing. The duties which flow from this form of bailment (in particular the bailee's duty of care and its attendant burden of proof, and the obligations of the bailor as to payment and fitness of the goods) are substantially the same as those which flow from mere custodial bailments.[349] The bailee is treated as a bailee for reward in regard to

---

[338] In this event, the immediate right to possession of the goods will ordinarily revert to the bailor, if it did not already reside with him: see *MCC Proceeds Inc v Lehmann Bros International (Europe)* [1998] 4 All ER 675, 686, CA, *per* Mummery LJ.

[339] *Lilley v Doubleday* (1881) 7 QBD 510; *Hain Steamship Co Ltd v Tate & Lyle Ltd* [1936] 2 All ER 597, HL.

[340] *Hain Steamship Co Ltd v Tate & Lyle Ltd* [1936] 2 All ER 597, HL.

[341] As to whether this consequence follows automatically or only on the construction of the particular agreement, see *Palmer on Bailment* (3rd edn, 2009) para 1-061 et seq; *Daewoo Heavy Industries Limited v Klipriver Shipping Limited, The Kapitan Petko Voivoda* [2002] EWHC 1306, [2002] 2 All ER (Comm) 560.

[342] As to common law particular liens, see 7.57.

[343] *Rushforth v Hadfield* (1806) 7 East 224, 103 ER 86; *Majeau Carrying Co Pty Ltd v Coastal Rutile Ltd* (1973) 129 CLR 48.

[344] *The Winkfield* [1902] P 42, CA; and see 7.25.

[345] Supply of Goods and Services Act 1982, s 15(1), which reflects the common law. What is reasonable is a question of fact: s 15(2).

[346] *Palmer on Bailment* (3rd edn, 2009) para 14-005. There is no authority in point.

[347] cf the consignor of goods to be carried: *The Giannis NK* [1998] 2 Lloyd's Rep 337, HL.

[348] *Palmer on Bailment* (3rd edn, 2009) para 15-001.

[349] See 7.49 and 7.54.

the custody of the goods even though there is no separate charge for safekeeping.[350] Several differences nevertheless exist.

(b) Bailee's obligations as to quality and result of work

7.56 In addition to his basic duty to take reasonable care in keeping the goods,[351] the bailee owes distinct obligations in regard to the work to be performed. He must carry out the work with reasonable care and skill[352] and (where no time for performance is agreed) within a reasonable time.[353] If the bailor relies on the bailee to produce goods that are fit for a particular purpose, a strict obligation to that effect may be implied,[354] similar to that affecting sales of goods.[355] Where the bailee, acting in the course of a business, supplies goods or materials in addition to his work (eg, where spare parts are fitted to a car, or an animal is injected with drugs) strict statutory obligations are implied into the agreement that the goods or materials are of satisfactory quality,[356] are reasonably fit for their purpose[357] and correspond with any sample by reference to which they are supplied.[358] Further strict statutory terms are implied (irrespective of the status of the bailee) to the effect that the bailee has the right to supply such goods or materials,[359] that the bailor will have quiet possession of them,[360] that they are free from any charge or encumbrance not disclosed or known to the bailor,[361] and that they comply with any description by which they are supplied.[362] These statutory terms as to goods and materials resemble closely those implied into contracts for the sale of goods. In contrast to the normal burden of proof in bailment,[363] and in common with that applying in contract, it is ordinarily for the bailor to show that the bailee has broken a particular obligation with regard to the work to be performed, rather than for the bailee to negative breach.[364]

(c) Bailee's lien

(i) Particular lien

7.57 The artificer bailee may have a common law particular lien over the goods if he improves them.[365] Examples of such improvement are the repair[366] or restoration (but not the mere

---

[350] *Sinclair v Juner* 1952 SC 35, 43, *per* the Lord President.

[351] See 7.49.

[352] Supply of Goods and Services Act 1982, s 13 (which applies to services supplied in the course of a business, but is reflected by a general common law rule applicable to all contracts for services: see *Smith v Eric S Bush* [1989] 2 All ER 514, 519–520, HL, *per* Lord Templeman; *Harmer v Cornelius* (1858) CB (NS) 236, 141 ER 94; *Metaalhandel JA Manus BV v Ardfields Transport Ltd* [1988] 1 Lloyd's Rep 197).

[353] Supply of Goods and Services Act 1982, s 14(1) (which applies to services supplied in the course of a business). A 'reasonable time' is a question of fact: s 14(2).

[354] cf *Greaves & Co (Contractors) Ltd v Baynham Meikle & Partners* [1975] 1 WLR 1095, CA (design of building).

[355] Sale of Goods Act 1982, s 14.

[356] Supply of Goods and Services Act 1982, s 4, as amended by the Sale and Supply of Goods Act 1994, s 7, Sch 2, para 6(3).

[357] Supply of Goods and Services Act 1982, s 4 (as amended).

[358] Supply of Goods and Services Act 1982, s 5 (as amended).

[359] Supply of Goods and Services Act 1982, s 2(1) (as amended).

[360] Supply of Goods and Services Act 1982, s 2(2)(b) (as amended).

[361] Supply of Goods and Services Act 1982, s 2(2)(a) (as amended).

[362] Supply of Goods and Services Act 1982, s 3 (as amended).

[363] See 7.50.

[364] *Fankhauser v Mark Dykes Pty Ltd* [1960] Victoria Reports 376.

[365] *Judson v Etheridge* (1833) 1 Cr & M 743, 149 ER 598; *Scarfe v Morgan* (1838) 4 M & W 270, 150 ER 1430; *Re Southern Livestock Producers Ltd* [1963] 3 All ER 801; *Re Witt, ex p Shubrook* (1876) 2 Ch D 489, CA; and see *Palmer on Bailment* (3rd edn, 2009) paras 15-077–15-078.

[366] *Tappenden v Artus* [1964] 2 QB 185, CA.

washing or servicing)[367] of a car, the treatment[368] or training of an animal, or the printing of a book on paper supplied by the bailor.[369] The 'cultural improvement' of an artistic or historic object (eg, a more authoritative attribution which increases the object's value) may suffice for this purpose.[370] The lien applies only to goods on which work is performed and not to goods with which work is to be performed.[371] Where goods are entrusted to an artificer by someone other than their owner, the artificer acquires a lien[372] only where the person entrusting them had the owner's actual or ostensible authority to create a lien.[373]

The particular lien is a common law 'self-help' remedy arising independently of contract.[374] **7.58** It entitles the bailee to retain possession of the goods as security for payment, but not to sell them, which would be conversion.[375] Nor does it generally entitle the artificer to charge for storage during the exercise of the lien,[376] though the position may differ where his keeping of the goods is substantially for the bailor's benefit.[377] While detaining the goods in exercise of his lien, the artificer must take reasonable care of them.[378] Where the bailor countermands the work before the bailee completes it, the bailee may at least have a lien for his fees in relation to the completed part of the work,[379] and may also be entitled to complete the work and exercise the lien for the full fee,[380] provided such completion does not require the bailor's co-operation and the bailee has a legitimate reason for completing.[381] The bailee acquires no lien if some

---

[367] *Hatton v Car Maintenance Co* [1915] 1 Ch 621; see also *Graham v Voight* (1989) 95 FLR 146, 153, *per* Kelly J.

[368] *Scarfe v Morgan* (1838) 4 M & W 270, 150 ER 1430, 1436.

[369] *Brown v Sommerville* (1844) 6 Dun 1 (Ct of Sess) 1267.

[370] *Spencer v S Franses Ltd* [2011] EWHC 1269 (QB).

[371] *Welsh Development Agency (Holdings) Ltd v Modern Injection Mouldings Ltd* (HC, 6 March 1986).

[372] See Halsbury's Laws of England (4th edn, Reissue) Vol 28, para 723. cf *Johnson Matthey & Co Ltd v Constantine Terminals Ltd* [1976] 2 Lloyd's Rep 215; not followed in *The Pioneer Container* [1994] 2 AC 324, PC.

[373] *Tappenden v Artus* [1904] 2 QB 185, CA; *Albemarle Supply Co Ltd v Hind & Co* [1928] 1 KB 307, CA.

[374] *Tappenden v Artus* [1964] 2 QB 185, 195, CA, *per* Diplock LJ; *Metall Market 000 v Vitorio Shipping Co Ltd* [2012] EWHC 844 (Comm), at [64], *per* Popplewell J.

[375] *Bolwell Fibreglass Pty Ltd v Foley* [1984] Victoria Reports 97. In this respect a lien is distinguishable from a pledge. As to the differences between lien and pledge, see *Re Cosslett (Contractors) Ltd* [1997] 4 All ER 115, 126, CA, *per* Millett LJ; cf *Marcq v Christie Manson & Woods Ltd* [2003] EWCA Civ 731, [2004] QB 286.

[376] *Somes v Directors of the British Empire Shipping Co* (1860) 8 HL Cas 388, 11 ER 459. Applied in *Morris v Beaconsfield Motors* (2001) unreported 24 June, CA, and in *Metall Market 000 v Vitorio Shipping Co Ltd* [2012] EWHC 844 (Comm), [2012] 2 Lloyd's Rep 73, at [64], *per* Popplewell J, in whose view: 'where a gratuitous bailee … is exercising a lien adversely to the goods owner, who is seeking possession, and that is his sole ground for denying possession to the owner who would otherwise be entitled to possession but for the lien, he has no such right. In the latter circumstance the exercise of the lien and the retention of possession adversely to the goods owner are treated as being solely for the benefit of the lienee, for which he is not entitled to be reimbursed, even if his costs include those of preserving the goods. Lien is an exercise in self help, and if the lienee is denying to the goods owner the possession which the latter seeks, he is not entitled to treat the preservation and caring for the cargo which he performs whilst exercising his option as being for the benefit of the goods owner.' But on appeal from Popplewell J [2013] EWCA Civ 650, [2014] QB 760 Rix LJ, allowing the appeal on a separate ground, distinguished *Somes v Directors of the British Empire Shipping Co* (1860) 8 HL Cas 388, 11 ER 459 (above), and allowed that decision to stand only on very narrow grounds. The judgment of Rix LJ reads as a clear invitation to a future court to abandon *Somes* when the direct opportunity arises. cf *ENE Kos I Ltd v Petroleo Brasileiro SA (No 2)* [2012] UKSC 17, [2012] 2 WLR 976, at [23], *per* Lord Sumption JSC.

[377] *China Pacific SA v Food Corp of India (The Winson)* [1982] AC 939, HL. cf *Morris v Beaconsfield Motors* (2001) unreported 24 June, CA.

[378] *Irving v Keen* (1995) unreported 3 March, CA, *per* Stuart-Smith LJ (obiter); *Nightingale v Tildsley* [1980] Current Law Year Book 134; *Angus v McLachlan* (1883) 23 Ch D 330.

[379] *Lilley v Barnsley* (1844) 1 Car & Kir 344, 174 ER 839.

[380] *Bolwell Fibreglass Pty Ltd v Foley* [1984] Victoria R 97.

[381] See *White & Carter (Councils) Ltd v McGregor* [1962] AC 413, HL, applied in *Bolwell Fibreglass Pty Ltd v Foley* [1984] Victoria R 97.

other aspect of the agreement is inconsistent with such security, eg a term providing for a periodic account,[382] or entitling the bailor to repossess the goods at will for his own purposes.[383] Both in their creation and in their continuation, particular common law liens depend on possession,[384] so none will arise where the artificer does not get possession, and an existing lien may expire where the bailee surrenders or loses possession.[385] In the latter event the later recovery of possession does not ordinarily revive the lien.[386] But a lien may be a transmissible security, assignable with the debt which it secures,[387] and it may also survive a sale of the goods by the bailor after the lien was created.[388] The common law lien also expires on payment or tender of the sum due.[389] All these characteristics can be varied by agreement.

(ii) General lien

7.59 A common law general lien may exist in regard to particular areas or trades.[390] Common law general liens are, as noted,[391] judicially unpopular and rarely discovered, but they are a common subject of express contractual provision.

(iii) Registration of lien

7.60 A possessory lien need not be registered.[392]

(3) Hire[393]

(a) Definition and character

7.61 Hire is a form of bailment under which the bailor (the 'lessor') permits the bailee (the 'lessee' or 'hirer') to use the goods for his own benefit in return for some advantage accruing to the lessor, and confers possession on the bailee for that purpose.[394] Both at common law and by statute the bailor's benefit may be either money or some other valuable advantage,[395] such as work performed for him by the bailee (whether with or without the bailed goods)[396] or

---

[382] *Wilson v Lombank Ltd* [1963] 1 WLR 1294.

[383] *Ward v Fielden* [1985] Current Law Yearbook 2000.

[384] *Protean Enterprises (Newmarket) Pty Ltd v Randall* [1975] Victoria Reports 327.

[385] *The Freightline One* [1986] 1 Lloyd's Rep 266, 270 (obiter); *Lickbarrow v Mason* (1973) 6 East 20n; *Krager v Wilcox* (1755) Amb 252, 27 ER 168; *Hathersing v Laing* (1873) LR Eq 92.

[386] *Jones v Pearl* (1723) 1 Stra 557; *Sweet v Pym* (1800) 1 East 4. cf *Euro Commercial Leasing Ltd v Cartwright & Lewis* [1995] 2 BCLC 618.

[387] *Bull v Faulkner* (1848) 2 De G & Sm 772, 64 ER 346; see now *Vered v Inscorp Holdings Ltd* (1993) 31 NSWLR 290.

[388] *The Freightline One* [1986] 1 Lloyd's Rep 266, 272, *per* Sheen J (obiter).

[389] *Caunce v Spanton* (1844) 1 C & P 575, 171 ER 1323.

[390] *Palmer on Bailment* (3rd edn, 2009) paras 15-090–15-092.

[391] See 7.53.

[392] *Trident International Ltd v Barlow* (1999) 2 BCLC 506; *Re Cosslett (Contractors) Ltd* [1997] 4 All ER 115, CA.

[393] See generally *Palmer on Bailment* (3rd edn, 2009) ch 21 and para A5-006. cf *TRM Copy Centres (UK) and others v Lanwall Services Ltd* [2009] UKHL 35, [2009] 1 WLR 1375, the agreements for the delivery of a photocopier to a bailee 'in return for a reward to the bailor, by way of a commission on all sums paid for the copies made by it, for being permitted to locate it on his premises' were held not to be consumer hire agreements under s 15 of the Consumer Credit Act 1974. Taking account of the commercial purpose of the agreements and their commercial reality at large, the agreements were not primarily conceived with the purpose of enabling retailers to whom the photocopiers were bailed to use the machines for their own advantage, those being the normal incidents of a bailment by way of hire. But Baroness Hale correctly observed that the distinction between the present case and a standard hire agreement was a fine one.

[394] See *Palmer on Bailment* (3rd edn, 2009) para 21-004. Bailments by way of hire are conventionally contractual and are construed by reference to normal contractual principles of construction (including the implication of terms). For a modern example see *Waite v Paccar Financial Plc* [2012] EWCA Civ 901.

[395] Supply of Goods and Services Act 1982, s 6.

[396] *Derbyshire Building Co Pty Ltd v Becker* (1962) 107 CLR 633.

some form of 'exchange bailment' by which the bailee counterbails (ie, creates a reciprocal bailment of his own goods) to the bailor.[397] The hirer gets a possessory interest defensible on normal principles against third parties who interfere with the goods without the authority of either the lessor or the hirer.[398] In cases, at least, where the hirer goes into possession of the goods, he may also be protected against eviction from the goods by a purchaser or other alienee of the lessor, where that alienee knew of the pre-existing hire and its terms.[399] These and other features of the hirer's position[400] have led commentators to speculate that the hirer has a proprietary interest.[401]

(b) Duties of the hirer

The hirer's duties, and the related burdens of proof, correspond substantially to those **7.62** affecting any other bailee for mutual advantage. The hirer must take reasonable care of the goods,[402] refrain from converting them, answer for the deliberate misconduct of those to whom he delegates possession and avoid deviating from the bailment.[403] The consequences of a breach of these obligations are essentially the same as for other bailments. In addition, and subject to the particular terms of the contract,[404] the hirer must make the goods available to the lessor at the end of the hiring period and bear the cost of retrieving them from any place in which they have become stranded through adverse events.[405] This obligation exists though the events in question were unforeseen and occurred irrespective of any lack of reasonable care on the hirer's part, though it may be displaced where the immobilization occurred through the fault of the lessor, or where the relevant events were sufficiently severe to frustrate the contract.[406]

(c) Right to hire and quiet possession

In other respects the position of the hirer (whose possession is for personal advantage) dif- **7.63** fers from that of a normal bailee (whose possession is to enable him to act in the service of his bailor). To take an obvious example, the hirer is under no duty to account to the lessor for profits made from the hiring, unless the hirer makes these through a breach of the bailment.[407] Moreover, and because the object of the transaction is to give the hirer the use and enjoyment of the goods, the normal bailee's estoppel against pleading the right of a third party gives way in favour of statutory implied terms that the bailor has the right to hire out

---

[397] *Bryce v Hornby* (1938) 82 Sol Jo 216; *Queen Sales and Service Ltd v Smith* (1963) 28 Maritime Provinces R 364; *Swann v Seal* (CA, 19 March 1999).
[398] See 7.25.
[399] This may be collected from *Port Line Ltd v Ben Line Steamers Ltd* [1958] 2 QB 146, 151, *per* Diplock J.
[400] eg *Wickham Holdings Ltd v Brookhouse Motors Ltd* [1967] 1 WLR 295, CA, applied in New Zealand to a simple lease: *NZ Securities & Finance Ltd v Wrightcars Ltd* [1976] 1 NZLR 77.
[401] *Palmer on Bailment* (3rd edn, 2009) paras A4-001–A4-053; *Bristol Airport v Powdrill* [1990] 2 WLR 1362, 1372, *per* Browne-Wilkinson V-C; *AL Hamblin Equipment Pty Ltd v Federal Commissioner of Taxation* [1974] ATC 4310, 4318, *per* Mason J; cf W Swadling, 'The Proprietary Effect of a Hire of Goods' in N Palmer and E McKendrick (eds), *Interests in Goods* (2nd edn, 1998).
[402] *Blackpool Ladder Centre v BWB Partnership* (2000) unreported, 13 November, CA; *Ludgate v Lovett* [1969] 1 WLR 1016, CA; *British Crane Hire Corp Ltd v Ipswich Plant Hire Ltd* [1975] 1 QB 303, 311–312, CA; cf *Coggs v Bernard* (1703) 2 Ld Raym 909, 92 ER 107, 111.
[403] *Roberts v McDougall* (1887) 3 TLR 666. But the hirer may, according to circumstances, be entitled to conclude a sub-hiring agreement with a third party, or to depute another to operate or take care of a hired machine.
[404] See generally *British Crane Hire Corp Ltd v Ipswich Plant Hire Ltd* [1975] 1 QB 303, CA.
[405] *British Crane Hire Corp Ltd v Ipswich Plant Hire Ltd* [1975] 1 QB 303.
[406] *British Crane Hire Corp Ltd v Ipswich Plant Hire Ltd* [1975] 1 QB 303.
[407] *Brambles Security Services Ltd v Bi-lo Pty Ltd* (1992) Aust Torts Reports 81–161, NSWCA, *per* Clarke JA.

the goods[408] and that the hirer will enjoy quiet possession of them.[409] It appears that similar terms existed at common law.[410]

(d) Quality and fitness of hired goods

7.64 The lessor is also bound by statutory implied terms as to the quality and fitness of the goods. In general, the goods must correspond with their description[411] and with any sample provided,[412] and must be reasonably fit for their purpose[413] and of satisfactory quality.[414] The term as to correspondence with description applies to both private and trade hiring, but the other terms are confined to cases where the lessor leases in the course of a business.[415] These terms (and the circumstances in which liability for breach of them can be excluded or restricted) are closely akin to the equivalent terms implied into contracts of sale of goods. Similar, but more vaguely formulated, terms were implied at common law.[416]

(e) Payment of hire charges

7.65 The hirer must pay the agreed hire at the agreed times.[417] Failure to pay may entitle the lessor to evict him from the goods and to resume possession.[418] This will occur where the breach is repudiatory according to general contractual principles (ie, where the hirer evinces by his non-payment an intention to be no longer bound by the contract)[419] or where the contract otherwise entitles the lessor to possession in the event occurring. A term of the contract which makes punctual payment of the essence of the contract is likely to be construed as a condition, in which case the non-payment of any instalment will be a repudiatory breach, enabling the lessor to set aside the contract and recover 'loss of bargain' damages, consisting of all future instalments both due and to become due, minus a rebate for accelerated performance.[420] Where, on the other hand, the hirer's non-payment is not a repudiation and the lessor relies on a term which does not make punctual payment a condition of the contract, but merely entitles him to terminate the contract in the event which has occurred, damages are limited to the sums outstanding at the time of termination, plus any loss the lessor has suffered through delayed payment.[421]

---

[408] Supply of Goods and Services Act 1982, s 7(1).

[409] Supply of Goods and Services Act 1982, s 7(2).

[410] *Lee v Atkinson and Brooks* (1609) Cro Jac 236, 79 ER 204; *Warman v Southern Counties Motors Ltd* [1949] 2 KB 576; *Australian Guarantee Corp Ltd v Ross* [1983] 2 Victoria Reports 319.

[411] Supply of Goods and Services Act 1982, s 8.

[412] Supply of Goods and Services Act 1982, s 10.

[413] Supply of Goods and Services Act 1982, s 9(5) as amended by the Sale and Supply of Goods Act 1994, s 7, Sch 2, para 6(7).

[414] Supply of Goods and Services Act 1982, s 9(2) as amended by the Sale and Supply of Goods Act 1994, s 7, Sch 2, para 6(7).

[415] Supply of Goods and Services Act 1982, s 9.

[416] *Palmer on Bailment* (3rd edn, 2009) paras A2-001–A2-016.

[417] *Palmer on Bailment* (3rd edn, 2009) para 22-006.

[418] The remedies available to the lessor in the event of non-payment, and the quantification of damages payable by the hirer, depend on the terms of the contract and the general law: *Bowmakers Ltd v Barnet Instruments Ltd* [1945] KB 65.

[419] eg where the failure to pay is persistent: *Interoffice Telephones Ltd v Robert Freeman Co Ltd* [1958] 1 QB 190; *Bowmakers Ltd v Barnet Instruments Ltd* [1945] KB 65.

[420] *Lombard North Central plc v Butterworth* [1987] QB 527, CA; cf *Financings Ltd v Baldock* [1963] 2 QB 104, CA.

[421] *Financings Ltd v Baldock* [1963] 2 QB 104, CA.

(f) Relief for defaulting hirer

Statute affords a measure of relief to certain classes of defaulting hirers.[422] The doctrine of **7.66**
equitable relief against forfeiture can also apply to hirers of goods[423] as to other holders
of rights in personal property.[424] The rule against penalties[425] can also relieve hirers from
contractual terms which purport to impose on them excessive liabilities in consequence of
breach.[426] But the rule against penalties does not protect the hirer against a term which
makes particular provisions (such as those requiring punctual payment) of the essence of the
contract, and therefore conditions of the contract.[427]

(4) Pledge

(a) Definition and character

Pledge is one of the four types of consensual security known to English law.[428] It arises where **7.67**
one person (the pledgor) confers possession of goods on another (the pledgee) as security for
the payment of a debt,[429] or for the performance of some other obligation,[430] owed by the
former to the latter. The pledgee's possession acts both as evidence of the debt between the
parties and as an advertisement of it to third parties. Partly for this reason, a true pledge does
not require registration under the Bills of Sale Acts or the Companies legislation.[431]

(b) Distinction from lien and mortgage

Pledge differs from lien in that the pledgee has an inherent power of sale to enforce the **7.68**
secured obligation. Both pledge and lien are, however, possessory securities and a lien (like a
pledge) need not be registered.[432] Moreover, it may be that a lien like a pledge can be assigned
to a third person.[433] Pledge differs from mortgage in that the secured party must get possession while the indebted party retains the general property in the goods. A further difference
is that pledgees have no power of foreclosure.

The securing of an obligation need not have been the original purpose of the bailment. A **7.69**
pledge can arise where parties to some other form of bailment (such as custody for reward)
agree that their relationship shall henceforth be one of pledgor and pledgee.[434] But an

---

[422] Consumer Credit Act 1974, ss 87–93.
[423] *Transag Haulage Ltd v Leyland DAF Finance plc* [1994] Consumer Credit LR 111. *On Demand Information v Michael Gerson (Finance) Plc* [2002] UKHL 13; [2003] 1 AC 368, HL. As to chattel leasing generally see *Bristol Airport v Powdrill* [1990] 2 WLR 1362.
[424] *Sport International Bussum BV v Inter-Footwear Ltd* [1984] 1 WLR 776; *BICC plc v Burndy Corp* [1985] Ch 232, CA.
[425] See EPL 18.163–18.167.
[426] *Ariston SRL v Charly Records Ltd* The Independent, 13 April 1990, CA; and see *Interfoto Picture Library Ltd v Stiletto Visual Programmes Ltd* [1989] QB 433.
[427] *Lombard North Central plc v Butterworth* [1987] QB 527, CA.
[428] *Re Cosslett (Contractors) Ltd* [1997] 4 All ER 115, 126, CA, *per* Millett LJ.
[429] *Halliday v Holgate* (1868) LR 3 Ex 299, 302, *per* Willes J.
[430] *Australia and New Zealand Banking Group Ltd v Curlett, Cannon and Galbell Pty Ltd* (1992) 10 Australian Company Law Cases 1292. But cf *Marq v Christie, Manson & Woods Ltd* [2003] EWCA Civ 731, [2004] QB 286, CA (delivery of a chattel to auction house for sale, and acceptance by auction house under contract giving auction house extensive powers of retention and sale designed to enforce obligations under-taken by the party delivering the chattel, held not to constitute a pledge of the chattel for purposes of the Torts (Interference with Goods) Act 1977, s 11(2)).
[431] *Waight v Waight and Walker* [1952] 2 All ER 290; and see n 392.
[432] *Re Hamlet International plc (in administration), Trident International Ltd v Barlow* (1999) 2 BCLC 506; *Re Cosslett (Contractors) Ltd* [1997] 4 All ER 115, CA.
[433] *Bull v Faulkner* (1848) 2 De G & Sm 772, 64 ER 346; see now *Vered v Inscorp Holdings Ltd* (1993) 31 NSWLR 290.
[434] *RA Barrett & Co Ltd v Livesey* (CA, 6 November 1980).

agreement that one party shall be entitled to take possession of another's goods on default of some obligation is not a pledge.[435] The essence of pledge is the delivery of goods as security against the non-performance of some future obligation. The conferment of possession must precede the crystallization of the right to possess.[436]

7.70 The pledgor can be any person who has an interest in the goods superior to that of the pledgee, and need not be the owner. Indeed, there may be a repledge of goods by an original pledgee to a third person, provided that the amount secured by the repledge does not exceed that secured by the original pledge;[437] where it does, the pledgee must yield up the goods to the original pledgor on tender of the sum secured by the original pledge.[438]

7.71 Pledge creates a proprietary interest (or 'special property')[439] in the pledgee and the security to which it gives rise is assignable. It survives a sale of the goods by the pledgor, so that the pledgee can resist the buyer's claim to possession of the goods and retain them until the debt is discharged;[440] the buyer, on the other hand, has the right to redeem the goods on payment of the sum originally secured.[441] In common with other bailees, the pledgee can sue third parties who maltreat or misappropriate the goods during his possession, and can at common law recover damages assessed according to the full value of the goods.[442] The pledgee has an insurable interest in the goods and can, under an appropriately worded policy, recover their full value in cases of loss, or the full depreciation in cases of damage.[443] This right, together with the pledgeor's general right to sue in tort for acts of negligence or conversion inflicted on the goods, applies even though his exposure under the pledge is less than the full value of the goods or the cost of depreciation, and even though he is not answerable to the pledgor for the misadventure.[444]

(c) General duties of the pledgee

7.72 The pledgee must take reasonable care of the goods[445] and must answer for any deliberate wrongdoing on the part of anyone to whom he has entrusted them. The burden of negativing these forms of fault is on him.[446] If he deviates from the terms of the entrustment to him (eg, by keeping the pledged goods somewhere other than agreed, or by retaining them longer than agreed, or by delegating custody to a third party) he is strictly answerable for all ensuing loss or damage.[447]

---

[435] *Re Cosslett (Contractors) Ltd* [1997] 4 All ER 115, 126, CA, *per* Millett LJ.
[436] *Re Cosslett (Contractors) Ltd* [1997] 4 All ER 115, 126, CA, *per* Millett LJ.
[437] *Donald v Suckling* (1866) LR 1 QB 585.
[438] *Donald v Suckling* (1866) LR 1 QB 585, 610, *per* Mellor J.
[439] *Donald v Suckling* (1866) LR 1 QB 585, 609, *per* Mellor J, 617, *per* Blackburn J.
[440] *Franklin v Neate* (1844) 13 M & W 481, 153 ER 200; *Halliday v Holgate* (1868) LR 3 Ex 299, 302, *per* Willes J.
[441] *Franklin v Neate* (1844) 13 M & W 481, 153 ER 200; *Rich v Aldred* (1705) 6 Mod 46, 87 ER 968.
[442] *The Winkfield* [1902] P 42, CA; and see 16.25.
[443] See 7.31.
[444] *The Jag Shakti* [1986] AC 337, PC. Otherwise, where the bailor has a mere reversionary interest in the goods and no immediate right to possession sufficient to enable him to sue for negligence or conversion. In that event he must prove enduring damage to his reversionary interest and will recover only to the extent of that permanent deprivation or impairment: *East West Corp v DKBS 1912* [2003] EWCA Civ 83, [2003] QB 1509, 1532–1534, *per* Mance LJ; *HSBC Rail (UK) Ltd v Network Rail Infrastructure Ltd* [2005] EWCA Civ 1437, [2006] 1 All ER 343, 349–351, *per* Longmore LJ.
[445] *Giles v Carter* (1965) 109 SJ 452; *Coggs v Bernard* (1703) 2 Ld Raym 909, 917, 92 ER 107, 112, *per* Holt CJ.
[446] *Giles v Carter* (1965) 109 SJ 452; see 7.50.
[447] *Coggs v Bernard* (1703) 2 Ld Raym 909, 916, 92 ER 107, 111, *per* Holt CJ; *The Odessa* [1916] AC 145, 149, HL, *per* Lord Mersey (semble).

(d) Pledgee's power of sale

On default of the secured obligation, the pledgee has a right of sale, which is inherent in **7.73** pledge and need not be expressly agreed in order to create a pledge.[448] In exercising the right, the pledgee must take reasonable care,[449] and it appears that he owes a similar duty to a guarantor of the debt.[450] The debt survives the sale and the pledgor remains liable for any shortfall.[451] Where the proceeds of sale exceed the debt, the pledgee holds the surplus on trust for the pledgor and must pay interest,[452] though he can set off from the surplus any other debts owed to him by the pledgor.[453] The pledgor has the right to redeem the goods at any time before the pledgee sells them.[454]

(e) Pledgor's duties: warranty as to title, duty of care

The pledgor warrants that he has title to the goods.[455] Where the pledgor is not the owner, **7.74** the undertaking is satisfied by showing that he had the right to pledge them to the pledgee.[456] An original pledgee who repledges to a third person is deemed to satisfy this obligation if repledge was not expressly or impliedly prohibited by the terms of the first pledge.[457] Ordinarily, no such prohibition will be discovered. The pledgor owes the pledgee a duty of care in respect of the goods and is answerable to the pledgee if he could by taking reasonable care have discovered and guarded against any unsafe condition in the goods which injures the pledgee or damages his property.[458] There is no case law suggesting any stricter liability, and statutes imposing strict liability on suppliers of goods exempt pledge from its provisions.[459]

(f) The role of possession

Possession is essential to pledge.[460] It must be received by the pledgee in order to create **7.75** a pledge and must remain with the pledgee in order to sustain a pledge. There are at least four exceptional cases, however, where a pledge can arise in favour of a person who does not receive or keep possession. These are: where the pledge arises by attornment,[461] where the pledgor obtains redelivery of the goods by fraud,[462] where the pledgee repledges to a third person,[463] and where the pledgee redelivers the goods to the pledgor for a limited period or purpose not inconsistent with the continuation of the pledge.[464] It is on the last of these exceptions that the trust receipt is founded.[465]

---

[448] *The Odessa* [1916] AC 145, 149, HL, *per* Lord Mersey (semble).
[449] *The Odessa* [1916] AC 145, 149, HL, *per* Lord Mersey (semble).
[450] *BCCI SA v Aboody* (HC, 30 September 1987), affd on a different point [1989] 2 WLR 759, CA.
[451] *South Sea Co v Duncomb* (1731) 2 Stra 919, 93 ER 942.
[452] *Mathew v TM Sutton Ltd* [1994] 4 All ER 793.
[453] *Young v Bank of Bengal* (1836) 1 Moo 150, 12 ER 771, PC.
[454] *Singer Manufacturing Co Ltd v Clark* (1879) 5 Ex D 37.
[455] *Cheesman v Exall* (1851) 6 Ex 341, 155 ER 574.
[456] This proposition follows from general principle and by analogy with the obligation owed by a seller of goods.
[457] *Donald v Suckling* (1866) LR 1 QB 585.
[458] This proposition follows from general principle; there is no specific authority on point. See generally 7.54.
[459] Sale of Goods Act 1979, s 62(4); Supply of Goods and Services Act 1982, s 1(2)(e).
[460] *Dublin City Distillery Ltd v Doherty* [1914] AC 823.
[461] *Askrigg Pty Ltd v Student Guild of Curtin University of Technology* (1989) 18 NSWLR 738.
[462] *Mocatta v Bell* (1857) 24 Beav 585, 53 ER 483; *TEA (1983) v Uniting Church (NSW) Trust Association* [1985] Victorian Reports 139, 141, *per* Brooking J.
[463] *Donald v Suckling* (1866) LR 1 QB 585.
[464] *Reeves v Capper* (1838) 5 Bing NC 136, 132 ER 1057, distinguished in *Dublin City Distillery Ltd v Doherty* [1914] AC 823, 845, HL, *per* Lord Atkinson; *Martin v Reid* (1862) 11 CB (NS) 730, 142 ER 982.
[465] *Re David Allester Ltd* [1922] 2 Ch 211.

7.76 The mere failure of the payment method used by the pledgor to redeem the goods does not, in the absence of clear words to the contrary, revive the pledge and entitle the pledgee to resume possession of the goods as continuing security. In Australia, where a cheque delivered in purported discharge of a debt was not met for insufficient funds, and certain bills previously delivered as security for the original debt had already been returned to the pledgor on delivery of the cheque, the pledgee was not entitled to recover possession of the bills in order to revive the pledge.[466] It has also been held in Australia that a pledge survived the delivery of the goods by the pledgee to his own bailee for some special purpose, and that this continuing pledge was not displaced by the purported creation of a direct and inconsistent security between the pledgor and the pledgee's bailee.[467]

7.77 A pledge may arise by delivery of a bill of lading, in which event the recipient of the bill may acquire an immediate right to the possession of the cargo and be treated as a pledgee of it. Where a third person converts the cargo, the pledgee with an immediate right of possession can at common law recover damages calculated by reference to the full market value of the goods and not merely (where this is less) the amount secured by the pledge.[468] It is a matter of intention and construction as to whether the pledge has become effective at the material time and whether any liminal condition to which the pledge is subject has been satisfied.[469] A claimant who knew, when the pledge to him was purportedly created, that the goods had already been dispersed on discharge from the vessel, cannot normally show the necessary possession of the goods or the necessary intention that the relevant bills of lading should confer constructive possession of the goods.[470]

F. Attornment, Sub-bailment, and Other Ambulatory Bailments

(1) Attornment

7.78 We have seen that a bailment can arise by attornment.[471] An attornment, for this purpose, is any overt and unequivocal demonstration by one person (the attornor) to another (the attornee) that the first person now holds goods in his possession as bailee of the second.[472] Attornment can have two effects: it may bring about the passing of a general or special property to the attornee, according to the nature of the transaction (sale or pledge) giving rise to the attornment;[473] and it may estop the attornor from denying the truth of the facts represented in the attornment.[474]

7.79 Very little may be needed to constitute an attornment, which may occur either orally or in correspondence, but attornment requires something more than the mere receipt of delivery

---

[466] *TEA (1983) v Uniting Church (NSW) Trust Association* [1985] Victorian Reports 139.
[467] *Gunnedah Municipal Council v New Zealand Loan and Mercantile Agency Ltd* [1963] NSWR 1229.
[468] *The Jag Shakti* [1986] AC 337, PC, subject to the Torts (Interference with Goods) Act 1977, s 8.
[469] *The Future Express* [1993] 2 Lloyd's Rep 542.
[470] *The Future Express* [1993] 2 Lloyd's Rep 542.
[471] See 7.03.
[472] See eg *Askrigg Pty Ltd v Student Guild of the Curtain University of Technology* (1989) 18 NSWLR 738; *Re London Wine Co (Shippers) Ltd* [1986] Palmer's Company Cases 121.
[473] *Maynegrain Pty Ltd v Compafina Bank* [1982] 2 NSWLR 141; reversed without reference to this point [1984] NSWLR 258, PC.
[474] *Maynegrain Pty Ltd v Compafina Bank* [1982] 2 NSWLR 141, 148, *per* Hope JA. For comparison of the proprietary effects of an attornment and the Sale of Goods Act 1979, s 20A, see L Gullifer, 'Constructive Possession after the Sale of Goods (Amendment) Act 1995' (1999) LMCLQ 93.

orders without objection,[475] or the alteration of the bailee's own records.[476] Once attornment occurs, the attornor owes the normal obligation of a bailee to the attornee, though any clauses qualifying his liability in the original bailment appear to be carried over into the new bailment.[477] At the same time, the attornor ceases to owe the obligation of a bailee to the original bailor. Attornments commonly occur where a seller of goods indicates to his buyer, to whom property but not possession have passed, that he now holds the goods on the buyer's behalf;[478] or where an owner of goods pledges them but retains possession and indicates to the pledgee that he now holds them as that person's bailee;[479] or where the bailees of either sellers[480] or pledgors[481] tell the buyers or pledgees that they now hold the goods as their bailees.

Where the goods comprised in the attornment are specific or ascertained, and the attornment arises on a sale, the attornment may pass property to the attornee, eg by constituting the necessary unconditional appropriation.[482] Where the goods are unascertained, and the bailee of a larger bulk merely attorns in respect of an undivided part of that bulk, the attornment will not normally pass property in any particular goods to the attornee, for the bulk remains undivided and the goods unascertained.[483] The bailee will, however, be estopped from denying that such a division and passing of property has occurred and may be answerable in damages for the loss suffered by the inaccuracy of the attornment;[484] it appears that this estoppel does not require acts of reliance by the attornee.[485] The obligation to which the estoppel gives rise is, however, personal to the parties to the attornment, and does not entitle the attornee to assert any general property in the goods exigible against third parties.[486] By statute, however, buyers of specified quantities of unascertained goods which form part of a bulk may gain property in an undivided share in the bulk and become owners in common with other persons whose interests are comprised in the bulk. For this purpose, the appropriate shares will be rated or abated proportionally according to the ratio which the quantity of goods paid for and due to the buyer out of the bulk bears to the quantity of goods in the bulk at any relevant time.[487] Further, buyers of specified quantities of unascertained goods which form part of a bulk may in certain circumstances gain property in the residue of that bulk once it is reduced to the specified quantity or to less than that quantity.[488] Moreover, where several depositors deliver generic fungible goods into a common store, on terms that they may later withdraw

7.80

---

[475] *Laurie and Morewood v John Dudin & Sons* [1926] 1 KB 223, CA.

[476] *Laurie and Morewood v John Dudin & Sons* [1926] 1 KB 223, CA.

[477] *HMF Humphrey Ltd v Baxter Hoare & Co Ltd* (1933) 149 LT 603; *Leigh and Sillivan Ltd v Aliakmon Shipping Co Ltd (The Aliakmon)* [1986] AC 785, 818, HL, *per* Lord Brandon; *The Captain Gregos (No 2)* [1990] 2 Lloyd's Rep 395, 405, CA, *per* Bingham LJ; and see *East West Corp v DKBS 1912* [2003] EWCA Civ 83, [2003] 1 Lloyd's Rep 239.

[478] *Gamer's Motor Centre (Newcastle) Pty Ltd v Natwest Wholesale Australia Pty Ltd* (1987) 163 CLR 236.

[479] *Askrigg Pty Ltd v Student Guild of Curtin University of Technology* (1989) 18 NSWLR 738.

[480] *Dublin City Distillery Ltd v Doherty* [1914] AC 823, HL.

[481] *Madras Official Assignee v Mercantile Bank of India Ltd* [1935] AC 58, PC; *Maynegrain Pty Ltd v Compafina Bank* [1982] 2 NSWLR 141.

[482] Sale of Goods Act 1979, s 18, r 5(1); *Maynegrain Pty Ltd v Compafina Bank* [1982] 2 NSWLR 141; reversed without reference to this point [1984] NSWLR 258, PC.

[483] Sale of Goods Act 1979, s 16; *Re London Wine Co (Shippers) Ltd* [1986] PCC 121; *Re Goldcorp Exchange Ltd* [1995] 1 AC 74, PC.

[484] *Maynegrain Pty Ltd v Compafina Bank* [1982] 2 NSWLR 141.

[485] *Maynegrain Pty Ltd v Compafina Bank* [1982] 2 NSWLR 141.

[486] *Re Goldcorp Exchange Ltd* [1995] 1 AC 74, 93, PC, *per* Lord Mustill; *Re London Wine Co (Shippers) Ltd* [1986] PCC 121; *Simms v Anglo-American Telegraph Co* (1879) 5 QBD 188.

[487] Sale of Goods Act 1979, ss 20A, 20B as inserted by the Sales of Goods (Amendment) Act 1995, s 1(3). See L Gullifer, 'Constructive Possession after the Sale of Goods (Amendment) Act 1995' (1999) LMCLQ 93.

[488] Sale of Goods Act 1979, s 18, r 5(3) as amended by the Sales of Goods (Amendment) Act 1995, s 1(2).

equivalent amounts, the depositors may (if that accords with their intention) be tenants in common, and thus bailors, of the overall amount in store.[489]

7.81 Where the attornment is made to an agent who acts for an undisclosed principal, the relevant passing of property and estoppel may operate in favour of either the agent or the principal, according to their election.[490]

(2) Sub-bailment

7.82 Sub-bailment arises where an original bailee of goods grants possession of them to a third person while retaining a right of possession against that person.[491] The third person becomes both a sub-bailee of the original bailor and a bailee of the original bailee.[492] It is said that, for this consequence to follow, the original bailee must continue to have a right of possession to the goods against the original bailor.[493] But in principle a sub-bailment should be capable of arising even where the grant of possession by the original bailee occurs without the original bailor's consent and thus involves a forfeiture of his right of possession against the original bailor.[494] The critical questions which depend on the existence of a sub-bailment are the liability of the bailee to the head bailor and the rights of the middle bailee against the ultimate bailee; in neither case is the legitimacy of the original bailee's right of possession against the original bailor decisive. It appears that the subsidiary bailee's lack of knowledge as to the identity of the original bailor does not normally prevent him from owing the original bailor the duties of a sub-bailee,[495] though the position may differ where the existence or identity of an original bailor is crucial to the subsidiary bailee's decision to accept possession, for such a misapprehension may mean that he is not voluntarily in possession with regard to the original bailor.[496]

---

[489] See eg *Mercer v Craven Grain Storage Ltd* [1994] CLC 328, HL.

[490] *Maynegrain Pty Ltd v Compafina Bank* [1982] 2 NSWLR 141, reversed without reference to this point [1984] NSWLR 258, PC.

[491] *China Pacific SA v Food Corp of India (The Winson)* [1982] AC 939, 959, HL, *per* Lord Diplock. see now also *Lotus Cars Ltd v Southampton Cargo Handling plc and Associated British Ports (The Rigoletto)* [2000] 2 Lloyd's Rep 532, CA; *Wincanton Ltd v P & O Trans European Ltd* [2001] EWCA Civ 227, *per* Dyson LJ (no sub-bailment, but rather substitutional bailment as to which see *Palmer on Bailment* (3rd edn, 2009) para 23-008). See also *Kamidian v Holt* [2008] EWHC 1483 (Comm); *Marcq v Christie Manson & Woods Ltd (t/a Christie's)* [2003] EWCA Civ 731, [2003] 3 WLR 980; *East West Corp v DKBS 1912* [2003] EWCA Civ 83, [2003] 1 Lloyd's Rep 239; *Sandeman Coprimar SA v Transitos y Transportes Integrales SL* [2003] EWCA Civ 113, [2003] QB 1270; *G Bosman (Transport) Ltd v LKW Walter International Transport-organisation AG* [2002] All ER (D) 13 (May), CA; *Jarl Tra AB v Convoys Ltd* [2003] EWHC 1488 (Comm); *Angara Maritime Ltd v Ocean Connect UK Ltd* [2010] EWHC 619 (QB).

[492] See 7.83. As to the principles of sub-bailment generally, see the important decision in *East West Corp v DKBS 1912* [2003] EWCA Civ 83, [2003] QB 1509, which confirms many of the propositions stated in the text of both this and the following paragraph, and indeed of the law of bailment generally. See also *Sandeman Coprimar SA v Transitos y Transportes Integrales SL* [2003] EWCA Civ 113, [2003] QB 1270; *G Bosman (Transport) Ltd v LKW Walter International Transportorganisation AG* [2002] All ER (D) 13 (May), CA; *Jarl Tra AB v Convoys Ltd* [2003] EWHC 1488 (Comm).

[493] *China Pacific SA v Food Corp of India (The Winson)* [1982] AC 939, 959, HL, *per* Lord Diplock; *Chapman v Robinson and Ferguson* (1969) 71 Western Weekly R 515. See now also *Marcq v Christie Manson & Woods Ltd (t/a Christie's)* [2003] EWCA Civ 731, [2003] 3 WLR 980.

[494] *Palmer on Bailment* (3rd edn, 2009) para 23-002, n 10; cf *Trancontainer Express Ltd v Custodian Security Ltd* [1998] 1 Lloyd's Rep 128, where the intermediate carriers brought no evidence of any right on their part to resume possession of the goods from the sub-carriers. See also *RM Campbell (Vehicle Sales) Pty Ltd v Machnig* (SC NSW, 22 May 1981); *The Anderson Group Pty Ltd v Tynan Motors Pty Ltd* [2006] NSWCA 22.

[495] *Balsamo v Medici* [1984] 1 WLR 951, 959, *per* Walton J.

[496] *The Pioneer Container* [1994] 2 AC 324, 342, PC, *per* Lord Goff. cf *Marcq v Christie Manson & Woods Ltd (t/a Christie's)* [2003] EWCA Civ 731, [2003] 3 WLR 980 (auctioneer who accepts stolen painting for sale is not a bailee of the true owner where he has no notice (or, it appears, no means of acquiring notice) of the existence of the owner's interest. In this case the theft of the work was registered on a professional register on stolen art).

A sub-bailee owes the normal common law duties of a bailee both to the original bailor **7.83** and to the original bailee.[497] In particular, he must take reasonable care of the goods[498] and answer to each of his bailors for any breach of this obligation.[499] He must also answer to both bailors for the deliberate wrongs of employees or independent contractors to whom he has entrusted the goods.[500] The burden of proof in each case corresponds with that applicable to a normal bailee by direct delivery.[501] In addition, the sub-bailee may be bound by the normal common law estoppel against contesting the title of both of his bailors,[502] and may claim against both of them for extraordinary expense incurred in discharging his duty of care, at least where the bailments are gratuitous.[503] But these obligations may be modified by agreement or by statute. The direct relations between original bailee and sub-bailee clearly enable the sub-bailee to impose exclusions or limitations of his normal responsibility to the original bailee, or to enlarge his commitments; these variations are normally but not necessarily contractual and may attract legislative control. The absence of direct relations between the normal head bailor and sub-bailee does not prevent the sub-bailee from positively undertaking to the head bailor some larger obligation than would otherwise obtain at common law, by means of some direct promise (whether contractual or otherwise) given to the head bailor as to the conduct of the sub-bailment.[504] Nor does this absence of direct relations necessarily prevent the sub-bailee from invoking the terms of the sub-bailment agreement between the original bailee and himself in defence to an action by the original bailor. In such an action, the sub-bailee can rely on any protective term contained in the sub-bailment agreement if the head bailor has expressly or impliedly consented to the sub-bailment on those terms,[505] or (probably) if the intermediate bailee had ostensible authority to sub-bail on those terms,[506] but not otherwise.[507]

---

[497] *The Pioneer Container* [1994] 2 AC 324, 338–342, PC, *per* Lord Goff; *Morris v CW Martin & Sons Ltd* [1966] 1 QB 716, CA; *China Pacific SA v Food Corp of India (The Winson)* [1982] AC 939, 957–959, HL, *per* Lord Diplock.

[498] *The Pioneer Container* [1994] 2 AC 324, PC; *Morris v CW Martin & Sons Ltd* [1966] 1 QB 716, CA; *China Pacific SA v Food Corp of India (The Winson)* [1982] AC 939, HL.

[499] cf *The Hamburg Star* [1994] 1 Lloyd's Rep 399.

[500] See 7.42 and 7.49. See now also *G Bosman (Transport) Ltd v LKW Walter International Transportorganisation AG* [2002] All ER (D) 13 (May), CA.

[501] *The Pioneer Container* [1994] 2 AC 324, 338–342, PC, *per* Lord Goff; *Morris v CW Martin & Sons Ltd* [1966] 1 QB 716, CA.

[502] *The Hamburg Star* [1994] 1 Lloyd's Rep 399, 405, *per* Clarke J (proposition at least arguable).

[503] *China Pacific SA v Food Corp of India (The Winson)* [1982] AC 939, HL; see 7.39.

[504] *Brambles Security Services Ltd v Bi-Lo Pty Ltd* (1992) Aust Torts Rep 81–161 and see also *City Television v Conference and Training Office Ltd* (CA, 29 November 2001), *per* Sedley LJ.

[505] *The Pioneer Container* [1994] 2 AC 324, 339–340, PC, *per* Lord Goff, following *Morris v CW Martin & Sons Ltd* [1966] 1 QB 716, 719–730, CA, *per* Lord Denning MR. See further *Lotus Cars Ltd v Southampton Cargo Handling plc (The Rigoletto); Southampton Cargo Handling plc v Associated British Ports* [2001] 2 Lloyd's Rep 532, CA; *Angara Maritime Ltd v Ocean Connect UK Ltd* [2010] EWHC 619 (QB). In exceptional cases the head bailor and the sub-bailee may occupy a direct contractual relationship, in which event the particular immunities and obligations arising under the terms of the sub-bailment might be directly enforced between those two parties: *Sandeman Coprimar SA v Transitos y Transportes Integrales SL* [2003] EWCA Civ 113, [2003] QB 1270; and cf *The Homburg Houtimport BV v Agrosin Private Ltd (The Starsin)* [2003] UKHL 12, [2004] 1 AC 705. But the head bailor's actual or ostensible consent to the terms of the sub-bailment can also (it appears) justify the direct enforcement of positive obligations between head bailor and sub-bailee, irrespective of whether they are contractually related: *Sandeman Coprimar SA v Transitos y Transportes Integrales SL* [2003] EWCA Civ 113, [2003] QB 1270; *Targe Towing Ltd v Marine Blast Ltd* [2004] EWCA Civ 346, [2004] 1 Lloyd's Rep 721 (consensual sub-bailment and contractual relationship between head bailor and sub-bailee are 'conceptually different').

[506] *The Pioneer Container* [1994] 2 AC 324, 341, 342, PC, *per* Lord Goff (obiter); *Westpac Banking Corp v Royal Tongan Airlines* (SC NSW, 5 September 1996).

[507] The decision in *Johnson Matthey & Co Ltd v Constantine Terminals Ltd* [1976] 2 Lloyd's Rep 215 that a sub-bailee could also rely on essential exculpatory terms in the sub-bailment to which the principal bailor

(3) Substitutional Bailment

7.84 Sub-bailment differs from substitutional bailment, which is in the relationship arising where an original bailee vacates possession in favour of a successor bailee and (if the successor is authorized and chosen with reasonable care) withdraws henceforth from the scheme of obligation.[508] In that event, the incoming bailee becomes the direct bailee of the bailor and owes his normal common law obligations as bailee exclusively to him.[509] This direct relationship may or may not be contractual and may be modified by agreement. The bailment by attornment which arises between a buyer and the seller's bailee is a typical substitutional bailment.[510]

(4) Quasi-bailment

7.85 This anomalous form of bailment arises where a person who is entitled to take possession of another's goods chooses instead to delegate the assumption of possession to a third person without taking possession personally.[511] If the delegation is unauthorized the person making the delegation owes to the bailor a strict liability similar to that of a deviating bailee.[512] If it is authorized, the person making the delegation remains answerable for the defaults of the third person, in much the same way as a normal bailee who sub-bails with authority.[513] He is also liable for any resulting loss or damage if he appointed the possessor negligently or contrary to instructions.[514] He probably does not, however, carry the same burden of proof as a normal bailee, so that fault must be positively proved;[515] the lack of possession makes this aspect of the bailee's liability inapposite.[516] The third person who gets possession ('the quasi-bailee') owes the normal common law duties of a bailee to the original bailor unless the original bailor has consented to the quasi-bailment on exculpatory terms[517] (in which

---

had not consented, at least where the duty on which the principal bailor was suing would not have arisen but for the fact of the sub-bailment, was not followed in *The Pioneer Container* [1994] 2 AC 324, 340–342, PC.

[508] The leading modern authorities are *China Pacific SA v Food Corp of India (The Winson)* [1982] AC 939, HL; *Wincanton Ltd v P & O Trans European Ltd* [2001] EWCA Civ 227, *per* Dyson LJ; and *Kamidian v Holt* [2008] EWHC 1483 (Comm) noted (2008) 13 Art Antiquity and Law 327. See also *Mayflower Foods Ltd v Barnard Bros Ltd* (HC, 9 August 1996).

[509] cf the new bailment which arose from the dealer's constructive delivery of goods held on title retention terms to a bona fide purchaser in *Gamer's Motor Centre (Newcastle) Pty Ltd v Natwest Wholesale Australia Pty Ltd* (1987) 163 CLR 236. See generally *East West Corp v DKBS 1912* [2003] 1 Lloyd's Rep 239; *Sandeman Coprimar SA v Transitos y Transportes Integrales SL* [2003] EWCA Civ 113, [2003] 3 All ER 108, [2003] 2 Lloyd's Rep 172, CA; *G Bosman (Transport) Ltd v LKW Walter International Transportorganisation AG* [2002] All ER (D) 13 (May), CA.

[510] See 7.79.

[511] *Palmer on Bailment* (3rd edn, 2009) paras 23-011–23-012. The term 'quasi-bailment' is used in *The Pioneer Container* [1994] 2 AC 324, 344–345, PC, *per* Lord Goff; *Metaalhandel JA Magnus BV v Ardfields Transport Ltd* [1988] 1 Lloyd's Rep 197, 202–203, *per* Gatehouse J.

[512] *Edwards v Newland & Co* [1950] 2 KB 534, CA.

[513] *Metaalhandel JA Magnus BV v Ardfields Transport Ltd* [1988] 1 Lloyd's Rep 197; *Hobbs v Petersham Transport Co Pty Ltd* (1971) 124 CLR 220.

[514] *Metaalhandel JA Magnus BV v Ardfields Transport Ltd* [1988] 1 Lloyd's Rep 197.

[515] *Metaalhandel JA Magnus BV v Ardfields Transport Ltd* [1988] 1 Lloyd's Rep 197, 203, *per* Gatehouse J.

[516] *Metaalhandel JA Magnus BV v Ardfields Transport Ltd* [1988] 1 Lloyd's Rep 197, 203, *per* Gatehouse J; *Hobbs v Petersham Transport Co Pty Ltd* (1971) 124 CLR 220, 232, *per* Barwick CJ, 242–243, *per* Windeyer J.

[517] *The Pioneer Container* [1994] 2 AC 324, 338, 342, PC, *per* Lord Goff. But Lord Goff ultimately left the point open as not needing decision. Where a quasi-bailor retains a possessory right to the goods, the quasi-bailee may owe the duties of a bailee to him as well as to the head bailor: *Edwards v Newland & Co* [1950] 2 KB 534, CA; cf *Transcontainer Express Ltd v Custodian Security Ltd* [1988] 1 Lloyd's Rep 128, CA (no possessory title shown); *The Hamburg Star* [1994] 1 Lloyd's Rep 399.

case those terms can probably be raised against the original bailor)[518] or unless perhaps the quasi-bailee was unaware of the identity of the original bailor and would not have consented to hold goods on his behalf [519] (in which case he may enjoy an immunity from duty of care similar to that of the involuntary bailee).[520]

G. Involuntary and Undisclosed Bailment

(1) Involuntary Bailment

An involuntary bailment can take one of two forms. An originally involuntary bailment arises where a person is put in possession of goods without his initial consent.[521] A typical example is the relationship between sender and recipient of unsolicited goods.[522] Such a relationship cannot strictly be called a bailment at all, because the possessor's consent is vital to bailment.[523] A subsequently involuntary bailment arises where a person who was originally a voluntary possessor of goods becomes an involuntary possessor by reason of passage of time, conduct of the bailor, or some other cause. This situation can arise where bailors of goods for repair, cleaning or some other service fail to collect them.[524] In cases of this type, courts are reluctant to find that the bailee has ceased to owe all responsibility for the goods, though they may well find that the duty of care has abated.[525]

7.86

Where possession is involuntary from its inception, the possessor owes no duty of care to protect the goods against loss or damage.[526] He must abstain from deliberate and (probably) reckless damage, and there are modern statements that he will be liable for gross negligence,[527] but beyond that he is not liable for the physical security of the goods.[528] He will be answerable to the owner in conversion if, without authority[529] and knowing that the goods are not his, he deliberately consumes them or otherwise deals with them in a manner

7.87

---

[518] *The Pioneer Container* [1994] 2 AC 324, 345, PC (point formally left open); *Lukoil-Kalingradmorneft plc v Tata Ltd* [1999] 1 Lloyd's Rep 365, 374, *per* Toulson J.

[519] cf *The Pioneer Container* [1994] 2 AC 324, 338, 342, PC, *per* Lord Goff; *Marcq v Christie, Manson & Woods Ltd* [2003] EWCA Civ 731, [2004] QB 286, at [50]–[51], *per* Tuckey LJ.

[520] See 7.87.

[521] cf the bailment by concealment, where the person in possession is unaware of the fact of his possession, or may be aware of his possession but unaware the goods belong to someone else. See 7.87.

[522] This is now governed by legislation: see the Unsolicited Goods and Services Act 1971.

[523] *The Pioneer Container* [1994] 2 AC 324, PC; and see 7.01.

[524] See 7.88.

[525] See eg *Mitchell v Davis* (1920) 37 TLR 68.

[526] *Lethbridge v Phillips* (1819) 2 Starke 544, 171 ER 731; *Howard v Harris* (1884) Cab & Ellis 258; *Neuwith v Over Darwen Co-operative Society Ltd* (1894) 63 LJ QB 290.

[527] *JJD SA (a company) v Avon Tyres Ltd* (CA, 23 February 2000), *per* Lord Bingham CJ; *Marcus v Official Solicitor* [1997] EWCA Civ 886; *Taylor v Diamond* [2012] EWHC 2900 (Ch), at [100], [103], [106].

[528] *Lethbridge v Phillips* (1819) 2 Starke 544, 171 ER 731; *Howard v Harris* (1884) Cab & Ellis 258; *Neuwith v Over Darwen Co-operative Society Ltd* (1894) 63 LJ QB 290 *JJD SA (a company) v Avon Tyres Ltd* (CA, 23 February 2000), *per* Lord Bingham CJ; *Marcus v Official Solicitor* [1997] EWCA Civ 886; *Taylor v Diamond* [2012] EWHC 2900 (Ch). But in recent years the Court of Appeal has cast the involuntary bailee's responsibility more generally as one to do what is right and reasonable: see *Da Rocha-Afodu and anr v Mortgage Express Ltd and anr* [2014] EWCA Civ 454, followed in *Campbell v Redstone Mortgages Ltd* [2014] EWHC 3081 (Ch), where this principle was held to justify the consignment of very low-value goods to refuse disposal facilities. In *Da Rocha*, Arden LJ relied on *Scotland v Solomon* [2002] EWHC 1886 (Ch), Deputy Judge David Kitchin QC at [23]; 'if persons are involuntary bailees and have done everything reasonable they are not liable to pay damages if something which they do results in the loss of the property. There is an obligation on the part of involuntary bailees to do what is right and reasonable'.

[529] eg under the Torts (Interference with Goods) Act 1977, ss 12 and 13.

contrary to the owner's right.[530] If he commits an innocent conversion of the goods (eg, by delivering them to someone whom he erroneously believes to be the owner) and the goods are lost to the owner in consequence, the possessor is liable only if, in doing the act, he acted without reasonable care.[531] An incoming occupier of land on which chattels have been left by an outgoing occupier may, from the moment the involuntary possessor realizes that there are potential owners of the goods about whose identity and whereabouts the possessor has insufficient information, owes a duty to institute inquiries in order to seek out such owners.[532] The involuntary bailee is probably entitled to do whatever is reasonable to rid himself of the goods[533] and to recover the reasonable costs of doing so, though the precise extent and rationale of these rights are uncertain.[534]

7.88 Where a bailee is left in possession of goods for a period longer than that contemplated, various doctrines may enable him to lessen his responsibility.[535] At one extreme, the court may find that he has become an involuntary bailee and no longer owes any duty to take care to safeguard the goods from theft or other physical hazard.[536] This conclusion will be easier to reach where the bailment was for a fixed period, though even in that event the court may imply a period of grace before the duties of the bailee determine. Where the period of the bailment was not fixed, the court may hold that possession was to be for a reasonable time and that the bailor's consent to possession has expired once such time has passed, relieving him of further responsibility.[537] Alternatively, it may conclude that the bailor has abandoned the property in the goods and can therefore no longer stand as bailor, in which case he cannot sue for any loss or damage occurring after that date.[538] But a defence of abandonment requires, at the least, proof of conduct from which one can infer an intention by the bailor to relinquish his property in the goods.[539] A period of inaction may be insufficient for this purpose.[540] In other cases, the appropriate conclusion may be that the bailment has changed

---

[530] *Foster v Juniata Bridge Co* 16 P St 393 (1851).

[531] *Elvin and Powell Ltd v Plummer Roddis Ltd* (1933) 50 TLR 158; *Motis Exports Ltd v Dampskibsselskabet AF 1912* [1999] 1 All ER (Comm) 571, 582–583, *per* Rix J; on appeal without reference to this point [2000] 1 Lloyd's Rep 211; *Scotland v Solomon* [2002] EWHC 1886 (Ch). cf *City Television v Conference and Training Office Ltd* (CA, 29 November 2001); *Marcq v Christie Manson & Woods Ltd (t/a Christie's)* [2003] EWCA Civ 731, [2004] QB 286.

[532] *Robot Arenas Ltd v Waterfield* [2010] EWHC 115 (QB), citing earlier authority. The duty would presumably be broken when the incoming occupier, having such realization, neglects to pursue reasonable inquiries. The failure to pursue reasonable and active inquiries might afford the setting for a liability in conversion if the failure is followed by an unauthorized disposal of the goods.

[533] *Da Rocha-Afodu and anr v Mortgage Express Ltd and anr* [2014] EWCA Civ 454; *Campbell v Redstone Mortgages Ltd* [2014] EWHC 3081 (Ch); *Pedrick v Morning Star Motors Ltd* (CA, 14 February 1979); *Haniotis v Dimitriou* [1983] 1 Victoria Reports 498; *Bowden v Lo* (1998) 9 BPR 16, 317, (1998) NSW Conv R 56, 807; *Robot Arenas Ltd v Waterfield* [2010] EWHC 115 (QB). And see n 528.

[534] Contrast *Nicholson v Chapman* (1793) 2 H Bl 254, 126 ER 536, *per* Eyre CJ with *Kolfor Plant Ltd v Tilbury Plant Ltd* (1977) 121 SJ 390.

[535] *Palmer on Bailment* (3rd edn, 2009) paras 13-030–13-059.

[536] *Maritime Coastal Containers Ltd v Shelburne Marine Ltd* (1982) 52 NSR (2d) 51; and see *Deakin and Wolf v Card Rax Ltd* [2011] EWPCC 3 at [117] per His Honour Judge Fysh QC (Patents County Court). cf the consensual but non-contractual bailment that arose on termination of the charterparty in *ENE Kos I Ltd v Petroleo Brasiliero SA (No 2)* [2012] UKSC 17, [2012] 2 WLR 976 (n 239). The relationship between owner and possessor might pass through several phases:*Marcus v Official Solicitor* [1997] EWCA Civ 886.

[537] *Maritime Coastal Containers Ltd v Shelburne Marine Ltd* (1982) 52 NSR (2d) 51.

[538] It is submitted that a chattel owner can divest himself of ownership by a means of abandonment: see A Hudson in *Palmer on Bailment* (3rd edn, 2009) paras 26-021–26-030; *Robot Arenas Ltd v Waterfield* [2010] EWHC 115 (QB); cf *Moorhouse v Angus and Robertson (No 1) Ltd* (1981) 1 NSWLR 700.

[539] *Moorhouse v Angus and Robertson (No 1) Ltd* (1981) 1 NSWLR 700. And see *Robot Arenas Ltd v Waterfield* [2010] EWHC 115 (QB) (conduct from which abandonment might be inferred).

[540] *Moorhouse v Angus and Robertson (No 1) Ltd* (1981) 1 NSWLR 700; *Robot Arenas Ltd v Waterfield* [2010] EWHC 115 (QB).

from a bailment for mutual advantage to a gratuitous bailment, with the bailee as the party deriving no benefit.[541] But modern decisions suggest that there is no difference in principle between the duties owed by a bailee for reward and those owed by a gratuitous bailee.[542]

Where no time is fixed for termination of the bailment, the courts will probably imply into **7.89** the bailment an obligation on the part of the bailor to collect the goods within a reasonable time.[543] Hitherto this approach has been confined to contractual bailments. Where the obligation is a condition of the contract,[544] the bailor's failure to collect the goods may entitle the bailee to contend that both contract and bailment are at an end and that his duty of care towards the goods has ceased.[545] Breach of such a term may also entitle the bailee to argue that remedial steps taken by him to relieve himself of the burden of the goods, such as removing an unwanted car to a public car park,[546] were a reasonable attempt to mitigate the loss which he would otherwise have suffered through the breach,[547] and not therefore wrongful.[548]

The bailee may be able to invoke statutory machinery for the disposal of uncollected goods. **7.90** Section 12(3) of the Torts (Interference with Goods) Act 1977 gives a general power of sale over goods bailed after commencement of the Act, but the bailee must give notice to the bailor of his intention to sell the goods.[549] Such a sale gives the buyer of the goods a good title as against the bailor alone.[550] Alternatively, the court may authorize the sale under section 13 of the Torts (Interference with Goods) Act 1977. A decision of the court authorizing a sale under section 13 of the Torts (Interference with Goods) Act 1977 is conclusive,[551] as against the bailor, of the bailee's entitlement to sell the goods, and gives a good title to the purchaser as against the bailor.[552]

---

[541] cf *Davis v Henry Birk & Sons Ltd* [1981] 5 Western Weekly R 559, on appeal (1983) 142 DLR (3d) 356.

[542] *Yearworth v North Bristol NH Trust* [2009] EWCA Civ 37, [2010] QB 1; *Graham v Voight* (1989) 95 Federal LR 146; *Mitchell v Ealing London Borough Council* [1979] QB 1; *Port Swettenham Authority v TW Wu & Co (M) Sdn Bhd* [1979] AC 580, PC; *Bowden v Lo* (1998) 9 BPR 16,317, (1998) NSW Conv R 56,807.

[543] *Pedrick v Morning Star Motors Ltd* (CA, 14 February 1979); *Ridyard v Roberts* (CA, 14 February 1979); *Davis v Henry Birk & Sons Ltd* [1981] 5 Western Weekly R 559, on appeal (1983) 142 DLR (3d) 356; *JJD SA (a company) v Avon Tyres Ltd* (HC, 19 January 1999); reversed on other grounds (CA, 23 February 2000).

[544] Or an innominate term whose breach deprives the bailee of substantially the whole of the expected contractual benefit.

[545] *Pedrick v Morning Star Motors Ltd* (CA, 14 February 1979); *Ridyard v Roberts* (CA, 14 February 1979); *Davis v Henry Birk & Sons Ltd* [1981] 5 Western Weekly R 559, on appeal (1983) 142 DLR (3d) 356; *JJD SA (a company) v Avon Tyres Ltd* (HC, 19 January 1999); reversed on other grounds (CA, 23 February 2000). There is authority that liability may be reduced or extinguished where the bailee sends to the bailor's last known address a notice of intention to dispose of the goods that can be deemed to have been accepted or acquiesced in by the bailor: *Sachs v Miklos* [1948] 2 QB 23, 40, *per* Lord Goddard CJ; *Infolines Public Networks Ltd v Nottingham City Council* [2009] EWCA Civ 708. But to infer acceptance would work unfairly against a bailor who had fallen out of contact through no fault of his own, and a bailee (in common with any other party to an agreement) cannot in any event impose acceptance by silence. cf *Irving v Keen* (1995) unreported, 3 March, CA. And see *Palmer on Bailment* (3rd edn, 2009) paras 13-050,13-058.

[546] *Pedrick v Morning Star Motors Ltd* (CA, 14 February 1979). See generally *Palmer on Bailment* (3rd edn, 2009) paras 13-032–13-033.

[547] eg in the form of storage costs, or lost business caused by the presence of the goods cluttering a workshop: see *Pedrick v Morning Star Motors Ltd* (CA, 14 February 1979); *Jeffersen Ltd v Burton Group Ltd* (HC, 13 April 1984).

[548] *Pedrick v Morning Star Motors Ltd* (CA, 14 February 1979); *Deakin and Wolf v Card Rax Ltd* [2011] EWPCC 3, at [117], *per* His Honour Judge Fysh QC (Patents County Court); and see *Robot Arenas Ltd v Waterfield* [2010] EWHC 115 (QB).

[549] Torts (Interference with Goods) Act 1977, s 12(3), Sch 1 Pt II. cf *Irving v Keen* (1995) unreported 3 March, CA (letters by bailee to owner ineffective as, even if received, they did not comply with the Act).

[550] Torts (Interference with Goods) Act 1977, s 12(6).

[551] Subject to any right of appeal.

[552] Torts (Interference with Goods) Act 1977, s 13(2).

(2) Undisclosed or Unconscious Bailment

7.91 A person who has possession of another person's goods but is unaware of the fact of his possession is not a bailee because he has not consented to possession.[553] Such a person is sometimes known as an unconscious bailee, his relationship with the owner being identified as one of undisclosed bailment. A further example of such a relation may arise where a person is aware of his possession of goods but mistakenly believes that they belong to him.[554] An undisclosed bailment of this sort may occur where the innocent purchaser of a stolen chattel takes possession without realizing that it still belongs to the person from whom it was stolen.

7.92 Like involuntary bailments[555] (where the possessor knows that he has possession but has not agreed to it) undisclosed bailments are not true bailments. The possessor does not ordinarily owe a duty of care in relation to the goods.[556] If, however, the unconscious bailee proposes to damage or destroy the goods, he owes a duty to take reasonable care to establish the fact of his ownership before doing so. If he fails to make this check he is answerable to the owner.[557] It may be assumed that a similar duty binds an unconscious bailee who proposes to dispose of the goods by sale or otherwise. A bailee who fails to perform this precaution, and who would have discovered the existence or ownership of the goods had he done so, may be deemed to be constructively aware of his possession of another person's goods, and thenceforth answerable for those goods in much the same way as an involuntary bailee.[558]

7.93 A person who finds goods on his land owes a duty to take them into his possession, to take reasonable steps to reunite them with their owner, and to take reasonable care of them meanwhile.[559]

---

[553] *Consentino v Dominion Express Co* (1906) 4 WLR 498; *Rolfe v Investec Bank (Australia) Ltd* [2014] VSCA 38 (containers alleged to contain three porsche cars; *Leld*, no bailment of the cars) and see *The Pioneer Container* [1994] 2 AC 324, 341–342, PC, *per* Lord Goff.

[554] *AVX Ltd v EGM Solders Ltd* (HC, 7 July 1982). A further category of undisclosed bailment might arise where the possessor mistakenly believes that the party delivering the goods to him is the owner, whereas the goods are stolen and the true owner is someone other than the party making the delivery: cf *Marcq v Christie Manson & Woods Ltd (t/a Christie's)* [2003] EWCA Civ 731, [2004] QB 286 (no duty of care to verify title).

[555] See 7.86.

[556] *Consentino v Dominion Express Co* (1906) 4 WLR 498; and see *Robot Arenas Ltd v Waterfield* [2010] EWHC 115 (QB); *Rolfe v Investec Bank (Australia) Ltd* [2014] VSCA 38; but cf *Awad v Pillai* [1982] RTR 266, CA.

[557] *AVX Ltd v EGM Solders Ltd* (HC, 7 July 1982) distinguished in *Marcq v Christie Manson & Woods Ltd (t/a Christie's)* [2003] EWCA Civ 731, [2004] QB 286 (auctioneer not liable for redelivering unsold chattel to party who had delivered it for sale, where that party was believed to be the owner; auctioneer owed no duty of care to verify that party's ownership either on taking original delivery from him or on making redelivery to him). See also to similar effect as *AVX v EGM, Robot Arenas Ltd v Waterfield* [2010] EWHC 115 (QB),

[558] *Palmer on Bailment* (3rd edn, 2009) para 6-006 et seq; *Robot Arenas Ltd v Waterfield* [2010] EWHC 115 (QB),

[559] *Parker v British Airways Board* [1982] QB 1004, 1017, 1018, CA, *per* Donaldson LJ; cf *Ngan v The Queen* [2007] NZSC 105; n 28.

8

SECURITY

A. Introduction

A security for an obligation is something that makes it more likely that the obligation will **8.01** eventually be fulfilled. It makes the creditor more secure. Like all developed legal systems, English law recognizes broadly two kinds of security: real security and personal security. The bulk of this chapter is concerned with real security. In real security, the creditor obtains a 'real right' or a proprietary right in one or more assets that belong to the debtor. This gives the creditor security for the obligation owed to him, in several ways. First, if the debtor defaults on the obligation, the creditor has enforcement rights that can be exercised in relation to the assets over which he has security. Depending on the kind of security, he may, eg, have the right to seize those assets and sell them in order to obtain the money that is owed to him. In most cases, he will be able to exercise these rights without going to court. These possibilities are not available to an ordinary unsecured creditor, whose only recourse is to sue his debtor on the debt. Secondly, if the debtor becomes insolvent or bankrupt, the security rights of a creditor who holds a real security will generally continue to be available. By contrast, the claims of unsecured creditors are reduced *pro rata* when the debtor is insolvent. Finally, the secured creditor's security rights will, in many cases, operate against third party transferees who acquire from the debtor the assets over which the secured creditor holds security. An unsecured creditor can only claim against the debtor.

Personal security for an obligation arises where one or more persons, other than the debtor, **8.02** agree that they will also be answerable for the obligation; eg, one person guarantees the obligation of another person. Here the creditor does not have any real rights, but he has security against the default of his primary debtor, because the guarantee means that he has an additional debtor who is liable. It is possible for a creditor to obtain both real security and personal security for the same obligation.

8.03   The structure of this chapter is as follows. The first two main sections discuss real security over land and real security over moveable property. Although there is some conceptual overlap between these two categories, there are a number of important differences due to the way that English law has developed historically. The next main section deals with priorities: ie, the resolution of disputes between the holder of a security interest and the holder of some other interest in the same property. Priority contests arise, eg, where the debtor grants two security interests in the same asset to two different creditors. They can also arise where the debtor has granted a security interest in an asset to a secured creditor, and the debtor then purports to sell the same asset to another party. Whether the secured creditor can continue to enforce his real security rights against the purchaser of the asset is a kind of priority contest. The final main section of the chapter addresses the principles of personal security.

B.   Real Security Over Land

(1)   Types of Security

8.04   The word 'mortgage' is used throughout this chapter, and it is necessary to say exactly what it means. There is a narrow sense of 'mortgage' which distinguishes it from other security interests, such as the 'charge'.[1] This strict sense is not used in this section, 'Real Security Over Land'. Instead, following common legal usage, 'mortgage' refers here to any interest in land held as security for a debt.[2] So, eg, this section will include some discussion of the idea of an equitable charge over land; for the purposes of this section, such a charge is merely one kind of mortgage of land. The 'mortgagor' is the debtor who grants this security interest, and the 'mortgagee' is the creditor who acquires it.[3]

8.05   Legal mortgages, meaning those in which the mortgagee holds a legal interest in the land, are explained separately from equitable mortgages, in which the mortgagee's interest is purely equitable.[4] They arise according to different principles, and the classification of a security interest as legal or equitable is often crucial when questions of priority arise.

(a)   Legal mortgages

8.06   The common law knew no interest in land which was by its nature a security interest. It had no concept of a charge or of a hypothec. It followed that if a creditor was to take a legal interest in land to secure a debt, the interest had to be an estate in the land, pressed into service as a security interest. Different types of estate could be used; the choice was governed partly by prevailing practice, and partly by the estate held by the debtor.[5] If he held the legal fee simple, he could transfer this to the mortgagee; or he could convey (demise) a legal leasehold estate to the mortgagee. If the mortgagor was himself a legal leaseholder, he could either assign his leasehold, or demise a sub-lease to the mortgagee. Historically, the written contract

---

[1] *Re Bond Worth Ltd* [1980] Ch 228, 250.

[2] This also corresponds to the definition in the Law of Property Act (LPA) 1925, s 205(1)(xvi). Note that this section is concerned with security over land, not over 'real property'; a leasehold interest in land is personal property, but security over such an interest falls within this section. For 'real property' and 'personal property', see EPL 4.14–4.16.

[3] In colloquial language, 'mortgage' is sometimes used to refer to a loan whose repayment is secured by an interest in land, or to the contract governing the relationship between borrower and secured lender. These colloquial senses are avoided here.

[4] See EPL 4.22–4.34 for more discussion of the distinction. Note that a mortgage is not classified as legal or equitable based on the kind of interest that the *mortgagor* holds. This is explained below.

[5] AWB Simpson, *A History of the Land Law* (2nd edn, 1986) 242–243. The idea of 'estates' is explained in EPL ch 4, 4.37ff.

governing the arrangement was always deceptive, in that it did not reveal the true nature of the legal relationship. It provided only for an obligation on the part of the mortgagee to retransfer the mortgaged estate upon payment of all sums due; in the case of a mortgage by demise, it provided for the determination of the lease held by the mortgagee. Moreover, until recently, it generally stipulated that the principal was due after six months, even though the parties had no intention that the loan would be repaid so soon.[6] In appearance, then, the mortgagor retained no property right in the land except in the case of a mortgage by demise; and even in that case, the mortgagor's interest in the land was subject to the estate demised to the mortgagee. Furthermore, if the mortgagor defaulted, then it appeared that he had no right to recover (or terminate, in the case of a lease) the mortgaged estate, even though that estate might be worth far more than the debt.

Of course the appearance was inaccurate.[7] The Court of Chancery was concerned to protect **8.07** the mortgagor, who was assumed always to be in a weaker position than the mortgagee. Moreover, it was willing to look beyond the form of the contract to its substance as a transaction for securing a debt. The most significant aspect of this intervention was that a mortgagor was allowed to 'redeem' the estate transferred to the mortgagee upon payment of the debt, even if the mortgagor had defaulted and so lost his estate under the terms of the contract.[8] No fixed limit of time was imposed upon the right to redeem, but each case was addressed individually. In so protecting the mortgagor, the Court of Chancery created and enforced for him a proprietary interest in the land. This interest became known as the 'equity of redemption'.[9] Its recognition entailed the possibility that at some point, the mortgagee should be able to close off or foreclose the prospect of redemption. This is why 'foreclosure' is the term still used for the process by which a mortgagee takes over the mortgaged estate for his own benefit. Once the equity of redemption was recognized, it was inevitable that parties would attempt to limit it by contractual provision; this was resisted in the strongest possible way.[10] Chancery developed the doctrine that there could be no 'clog on the equity of redemption', and this has important repercussions in the modern law.[11]

The comprehensive reform of land law which took effect in 1926 has simplified the possibili- **8.08** ties for the creation of legal mortgages. Land in England and Wales is held under two systems, registered and unregistered. Most land is now registered. In unregistered land, there are now only two conceptual possibilities for creating legal mortgages: (i) a mortgage by demise and (ii) a legal charge, called in the legislation a 'charge by way of legal mortgage'.[12] Any transaction which purports to be a conveyance of a legal fee simple by way of mortgage takes effect

---

[6] Modern forms of mortgage agreement usually stipulate more accurately the obligations of the parties. They may provide for blended payments of interest and principal which, over the term of the loan, will retire the debt; or they may provide for the payment of interest only, the principal to be payable in a lump sum at the end of the term, but with the term reflecting the genuine intention of the parties.

[7] Lord Macnaghten famously said, 'no one, I am sure, by the light of nature ever understood an English mortgage of real estate': *Samuel v Jarrah Timber & Wood Paving Corp Ltd* [1904] AC 323, 326, HL.

[8] In a mortgage by demise or sub-demise, redemption would entail the determination of the leasehold held by the mortgagee. In a mortgage by conveyance, it would entail a specifically enforceable right of reconveyance.

[9] So it remains colloquial for a person to describe as his 'equity' in his house the difference between the unencumbered value of the estate he holds and the outstanding secured debt. This also appears to be the root of the term 'equity' in corporate finance, where it identifies financing which (unlike debt) carries with it an indirectly beneficial interest in the enterprise.

[10] AWB Simpson, *A History of the Land Law* (2nd edn, 1986) 246: 'in no branch of the law was the sanctity of agreement less regarded'.

[11] Discussed in 8.21ff. 'Clog' here does not refer to a blockage but to a restraint; the word 'clog' has a (somewhat archaic) sense of a piece of wood which is attached to an animal to restrain its movement.

[12] LPA 1925, ss 85(1), 86(1).

as a mortgage by demise with a term of 3,000 years.[13] A transaction which purports to be an assignment of a leasehold estate by way of mortgage takes effect as a mortgage by sub-demise, with a term ten days less than the term expressed to be assigned.[14] These provisions operate not only when the transaction's nature as a mortgage is clear from its terms, but also when an apparently absolute transfer is proved by extrinsic evidence to be, in substance, the creation of a mortgage.[15] In registered land, since the coming into force of the Land Registration Act (LRA) 2002, there is only one possibility, and that is the legal charge.[16] A person holding a legal charge over registered land has the power to create a sub-charge over his charge.[17]

8.09 The legal charge is a creature of statute. Because it is, in essence, a security interest and not an estate in land, it is conceptually different from the mortgage by demise or sub-demise; but its legal incidents are defined 'as if' the mortgagee had taken exactly that kind of mortgage.[18] The legislative intention was to simplify the creation of legal mortgages by dispensing with the creation of the lease, but it was not intended to produce a security interest with different features.[19] There may, however, remain some minor differences between legal charges and mortgages by demise. In particular, if the mortgagor is a leaseholder, the lease will probably stipulate that the creation of a sub-lease requires the consent of the landlord;[20] such a stipulation would not necessarily apply to the creation of a legal charge.[21]

8.10 The effect is that when any legal mortgage is given, the mortgagor does not part with his legal estate in the land. The concept of the equity of redemption, however, remains just as important as before. If the holder of a legal fee simple estate grants a legal mortgage, he retains the fee simple; but the mortgagee either holds a long leasehold interest in the land, or is treated as if he held such an interest. At common law, the mortgagor's fee simple is subject to the leasehold interest. The concept of the equity of redemption still performs its traditional function of ensuring that the mortgagee's interest shall be effective only as a security interest, and that the economic benefits of ownership shall remain in the mortgagor.

(b) Equitable mortgages

8.11 For reasons relating to the effectiveness of the security against third parties, a mortgagee is often best protected if the interest he holds in the land is a legal interest. It is, however, possible to create a mortgage in which the mortgagee's security interest is purely equitable. In some cases an equitable mortgage is entirely satisfactory for the parties' needs; in some cases it is the only kind of mortgage which can be created.

8.12 Before 1926, if a mortgage was created by the conveyance of the mortgagor's legal estate, then the only interest retained by the mortgagor would be the equity of redemption. This

---

[13] LPA 1925, s 85(2). Second and subsequent mortgages take effect as mortgages by demise of a lease ending one day after the lease demised to the prior mortgagee.

[14] LPA 1925, s 86(2). Again, second and subsequent mortgages take effect as mortgages by subdemise of a lease ending one day after the lease subdemised to the prior mortgagee.

[15] *Grangeside Properties Ltd v Collingwoods Securities Ltd* [1964] 1 WLR 139, CA.

[16] LRA 2002, ss 23(1), 51.

[17] LRA 2002, s 23(2).

[18] LPA 1925, s 87: if the mortgagor holds a fee simple estate, the mortgagee is put in the same position as if a mortgage by demise with a term of 3,000 years had been granted; if the mortgagor holds a leasehold, the mortgagee is treated as though he had been granted a mortgage by sub-demise with a term one day shorter than the term of the mortgaged lease.

[19] *Grand Junction Co Ltd v Bates* [1954] 2 QB 160, 168; approved *Regent Oil Co Ltd v JA Gregory (Hatch End) Ltd* [1966] Ch 402, 431, CA.

[20] Although LPA 1925, s 86(1) provides that permission to create a sub-lease by way of mortgage shall not be unreasonably refused.

[21] *Grand Junction Co Ltd v Bates* [1954] 2 QB 160, 168.

could itself be mortgaged to a second mortgagee, but necessarily this second mortgagee (and any subsequent mortgagee) would hold only an equitable mortgage.[22] Similarly, in any case where the mortgagor held only an equitable interest, only an equitable mortgage of that interest could be created; eg, if the mortgagor was the beneficiary of a trust of land. This remains true in the modern law.

Even where the mortgagor holds a legal interest, an equitable mortgage can be created. An **8.13** equitable mortgage will arise by operation of law upon the making of an enforceable agreement to create a legal mortgage, once the loan has been advanced. This occurs via the same principle by which an agreement to create a legal lease will create an equitable lease.[23] One implication is that if parties contract, for value given and received, for the creation of a legal mortgage, but they fail to take all the required steps to create one, nonetheless an equitable mortgage will arise.[24] Another implication is that if there is a contract for value to grant a mortgage (whether legal or equitable) over land that the debtor does not yet hold, an equitable mortgage will arise at the moment the debtor acquires an interest in the land, without any new legal act.[25] This doctrine also used to allow for the creation of equitable mortgages of land without any formal documentation. Until 1989, the physical deposit of the documents of title to land ('title deeds') in the hands of the mortgagee could, without the need for any writing, create an equitable mortgage of the land if the deposit was intended to be by way of security.[26] The parties must have intended the deposit to be by way of security, but this is the inference to which such a deposit usually gives rise.[27] The deposit was also treated as part performance of the agreement to create a mortgage, which obviated the need for the agreement to be evidenced in writing, under the law as it was before 1989. Since 1989, any agreement for the sale or disposition of an interest in land is of no legal effect in the absence of the required writing;[28] and so the mere deposit of title deeds no longer creates an equitable mortgage.[29] It is still possible to create an equitable mortgage via an agreement to

---

[22] By contrast if a mortgage was created by demise of a lease, second and subsequent mortgages could be created by the creation of further (legal) leases. In the modern law, second and subsequent mortgages can always be legal, since the first mortgage is either a legal charge or a mortgage by demise.

[23] See EPL 4.32–4.34, 4.106–4.108. In this context the principle only operates once the loan has been advanced, because the contract is not specifically enforceable: EH Burn and J Cartwright, *Cheshire and Burn's Modern Law of Real Property* (18th edn, 2011) 807.

[24] It may be that following the agreement and loan, there is some defect in the attempt to create a legal mortgage, such as the failure to execute a deed (in the case of unregistered land) or the failure to register the mortgage (in the case of registered land; see eg *Swift 1st Ltd v Colin* [2011] EWHC 2410, [2011] Ch 206). Alternatively, it may be that even though there is an agreement to create a legal mortgage, the mortgagee is content to rely on his rights under the equitable mortgage.

[25] Conversely, if the parties wish to create a legal mortgage over that land, the required formal steps will have to be taken.

[26] *Russel v Russel* (1783) 1 Bro CC 269, 28 ER 1121.

[27] See however *Re Alton Corp* [1985] BCLC 27, in which the inference was not drawn, partly because other adequate security had been given for the loan.

[28] Law of Property (Miscellaneous Provisions) Act 1989, s 2 requires a written agreement which is signed by both parties and incorporates all the agreed terms. This is a formal requirement that applies to the agreement to create the mortgage, as opposed to the formalities attached to the creation of a legal mortgage as such (*Helden v Strathmore Ltd* [2011] EWCA Civ 542, at [27]–[28]). The principles of equitable mortgages can dispense with the latter, but not the former.

[29] *United Bank of Kuwait plc v Sahib* [1997] Ch 107, CA. The decision depends upon the holding that since the 1989 Act denies any legal effect to an agreement which does not comply with its terms, therefore the doctrine of part performance has no longer any role to play. See however *Yaxley v Gotts* [2000] Ch 162, CA, holding that the 1989 does not preclude the operation of proprietary estoppel, and suggesting that it may not preclude the operation of part performance.

create a legal mortgage, but only if the agreement to create the mortgage satisfies the required formalities.[30]

8.14 Equity has always recognized the charge as a security interest which can be created in any kind of asset. It does not require that the creditor (chargee) take possession of the charged asset, or of title deeds to it. Subject to requirements of writing and registration, discussed below, such a charge may be created over any kind of interest in land. Sometimes equitable charges arise or are imposed without the consent of the holder of the charged asset. Such a charge can be imposed judicially to secure a judgment debt.[31] It can also be obtained under certain statutes, upon the application of a person who has spent money in a way related to the land.[32] One example of a charge that arises by operation of law is the unpaid vendor's lien, which arises upon the making of a contract for the sale of land unless expressly excluded.[33] Moreover, a lender whose money is used to pay a debt secured by a charge may be subrogated to that charge, if a subsequent lender would otherwise be unjustly enriched.[34] A charge can also arise where trust property is disposed of without authority. The trust beneficiary who can trace into the proceeds of disposition can treat those proceeds as trust property, or can assert a charge over them to secure his claim for breach of trust.[35] A trustee has a lien over the trust property to secure the recovery of expenses properly incurred in the administration of the trust.[36] There are also charges which arise by operation of law under various statutes.[37]

(2) Creation

(a) Formalities for creation

8.15 In unregistered land, legal mortgages are created either by the grant of a leasehold interest or the creation of a legal charge. A deed is required in each case.[38] A deed involves certain

---

[30] Law of Property (Miscellaneous Provisions) Act 1989, s 2. The deposit of title deeds with the mortgagee may still be relevant in unregistered land, as it may affect the registrability of the mortgage (8.19), and in any event it provides practical security since it hinders the mortgagor's ability to deal with the land. In registered land, any document is merely evidence of the state of the register and is not a true title deed; possession of such an extract from the register has no effect on registrability of a mortgage, and is not required to make a registered disposition.

[31] Charging Orders Act 1979. See EPL 22.126. A court can also impose a charge on land to secure unpaid property tax under the Local Government Finance Act 1992, Sch 4, para 11.

[32] Examples include charges arising under the Landlord and Tenant Act 1927, s 12 and Sch 1; Agricultural Holdings Act 1986, ss 85–86.

[33] *Barclays Bank plc v Estates & Commercial Ltd* [1997] 1 WLR 415, CA. The lien allows the unpaid vendor to remain in possession of the land until fully paid. Even if he gives up possession, he retains an interest in the nature of a charge over the land to secure the full payment of the price. There is also a purchaser's lien over the property to secure the repayment of any deposit paid, where the purchaser lawfully terminates the contract: *Lee-Parker v Izzet* [1971] 1 WLR 1688. On the terminological difference between 'charge' and 'lien', see 8.87.

[34] *Anfield (UK) Ltd v Bank of Scotland plc* [2010] EWHC 2374, [2011] 1 WLR 2414. For more detail, see EPL 18.278–18.282.

[35] See EPL 18.239–18.246, 18.267, and 18.274–18.275.

[36] *Stott v Milne* (1884) 25 ChD 710, 715, CA. The trustee may secure a declaration of the lien even in respect of contingent or future liabilities, allowing him to retain in trust property which he would otherwise be obliged to distribute, until the extent of liability becomes clear: *X v A* [2000] 1 All ER 490.

[37] Examples include a 'limited owner's charge,' which can arise under the Inheritance Tax Act 1984, s 212(2) upon the payment by a life tenant of inheritance tax owing in respect of the land; an 'Inland Revenue charge' which can arise under the same Act, s 237, in respect of unpaid inheritance tax; and some of the miscellaneous 'local land charges' enumerated in Local Land Charges Act 1975, s 1(a). These are not discussed herein, being of a public law character, but they may bind both registered and unregistered land and they are to be registered in registers kept by local government authorities. See EH Burn and J Cartwright, *Cheshire and Burn's Modern Law of Real Property* (18th edn, 2011) 1066–1067, 1102–1104.

[38] LPA 1925, ss 52, 87.

formalities. It must make clear that it is intended by the parties to it to be a deed, and it must be executed by all of them.[39] For an individual this requires a witnessed signature, and delivery as a deed.[40] For a company, authentication may be by its seal or by signatures; delivery as a deed is also required.[41] In registered land, the only legal mortgage is a registered legal charge.[42] Again, a deed is required;[43] but the charge does not create a legal interest in the mortgagee until it is registered.[44] In the future it will be possible to create a charge on registered land electronically, without any paper documentation; but even in this case, it is provided that a registered charge has the same effects as if it had been made by a deed.[45] This ensures the activation of the mortgagee's powers under LPA 1925, section 101, including the power of sale.[46]

For an equitable mortgage which takes effect by the transfer of an equitable interest to the mortgagee, the transfer must be in writing, signed by the transferor or his agent.[47] Where the mortgage takes the form of an equitable charge created consensually by the chargor, the same kind of writing is required.[48] However, equitable interests which arise by operation of law are excluded. This exclusion saves not only charges arising without any element of consent;[49] it also applies to the equitable mortgage which arises upon the making of an enforceable agreement, for value given, to create a legal mortgage. Here a different formality is required, in order to make the *agreement* to create a legal mortgage enforceable. A contract for the sale or disposition of an interest in land can only be made in writing, signed by or on behalf of each party.[50] 'Interest in land' here means any estate, interest or charge in or over land.[51] Hence any agreement for any kind of mortgage must be in this form, or it will have no legal effect as an agreement. This is why the mere deposit of title deeds no longer creates an equitable mortgage.[52]

8.16

(b) Defective creation

The transaction by which the mortgage is created may be defective if the mortgagor did not properly understand it.[53] More commonly, the mortgagor will argue that the transaction was induced by misrepresentation or undue influence,[54] or that it resulted from an unconscionable use of bargaining power.[55] Rarely, the problem is said to have originated with the lender.[56]

8.17

---

[39] Law of Property (Miscellaneous Provisions) Act 1989, s 1(2).

[40] Law of Property (Miscellaneous Provisions) Act 1989, s 1(3). 'Delivery' does not refer to a transfer of possession in this context, but means any unilateral act or statement signifying that the person adopts the deed irrevocably: *Xenos v Wickham* (1867) LR 2 HL 296, 312.

[41] Companies Act (CA) 2006, ss 44–46. For other kinds of corporations, see Law of Property Act 1925, s 74–74A.

[42] LRA 2002, s 23(1)(a).

[43] LPA 1925, s 85(1), 87.

[44] LRA 2002, s 27.

[45] LRA 2002, ss 51, 91(5).

[46] Discussed in 8.46ff.

[47] LPA 1925, s 53(1)(c).

[48] LPA 1925, s 53(1)(a).

[49] Some examples are given in 8.14.

[50] Law of Property (Miscellaneous Provisions) Act 1989, s 2.

[51] Law of Property (Miscellaneous Provisions) Act 1989, s 2(6).

[52] See 8.13.

[53] See EPL 8.149–18.152 (*non est factum*).

[54] For the general law of misrepresentation and undue influence, see EPL 8.159–8.210.

[55] *Alec Lobb (Garages) Ltd v Total Oil GB Ltd* [1983] 1 WLR 87, 94–95; *Crédit Lyonnais Bank Nederland NV v Burch* [1997] 1 All ER 144, 151, 152–153, CA. Unconscionability can also be used to set aside particular terms of a mortgage agreement, rather than the whole transaction: 8.28. For discussion of the general law of unconscionable transactions, see EPL 8.208, EPL 18.71–18.75.

[56] *Lloyds Bank Ltd v Bundy* [1975] QB 326, CA (transaction set aside); *National Westminster Bank plc v Morgan* [1985] AC 686, HL (transaction upheld).

More often, it originates from someone else, usually a spouse or other cohabitant of the mort-gagor.[57] Because of the need to protect spouses in such situations, particular principles have been developed which require the mortgagee to take steps to ensure that the mortgage will be valid.[58] Sometimes, these protective principles lead to the creation of an equitable mortgage over a share of the land. As noted above, if there is a valid and enforceable agreement to create a legal mortgage, but there is some defect in the actual creation of that legal mortgage, an equi-table mortgage will arise by operation of law.[59] One effect is that in a mortgage of co-owned land, if the consent of one co-owner is ineffective (whether due to misrepresentation, undue influence, forgery or any other reason), the mortgage can be effective as an equitable mortgage of the interest of the other co-owner.[60]

(c) Registration

8.18 Under the registered land system, a legal charge comes into existence when it is registered. Before registration, 'it does not operate at law'.[61] This means that an unregistered charge may take effect as an equitable mortgage.[62] It remains possible to create voluntarily a mortgage which is only equitable;[63] but this is no longer of practical importance.[64] Again, it is possible for a person to hold an equitable mortgage in registered land, where the mortgage arises by operation of law.[65] Since equitable mortgages of registered land are not registered, they cannot benefit from the governmental guarantee that protects all registered interests.[66] They are valid, however, and it is possible to protect them by making a suitable *entry* in the land register. The idea of an entry in the register is distinct from the idea of the registration of an interest. An entry is made in relation to a particular registered interest, but the entry is not itself a regis-tered interest. Entries are either notices or restrictions. A restriction is an entry in the register that regulates dealings with a registered interest, while a notice is an entry in respect of an unregistered interest affecting a registered interest. A notice of an interest does not guarantee that the interest noted has any validity; but, if it is valid, the notice will preserve the priority of the interest noted, in the face of subsequent dispositions of the affected registered interest.[67] Notices may be entered unilaterally. Finally, it can be observed that an equitable mortgage of an equitable interest in registered land is not registrable, nor can it be protected by any entry on the register, because the equitable interest of the mortgagor cannot itself be registered.[68]

8.19 If the mortgaged land is unregistered, some mortgages can nonetheless be registered in the Land Charges Register.[69] This is a completely separate register from the register of registered

---

[57] Often in such cases there is, instead of or in addition to a mortgage, a guarantee.
[58] See EPL 8.210.
[59] See 8.13, 8.16.
[60] *First National Bank plc v Achampong* [2003] EWCA Civ 487.
[61] LRA 2002, s 27.
[62] *Swift 1st Ltd v Colin* [2011] EWHC 2410, [2011] Ch 206.
[63] LRA 2002, s 23(2).
[64] The main attraction of equitable mortgages was the possibility of creating them informally; for the reasons discussed in 8.13, this is no longer possible.
[65] See 8.14.
[66] Some of them—unregistered legal mortgages—could be registered; but then they would become legal mortgages. Other equitable mortgages cannot be registered.
[67] Priority contests in registered land are discussed at 8.131–8.135.
[68] LRA 2002, s 2. It might be possible to protect the *mortgagor's* equitable interest by restriction or notice, entered in relation to the affected registered legal estate.
[69] Land Charges Act 1972, s 1(1)(a). Note that many dispositions in relation to unregistered land trigger a compulsory registration of the land, including the granting of a first legal mortgage with deposit of title deeds: LRA 2002, s 4(1)(g), (8). If such a legal mortgage is granted over unregistered land and the mortgaged estate is registered as required, then of course the mortgage has to be registered as discussed in the previous para-graph. If the mortgaged estate is not registered as required, the mortgage will take effect only as an equitable interest (LRA 2002, s 7). The goal is to ensure a continual rise in the proportion of land that is registered.

land, although it is maintained by the same Land Registrar. It is organized by the name of the proprietor rather than by the location of the land. Registration is not required for validity, but improves the enforceability of the mortgagee's interest against third parties.[70] The holder of a legal mortgage who also has possession of the title deeds to the mortgaged estate cannot register his interest; but he has no need to do so, since the mortgagor is unable to make any further disposition of a legal interest without this mortgagee's consent. A legal mortgage whose holder does not have the title deeds is registrable;[71] so too are equitable charges not secured by deposit of title deeds, including the unpaid vendor's lien,[72] and, it seems, the kind of equitable mortgage which arises when value is given pursuant to an enforceable agreement to grant a legal mortgage.[73] However, an equitable mortgage of an equitable interest in land is not registrable.[74]

Where a company mortgages land, the mortgage agreement and the prescribed details of the mortgage must be submitted to the Registrar under the Companies Act 2006.[75] Failure to register within 21 days of execution makes the mortgage void as against a liquidator or administrator of the company, or a secured or execution creditor.[76] It also makes the money secured by the mortgage payable immediately.[77] In general, registration under the Companies Act does not dispense with any requirement to register in the relevant land registry. The exception is the case of unregistered land covered by a company's floating charge; here, the mortgagee is protected by Companies Act registration, without any registration in the Land Charges Registry.[78]   **8.20**

(3) Protection of the Mortgagor

There is a long tradition in English law of controlling the parties' freedom in relation to the terms of the contract governing the mortgage. The root of much of this intervention was the recognition of the equity of redemption, by which the mortgagor was allowed to redeem the mortgage even if, according to the terms of the contract, he had lost it. By the early seventeenth century, redemption was allowed as a matter of course, without the requirement of showing any particular hardship.[79] This led, by the end of that century, to the recognition   **8.21**

---

[70] See 8.136–8.140.

[71] Land Charges Act 1972, s 2(4)(i). Such a mortgage is called a 'puisne mortgage', because in practice it will be a second or subsequent mortgage. 'Puisne' is derived from the French *puis né* but in English it is pronounced the same as 'puny', which indeed is a later evolution of the same word.

[72] Land Charges Act 1972, s 2(4)(iii).

[73] Land Charges Act 1972, s 2(4)(iv); see EH Burn and J Cartwright, *Cheshire and Burn's Modern Law of Real Property* (18th edn, 2011) 886. This section does not specifically exclude the case of a mortgage of this type where the mortgagee holds the title deeds, and it has been suggested that such a mortgage may be registrable: C Harpum, S Bridge and M Dixon, *Megarry and Wade: The Law of Real Property* (8th edn, 2012) 1229–1230. This would be inconsistent with the scheme of the Act, which appears to be that any mortgage, legal or equitable, which is protected by a deposit of title deeds is not registrable: Burn and Cartwright, 886–887; Harpum, Bridge and Dixon.

[74] By the Land Charges Act 1972, s 3 registration is made under the name of the 'estate owner' (mortgagor) and this includes only the holder of a legal estate: Land Charges Act 1972, s 17(1); LPA 1925, s 205(1)(v).

[75] CA 2006, ss 859A–859B, 860–861. The word 'charge' in this Chapter of the Act includes a mortgage: CA 2006, ss 859A(7), 861(5).

[76] CA 2006, ss 859H, 874. See 8.105 and 8.142–8.144.

[77] CA 2006, ss 859(4) 874(3).

[78] Land Charges Act 1972, s 3(7). This is effective even if the company is not the holder of the freehold estate, so that the Companies Act registration is under a different name than the registration that would otherwise need to be made under the Land Charges Act 1972: *Property Discount Corp Ltd v Lyon Group Ltd* [1981] 1 WLR 300, CA, dealing with the situation for mortgages made before 1970, when the Companies Act registration sufficed even if the charge was not floating.

[79] AWB Simpson, *A History of the Land Law* (2nd edn, 1986) 244.

of the equity of redemption as a form of property with which the mortgagor could deal like any other. This was carried forward into a far-reaching prohibition against creating any 'clog or fetter' on the equity of redemption. All of these doctrines are said to stem from the fact that regardless of its form or its precise terms, equity looked to the substance of a mortgage transaction as the creation of a security interest only, with the beneficial ownership of the land remaining in the mortgagor.[80] This is said to justify the courts in refusing to enforce any term seen as inconsistent with the nature of the transaction as one that gives the mortgagee security for a debt, but no more than that.[81]

(a) Excluding or postponing the right to redeem

8.22   The starting point is that even though the contract may appear to provide for redemption only upon payment within a particular time, this governs only the position at common law; the equitable right to redeem is indefinite in duration. For many years the standard form of mortgage purported to require payment of the full debt within six months, even though such payment was not actually contemplated by either party.[82] The implication was that redemption by the mortgagor could not occur unless the debt was repaid within six months; but this was misleading and it certainly could. This shows that any term that would preclude redemption is void to that extent, no matter how clearly expressed. This principle has been extended even to a term which might have the effect of preventing redemption. In *Samuel v Jarrah Timber & Wood Paving Corp Ltd*,[83] the agreement gave the mortgagee an option to purchase the mortgaged property within one year of the date of the loan.[84] The option was held to be void. The speeches show some reluctance, however, in applying the traditional rules to what was a commercial transaction between two competent parties of equal bargaining power. This is especially clear when it is observed that if the option is part of a separate contract, it will be valid.[85] But it is not enough that the option is created by a separate document. In *Lewis v Frank Love Ltd*[86] the mortgagor had defaulted and the mortgagee had obtained judgment for £6,070. The defendant agreed to lend £6,500 to the mortgagor on the terms that the defendant would have the option to acquire the fee simple in part of the mortgaged land. The defendant paid the debt owing to the original mortgagee and took an assignment of the mortgage, and the mortgagor contemporaneously granted the option.[87] When the defendant

---

[80] 'Once a mortgage, always a mortgage': *Seton v Slade* (1802) 7 Ves 265, 273, 32 ER 108, 111; '... and nothing but a mortgage': *Noakes & Co Ltd v Rice* [1902] AC 24, 33, HL. The converse of this regard for substance over form is that even if a transaction is in the form of a mortgage, the court may conclude that it is not in substance a mortgage, with the result that the principles discussed here will not apply: *Brighton & Hove City Council v Audus* [2009] EWHC 340, [2010] 1 All ER (Comm) 343.

[81] *Jones v Morgan* [2001] EWCA Civ 995, [2002] EGLR 125, at [55]. This was cogently criticized in GL Williams, 'The Doctrine of Repugnancy–III: "Clogging the Equity" and Miscellaneous Applications' (1944) 60 LQR 190, 190–193. Williams argued that while the control of mortgage contract terms might be justified on the basis that the terms were oppressive, there is no logic in the traditional position, that they are inconsistent with the nature of a mortgage.

[82] Modern forms of mortgage contract usually state more accurately the rights of the parties, including the mortgagee's right to payment and the mortgagor's right to redeem. In this case the mortgagor probably does not need to rely on the equitable right to redeem; this will be coextensive with his legal rights as set out in the contract. The equity of redemption retains its importance, however, in giving proprietary effect to the mortgagor's rights under the contract.

[83] [1904] AC 323, HL.

[84] The property in question here was debenture stock, not land, but the applicable principles are the same.

[85] *Reeve v Lisle* [1902] AC 461, HL, where an agreement which contemplated the possible acquisition by the mortgagee of part of the mortgaged property was made two weeks after the mortgage; it was held to be enforceable.

[86] [1961] 1 WLR 261.

[87] The defendant did not, however, advance the additional £430 which the transaction contemplated.

tried to exercise the option, the mortgagor successfully brought proceedings for a declaration that it was invalid as a clog on the equity of redemption.[88] The question in each case is one of characterization of the substance of the transaction.[89] It is possible that if the House of Lords were faced today with the agreement in *Samuel v Jarrah Timber & Wood Paving Corp Ltd*, it would uphold the validity of the option.[90]

Terms which delay the mortgagor's ability to redeem are not viewed in so absolute a light   **8.23** as those which could preclude it. The old standard form of mortgage required repayment of the loan after six months. As has been discussed, this was largely illusory and the mortgagor could redeem at any time during the subsistence of the mortgage. But one effect of the six-month term was that the mortgagor could not unilaterally redeem until the end of that period; moreover, if he wished to redeem outside that period, he was required as a rule of equity to give six months' notice to the mortgagee, or to pay six months' interest in lieu of notice.[91] So clearly some postponement of redemption has always been permissible.

Sometimes the agreement purports to impose a much longer postponement. The leading case   **8.24** is *Knightsbridge Estates Trust Ltd v Byrne*,[92] in which an agreement precluding redemption for a period of 40 years was held to be valid. The court in that case said that a mortgage will not be reformed because it is unreasonable; a delay in the right to redeem would be unenforceable only if it was oppressive or unconscionable,[93] or if it made the right to redeem 'illusory'. This latter concept was used by the court to explain the decision in *Fairclough v Swan Brewery Co Ltd*,[94] which illustrates that the effect of a postponement of redemption can cause more concern where the mortgaged estate is a leasehold, because the postponement may be such that very little of the term of the lease will remain to the mortgagor. In that case the mortgaged estate was a leasehold with over seventeen years to run, but the agreement did not permit redemption until only six weeks of the lease remained. The Privy Council held that the term postponing redemption was void. The decision is, however, inconsistent with an earlier decision of the Court of Appeal,[95] and is regarded by some commentators as open to review.[96]

The concern expressed in *Samuel v Jarrah Timber & Wood Paving Corp Ltd*,[97] that commercial   **8.25** agreements between equal parties should not be lightly upset, may now have been met by statute. A company may create 'debentures' which are irredeemable, or redeemable only on

---

[88] Similar is *Jones v Morgan* [2001] EWCA Civ 995, [2002] EGLR 125, in which the mortgage was created in 1994; the mortgagee acquired a right to part of the mortgaged property in an agreement in 1997; this right was held to be void as a clog, by a majority of the Court.

[89] *Warnborough Ltd v Garmite Ltd* [2003] EWCA Civ 1544, at [73].

[90] Some academic commentary is hostile to the case: F Pollock (1903) 19 LQR 359; PV Baker (1961) 77 LQR 163; EH Burn and J Cartwright, *Cheshire and Burn's Modern Law of Real Property* (18th edn, 2011) 818. In *Jones v Morgan* [2001] EWCA Civ 995, [2002] EGLR 125, Lord Phillips MR agreed that the impugned term was void as a clog, but said at [86], '... the doctrine of a clog on the equity of redemption is, so it seems to me, an appendix to our law which no longer serves a useful purpose and would be better excised.' See also *Warnborough Ltd v Garmite Ltd* [2003] EWCA Civ 1544, at [72].

[91] But if the mortgagee demanded payment, he was not entitled to this interest: *Centrax Trustees Ltd v Ross* [1979] 2 All ER 952; nor if he entered into possession of the land: *Bovill v Endle* [1896] 1 Ch 650.

[92] [1939] Ch 441, CA, affd on different grounds [1940] AC 613, HL, on which see 8.25.

[93] On which see 8.28.

[94] [1912] AC 565, PC.

[95] *Santley v Wilde* [1899] 2 Ch 474, CA, upholding a term which required the mortgagor to share with the mortgagee the business profits earned during the ten years remaining in the mortgaged lease. This meant that there could be no redemption during the term of the lease.

[96] EH Burn and J Cartwright, *Cheshire and Burn's Modern Law of Real Property* (18th edn, 2011) 820. *Santley v Wilde* was questioned in *Noakes & Co Ltd v Rice* [1904] AC 24, 31, 34, HL; but there was veiled criticism of the *Fairclough* case in *Kreglinger v New Patagonia Meat and Cold Storage Co Ltd* [1914] AC 25, 53, HL.

[97] [1904] AC 323, HL.

a contingency (however remote) or after a period of time (however long).[98] On the basis of surrounding legislative provisions, the word 'debenture' might be thought to be confined to investment securities secured on the undertaking of the company; but in *Knightsbridge Estates Trust Ltd v Byrne*,[99] it was held to cover an ordinary mortgage of land.[100] This implies that the rules discussed in this section have no application where the mortgagor is a company. In any event, in modern practice mortgagees more often protect themselves by requiring monetary penalties for early redemption. Such penalties do not interfere with the right to redeem, but they may be challenged on other grounds, as discussed below.

(b) Collateral advantages

8.26 The idea that a mortgage can never be anything but a mortgage generated the doctrine of 'collateral advantages', by which it is meant that the court may invalidate a term of the mortgage agreement under which some advantage accrues to the mortgagee, beyond recovery of the debt with interest. At the turn of the twentieth century the doctrine took on a more modern cast, with the courts refusing to invalidate terms so long as the advantage in question was not expressed to continue in force after redemption.[101] To the extent, however, that an advantage was expressed to survive redemption, it was not enforceable, even by way of damages.[102] As in the decisions relating to options, the cases show an increasing awareness of the tension between the old protective approach of equity and the recognition that many mortgagors are not particularly in need of paternalistic care. In *Kreglinger v New Patagonia Meat and Cold Storage Co Ltd*,[103] the agreement purported to give the lender a right of first refusal and a right of commission in respect of some assets which the borrower was in the business of selling. The House of Lords upheld the validity of these terms even after the discharge of the security, on the ground that they were effectively terms of a separate agreement.[104] If this can be taken to represent the modern law, then the doctrine of collateral advantages is now of little importance.[105]

(c) Other doctrines

8.27 There are a number of other bases on which terms in mortgage agreements may be invalidated. These, however, derive from more general principles, rather than from the particular approach of equity to mortgage transactions. For this reason they will be dealt with more briefly.

(i) Unconscionability

8.28 In a number of cases, particular terms have been invalidated as unconscionable. Historically, equity has been more willing to intervene on this ground in mortgage transactions than in general; as discussed above, the mortgagor was traditionally seen as being in need of special

---

[98] CA 2006, s 739.

[99] [1940] AC 613, HL.

[100] Relying on the definition now in the CA 2006, s 738, that the word includes 'debenture stock, bonds and any other securities of a company, whether or not constituting a charge on the assets of the company'.

[101] *Biggs v Hoddinott* [1898] 2 Ch 307, CA. This perspective fits with the holding in *Santley v Wilde* [1899] 2 Ch 474, CA, where the advantage in question accrued only during the term of the mortgage.

[102] *Noakes & Co Ltd v Rice* [1902] AC 24, HL; *Bradley v Carritt* [1903] AC 253, HL.

[103] [1914] AC 25, HL.

[104] The security was not a mortgage of land but a floating charge over the assets of the debtor. Their Lordships rejected an argument that different principles applied to such a charge.

[105] The *Kreglinger* case was applied in *Re Petrol Filling Station, Vauxhall Bridge Road, London* (1968) 20 P & CR 1 in upholding a term which required the mortgagor to purchase stock-in-trade only from the mortgagee even after redemption. The conclusion was assisted by the fact that the purchase agreement preceded the mortgage agreement; but the judge said that the purchase agreement would have been enforceable after redemption as a separate agreement from the mortgage, even if the two agreements were properly viewed as parts of a single transaction.

protection. Unlike rules relating to the equity of redemption, however, the unconscionability jurisdiction does not arise from any particular feature of mortgage transactions.[106] The courts have said repeatedly that it is not sufficient for a term to be unreasonable.[107] In one case, the mortgagor borrowed £2,900 and agreed to repay £4,553 by instalments over six years.[108] The mortgagor's default triggered a clause making the full debt payable immediately, creating an effective interest rate of 38 per cent. The court held that the agreement was not enforceable on its terms, because they destroyed any possibility that there would be any surplus for the mortgagor. It was held that the mortgagee could recover the amount of the advance together with interest at the rate of 7 per cent. The basis of the jurisdiction was clarified in *Multiservice Bookbinding Ltd v Marden*.[109] The mortgagee wanted to be secure against any decline in the value of sterling. The agreement provided for a floating rate of compound interest, and for the sums payable to be indexed to the value of the Swiss franc. At the end of the ten-year term, the effective interest rate was 16 per cent. Browne-Wilkinson J held that although the terms of the agreement were unreasonable, they were enforceable. He said:

> ...in order to be freed from the necessity to comply with all the terms of the mortgage, the plaintiffs must show that the bargain, or some of its terms, was unfair and unconscionable: it is not enough to show that, in the eyes of the court, it was unreasonable. In my judgment a bargain cannot be unfair and unconscionable unless one of the parties to it has imposed the objectionable terms in a morally reprehensible manner, that is to say, in a way which affects his conscience.

> The classic example of an unconscionable bargain is where advantage has been taken of a young, inexperienced or ignorant person to introduce a term which no sensible well-advised person or party would have accepted. But I do not think the categories of unconscionable bargains are limited; the court can and should intervene where a bargain has been procured by unfair means.

(ii) Restraint of trade

Many cases involve mortgage agreements containing terms by which the mortgagor must **8.29** deal exclusively with the mortgagee, usually in acquiring stock-in-trade for business. In order to preserve the validity of these 'ties', such agreements commonly postponed the mortgagor's right to redeem; this was to ensure that the restriction was not struck down as a collateral advantage, but it also underpinned the argument that the restriction was more justifiable where the tied party owed money to the other. It was decided in *Esso Petroleum Co Ltd v Harper's Garage (Stourport) Ltd*[110] that the principles of public policy which governed the validity of such ties were the same whether or not there was a mortgage agreement in place.[111] Where the tie is void as contrary to public policy, a postponement of redemption which was inserted to protect the tie is probably also invalid.[112]

(iii) Implied terms

Many mortgage agreements (and many unsecured lending arrangements) have a variable **8.30** interest rate. It is the lender, of course, that has the power to vary the rate. It has been held that

---

[106] For discussion of the general law of unconscionable transactions, see EPL 8.208, 18.71–18.75. It is also possible that the whole mortgage agreement is voidable for unconscionability: see 8.17.

[107] *Knightsbridge Estates Trust Ltd v Byrne*, [1939] Ch 441, CA, aff'd on different grounds [1940] AC 613, HL; *Multiservice Bookbinding Ltd v Marden* [1979] Ch 84.

[108] *Cityland & Property (Holdings) Ltd v Dabrah* [1968] Ch 166.

[109] [1979] Ch 84. This case also established that it is permissible for a mortgage agreement to make the principal debt variable according to some index.

[110] [1968] AC 269, HL.

[111] For a discussion of the principles see EPL 8.238–8.248.

[112] [1968] AC 269, 314, 321, 342, HL.

this power is controlled by an implied term of the contract. The implied term is that the power may not be used dishonestly, for an improper purpose, capriciously or arbitrarily; nor may it be used in a way in which no reasonable mortgagee, acting reasonably, would use it.[113]

(iv) Legislative intervention

8.31   Certain legislative interventions are relevant to the control of mortgage terms. In the case of most first residential mortgages, mortgage lenders are subject to regulation under the Financial Markets and Services Act (FSMA) 2000, as are mortgage brokers and mortgage advisors.[114] This means that lenders must be authorized to do business, and there is detailed regulation of advertising and other aspects of seeking and doing business. This is public law regulation, that does not have direct effect on contracts. The Consumer Credit Act (CCA) 1974 provides many protections for consumer debtors, and these often do have direct effect on contracts; but in general, the CCA 1974 will not apply where the FSMA 2000 applies. Many of the provisions of the CCA 1974 apply only to 'regulated agreements'. An agreement is a regulated agreement only if the debtor is an individual.[115] But some agreements are not regulated under the CCA 1974 because they are 'exempt', and these exemptions include any mortgage that is regulated under the FSMA 2000.[116] One exceptional case may be noted. The CCA 1974 provides that if a land mortgage is a regulated agreement, there can be no extrajudicial enforcement;[117] exceptionally, this provision applies even to a mortgage agreement that is otherwise regulated only under the FSMA 2000.[118]

8.32   The CCA 1974, therefore, could apply to a mortgage where the mortgagor is an individual, and either the mortgage is over non-residential property, or it is a second or later mortgage on a residence. The Act allows the debtor in a regulated agreement to repay the loan at any time regardless of its terms;[119] this would override any term postponing the right to redeem. The Act imposes requirements of form and procedure for the making and enforcement of agreements. The sanction for non-compliance by the lender is generally that the agreement cannot be enforced without a court order.[120] As previously noted, a court order is always required for enforcement of a land mortgage.[121] The Act also includes public law regulation requiring the authorization of commercial lenders, and regulating advertising and other aspects of seeking business.

8.33   Under CCA 1974, sections 140A–140D, the court can reopen and revise a credit agreement if it determines that the relationship between the debtor and the creditor, arising out of the agreement, is unfair to the debtor.[122] These provisions apply even to agreements that are not 'regulated agreements'; but this does not significantly widen their scope in the mortgage

---

[113] *Paragon Finance plc v Nash* [2001] EWCA Civ 1466, [2002] 1 WLR 685, CA; *Paragon Finance plc v Pender* [2005] EWCA Civ 760, [2005] 1 WLR 3412, CA.

[114] Sections 19, 22(1), and Sch 2, paras 1, 2(1), 3, 7, 10, 23, 23A; Financial Services and Markets Act 2000 (Regulated Activities) Order 2001, SI 2001/544, especially arts 25E, 61. Basically, the FSMA regime applies in cases where the debtor is an individual, the mortgage is a first mortgage, and the debtor or his family will be living in the mortgaged property. It also applies to 'sale and rent back' transactions in which the lender purchases the borrower's residence and agrees to let the borrower remain as a tenant.

[115] Sections 8, 189(1).

[116] The exemptions are in ss 16–16B; by s 16(6C), the CCA 1974 does not regulate a mortgage where the lender is regulated under the FSMA 2000.

[117] Section 126.

[118] Section 16(6D).

[119] FSMA 2000, s 94.

[120] eg ss 65(1), 105(7), 111(2). By s 113, any security is only enforceable to the extent of such an order, even if otherwise it would be effective against a third party.

[121] Section 126.

[122] Unfairness may be present where the amount of a commission was not disclosed, even if the consumer was informed that a commission was being charged: *Plevin v Paragon Personal Finance Ltd* [2014] UKSC 61,

context, because they only apply to individual debtors, and they do not apply to mortgage agreements regulated by FSMA 2000.[123] The creditor is required to disprove any allegation that a relationship is unfair.[124]

In insolvency, whether of a company or an individual, the court may, on the application of **8.34** the insolvency officer, reopen and revise a credit transaction that is 'extortionate' if it was entered into within three years before the insolvency.[125] This jurisdiction exists to protect other creditors of the insolvent person from the extortionate transaction that one creditor has made. Where the insolvency officer alleges that a transaction is extortionate, the creditor is required to disprove the allegation.[126]

Part 2 of the Consumer Rights Act (CRA) 2015 gives effect to the Directive on Unfair Terms **8.35** in Consumer Contracts.[127] These provisions are confined to cases where one party is acting in the course of its business and the other is acting as a consumer.[128] They permit a contract term to be assessed as to whether it is fair; a term is unfair if 'contrary to the requirement of good faith, it causes a significant imbalance in the parties' rights and obligations under the contract to the detriment of the consumer'.[129] If it is unfair, a term is not enforceable against the consumer.[130] There is, however, a further limitation in that a term (provided that it is transparent and prominent) may not be assessed for fairness to the extent that it specifies the main subject matter of the contract, or the assessment is of the appropriateness of the the price payable by comparison to what is being supplied.[131] The practice of having variable interest rates is, in general, protected from review for fairness, so long as there is a 'valid reason' for the variation, a requirement to notify the consumer, and a right on the part of the consumer to dissolve the contract immediately.[132] The Financial Conduct Authority issues guidance on its views as to fairness of variation clauses.[133] Part 1 of the CRA 2015 also regulates terms in consumer contracts, and Chapter 4 applies to contracts for services. However, these provisions are unlikely to be relevant to lending contracts.

The Unfair Contract Terms Act 1977 is now concerned only with non-consumer contracts. **8.36** Moreover, it is concerned with exemption clauses and therefore is not likely to have much impact on mortgage contracts.[134]

[2014] 1 WLR 4222. The decision whether the agreement is unfair may take into account misrepresentations made by someone other than the creditor: *Scotland v British Credit Trust Ltd* [2014] EWCA Civ 790, [2015] 1 All ER 708. Because the court's jurisdiction is based on the relationship arising out of the agreement, and not on the agreement itself, these provisions create a continuing cause of action; a limitation period will only start to run after the relationship ends: *Patel v Patel* [2009] EWHC 3264, [2010] 1 All ER (Comm) 864.

[123] CCA 1974, ss 140C(1), 140A(5).

[124] CCA 1974, s 140B(9).

[125] Insolvency Act 1986, ss 244, 343. 'Extortionate' is defined as requiring that the transaction provides for payments which are 'grossly exorbitant', or that it otherwise 'grossly contravenes ordinary principles of fair trading' (ss 244(3), 343(3)).

[126] Insolvency Act 1986, ss 244(3), 343(3).

[127] Council Directive (EEC) 93/13 [1993] OJ L095/29.

[128] CRA 2015, s 61(1).

[129] CRA 2015, s 62(4).

[130] CRA 2015, s 62(2).

[131] CRA 2015, s 64(1).

[132] CRA 2015, Sch 2, para 22.

[133] The FCA is the regulator for contracts governed by the FSMA 2000 (which includes most first residential mortgages: see 8.31) and also for agreements governed by the CCA 1974. This means that it administers the public law aspects of the legislation.

[134] In *Paragon Finance plc v Nash* [2001] EWCA Civ 1466, [2002] 1 WLR 685, CA, the mortgage agreement had a floating rate of interest. The mortgagors argued that the failure of the mortgagees to lower the

(4) Enforcement

8.37 The primary focus here is on the rights arising from the mortgage itself. There will of course be a personal obligation created by the transaction, and the mortgagee will have a right to recover the debt owed to it, as stipulated in the mortgage agreement. The personal obligation can generally be cumulated with any other enforcement measure.[135] In other words, if the mortgagee takes steps to enforce the mortgage and there is still a deficiency, so that the mortgagee is still owed money after that enforcement measure, an action may be brought on the personal obligation.[136] A claim to enforce the mortgage which does not also disclose a claim on the personal obligation does not prevent the mortgagee from later making a claim on the personal obligation.[137] Similarly, even if the mortgage as such is effectively unenforceable, the lender may proceed to judgment on the personal claim, which may lead to bankruptcy proceedings and, eventually, realization (on behalf of all creditors) of the mortgagor's interest in the mortgaged land.[138]

(a) Possession

8.38 Subject to any contractual stipulation, a legal mortgagee has the right to take possession of the land.[139] This does not depend on any default, but is simply an incident of the legal estate which he holds.[140] Equity did not intervene in this regard, because the mortgagee's right to possession is not inconsistent with the security nature of his interest in the land.[141] It has been held, however, that the right to take possession may only be exercised *bona fide* and reasonably for the purpose of enforcing the security, and not for an ulterior purpose such as evading legislation governing security of tenure.[142]

---

rates, as interest rates fell in the general lending market, was a violation of s 3(2)(b) of the Unfair Contract Terms Act 1977, which limits the ability of a party to be excused from performance of its obligations. The court rejected this argument on the basis that the setting of interest rates by the creditor is not a performance by the creditor of its obligation. Note also that some aspects of land mortgage agreements may be outside the Act, since it does not apply to 'any contract so far as it relates to the creation or transfer of an interest in land, or to the termination of such an interest': s 1(2); Sch 1, para 1(b).

[135] *Gordon Grant & Co Ltd v Boos* [1926] AC 781, PC. If the mortgagee has foreclosed the equity of redemption and acquired the mortgaged property beneficially, any claim on the personal obligation requires the mortgagee to allow the mortgagor once again to redeem (at 785). Foreclosure followed by sale to a third party, however, precludes any claim on the personal obligation. For more detail, see 8.53.

[136] The limitation period on the personal obligation is twelve years from the date of breach: Limitation Act 1980, s 20; *West Bromwich BS v Wilkinson* [2005] UKHL 44, [2005] 1 WLR 2303.

[137] In *UCB Bank plc v Chandler* (1999) 79 P & CR 270, CA, an argument that the mortgagee was estopped (see EPL 22.120–22.124) was rejected.

[138] *Alliance and Leicester plc v Slayford* [2001] Bankruptcy and Personal Insolvency Rep 555, CA. In this case the mortgagee could not obtain a possession order against the mortgagor because the mortgage was not effective against mortgagor's wife, who also lived in the house. However the mortgagee could obtain personal judgment against him, leading to bankruptcy and probably the eventual sale of the house.

[139] *Four-Maids Ltd v Dudley Marshall (Properties) Ltd* [1957] Ch 317. A term restricting this right will not be readily implied: *National Westminster Bank plc v Skelton* [1993] 1 WLR 72, 77, CA.

[140] *Four-Maids Ltd v Dudley Marshall (Properties) Ltd* [1957] Ch 317; *National Westminster Bank plc v Skelton* [1993] 1 WLR 72, 77, CA; *Paragon Finance plc v Pender* [2005] EWCA Civ 760, [2005] 1 WLR 3412, CA. Before 1926 he might take a conveyance of the mortgagor's estate, or a lease granted by the mortgagor; either way, at law he had a better right to possession than the mortgagor. After 1925 the mortgagee's rights are, or are treated as, those of a lessee from the mortgagor, with the same effect. In particular, in providing that the holder of a legal charge has the same protection as if granted a lease, LPA 1925, s 87(1) expressly mentions the mortgagee's right to possession.

[141] Where the mortgagee has the right to possession, the mortgagor's possession of the land can be adverse possession capable of extinguishing the mortgagee's right to recover the land: *National Westminster Bank Plc v Ashe* [2008] EWCA Civ 55, [2008] 1 WLR 710. A mortgagee who has a right to possession does not lose it merely by executing a sub-mortgage, unless the terms of that contract transfer the right to possession to the sub-mortgagee: *Credit & Mercantile plc v Marks* [2004] EWCA Civ 568, [2005] 1 Ch 81.

[142] *Quennell v Maltby* [1979] 1 WLR 318, CA; approved in *Albany Home Loans Ltd v Massey* [1997] 2 All ER 609, CA.

In practice the right to take possession is used only as a means of enforcement. The mortga- **8.39**
gee will almost always take possession before exercising the power to sell, because it will be
impossible to get the best price unless vacant possession is offered.[143] Possession is less commonly taken for other reasons. Eg, the mortgagee might wish to lease the land so that the
profits can be applied against the mortgagor's obligations under the mortgage agreement.[144]
The drawback of taking possession is that a mortgagee in possession is required to account
'strictly'.[145] This means he must account to the mortgagor for all profits which were, or ought
reasonably to have been, realized from the land.[146] If a mortgagee is concerned to preserve
the income from a property, it is usually wiser to appoint a receiver.[147]

Proceedings for possession are usually therefore the first stage in the sale of the property; for **8.40**
this reason, such proceedings often serve as the occasion for determining the validity of a
mortgage.[148] In the case of most mortgages granted by individual debtors, an order of the
court will be required for the mortgagee to take possession.[149] Otherwise, possession can be
taken extrajudicially, but mortgagees usually seek a court order unless the occupier is willing
to give up the premises. Forcible entry constitutes an offence if there is an occupier resisting
that entry.[150] In the case of residential premises, unlawful eviction is an offence even if it is
peaceable.[151]

The mortgagor can be protected from this seemingly Draconian power of the mortgagee in **8.41**
various ways. First, the right to take possession can be excluded contractually, and in the case
of most modern residential mortgages it is usual to exclude the right to take possession before
default. Such an exclusion could be implied, but at least in commercial transactions, the
courts will not quickly draw the conclusion that this has been done. For example, the mere
fact that the mortgage agreement provides for payments by instalment does not mean that
the mortgagee's right to take possession is excluded in the absence of default.[152] Similarly,
a mortgage agreement which contemplates no payments of either interest or capital for ten
years does not, by that reason alone, exclude the right to possession during the ten-year
period.[153]

More significant for the residential mortgagor are the statutory interventions which control **8.42**
the right to take possession. The Administration of Justice Act 1970, section 36, applies
where the mortgaged premises consist of or include a dwelling-house,[154] and the mortgagee

---

[143] See however *Ropaigealach v Barclays Bank plc* [1998] EWCA Civ 1960, [2000] 1 QB 263; *Horsham Properties Group Ltd v Clark* [2008] EWHC 2327 (Ch), [2009] 1 WLR 1255. In the latter case it was held that the possibility of sale without a prior order for possession is not inconsistent with art 1 of the First Protocol (Paris, 1952) to the Convention for the Protection of Human Rights and Fundamental Freedoms (Rome, 1950), implemented in English law by the Human Rights Act 1998, s 1.

[144] *White v City of London Brewery Co* (1889) 42 ChD 237, CA.

[145] The taking of possession by the mortgagee also gives the mortgagor an immediate right to redeem, even if the legal date for redemption has not arrived: *Bovill v Endle* [1896] 1 Ch 648.

[146] *White v City of London Brewery Co* (1889) 42 ChD 237, CA.

[147] See 8.54.

[148] As eg in *Barclays Bank plc v O'Brien* [1994] 1 AC 180, HL.

[149] If the mortgage agreement is a 'regulated agreement' within the CCA 1974 (on which see 8.31), then an order of the court is required for possession: CCA 1974, s 126; by s 16(6D), s 126 applies even where the mortgage is one that is otherwise regulated by the FSMA 2000 rather than the CCA 1974.

[150] Criminal Law Act 1977, s 6; by s 6(2), a right to possession of the premises does not excuse this offence.

[151] Protection from Eviction Act 1977, s 1. If the eviction is both peaceable and lawful, there is no offence, but a prudent mortgagee will often seek a court order to avoid any doubt.

[152] *Esso Petroleum Co Ltd v Alstonbridge Properties Ltd* [1975] 1 WLR 1474, 1484.

[153] *Western Bank Ltd v Schindler* [1977] Ch 1, CA.

[154] Under the Administration of Justice Act 1970, s 39(1), 'dwelling house' is defined as property 'used' for a dwelling. In *Royal Bank of Scotland v Miller* [2001] EWCA Civ 344, [2002] QB 255, the mortgaged premises included a residential flat; at the time of the granting of the mortgage, this was unoccupied, but at

brings an action for possession, not being an action for foreclosure.[155] The section provides that in such a case, the court may adjourn the proceedings, or suspend or postpone the possession order:

> if it appears to the court that in the event of its exercising the power the mortgagor is likely to be able within a reasonable period to pay any sums due under the mortgage or to remedy a default consisting of a breach of any other obligation arising under or by virtue of the mortgage.[156]

8.43 It is usual for instalment mortgages to have an 'acceleration clause' by which, in the event of a default, the whole of the principal and interest become payable. In such a case, for the purposes of section 36, the amount due is to be taken to mean the amount that would be due if there had been no acceleration clause.[157] However, if the debt is payable on demand from the outset, then upon demand being made, the amount due for the purposes of section 36 is the full debt.[158] It was argued by some that the effect of section 36 was impliedly to abrogate the mortgagee's right to take possession extrajudicially, so that possession could be taken only with judicial approval and subject to the statutory discretion. However, it has been held, reading the section literally, that it only applies where there is an *action* for possession. The court cannot interfere if the mortgagee lawfully takes possession extrajudicially.[159]

8.44 Some guidelines have been laid down for the application of section 36. If the mortgagor proposes to pay the arrears in instalments, the court will take into account such factors as the mortgagor's financial means, the prospects for their improvement, and the reasons for the default; the remaining term of the mortgage and its other terms; and the possibilities for paying the arrears, such as different repayment schedules or the capitalization of unpaid interest.[160] If the mortgagor proposes to sell the land, the relevant considerations will include the adequacy of the land as security for the debt, and the time required to effect a sale.[161] If the court is exercising its discretion under section 36, then if the mortgagee is also seeking a judgment on the mortgagor's personal obligation, the court will normally also suspend any such judgment in line with the suspension of the possession order pursuant to section 36.[162]

---

the time that the mortgagee sought possession, it was alleged to be occupied, albeit by someone other than the mortgagor, which would be a breach of a term of the mortgage contract. Nonetheless, it was held that if it was established that the flat was occupied at the time possession was sought, s 36 would apply.

[156] On a literal reading s 36 would only apply where there has been a default by the mortgagor, so that if the mortgagee took proceedings for possession in the absence of default, the court would have no discretion to postpone possession. It was held by a majority in *Western Bank Ltd v Schindler* [1977] Ch 1, CA, that the section must be interpreted to apply even if there has been no default under the mortgage agreement.

[157] Section 36(1). By s 36(3), the court may attach conditions to the suspension of a possession order, and such conditions need not be confined to the 'reasonable period' referred to in s 36(1), but can operate during the remaining life of the mortgage: *Bank of Scotland plc v Zinda* [2011] EWCA Civ 706, [2012] 1 WLR 728. By s 38A, s 36 does not apply to an agreement which is a regulated agreement under the CCA 1974 (on which see 8.31); but in such a case an order of the court is required for possession: CCA 1974, s 126.

[158] Administration of Justice Act 1973, s 8(1). This section applies whether the mortgage is a 'repayment mortgage' (which involves blended payments of interest and principal) or an 'endowment mortgage' (in which only interest is payable by instalments and the capital is payable in a lump sum at the end of the term): *Governor and Company of the Bank of Scotland v Grimes* [1985] QB 1179, CA; *Royal Bank of Scotland v Miller* [2001] EWCA Civ 344, [2002] QB 255. It also applies to the older style of mortgage which provided on its face for full payment of principal after six months, but which really had an indefinite term for the repayment of capital: *Centrax Trustees Ltd v Ross* [1979] 2 All ER 952.

[158] *Habib Bank v Tailor* [1982] 1 WLR 1218, CA.

[159] *Ropaigealach v Barclays Bank plc* [1998] EWCA Civ 1960, [2000] 1 QB 263.

[160] *Cheltenham and Gloucester BS v Norgan* [1996] 1 WLR 343, CA.

[161] *Bristol and West BS v Ellis* (1996) 73 P & CR 158, CA; if the security is inadequate, possession will not be postponed: *Cheltenham and Gloucester plc v Krausz* [1997] 1 All ER 21, CA.

[162] *Cheltenham and Gloucester BS v Grattidge* (1993) 25 Housing LR 454, CA.

The foregoing has been concerned with the case of a legal mortgage. If the mortgagee holds **8.45** an equitable charge, it seems clear that there is no right to possession except in so far as it may arise by contract or court order;[163] this is because the right to possession arises from the holding of an estate in the land, and the chargee has no such estate, nor any right to one. It is generally said that the holder of an equitable mortgage (in the narrow sense which excludes a charge) also has no right to possession except by agreement or court order, but the point is arguable.[164]

(b) Sale

(i) Mortgagee's statutory power of sale

In the case of a mortgage made by deed, the mortgagee obtains a power of sale by operation **8.46** of law.[165] This will apply to all legal mortgages of unregistered land, and to any registered legal charge over registered land, since these mortgages must be created by deed.[166] It also applies to any equitable mortgage created by a deed.[167] The power arises 'when the mortgage money has become due'.[168] This refers to the principal, and was apparently drafted with reference to the traditional mortgage, which made the full principal legally due after six months. It is harder to apply to modern forms of mortgage, but they usually provide that for the purposes of this power, the mortgage money is due immediately or after six months, so ensuring that the power of sale has arisen.[169]

The power, having arisen, may not however be properly exercisable. It is properly exercisable **8.47** upon the occurrence of the first of three events:[170]

(1) the mortgagor's failure to pay the mortgage money on three months' notice in writing;[171]
(2) the mortgagor's falling at least two months in arrears on payments of interest;
(3) breach by the mortgagor of an obligation contained in the mortgage agreement or the LPA 1925.

If the power has arisen, but is not properly exercisable, then the purchaser of the land will **8.48** nonetheless take a good title; the mortgagor's remedy is against the mortgagee.[172] In the case of unregistered land, this is qualified in that a sale to a purchaser who has notice of some impropriety in the mortgagee's exercise of the power of sale can be impeached by the mortgagor.[173] In registered land, however, the purchaser always takes an unimpeachable title, unless perhaps he commits some independent wrong such as conspiracy or dishonest

---

[163] LPA 1925, s 90 empowers the court to make an order vesting a legal estate in any equitable mortgagee (including a chargee) 'to enable him to carry out the sale', as if the mortgage was a legal one; this would entitle the mortgagee to possession.

[164] HWR Wade, 'An Equitable Mortgagee's Right to Possession' (1955) 71 LQR 204.

[165] LPA 1925, s 101(1)(i). A sale by a mortgagee is deemed to be made pursuant to the statutory power unless express provision to the contrary is made: LPA 1925, s 104(3). Because of the safeguards which the statutory power provides for ensuring the effectiveness of the sale, it is usual to rely on it.

[166] 8.15.

[167] *Swift 1st Ltd v Colin* [2011] EWHC 2410, [2011] Ch 206. This includes an equitable charge made by a deed: C Harpum, S Bridge and M Dixon, *Megarry and Wade: The Law of Real Property* (8th edn, 2012) 1166.

[168] LPA 1925, s 101(1)(i).

[169] *West Bromwich BS v Wilkinson* [2005] UKHL 44, [2005] 1 WLR 2303, at [25].

[170] LPA 1925, s 103.

[171] LPA 1925, s 196(1) requires that the notice be in writing.

[172] LPA 1925, s 104(2).

[173] *Lord Waring v London & Manchester Assurance Co Ltd* [1935] Ch 310, 318; *Corbett v Halifax BS* [2002] EWCA Civ 1849, [2003] 1 WLR 964. Section 104(2) protects a 'purchaser' and by s 205(1)(xxi), this means a purchaser in good faith.

assistance in a breach of trust.[174] The power enables the mortgagee to sell the mortgaged property, even though the mortgagee does not (except in an equitable mortgage of an equitable interest) himself hold that property; the purchaser takes free of the interest of the mortgagor, and of any mortgagees subsequent to the one exercising the power of sale.[175] Assuming the power of sale has become exercisable, the mortgagor loses his ability to redeem upon the making of the contract.[176] After conveyance to the purchaser, the mortgagee is a trustee of the purchase money and is required to pay, in this order, the expenses of the sale; the principal, interest and costs due to himself; and then, if there is any surplus, the mortgagor or the next mortgagee if there is one.[177] If there is a deficiency, the mortgagee can normally proceed against the mortgagor as an unsecured creditor.[178] The mortgagor has no grounds for complaint if the first mortgagee pays itself less than it is owed and pays the balance to a subsequent mortgagee, even if the mortgagor takes the view that its position would have been better if the first mortgagee had paid itself all of what it was owed.[179]

8.49   If the mortgagor is not content that the property be sold, or wishes to sell the property himself, the wisest course is to dispute the matter when the mortgagee seeks possession; as discussed above, if the property includes a dwelling-house and the mortgagee seeks possession through legal proceedings, the court has a discretion to postpone the taking of possession.[180] In the case of mortgages given by individuals that are 'regulated agreements' under the CCA 1974, a court order is required for sale.[181] Otherwise, the power of sale can be exercised extrajudicially, and it is for the mortgagee to choose the time and the mode of sale, whether

---

[174] LRA 2002, s 52. A mortgagor who exercises a power of sale cannot generally be made liable in tort for causing the mortgagee to breach its contractual obligations: *Meretz Investments NV v ACP Ltd* [2007] EWCA Civ 1303, [2008] Ch 244.

[175] LRA 2002, s 104(1); *Horsham Properties Group Ltd v Clark* [2008] EWHC 2327 (Ch), [2009] 1 WLR 1255. Similarly, the mortgagee can sell free of the interest held by a purchaser who has contracted to buy the land from the mortgagor: *Duke v Robson* [1973] 1 WLR 267, CA. In the case of an equitable mortgage of a legal estate, it seems that this section empowers the mortgagee to convey the legal estate (*Re White Rose Cottage* [1965] Ch 940, 951, CA; *Swift 1st Ltd v Colin* [2011] EWHC 2410, [2011] Ch 206) although some commentators still take the view that the mortgage deed in such a case should contain provisions (such as an irrevocable power of attorney or a declaration of trust) to ensure that the mortgagee will be able to do so (C Harpum, S Bridge and M Dixon, *Megarry and Wade: The Law of Real Property* (8th edn, 2012) 1164–1165). In the case of legal mortgages, the estate held as security by the mortgagee himself is extinguished: LRA 2002, ss 88, 89.

[176] *Lord Waring v London & Manchester Assurance Co Ltd* [1935] Ch 310; *National Provincial BS v Ahmed* [1995] 2 EGLR 127, CA.

[177] LPA 1925, s 105. LRA 2002, s 54, provides that for the purposes of LPA 1925, s 105, the mortgagee of registered land is taken to have notice of anything in the register immediately prior to the sale. This bridges the gap between the registration system, which does not generally use the equitable idea of 'notice' of an interest, and the provisions of LPA 1925, s 105, which is drafted in terms of a trust and does not refer to any register. The idea is to create a requirement that a selling mortgagee search the register for other subsequent mortgages, and notices and restrictions, before transferring any surplus proceeds to the mortgagor.

[178] See 8.37.

[179] *Raja v Lloyds TSB Bank plc* [2001] 19 EG 143, leave to appeal this point denied [2001] EWCA Civ 210.

[180] See 8.42–8.44. However, as noted in n 142, the mortgagee is not bound to take possession before exercising the power of sale. An example is *Horsham Properties Group Ltd v Clark* [2008] EWHC 2327 (Ch), [2009] 1 WLR 1255, in which it was held that the possibility of sale without a prior order for possession is not inconsistent with art 1 of the First Protocol (Paris, 1952) to the Convention for the Protection of Human Rights and Fundamental Freedoms (Rome, 1950), implemented in English law by the Human Rights Act 1998, s 1. In *Duke v Robson* [1973] 1 WLR 267, CA, the mortgagee had obtained a possession order but had not sought to enforce it; the mortgagor contracted to sell the land to the claimant; the mortgagee then took possession. It was held that the claimant could not interfere with the mortgagee's power of sale.

[181] CCA 1974, s 126. As noted in 8.31, this provision applies even to mortgages that are otherwise regulated under FSMA 2000 rather than under CCA 1974. The current monetary limitation in the definition of 'regulated agreement' means that most mortgages are not regulated agreements; however, this monetary limitation was removed by amendments made in the CCA 2006, which are expected to come into force in 2008.

private or by public auction.[182] The mortgagee holds the power for his own benefit, and is not a trustee of the power.[183] This means that he has no duty to try to improve the value of the property, or to wait for the most propitious time to sell.[184] In carrying out the sale, however, the mortgagee has certain duties; these are owed to the mortgagor, to any subsequent mortgagees,[185] and anyone else with a financial interest in the equity of redemption;[186] and, to any guarantor of the mortgage debt.[187] Where the mortgagor is a trustee of the land, however, no duty is owed directly to the beneficiary of the trust, even if the mortgagee is aware of the trust; the remedies for improper exercise of the power of sale must be exercised by the trustee mortgagor.[188] The content of the duty may be expressed as follows:

> The mortgagee…must show that the sale was in good faith and that the mortgagee took reasonable precautions to obtain the best price reasonably obtainable at the time. The mortgagee is not however bound to postpone the sale in the hope of obtaining a better price or to adopt a piecemeal method of sale which could only be carried out over a substantial period at some risk of loss.[189]

If the mortgagee breaches the duty to act reasonably in selling, the loss caused is to be measured by the difference between the sale price actually obtained and the price which would have been obtained had the mortgagee acted reasonably.[190] A mortgagee who breaches this duty cannot reduce its liability to the mortgagor by arguing that if it had realized a higher price, the extra money would in any event have been paid to a subsequent mortgagee.[191] Except via a court-ordered sale, discussed below, it is not possible for the mortgagee to sell to itself, as that is not considered a sale; but there is no absolute bar to selling to a company in which the mortgagee is financially interested. In such a case, however, the sale will be closely examined.[192]

(ii) Court-ordered sale

In an action for foreclosure, redemption or sale, brought by any interested party, the court **8.50** has the power to order a sale on the application of the mortgagor or any mortgagee.[193] This means that even if the statutory power of sale does not arise, a sale may be ordered in an action brought by the mortgagee. In this way, the holder of an equitable mortgage which was not created by deed can effect a sale of the mortgaged property.[194] Similarly, a sale may be ordered where the statutory power fails to arise due to the defective drafting of a legal

---

[182] LPA 1925, s 101(1)(i).

[183] *Cuckmere Brick Co Ltd v Mutual Finance Ltd* [1971] Ch 949, 965, CA.

[184] *Silven Properties Ltd v Royal Bank of Scotland plc* [2003] EWCA Civ 1409, [2004] 1 WLR 997.

[185] *Downsview Nominees Ltd v Mutual Finance Corp Ltd* [1993] AC 295, PC.

[186] *Freeguard v Royal Bank of Scotland plc* [2002] EWHC 2509 (Ch).

[187] *Standard Chartered Bank Ltd v Walker* [1982] 1 WLR 1410, CA; *Barclays Bank plc v Kingston* [2006] EWHC 533, [2006] 1 All ER (Comm) 519. The latter case addressed the possibility of the contractual exclusion of liability for breach of this duty, and accepted that it was possible but held that it was not established on the wording of the particular guarantee.

[188] *Parker-Tweedale v Dunbar Bank plc* [1991] Ch 12, CA. The mortgagor's claim will be held for the benefit of the beneficiary, who may, on general principles, require him to exercise it.

[189] *Tse Kwong Lam v Wong Chit Sen* [1983] 1 WLR 1349, PC.

[190] *Skipton BS v Stott* [2001] QB 261, CA. The limitation period for a breach of the duty to act reasonably in selling is six years: *Raja v Lloyds TSB Bank plc* [2001] EWCA Civ 210.

[191] *Adamson v Halifax plc* [2002] EWCA Civ 1134, [2003] 1 WLR 60. However, if there is a serious prospect that the selling mortgagee may be sued by the subsequent mortgagee, the court may order that the money be paid into court against such a possibility.

[192] *Tse Kwong Lam v Wong Chit Sen* [1983] 1 WLR 1349, PC.

[193] LPA 1925, s 91(2).

[194] The court which orders the sale can make various orders to permit the legal estate (held by the mortgagor) to be transferred to the purchaser: LPA 1925, s 90(1).

mortgage.[195] Even if the statutory power has arisen, but the mortgagor is impeding its exercise by threatening proceedings against potential purchasers, the court may order a sale to ensure that the purchaser's title will be unimpeachable.[196] On the other hand, the mortgagor may apply for a court-ordered sale, even where the mortgagee wants to retain the property. In *Palk v Mortgage Services Funding plc*,[197] the mortgaged home was worth less than the mortgage debt. The mortgagee wanted to take possession of the mortgaged home and lease it, hoping the value of the home would improve. The court granted the mortgagors' request for an order for sale, because the income from the lease would not cover the interest as it accrued and the debt would increase. In *Cheltenham and Gloucester plc v Krausz*,[198] however, the Court of Appeal made it clear that where a mortgagor is resisting the mortgagee's attempt to gain possession on the ground that the mortgagor wishes to sell the property, the mortgagor should be allowed to retain possession only if it is clear that the sale proceeds will be sufficient to discharge the debt. The court can authorize the mortgagee itself to bid on the property; although this creates an obvious conflict of self-interest and duty, the sale is under the control of the court, which will not approve an inadequate price.[199]

8.51 Another situation in which court-ordered sale may be sought is where land is held on trust. In English law, any case of joint land ownership usually involves a trust of land.[200] Mortgagees usually wish to take a legal mortgage, and this requires the trustees of the trust to act together. It is possible, however, for a beneficiary, acting alone, to create a mortgage over his beneficial interest alone. This will necessarily be an equitable mortgage.[201] If the mortgagee seeks to enforce, the other beneficiary or beneficiaries are naturally potentially affected. The problem is similar to the case in which joint owners disagree as to whether to sell the land or not. The court has a discretion whether to order the trustees to comply with the wishes of the equitable mortgagee, but the mortgagee's rights will not be ignored.[202]

(c) Foreclosure

8.52 As long as the mortgagor has the legal right to redeem under the terms of the mortgage agreement, there is no possibility of foreclosure. Once the mortgagor has committed some default, so that he has no right of redemption under the express terms of the agreement, then his only right of redemption is equitable. At this point, it becomes possible for the mortgagee to apply to the court to foreclose this equitable right of redemption.[203] Foreclosure will terminate the

---

[195] *Twentieth Century Banking Corp Ltd v Wilkinson* [1977] Ch 99, leaving open whether the jurisdiction requires that the mortgagee have a right of foreclosure.

[196] *Arab Bank plc v Mercantile Holdings Ltd* [1994] Ch 71.

[197] [1993] Ch 330, CA.

[198] [1997] 1 All ER 21, CA.

[199] *Gordon Grant & Co Ltd v Boos* [1926] AC 781, 787, PC; *Palk v Mortgage Services Funding plc* [1993] Ch 330, 339–341, CA.

[200] EPL 4.394ff.

[201] The typical scenario is a couple who live in a jointly owned house. They are legal joint tenants of the fee simple estate, holding it on a trust of land for themselves as equitable joint tenants. The husband fraudulently purports to grant a legal mortgage over the fee simple estate. Acting alone, he is incapable of doing so. The effect is that he succeeds in giving an equitable mortgage over his beneficial share of the house: *First National Bank plc v Achampong* [2003] EWCA Civ 487.

[202] The governing legislation is Trusts of Land and Appointment of Trustees Act 1996, ss 14–15, which require the court to take account of the creditor's interests but also those of any children occupying the land. For discussion, see *Mortgage Corp v Shaire* [2001] Ch 743; *First National Bank plc v Achampong* [2003] EWCA Civ 487; *Edwards v Lloyds TSB Bank plc* [2004] EWHC 1745, [2004] Bankruptcy and Personal Insolvency Rep 1190, [2005] 1 Family Court Rep 139, in which the court made an order for sale but postponed its effect until the children reached the age of 18.

[203] *Twentieth Century Banking Corp Ltd v Wilkinson* [1977] Ch 99. The concept of redemption has never applied to the case of an equitable charge, and so likewise there is no possibility of foreclosure: *Tennant v Trenchard* (1869) 4 Ch App 537, 542, HL.

mortgage relationship and the equity of redemption, and leave the mortgagee holding beneficially the interest which the mortgagor used to hold in the land.[204] For foreclosure to be
effective, the interest of any mortgagee subsequent to the foreclosing mortgagee must also be
extinguished; any such party must therefore be made a party to the proceeding, and be given
the opportunity to redeem the mortgagor's interest.[205]

It has never been possible to foreclose extrajudicially.[206] For the same reasons that the Court **8.53**
of Chancery controlled the terms of the mortgage agreement, it also controlled the process of
foreclosure. The concern was that the mortgagee should not be unjustly enriched by acquiring the benefit of an estate which he was only intended to hold as security. The process
therefore proceeds in stages, with the initial 'order nisi' giving the mortgagor six months to
pay the debt and redeem the mortgage. Only on the failure of the mortgagor to raise the
required funds will the court make the 'order absolute'. Even after that, the mortgagor can
apply to open the foreclosure and recover his estate by paying the debt; rarely, this can occur
even where the mortgagee has sold the estate to a third party.[207] Furthermore, at the application of the mortgagor or another interested party, the court may order a sale of the property
instead.[208] A mortgagee who forecloses is not under any duty to the mortgagor regarding
the subsequent sale of the land. Conversely, following such a sale the mortgagee is unable to
sue the mortgagor for any sum still owing on the personal obligation which the mortgage
secured, since he has put it beyond his power to allow the mortgagor to redeem.[209] For all of
these reasons, foreclosure is rarely used today.[210]

(d) Appointment of a receiver

The mortgagee, whether in or out of possession, may appoint a receiver to take control of the **8.54**
mortgaged property and receive the income therefrom.[211] In the case of a mortgage by deed,

---

[204] If a mortgage was created by the conveyance of the mortgagor's estate to the mortgagee, foreclosure
simply cuts off the mortgagor's ability to get back the estate he conveyed. (After 1925, in relation to land, this
is only possible if the mortgagor's interest is equitable.) If a mortgage was created by demise, or by sub-demise,
or by statutory legal charge, the decree of foreclosure effects a transfer to the mortgagee of the mortgagor's
estate: LPA 1925, ss 88(2), 89(2). If there is an equitable mortgage of a legal estate, the foreclosure order
will direct the conveyance of the legal estate: *Marshall v Shrewsbury* (1875) 10 Ch App 250, 254, DC. If the
land is registered then consequent amendments to the register are required: LRA 2002, s 65 and Sch 4; Land
Registration Rules 2003, SI 2003/1417, r 112.

[205] In other words, where there are multiple mortgages the principle governing foreclosure is 'foreclose
down': not only the mortgagor but all subsequent mortgagees must be foreclosed. Conversely, in redemption
the maxim is 'redeem up, foreclose down': if an intermediate mortgagee wishes to preserve its interest against
a foreclosure attempt by a superior mortgagee, it must redeem that mortgage (and any others superior to its
own), while foreclosing the mortgagor and any inferior mortgagee. See C Harpum, S Bridge, and M Dixon,
Megarry and Wade: The Law of Real Property (8th edn, 2012) 1191–1192.

[206] *Re Farnol Eades Irvine & Co Ltd* [1915] 1 Ch 22, 24.

[207] *Campbell v Holyland* (1877) 7 Ch D 166, 172, *per* Jessel MR: 'it is impossible to say a priori what are
the terms' on which a foreclosure might be reopened by the court.

[208] LPA 1925, s 91(2). In foreclosure proceedings this order will only be made if the mortgagee's interests
can be protected: *Woolley v Colman* (1882) 21 Ch D 169; *Merchant Banking Co of London v London and
Hanseatic Bank* (1886) 55 LJ Ch 479.

[209] *Kinnaird v Trollope* (1888) 39 Ch D 636, 642. On the same principle, if the mortgagee has foreclosed
but still holds the property, he cannot sue on the personal obligation unless he opens the foreclosure and offers
to allow redemption: *Gordon Grant & Co Ltd v Boos* [1926] AC 781, 785, PC.

[210] In *Palk v Mortgage Services Funding plc* [1993] Ch 330, 336, CA, Nicholls V-C said, 'So far as I am
aware, foreclosure actions are almost unheard of today and have been so for many years.'

[211] If the mortgage is a floating charge over all or substantially all of the assets of the mortgagor, the
appointment of a receiver has such serious implications for other creditors that it is regulated by the
Insolvency Act 1986: see 9.18–9.20. The receiver will usually be characterized as an 'administrator' under
that Act.

such a power arises and is exercisable on the same conditions as the statutory power of sale.[212] The receiver is deemed to act as the agent of the mortgagor;[213] this means that if he commits a tort, it is the mortgagor and not the mortgagee who is vicariously liable. This generally makes the appointment of a receiver a more attractive option than taking possession in cases where the mortgagee does not intend to sell. The fact that the receiver is the agent of the mortgagor does not, however, mean that he acts primarily in the interests of the mortgagor.[214] On the contrary, his primary duty is to the mortgagee, to bring about the payment of the debt; at the same time, the receiver owes certain duties to the mortgagor, and to anyone else with an interest in the equity of redemption.[215] His general duty is to act in good faith; this duty will not be breached in the absence of dishonesty or improper motive.[216] Unlike a mortgagee, a receiver, once appointed, cannot be totally passive if that course would be damaging to the interests of the mortgagor or mortgagee.[217] If the mortgaged property includes a business, the receiver may choose to manage it, but he is not required to do so; if he does, he must act with due diligence, which requires the taking of reasonable steps.[218] If he chooses to sell any part of the mortgaged property, he is subject to the same duties as a mortgagee exercising the power of sale.[219] A receiver appointed under the statutory power is bound to apply money he receives in the order set out by the statute: taxes; payments having priority to the mortgage; his own fee, and insurance; interest on the mortgage debt; and, if directed, principal of the mortgage debt. Any surplus goes to the mortgagor.[220] In the case of an equitable mortgage (including a charge) not created by deed, there is no statutory power, but a receiver may be appointed under the terms of the agreement, or by the court.[221]

(5) Miscellaneous Features

8.55 In this section a number of other features of the mortgage relationship are mentioned, although they are not discussed in detail.

(a) Leases

8.56 Subject to the terms of the mortgage agreement, whichever of the mortgagor or the mortgagee is in possession of the mortgaged land is given a statutory power to grant certain leases.[222] The power is constrained in certain ways, in particular as to the length of the lease.[223] A mortgagor in possession may make an unauthorized lease, being either inconsistent with the statutory power, or inconsistent with the terms of the mortgage agreement.[224] It has been

---

[212] LPA 1925, s 101(1)(iii) (power arises); s 109(1) (power exercisable). For the details see 8.46–8.47. By s 109(4), one who pays a receiver need not be concerned whether the power to appoint him was exercisable.

[213] LPA 1925, s 109(2).

[214] *Silven Properties Ltd v Royal Bank of Scotland plc* [2003] EWCA Civ 1409, [2004] 1 WLR 997.

[215] *Medforth v Blake* [2000] Ch 86, 102, CA.

[216] *Medforth v Blake* [2000] Ch 86, 102, CA.

[217] *Silven Properties Ltd v Royal Bank of Scotland plc* [2003] EWCA Civ 1409, [2004] 1 WLR 997.

[218] *Medforth v Blake* [2000] Ch 86, 102, CA.

[219] *Downsview Nominees Ltd v Mutual Finance Corp Ltd* [1993] AC 295, PC; 5.49. This means that like a selling mortgagee, the receiver has no duty to try to improve the value of the property, or to wait for the most propitious time to sell: *Silven Properties Ltd v Royal Bank of Scotland plc* [2003] EWCA Civ 1409, [2004] 1 WLR 997.

[220] LPA 1925, s 109(8).

[221] Supreme Court Act 1981, s 37.

[222] LPA 1925, s 99. By s 100, there is also a power to accept the surrender of a lease in order to grant a new lease. If the mortgagor's power to grant a lease is not excluded by a mortgage agreement, the exercise of the power is usually made conditional on the consent of the mortgagee.

[223] Agricultural or occupation leases may be for up to 50 years; building leases (in which, by LPA 1925, s 99(9), the lessee builds or improves buildings on the land) for up to 999 years.

[224] In particular the agreement is likely to require the written consent of the mortgagee to the granting of a lease by the mortgagor.

held that in such a case, the lease is not enforceable against the mortgagee.[225] He may treat the lessee as a trespasser or accept him as his own tenant; such acceptance may be inferred from conduct.[226]

(b) Other profits

Subject to the terms of the mortgage agreement, a mortgagee in possession under a mortgage created by deed has a statutory power to cut and sell timber, within certain limits.[227] **8.57**

(c) Insurance

If the mortgage was created by deed, then the mortgagee has a statutory power to insure the property against fire, the costs being chargeable to the mortgagor with the same priority as the sums due under the mortgage agreement.[228] The power is subject to the terms of the mortgage agreement and to a limit as to amount, and does not arise if the mortgagor has insured the property with the consent of the mortgagee.[229] **8.58**

(d) Possession of title deeds

In the classic legal mortgage by conveyance, the mortgagee would hold the title deeds to the mortgagor's estate in the land, having taken a conveyance of that estate. This provided an invaluable safeguard against any unauthorized further dealings by the mortgagor. A mortgage by demise or sub-demise did not, however, give any right at common law to possession of the title deeds, since the estate held by the mortgagee was not the same as that held by the mortgagor; and all legal mortgages are now mortgages by demise or sub-demise, or are treated as such.[230] It is therefore provided by statute that the first legal mortgagee shall have the same right to possession of the title deeds as if his mortgage had been by conveyance of the mortgagor's estate.[231] Upon discharge of the mortgage they must be returned to the mortgagor, or any subsequent mortgagee of which the mortgagee is aware.[232] If an equitable mortgage is protected by deposit of the title deeds, the mortgagee has the right to retain those deeds until the debt is paid. **8.59**

In registered land, however, the idea of title deeds has become obsolete. The LRA 2002 abolishes the 'land certificate' that used to be issued to the holder of a registered title and the 'charge certificate' that used to be issued to the holder of a registered legal charge.[233] The Land Registry will issue 'title information documents', showing the content of the register at a given time. These, however, are not documents of title; they are not needed in order to effect subsequent registered dealings with the land. These changes pave the way **8.60**

---

[225] *Britannia BS v Earl* [1990] 1 WLR 422, CA. Exceptionally in the case of agricultural land, by LPA 1925, s 99(13A), an unauthorized lease is enforceable against the mortgagee, if the lease was granted after 1 March 1948 but before 1 September 1995, and if the other requirements of the LPA 1925, s 99 are satisfied. Of course, if the mortgage is not registered, it may be subordinate to the interest of the lessee. This is effectively a priority contest. For an example decided under the prior land registration statute, see *Barclays Bank plc v Zaroovabli* [1997] Ch 321.

[226] *Chatsworth Properties Ltd v Effiom* [1971] 1 WLR 144, CA; *Nijar v Mann* (CA, 18 December 1998).

[227] LPA 1925, s 101(1)(iv).

[228] LPA 1925, s 101(1)(ii).

[229] LPA 1925, s 108.

[230] See 8.08.

[231] LPA 1925, ss 85(1), 86(1). The mortgagor has the right to inspect and make copies of the title deeds: LPA 1925, s 96(1). However, a first legal mortgage of unregistered land with the deposit of title deeds will now trigger compulsory registration of the land: LRA 2002, s 4(1)(g), (8).

[232] Although registration of a subsequent mortgage of unregistered land is treated as giving notice of it to all parties (LPA 1925, s 198(1)), this rule is overridden in this context (LPA 1925, s 96(2)).

[233] Land Registration Act 2002 (Transitional Provisions) Order 2003, SI 2003/1953, art 24.

for electronic conveyancing, and they make obsolete the mortgagee's right to possession of title deeds.

(e) Consolidation

8.61 Consolidation is an old doctrine by which a mortgagee who holds more than one mortgage, granted by the same mortgagor but on different properties in respect of more than one loan, may resist the redemption of one mortgage until the other debt or debts are also paid. The mortgagee is allowed to consolidate the separate transactions and treat them as one. The matter is complex (and arguably unfair) because the right may be asserted even against a transferee from the original mortgagor, who has no knowledge of the other transaction or transactions. It is only necessary that the right to consolidate be reserved in at least one of the mortgage agreements.[234] Details of the doctrine may be found in specialized texts.[235]

(6) Discharge

8.62 When a mortgage of unregistered land is to be discharged, it is not generally necessary for the mortgagee to reconvey the interest he holds, or in the case of a mortgage by demise or sub-demise, to surrender the leasehold interest he holds. If he signs a receipt on or annexed to the document by which the mortgage was created, then such a reconveyance or surrender will occur by operation of law.[236] It is, however, still possible to discharge the mortgage by a reconveyance or surrender,[237] and this will be necessary if the mortgage is being discharged as to only part of the mortgaged property.

8.63 In the context of registered land, these provisions also apply to equitable mortgages, which are not registered. They do not, however, apply to registered charges on registered land.[238] In that context, the registrar must amend the register to show the discharge of a registered charge upon the request of the charge holder, or upon proof of the satisfaction of the charge.[239]

C. Real Security Over Moveables

8.64 This section, 'Real Security Over Moveables', will examine in turn each of the different kinds of security over moveable property, describing for each one the rules for creation, registration and enforcement. Broadly speaking, the principles discussed in the previous section apply here as well. This is true for principles developed from the case law, such as the prohibition on clogging the equity of redemption, or the principles on unconscionable bargains. As for statutory provisions, consumer protection statutes are generally applicable in both contexts.[240] The

---

[234] LPA 1925, s 93. In registered land, a right to consolidate can be noted on the register pursuant to LRA 2002, s 57; Land Registration Rules 2003, SI 2003/1417, r 110.

[235] eg C Harpum, S Bridge, and M Dixon, *Megarry and Wade: The Law of Real Property* (8th edn, 2012) 1169–1174; EH Burn and J Cartwright, *Cheshire and Burn's Modern Law of Real Property* (18th edn, 2011) 867–870.

[236] LPA 1925, s 115(1). The receipt must state the name of the person who paid the money, and if it is not the person entitled to the equity of redemption, then the receipt generally operates instead as a transfer of the mortgage to the payor: LPA 1925, s 115(2). This provision however does not operate in the case of a mortgage held by a building society: see Building Societies Act 1986, Sch 2A, para 1(2).

[237] LPA 1925, s 115(4).

[238] LPA 1925, s 115(10).

[239] LRA 2002, s 65 and Sch 4.

[240] This includes many of the statutory protections discussed in 8.31–8.36. The FMSA 2000 will not usually apply to transactions involving security over moveables, but the CCA 1974 may well do (but CCA 1974, s 126 applies only to security over land).

statutory protections for residential mortgagors are, however, confined to land mortgages.[241] The statutory powers that are granted by the LPA 1925, where the mortgage is granted by deed and the deed does not otherwise provide, can also apply to security over moveables.[242] In security over moveable property, however, there are many differences related to the formalities for creation and for registration. There is also a difference in terminology between this section and the previous one. In the section on security over land, 'mortgage' was used to include any security interest in land. In this section, it is more important to distinguish between a transfer of title for security and other means of creating a security interest, and so here 'mortgage' is used in the narrower sense of a transfer of title by way of security. Other security interests (such as the charge or the pledge) are always referred to by their precise names. This follows common legal usage in relation to moveables.

(1) Legal Security

Unlike the position in relation to land, the common law (as distinct from equity) did recognize certain interests in moveables which were, by their nature, security interests: the pledge and the lien. These security interests depend upon possession by the creditor, which limits their commercial utility. As in the law of land mortgages, there is also a long tradition of using legal ownership as a security interest, especially since this makes it possible to leave the debtor in possession.

8.65

(a) Pledge

Pledge is a transaction in which the debtor (pledgor) transfers possession of a thing to the creditor (pledgee) to hold as security.[243] The focus on possession limits the transaction to tangible assets.[244] In general, no formalities are required beyond the transfer of possession.[245] Upon constitution of the pledge, the pledgee acquires a real right in the pledged thing; the pledgor retains ownership,[246] but does not have a right to possession until the debt secured is paid.[247] The pledgee's interest may be transferred or sub-pledged.[248] It carries with it a power of sale which arises by operation of law upon default by the

8.66

---

[241] This includes the criminal law protections against eviction (8.40) and the judicial discretion to postpone the taking of possession by a mortgagee (8.41–8.43), and CCA 1974, s 126, which forbids any extrajudicial enforcement of a land mortgage within its scope (on which see 8.31).

[242] These include the power of sale, the power to appoint a receiver, and the power to insure (8.46–8.49, 8.54, 8.58). Regardless of whether there is a deed, the court's power to order sale (8.50) is triggered by any mortgage litigation.

[243] Further discussion in 7.67–7.77. Where the pledgor is an individual the transaction is often called 'pawn' and the pledgee who enters into such transactions in the course of his business is called a 'pawnbroker'. Like anyone whose business involves lending money to consumers, a pawnbroker is required to be licensed under the CCA 1974; failing this, he commits an offence and the transaction is likely to be unenforceable against the debtor: ss 39–40.

[244] This can include documentary intangibles (on which see 8.75), including securities in bearer form (*Carter v Wake* (1877) 4 Ch D 605); but securities in registered form are considered entirely intangible. A security interest in registered securities can only be taken by way of mortgage or charge: *Harrold v Plenty* [1901] 2 Ch 314; *Stubbs v Slater* [1910] 1 Ch 632, CA.

[245] Again the situation is different in the case of a pawnbroker. He commits an offence if he fails to provide the pledgor with prescribed documentation (CCA 1974, s 115) and the agreement may be unenforceable.

[246] *The Odessa* [1916] 1 AC 145, 158–9, PC. The pledgor may transfer his ownership to another, who will have the same rights against the pledgee as the original pledgor did: *Franklin v Neate* (1844) 13 M & W 481, 153 ER 200.

[247] *Donald v Suckling* (1866) LR 1 QB 585; *Halliday v Holgate* (1868) LR 3 Ex 299, Exch Ch.

[248] Although such a disposition may be a breach of the contract with the pledgor: *Donald v Suckling* (1866) LR 1 QB 585. In the case of a sub-pledge the pledgor will be entitled to recover the goods from the sub-pledgee on tendering the amount due from the pledgor to the original pledgee: *Donald v Suckling*.

pledgor;[249] it may, however, amount to a breach of contract for the pledgee to sell the goods without first giving notice to the pledgor.[250] What counts as a default is a matter of agreement between the parties.[251] Subject to agreement, the pledgor may redeem the pledge by paying the full debt with interest, at any time before sale has occurred. The pledgee need not sell the goods but can sue the pledgor on the debt; and if, after sale, there is a deficiency, the pledgee can sue for this.[252] If there is a surplus, it is held on trust for the pledgor; it must be repaid with interest, and if it has been used in business the pledgee will have to account to the pledgor for profits earned.[253]

8.67 In order to create the pledge, possession of the goods must be transferred to the pledgee.[254] If the goods are held by a third party, the transfer may be by attornment of that party.[255] A formal attornment is not needed if the goods are represented by a document of title. Transfer of possession of a bill of lading, with any necessary endorsement, has always been treated (where the parties so intended it) as equivalent to an attornment to the transferee by the issuer of the bill.[256] Goods may therefore be pledged by the transfer to the pledgee of the bill of lading.[257] At least in the case of a pledgor who is a mercantile agent of the owner, this possibility has been extended by statute to a range of other documents, the transfer of which, at common law, was not apt to transfer a right to possession without an actual attornment from the third party.[258]

8.68 Possession by the pledgor himself might be thought to be inconsistent with the nature of the transaction. The transfer of possession to the pledgee serves the purpose of removing the asset from the apparent ownership of the pledgor, thereby reducing the potential for problems relating to the deception of third parties. Nonetheless, it has been suggested that a pledge

---

[249] In the case of pawnbrokers, the CCA 1974, s 120 provides that in the case of debts under £75, a power of sale does not arise but rather the ownership of the pledged goods passes to the pawnee.

[250] *Halliday v Holgate* (1868) LR 3 Ex 299, Exch Ch. In the case of pawnbrokers, the period and form of notice are governed by the statute: CCA 1974, s 121.

[251] If the agreement did not stipulate a date for repayment, the pledgee may demand payment upon reasonable notice: *Ex p Hubbard* (1886) 17 QBD 690, 698, CA; *Deverges v Sandeman, Clark & Co* [1902] 1 Ch 579, 589, CA. In the case of pawnbrokers the pawnor must be given at least six months in which to redeem the pawn: CCA 1974, s 116.

[252] *Jones v Marshall* (1889) 24 QBD 269, DC.

[253] *Mathew v TM Sutton Ltd* [1994] 4 All ER 793.

[254] There is a general equitable principle that if value has been given for a promise to create or transfer a legal interest, a corresponding equitable interest arises immediately: see 8.13. This principle does not apply to a promise to give a pledge, and so such a promise creates no real rights in the creditor: 'there was no such thing as equitable possession': RM Goode and E McKendrick, *Goode on Commercial Law* (4th edn, 2009) 669.

[255] See 7.78–7.81. An attornment is a bailee's acknowledgement to a third party, made with the bailor's authority, that the bailee now holds for the third party. It is an exception to the basic principle that possession cannot pass by intention and words alone.

[256] Goode and McKendrick, (n 254) 980–982.

[257] *Meyerstein v Barber* (1870) LR 4 HL 317. Even if the bill of lading is endorsed to the pledgee, he does not thereby become the owner of the goods, but only has the limited interest of a pledgee: *Sewell v Burdick* (1884) 10 App Cas 363, HL.

[258] The Factors Act 1889, s 2(4), defines 'document of title' to include 'any bill of lading, dock warrant, warehouse-keeper's certificate, and warrant or order for the delivery of goods, and any other document used in the ordinary course of business as proof of the possession or control of goods, or authorizing or purporting to authorize, either by endorsement or by delivery, the possessor of the document to transfer or receive goods thereby represented'; and s 3 provides, 'A pledge of the documents of title to goods shall be deemed to be a pledge of the goods'. In *Inglis v Robertson* [1898] AC 616, HL, it was held under the Scots statute (whose wording was identical) that s 3 only applied to transactions made by a mercantile agent. *Inglis* was apparently approved in *Official Assignee of Madras v Mercantile Bank of India Ltd* [1935] AC 53, 60, PC, although Lord Wright observed that it was 'curious and anomalous' that a mercantile agent should be able to make an effective pledge using one of these documents in the absence of any attornment, while the owner of the goods could not.

can be created by the pledgor himself attorning to the pledgee, making himself the pledgee's bailee.[259] In any event, once a pledge has been created, it has been held that it is not destroyed by a retransfer of possession to the pledgor, so long as this is done for a limited purpose only.[260] In modern commercial practice it is often necessary for financial institutions, which are pledgees of bills of lading, to release them to the pledgor for the purpose of selling the goods; the debt is paid out of the proceeds of the sale. This is usually done under the terms of a 'trust receipt', by which the pledgor takes possession as trustee for the benefit of the pledgee; because the transfer of possession is for a limited purpose, the pledge is not destroyed.[261]

(b) Lien

A common law lien is a right to retain possession of a tangible moveable until a debt is paid.[262] Like the pledge, it is a possessory security, but there are several important differences. The lien may arise by agreement, but unlike the pledge it may also arise by operation of law. Another difference is that 'in the case of a pledge the owner delivers possession to the creditor as security, whereas in the case of a lien the creditor retains possession of goods previously delivered to him for some other purpose'.[263] The lien does not give rise to any power of sale but only permits retention.[264] Finally, the interest of the holder of a lien is not transferable; the lien is lost when possession is lost. **8.69**

Many liens arise by operation of law, or from recognized usage. A 'common carrier' is one who advertises his services to the public, and as a result is obliged by law to accept goods for carriage; as a kind of recompense, such a carrier has a lien on his customers' goods for carriage charges when they become due. A sea carrier also has a lien on cargo for carriage charges, and on passengers' luggage for their fares. The innkeeper, who also follows a common calling, has a lien on the belongings of guests to secure payment for their food and lodging.[265] The common law also grants a lien to anyone to whom goods are entrusted in order that he can employ his work or skill on them, so long as they are thereby improved.[266] Under maritime law, liens may arise against a ship in respect of work done, or for damage **8.70**

---

[259] *Dublin City Distillery Co Ltd v Doherty* [1914] AC 823, HL; although, if the attornment is effected via a document, it may well be registrable as a bill of sale. See 8.76.

[260] *Reeves v Capper* (1838) 5 Bing NC 136, 132 ER 1057; *Mercantile Bank of India Ltd v Central Bank of India Ltd* [1938] AC 287, PC. This is true even though (as in both of these cases) this situation permits the pledgor to mislead others, by whom the pledgee's legal security interest is undetectable.

[261] *North Western Bank Ltd v John Poynter, Son & Macdonalds* [1895] AC 56, 68; *Re David Allester Ltd* [1922] 1 Ch 211, 216. Because it is said that the pledge continues, the security is not registrable as a bill of sale or charge. Although this will protect the pledgee on the pledgor's insolvency, it may not protect him against a subsequent pledge of the same document of title; the subsequent pledgee may be able to rely on the Factors Act 1889, s 2 (on which see 2.25): *Lloyds Bank Ltd v Bank of America National Trust and Savings Association* [1938] 2 KB 147, CA.

[262] Excluded from consideration here is the *equitable* lien, a non-possessory security interest in the nature of a charge, the best known example of which is held by the unpaid seller of land: 8.92.

[263] *Re Cosslett (Contractors) Ltd* [1998] Ch 495, 508, CA.

[264] Note however that in common with anyone who is in possession of another's goods, the holder of a lien may be able to sell uncollected goods under the terms of the Torts (Interference with Goods) Act 1977, ss 12–13. An innkeeper may be authorized to sell goods under the Innkeepers Act 1878, s 1, and an unpaid seller of goods is given the right to resell them by the Sale of Goods Act 1979, s 48.

[265] There is a power of sale under the Innkeepers Act 1878, s 1. By the Hotel Proprietors Act 1956, s 2(2), the lien does not extend (as it did at common law) to the guest's vehicle, nor to any live animal.

[266] *Tappenden v Artus* [1964] 2 QB 185, CA. Because of the requirement of improvement, there is no lien for the maintenance of an animal: *Re Southern Livestock Producers Ltd* [1964] 1 WLR 24. However, a lien will arise in relation to work in the nature of research that gives to an object an increased market value, even though the object itself is unchanged: *Spencer v S Franses Ltd* [2011] EWHC 1269. The judgment also states (at [264]–[267]) the general principle that a lien holder must provide the debtor with the amount of the claim, or the means to calculate it.

done by it; and against a ship or goods, in respect of salvage; but the principles apply only in tidal waters.[267]

8.71 All of these may be classified as 'particular' liens, which allow the goods to be retained only against payment of obligations which are referable to goods in question. Other liens are 'general', meaning that they allow the goods to be retained until all obligations are discharged. In litigation raising the issue whether accountants have a lien over their clients' papers, Lawton LJ summarized the position for many professionals:

> The kind of work [accountants] do may be very different from that of a craftsman who is making or repairing a chattel (the kind of work which gave rise to the common law concept of particular liens); but since the beginning of the 19th century arbitrators, architects, conveyancers and parliamentary agents have been adjudged capable of having particular liens…Solicitors, bankers, factors, stockbrokers and insurance brokers have long enjoyed the right to general liens.[268]

8.72 Liens also arise by statute. The seller of goods has a lien over them until he is paid.[269] An airport has a lien over an aircraft for airport charges and fuel supplied.[270] A garage which, acting as the agent of the police, recovers an abandoned car has a lien over it until it has been paid for its services.[271]

8.73 Finally, a lien may be created by agreement, or an agreement can modify the lien which would otherwise arise. Carriers commonly stipulate for a general lien,[272] as do warehousemen.[273] Such a lien will not amount to a mortgage or charge (which would require registration for effectiveness in insolvency), even if it is coupled with a power of sale.[274]

(c) Legal ownership as security

(i) Mortgage

8.74 **General.** As with land, one way to secure a debt is to transfer ownership of moveables to the creditor, with an agreement for retransfer upon payment.[275] Equity will intervene, as in the case of land, to elevate the mortgagor's contractual rights to a proprietary interest or 'equity of redemption'. The advantage of this transaction over a pledge is that the debtor can remain in possession of the asset. However, the common law developed differently in relation to moveables. Since there are generally no documents of title for tangible moveables, a transfer of ownership, with the transferor remaining in possession, creates an appearance of unfettered ownership in the transferor which potentially misleads his other

---

[267] *The Goring* [1988] 1 AC 831, HL.

[268] *Woodworth v Conroy* [1976] QB 884, 890, CA. It was held that accountants have at least a particular lien, the question whether they have a general one being left open.

[269] Sale of Goods Act 1979, ss 41–43, with a power of sale in s 48.

[270] Civil Aviation Act 1982, s 88, as interpreted in *Bristol Airport plc v Powdrill* [1990] Ch 744, CA.

[271] Road Traffic Regulation Act 1984, s 101, as interpreted in *Service Motor Policies at Lloyds v City Recovery Ltd* [1997] EWCA Civ 2073; *Surrey Breakdown Ltd v Knight* [1999] RTR 84, CA.

[272] *George Barker (Transport) Ltd v Eynon* [1974] 1 WLR 462, CA.

[273] *Chellaram & Sons (London) Ltd v Butlers Warehousing and Distribution Ltd* [1978] 2 Lloyd's Rep 412, CA.

[274] *Great Eastern Rly Co v Lord's Trustee* [1909] AC 109, HL; *Trident International Ltd v Barlow* [1999] 2 BCLC 506, CA. But a contractual right to *take* possession of the debtor's goods to answer to a debt will be characterized as a charge: *Re Cosslett (Contractors) Ltd* [1998] Ch 495, 508–509; *Online Catering Ltd v Acton* [2010] EWCA Civ 58, [2011] QB 204.

[275] As discussed earlier (8.06), a legal mortgage of land could be created granting a legal leasehold estate in the land, and the modern 'charge by way of legal mortgage' over land is defined by reference to this transaction (8.08–8.09). A legal mortgage of moveables is always created by the transfer of ownership, since the doctrine of estates is said not to apply to moveables.

creditors; and such a transaction was almost invariably viewed as a fraud on those creditors, and so void.[276] This left the transferee with no real rights and so no security. For tangible moveables, the mortgage could only succeed if possession were transferred to the mortgagee. The 'chattel mortgage' was therefore not viable in its non-possessory form until the creation of a public registration system for documents by which such mortgages were created.[277] This legislation, the Bills of Sale Acts 1878 and 1882, continues to impose restrictions which limit the commercial utility of the transaction.[278] It does not, however, apply to companies or limited liability partnerships.[279] They are subject to a different registration system which allows them to use the chattel mortgage more flexibly.[280]

Intangibles need to be considered in two categories. A 'documentary intangible' is a right **8.75** represented by a document which is apt to transfer the right by delivery, possibly with indorsement.[281] The common law treats it as a tangible, and so it is the proper subject matter of a pledge. It may, however, also be mortgaged. A 'pure intangible' is a right which is not represented by such a document. These could not be assigned at common law, although an attempted assignment would take effect in equity.[282] By statute it is now possible to make a legal assignment of a pure intangible, and in this way a legal mortgage of such an intangible is possible.[283] Some pure intangibles are assigned according to particular statutory rules.[284]

---

[276] Under the Statute of Fraudulent Conveyances 1571, now repealed. The situation was different where there was a register of ownership, as in the case of ships.

[277] Initially the Bills of Sale Act 1854; now, the Bills of Sale Act 1878 and the Bills of Sale Act (1878) Amendment Act 1882, together cited as the Bills of Sale Acts 1878 and 1882. It is a peculiar feature of English law, explicable historically, that the term 'bill of sale' primarily refers not to a document evidencing a sale of goods but rather to one creating a chattel mortgage: see AP Bell, *Modern Law of Personal Property in England and Ireland* (1989) 189.

[278] In particular, the Acts make it impossible to create a transaction which will give the mortgagee even an equitable mortgage in property acquired after the transaction.

[279] Bills of Sale Act (1878) Amendment Act 1882, s 17; *Re Standard Manufacturing Co* [1891] 1 Ch 627, CA; *Online Catering Ltd v Acton* [2010] EWCA Civ 58, [2011] QB 204. In *NV Slavenburg's Bank v Intercontinental Natural Resources Ltd* [1980] 1 WLR 1076, Lloyd J held that the Bills of Sale Acts do not apply to any corporation. That case concerned a foreign company charging property in England; this situation has been more clearly addressed under CA 2006 but is not discussed here. Lloyd J did not refer to *Re North Wales Produce and Supply Society* [1922] 2 Ch 340 in which it was held that a Welsh industrial and provident society (a co-operative), which is a corporation not formed under the Companies Acts, was subject to the Bills of Sale Acts. It is now provided that if such societies do register charges that they give, the Bills of Sale Acts do not apply: Agricultural Credits Act 1928, s 14 (in the case of a charge over farming stock); Industrial and Provident Societies Act 1967, s 1 (in the case of other charges). These registrations, however, appear to be optional, and the Bills of Sale Acts will otherwise apply to charges given by such societies.

[280] 8.77.

[281] RM Goode and E McKendrick, *Goode on Commercial Law* (4th edn, 2009) 52–53.

[282] The common law did recognize the assignment of debts due to and from the Crown.

[283] LPA 1925, s 136(1). The provision applies only to 'an absolute assignment... (not purporting to be by way of charge only)' but it has been held that this does not exclude an assignment by way of mortgage: *Tancred v Delagoa Bay and East Africa Rly Co* (1889) 23 QBD 239, approved in *Durham Brothers v Robertson* [1898] 1 QB 765, 772, CA. It may be difficult to distinguish a mortgage of an intangible from a sale: see 8.98–8.101.

[284] Shares in a company are transferred by amendment of the company's shareholder register (which may or may not require a written form of transfer: CA 2006, s 544; Stock Transfer Act 1963, s 1; Stock Transfer Act 1982; Uncertificated Securities Regulations 2001, SI 2001/3755, as amended). Life assurance policies are assigned under the Policies of Assurance Act 1867; copyright and related rights, under the Copyright, Designs and Patents Act 1988, ss 90, 191B, 222; patents, under the Patents Act 1977, ss 30–33; registered trade marks, under the Trade Marks Act 1994, ss 24–25; registered designs, under the Registered Designs Act 1949, s 19.

8.76 **Creation.** The creation of a mortgage involves the making of an agreement and the convey-ance of ownership of the mortgaged moveables. In the case of a mortgage of tangible move-ables by an individual or a partnership, the Bills of Sale Acts 1878 and 1882 will generally apply.[285] The document evidencing the agreement will be absolutely void (even against the borrower) unless it is in the form required by the Acts.[286] It must be in writing in the pre-scribed form, attested by at least one witness.[287] The document must also be registered under the Acts within seven days of execution; if this is not done, the security is unenforceable, even against the borrower, although the loan agreement is not affected.[288] The bill must list all of the property covered by it; this means that it is impossible to create a security which will extend to property acquired later.[289] These Acts do not apply to a mortgage of intangibles, which can be created without formality, except in so far as the conveyance of the intangible requires it.[290]

8.77 In the case of a company or a limited liability partnership, there is no prescribed form for the document creating the mortgage. Unlike the situation under the Bills of Sale Acts, these entities can create a mortgage that will extend (at least in equity) to after-acquired property as soon as it is acquired.[291] A different registration system applies: certain mortgages must be submitted, along with prescribed particulars, to the Registrar of Companies under the CA

---

[285] There are exceptions, including assignments for the benefit of creditors, marriage settlements, ship mortgages, and 'transfers of goods in the ordinary course of business of any trade or calling': Bills of Sale Act 1878, s 4. The 'ordinary course' exemption will cover absolute sales of goods (*Stephenson v Thompson* [1924] 2 KB 240, CA), but it has been interpreted narrowly in the context of transfers by way of security for loans (*Charles Tennant, Sons & Co v Howatson* (1888) 13 App Cas 489, PC; *Re Hall* (1884) 14 QBD 386, 394; *Ian Chisholm Textiles Ltd v Griffiths* [1994] 2 BCLC 291, [1994] BCC 96). The Acts do not apply to an agricul-tural charge given by a farmer (Agricultural Credits Act 1928, s 8(1); see 8.102), nor to aircraft mortgages (Mortgaging of Aircraft Order 1972, SI 1972/1268, art 16(1)). There is also an exception for security on imported goods before they are warehoused or reshipped: Bills of Sale Act 1890, s 1; this is probably confined to excepting trust receipts (on which see 8.68), and does not except a document granting security over future goods: *NV Slavenburg's Bank v Intercontinental Natural Resources Ltd* [1980] 1 WLR 1076.

[286] *Online Catering Ltd v Acton* [2010] EWCA Civ 58, [2011] QB 204, at [25]. Money advanced will be recoverable in unjust enrichment: *North Central Wagon Finance Co Ltd v Brailsford* [1962] 1 WLR 1288. The Acts deal in documents and not in transactions; they require documents to be in the correct form and registered, but do not state that a document is essential. It has been suggested that a purely oral mortgage of moveables could therefore be created: RM Goode and E McKendrick, *Goode on Commercial Law* (4th edn, 2009) 689 fn 2. Given the policies which motivated the Acts, however, it is probably true that unless posses-sion were transferred to the mortgagee, the attempted conveyance would be ineffectual in such a case.

[287] Bills of Sale Act (1878) Amendment Act 1882, ss 9–10. Any bill made in consideration of less than £30 is void in any event: s 12.

[288] Bills of Sale Act (1878) Amendment Act 1882, s 8. Registration is with a Master of the Queen's Bench Division of the High Court of Justice: Bills of Sale Act 1878, s 13. In addition to the bill of sale and all attach-ments in duplicate, an affidavit is required: Bills of Sale Act 1878, s 10(2).

[289] Bills of Sale Act (1878) Amendment Act 1882, s 4; it is void (except against the borrower) in respect of property not listed. This means that as against third parties, not even an equitable mortgage could be claimed in such property. Even if the schedule specifies the after-acquired property, it is to this extent void (again, except against the borrower): Bills of Sale Act (1878) Amendment Act 1882, s 5.

[290] This follows from the definition of 'personal chattels' in the Bills of Sale Act 1878, s 4. There is authority suggesting that if a document grants security over both property that is within the Acts and property that is not, it may be valid as to the property outside the Acts: *Re North Wales Produce and Supply Society* [1922] 2 Ch 340. Note however that by the Insolvency Act 1986, s 344, certain general assign-ments of 'book debts' (accounts receivable arising in the course of business) are void against a trustee in bankruptcy unless they are registered under the Bills of Sale Act 1878 as if they were absolute assignments (whether the assignment is indeed absolute, or by way of security). In this case a schedule of property is not required. See 9.84.

[291] 8.81.

2006.[292] The list of registrable mortgages is such that in practice almost every mortgage is registrable.[293] Failure to register within 21 days of execution makes the mortgage void against a liquidator, an administrator and any creditor of the company.[294] It also makes the money secured by the mortgage payable immediately.[295]

There are other registers for mortgages of particular kinds of asset. They include mortgages **8.78** of ships[296] and aircraft,[297] and of patents,[298] trade marks,[299] and registered designs.[300] In these systems a failure to register does not invalidate the mortgage, although it will affect its priority. These requirements are, however, cumulative with those of the Companies Acts,[301] and so if the mortgagor is a company the mortgage is subject to avoidance if the Companies Act registration is not made in time.

In any case, the nature of the property mortgaged will dictate what is required for the convey- **8.79** ance. In a mortgage transaction, legal title to tangible moveables will pass when the parties so intend, without the need for delivery.[302] The legal assignment of a pure intangible must be in writing, and there must be notice in writing to the debtor.[303] In the case of registered securities, the appropriate steps must be taken to bring about the amendment of the relevant register. Other intangibles may be governed by special rules.[304]

Enforcement. The features of a legal mortgage of moveables are essentially the same as **8.80** those of a mortgage of land. The right to take possession is the same, except in the case of mortgages governed by the Bills of Sale Acts 1878 and 1882, where it is restricted.[305] Unlike in the case of land, a power of sale arises at common law in the case of intangibles,[306] and may also do so for tangible moveables.[307] A power of sale may arise by agreement; if the mortgage was created by deed, then the statutory power which arises under every mortgage so

---

[292] CA 2006, ss 859A, 860, 861(5). For the applicability to limited liability partnerships, with minor amendments, see Limited Liability Partnerships (Application of Companies Act 2006) Regulations 2009, SI 2009/1804, r 32.

[293] CA 2006, ss 859A, 860. For more detail, see 8.103.

[294] CA 2006, ss 859A(4), 859H(3), 870, 874(1); for the effects of non-registration, see 8.105 and 8.142.

[295] CA 2006, ss 859H(4) 874(3).

[296] Merchant Shipping Act 1995, Sch 1, para 7, with requirements as to form. Note however that these provisions do not apply to all ships; the matter turns on how the ship itself is registered. See Merchant Shipping Act 1995, s 16(2); A Clarke, 'Ship Mortgages' in N Palmer and E McKendrick (eds), *Interests in Goods* (2nd edn, 1998). Because the Bills of Sale Acts 1878 and 1882 do not apply to ship mortgages (Bills of Sale Act 1878, s 4), it follows that if a legal mortgage is given by an individual over an unregistered ship, the mortgage is not registrable but it nonetheless binds a good faith purchaser of the ship: *British Credit Trust Ltd v The Owners of the Shizelle (The Shizelle)* [1992] 2 Lloyd's Rep 444.

[297] Mortgaging of Aircraft Order 1972, SI 1972/1268. A floating charge which extends to an aircraft is not registrable under this Order: art 2(2). The Bills of Sale Acts 1878 and 1882 are not applicable to a mortgage of an aircraft by an individual: 1972 Order, art 16(1). The UK has signed, but not ratified, the Convention on International Interests in Mobile Equipment and the Protocol on Matters Specific to Aircraft Equipment (Cape Town, 2001).

[298] Patents Act 1977, s 33.

[299] Trade Marks Act 1994, s 25.

[300] Registered Designs Act 1949, s 19.

[301] See CA 2006, ss 860(7)(h), (i), 861(4).

[302] See AP Bell, *Modern Law of Personal Property in England and Ireland* (1989) 184.

[303] LPA 1925, s 136(1).

[304] See n 284.

[305] The Bills of Sale Act (1878) Amendment Act 1882, s 7, allows seizure only in specified circumstances, such as default, bankruptcy or other events evidencing insolvency, or fraudulent removal of the goods.

[306] *Stubbs v Slater* [1910] 1 Ch 632, CA.

[307] There was disagreement on this point in *Re Morritt* (1886) 18 QBD 222, 233, 235, CA, and it was said to be an open question in *Deverges v Sandeman, Clark & Co* [1902] 1 Ch 579, 589, CA.

created will generally be available.[308] The duties of a mortgagee exercising a power of sale are the same as in mortgages of land.[309] Sale can be authorized by the court.[310] If the mortgage was created by deed, there will be a statutory power to appoint a receiver,[311] but again this can also be stipulated in the agreement. The mortgagee can foreclose on application to the court.[312]

8.81 **Limitations of legal mortgages.** In the context of moveables, one deficiency of the legal mortgage relates to after-acquired property. The mortgagor might promise to transfer owner-ship of property which he will later acquire, but this promise will not convey the legal own-ership when the property is acquired. However, a promise, for value given, to create a legal mortgage will create an immediate equitable mortgage if that is consistent with the intention of the parties.[313] In this context, this principle means that as soon as the mortgagor acquires property which is within the scope of the promise given earlier, it will be immediately subject to an *equitable* mortgage, even before the mortgagee transfers legal ownership, or even if he never does. The equitable mortgage will be discussed below, but so long as it is properly reg-istered, an equitable mortgage arising in the circumstances just mentioned will usually differ from a legal one only in respect of priorities.[314]

(ii) Retention of ownership

8.82 A legal mortgage is a *transfer* of ownership by way of security. In some situations, a creditor who is the owner of a moveable thing may instead retain ownership until he is paid in full. This interest is not a security interest by nature; and, unlike a mortgage, the transaction is not a security transaction by its nature. But ownership can function economically as a security interest; and, in the absence of any register of title for moveables, it can raise difficult ques-tions of policy due to problems of apparent ownership.

8.83 **Forms.** There are a number of transactional structures in which ownership of a moveable is separated from possession, while there are obligations owing from the possessor to the owner. In general, such transactions are not treated as security transactions; and this is so whether the parties intend that the owner will ultimately recover possession of the thing (as in an operating lease), or whether they intend the opposite, so that ownership is effectively used as

---

[308] LPA 1925, ss 101(1)(i) (power arises); 103 (power exercisable); 205(1)(xvi), (xx) (showing applicabil-ity to moveables). For the distinction between the power's arising and being exercisable, see 8.46–8.47. It was held that where the transaction is governed by the Bills of Sale Acts 1878 and 1882, the Bills of Sale Act (1878) Amendment Act 1882, s 7 excluded the statutory power of sale arising under the Conveyancing Act 1881, s 19, which was the predecessor of LPA 1925, s 101: *Re Morritt* (1886) 18 QBD 222, CA. It is not clear whether this holding survives the re-enactment of the power of sale in LPA 1925, s 101: AP Bell, *Modern Law of Personal Property in England and Ireland* (1989) 187. A minority of the judges, however, held that a power of sale impliedly arose under s 7. Note also that by Bills of Sale Act (1878) Amendment Act 1882, s 13, the mortgagee may not sell the goods until they have been held for five days; there is more protection for consumer debtors (see 8.31–8.36).

[309] *Den Norske Bank ASA v Acemex Management Company Ltd* [2003] EWCA Civ 1559, [2004] 1 All ER (Comm) 904, [2004] 1 Lloyd's Rep 1; 8.49.

[310] LPA 1925, s 91(2).

[311] LPA 1925, s 101(1)(iii) (power arises); s 109(1) (power exercisable).

[312] There is the possibility for extrajudicial foreclosure in one context, where there is a mortgage (legal or equitable) of financial instruments to which Council Directive (EC) 2002/47 [2002] OJ L168/43 on finan-cial collateral arrangements applies, via the Financial Collateral Arrangements (No 2) Regulations 2003, SI 2003/3226, r 17; however, the Court still has the jurisdiction to protect the equity of redemption by ordering relief against forfeiture on terms. See *Cukurova Finance International Ltd v Alfa Telecom Turkey Ltd* [2009] UKPC 19, [2010] All ER (Comm) 1173; [2013] UKPC 2, [2013] UKPC 20, [2013] UKPC 25, [2015] 2 WLR 875, PC.

[313] See 8.13.

[314] Equitable mortgages: 8.88; priorities: 8.126ff. Note, however, that after-acquired property cannot be mortgaged if the Bills of Sale Acts 1878 and 1882 apply: 8.76.

a security interest. The clearest example is a sale of goods in which the buyer takes possession, but ownership is retained by the seller until the price is paid. This is not treated as a security interest; it is merely a postponement of one of the stages involved in any sale, namely the conveyance of the property sold.[315] The same conclusion follows even if the passage of ownership is delayed until the satisfaction of obligations other than the purchase price of the goods.[316] Similarly in a lease of goods, the lessor's ownership is not viewed as a security interest, even in the case of a 'finance lease', where the term of the lease approximates the anticipated useful life of the goods. The same is true in a hire-purchase, which is a lease coupled with an option to purchase, exercisable by the lessee at the end of the lease period.

Characterization. The situation may be different, however, if the ownership of the goods **8.84** was originally in the party who later leases them back, or buys them with retention of ownership. Here ownership has been transferred, and not just retained, so that it can be used as security. If the court finds that the substance of the transaction was the creation of a non-possessory security interest, then, looking at the substance over the form, it will so characterize the interest of the creditor.[317] When this will be done is not wholly clear. The courts say that they look for the 'true nature' of the transaction, but do not spell out what this means. They do not look directly to the economic function of the transaction, or else all such transactions would be viewed as secured lending. It appears that if the credit which is effectively advanced is secured by an asset which previously belonged absolutely to the debtor, the form of the transaction is more likely to be ignored.[318] In these cases, there are really only two parties, with the debtor offering the asset as security to the creditor; if a third party is employed, it is for no commercial purpose. On the other hand, if the credit is advanced for the initial acquisition by the debtor of the asset in question, then the transaction is more likely to be effective.[319]

Proceeds and products. The effectiveness of the retention of legal ownership has led sup- **8.85** pliers of goods to attempt to extend their security further. Often, they authorize the buyer to resell the goods in question, or (depending on the nature of the business) to use them in the manufacture of some other product. In such cases the terms of the contract may stipulate that the supplier shall be the owner (or trust beneficiary) of the proceeds of sale, or of the manufactured products. Considering proceeds first, the approach of the courts is to observe that the interest of the supplier in the proceeds is defeasible upon payment of the price of the original goods; hence, regardless of the contractual language, it is properly characterized as an equitable charge.[320] As to products, the courts are likely to conclude that the parties did not

---

[315] *Clough Mill Ltd v Martin* [1985] 1 WLR 111, CA. By Sale of Goods Act 1979, s 17, ownership passes when the parties intend it to pass.

[316] *Armour v Thyssen Edelstahlwerke AG* [1991] 2 AC 339, HL.

[317] eg, *Re Watson* (1890) 25 QBD 27, CA (bill of sale); *Polsky v S & A Services* [1951] 1 All ER 185, affd [1951] 1 All ER 1062, CA (bill of sale); *Re Curtain Dream plc* [1990] BCLC 925, [1990] BCC 341 (charge). Whether the interest is characterized as a charge or the agreement is characterized as a bill of sale, registration is required.

[318] As in the cases cited in n 317. Such a transaction was held valid in *Yorkshire Wagon Co v Maclure* (1882) 21 ChD 309, CA; it might be relevant that in this case, it was legally impossible for the transaction to be structured as a simple loan with security.

[319] *Staffs Motor Guarantee Ltd v British Wagon Ltd* [1934] 2 KB 305; *Pacific Motor Auctions Pty Ltd v Motor Credits (Hire Finance) Ltd* [1965] AC 867, PC. In such a case, there are genuinely three parties involved (debtor, supplier, and creditor), and it is only some practical difficulty which prevents the adoption of the unchallengeable structure in which the creditor buys the goods from the original supplier and then agrees to sell or lease them to the debtor.

[320] Since it is also seen as consensually created, it is therefore registrable: 8.102–8.103. See *E Pfeiffer Weinkellerei-Weineinkauf GmbH & Co v Arbuthnot Factors Ltd* [1988] 1 WLR 150; *Tatung (UK) Ltd v Galex Telesure Ltd* [1989] BCC 325; *Compaq Computer Ltd v Abercorn Group Ltd* [1993] BCLC 602, [1991] BCC 484. It is unlikely to have been registered; even if it has been, it will almost certainly be subject to a prior

intend the supplier to be the owner of a product whose value has greatly increased due to the processing, so again the interest will be characterized as a charge.[321] Where the processing leads to the creation of a new thing, the conclusion that the supplier's interest is only a charge is even stronger.[322] The cases are not always consistent in their analysis, but in this context the courts look more directly to the economic function of the transaction. They seem driven by a policy of minimizing hidden security interests in proceeds and products.[323]

8.86 **Enforcement.**   A creditor who holds legal ownership can, in general, take any step that any legal owner can take, including taking possession of the goods and selling them.[324] In some respects, however, courts may be willing to take notice of the security aspect of the transaction and thereby limit the steps which the creditor may take.[325]

(2) Equitable Security

(a) Equitable lien

8.87 There is no such thing as an equitable pledge, but there are equitable liens. They differ from common law liens in that they do not depend on possession by the creditor, and for this reason are not readily distinguishable from equitable charges, discussed below.[326]

(b) Equitable mortgage

8.88 There are several ways to create an equitable mortgage, being a mortgage in which the mortgagee's interest is purely equitable. The first is where the mortgagor's interest is itself purely equitable. This would include the mortgage of a beneficiary's interest under a trust, but also the case where the mortgagor had already granted a legal mortgage and wished to grant a second mortgage; after granting the first mortgage, his only interest is the equity of redemption. Another situation where only an equitable mortgage can be created is where the mortgagor has a legal interest, but is not able to transfer that legal interest. This is illustrated by the case of the mortgage of a pure intangible. At common law this could not be assigned and therefore could not be the subject of a legal mortgage. It was, however, possible to assign a pure intangible in equity, and therefore it could be the subject matter of an equitable mortgage.[327] Furthermore, equitable mortgages can be used even where a legal mortgage is possible. Any

---

registered charge. The proceeds clause was effective in *Aluminium Industrie Vaassen BV v Romalpa Aluminium Ltd* [1976] 1 WLR 676, CA, but no argument was made as to there being a charge, and the result has never been followed.

[321] *Clough Mill Ltd v Martin* [1985] 1 WLR 111, CA; *Re Peachdart Ltd* [1984] 1 Ch 131.

[322] *Modelboard Ltd v Outer Box Ltd* [1992] BCC 945.

[323] See S Worthington, *Proprietary Interests in Commercial Transactions* (1996) 7–42.

[324] If the transaction is regulated under the CCA 1974, enforcement is strictly regulated. See especially ss 90–91.

[325] It has been said that a seller who retains title and who recovers the goods on a breach by the buyer must account for the part of the price which has been paid (subject, of course, to any claim for compensation for breach of contract): *Stockloser v Johnson* [1954] 1 QB 476, CA; *Clough Mill Ltd v Martin* [1985] 1 WLR 111, 117–118, 124, 125–126, CA. In hire purchase and finance lease transactions, the courts may recognize that the debtor acquires an interest in the goods, similar to the equity of redemption in mortgages, that is protected by the doctrine of relief against forfeiture: *Transag Haulage Ltd v Leyland Daf Finance plc* [1994] 2 BCLC 88, [1994] BCC 356; *On Demand Information plc v Michael Gerson (Finance) plc* [2002] UKHL 13, [2003] 1 AC 368; L Smith, 'Relief Against Forfeiture: A Restatement' (2001) 60 CLJ 178.

[326] Some say that an equitable lien arises by operation of law (*Re Bond Worth* [1980] 1 Ch 228, 250–251), but the word 'charge' is often used of an equitable security interest so arising; and since a common law lien can arise by agreement, there seems to be no stable terminological difference between 'charge' and 'lien'.

[327] As noted in 8.75, a legal assignment (and therefore a legal mortgage) of a pure intangible is now possible by statute, but the possibility of an equitable mortgage remains where only an equitable assignment is made (and this includes the case in which the debtor has promised for value to create a legal mortgage). It may be difficult to distinguish a mortgage or charge of an intangible from a sale: see 8.98–8.101.

asset can be made the subject of an equitable mortgage by the making of an enforceable agreement for the giving of a legal mortgage.[328] Once the loan has been advanced, an equitable mortgage will arise by operation of law.[329] The mere deposit with the creditor of documentary evidence of an asset may be enough to permit the conclusion that there was an agreement for the creation of a legal mortgage.[330] This principle can apply so as to make property acquired after the date of the agreement subject to the mortgage, at the moment of its acquisition and without any further legal act, if the parties so intended.[331]

The formalities required for the creation of equitable mortgages are the same as those for legal mortgages.[332] The conveyance to the mortgagee of the property which is the subject of the mortgage may itself require writing, eg in the case of the transfer of an equitable interest.[333] **8.89**

The possibilities for the enforcement of an equitable mortgage are much the same as those for a legal mortgage.[334] As with land, it is doubtful whether the equitable mortgagee has a right to take possession by operation of law, but the agreement will generally provide for this on default by the mortgagor. A statutory power of sale, and a power to appoint a receiver, will arise if the mortgage was created by deed.[335] These powers can also be created by agreement, and in any event sale can be authorized by the court.[336] **8.90**

(c) Equitable charge

An equitable charge is a security interest in an asset. 'It is of the essence of a charge that a particular asset or class of assets is appropriated to the satisfaction of a debt or other obligation of the chargor or a third party, so that the chargee is entitled to look to the asset and its proceeds for the discharge of the liability.'[337] It may arise by agreement or by operation of law. **8.91**

(i) Arising by operation of law

As in the case of land, equitable charges can arise without the consent of the holder of the charged asset. A charge can be imposed judicially to secure a judgment debt.[338] Some charges arise by operation of law; these are often called 'equitable liens'. Just as in the case of land, an unpaid vendor's lien arises by operation of law upon the making of a contract for the sale of moveables, other than goods.[339] A charge can also arise where trust property is disposed of **8.92**

---

[328] See 8.13. It may be that following the agreement and loan, there is some defect in the attempt to create a legal mortgage; alternatively, it may be that even though there is an agreement to create a legal mortgage, the mortgagee is content to rely on his rights under the equitable mortgage.

[329] In this context the principle only operates once the loan has been advanced, because the contract is not specifically enforceable: RM Goode and E McKendrick, *Goode on Commercial Law* (4th edn, 2009) 668.

[330] *Harrold v Plenty* [1901] 2 Ch 314 and *Stubbs v Slater* [1910] 1 Ch 632, CA show that the deposit of share certificates for registered shares cannot create a pledge; the relevant asset is the share, a pure intangible, and not the certificate, which is mere evidence. The deposit can, however, create an equitable mortgage of the shares, without the need for any amendment to the share register (which would be required for a legal mortgage).

[331] However in the case of an individual or partnership, it would be impossible to comply with the requirements of the Bills of Sale Acts 1878 and 1882 in respect of after-acquired property: see 8.76.

[332] See 8.76–8.78.

[333] LPA 1925, s 53(1)(c).

[334] See 8.80.

[335] LPA 1925, ss 101(1)(i), (iii) (power arises); 103 (power exercisable); 205(1)(xvi), (xx) (showing applicability to moveables). For the distinction between the power's arising and being exercisable, see 8.46–8.47. For the position where the transaction is governed by the Bills of Sale Acts 1878 and 1882, see n 308.

[336] LPA 1925, s 91(2).

[337] *Re Cosslett (Contractors) Ltd* [1998] Ch 495, 508, CA.

[338] Charging Orders Act 1979. See EPL 22.126.

[339] AP Bell, *Modern Law of Personal Property in England and Ireland* (1989) 180–181. It was suggested in *Re Bond Worth* [1980] Ch 228, 251 that the lien may only arise if the contract was specifically enforceable. In the case of goods, the unpaid vendor has a possessory lien under the Sale of Goods Act 1979, ss 41–43, and

without authority. The trust beneficiary who can trace into the proceeds of disposition can treat those proceeds as trust property, or can assert a charge over them to secure his claim for breach of trust.[340] A trustee has a lien over the trust property to secure the recovery of expenses properly incurred in the administration of the trust.[341] Where an insurer indemnifies its insured, and the insured recovers from a wrongdoer in respect of the loss suffered, the insurer has a lien over the funds received to secure its claim against the insured.[342] Charges on moveables arising by operation of law do not need to be registered.

(ii) Arising by consent

8.93 **Fixed and floating charges.** A fixed charge is one in which the chargor is not authorized to dispose of the charged property without the consent of the chargee.[343] By contrast, a floating charge is one in which the chargor is authorized by the chargee to dispose of the charged asset in the ordinary course of the chargor's business.[344] It has often been said that a characteristic feature of the floating charge is that the pool of assets subject to the charge fluctuates and changes.[345] While this is true of almost every floating charge, as the law has developed it is now true of some fixed charges as well: just as in the case of equitable mortgages, property acquired after the date of the agreement can be automatically subjected to the charge at the moment of its acquisition, if the parties so intended.[346] The definitional difference between fixed and floating charges is that a charge is a floating charge if the debtor is authorized to dispose of the charged assets in the ordinary course of its business.[347]

8.94 The distinction between fixed and floating charges is crucial for the resolution of priority disputes and for other issues.[348] In general, the chargee is better protected by holding a fixed charge. It is not always clear, however, where the boundary lies. The label attached to the charge by the parties in their agreement is not determinative.[349] Some restriction on the chargor's liberty to deal with the asset is consistent with the existence of a floating charge.[350] On the other hand, some liberty on the part of the chargor to deal with the charged asset is

---

this is generally understood to exclude the equitable lien. The purchaser's lien to secure the repayment of any deposit paid also appears to apply to moveables other than goods: Bell 181–182.

[340] See EPL 18.239–18.246, EPL 18.267 and EPL 18.274–18.275. If property subject to a charge were disposed of without authority, the chargee would also be able to assert a charge in the traceable proceeds.

[341] *Stott v Milne* (1884) 25 ChD 710, 715, CA. The trustee may secure a declaration of the lien even in respect of contingent or future liabilities, allowing him to retain in trust property which he would otherwise be obliged to distribute, until the extent of liability becomes clear: *X v A* [2000] 1 All ER 490.

[342] *Lord Napier and Ettrick v Hunter* [1993] AC 713, HL.

[343] This does not mean that the chargor is unable to dispose of the asset clear of the charge, only that it is unlawful to do so.

[344] It is possible to have a floating mortgage if the same kind of authority is provided. In practice there is little distinction between an equitable mortgage and a charge; the theoretical differences are largely as to enforcement, but these differences will usually be removed by agreement.

[345] See eg *Re Yorkshire Woolcombers Assoc Ltd* [1903] 2 Ch 284, 295 CA; aff'd *sub nom Illingworth v Houldsworth* [1904] 355, HL.

[346] See 8.88. However in the case of an individual or partnership, it would be impossible to comply with the requirements of the Bills of Sale Acts 1878 and 1882 in respect of after-acquired property: 8.76.

[347] *Re Cosslett (Contractors) Ltd* [1998] Ch 495, 510, CA; *Agnew v Commissioner of Inland Revenue* [2001] UKPC 28, [2001] 2 AC 710; *Re Spectrum Plus Ltd* [2005] UKHL 41, [2005] 2 AC 680.

[348] eg, some fixed charges need not be registered; see 8.102ff. Some other differences: floating charges given near the onset of insolvency may be avoided by Insolvency Act 1986, s 245 (see 9.162–9.164); the holder of a floating charge over all (or substantially all) of a company's assets may be able to appoint an administrator of the company, under Insolvency Act 1986, s 8 and Sch B1, paras 14–21(see 9.104ff); and floating (but not fixed) charges are subordinated to preferential creditors (see 9.104).

[349] *Agnew v Commissioner of Inland Revenue* [2001] UKPC 28, [2001] 2 AC 710; *Re Spectrum Plus Ltd* [2005] UKHL 41, [2005] 2 AC 680.

[350] *Re Brightlife* [1987] Ch 200, 209; *Re Spectrum Plus Ltd* [2005] UKHL 41, [2005] 2 AC 680, at [140]. In particular, it is common for the agreement to restrict the chargor's ability to create any other charge on

consistent with the existence of a fixed charge. This is most clearly seen in the cases involving charges over the accounts receivable or 'book debts' of the chargor company. Here the company must have liberty to deal with the charged assets, at least to the extent of collecting the debts in the ordinary course of business, and it was at one time thought that this meant that a charge over book debts must be a floating charge.[351] It has now been held that a fixed charge can be created over a fluctuating body of book debts, so long as the chargor is not free to deal with the proceeds, once collected, in the ordinary course of business.[352] This requires not just a right in the chargee to take control of the proceeds, but an actual ongoing control over the collected proceeds.[353] In most cases, the chargor is free to deal with the proceeds as part of its cash flow, which means that the charge on book debts will be a floating charge.

Crystallization of floating charges.   Upon the happening of certain events, a floating   **8.95** charge 'crystallizes' and becomes a fixed charge. The nature of the chargee's interest before that event is a matter of some academic dispute. On one view, the chargee has no proprietary rights in the charged assets until crystallization.[354] Another view is that the chargee holds some proprietary rights before crystallization, but that these rights are not held in specific assets; they are rights in a 'fund'.[355] A third view is that the chargee's proprietary interest is the same whether it is a fixed charge or an uncrystallized floating charge; the only difference is that in the latter case, there is a licence to deal with the assets, which terminates on crystallization.[356] These and other views continue to be tenable, although the last one seems to be the simplest, since the courts have come to the view that the very essence of the difference between fixed and floating charges is the chargor's ability lawfully to deal with charged assets, not some difference in the interest held by the chargee.

Whether or not crystallization alters the proprietary rights of the chargee, it certainly termi-   **8.96** nates the authority of the chargor to deal with the charged assets in the ordinary course of business; it converts the floating charge into a fixed charge. Third parties who might have taken free of the charge while it was floating may take subject to the charge once it has crystallized.[357] Crystallization occurs when the management powers of the directors of the chargor company are lost to a receiver or administrator or liquidator, or when the chargor ceases to carry on business.[358] In order to protect the chargee, the agreement may provide for crystallization upon the giving of a notice by the chargee, and also for 'automatic crystallization' upon certain events such as the failure of the chargor to make a payment when due.[359] These provisions cause some concern since they potentially affect third parties who may be unaware of the crystallization; but in deference to the principle of freedom of contract, it has been held that crystallization by notice is effective, and the reasoning implies that automatic

---

the same property which ranks prior or equivalent to the charge; although this is regarded as a dealing in the ordinary course of business, this in itself will not make the charge a fixed charge.

[351] *Re Yorkshire Woolcombers Assoc Ltd* [1903] 2 Ch 284, 295 CA; aff'd *sub nom Illingworth v Houldsworth* [1904] 355, HL.

[352] *Agnew v Commissioner of Inland Revenue* [2001] UKPC 28, [2001] 2 AC 710; *Re Spectrum Plus Ltd* [2005] UKHL 41, [2005] 2 AC 680.

[353] *Agnew v Commissioner of Inland Revenue* [2001] UKPC 28, [2001] 2 AC 710, at [48]; *Re Spectrum Plus Ltd* [2005] UKHL 41, [2005] 2 AC 680, at [55]–[58], [116]–[119], [140].

[354] WJ Gough, *Company Charges* (2nd edn, 1996) ch 13.

[355] RM Goode and E McKendrick, *Goode on Commercial Law* (4th edn, 2009) 722–726; *Re Spectrum Plus Ltd* [2005] UKHL 41, [2005] 2 AC 680, at [139].

[356] S Worthington, *Proprietary Interests in Commercial Transactions* (1996) 82–100.

[357] See 8.144.

[358] *Re Woodroffe's Musical Instruments Ltd* [1986] 1 Ch 366; *National Westminster Bank plc v Jones* [2001] EWCA Civ 1541, [2002] 1 BCLC 55; WJ Gough, *Company Charges* (2nd edn, 1996) ch 8.

[359] Crystallization by giving notice is specifically contemplated for floating agricultural charges in the Agricultural Credits Act 1928, s 7(1)(a)(iv).

crystallization would be effective as well.[360] One approach which preserves the parties' free-dom of contract while yet respecting third party interests is that while the crystallization may be effective to terminate the chargor's actual authority to deal with the charged assets free of the charge, third parties who are unaware of it will be able to rely on the chargor's ostensible authority.[361] Another approach would be to say that the question whether a charge has crys-tallized is simply the question whether the charge remains floating or has become fixed; and the courts have already held that this issue is determined not by the parties' own labelling, but by whether the chargee actually restricts the chargor's control of the assets.[362]

8.97   **Negative pledge.**   Similar issues arise in the case of the negative pledge clause. The chargor's ability to deal in the ordinary course of business with the assets subject to a floating charge is understood to include an ability to grant fixed charges over those assets which have prior-ity over the floating charge.[363] The negative pledge is a typical term in the charge agreement which excludes this ability; the chargor promises not to create any charge over the charged assets which would rank prior to (or equally with) the floating charge. When such clauses are inserted in agreements governing unsecured lending, they are generally understood to have only personal effects.[364] The matter is not so clear where the clause is inserted in an agree-ment governing a charge. It has been held that here as well, the clause has only personal and not real effects;[365] but academic commentary is generally opposed to this, suggesting that the clause would have proprietary effect against a third party who had actual notice of it.[366]

8.98   **Charge or sale.**   In most cases there is no difficulty in distinguishing between a charge over an asset, granted to secure a loan, and a sale of that asset. In the case of accounts receivable, the distinction may be less clear since the economic effects of the transactions may be very similar and since there is no tangible asset involved. The difference between a mortgage and a sale is obscure because in both transactions the intangible receivable is assigned to the

---

[360]   *Re Brightlife Ltd* [1987] 1 Ch 200. The court rejected an argument that crystallizing events were fixed by law as (1) winding up, (2) appointment of a receiver and (3) ceasing to carry on business, and held instead that it was for the parties to stipulate the crystallizing events.

[361]   RM Goode and E McKendrick, *Goode on Commercial Law* (4th edn, 2009) 730–731; on ostensible authority, see 1.60–1.71. See however WJ Gough, *Company Charges* (2nd edn, 1996) 254–256, casting doubt on this explanation; eg, noting that mere possession of goods by a debtor has never been understood as pre-cluding others from asserting their rights in those goods.

[362]   8.94.

[363]   *Wheatley v Silkstone and Haigh Moor Coal Co* (1885) 29 Ch D 715.

[364]   This is so even if the clause is an 'affirming negative pledge', in which the debtor promises that should it grant security to another creditor, it will provide equal security to the hitherto unsecured creditor. See RM Goode and E McKendrick, *Goode on Commercial Law* (4th edn, 2009) 653–654; J Maxton, 'Negative Pledge and Equitable Principles' [1993] JBL 458. The third party may, if it had knowledge of the clause, be liable in tort for inducing a breach of contract.

[365]   *Griffiths v Yorkshire Bank Ltd* [1994] 1 WLR 1427.

[366]   RM Goode and E McKendrick, *Goode on Commercial Law* (4th edn, 2009) 734; Gough, *Company Charges* (2nd edn, 1996) 225–231. There is however a dispute about whether constructive notice could suf-fice, and if so what would constitute that. A dictum in *Ian Chisholm Textiles Ltd v Griffiths* [1994] 2 BCLC 291, [1994] BCC 96, drawn from the context of land conveyancing, suggests that notice of the existence of the prior floating charge is constructive notice of the negative pledge, but this is inconsistent with the consid-ered holding to the contrary in *Siebe Gorman & Co Ltd v Barclays Bank Ltd* [1979] Lloyd's Rep 142. (*Siebe Gorman* was itself overruled in *Re Spectrum Plus Ltd* [2005] UKHL 41, [2005] 2 AC 680, but only on the question whether the charge agreement created a fixed or a floating charge.) The 'particulars' which must be registered under CA 2006, ss 860, 869, do not include whether or not there is a negative pledge clause, but the registrar will permit it to be noted; the effect is unclear: Goode 705. One commentator has argued that given the prevalence of such clauses, registration of the charge should now be treated as giving notice of the clause to anyone who could reasonably be expected to search the register: JH Farrar 'Floating Charges and Priorities' (1974) 38 Conveyancer and Property Lawyer (New Series) 315, 322, but this is a minority view. For charges created by a written instrument on or after 6 April 2013, the 'particulars' will include a notice

mortgagee or buyer. Of course, a mortgage is associated with a loan and a debt, while a sale is associated with the payment of a price; but in the case of receivables this distinction is not so clear, because in both transactions, it is common that the debtors are not notified, and the seller or mortgagor of the receivables continues to collect them and then to account to the buyer. The distinction is further blurred because while in a sale of tangible assets the price is usually fixed, in a sale of receivables it is common for the agreement to provide for recourse by the buyer against the seller in respect of non-performing receivables. The difference between a sale and a charge might seem clearer, but this is not so because in the case of receivables a mortgage and a charge are also difficult to distinguish except in abstract terms. While in a charge there is no assignment of the receivables, it is typical for the chargor to grant to the chargee not only a power to appoint a receiver, but also an irrevocable power of attorney to effect an assignment of the charged receivables to the chargee.

Although the economic effects are very similar, the legal incidents are quite different. A mort- **8.99** gage or charge of receivables by a company must be registered;[367] a sale is not registrable.[368] Conversely, a registrable charge or mortgage which was not registered is void against a subsequent chargee or mortgagee; it is not void against a subsequent purchaser of the mortgaged or charged asset.[369] The accounting treatment may also be different, since, unlike a loan, a sale does not generate a liability, and it removes an asset from the seller's balance sheet.[370] A sale may attract value added tax. In some cases a company may be at liberty to sell receivables while it might not be at liberty to charge them, eg under the terms of an earlier loan agreement.

In deciding whether a transaction is a sale or secured loan, the courts purport to look at the **8.100** substance and not the form, but this does not mean that they look directly to the economic function.[371] The form of a transaction will be ignored if it is a 'sham', meaning that none of the parties to it intended to conduct themselves in accordance with its terms.[372] It is also possible that the parties have, by their conduct, replaced their formal agreement with another one.[373] Beyond that, the matter is less clear. It has been said that there are some distinguishing factors:[374] in a sale, the seller has no right or obligation to recover the sold asset, while in a secured loan he is obliged to repay the loan and thereby recovers the charged asset. It is, however, acceptable in sales of receivables for the seller to be required to repurchase non-performing receivables;[375] and a seller's option to repurchase does not make a sale into a charge.[376] In a secured loan, the borrower is entitled to any surplus realized from the security, and is liable for any deficiency; while in a sale, the buyer is entitled to the full value of the asset bought, and must bear the risk of its being worth less than the price. But it is

---

of any negative pledge: CA 2006, 859D(2)(c); Companies Act 2006 (Amendment of Part 25) Regulations 2013, reg 6. This is presumably intended to give constructive notice.

[367] CA 2006, ss 859A, 860(7)(f), 861(5). On the meaning of 'book debts', see n 389.

[368] But see, for individuals, Insolvency Act 1986, s 344; see 9.84.

[369] CA 2006, ss 859H, 874; *Stroud Architectural Systems Ltd v John Laing Construction Ltd* [1994] 2 BCLC 276, [1994] BCC 18.

[370] But under current accounting standards, a sale of receivables with recourse will leave the receivables on the seller's balance sheet, since in economic terms it is only a loan.

[371] *Lloyds and Scottish Finance Ltd v Cyril Lord Carpets Ltd* (1979) [1992] BCLC 609, HL; *Welsh Development Agency v Export Finance Co Ltd* [1992] BCLC 148, [1992] BCC 270, CA.

[372] *Snook v London and West Riding Investments Ltd* [1967] 2 QB 786, 802, CA.

[373] *Lloyds and Scottish Finance Ltd v Cyril Lord Carpet Sales Ltd* (1979) [1992] BCLC 609, HL; *Orion Finance Ltd v Crown Financial Management Ltd* [1996] 2 BCLC 78, [1996] BCC 621, CA.

[374] *Re George Inglefield Ltd* [1933] Ch 1, CA.

[375] *Lloyds and Scottish Finance Ltd v Cyril Lord Carpet Sales Ltd* (1979) [1992] BCLC 609, HL.

[376] Even if the repurchase price is calculated by reference to the original sale price plus interest since the date of the original sale: *Orion Finance Ltd v Crown Financial Management Ltd* [1996] 2 BCLC 78, 84, [1996] BCC 621, CA.

acceptable in sales of receivables for the buyer to have recourse against the seller in respect of non-performing receivables, and for there to be adjustments to the sale price after the receivables have been collected, and so these indicia are not determinative.[377]

8.101   English law has historically attached a high importance to the intention of the parties, allowing it to be determinative even where third parties may have been misled. In one case, a company wanted to convert its receivables into cash, without creating a registrable charge in favour of the financier. Under a master agreement with the financier, when the company had agreed a sale of goods with a customer, it actually sold the goods to the financier for cash; it then proceeded to sell the goods to the customer as undisclosed agent of the financier, so that the receivable owing from the customer vested in the financier. A subsequent secured creditor lent money to the company, taking a charge over its book debts and registering that charge. On the insolvency of the company, this subsequent secured creditor argued that the financier's interest in receivables was by way of a charge, which was unregistered and therefore void against the subsequent creditor. This argument was rejected, and the agency arrangement upheld.[378] This suggests that the language which the parties use in their agreement is more important than its economic effect or its implications for third parties.[379] Recently, however, on the issue of whether a charge is fixed or floating, it has been held that the intention of the parties cannot be determinative where the interests of third parties are affected.[380] In the future it will probably be held, by parity of reasoning, that the question whether a transaction was a sale or a secured loan is not one that is determined by the intentions of the parties.

(iii) Registration

8.102   Many, but not all, charges require registration.[381] In the case of a charge created by an individual or a partnership, registration may be required under the Bills of Sale Acts 1878 and 1882. These provisions, which also regulate the form of the document evidencing the agreement, apply only to interests in tangible moveables.[382] The Acts do not apply in the case of an 'agricultural charge', given to a bank by a farmer on all or any of his farming stock.[383] Agricultural charges must be registered in a special register, or else they will be void against anyone except the farmer.[384]

---

[377] *Welsh Development Agency v Export Finance Co Ltd* [1992] BCLC 148, [1992] BCC 270, CA; *Orion Finance Ltd v Crown Financial Management Ltd* [1996] 2 BCLC 78, [1996] BCC 621, CA.

[378] *Welsh Development Agency v Export Finance Co Ltd* [1992] BCLC 148, [1992] BCC 270, CA.

[379] *Lloyds and Scottish Finance Ltd v Cyril Lord Carpet Sales Ltd* (1979) [1992] BCLC 609, HL; *Orion Finance Ltd v Crown Financial Management Ltd* [1996] 2 BCLC 78, [1996] BCC 621, CA.

[380] *Re Spectrum Plus Ltd* [2005] UKHL 41, [2005] 2 AC 680. This case overruled *Re New Bullas Trading Ltd* [1994] 1 BCLC 485, [1994] BCC 36, CA, which had held that the parties' intention could be determinative on the question whether a charge was fixed or floating.

[381] Charges on moveables arising by operation of law are never registrable.

[382] For details, see 8.76. This legislation requires a listing of the moveables in which the creditor holds a security interest, and this precludes the creation by an individual or partnership of a security interest extending to after-acquired property.

[383] Agricultural Credits Act 1928, s 5(1) permits the charge, and s 5(2) provides that it may be fixed or (unlike security interests registrable under the Bills of Sale Acts 1878 and 1882) floating or both. Agricultural Credits Act 1928, s 5(7) indicates that the farmer must generally be an individual, while the chargee must generally be a bank; it clarifies the permissible subject matter of the charge as being tangible and certain intangible moveables relating to the business of farming. Section 8(1) disapplies the Bills of Sales Acts. By s 14, an industrial and provident society (a co-operative), which is a corporation not formed under the Companies Acts, may also give an agricultural charge, and if it registers it under the Agricultural Credits Act 1928 then the Bills of Sale Acts will not apply.

[384] Agricultural Credits Act 1928, s 9.

Where a company or limited liability partnership creates a charge, registration will usually **8.103**
be required by the Companies Act 2006.[385] The following charges, if created before 6 April
2013, must be registered:[386]

(1) a charge on land or any interest in land, other than a charge for any rent or other periodical sum issuing out of land;[387]
(2) a charge created or evidenced by an instrument which, if executed by an individual,
would require registration as a bill of sale;[388]
(3) a charge for the purposes of securing any issue of debentures;
(4) a charge on uncalled share capital of the company;
(5) a charge on calls made but not paid;
(6) a charge on book debts of the company;[389]
(7) a floating charge on the company's property or undertaking;
(8) a charge on a ship or aircraft, or any share in a ship;[390]
(9) a charge on goodwill or on any intellectual property.[391]

An example of a charge created by a company that is not registrable is a fixed charge it grants
over the shares it holds in a subsidiary company.[392]

Registration is also required where a company acquires property which is already subject to **8.104**
a registrable charge.[393] The Companies Act register performs a dual function, giving notice
of security interests but also revealing the financial position of the company, eg to potential
shareholders. This is why each company is required to keep its own register of charges it

---

[385] For the applicability to limited liability partnerships, with minor amendments, see Limited Liability
Partnerships (Application of Companies Act 2006) Regulations 2009, SI 2009/1804, r 32. If an industrial and
provident society creates a charge that is not an agricultural charge, then it may optionally register that charge
with its regulator (which may be the FCA or the Prudential Regulatory Authority), in which case the Bills of
Sale Acts will not apply (Industrial and Provident Societies Act 1967, s 1); if it does not, the Bills of Sale Acts
will apply: *Re North Wales Produce and Supply Society* [1922] 2 Ch 340.
[386] CA 2006, s 860(7). For charges created on or after 6 April 2013, the law is different and all charges
must be registered, subject to a short list of exclusions: CA 2006, s 859A; Companies Act 2006 (Amendment
of Part 25) Regulations, reg 6. The new regulations permit electronic registration.
[387] A charge on land created by a company may need to be registered in the relevant land register as well as
in the Companies Act register; although a charge on unregistered land which would otherwise be registrable
in the Land Charges Registry need not be registered there if it is a floating charge *and* it is registered in the
Companies Act register: Land Charges Act 1972, s 3(7).
[388] This provision means that all of the law relating to the Bills of Sale Acts 1878 and 1882 is relevant in
determining which company charges must be registered.
[389] A 'book debt' is understood to mean a claim arising in the course of the company's business, and a fixed
charge on such debts is registrable even if it is over future book debts: *Independent Automatic Sales Ltd v Knowles &
Foster* [1962] 1 WLR 974; but a contingent debt is not a book debt: *Paul and Frank Ltd v Discount Bank (Overseas)
Ltd* [1967] Ch 348. The term appears to exclude a bank account: *Re Bank of Credit and Commerce International
SA (No 8)* [1998] AC 214, 227, HL. It was held in this case that it is possible for a bank to take a charge over a
bank account to secure a loan to the customer even where the bank is itself the debtor on the charged account.
[390] Charges on aircraft and ships may also require another registration, whether or not the chargor is a
company: see 8.78. All of those registers apply to consensually created charges as well as mortgages.
[391] 'Intellectual property' means a patent, trade mark, service mark, registered design, copyright or design
right, or any licence thereof: CA 2006, s 861(4). Charges over patents, trade marks and registered designs will
require another registration, whether or not the chargor is a company: see 8.78.
[392] *Arthur D Little Ltd v Ableco Finance LLC* [2002] EWHC 701, [2003] Ch 217, applying CA 1985,
s 410 which applied to Scottish companies. However the same result would follow under CA 2006, s 860,
unless the charge secured an issue of debentures. Such a charge would not be registrable as a bill of sale, if
granted by an individual, because that legislation does not apply to security in intangible assets. However, if
it were created on or after 6 April 2013, it would be registrable: n 386.
[393] CA 2006, ss 859C, 862.

has granted, in addition to the central public register maintained under the Act.[394] It also explains why in many cases, a registration under the Companies Act is required even though there is some other system for giving notice of the security interest, which applies whether or not the debtor is a company.[395] In such cases, the requirements of the Companies Act are cumulative with the other requirements.[396]

8.105 Registration is effected by delivering to the Registrar of Companies a form listing the 'prescribed particulars' of the charge, and the original instrument by which the charge is created or evidenced.[397] This may be done either by the chargor or the chargee.[398] It must be done within 21 days of the creation of the charge, or else the charge will become void as against a liquidator or administrator of the company, or a secured or execution creditor.[399] If this failure to register occurs, the debt secured by the charge becomes payable immediately.[400] It is possible to obtain leave from the court to register outside the permitted time;[401] this will usually be permitted if other creditors will not be affected.[402] A certificate of registration from the Registrar is conclusive evidence that the requirements of the Act have been fulfilled.[403] Although there is no obligation to do so, a company may notify the Registrar when the obligation secured has been satisfied, or when it no longer owns the charged property; and this will be noted on the register.[404]

(iv) Enforcement

8.106 If the charge was created by deed, then a statutory power of sale will generally be available.[405] A power of sale will usually be created by agreement, and in any event sale can

---

[394] CA 2006, s 876. This obligation extends to every charge, not just those that must be publicly registered. The failure to maintain either register is an offence. However, the obligation to keep a company register does not apply to charges created on or after 6 April 2013, and the offence for failure to register has now been removed: n 389. The company must also keep a copy of every instrument creating a registrable charge: CA 2006, ss 859P, 875.

[395] Similarly, the requirement of registration applies even to property situated abroad, even though the validity of the security interest is likely to be governed by the law of that place: CA 2006, ss 859A, 866.

[396] There are some exceptions. A floating charge which extends to an aircraft is not registerable under the Mortgaging of Aircraft Order 1972, SI 1972/1268: art 2(2); similarly, a charge that extends to unregistered land, which would otherwise be registrable in the Land Charges Registry, need not be registered there if it is a floating charge and it is registered under the Companies Acts: Land Charges Act 1972, s 3(7). A charge on unregistered land may be unregistrable under the Land Charges Act 1972, because the creditor holds the title deeds: 8.19; nonetheless, it will probably need to be registered under the CA 2006, ss 859A, 860(7)(a).

[397] CA 2006, ss 859D, 860(1). The particulars include the date the charge was created, the amount secured, the property charged, and the identity of the chargee. A copy of the document creating the charge is acceptable in place of the original if (a) the charge is over property situated outside the United Kingdom (CA 2006, s 866(1)) or (b) the charge is over property in Scotland or Northern Ireland and has been registered there (CA 2006, s 867). For charges created on or after 6 April 2013 (see n 389), a certified copy of the instrument must always be delivered.

[398] CA 2006, ss 859A(2), 860(1)–(2).

[399] CA 2006, ss 859A, 869H(3), 870, 874(1); see further 8.142. The charge is not void against the chargor company if it is not in liquidation or administration (*Smith (as Administrator of Cosslett (Contractors) Ltd) v Bridgend County Borough Council* [2001] UKHL 58, [2002] 1 AC 336; *Online Catering Ltd v Acton* [2010] EWCA Civ 58, [2011] QB 204, at [23], [32]); hence, an unsecured creditor has no standing to attack the unregistered charge (*Re Ehrmann Bros Ltd* [1906] 2 Ch 697, CA).

[400] CA 2006, ss 859H(4), 874(3).

[401] CA 2006, ss 859F, 873.

[402] RM Goode and E McKendrick, *Goode on Commercial Law* (4th edn, 2009) 711–712.

[403] CA 2006, ss 859I, 885(5).

[404] CA 2006, ss 859L, 887.

[405] LPA 1925, s 101(1)(i) (power arises); s 103 (power exercisable); s 205(1)(xvi), (xx) (showing applicability to moveables). For the distinction between the power's arising and being exercisable, see 8.46–8.47. For the position where the transaction is governed by the Bills of Sale Acts 1878 and 1882, see n 308. Agricultural charges import a power of sale, which must be by auction unless the agreement provides otherwise, and which cannot be exercised until five days after seizure unless the agreement provides otherwise: Agricultural Credits Act 1928, s 6(1)(b).

be authorized by the court.[406] If the charge was created by deed, there will be a statutory power to appoint a receiver;[407] again, most agreements will provide for such an appointment.[408] The agreement will also generally provide for the taking of possession by the chargee in the event of default. In the case of a charge over receivables, the chargor will commonly grant to the chargee an irrevocable power of attorney to effect an assignment of the charged receivables to the chargee, which will allow them to be collected directly by the chargee if the chargor defaults.

(d) Trust

A beneficiary's interest under a trust is not considered a security interest; but just as legal owner- **8.107** ship can be used to perform the function of a security interest, so too can a trust interest. The creation of trusts, and the rights of beneficiaries, are considered elsewhere.[409] An interest under a trust, as such, is never registrable. Attempts to use the trust to secure obligations are not, however, guaranteed to succeed. It is possible to secure the purchase price of supplied goods by reservation of legal title, allowing the seller to retain a real right which does not require registration.[410] It is not, however, possible to 'reserve' equitable title to achieve a similar effect; any equitable interest held by the seller must have been granted by the buyer.[411] Moreover, the court will examine the features of the seller's interest; since it is defeasible upon the payment of the relevant debt, it is likely to be characterized as a charge, which is almost certainly registrable.[412] The same line of reasoning would apply where the seller attempts to assert a trust interest in the proceeds of sale of the supplied goods, or in the products made from them.[413] The interest might be upheld as a true trust interest only if the buyer was not allowed to deal with the proceeds or products on its own account, and such an arrangement is not usually commercially practicable.

Where money (or perhaps other property) is advanced for a particular purpose, the **8.108** *Quistclose* trust lends itself to utilization as a security device.[414] In this transaction, the one who receives the money holds it in trust for the one who advanced it; but the former has the power and authority to apply the money for the agreed purpose.[415] This will allow the money to be recovered in full if the purpose is not fulfilled and the value advanced can be traced. If the money is applied for the agreed purpose, though, the trust interest will be at an end, and another device will be needed if the provider of the money is to have real security.

---

[406] LPA 1925, s 91(2).

[407] LPA 1925, s 101(1)(iii) (power arises); s 109(1) (power exercisable).

[408] In any event the court has jurisdiction to appoint a receiver: Supreme Court Act 1981, s 37. If a receiver is appointed in respect of a company's property, the Registrar of Companies must be notified and he will note this on the register: CA 2006, ss 859K, 871. A creditor whose floating charge relates to all or substantially all of a company's property may appoint an administrator, who will be regulated by the Insolvency Act 1986, s 8 and Sch B1, esp paras 14–21 (see 9.19, 9.87).

[409] See EPL 4.140ff.

[410] See 8.82–8.86.

[411] *Re Bond Worth Ltd* [1980] Ch 228, 253–256; *Stroud Architectural Services Ltd v John Laing Construction Ltd* [1994] 2 BCLC 276, [1994] BCC 18.

[412] *Re Bond Worth Ltd* [1980] Ch 228, 248–249. The charge is unlikely to have been registered; even if it has been, it will probably be subject to a prior registered charge.

[413] *Re Peachdart Ltd* [1984] Ch 131; *Compaq Computer Ltd v Abercorn Group Ltd* [1993] BCLC 602, [1991] BCC 484; *Stroud Architectural Services Ltd v John Laing Construction Ltd* [1994] 2 BCLC 276, [1994] BCC 18.

[414] *Barclays Bank v Quistclose Investments Ltd* [1970] AC 567, HL; see EPL 18.98–18.100.

[415] *Twinsectra Ltd v Yardley* [2002] UKHL 12, [2002] 2 AC 164.

D. Priorities in Real Security

(1) Introduction

8.109 The law governing the priority of security interests is not simple.[416] It is a mosaic of general rules of property law, conditioned by principles which respond to fault, modified in many cases by particular statutory provisions. It is usually impossible to solve cases with general principles, as the following example illustrates. A customer C buys a car from a trader, T Ltd, taking possession of the car and giving value in good faith and without any knowledge of prior dealings. If, before the sale, T Ltd had sold the car to someone else, then C will prevail.[417] If, before the sale, T Ltd had given to someone else an equitable charge over the car, then again C will prevail, even if the charge was properly registered.[418] But an intermediate case would be that T Ltd had earlier granted to someone else a legal mortgage over the car. Here, illogically, it appears that C's interest is subject to the mortgagee's interest, even if the mortgage was not properly registered.[419] The situation is made even more complicated by the fact that there are many registration systems for security interests in English law.[420] A security interest may be registrable in none of them, or one of them, or more than one of them. Whether registration is required, and the effects of registration or failure to register, are not uniform across these systems.

8.110 Priorities may be modified by agreement among secured creditors, and this does not require the consent of the debtor.[421] When a security interest has been discharged, any subordinate security interests are automatically promoted; the debtor cannot keep the prior interest alive for transfer to another creditor.[422]

(2) General Principles

8.111 In general, the first step in solving any priority contest is to characterize the competing interests. Interests may be beneficial or by way of security.[423] If a beneficial interest prevails, then

---

[416] In this section, as in the earlier text, in the context of land the word 'mortgage' is used to include all interests by way of security: 8.04. In the context of moveables the word is confined to its technical sense: 8.64.

[417] Factors Act 1889, s 8; Sale of Goods Act 1979, s 24.

[418] If the charge was a floating one, then the trader would have been authorized to sell stock in the ordinary course of business so that buyers take free of the charge. Even if the charge was fixed, C would be able to take advantage of the rule that a bona fide purchaser of a legal interest for value takes free of a pre-existing equitable interest of which he did not have notice. The registration of the charge would not be treated as giving C constructive notice. All of these points are developed later.

[419] Because the mortgage was legal, C cannot invoke the doctrine of bona fide purchase of a legal interest for value without notice of a pre-existing equitable interest. Because the mortgage was not a sale, C cannot invoke Factors Act 1889, s 8 or Sale of Goods Act 1979, s 24. Moreover, although there is an obligation to register the mortgage under the CA 2006, ss 859A, 860–861, failure to do so does not avoid the charge as against a purchaser of the charged asset. The point is illustrated by *British Credit Trust Ltd v The Owners of the Shizelle (The Shizelle)* [1992] 2 Lloyd's Rep 444, where the mortgagor was an individual but the mortgage was not registrable.

[420] These include the Land Register for registered land; the Land Charges Register for mortgages on unregistered land, which is also kept by the Land Registrar; the Companies Act register kept by the Registrar of companies; the register of agricultural charges, kept by the Land Registrar; the register for bills of sale, kept at the High Court; the registers for industrial and provident societies, kept by the FCA and the PRA; the register for ship mortgages; the register for aircraft mortgages; the register for patents; the register for registered trade marks; and the register for registered designs. All of these are discussed in what follows. Furthermore, each local authority keeps a register of 'local land charges'; these are not discussed herein; see n 37.

[421] *Cheah Theam Swee v Equiticorp Finance Group Ltd* [1992] 1 AC 472, PC; see P Wood, *The Law of Subordinated Debt* (1990). In relation to registered land, registration may be required if the alteration of priorities is to affect third parties: LRA 2002, s 48(2); Land Registration Rules 2003, SI 2003/1417, r 102.

[422] *Grierson v National Provincial Bank of England Ltd* [1913] 2 Ch 18.

[423] Retained ownership can be used as a kind of security interest: 8.82–8.86; but even so it is a beneficial interest in this context. Ownership transferred by way of mortgage is a security interest.

the losing interest (whether beneficial or security) will be ineffective; but if a security interest prevails, then the other interest can subsist, merely being postponed to the prior security. Interests can also be legal or equitable, and this may affect the priority contest. The next step is to understand how the general principles of property law will provide a prima facie answer to the contest. These principles are modified in important ways by statute. In particular, they are least likely to be determinative in cases involving land, but they still serve as the starting point. Even for moveables, those principles which involve notice are subject to modification where there is a registration system, since registration may generate constructive notice.

(a) First in time generally prevails

The basic principle is *nemo dat quod non habet;* one cannot give what one does not have, **8.112** which in this context means that interests are ranked in the order of their creation. There are a number of crucial modifications to this basic rule.

(b) Authority to grant later interest

If the holder of the earlier interest consented to the creation of a subsequent interest having **8.113** priority over his earlier interest, this will be effective. For example, if a mechanic repairs a car and then discovers that the party who delivered the car to him is not the owner, the question will arise whether the mechanic can assert his lien against the owner; the crucial question will be whether the owner authorized the repairs.[424] The most important application of this principle in its pure form is the case where the earlier interest is under a floating charge.[425] The essence of this interest is that the chargee grants authority to the chargor to deal with the charged assets in the ordinary course of business. If the chargor takes an asset which he holds, subject to the charge, as stock in trade, and sells it in the ordinary course of business to a customer, then the customer takes free of the charge, without the need for reliance on any principle of good faith purchase. The asset is taken free of the charge because the disposition was authorized by the chargee.

(i) Ostensible authority

Just as actual authority from the holder of an earlier interest can allow a later interest to **8.114** take priority, so too can ostensible or apparent authority.[426] This may allow an artificer to maintain his lien against the owner of goods even if the owner did not actually authorize the repair, on the ground that the owner held out another person as having the authority to order repairs.[427] Again, in floating charges, the contract between the chargor and the chargee will determine which dispositions the chargor is actually authorized to make. Even beyond that actual authority, however, the chargor may have ostensible authority to make dispositions that are ordinarily authorized by floating chargees as being in the ordinary course of business, so long as the party taking under that disposition did not have notice of any limitation on the chargor's authority. For example, the granting of subsequent fixed charges having priority over the earlier floating charge is understood to be a disposition in the ordinary course of business.[428] The result is that even if the floating charge agreement prohibits the granting of a fixed charge with priority over the floating charge, the prohibition is generally understood

---

[424] *Tappenden v Artus* [1964] 2 QB 185, CA.

[425] The analysis here assumes that the floating charge was still floating when the subsequent interest was created. If, at that time, the floating charge had crystallized, then it was no longer floating but had become fixed: 8.95. If, however, the crystallization was 'automatic,' then the effectiveness of that crystallization may be overridden by considerations of ostensible authority on the same principles as those discussed here: 8.96.

[426] See 1.60–1.71 and 2.25.

[427] *Albemarle Supply Co Ltd v Hind and Co* [1928] 1 KB 307, CA.

[428] *Wheatley v Silkstone and Haigh Moor Coal Co* (1885) 29 Ch D 715.

to be ineffective unless the subsequent fixed chargee had notice of it.[429] Similarly, even if, by the terms of the agreement, there has been an automatic crystallization of the floating charge, this crystallization will be ineffective against third parties who lack notice of the terms of the agreement.[430]

8.115 This result is usually understood as based on ostensible authority. That is, the actual terms of the charge delimit the chargor's actual authority; but in allowing the chargor to operate under a floating charge, the chargee is understood to be holding out the chargor as having the authority which the chargor normally has under a floating charge. One difficulty with this analysis is that the ostensible authority appears to be based not on the level of actual authority which chargors normally have now, but on that which they normally had when floating charges were developing, in the late nineteenth and early twentieth centuries. It is not surprising that it was held that a floating chargor generally lacks authority to create a second floating charge ranking in priority to the first;[431] and so it follows that there will be no ostensible authority for such an act. On the other hand, it was held that a floating chargor had actual authority to create a subsequent fixed charge ranking in priority to the floating charge.[432] Today floating charges almost universally prohibit this as a matter of actual authority, but the law still permits it unless the second chargee has actual knowledge of the prohibition.[433] Basing this result on a theory of ostensible authority derived from 'holding out' may therefore be artificial.[434] Another difficulty with the estoppel theory is the case of the execution creditor. If such a creditor completes his execution before the charge crystallizes, he has priority over the charge. It is hard to understand how an execution creditor can be said to rely on a holding out by the chargee, or indeed how execution on a judgment can be understood as a transaction in the ordinary course of business.[435] It might be more logical to say that the priority of subsequent fixed chargees, or of execution creditors, is an incident of the floating charge that is not subject to freedom of contract.[436]

8.116 The principle of ostensible authority can also apply in relation to mortgages of land.[437]

(c) Fault

8.117 If the priority conflict has arisen due to the fault of the earlier party, who prima facie has priority, he may be postponed to the later party. This principle has primarily been developed in the context of mortgages of land, and in particular in relation to carelessness by the earlier

---

[429] See 8.97. Note however that in the case of agricultural charges, by the Agricultural Credits Act 1928, s 8(3), a subsequent bill of sale or fixed agricultural charge is void against an earlier floating agricultural charge.

[430] 8.96.

[431] *Re Benjamin Cope & Sons Ltd* [1914] 1 Ch 800. In *Re Automated Bottle Makers Ltd* [1926] Ch 412, CA, it was held that the chargor could effectively create, over a part of the charged assets, a subsequent floating charge which had priority over the earlier charge; but the creation of such a charge was expressly authorized by the earlier charge. The decision must be based on that actual authority, not on the fact that the second charge covered only part of the assets; and such actual authority will be most uncommon.

[432] *Wheatley v Silkstone and Haigh Moor Coal Co* (1885) 29 Ch D 715.

[433] See 8.97.

[434] See JH Farrar 'Floating Charges and Priorities' (1974) 38 Conveyancer (New Series) 315, 322, effectively arguing that the content of ostensible authority must respond to changing commercial realities.

[435] WJ Gough, *Company Charges* (2nd edn, 1996) 255–256 doubts whether estoppel can apply in favour of such a creditor, but argues (320–321) that the seizure of a debtor's assets in execution of a judgment is within the debtor's ordinary course of business.

[436] In *Re Spectrum Plus Ltd* [2005] UKHL 41, [2005] 2 AC 680, the House of Lords held that the question whether a charge is fixed or floating is determined by the law and is not subject to freedom of contract. This is because it has effects on third parties. The same is true of the priority of the charge as against subsequent interests.

[437] *Brocklesby v Temperance Permanent BS* [1895] AC 173, HL.

mortgagee regarding the title deeds, which he was entitled to possess.[438] A failure to obtain the deeds might, if it amounted to gross negligence, lead to a legal mortgagee's being postponed to an interest created later.[439] Similarly, if the title deeds had been obtained, then it was possible that gross negligence regarding their custody could lead to the mortgagee's being postponed to a later interest.[440]

(d) Exceptional assets

Some kinds of assets are subject to exceptional rules which can displace the normal rule that **8.118** the earliest interest prevails.

(i) Money and negotiable instruments

If the asset in question is a form of money, then a party who acquires it as currency, for **8.119** value, in good faith, and without notice of any earlier interest held by someone other than the transferee, will take free of that earlier interest. This is a defence which the later party must establish. For coins this is a rule of the common law,[441] and it was so for bank notes as well,[442] although bank notes are now dealt with by the Bills of Exchange Act 1882.[443] Under that Act, the defence as applicable to bills of exchange and promissory notes is codified as the status of 'holder in due course'.[444] The uncodified version of the defence is available to holders of a number of other instruments, namely those recognized by the courts (taking notice of commercial usage) as 'negotiable'.[445] Some examples are share warrants, negotiable certificates of deposit, and bearer bonds.[446] For the purposes of this defence, the value which must be given includes any consideration which would support a contract.[447]

(ii) Assignments of trust interests and debts

If an interest in a trust (whether of land or moveables)[448] is charged or assigned more **8.120** than once, whether absolutely or by way of security, then priority goes to the assignee who

---

[438] Gross negligence by a legal mortgagee might also mean that he would not be allowed to take free of a prior equitable interest, but that principle is not an exception to the *nemo dat* principle; it is discussed in 8.112.

[439] *Farrand v Yorkshire Banking Co* (1888) 40 Ch D 182; *Grierson v National Provincial Bank of England Ltd* [1913] 2 Ch 18. Fraud is a fortiori.

[440] *Waldron v Sloper* (1852) 1 Drew 193, 61 ER 425; *Northern Counties of England Fire Insurance Co v Whipp* (1884) 26 Ch D 482, CA, holding carelessness is not enough. It is unclear whether the priority of a prior equitable mortgagee was more easily displaced by his carelessness than that of a prior legal mortgagee; see EH Burn and J Cartwright, *Cheshire and Burn's Modern Law of Real Property* (18th edn, 2011) 878.

[441] *Moss v Hancock* [1899] 2 QB 111, DC.

[442] *Miller v Race* (1758) 1 Burr 452, 97 ER 398.

[443] By s 89 the provisions of the Act for bills of exchange also apply, with necessary modifications, to promissory notes. By the Currency and Bank Notes Act 1954, a bank note is a bearer promissory note.

[444] Bills of Exchange Act 1882, s 29(1). The same status can attach to one who has a lien over a bill (Bills of Exchange Act 1882, s 27(3)). Note that for many bills of exchange (of which cheques are a subset) a transfer requires not only delivery but endorsement. In English law a forged endorsement is a nullity (Bills of Exchange Act 1882, s 24, codifying the common law rule; although there is special protection for bankers in the case of cheques: Bills of Exchange Act 1882, ss 60, 80; Cheques Act 1957, s 1). This means that in the case of instruments which require endorsement, the ability to take free of defects in the transferor's title is much more limited than in the case of bearer instruments, where even a thief can give a good title.

[445] This word is sometimes used to designate an instrument transferable by delivery, with any necessary endorsement. In this wider sense it does not connote the possibility that the transferor be able to give a better title than he has. See RM Goode and E McKendrick, *Goode on Commercial Law* (4th edn, 2009) 53 fn 166.

[446] For a full list, see LS Sealy and RJA Hooley, *Commercial Law* (4th edn, 2008) 525–526.

[447] Bills of Exchange Act 1882, s 27(1)(a). At common law and under the statute, this includes an unconditional promise to pay money (*Ex p Richdale* (1882) 19 Ch D 409, 417, CA; *Royal Bank of Scotland v Tottenham* [1894] 2 QB 715, CA).

[448] LPA 1925, s 137(1).

first gives notice of the charge or assignment to the trustees.[449] This is the rule in *Dearle v Hall*.[450] Notice is not necessary to *constitute* the charge or assignment;[451] but written notice is determinative of priority in the case of multiple dispositions.[452] The later chargee or assignee can take priority over the earlier one by giving the first notice only if, at the time that he gave value for his assignment, the later assignee did not have notice of the earlier disposition.[453]

8.121 At common law a debt (not represented by an instrument) could generally be assigned only in equity. In a case of multiple equitable assignments, the rule in *Dearle v Hall* applies. Again, the *validity* of an equitable assignment does not depend on notice to the debtor,[454] but such notice is determinative of priority among multiple assignments; and this is so whether the assigned debts themselves are legal or equitable.[455] The notice must be unequivocal but (unlike in the case of trust interests) it need not be in writing.[456] It is possible by statute to make a legal assignment of a debt; in this case, the assignment must be in writing, and written notice to the debtor is required to constitute the assignment.[457] As in the case of an equitable assignment, that written notice will determine priority in a case of multiple assignments.[458] In both cases, as in assignments of trust interests, the later assignee cannot acquire priority if, at the time he advanced value for his assignment, he had notice of the earlier assignment.[459]

8.122 It appears that if a trust of a debt is created, this does not attract the rule in *Dearle v Hall* and so the beneficiary of the trust is not required to give notice to the debtor to protect his

---

[449] If there are multiple trustees and all are notified, the notice is effective from that date even if some or all of the trustees later leave office (*Re Wasdale* [1899] 1 Ch 163). If not all of the trustees are notified, then the notice is effective only in respect of subsequent notifications made while one of those earlier notified remains in office (*Ward v Duncombe* [1893] AC 369, HL; *Re Phillips' Trusts* [1903] 1 Ch 183). Notice of a trustee who is himself the mortgagor is ineffective (*Lloyds Bank v Pearson* [1901] 1 Ch 865). LPA 1925, s 138 allows a trust settlor, trustees, or the court to nominate a trust corporation as the proper party to receive such notices. Failing this, s 137(2) specifies to whom notice should be given in trusts of or relating to land, although it appears to leave untouched the common law rules regarding multiple trustees. The Act also provides (s 137(4)–(6)) for the giving of notice by endorsement upon the trust instrument, in cases where the giving of notice to trustees is impossible or impracticable; these provisions apply to trusts of land and moveables.

[450] (1823) 3 Russ 1, 38 ER 475, MR; aff'd (1828) 3 Russ 48, 38 ER 492, LC. The crucial time is that when the notice was received, not sent.

[451] eg, it appears that a consensual chargee who did not give notice takes priority over a subsequent holder of a charging order, who was treated as a chargee not for value and therefore was unable to take advantage of the rule in *Dearle v Hall*: *United Bank of Kuwait plc v Sahib* [1997] Ch 107, 118–120, aff'd on other grounds [1997] Ch 107, CA.

[452] *Ward v Duncombe* [1893] AC 369, 392, HL. The notice must be written under LPA 1925, s 137(3). The assignment of an equitable interest must itself be in writing under LPA 1925, s 53(1)(c).

[453] *Re Holmes* (1885) 29 Ch D 786, CA. An assignee otherwise than for value cannot be promoted over an earlier assignment by being the first to give notice: *United Bank of Kuwait plc v Sahib* [1997] Ch 107, at 119–120, aff'd on other grounds [1997] Ch 107, CA.

[454] eg, it is effective in an insolvency against the liquidator: *Gorringe v Irwell India Rubber and Gutta Percha Works* (1886) 34 Ch D 128, CA (although for individuals, see Insolvency Act 1986, s 344; see 9.84).

[455] *Compaq Computer Ltd v Abercorn Group Ltd* [1993] BCLC 602, [1991] BCC 484.

[456] *James Talcott Ltd v John Lewis & Co Ltd* [1940] 3 All ER 592, CA.

[457] LPA 1925, s 136(1).

[458] *E Pfeiffer Weinkellerei-Weineinkauf GmbH & Co v Arbuthnot Factors Ltd* [1988] 1 WLR 150; *Compaq Computer Ltd v Abercorn Group Ltd* [1993] BCLC 602, [1991] BCC 484. There is academic argument to the effect that where a statutory assignment has been made, the rule in *Dearle v Hall* should not apply, but rather the rule that a later legal interest, acquired for value and in good faith without notice of an earlier equitable interest, takes priority over that interest: F Oditah, 'Priorities: Equitable versus Legal Assignments of Book Debts' (1989) 9 OJLS 521.

[459] Including constructive notice: *Spencer v Clarke* (1878) 9 Ch D 137. Similarly, a later assignee will be unable to gain priority over an earlier charge on the debt if, at the time he gave value, he had notice of the charge.

priority against a later assignee of the debt.[460] Moreover, if a party's interest in a debt is a charge which arose by operation of law, then again the rule probably does not apply. The rule can, however, apply to a consensually created charge, and can subordinate the chargee's interest to that of a later assignee.[461] Furthermore, if a party has an interest in a debt because it had an interest in goods which were sold to generate that debt, the interest in the debt is likely to be characterized as a charge which arose by agreement, and so the rule will apply.[462]

(e) Exceptional transactions

There is no general principle in English law that a party in good faith is entitled to rely on another party's possession of a thing as indicative that the other party is the owner of that thing. There are, however, a number of situations where particular rules or principles have that effect, and give a later interest priority over an earlier one.[463] These are dealt with in detail elsewhere, but their impact on priorities will be outlined here.

8.123

Where goods are sold and the seller retains ownership to secure the price, the buyer in possession will often be in a position to give to another party whatever title the seller had.[464] Partly for this reason, much secured finance is done by hire purchase. Here the principle is much narrower, although a hirer of a motor vehicle may be able to give title to a private purchaser.[465] Returning to the case of a sale of goods with retention of ownership, the buyer in possession will also generally be in a position to give a pledge of the goods which will have priority over the seller's ownership.[466] Similarly, if goods are entrusted to a mercantile agent for sale, the agent will be in a position to create a pledge which will have priority over the owner's interest.[467] This provision has also been used to resolve a contest between multiple pledges. A pledgee of a document of title to goods may release it to the pledgor under a 'trust receipt', which allows the pledge to subsist; but where the pledgor created another pledge, the second one had priority.[468]

8.124

A party can sometimes enforce a lien against the owner of goods even if they were deposited by someone else. This may be because the deposit was with the actual or ostensible authority of the owner.[469] Where the creditor follows a common calling,[470] however, he will be able to assert his lien even if there is no actual or ostensible authority, as where the deposited goods

8.125

---

[460] *BS Lyle Ltd v Rosher* [1959] 1 WLR 8, 22–23, HL.

[461] The holder of a charge over a debt is not, as such, in a position to secure his priority by giving notice of assignment to the debtor, because the charge is not an assignment and the chargee has no right to payment from the debtor. Registration of the charge may, however, amount to constructive notice of it, preventing a subsequent assignee from taking priority: 8.143. Also, a consensual charge over a debt is usually combined with a power in the chargee to convert the charge into a mortgage, that is an assignment by way of security: 8.98. Upon the exercise of that power, the chargee becomes an assignee and can give notice.

[462] On such facts, the court will probably reject attempts to characterize the interest as a trust or as a charge arising by operation of law: *Compaq Computer Ltd v Abercorn Group Ltd* [1993] BCLC 602, [1991] BCC 484; 8.85.

[463] Factors Act 1889, ss 2, 8, 9; Sale of Goods Act 1979, ss 24, 25; Hire Purchase Act 1964, Part III; see 10.25.

[464] Factors Act 1889, s 9; Sale of Goods Act 1979, s 25; *National Employers' Mutual General Insurance Assoc Ltd v Jones* [1990] 1 AC 24, HL.

[465] Hire Purchase Act 1964, Part III.

[466] Factors Act 1889, s 9; Sale of Goods Act 1979, s 25.

[467] Factors Act 1889, s 2. This provision also allows him to sell the goods free of the principal's interest, but the focus here is on contests where at least one of the competing interests is by way of security.

[468] *Lloyds Bank Ltd v Bank of America National Trust and Savings Association* [1938] 2 KB 147, CA. Because of the language of s 2, it can generate this result only where the pledgor is a mercantile agent and where the goods or document of title were delivered to him in that capacity.

[469] See 8.113–8.114.

[470] eg, a common carrier or an innkeeper.

were stolen,[471] or where, to his knowledge, they belong to someone else.[472] This is because such a party is obliged to accept the goods and to provide the relevant services.[473]

(f) Superiority of legal interests

8.126 It is important to know whether a party's interest is legal or equitable because there is a general principle, albeit modified by statute in many situations, that may permit a later legal interest to prevail over an earlier equitable one. The principle is that if one acquires a legal interest in good faith and for value, and without notice of the prior equitable interest, then one takes free of that interest. In the context of this doctrine of equity, 'value' means money or money's worth, or marriage consideration. It includes the satisfaction of an antecedent debt owed to the purchaser;[474] but it must be executed, and so it excludes a promise made by the purchaser to pay money or transfer property.[475]

8.127 The notice may be actual, constructive or imputed. Constructive notice exists where actual notice is absent but would have been present had the purchaser acted reasonably. The scope of constructive notice has always been much broader in transactions involving immoveables, where there are established procedures for investigating title; one who fails to follow them will be said to have constructive notice of that which he would have discovered had he followed them.[476] This context also generated the concept of imputed notice; a party has imputed notice of any interest which was or would have been discovered by his conveyancing solicitor or other agent, had the agent acted competently. This general doctrine regarding notice is now of much less importance for interests in land, because of the statutory priority rules now in place.[477] Constructive notice remains relevant in cases involving moveables, although in the absence of established machinery for searching titles its scope is necessarily narrower.[478]

8.128 The crucial time for determining whether the holder of the legal interest had notice of the equitable interest is not the time at which the legal interest was acquired, but rather the time at which the holder of the legal interest gave value. Assume that the debtor granted equitable mortgages or charges to A and then to B, so that A's interest had priority to B's, but that B lacked notice of A's interest at the time B made his advance. If B were able to acquire a legal interest in the mortgaged asset, eg by exercise of a power to convert his mortgage into a legal mortgage, then B would acquire priority, even if by that time he was aware of A's interest.[479] One aspect of this general doctrine has been abrogated by statute, namely where the legal interest in question is acquired from someone who was himself a mortgagee. If a legal mortgage were given to A, and then equitable mortgages to B and to C, then C's interest ranks

---

[471] *Marsh v Police Commissioner* [1945] KB 43, CA.

[472] *Robins & Co v Gray* [1895] 2 QB 501, CA.

[473] Although an innkeeper might not be obliged to accept 'a tiger or a package of dynamite': *Robins & Co v Gray* [1895] 2 QB 501, 504, CA.

[474] *Taylor v Blakelock* (1886) 32 Ch D 560, CA.

[475] *Story v Windsor* (1743) 2 Atk 630, 26 ER 776.

[476] *Berwick & Co v Price* [1905] 1 Ch 632. For details, see C Harpum, S Bridge, and M Dixon, *Megarry and Wade: The Law of Real Property* (8th edn, 2012) 264–270.

[477] See 8.131–8.139. There is still some role for constructive and imputed notice, in cases involving unregistrable interests in unregistered land: LPA 1925, s 199(1)(ii); but these doctrines have no role to play for registered land: *Williams & Glyn's Bank Ltd v Boland* [1981] AC 487, 503–504, HL; see however n 491.

[478] *Eagle Trust plc v SBC Securities Ltd* [1993] 1 WLR 484, 504–506. There can, however, be constructive notice by registration: 8.143.

[479] *Bailey v Barnes* [1894] 1 Ch 25, CA; *McCarthy & Stone Ltd v Julian S Hodge & Co Ltd* [1971] 1 WLR 1547; *MacMillan Inc v Bishopsgate Investment Trust plc (No 3)* [1995] 1 WLR 978, 1003, aff'd on other grounds [1996] 1 WLR 387, CA. If, to the knowledge of B, the later conveyance of the legal interest is a breach of trust on the part of the debtor, then B cannot prevail (*Mumford v Stohwasser* (1874) LR 18 Eq 556); and the cases suggest that this result will follow even if neither the debtor nor B knew that the conveyance was a breach of trust.

last. By the general law, if C had no notice of B's interest at the time C made his advance, C would be able to upgrade his priority by purchasing A's mortgage interest and so acquiring a legal interest in the mortgaged asset, even if, at the time of purchasing A's interest, C was aware of B's. This would allow C to recover the amount originally owed to A, and the amount which C had advanced, all in priority to B's interest. This particular application of the general law has been abolished so that the ranking of the three mortgages would be unaffected by C's purchase.[480]

The general doctrine by which a legal interest can prevail over an earlier equitable interest **8.129** is subject to many of the principles which have been set out above. For example, gross negligence by the holder of a legal interest might mean that he will be postponed to an earlier equitable interest.[481] Where the subject matter of the priority contest is a debt, then there is no room for the doctrine which gives priority to legal interests; even in the case of a legal assignment of a legal debt, the rule in *Dearle v Hall* governs the contest.[482]

(3) Particular Priority Contests

The application of these general principles to particular situations is modified by statutory **8.130** interventions.

(a) Registered land

(i) Where the mortgaged estate is legal

If a mortgagee wishes to have a registered charge on registered land, he must take a charge **8.131** by way of legal mortgage and register it in the Land Registry.[483] Such registered charges rank according to the order in which they are entered on the register, not the order of the execution of the documents.[484]

If a legal mortgagee fails to register his interest, it takes effect only in equity.[485] Similarly, if **8.132** a mortgagee takes only an equitable mortgage on a legal estate, this cannot be registered as a charge. Equitable mortgages can be protected by entering a notice in the Land Registry.[486]

A registered charge, or any other registered disposition, which is made for value, will gen- **8.133** erally take priority over a prior interest that is unregistered, even if the purchaser of the

---

[480] LPA 1925, s 94(3), which appears to apply to moveables as well as land (RM Goode and E McKendrick, *Goode on Commercial Law* (4th edn, 2009) 699). On facts such as these, C's goal is said to be to 'tack' his own advance on to the prior interest of A, and s 94(3) abolishes all forms of 'tacking' not specifically preserved by s 94(1), (2) (which are discussed in 5.154–5.157); but it did not abolish the general rules regarding the subsequent acquisition of a legal interest: *McCarthy & Stone Ltd v Julian S Hodge & Co Ltd* [1971] 1 WLR 1547, 1556; *MacMillan Inc v Bishopsgate Investment Trust plc (No 3)* [1995] 1 WLR 978, 1002–1005, aff'd on other grounds [1996] 1 WLR 387, CA.

[481] *Oliver v Hinton* [1899] 2 Ch 264, CA. The holder of the legal title made no inquiries about the title deeds; if he had, he would have learned of the earlier equitable mortgage, whose mortgagee held the deeds. The equitable mortgage was given priority. One might have said that the carelessness of the holder of the legal title gave him constructive notice of the equitable interest, so that the basic rule applied, with priority going to the earliest interest: EH Burn and J Cartwright, *Cheshire and Burn's Modern Law of Real Property* (18th edn, 2011) 875 fn 499.

[482] See 8.121.

[483] See 8.18.

[484] LRA 2002, s 48. An intending mortgagee who obtains a clear search of the register may be concerned that another interest may be registered before the mortgagee completes his own registration. He may protect himself by making an 'official search with priority', which will guarantee priority if the mortgage is registered within 30 days: Land Registration Rules 2003, SI 2003/1417, rr 131, 147–154.

[485] LRA 2002, s 27(1).

[486] 8.18.

charge is aware of that interest.[487] There are two main exceptions, in which a registered disposition will not take priority over a prior unregistered interest. It will not do so if, at the time of the registration of the disposition, the unregistered interest was protected by a notice. Nor will it do so if the unregistered interest is an 'overriding interest', one that is protected even without registration.[488] As between themselves, unregistered interests rank by the order of their creation, whether or not they are protected;[489] although this is subject to the principle that the earlier mortgagee can be subordinated where fault is attributable to him.[490] In effect, protection of an unregistered interest on the register protects it against later interests, but (unlike full registration) does not improve the interest's priority against existing interests.

8.134 A priority contest may arise between a mortgagee and the beneficiaries of a trust of land; eg, if the trustees (who hold the registered title to the land) grant a registered charge on the land contrary to the terms of the trust. Beneficiaries have always been protected by the principles of equity, including the doctrine of notice; but too much protection of this kind meant that purchasers or mortgagees from trustees had to conduct very extensive inquiries as to the terms of a trust in order to be certain that they would get a clear title. The legislative solution is the principle that a mortgagee or other purchaser of a legal interest takes free of a pre-existing trust interest (even if he is aware of the trust, and even if the trustee is acting in breach of trust) so long as the mortgage advance is paid either to two or more individual trustees, or to a trust corporation.[491] The idea underlying these 'overreaching' provisions is that the beneficiaries are sufficiently protected against breach of trust by the requirement of multiple trustees or a trust corporation. If these provisions are complied with, then the mortgagee will have priority over even an overriding beneficial interest.[492] The overreaching provisions are reinforced by requiring that in trusts of land, there should be a restriction on the register that does not allow the trustees to make a disposition except one that will satisfy the overreaching provisions, guaranteeing that the purchaser will take a clear title.[493] In the case of a trust arising by operation of law, eg between married or unmarried cohabitants, this may be impossible since there may be only one individual trustee. In such a case, the statutory overreaching provisions cannot operate.[494] The beneficiary's interest will be protected if

---

[487] LRA 2002, ss 28–30. Actual notice does not affect priorities in respect of registered land.

[488] These are listed in LRA 2002, Sch 3. One of the most important (para 2) is an 'interest belonging at the time of the disposition to a person in actual occupation'; this protects, eg, the equitable interest of a person under a trust arising by operation of law, so long as they occupy the land (*Williams & Glyn's Bank Ltd v Boland* [1981] AC 487, HL). The result is that although the old concept of 'notice' does not apply to registered land, a prudent purchaser must not only inspect the register, but must ascertain what rights the occupants may have. However, the interest must be a proprietary right and not merely a personal right: *Southern Pacific Mortgages Ltd v Scott* [2014] UKSC 52, [2015] AC 385.

[489] LRA 2002, s 28. See, under the LRA 1925, *Barclays Bank Ltd v Taylor* [1974] Ch 137, CA and *Mortgage Corp Ltd v Nationwide Credit Corp* [1994] Ch 49, CA.

[490] See, under the LRA 1925, *Freeguard v Royal Bank of Scotland plc* (1998) 79 P & CR 81, CA.

[491] LPA 1925, ss 2(1)(ii), 27. Not any corporation qualifies as a trust corporation: LPA 1925, s 205(xxviii). Note that because of the way 'purchaser' is defined (s 205(1)(xxi)), for the purposes of ss 2 and 27, a purchaser need not be in good faith. The consensus is that these provisions of LPA 1925 apply to registered as well as unregistered land; see however N Jackson, 'Overreaching in Registered Land' (2006) 69 MLR 214.

[492] *City of London BS v Flegg* [1988] AC 54, HL. In *State Bank of India v Sood* [1997] Ch 276, CA, it was held that the mortgagee takes priority even where no money was advanced at the time the mortgage was taken, as where it is taken to secure existing and future advances.

[493] LRA 2002, ss 40–47; Land Registration Rules 2003, SI 2003/1417, rr 91–99 and Forms A, B, C.

[494] It is of course possible for a clear title to be conveyed, either with the consent of the beneficiary or by the appointment of a new trustee. The problem discussed in the text arises where the single individual trustee attempts to make a disposition without the consent of a beneficiary. The beneficiary who becomes aware of this possibility in advance can enter a restriction.

he is in actual occupation;[495] or, if it is protected by a restriction on the register; otherwise a subsequent registered charge will take priority under the general rules.[496]

(ii) Where the mortgaged interest is equitable

If the mortgaged interest is equitable, eg an interest under a trust of land, then only an equi- **8.135** table mortgage can be created, and it cannot be registered or protected.[497] Priorities among such mortgages are resolved by the rule in *Dearle v Hall*.[498] There are important statutory provisions governing how notice may be given so as to secure priority under this rule.[499]

(b) Unregistered land

(i) Where the mortgaged estate is legal

There may be multiple legal mortgages of a legal estate. Only the holder of the first one is **8.136** entitled to possession of the title deeds; the consequence is that this mortgage is not regis- trable in the Land Charges Register.[500] Later legal mortgages are registrable, as are equitable mortgages not protected by a deposit of title deeds.[501] Among these registrable mortgages, the general rule is that mortgages rank by the order of their registration.[502] The exception is that a registrable mortgage which was not registered when another interest was subsequently acquired for value is void against the holder of that interest.[503] This means that a subsequent registered mortgage defeats an earlier unregistered one, but it also has a less obvious effect. If A takes a registrable mortgage, and then B takes a registrable mortgage for value, and then A registers, and then B registers, B has priority, since A's interest is void against B.[504] A

---

[495] LRA 2002, Sch 3, para 2; *Williams & Glyn's Bank Ltd v Boland* [1981] AC 487, HL.

[496] LRA 2002, s 30.

[497] Because the equitable interest of the mortgagor cannot itself be registered: LRA 2002, s 2.

[498] Land Registration Act 1986, s 5(1)(b). The rule is explained in 8.120. If the mortgaged equitable interest is not an interest in a trust (eg, an estate contract) then it appears that the rule in *Dearle v Hall* does not apply: LPA 1925, s 137(10); *Property Discount Corp Ltd v Lyon Group Ltd* [1981] 1 WLR 300, CA. This means that priority will be determined by order of creation, subject to the rules about fault.

[499] LPA 1925, ss 137, 138; n 452.

[500] Recall, however, that the creation of such a mortgage now triggers compulsory registration of the mort- gaged estate, meaning that the land becomes registered land and the mortgage itself will need to be registered: LRA 2002, s 4(1)(g), (8).

[501] See 8.19.

[502] LPA 1925, s 97. To the extent that notice may be relevant, by s 198(1) registration constitutes notice to all parties from the date of registration. An intending mortgagee who obtains a clear search of the register may be concerned that another interest may be registered before the mortgagee completes his own registra- tion. If he makes an official search, however, and completes the transaction within 15 days, then he will not be affected by any registration made between search and completion: Land Charges Act 1972, s 11(5). An intending mortgagee may also enter in the register a priority notice at least 15 days before registering his mortgage (Land Charges Act 1972, s 11(1)–(3)); if he registers within 30 days from entering the priority notice, then the date of creation of the mortgage is treated as the date of registration.

[503] Land Charges Act 1972, s 4(5); the subsequent interest may be a mortgage or a beneficial interest: Land Charges Act 1972, s 17(1). Section 4(5) covers Class C land charges (other than estate contracts); that includes second and subsequent legal mortgages, and equitable mortgages of legal interests, except equitable mortgages arising from an agreement to give a legal mortgage, which are a type of estate contract. Other types of charges are dealt with by other parts of s 4, and generally the same rule applies, except under s 4(6) which governs estate contracts and Class D land charges (Inland Revenue charges, restrictive covenants, and equi- table easements). Here the unregistered interest is only void where the subsequent interest is a legal interest, acquired for money or money's worth (which expression excludes marriage consideration); thus if the second interest is equitable (or a legal interest acquired as a gift) the general law applies, and the earlier unregistered interest will usually prevail (subject to the rules about fault, and the possibility that the holder of the later interest has acquired a legal estate without notice): *McCarthy & Stone Ltd v Julian S Hodge & Co Ltd* [1971] 1 WLR 1547.

[504] The default rule, giving priority to A as the first to register (LPA 1925, s 97), seems inapplicable because A's interest is void against B: EH Burn and J Cartwright, *Cheshire and Burn's Modern Law of Real Property* (18th edn, 2011) 887. Depending on the timing, A could avoid the outcome by the use of a priority

registrable mortgage which is made void by non-registration against the holder of a subsequent interest is void even if the latter was aware of the earlier interest.[505]

8.137 Where a mortgage is protected by deposit of the title deeds, that mortgage is not registrable. Priorities are determined by the general principles discussed above; in particular, that interests are generally ranked by the order of their creation, but that this can be displaced by carelessness with title deeds,[506] and by the superiority of legal interests.[507] So if the first interest is protected by the title deeds, it will be important to know whether it is legal or equitable. If it is legal, then the only way the later interest could prevail would be if the first mortgagee was grossly negligent with the title deeds, eg giving up possession of them and so allowing the later mortgagee to be deceived. If the first mortgage, protected by the deeds, is equitable, then a later legal interest not so protected might take priority as the acquisition of a legal interest in good faith, for value and without notice of the earlier equitable interest. The inability of the mortgagor to produce the title deeds, however, might well give the legal mortgagee constructive notice of the earlier interest, so that the basic rule of first in time would govern.[508] If the second mortgage is equitable as well as the first, then again only gross negligence could displace the normal rule ranking the interests by the time of creation.

8.138 On the other hand, it might be that the second interest is the one protected by the title deeds. This implies that the first interest is registrable, and if it was registered before the second interest was granted, then the second mortgagee is treated as having notice of the first, and so the first takes priority.[509] This would be true even if the first mortgage was equitable and the second was legal, since the legal mortgagee could not claim to have acquired his interest without notice of the other. Only gross negligence could possibly postpone the earlier mortgage. If, on the other hand, the first interest was not registered before the second was granted, the first interest is void against the holder of the second, which therefore takes priority.[510]

8.139 As in registered land, a mortgage granted by trustees may come into conflict with an earlier beneficial interest under a trust of land. The principles of statutory overreaching, discussed above, apply also to unregistered land.[511] In unregistered land, the beneficiary's interest is not registrable, nor can it be protected on any register. A subsequent legal mortgagee can take priority only as a bona fide purchaser for value without notice of the trust. The mortgagee may have actual, constructive or imputed notice of the trust via the beneficiary's occupation

---

notice (n 505). The interaction of the Land Charges Act 1972, s 4(5) and LPA 1925, s 97 is generally considered unsatisfactory; apart from the result mentioned in the text, the scheme can also produce circular priorities where there are more than two interests. The voidness of A's interest against B also means that if neither interest was registered, B would still prevail even though later in time.

[505] LPA 1925, s 199(1)(i); *Coventry Permanent Economic BS v Jones* [1951] 1 All ER 901; *Midland Bank Trust Co Ltd v Green* [1981] AC 513, HL. If the earlier interest is not made void by non-registration, as where it is an estate contract and the later interest is equitable (see n 506), then the non-statutory rules apply: first in time generally prevails, subject to the rule about the superiority of a legal estate acquired for value without notice of the earlier equitable interest: LPA 1925, s 199(1)(ii); *McCarthy & Stone Ltd v Julian S Hodge & Co Ltd* [1971] 1 WLR 1547.

[506] See 8.117. LPA 1925, s 13, makes it clear that these principles remain applicable.

[507] See 8.126–8.129.

[508] The relevance of constructive and imputed notice in this context is preserved by LPA 1925, s 199(1)(ii). Those doctrines are displaced only when the earlier interest is made void by non- registration: LPA 1925, s 199(1)(i).

[509] LPA 1925, s 198.

[510] Land Charges Act 1972, s 4. If, however, the first interest was an equitable mortgage arising from an agreement to grant a legal mortgage, then under s 4(6) it would not be void if the second interest was equitable.

[511] 8.134.

of the land.[512] He is relieved, however, from inquiring into whether the trustees have fulfilled all of their trust obligations, unless he has actual notice that they have not.[513]

(ii) Where the mortgaged interest is equitable

If the mortgaged interest is equitable, eg an interest under a trust of land, then only an equi- **8.140**
table mortgage can be created, and it is not registrable.[514] As in registered land, priorities
among such mortgages are resolved by the rule in *Dearle v Hall*.[515]

(c) Moveables

For moveables, the general principles set out above remain of primary importance. For posses- **8.141**
sory security interests, such as liens and pledges, they are determinative. For non-possessory
interests, such as mortgages and charges, statutory registration requirements are usually applicable.[516] The registration systems can modify the general principles in different ways. First,
failure to register an interest may make it void; secondly, registration may constitute notice of
the registered interest, which has implications for some priority rules; thirdly, priority among
registered interests may be determined by the time of registration. But there is no consistent
policy or legislative technique across the many registers; in particular, in the crucial case of
company charges, the time of registration does not determine priorities.

(i) Company charges and mortgages

If a charge or mortgage is registrable by a company, and it is not registered within 21 days **8.142**
of its creation, the charge will become void as against a liquidator or administrator of the
company, or a secured or execution creditor.[517] Clearly, as between two registrable charges,
a registered charge prevails against an unregistered one; if neither is registered, the later will
have priority, as the earlier one will be void against the later one.[518] Despite the wording of
the section, an unregistered charge is not void against an *unsecured* creditor, unless he has
completed an execution process.[519] In the absence of a subsequent secured or execution
creditor, or a liquidation or administration, there will be no one with standing to prevent the
chargee from enforcing an unregistered charge. A registrable but unregistered charge is not
void against a purchaser of the asset,[520] although the purchaser might take free of the charge
under the general law, for instance if the disposition was authorized under a floating charge,
or if he purchased a legal interest for value, in good faith and without notice of the charge. It
has also been held that where a charge is void, rights arising out of the contract which created
the charge are still enforceable if they are not part of the charge itself; so where a company
charged machinery and the charge was void for non-registration in the liquidation of the

---

[512] LPA 1925, s 199(1)(ii); *Kingsnorth Trust Ltd v Tizard* [1986] 1 WLR 783.

[513] Trusts of Land and Appointment of Trustees Act 1996, s 16.

[514] By Land Charges Act 1972, s 3(1) registration is in the name of the 'estate owner' (mortgagor) and this includes only the holder of a legal estate: Land Charges Act 1972, s 17(1); LPA 1925, s 205(1)(v).

[515] 8.135.

[516] There are however some gaps, such as a mortgage given by an individual over an unregistered ship: *British Credit Trust Ltd v The Owners of the Shizelle (The Shizelle)* [1992] 2 Lloyd's Rep 444.

[517] CA 2006, ss 859H(3), 874(1). In the remainder of this section, 'Company charges and mortgages', the word 'charge' should be read to include 'mortgage' (CA 2006, ss 859A(7), 861(5)). For the charges which are registrable, manner of registration, and the effect of non-registration between debtor and creditor, see 8.103–8.105. The same provisions apply, with minor amendments, to limited liability partnerships: Limited Liability Partnerships (Application of Companies Act 2006) Regulations 2009, SI 2009/1804, r 32.

[518] RM Goode and E McKendrick, *Goode on Commercial Law* (4th edn, 2009) 711; for the similar position in unregistered mortgages of unregistered land, see 8.136.

[519] *Re Ehrmann Bros Ltd* [1906] 2 Ch 697, CA; RM Goode and E McKendrick, *Goode on Commercial Law* (4th edn, 2009) 709–710.

[520] *Stroud Architectural Services Ltd v John Laing Construction Ltd* [1994] BCC 18.

company, this did not prevent the chargee from exercising its right under the contract to continue to make use of the machinery, as that right was held not to be part of the charge.[521]

8.143 If the charge is properly registered, then its priority is governed by the general rules, modified by the fact that the registration may constitute notice of the registered interest. There is no principle that the priority of registered charges is determined by the order of registration.[522] Registration does not, as it does in the case of unregistered land, constitute notice to everyone, since acquisitions of interests in moveables cannot always be preceded by registry searches. The legislation does not clarify the point, but the best view appears to be that registration constitutes notice of the charge to any party who could reasonably be expected to conduct a search.[523] This would seem to include a subsequent secured lender or a purchaser of book debts. A registered charge over book debts should therefore have priority over a subsequent assignment of the debts under the rule in *Dearle v Hall*, not because the chargee gives notice to the debtors, but because the later assignee will have constructive notice of the earlier charge.[524] A purchaser of a single asset in the ordinary course of business would not, however, have constructive notice of a registered charge over the asset. Such a purchaser might therefore be able to rely on the doctrine which allows the good faith purchaser for value of a legal interest to take free of a prior equitable interest if he did not have notice of it.[525]

8.144 A floating charge, even if it be properly registered, will often be subordinate to a later interest. The holder of the later interest can rely on the authority granted to the chargor company to dispose of the charged goods in the ordinary course of business. This reasoning applies even if the holder of the subsequent interest has actual or constructive notice of the earlier charge. Moreover, the relevant authority extends beyond actual authority to ostensible authority, making effective any disposition which is usually authorized under a floating charge, even if the terms of the particular floating charge forbid it.[526] This ostensible authority would extend to the granting of a fixed charge following the floating charge but with priority over it.[527] Similar reasoning makes effective a disposition occurring after the floating charge crystallized, if the crystallization did not occur by one of the events which give notice to the world that the chargor's authority to deal with its assets is at an end.[528]

(ii) Bills of sale

8.145 If a document creating a security interest is registrable as a bill of sale, and it is not properly registered within seven days of execution, the security is unenforceable, even against the debtor.[529] As between the interests of secured creditors under properly registered bills,

---

[521] *Re Cosslett (Contractors) Ltd* [1998] Ch 495, CA. However, in a later round of litigation it was held that the chargee's right under the contract to sell the charged property was part of the charge and was therefore void: *Smith (as Administrator of Cosslett (Contractors) Ltd) v Bridgend County Borough Council* [2001] UKHL 58, [2002] 1 AC 336.

[522] If, however, the charges are registrable under another system, such as ship mortgages, then such a rule may be imposed by that system.

[523] RM Goode and E McKendrick, *Goode on Commercial Law* (4th edn, 2009) 705, 709. It appears, however, that those who have actual or constructive notice of the existence of a charge do not have constructive notice of particular terms of the charge, beyond the particulars which are required to be filed: see n 366.

[524] On charges over book debts, see 8.98. On the rule in *Dearle v Hall*, see 8.121.

[525] This would not, however, be possible if the registered 'charge' was actually a legal mortgage; in that case, both interests are legal.

[526] Constructive notice of the charge does not constitute constructive notice of all of its terms: see n 366. It seems that only actual notice of the restriction can prevent the subsequent party from relying on ostensible authority.

[527] 8.114.

[528] See 8.96. Note also that, in insolvency proceedings, a floating charge is subordinated to preferential debts; and, since 2002, some assets that would otherwise fall within a floating charge must be set aside to help meet the claims of unsecured creditors. See 9.103–9.112.

[529] Bills of Sale Act (1878) Amendment Act 1882, s 8.

priority goes to the first to register, displacing the basic rule giving priority to the first interest created.[530] Purchasers may be able to take free of the creditor's security interest even if it is properly registered, since registration does not constitute constructive notice.[531] If the creditor's interest is by way of equitable charge or mortgage, then a purchaser might be able to rely on the doctrine which allows the good faith purchaser for value of a legal interest to take free of a prior equitable interest if he did not have notice of it.[532]

(iii) Agricultural charges

An agricultural charge is void against everyone except the chargor if not properly registered **8.146** within seven days of creation.[533] As between multiple agricultural charges, priority goes to the earliest registered, again displacing the basic rule giving priority to the first created.[534] Unlike in the case of company charges, a registered floating agricultural charge always takes priority over a later agricultural charge, even if the latter is fixed.[535] Registration of the charge constitutes notice to all persons and for all purposes.[536] However, a purchaser of charged assets can take free of the charge, even if it is a fixed charge, and even if he is aware of it.[537]

(iv) Charges given by industrial and provident societies

An industrial and provident society is a corporation in the nature of a co-operative.[538] Such a **8.147** society may give an agricultural charge, and if it does, it may register it as such.[539] If it gives any other charge, it may register the charge with its regulator (the FCA or the PRA).[540] If it makes either one of these registrations, the Bills of Sale Acts will not apply to the transaction; otherwise, they will.[541] Beyond this, it appears that general principles govern.[542]

(v) Other registers

There are other registers for particular kinds of assets. If the charge or mortgage is given by **8.148** a company, then the requirements of the Companies Act are generally cumulative.[543] The

---

[530] Bills of Sale Act 1878, s 10. This is also true if an 'absolute' bill is granted after a security bill, an absolute bill being a bill of sale conveying an interest which is not by way of security. If, however, a security bill is granted after an absolute bill, then the security bill will be void (except as against the grantor) whether or not the absolute bill was registered: Bills of Sale Act (1878) Amendment Act 1882, s 5. The latter act does not apply to absolute bills: Bills of Sale Act 1878, s 3.

[531] *Joseph v Lyons* (1884) 15 QBD 280, 286, CA.

[532] This would not, however, be possible if the secured creditor had taken a legal mortgage; in that case, both interests are legal.

[533] Agricultural Credits Act 1928, s 9(1), providing for extension of time by the court. The register is kept by the Land Registrar, but, unlike the Land Registry of registered land, it is not organized by the location of the land. The register of agricultural charges is organized by the name of the debtor.

[534] Agricultural Credits Act 1928, s 8(2).

[535] Agricultural Credits Act 1928, s 8(3), also giving the floating charge priority over an interest created under a bill of sale. An agricultural charge can only be given to a bank (Agricultural Credits Act 1928, s 5(1)), so a charge given by the farmer to any other creditor would probably be registrable as a bill of sale.

[536] Agricultural Credits Act 1928, s 9(8).

[537] Agricultural Credits Act 1928, s 6(3), which does not even specify that the sale must be in the ordinary course of business. The ability to take clear of a floating charge is governed by the general law (Agricultural Credits Act 1928, s 7(1)), which would impose such a limitation.

[538] EPL 3.92–3.93.

[539] Agricultural Credits Act 1928, s 14.

[540] Industrial and Provident Societies Act 1967, ss 1–2.

[541] *Re North Wales Produce and Supply Society* [1922] 2 Ch 340.

[542] eg, a society might grant a charge over intangible property that it holds, and fail to register it, and then grant another charge over the same property, and register the second charge with the FCA. Registration with the FCA is optional, and failure to register does not have any consequence except to bring in the Bills of Sale Acts. Those Acts apply to the first charge, but intangible property is not affected by them so the first charge is valid. It would appear that the unregistered first charge would have priority over the registered second charge.

[543] 8.104, noting some exceptions.

charge may therefore be avoided by that Act, even if the particular registration system does not avoid it.

8.149   Ships.   Ship mortgages (including charges) have their own registration system, although it does not apply to every ship mortgage.[544] Where it does apply, it ranks registered mortgages by the time of their registration.[545] An unregistered mortgage is not void, but is subordinate to a registered mortgage, even one created later and with notice of the earlier unregistered mortgage.[546] Outside these cases, it appears that general principles govern.[547]

8.150   Aircraft.   Aircraft mortgages and charges also have their own registration system.[548] It ranks registered mortgages by the time of registration.[549] As in ship mortgages, an unregistered mortgage is not void, but is subordinate to a registered one, even if created later and with notice.[550] Registration of a mortgage is treated as giving notice of it to all parties.[551] Again, it appears that general principles govern other cases.

8.151   Patents.   A mortgage or charge on a patent may be registered.[552] Here a registered interest takes priority over an earlier interest only if the earlier interest was unregistered, and the holder of the later interest did not know of the earlier transaction.[553] As between unregistered interests, it appears that the one created first will prevail; and the same principle will govern as between registered interests, there being no provision making priority depend upon order of registration.

8.152   Registered trade marks.   A mortgage or charge on a registered trade mark may be registered.[554] Under this system, an unregistered interest is ineffective against anyone who acquires a conflicting interest, in ignorance of the earlier interest.[555] This seems to mean that an unregistered interest will be subordinated to a later interest, whether registered or unregistered. But registered interests will take priority by time of creation, there being no provision making priority depend upon order of registration.

8.153   Registered designs.   A mortgage or charge on a registered design is required to be registered.[556] Until this is done, the document by which it is created is inadmissible in evidence.[557] By this unusual legislative technique, it appears that any registered mortgage will prevail over any unregistered disposition, even if the registered mortgagee is aware of the earlier unregistered disposition, because it will be impossible to prove the unregistered disposition. In a dispute as between unregistered interests, neither party will be able to prove the

---

[544] Merchant Shipping Act 1995, Sch 1; as to scope, see n 296. Where the system does not apply, general principles are determinative.

[545] Merchant Shipping Act 1995, Sch 1, para 8. There is a system of priority notices (para 8(2)).

[546] *Black v Williams* [1895] Ch 408.

[547] A Clarke, 'Ship Mortgages' in N Palmer and E McKendrick (eds), *Interests in Goods* (2nd edn, 1998) 684.

[548] Mortgaging of Aircraft Order 1972, SI 1972/1268. The UK has signed, but not ratified, the Convention on International Interests in Mobile Equipment and the Protocol on Matters Specific to Aircraft Equipment (Cape Town, 2001).

[549] Mortgaging of Aircraft Order 1972, SI 1972/1268, art 14(2), with a priority notice system.

[550] Mortgaging of Aircraft Order 1972, SI 1972/1268, art 14(1), (4).

[551] Mortgaging of Aircraft Order 1972, SI 1972/1268, art 13. It also activates a system that indemnifies anyone who suffers a loss due to an error in the register: art 18.

[552] Patents Act 1977, s 33(3)(b).

[553] Patents Act 1977, s 33(1),(2).

[554] Trade Marks Act 1994, s 25(2)(c).

[555] Trade Marks Act 1994, s 25(3).

[556] Registered Designs Act 1949, s 19(1).

[557] Registered Designs Act 1949, s 19(5).

creation of its interest. On the other hand, registered interests will take priority by time of creation, there being no provision making priority depend upon order of registration.

(4) Future Advances

The problem of future advances arises where A has a security interest with priority to that of **8.154** B, and A advances further funds to the debtor. Does the priority of A's security extend to the further advance? An affirmative answer can be given in four cases.[558]

(a) Arrangement

If, pursuant to an arrangement between them, A shall have priority for the further advance, **8.155** this is effective.[559]

(b) Lack of notice

If, at the time he made his further advance, A lacked notice of B's interest, A's prior- **8.156** ity extends to the further advance.[560] In unregistered land, if B's interest is a registered mortgage, then B's registration of his mortgage generally constitutes constructive notice to A, reversing the priorities.[561] If, however, A's security is expressly taken to secure future advances, or to secure a current account, then A will not have constructive notice by B's registration, unless B's registration was in place at the later of the time of A's registration and the time of A's last search of the register.[562] It is therefore general practice for a mortgage agreement to stipulate that the mortgage will secure further advances, while a subsequent mortgagee will be careful to give actual notice to the prior mortgagee. Where A's interest is a registered charge on registered land, the position is slightly different.[563] The basic rule is that A has priority until he has notice of B's registered charge; but A is deemed to receive that notice after a fixed amount of time, depending upon how the notice is sent.[564] In the case of company charges, although there is no express provision regarding the effect of registration, it appears again that B's registration will not constitute constructive notice to A, at least in the case where A is a bank making further advances on a current account, since

---

[558] The matter is governed by LPA 1925, s 94, which appears to apply to moveables as well as unregistered land (RM Goode and E McKendrick, *Goode on Commercial Law* (4th edn, 2009) 699), and LRA 2002, s 49 for registered land. Perhaps by an oversight, the wording of these sections is such that they do not seem to apply to the case where A has not made even his initial advance before B's interest is taken. Here it seems the common law rule, which these provisions otherwise replace, continues to apply: RM Goode and E McKendrick, *Goode on Commercial Law* (4th edn, 2009) 700–701. That rule says that A's advance cannot have priority if A's mortgage is equitable, and even if it is legal, A loses his priority once he has notice of B's interest; this is the case even if A is contractually obliged to make the advance: *Hopkinson v Rolt* (1861) 9 HL Cas 514, 11 ER 829; *West v Williams* [1899] 1 Ch 132, CA.

[559] LPA 1925, s 94(1)(a). LRA 2002, s 48 allows mortgagees of registered land to modify priorities; registration is required for third parties to be affected: LRA 2002, ss 48(2), 49(6); Land Registration Rules 2003, SI 2003/1417, r 102.

[560] LPA 1925, s 94(1)(b); LRA 2002, ss 48(1).

[561] LPA 1925, s 198(1).

[562] LPA 1925, s 94(2). A similar principle operates for agricultural charges: Agricultural Credits Act 1928, s 9(8).

[563] LPA 1925, s 94 does not apply to any mortgages on registered land (s 94(4)); LRA 2002, s 49 dictates when registered mortgages on registered land have priority for future advances. It would appear that s 49 applies if A's interest is registered but B's is unregistered; if both are unregistered, it would appear that the common law rules govern (n 561).

[564] LRA 2002, s 49(2); Land Registration Rules 2003, SI 2003/1417, r 107. eg, if a notice is sent by post, it is deemed to be received on the second day after posting and A will lose priority to B for any advances made after that, even if A never actually receives the notice. When electronic conveyancing is implemented, such a notice will be sent electronically.

it would not be reasonable to require the bank to make a search every time a cheque was presented for payment.[565]

(c) Obligation to make further advance

8.157 Even if A has notice of B's interest, nonetheless if A was obliged by his agreement with the debtor to make the further advance, then his priority extends to the further advance.[566]

(d) Advances within registered upper limit

8.158 In registered land only, even if A has notice of B's interest, and even if A was not obliged to make the further advance, A's further advance can still have priority if A's mortgage was taken to secure advances up to a stated maximum amount and that fact is noted in the register.[567]

(5) After-Acquired Property and Purchase Money Finance

8.159 An equitable mortgage or charge can apply to property acquired by the debtor after the date of the agreement, automatically and without any further legal act.[568] If such a charge has been created in favour of A, the question arises whether a later creditor B can advance money to allow the debtor to purchase an asset which is within A's security, in such a way that B will have priority to that asset. Although in general terms a later security interest is subordinate to an earlier one, in the case where the later creditor is advancing 'purchase money' finance for an asset, there are good reasons for allowing priority in relation to that asset. This will remove what would otherwise be A's credit monopoly; at the same time, it does not materially harm A, since the loss of priority is only in respect of an asset which would not have been acquired but for B's advance.

8.160 If B is actually the seller of the asset, then he can obtain priority by retaining legal ownership of it. As long as B is the owner, the asset does not belong to the debtor, and so it cannot be subject to A's security. If, however, B is merely providing the finance to permit the debtor to acquire the asset, this is not possible; B must take a security interest, such as a mortgage or charge. On one view, it is logically necessary for the debtor to acquire the asset before B's interest can be granted to B; but at the moment the debtor acquires the asset, it will become subject to A's interest.[569] It has been held, however, that if, before the debtor acquired the asset, he had agreed with B that it would be charged to B, then B's interest will take priority.[570] When the purchase of land is being financed, such an agreement will almost always be found; however, the difficulty with making B's priority turn on an agreement is that an agreement to give a charge over land is now of no legal effect unless it is in writing and signed by both parties.[571] If B is to continue to have priority over A, this result must now

---

[565] RM Goode and E McKendrick, *Goode on Commercial Law* (4th edn, 2009) 699 fn 80, 708–709.

[566] LPA 1925, s 94(1)(c); LRA 2002, s 49(3). In registered land, A's obligation must be entered in the register (Land Registration Rules 2003, r 108).

[567] LRA 2002, s 49(4); Land Registration Rules 2003, r 109. Although the LRA does not state this clearly, presumably A's priority extends only to advances up to the registered limit.

[568] See 8.13, 8.88, 8.93.

[569] *Church of England BS v Piskor* [1954] Ch 553, CA.

[570] *Abbey National BS v Cann* [1991] 1 AC 56, 92, 101–102, HL, overruling *Church of England v Piskor*. In *Southern Pacific Mortgages Ltd v Scott* [2014] UKSC 52, [2015] AC 385, it was held that *Cann* stands for the principle that the conveyance of an interest in land is indivisible from the grant of the security interest that was necessary to finance the acquisition; thus, the purchaser does not have a juridical moment in which to grant another interest that could take priority over the interest of the secured lender. Two of the five judges would have held that *Cann* stands for a wider proposition, that the contract between the vendor and the purchaser of the interest is also part of the indivisible transaction. The other judges disagreed. This point was not essential for the decision.

[571] Law of Property (Miscellaneous Provisions) Act 1989, s 2(1); RM Goode and E McKendrick, *Goode on Commercial Law* (4th edn, 2009) 713–714.

be understood to flow from the status of his interest as a purchase money security interest. The implications for security in moveables of the reasoning based on agreement has not been fully worked out.[572]

E. Personal Security

(1) Types of Security

(a) Guarantees and indemnities

A guarantee is a contract to answer for the default of another. As such, it imposes an obliga- **8.161** tion which is *secondary* to that of a primary debtor, meaning that the guarantor's liability depends upon default by the primary debtor. The guarantor's obligation is also *accessory* to that of the primary debtor, meaning that it is enforceable only to the extent that the obligation of the primary debtor is enforceable. A guarantee must be distinguished from an indemnity, where one party is obliged to keep another harmless from loss. The obligation assumed in an indemnity is primary and so does not depend on another's default, nor is it affected by any inability to enforce some other obligation. The question whether a particular contract is a guarantee or an indemnity is one of construction of the contract.[573] The court must decide whether the parties did or did not intend that the liability should be secondary and accessory. Moreover, if the liability was undertaken in a free-standing transaction, it is more likely to be characterized as a guarantee, while if it is undertaken as part of a larger transaction, in which the 'guarantor' has a direct interest, it is more likely to be characterized as an indemnity.[574]

The wide freedom of contract granted by English law means that the boundary between **8.162** guarantee and indemnity is difficult to draw. For example, an agreement may be a guarantee even though it stipulates that the guarantor is liable as a principal debtor, if the agreement as a whole shows an intention that the obligation be a guarantee.[575] It should also be noted that it is possible to provide real security for another's debt, without incurring any personal liability;[576] even though this is a form of real security, nonetheless if it is provided as a guarantee then the principles governing guarantees will apply.[577]

---

[572] eg, attempts by reservation of title sellers to secure an interest in the proceeds of sub-sales usually fail, because the interest is characterized as a charge created by the company, and is not registered: 8.85. It is not always practicable for such sellers to make a registration; even where it is, as in a high-value sale, it might be thought to be pointless if the charge would be subordinate to any earlier charge in favour of an institutional creditor. If, however, the reasoning in *Abbey National BS v Cann* [1991] 1 AC 56, HL, applied to such charges over proceeds, the position of such sellers would be materially improved.

[573] *Yeoman Credit Ltd v Latter* [1961] 1 WLR 828, CA; *Marubeni Hong Kong and South China Ltd v Mongolian Government* [2005] EWCA Civ 395, [2005] 1 WLR 2497.

[574] *Pitts v Jones* [2007] EWCA Civ 1301, [2008] QB 706. In this case the Court of Appeal did not refer to its earlier decisions in *Yeoman Credit Ltd v Latter* [1961] 1 WLR 828, CA; *Marubeni Hong Kong and South China Ltd v Mongolian Government* [2005] EWCA Civ 395, [2005] 1 WLR 2497, but only to older authorities.

[575] *Heald v O'Connor* [1971] 1 WLR 497, 503. Such a term can however have legal effects. It may mean that the guarantor is not discharged, as he normally is, by a release of the primary debtor: *General Produce Co v United Bank Ltd* [1979] 2 Lloyd's Rep 255; it may mean that the creditor is relieved of the usual requirement that he make a demand on the guarantor before the latter is liable: *MS Fashions Ltd v Bank of Credit and Commerce International SA* [1993] Ch 425, CA.

[576] *Smith v Wood* [1929] 1 Ch 14, CA; *Re Bank of Credit and Commerce International SA (No 8)* [1998] AC 214, HL.

[577] *Smith v Wood* [1929] 1 Ch 14, CA.

(b) Other personal securities

8.163 The same freedom of contract permits the creation of agreements which are guarantees in form, but in effect are closer to indemnities. It is common in substantial projects for a party who owes non-monetary obligations to a creditor to procure, for the benefit of that creditor, a performance guarantee from a third party. Such a document may be a true guarantee;[578] but it may instead be a guarantee in form only. In this latter case, the contract is often called a 'first demand guarantee', and the 'guarantor' is usually a bank or other financial institution.[579] Apart from its name, such a contract shares with a true guarantee only the feature that the 'guarantor's' liability is intended to be secondary, so that the guarantee is not to be enforced except in a case of default by the primary debtor. But the 'guarantor's' liability is not accessory, and the default of the primary debtor need not be proved as such; in the usual case, the 'guarantor' is obliged to pay a fixed amount of money upon the presentation by the creditor of a certificate that the primary debtor is in default, or merely upon demand. For this reason, such contracts have more in common with letters of credit than with true guarantees.[580] For example, as in letters of credit, the courts have applied the principle that the bank must pay when the requisite documents are presented unless it has knowledge of fraud; this reflects the parties' intention that the bank's liability is not accessory.[581] On the other hand, as between primary debtor and creditor, it is recognized that the contract is intended to provide a security function, and so it is likely to be construed such that after the creditor is paid under the guarantee, he may recover from the primary debtor any further loss he has suffered, but must also account for any surplus he gained.[582] Still another kind

---

[578] *Trafalgar House Construction (Regions) Ltd v General Security and Guarantee Co Ltd* [1996] AC 199, HL. In this case the guarantee, which may be called a 'performance bond', is usually issued by an insurance company. If the transaction is international, the parties may well incorporate the International Chamber of Commerce's *Uniform Rules for Contract Bonds* (1993).

[579] The terminology is somewhat unstable. The contract may also be called a 'demand' or 'on-demand' guarantee, or the adjectives 'demand', 'first demand' or 'on-demand' may be applied instead to the names 'performance bond' or 'performance guarantee'. Although the 'guarantor' is usually a financial institution, this interpretation may also apply in the case of an individual, if the contract is sufficiently clear: *IIG Capital LLC v Van Der Merwe* [2008] EWCA Civ 542, [2008] 2 All ER (Comm) 1173. However, outside the banking context, there is a presumption against interpreting the agreement in this way: *IIG Capital LLC v Van Der Merwe* [2008] EWCA Civ 542, [2008] 2 All ER (Comm) 1173; *Carey Value Added SL v Grupo Urvasco SA* [2010] EWHC 1905 (Comm), [2011] 2 All ER (Comm) 140; *North Shore Ventures Ltd v Anstead Holdings Inc* [2011] EWCA Civ 230, [2012] 1 Ch 31; *Vossloh Aktiengesellschaft v Alpha Trains (UK) Ltd* [2010] EWHC 2443, [2010] 1 All ER (Comm) 343.

[580] The parties may choose to apply the International Chamber of Commerce's *Uniform Rules for Demand Guarantees* (2010), as in *Meritz Fire & Marine Insurance Co Ltd v Jan De Nul NV* [2011] EWCA Civ 827, [2011] 2 Lloyd's Rep 379. As in letters of credit, in some transactions there may be two banks and four parties: the primary debtor having secured a bank to issue the guarantee, commonly another bank in the jurisdiction of the creditor will agree with the first bank to make the same promise to the creditor with an arrangement for reimbursement. It may also be noted that if the obligation of the primary debtor is a monetary one, the document may well be styled a 'standby letter of credit', which emphasizes the functional affinity of the first demand guarantee with the letter of credit. The ICC's *Uniform Customs and Practice for Documentary Credits* (2006) have been extended to cover standby letters of credit. The ICC has also promulgated a set of *Rules on International Standby Practices* (1998). The UK has not acceded to the 1995 UN Convention on Independent Guarantees and Standby Letters of Credit (New York, 1995).

[581] To maintain its reputation the bank will usually pay unless the primary debtor can obtain an injunction; such an injunction will be granted only if the court considers that the only realistic inference to draw is that of fraud: *Edward Owen Engineering Ltd v Barclays Bank International Ltd* [1978] QB 159, CA. But if a bank resists a claim on a 'demand guarantee' on the basis that the agreement itself is voidable for fraud, and the claimant seeks summary judgment, the test to be applied is whether the bank has shown 'a reasonable or real prospect' that the relevant bond was voidable: *Solo Industries UK Ltd v Canara Bank* [2001] EWCA Civ 1041, [2001] 1 WLR 1800.

[582] *Cargill International SA v Bangladesh Sugar and Food Industries Corp* [1998] 1 WLR 461, CA.

of transaction is a policy of indemnity insurance that a creditor may take out against the risk of a debtor's default.[583]

(2) Creation

A guarantee is a contract and its formation is governed by the normal rules.[584]   **8.164**

(a) Parties

The contract may be a tripartite one including the primary debtor, guarantor and credi-   **8.165**
tor, but this is unusual. Most commonly, the parties to the contract are the guarantor and the creditor, although usually the primary debtor has requested the guarantor to enter the contract.[585] If two debtors contract as principal debtors with the creditor, then they may agree between themselves that one shall be primarily liable and the other shall be guarantor; in this case, there is a contract of guarantee only as between the debtors.[586] If, however, the creditor later becomes aware of the understanding between the debtors, then the liability of the guarantor will be subject to the principles governing guarantees; and this is so even if the debtors themselves only came to this understanding after the relevant contracts were formed.[587]

The parties to a contract of guarantee may change if the creditor or the primary debtor assign   **8.166**
their rights to some other party. This has caused particular complications in guarantees of covenants contained in leases of land. If a guarantor guaranteed the obligations of a tenant, and the tenant assigned his leasehold interest to another, then the guarantor might well be liable for the defaults of the assignee. The law has been modified by statute.[588]

(b) Formation

(i) Consideration

The agreement is often in the form of a deed.[589] If it is not, then the guarantor's promise   **8.167**
must be supported by consideration.[590] As in any contract, this may either be a promise, or some act or forbearance requested by the guarantor. In this context, there may be a promise to advance funds to the primary debtor, or there may be the fact of an advance which was requested by the guarantor. If the guarantee is for an existing debt, then there must either be a promise to forbear from suing on the debt, or actual forbearance at the request of the guarantor.[591]

---

[583] *Arab Bank plc v John D Wood Commercial Ltd* [2000] 1 WLR 857, CA, noted D Friedmann (2000) 116 LQR 365.

[584] See eg *Capital Bank Cashflow Finance Ltd v Southall* [2004] EWCA Civ 817, [2004] 2 All ER (Comm) 675.

[585] If he has not, this can affect the guarantor's rights against the primary debtor: 8.182.

[586] *Duncan, Fox & Co v North and South Wales Bank* (1880) 6 App Cas 1, 11–12, HL.

[587] *Rouse v Bradford Banking Co* [1894] AC 586, HL.

[588] Landlord and Tenant (Covenants) Act 1995. The Act renders void any attempt to impose, by contract, those obligations which of which it relieves guarantors: *Good Harvest Partnership LLP v Centaur Services Ltd* [2010] EWHC 330, [2010] Ch 426; *K/S Victoria Street (A Danish Partnership) v House of Fraser (Stores Management) Ltd* [2011] EWCA Civ 904, [2012] Ch 497. The Act also deals with the case in which the landlord assigns his interest, generally ensuring that the assignee will have the benefit of the obligations of the tenant and any guarantor. The most significant changes only apply to leases created after 1995; see C Harpum, S Bridge, and M Dixon, *Megarry and Wade: The Law of Real Property* (8th edn, 2012) 973–994.

[589] Usually the deed is executed by the guarantor and the creditor. If the parties so intend, even a deed executed by the primary debtor and the guarantor may create a guarantee enforceable by the creditor: *Moody v Condor Insurance Ltd* [2006] EWHC 100 (Ch), [2006] 1 WLR 1847.

[590] *Pitts v Jones* [2007] EWCA Civ 1301, [2008] QB 706.

[591] *Crears v Hunter* (1887) 19 QBD 341, CA.

(ii) Offer and acceptance: continuing guarantees

8.168 It is possible to guarantee future liabilities of the debtor, whether on a particular account or arising generally. In this situation, the guarantor's liability fluctuates with the balance owing to the creditor, although it may be subject to a limit in the guarantee. Such contracts are usually understood as unilateral contracts, in which the guarantor leaves open an offer to guarantee future advances, and the creditor accepts each time an advance is made. On this analysis, the guarantor can always terminate the guarantee as to future advances. Such guarantees often provide for termination of the guarantee after a period of notice. In the absence of a deed, it is not clear whether the guarantor is bound by the promise to give a period of notice; if the guarantee is understood as a standing offer, then he is not, since an offer can always be withdrawn unless it is itself supported by consideration.[592]

8.169 Even if the guarantor is bound to give notice, the effect of the notice may be a difficult issue. In *National Westminster Bank plc v Hardman*,[593] the defendant gave a continuing guarantee to pay on demand, determinable on three months' notice. The creditor did not make a demand on the guarantor during the three months after the notice was given, and it was held that there was no liability. The events were similar in *Bank of Credit and Commerce International SA v Simjee*,[594] but based on different wording, it was held that the effect of the expiry of the notice was only to fix the amount of the guarantor's liability. The creditor could still make a demand and so make the guarantor liable for the amount owing from the primary debtor at the time that the notice expired.

(iii) Vitiating factors

8.170 The guarantee may be vitiated by any of the factors which affect any contract, such as a fundamental mistake.[595] The guarantor may argue that he did not understand the nature of the transaction.[596] More commonly, the guarantor will argue that the transaction was induced by misrepresentation or undue influence,[597] or that it resulted from an unconscionable use of bargaining power.[598] Rarely, the problem is said to have originated with the creditor.[599] More often it originates from the primary debtor, who is often the spouse or cohabitant of the guarantor. Particularly protective principles have been developed which require the creditor to take steps to ensure that the guarantee will be valid in such a case.[600]

(iv) Duty of disclosure

8.171 In addition to the normal rules of misrepresentation, there is also a limited positive duty of disclosure on the creditor. If there are features of the transaction between the creditor and the

---

[592] In some continuing guarantees the creditor will have entered into an irrevocable and indivisible transaction, such as appointing the primary debtor to an office (*Re Crace* [1902] 1 Ch 733); this can amount to consideration, making enforceable a promise by the guarantor to give notice.

[593] [1988] FLR 302, CA.

[594] CA, 3 July 1996.

[595] *Associated Japanese Bank (International) Ltd v Crédit du Nord SA* [1989] 1 WLR 255.

[596] In *Lloyds Bank plc v Waterhouse* [1993] 2 FLR 97, CA, one judge (Purchas LJ) would have excused the guarantor on this basis. See EPL 8.149–8.152 (*non est factum*).

[597] For the general law of misrepresentation and undue influence, see EPL 8.159–8.210.

[598] *Alec Lobb (Garages) Ltd v Total Oil GB Ltd* [1983] 1 WLR 87, 94–95; *Crédit Lyonnais Bank Nederland NV v Burch* [1997] 1 All ER 144, at 151, 152–3, CA. For discussion of the general law of unconscionable transactions, see EPL 8.208, 18.71–18.75.

[599] *Lloyds Bank Ltd v Bundy* [1975] QB 326, CA; *Lloyds Bank plc v Waterhouse* [1993] 2 FLR 97, CA; *Barton v County Natwest Ltd* [1999] Lloyd's Rep Bank 408, CA.

[600] See EPL 8.210.

[601] *Levett v Barclays Bank plc* [1995] 1 WLR 1260, followed in *Crédit Lyonnais Bank Nederland v Export Credit Guarantee Department* [1996] 1 Lloyd's Rep 200, affd on other grounds [1998] 1 Lloyd's Rep 19, CA, and [1999] 2 WLR 540, HL; *North Shore Ventures Ltd v Anstead Holdings Inc* [2011] EWCA Civ 230, [2012] 1 Ch 31.

primary debtor which make it materially different from what the guarantor would naturally expect, in a way which is potentially disadvantageous to him, then the creditor must disclose these arrangements. This does not extend to background facts about the primary debtor which might be relevant to the credit risk.[601] Breach of the duty permits rescission of the guarantee.

(v) Formalities

A guarantee is not enforceable unless the agreement, or some memorandum or note thereof, **8.172** is in writing and signed by the guarantor or his agent.[602] This provision does not apply to indemnities, and indeed this is the origin of the need to make the distinction between the two transactions. The note or memorandum can be created after the formation of an oral guarantee.[603] All the material terms must be stated, including the identity of the primary debtor and the limit, if any, of the guarantor's liability;[604] but the consideration for which the guarantee was given need not be stated.[605] Failure to comply with this requirement makes the guarantee unenforceable, but not void.[606] If the required writing exists, then extrinsic evidence may be admissible in the interpretation of the contract, according to the normal rules.[607]

Any credit agreement involving an individual debtor may be subject to regulation under the **8.173** CCA 1974.[608] This Act can govern the required form for guarantees and indemnities relating to regulated agreements.[609] It also requires certain information to be made available to guarantors and primary debtors.[610] A guarantee given by an individual may also be subject to the Consumer Rights Act 2015.[611]

---

[602] Statute of Frauds 1677, s 4; *Pitts v Jones* [2007] EWCA Civ 1301, [2008] QB 706; *Fairstate Ltd v General Enterprise & Management Ltd* [2010] EWHC 3072, [2011] 2 All ER (Comm) 497 (noting that rectification of a guarantee document may be available despite the Statute of Frauds). In *J Pereira Fernandes SA v Mehta* [2006] EWHC 813 (Ch), [2006] 2 All ER 891, it was held that while an email could be sufficient writing, the mere inclusion of the sender's return email address in the header did not constitute a 'signature' within the Statute; a signature must be inserted in a way that shows that it 'governs' the whole document. In *Golden Ocean Group Ltd v Salgaocar Mining Industries PVT Ltd* [2011] EWHC 56, [2011] 1 WLR 2575, the claimant was allowed to argue that a series of emails could be considered together as satisfying the Statute. In *Actionstrength Ltd v International Glass Engineering IN.GL.EN SpA* [2003] UKHL 17, [2003] 2 AC 541 it was held that an argument based on estoppel (on which see EPL 8.53–8.57) could not be used to circumvent the requirement of writing.

[603] *Elpis Maritime Co Ltd v Marti Chartering Co Inc (The Maria D)* [1992] 1 AC 21, HL.

[604] *State Bank of India v Kaur* [1996] 5 Banking LR 158, CA.

[605] Mercantile Law Amendment Act 1856, s 3.

[606] *Maddison v Alderson* (1883) 8 App Cas 467, HL; for the significance of this distinction, see 8.182 and EPL 8.72–8.81.

[607] *Perrylease Ltd v Imecar AG* [1988] 1 WLR 463.

[608] On the scope of the CCA 1974, see 8.31. The Act has provisions that allow the court to reopen credit agreements that are substantively unfair even if they are not otherwise regulated: see 8.33.

[609] CCA 1974, s 105 and the Consumer Credit (Guarantees and Indemnities) Regulations 1983, SI 1983/1556 thereunder; failure to comply makes the agreement void (s 106). Other violations of the Act may also avoid a guarantee or indemnity (s 113(3)).

[610] CCA 1974, ss 107–111.

[611] On the scope of these provisions, see 8.35. The CRA 2015 applies to a contract between a supplier and a consumer; and a supplier is defined to be one acting in the course of his business. If the service provided is the guarantee, then it is arguable that the provisions would only apply where the consumer is the creditor and the supplier is giving a guarantee in the course of its business. For discussion, see H Beale (gen ed), *Chitty on Contracts* (31st edn, 2012) para 44–149. The Unfair Contract Terms Act 1977 now applies only to non-consumer contracts; moreover, it is concerned with exemption clauses and therefore is unlikely to have an impact on guarantees. For discussion of this Act, see EPL 8.110–8.118.

(3) Scope of Liability

(a) Co-extensiveness

8.174   The co-extensiveness principle is that the guarantor's obligation is to see to it that the primary debtor performs his own obligation.[612] This means that the guarantor is liable not only for the obligation guaranteed, but also for damages arising from the primary debtor's breach of that obligation.[613] Conversely, it generally means that the guarantor cannot be liable except to the extent that the primary debtor is liable.[614] At common law, if the contract with the primary debtor was void or unenforceable due to the primary debtor's infancy, then so too was the guarantee;[615] this rule has now been changed by statute.[616] The common law principle implies that the same result would follow where the primary debtor is a company, whose contract is void for lack of capacity; but the cases suggest that this may not be so, at least in the case of a guarantor who is a director of that company.[617]

(b) Discharge

8.175   The guarantor's obligations can be discharged in a number of ways. Most obviously, he may pay the creditor what is owed under the guarantee and so be discharged by performance. Other possibilities follow from the normal rules of contract. If the guarantee is limited in time, or can be terminated on notice, then of course the guarantor can be discharged in these ways.[618] If the creditor owes obligations to the guarantor under the contract of guarantee, then the creditor may commit a breach which permits the guarantor to terminate the guarantee.[619]

(i) Discharge of primary debtor

8.176   It follows from the co-extensiveness principle that the guarantor can be discharged through the discharge of the primary debtor's obligation, whether by the primary debtor's performance,[620] or by the lawful termination of the obligations owed by the primary debtor to the creditor,[621] or by frustration of the contract between primary debtor and contractor.[622] If, however, the obligation of the primary debtor is terminated in a situation which generates a secondary obligation to pay damages, then the guarantor is liable for such damages.[623]

---

[612] The obligation of one who gives an indemnity (8.161) is not subject to this principle.

[613] *Moschi v Lep Air Services Ltd* [1973] AC 331, HL.

[614] In *Hyundai Heavy Industries Co Ltd v Papadopoulos* [1980] 1 WLR 1129, 1137, HL, Viscount Dilhorne suggested that in some cases a guarantor would be liable to pay an instalment even though the primary debtor was not; this is strongly doubted by commentators (see eg G Andrews and R Millett, *Law of Guarantees* (6th edn, 2011) 312).

[615] *Coutts & Co v Browne-Lecky* [1947] KB 104; but not an indemnity: *Yeoman Credit Ltd v Latter* [1961] 1 WLR 828, CA.

[616] Minors' Contracts Act 1987, s 2.

[617] J Steyn, 'Guarantees: The Co-Extensiveness Principle' (1974) 90 LQR 246, 248–251, explaining *Gerrard v James* [1925] 1 Ch 616 and other cases, but noting that if the result follows because the 'guarantor' agreed to be liable regardless of the company's capacity, then the contract is probably better understood as an indemnity. In *Communities Economic Development Fund v Canadian Pickles Corp* [1991] 3 SCR 388, 85 DLR (4th) 88, the incapacity was on the part of the creditor, which lent money to the primary debtor. Although the primary debtor would have been liable in unjust enrichment, it was held that the guarantor was not liable.

[618] As to the effect of a provision permitting termination of a continuing guarantee by notice, see 8.169.

[619] Under normal principles, however, a less serious breach may only give the guarantor a claim in damages for loss suffered: *Bowmaker (Commercial) Ltd v Smith* [1965] 1 WLR 855, CA.

[620] If there are multiple obligations between the creditor and the primary debtor, the normal rules of appropriation of payments apply to determine whether the primary debtor has paid the guaranteed debt.

[621] *Western Credit Ltd v Alberry* [1964] 1 WLR 945, CA.

[622] Because this is a consequence of the principle of co-extensiveness, the results could be different under an indemnity.

[623] *Moschi v Lep Air Services Ltd* [1973] AC 331, HL. In the English tradition of freedom of contract, Lord Reid left open the possibility of a guarantee which extended to primary obligations only.

If the primary debtor is discharged through a binding agreement with the creditor, then the **8.177**
guarantor is also discharged,[624] unless the creditor reserved his rights against the guarantor.[625] Discharge of the primary debtor by bankruptcy does not, however, discharge the
guarantor.[626] Similarly, if a debtor company is wound up and ceases to exist, a guarantor of
its debts remains liable.[627]

(ii) Discharge by creditor's conduct

Variation of contract between creditor and primary debtor. There is a strict principle **8.178**
that any variation of the contract between the creditor and the primary debtor, which could
have the effect of increasing the risk that the guarantor bears, will discharge the guarantor
completely. This is so even if later events show that the guarantor was not in fact harmed by
the variation.[628] A binding agreement to give the primary debtor further time to pay is a
variation which will discharge the guarantor.[629] The same principle will apply to the release
by the creditor of a co-guarantor,[630] or the release of real security given by a co-guarantor[631]
or by the primary debtor.[632] Upon discharge the guarantor is entitled to recover any real
security he provided.[633]

The principle which discharges the guarantor will not apply if the guarantee excludes it, and **8.179**
commercial guarantees commonly do so.[634] It is also excluded if the guarantor consents to
the variation at the time it is made. At least in the case where the variation is an extension
of time, it is excluded if, at the time the variation is made, the creditor notifies the primary
debtor that he reserves his rights against the guarantor.[635]

The principle does not rise to the level of a general duty of care owed by the creditor to the **8.180**
guarantor, although particular duties have been recognized.[636] The creditor owes a duty to
the guarantor to act reasonably in selling a real security held for the debt, whether it belongs

---

[624] *Commercial Bank of Tasmania v Jones* [1893] AC 313, PC.
[625] *Cole v Lynn* [1942] 1 KB 142, CA. The guarantor is also not discharged if the terms of the guarantee
preserve his liability in such a case, or if he so agreed at the time the primary debtor was discharged. Like
in the situation where a creditor has multiple co-debtors, the guarantor's liability may be preserved where
the creditor does not release the primary debtor but merely agrees not to sue him; however, the distinction between a release and an agreement not to sue has recently been questioned in the context of multiple co-debtors: *Johnson v Davies* [1999] Ch 117, CA. If this distinction were abandoned in the context of
guarantees, the only question would be whether the creditor had reserved his rights against the guarantor.
[626] Insolvency Act 1986, s 281(7).
[627] *Re Fitzgeorge* [1905] 1 KB 462; *Ali Shipping Corp v Jugobanka DD Beograd* [1997] EWCA Civ 2705.
[628] *Holme v Brunskill* (1878) 3 QBD 495, CA.
[629] *Polak v Everett* (1876) 1 QBD 669, CA.
[630] *Mercantile Bank of Sydney v Taylor* [1893] AC 317, PC. This increases the guarantor's risk because there
is a right of contribution among co-guarantors: 8.185. If the co-guarantors are only severally and not jointly
liable, it has been held that release of one does not discharge the others fully, but only to the extent that they
are harmed by it: *Ward v National Bank of New Zealand Ltd* (1883) 8 App Cas 755, PC.
[631] *Smith v Wood* [1929] 1 Ch 14, CA.
[632] *Re Darwen & Pearce* [1927] 1 Ch 176. It has been suggested the guarantor will not be discharged fully
(but only *pro tanto*) by the creditor's releasing securities acquired by the creditor only after the guarantee was
given: *Polak v Everett* (1876) 1 QBD 669, 676, CA.
[633] *Bolton v Salomon* [1891] 2 Ch 48; *Smith v Wood* [1929] 1 Ch 14, CA.
[634] A guarantee given by an individual which contained such a term might be subject to review under the
CRA 2015; but see n 611.
[635] J O'Donovan and J Phillips, *The Modern Contract of Guarantee* (2nd English edn, 2010) 472–473,
suggesting that the primary debtor must agree to the preservation of the guarantor's liability; and that in
such a case, the guarantor will not be bound by the extension of time when exercising his rights against the
primary debtor.
[636] *China and South Sea Bank Ltd v Tan Soon Gin* [1990] 1 AC 536, PC.

beneficially to the guarantor or to the primary debtor.[637] But a breach of this duty does not discharge the guarantor; it only reduces his liability by the difference between the price actually obtained by the creditor, and the price it would have obtained had it acted reasonably.[638] Also, if the creditor causes loss to the guarantor by carelessly failing to perfect a real security, the guarantor will be discharged to the extent of the resultant loss.[639]

8.181 **Material alteration to the guarantee.** In line with general principles of contract law, a guarantee may be avoided by alteration. If, after the guarantee has been created, the creditor makes a material alteration to the written document in which it is embodied, the guarantor is discharged. An alteration is material if it affects the whole character of the document, but also if it is potentially prejudicial to the guarantor's legal position; actual prejudice need not be shown.[640]

(4) Guarantor's Rights Against Primary Debtor

(a) Indemnity

8.182 Upon payment to the creditor, the guarantor has a right of indemnity against the primary debtor.[641] If the guarantor has become liable, but has not yet paid, he may secure a declaration of his right of indemnity, and an order that the primary debtor pay the creditor.[642] The right to indemnity arises even if the guarantee was unenforceable for lack of evidence in writing.[643] There is authority that if the guarantee was not given at the request of the primary debtor, then no right of indemnity arises.[644]

(b) Subrogation

8.183 A guarantor who has paid the guaranteed debt is entitled to be subrogated to the rights formerly held by the creditor, irrespective of whether or not the guarantor was aware of them and of whether they were acquired before or after the guarantee was given.[645] This includes not only rights of real security, but also personal rights which the creditor held, which may carry a preferential status.[646] Subrogation operates even in respect of rights which would otherwise have been extinguished when the creditor was paid. To the extent that any right held by the creditor cannot be assigned by operation of law, the guarantor is entitled to demand an express assignment of it;[647] and even if such an assignment has not been taken, he can use the name of the creditor to enforce it for his own benefit.[648]

---

[637] See 8.49, noting that the duty may be modified by the terms of a guarantee.

[638] *Skipton Building Society v Stott* [2001] QB 261, CA.

[639] *Wulff v Jay* (1872) LR 7 QB 756.

[640] *Raiffeisen Zentralbank Osterreich AG v Crossseas Shipping Ltd* [2000] 1 WLR 1135, CA. Hence if the alteration is beneficial to the guarantor, this doctrine cannot be invoked: *Bank of Scotland v Henry Butcher & Co* [2003] EWCA Civ 67, [2003] 1 BCLC 575, at [72]–[74].

[641] *Re A Debtor (No 627 of 1936)* [1937] Ch 156, CA.

[642] *Ascherson v Tredegar Dry Dock and Wharf Co Ltd* [1909] 2 Ch 401. In *Thomas v Nottingham Incorporated Football Club Ltd* [1972] Ch 596, it was held that the guarantor may obtain this order even though no demand has yet been made upon him as required by the terms of the guarantee. The requirement of the demand is for the benefit of the guarantor and may be waived by him.

[643] *Alexander v Vane* (1836) 1 M & W 511, 150 ER 537; or even if both the guarantee and the primary debtor's obligations were unenforceable: *Re Chetwynd's Estate* [1938] Ch 13, CA, applied in *Argo Caribbean Group Ltd v Lewis* [1976] 2 Lloyd's Rep 289, CA.

[644] *Owen v Tate* [1976] 2 QB 402, CA. The case has been criticized: see EPL 18.109.

[645] *Forbes v Jackson* (1882) 19 Ch D 615.

[646] *Re Lord Churchill* (1888) 39 Ch D 174; *Re Lamplugh Iron Ore Co Ltd* [1927] 1 Ch 308.

[647] Mercantile Law Amendment Act 1856, s 5.

[648] Mercantile Law Amendment Act 1856, s 5; *Re M'Myn* (1886) 33 Ch D 575; *Re Lamplugh Iron Ore Co Ltd* [1927] 1 Ch 308.

Unlike the right of indemnity discussed above, the right of subrogation does not arise until **8.184** the guarantor pays the full amount of the indebtedness to which his guarantee relates. This raises a point of construction when a guarantee is limited in amount, as is usually the case. If it is a guarantee of the whole debt, but subject to a limit as to the guarantor's liability, then there can be no subrogation until the whole debt is paid, even if it exceeds the guarantor's liability.[649] If, on the other hand, the effect of the limit is to create a guarantee as to only a proportion of the debt, then when the guarantor has paid that proportion, he is entitled to subrogation as to the relevant proportion of any securities.[650]

(5) Guarantor's Rights Against Co-Guarantors

Subject to a contrary agreement among them, co-guarantors of the same debt bear the bur- **8.185** den of their obligations equally. This means that they have rights of contribution against one another.[651] They also have rights of subrogation, if the creditor held real security to secure the obligations of co-guarantors.[652] These rights arise even if a co-guarantor was not aware, at the time he gave his guarantee, of the other co-guarantors. Where the guarantees were of the same debt but had different limits, the guarantors will share the burden in proportion to the limits.[653]

As with indemnity against the primary debtor, a co-guarantor may obtain a declaration **8.186** of another co-guarantor's liability to contribute even before he has paid, so long as he has become liable.[654] A co-guarantor can also be liable to contribute even if his co-guarantor paid the creditor in the absence of a demand which was required to generate liability under the guarantee. Such a requirement being for the guarantor's benefit, it may be waived by him; and contribution will be ordered so long as the payment to the creditor was not officious.[655]

---

[649] This is the normal form for a limited guarantee.

[650] *Re Butler's Wharf Ltd* [1995] 2 BCLC 43, [1995] BCC 717.

[651] Whether they are jointly, severally, or jointly and severally liable, and whether on the same or more than one document, without the need for any agreement: *Dering v Earl of Winchelsea* (1787) 2 B & P 270, 126 ER 1276, 1 Cox Eq 319, 29 ER 1184; *Caledonia North Sea Limited v British Telecommunications Plc (Scotland)* [2002] UKHL 4, [2002] 1 Lloyd's Rep 553, at [12]. If the liability of the claimant co-guarantor arises out of 'damage suffered' by him in paying the creditor, then his claim for contribution must be founded on the Civil Liability (Contribution) Act 1978, s 1. This will be the ordinary construction of most guarantees (see 8.174), but it leads to a two-year limitation period for the contribution claim (Limitation Act 1980, s 10): *Hampton v Minns* [2002] 1 WLR 1. In that case, however, it was held that the correct construction of some guarantees is that the claimant co-guarantor is liable for a debt, not 'damage'; in that case, the limitation on the contribution claim is six years (Limitation Act 1980, s 5). The distinction is difficult to support.

[652] *Smith v Wood* [1929] 1 Ch 14, 21–22, CA. If the creditor held real security from the primary debtor, and a co-guarantor has acquired it, he must share the benefit in order to claim contribution: *Steel v Dixon* (1881) 17 Ch D 825; *Berridge v Berridge* (1890) 44 Ch D 168.

[653] *Ellesmere Brewery Co v Cooper* [1896] 1 QB 75, DC. In *Hampton v Minns* [2002] 1 WLR 1 the claimant and the defendant were co-guarantors of the debts of a company. The claimant discharged the debt and sought contribution. The defendant argued that he should be liable only as to 20%, since he held 20% of the shares of the debtor company, while the claimant held 80%. The court held that the normal rule of equal contribution applied.

[654] *Wolmershausen v Gullick* [1893] 2 Ch 514.

[655] *Stimpson v Smith* [1999] Ch 340, CA.

9

INSOLVENCY

A. Introduction: Structure and Process

(a) Scope of chapter

Bankruptcy is concerned with the insolvency of individuals, and liquidation, or winding-up, **9.01** with the insolvency of companies.[1] Both are collective procedures. Bankruptcy and company liquidation have evolved separately with, at times, bankruptcy law being applied by way of analogy to liquidation. Since the insolvency legislation of the mid-1980s, the two subjects have been treated in parallel in a single statute, now the Insolvency Act 1986,[2] under which common rules, the Insolvency Rules,[3] have been made.[4] So far as possible, the two subjects will be covered together in this chapter. The various forms of corporate restructuring, however, remain outside the scope of this chapter.

Company administration is also dealt with in this chapter. It frequently, but not necessar- **9.02** ily, precedes a winding-up. Sometimes administration leads into a voluntary arrangement between a company and its creditors. Although technically a collective procedure, administration may also, since the Enterprise Act 2002, be invoked out of court by certain secured creditors in place of administrative receivership, confined now to a limited number of cases.[5] Receivership, including administrative receivership will also receive some coverage.

The focus of this chapter is on insolvency principles rather than the details of insolvency **9.03** procedure. Since there is little scope for compromise in insolvency cases, principles of law are tested to their limits.

---

[1] The subject of insolvent partnerships is left to specialist texts.

[2] References below to statutory sections are to the Insolvency Act 1986 unless otherwise stated. For commentary on its provisions, see L Sealy and D Milman, *Annotated Guide to Insolvency Legislation* (15th edn, 2012).

[3] References below to rules are to the Insolvency Rules 1986, SI 1986/1925, unless otherwise stated.

[4] By the Lord Chancellor with the concurrence of the Secretary of State pursuant to powers under ss 411–12. See SI 1986/1925.

[5] Administrative receivers are a sub-category of receivers (sometimes referred to as receivers or managers).

(b) Definition and effects of insolvency

9.04 Insolvency is a financial condition, not a legal status, that can lead to the winding-up of a company and to the bankruptcy of an individual. A company need not be insolvent when it is wound up; if it is not, any surplus assets after a company's creditors have been paid in full are then returned to its former members.[6] If a surplus is left when a bankrupt's creditors have been paid, it will be paid to the bankrupt himself.[7] Unlike companies that have been wound up, bankrupt individuals survive bankruptcy[8] and a discharged bankrupt may subsequently become bankrupt again, which creates a need for separate statutory provision.[9]

9.05 Insolvency is an inability to pay one's debts,[10] and is one of a number of grounds on which the court may order a company to be wound up.[11] For bankruptcy, there is only one ground on which a bankruptcy petition may be presented, the debtor's inability to pay his debts.[12] This is defined as a failure for three months to respond to a creditor's statutory demand for payment, or a failure to satisfy execution.[13] A creditor's bankruptcy petition is restricted to liquidated sums above a statutory amount,[14] and the debtor must either be unable to pay or have no reasonable prospect of making payment.[15]

9.06 The Insolvency Act provides that a number of different events are deemed to amount to a company's inability to pay its debts for the purpose of compulsory winding-up: a statutory demand for a debt of at least £750 is not paid; or an execution remains unsatisfied; or the company is unable to pay its debts as they fall due.[16] This last case includes a company whose assets are less than its liabilities; hence, both cash flow and balance sheet insolvency fall within the definition of inability to pay. The first two cases reveal that compulsory winding-up can be used to control abusive debtor behaviour.

9.07 A company may be wound up voluntarily if it resolves by special resolution to do so.[17] In the case of a members' voluntary winding-up, the company's directors have to make a statutory declaration of solvency that the company will be able to pay its debts in full within a stipulated period not to exceed 12 months.[18] The prospect of the directors' personal liability for fraudulent and wrongful trading[19] is an inducement to wind up a company facing a hopeless future.

(c) The bankruptcy and liquidation process

(i) Bankruptcy

9.08 The estate of insolvent individuals is dealt with by the trustee-in-bankruptcy and that of companies by the liquidator. Bankruptcy was modernized in the 1980s[20] and further reformed

---

[6] Section 107.

[7] Section 330(5).

[8] *Re Rae* [1995] BCC 102.

[9] See, eg, ss 334–335, Sch 11 para 16 and Insolvency Rules, rr 6.225–6.228.

[10] On which, see *Byblos Bank SAL v Al-Khudairy* (1986) 2 BCC 99, 549, CA. Genuinely disputed debts are excluded: see, eg, *Re Janeash Ltd* [1990] BCC 250.

[11] Section 122(1)(f).

[12] Section 272.

[13] Section 268(1). For the definition of the absence of a reasonable prospect to pay, see s 268(2).

[14] £750.

[15] Section 267.

[16] Section 123. The debts in question may include future debts, and inability, for a company with deferred liabilities, does not turn simply on whether the debtor has 'reached the point of no return'. Rather the court should make a more cautious assessment of the position based on a case by case analysis: *BNY Corporate Trustee Services Ltd v Eurosail-UK 2007-3BL plc* [2013] UKSC 38. See also *Re Casa Estates (UK) Ltd* [2014] EWCA Civ 383, [2014] BCC 269.

[17] Section 84 (also by ordinary resolution if a period fixed for its duration has expired).

[18] Section 89.

[19] Sections 213–214. On disqualification of directors, see A Mithani, *Directors' Disqualification* (2nd edn, looseleaf).

[20] eg, the act of bankruptcy and reputed ownership doctrines and the interim receivership procedure were abolished.

in 2002.[21] The bankruptcy process begins with the presentation of a petition by either the debtor, one or more creditors, or the supervisor of an individual voluntary arrangement.[22] Prior to the appointment of a trustee, and upon the making of a bankruptcy order, the official receiver administers the bankrupt's affairs[23] and, unless the debtor is himself the petitioner, will receive from the bankrupt a statement of his affairs[24] and will investigate the conduct and affairs of the bankrupt.[25] The trustee, once appointed, will be subject to the supervision of a creditors' committee[26] and the control of the court.[27] The bankrupt has a duty to inform and co-operate with the trustee[28] and is also required to refrain from committing bankruptcy offences, such as the concealment of property and records and the fraudulent disposal of property.[29]

The bankrupt is normally discharged after a maximum period of one year from the making of the bankruptcy order.[30] The period is subject to the court's power to annul a bankruptcy order,[31] as it may do eg where the bankruptcy debts and expenses have been paid in full. With certain exceptions, discharge of a bankrupt releases him from all the bankruptcy debts.[32] **9.09**

(ii) Winding-up

As stated above, there are two types of winding-up: compulsory and voluntary. Voluntary **9.10** winding-up may be either a members' or a creditors' voluntary winding-up. Only the latter is truly an insolvency process. A members' voluntary winding-up can take place only if the directors make a statutory declaration of solvency.[33] Provision is also made for converting a members' into a creditors' winding-up.[34]

A voluntary winding-up begins with a resolution to wind up which is then published.[35] The **9.11** commencement of the winding-up is deemed to begin at the date the resolution is passed,[36] whereupon the company is to cease to carry on business except as required for its beneficial winding-up[37] with no more changes in the membership of the company.[38] In a creditors' voluntary winding-up, the company has to summon a meeting of its creditors, before whom the directors lay a statement of the company's affairs.[39] In the appointment of a liquidator, the

---

[21] Enterprise Act 2002.

[22] Section 264 (which also deals with the criminal bankruptcy process). On the court's unfettered power to dismiss or adjourn a bankruptcy petition, see *Re Micklethwait* [2002] EWHC 1123, [2003] BPIR 101.

[23] Section 287. The provisions dealing with official receivers are to be found at s 399 et seq.

[24] Section 288.

[25] Section 289.

[26] Section 301.

[27] Section 303.

[28] Section 333.

[29] Section 350 et seq. In extreme cases, a bankrupt may be committed to prison for contempt of court.

[30] Section 279 as added by s 256 of the Enterprise Act 2002. The 2002 Act also contains a number of provisions that diminish post-bankruptcy restrictions on a bankrupt's activities and that reduce the number of bankruptcy offences (ss 257 and 265–288 and Schs 20–21, variously amending the Insolvency Act). Bankruptcy restrictions, which can last for up to 15 years, can be used to inhibit rogue directors from seeking sole trader status.

[31] Sections 279(4) and 282. The court has a broad discretion: *Harper v Buchler (No 2)* [2005] BPIR 577.

[32] Section 281. Discharge does not affect the rights of secured creditors (s 281(2)) and does not extend to debts arising out of 'fraud or fraudulent breach of trust' (s 281(3)).

[33] Sections 89–90.

[34] Section 96.

[35] Sections 84–85.

[36] Section 86.

[37] Section 87.

[38] Section 88.

[39] Sections 98–99.

creditors have the decisive voice.[40] If a liquidation committee is formed, both creditors and company may appoint members.[41] The committee may sanction the continuing exercise by the directors of their powers, which otherwise cease on the appointment of the liquidator.[42]

9.12 A compulsory winding-up usually begins with a petition presented by the company, its directors, one or more creditors or one or more contributories.[43] In the meantime, proceedings pending against the company may be stayed or restrained[44] and there are further powers regarding the protection of the company's property after the commencement of a winding-up[45] and the control of proceedings against the company after the order has been made.[46] There may then follow an investigation of the company's affairs and an examination of its officers by the official receiver.[47] The court may appoint a provisional liquidator[48] before meetings are held by creditors and contributories separately for the appointment of a liquidator and for the (optional) appointment of a liquidation committee.[49] The liquidator's function is to get in, realize and distribute the company's property and to co-operate where necessary with the official receiver.[50] Upon the conclusion of the winding-up, the liquidator summons a final meeting of the creditors to receive his report and release him.[51] After its winding-up, the company is formally dissolved.[52]

9.13 There is no true corporate equivalent of the discharge of individuals from bankruptcy. Occasionally, however, a wound up company will be restored to the register upon application by the liquidator or other interested person.[53] This revival of the company's legal personality permits an injured claimant's access to the company's liability insurer in accordance with the statutory scheme.[54]

(d) Voluntary arrangements

9.14 Voluntary arrangements are schemes for the composition of indebtedness that are an alternative to bankruptcy and liquidation[55] and that, by pre-empting the latter procedures, are designed to salvage a debtor in financial distress. Corporate voluntary arrangements (CVAs) have proved to be less successful than individual voluntary arrangements (IVAs).

(i) CVAs

9.15 The rules concerning CVAs are in Part I of the Insolvency Act. A CVA is a matter of contract for those party to it[56] and need not entail a composition of claims.[57] Except for small companies, a CVA does not impose a moratorium on proceedings against the company[58] or on the

---

40 Section 100.
41 Section 101.
42 Section 103.
43 Section 124.
44 Section 126.
45 Section 127, discussed at 9.69–9.80.
46 Section 130(2).
47 Sections 131–134.
48 Section 135.
49 Sections 139 and 141.
50 Section 143.
51 Section 146.
52 Section 201 et seq.
53 Companies Act 2006, s 1029. See *Peaktone v Joddrell* [2012] EWCA Civ 1035.
54 Third Parties (Rights Against Insurers) Act 1930.
55 Hence they are taken before these procedures in the Insolvency Act and also do not require the company or individual to be insolvent as defined by the Act.
56 *Johnson v Davies* [1998] EWCA Civ 483, [1999] Ch 117.
57 See *Commissioners of Inland Revenue v Adam & Partners* [2001] 1 BCLC 222, CA.
58 See *Alman v Approach Housing Ltd* [2001] 1 BCLC 530.

exercise of rights by secured creditors. Prior to liquidation and administration, only the directors of the company, and not the members or creditors, may propose an arrangement,[59] and thereafter only liquidators and administrators may do so. In the case of a directors' proposal, a nominee will be appointed to supervise the arrangement and may act in the character of 'trustee or otherwise'.[60] This nominee is obliged first to report to the court[61] before summoning separate meetings of the company's members and of all of its creditors.[62] Liquidators and administrators may proceed directly to the summoning of the meetings.[63] An agreed arrangement, which turns upon majority voting,[64] binds all of the company's members and its creditors with notice of the meeting.[65] Nevertheless, the concurrence of secured creditors[66] and of preference creditors is required if their rights are to be affected by the arrangement,[67] which reveals the limitations of the CVA process. The two meetings of members and creditors must approve the same arrangement.[68] For small companies, the above moratorium is available. A small company is one that meets at least two of the requirements for a small company laid down in the Companies Act 2006.[69]

For companies other than small companies, the prospects of an arrangement are improved in the case of administration and liquidation by the moratorium on the taking of proceedings and (in the case of administration only) the enforcement of security against the company.[70] **9.16**

(ii) IVAs

The rules concerning IVAs,[71] which have proved to be popular with debtors and to leave creditors with more than the bankruptcy process, are to be found in Part VIII of the Act.[72] They are *mutatis mutandis* the same as for CVAs. In those cases where an application is made for an interim order and is pending, there is a moratorium in the form of a stay of proceedings.[73] This is followed by the order itself whose effect is to prevent or discontinue bankruptcy petitions and to require the leave of the court for other proceedings, legal process and **9.17**

---

[59] Section 1(1), (3).

[60] Section 1(2). The conduct of the supervisor is open to review and the supervisor himself may apply for directions: s 7. Whether there is a trust over the CVA moneys is, like the range of assets included in the CVA, a matter of construction of the CVA: *Re Kudos Glass Ltd* [2001] 1 BCLC 390; *NT Gallagher & Son Ltd v Tomlinson* [2002] EWCA Civ 404, [2002] 1 WLR 2380.

[61] Members and unsecured creditors may challenge the arrangement in court where there has been unfair prejudice or material irregularity in the conduct of meetings: s 6.

[62] Sections 2–3. Creditors include those with contingent and unquantified claims: *Doorbar v Alltime Securities Ltd* [1996] 1 WLR 456, CA.

[63] Section 3(2).

[64] Rule 1.19 (three-quarters in value of debt owed to creditors present in person or by proxy and voting); r 1.20 (one-half in value of members present in person or by proxy and voting).

[65] Section 5(2)(b).

[66] Who do not include landlords forfeiting a lease: *Razzaq v Pala* [1997] 1 WLR 1336 (which is consistent with *Re Park Air Services plc* [2000] 2 AC 172, HL). See also *Thomas v Ken Thomas Ltd* [2006] EWCA Civ 1054, [2007] Bus LR 429, from which may be inferred that the owner of goods the subject of a finance or equipment lease is an unsecured creditor for present purposes.

[67] Section 4(3), (4).

[68] Section 5(1) (modifications to proposed scheme). For the power of the court to reconcile differences between the two meetings, see Insolvency Act (as amended by Sch 2 to the Insolvency Act 2000), s 4A.

[69] Section 382(3).

[70] Discussed at 9.87–9.91.

[71] Certain changes were introduced by Sch 3 to the Insolvency Act 2000 and, for post-bankruptcy IVAs, the Enterprise Act 2000 (s 264, amending the Insolvency Act, creating a fast-track procedure where the Official Receiver is the nominee).

[72] The procedure under the Deeds of Arrangement Act 1914 is different and mutually exclusive (s 260(3) of the 1986 Act) and, though still extant, barely used.

[73] Section 254.

execution against the debtor or his property.[74] The debtor himself may apply for an interim order, as well as, in the case of an undischarged bankrupt, his trustee or the official receiver.[75] A nominee must be appointed to act as trustee or otherwise supervise the arrangement.[76] There follows the nominee's report, a summoning of a meeting of creditors if the report favours this and a decision of the meeting.[77]

(e) Other insolvency procedures for company debtors: receivership and administration

(i) Receivers

9.18 Receivership, and its sub-category, administrative receivership, are dealt with at length in the Insolvency Act. A standard bank debenture[78] will authorize the creditor in stated circumstances, under the terms of an irrevocable power of attorney, to act in the name of the company by appointing a receiver whose function is to pay down the debt. The creditor is entitled to pursue self-interest when exercising this power.[79] Unlike most other legal systems, English law permits secured creditors to take steps to enforce their rights with minimal interference from company liquidators and trustees-in-bankruptcy. Whilst advancing the creditor's self-interest, receivership is widely credited as having saved many businesses. The receiver will be given broad powers of management in the debentures, which are presumed by the Act in the case of administrative receivership.[80] The receiver acts as the agent of the company,[81] which the Act explicitly treats as being the case for administrative receivers prior to the liquidation of the company.[82] Administrative receivers are those appointed pursuant to a debenture secured by a charge or charges, including a floating charge, extending to at least substantially the whole of a company's property (a qualifying charge).[83] They have special powers of contracting and of investigation[84] which takes them out of the realm of ordinary debt enforcement, hence their prominent treatment in insolvency legislation. Since the Enterprise Act 2002, an administrative receiver may be appointed only in the case of designated transactions.[85]

(ii) Administrators

9.19 The Cork Report[86] proposed, in cases where there was no debenture holder to appoint a receiver or manager, that a statutory power be granted to appoint an administrator able to achieve the same rescue goal as receivership. This led to the enactment of Part II of the Insolvency Act. The Act conferred on the administrator the same powers as those deemed

---

[74] Section 252. The Insolvency Act 2000 extended this to include the levying of distress and re-entry by the landlord. For the assets subject to an IVA, see *Welburn v Dibb Lupton Broomhead* [2002] EWCA Civ 1601, [2003] BPIR 768.

[75] Section 253(3).

[76] Section 253(2).

[77] Sections 256–258.

[78] The statutory power of a chargee or mortgagee to appoint a receiver under ss 101 and 109 of the Law of Property Act 1925 is very similar.

[79] *Shamji v Johnson Matthey* [1986] BCLC 278, CA.

[80] See s 42 and Sch 1.

[81] It is an unusual type of agency: *Gomba Holdings UK Ltd v Minories Finance Ltd* [1989] BCLC 115, 117, CA. Under s 109(2) of the Law of Property Act 1925, a receiver appointed thereunder is also the agent of the mortgagor or chargor.

[82] Section 44(1)(a).

[83] Section 29(2).

[84] Discussed at 9.169.

[85] Section 249, adding ss 72B–G of the Insolvency Act (major capital market and financial market transactions, utility transactions and public-private finance transactions).

[86] *Report of the Review Committee on Insolvency Law and Practice* (Cmnd 8558, 1982).

to exist in the debentures giving rise to the appointment of an administrative receiver.[87] In addition, Part II provided for a moratorium on the exercise of proprietary rights by secured creditors and title-retainers that did not exist for administrative receivership.[88] Initially, administrators were appointed only by the court. Since the Enterprise Act,[89] they may now also be appointed out of court by the holder of a qualifying charge, defined as required for administrative receivership, when empowered expressly or impliedly to do so by the company.[90] Administrators may also be appointed by the debtor company or its directors. In all cases, the administrator is an officer of the court.[91] The purpose of administration is, in order, first, to rescue the company as a going concern;[91a] secondly, to achieve a better result for the creditors as a whole than liquidation; thirdly, to realize property for distribution to secured or preference creditors.[92] Since the salvage of value depends heavily on an administrator's speed of action, it is common for administrators to be appointed with a pre-packaged plan of action,[92a] which at times has given rise to judicial concerns about the possibilities of abuse.[93]

Administrators are appointed by the court if the company is unable to pay its debts and if the court is satisfied that one or other purpose of administration will be served by the appointment.[94] They may be appointed by the holder of a qualifying charge if it provides for the appointment of an administrator (or an administrative receiver). The power of a company or its directors to appoint an administrator is essentially unrestricted,[95] except that the floating chargee is in the driving seat and can pre-empt an appointment by either of the other two means.[96] Administrators appointed out of court under a qualifying charge are required to exercise their functions in the interests of creditors as whole[97] and have certain responsibilities when carrying out their functions and reporting to creditors. Nevertheless, there is likely to be little practical difference in outcome between administrative receivership and an out of court administration. **9.20**

(f) Legislative background and sources

The statutory material on insolvency is mainly found in the Insolvency Act together with its accompanying Insolvency Rules. The 1986 Act was a consolidation measure following close **9.21**

---

[87] Schedules 1 and B1, para 60. Although administration displaces company directors from the exercise of management powers, other powers remain, such as the power to challenge the administrator's appointment: *Closegate Hotel Development (Durham) Ltd v McLean* [2013] EWHC 3237 (Ch), [2014] Bus LR 405.

[88] Discussed at 9.86–9.89.

[89] See now Sch B1 of the Insolvency Act.

[90] Schedule B1, para 14.

[91] Schedule B1, para 5.

[91a] Whether a company has in fact been rescued turns on its cash flow solvency and the probability that it can pay its debts as they fall due: *Nimmo and Fraser, Joint Administrators of Station Properties Ltd* [2013] CSOH 120.

[92] Schedule B1, para 3(1). For the use of administration to reorganize a business, see *Re British American Racing (Holdings) Ltd* [2004] EWHC 2947 (Ch), [2005] 2 BCLC 324. Administrators are empowered to distribute to secured and preferential creditors and, usually with the leave of the court, to other creditors: Schedule B1, paras 65–66; Insolvency Rules, rr 2.68–2.71.

[92a] For a recent example, see *Re Christophorus 3 Ltd* [2014] EWHC 1162 (Ch).

[93] eg, *Re Kayley Vending Ltd* [2009] EWHC 904 (Ch), at [2]; *Clydesdale Financial Services Ltd v Smailes* [2009] EWHC 1745 (Ch), at [6]. A court order providing for a pre-packaged administration will nevertheless be made if the administration is not obviously abusive, since the administrator's decisions are open to challenge by the creditors: *Re Hibernia (2005) Ltd* [2013] EWHC 2615 (Ch). A ministerial statement was made on 16 June 2014 that regulatory measures would be made to deal with pre-packaged administration if Parliamentary time allowed.

[94] Schedule B1, para 11.

[95] Schedule B1, para 22.

[96] Schedule B1, para 7 (and the floating chargee's ability to move at speed).

[97] Schedule B1, para 3.

on the heels of the Insolvency Act 1985, which effected major reforms of individual and corporate insolvency. The two Acts brought corporate and individual insolvency under the same statutory roof. The former had previously been located in the Companies Acts and the latter in the Bankruptcy Acts. The main influence behind the Insolvency Acts of 1985 and 1986 was the Cork Report.[98] The Cork Committee had been given broad terms of reference extending to a review of the law and practice of insolvency, bankruptcy, liquidation and receivership, as well as the consideration of a comprehensive insolvency system.

9.22 Notwithstanding their shared statutory parentage, the individual and corporate insolvency regimes are by no means identical in their content. Parts I to VII of the 1986 Act deal with corporate insolvency, while Parts VIII to XI deal with individual insolvency and Parts XII to XIX are common to both regimes.

B. The Estate of the Insolvent and Its Distribution

(1) The Estate of the Insolvent in the Insolvency Process

(a) The content of the insolvent's estate

9.23 Prior to any distribution, the insolvent's estate must first be gathered in.[99] The property of bankrupt individuals first vests automatically in the trustee upon his appointment taking effect.[100] Before the changes of the 1980s, under the reputed ownership doctrine, it included '[a]ll goods...in the possession, order or disposition of the bankrupt, in his trade or business, by the consent of the true owner'.[101] Bankruptcy differs from liquidation in that a portion of the property of the bankrupt is retained for his beneficial enjoyment and does not vest in the trustee.[102] There is provision in the case of compulsory (but not voluntary) liquidation for the liquidator to apply for a vesting order[103] but there is little practical need since the distribution of the estate can be accomplished through the powers conferred on the liquidator[104] after the liquidator has performed his statutory task of gathering in the property of the company.[105] The property of the company does not vest in

---

[98] Cmnd 8558 (1982).

[99] For the powers of administrative receivers, administrators and liquidators to take possession of company property and its papers, see s 234 and *Walker Morris v Khalastchi* [2001] 1 BCLC 1. For bankruptcy, see s 312. For immunity from liability in conversion when the office holder reasonably believes that property belongs to the company, see *Re Euromex Ventures Ltd* [2013] EWHC 3007 (Ch). For guidance given to administrators handling reservation of title claims, see *Blue Monkey Gaming Ltd v Hudson* [2014] All ER(D) 222.

[100] Section 306. This vesting rule is compatible with the European Convention on Human Rights: *Young v Official Receiver* [2010] EWHC 1591 (Ch), [2010] BPIR 1477. As in the case of a winding-up, the property of the bankrupt will be impressed with a trust in favour of his creditors: *Ayerst v C&K (Construction) Ltd* [1976] AC 167, HL; *Re Yagerphone Ltd* [1935] Ch 392; *Re MC Bacon Ltd* [1991] Ch 127.

[101] Bankruptcy Act 1914, s 38(2)(c). The reputed ownership doctrine never applied to companies.

[102] Namely, essential personal and vocational items (s 283) and personal rights of action: discussed at 9.34. With regard to the bankrupt's home, see ss 283A (vesting the property interest in the bankrupt after three years if the trustee does not realize the interest) and 313A (low value homes) of the Insolvency Act.

[103] Section 145.

[104] Sections 165 and 167, Sch 4. See *Smith v Bridgend County Borough Council* [2001] UKHL 58, [2002] 1 AC 336.

[105] Section 144. It is the function of trustees to 'get in' the bankrupt's estate (s 305(2)). Like a compulsory liquidator, the administrator takes into custody the company's property (Insolvency Act, Sch B1, para 67). No similar duty is laid down in the Act for voluntary liquidators: their functions will be set out in the terms of their appointment. An administrative receiver is empowered to 'take possession of, collect and get in' the company's property (Sch 1, para 1).

an administrator, nor does it vest in an administrative receiver, both of whom enjoy broad powers in respect of the property.[106]

(i) The 'property' of the insolvent

Under section 436, the word 'property' embraces 'every description of property wherever **9.24** situated and also obligations and every description of interest, whether present or future or vested or contingent, arising out of, or incidental to, property'.[107] It is hard to imagine a wider definition.[108] Indeed, an item need not have realizable value or be capable of being beneficially enjoyed by the creditors of the insolvent for it to be property.[109]

In the case of bankruptcy, the date for testing when an item is property is the date of appoint- **9.25** ment of the trustee when the vesting occurs. Items purely personal to the bankrupt[110] at that time will not vest in the trustee. Thus the personal correspondence of the bankrupt, even if valuable, is excluded since the opposite conclusion would entail a 'gross invasion of privacy'.[111] Although an action for breach of contract for wrongful dismissal, occurring before the vesting date, will vest in the trustee,[112] the rights of a bankrupt under a continuing personal services contract will not. Nevertheless, if property rights of the bankrupt can be enjoyed only by him but entail expenditure that will affect the dividend available to his creditors, they are treated as property of the estate for the purpose of the trustee's disclaimer power.[113]

Property is defined widely in the insolvency process because, apart from gathering in **9.26** an estate so that the maximum is available for distribution, its existence is a precondition for the exercise by a liquidator or trustee of the power of disclaimer. The exercise of this power[114] permits the removal from the estate of items that are worthless or even, because their burdens outweigh their benefits, possess negative value. Value, therefore, is not a precondition for the treatment of an item as property.[115] The meaning of property may depend upon its context,[116] but there is just one definition of property in the Insolvency Act and no justification for giving the word one interpretation when dealing

---

[106] Insolvency Act, Schs 1 and B1.

[107] That value may be indirectly realized. See *Re Rae* [1995] BCC 102 (fishing licences terminated on bankruptcy but the Ministry recognized bankrupt's 'entitlement' to apply for new licences).

[108] *Bristol Airport plc v Powdrill* [1990] Ch 744, 759, CA: *Re Rae* [1995] BCC 102, 113. Hence 'property' can include rights of pre-emption (*Dear v Reeves* [2001] EWCA Civ 277, [2002] Ch 1), discretionary payments under a pension scheme (*Patel v Jones* [2001] EWCA Civ 779, [2001] BPIR 919); and the benefit of a proprietary estoppel (*Webster v Ashcroft* [2011] EWHC 3848 (Ch), [2012] 1 WLR 1309).

[109] See *De Rothschild v Bell* [2000] QB 33, CA (continuation tenancy which could not be turned into money for the benefit of the bankrupt's creditors); *Morgan v Morris* [1998] BPIR 764 (vesting of moneys in an offshore trust).

[110] Life insurance policies, purchased with premiums that would otherwise have gone to the estate, are not personal: *Cork v Rawlins* [2001] EWCA Civ 197, [2001] Ch 792.

[111] *Haig v Aitken* [2001] Ch 110, 118.

[112] *Bailey v Thurston & Co Ltd* [1903] 1 KB 137, CA. Any sums the bankrupt recovers in proceedings for a breach arising after the date of the trustee's appointment will be subject to the provisions on after-acquired property, discussed at 9.32–9.33. The approach in *Bailey v Thurston & Co Ltd* does not readily lend itself to corporate insolvency.

[113] *De Rothschild v Bell* [2000] QB 33, CA.

[114] Discussed at 9.40–9.48. An unprofitable contract can be disclaimed (ss 178(3)(a), 315(2)(a)); it should make no difference that the contract contains a no-assignment clause (see *De Rothschild v Bell* [2000] QB 33, CA).

[115] Whether in the actual sense (Is this in fact worth anything?) or in its potential sense (Is this capable of having value attributed to it?).

[116] *Nokes v Doncaster Amalgamated Collieries* [1940] AC 1014, 1051, HL.

with disclaimer, another when dealing with the gathering in and distribution of the estate and another when dealing with the enforcement of security over the property of a company in administration.[117]

9.27 Consequently, the definition of property is capable of including causes of action, in so far as their assignment does not infringe rules of public policy against champerty and maintenance.[118] It includes anything that can be held subject to the terms of a trust,[119] such as the benefit of a non-assignable contract,[120] and carbon trading allowances.[121] As long as there is a framework of entitlement, it also includes items of value that cannot be transferred by the insolvent, such as a waste management licence,[122] and items that can be transferred only by very indirect means, such as a milk quota.[123]

(ii) Beneficial property rights

9.28 The property available for distribution to creditors comprises only assets that are beneficially owned by the insolvent.[124] It does not extend to property held on trust,[125] or to property the subject of a reservation of title clause or of a security interest[126] by way of charge or mortgage. The insolvent's equity of redemption[127] is available for distribution but the liquidator or trustee may not prevent the realization of the security, any more than he may prevent the exercise of a lien, a right of retention or a right of stoppage of goods in transit.[128]

9.29 The immunity of trust property from distribution to the creditors of an insolvent trustee is not infringed in a case where the trustee, a bank that becomes insolvent, lawfully deposits trust money with itself so as to leave the trust with an unsecured claim in its insolvency.[129] The trust estate now comprises the personal debt claim against the trustee instead of the former trust money.

(iii) Trusts

9.30 Various forms of constructive and invented trusts are capable of affecting the size of the insolvent's estate. First of all, the growth of restitutionary *in rem* claims, without regard to the effect of their creation on other creditors of the insolvent defendant, threatens to disrupt the system of rateable insolvency distribution. The so-called *Quistclose* trust, whether it takes

---

[117] *Bristol Airport plc v Powdrill* [1990] Ch 744, CA (interest of lessee in aircraft).

[118] Discussed at 9.49–9.54. But a bare right of appeal is not a thing in action capable of being property under the Act: *Re GP Group Aviation International Ltd* [2013] EWHC 1447 (Ch), [2014] 1 WLR 166.

[119] See *Swift v Dairywise Farms Ltd* [2000] 1 WLR 1177, aff'd [2001] EWCA Civ 145, [2003] 1 WLR 1606 (Note).

[120] See *King (Don) Productions Inc v Warren* [1998] 2 All ER 608, aff'd [2000] Ch 291, CA.

[121] *Armstrong DLW GmbH v Winnington Networks Ltd* [2012] EWHC 10 (Ch), [2012] Bus LR 1199.

[122] *Re Celtic Extraction Ltd* [2001] Ch 475, CA (a disclaimer case).

[123] *Swift v Dairywise Farms Ltd* [2000] 1 WLR 1177, aff'd [2001] EWCA Civ 145, [2003] 1 WLR 1606 (Note).

[124] Section 283(3)(a) (bankruptcy, but references in the Act to getting in and distributing company property impliedly recognize the rights of beneficiaries).

[125] *Mountney v Treharne* [2002] EWCA Civ 1174, [2003] Ch 135.

[126] See s 283(5). Even if it has not been realized, the security also remains in existence after the discharge of the bankrupt: s 281(2).

[127] Although a charge is merely an encumbrance and no property interest is conveyed to the chargee, it is common to say loosely that the chargor has, like the mortgagor, an equity of redemption in the property charged: see, eg, *Re Bank of Credit and Commerce International SA (No 8)* [1998] AC 214, HL.

[128] But note that a lien over a company's books, papers and records (excepting documents of title) is unenforceable against an administrator or liquidator: s 246(2), (3). For the moratorium on the exercise of lien, security and related rights in administration, see 9.87.

[129] *Space Investments Ltd v Canadian Imperial Bank of Commerce Trust Co (Bahamas) Ltd* [1986] 1 WLR 1072, PC.

the form of a trust attaching to money because of the terms on which it is paid[130] or of a trust declared by the payee upon the receipt of money,[131] has a particular impact in insolvency cases.[132] Other examples of equitable proprietary interests also exist, which prefer the claimant in the defendant's insolvency.[133] Nevertheless, there is some reluctance to allow equitable proprietary interests to take root in the insolvency process.[134]

(iv) Clauses determining property interests

The estate of an insolvent may in effect be diminished by clauses in a will, contract, assignment or similar instrument conferring a limited interest and determining that interest in the event of the holder's insolvency.[135] Such clauses are valid[136] provided there is no repugnancy between a clause of this nature and a clause in the same instrument that purports to assign property in absolute terms.[137] Nevertheless, a clause in an instrument is void, on the ground that it infringes the so-called anti-deprivation rule, if it forfeits an unlimited interest in the event of insolvency.[138] The distinction thus drawn is notoriously difficult to justify.[139] The anti-deprivation rule, one of public policy, is not stated in general terms in the Insolvency Act. The Supreme Court in *Belmont Park Investments Pty Ltd v BNY Corporate Trustee Services Ltd*,[140] a case involving a complex financial markets transaction, concluded that the rule should not apply in 'borderline' cases where a transaction had been concluded for bona fide commercial reasons and without any intention of evading insolvency rules.[141] **9.31**

(v) Bankrupts, pensions, and after-acquired property

As stated above, not all of a bankrupt's property vests in the trustee for distribution,[142] though the vesting net is particularly wide in bankruptcy to compensate for the advantage the bankrupt receives from being forever released from personal payment obligations.[143] **9.32**

---

[130] See eg *Barclays Bank Ltd v Quistclose Investments Ltd* [1970] AC 567, HL; *Re EVTR Ltd* [1987] BCLC 646, CA; *Re Chelsea Cloisters Ltd* (1980) 41 P&CR 98, CA; *Carreras Rothmans Ltd v Freeman Mathews Treasure Ltd* [1985] Ch 207; *Re Lewis's of Leicester Ltd* [1995] 1 BCLC 428; *Twinsectra Ltd v Yardley* [2002] UKHL 12, [2002] 2 AC 164 (Lord Millett). The imposition of restrictions on the use of money is not sufficient to establish the purpose that is necessary for the inference of a *Quistclose* trust: *Re Griffin Trading Co* [2000] BPIR 256.

[131] See *Re Kayford Ltd* [1975] 1 WLR 279.

[132] See *Twinsectra Ltd v Yardley* [2002] UKHL 12, [2002] 2 AC 164; *Bellis v Challinor* [2015] EWCA Civ 59; M Bridge, 'The Quistclose Trust in a World of Secured Transactions' (1992) 12 OJLS 333.

[133] See eg *Chase Manhattan Bank SA v Israel-British Bank (London) Ltd* [1981] Ch 105; *Re Fleet Disposal Services Ltd* [1995] 1 BCLC 345; *Neste Oy v Lloyd's Bank plc* [1983] 2 Lloyd's Rep 658.

[134] See *Re Wait* [1927] 1 Ch 606, CA and *Re Goldcorp Exchange* [1995] 1 AC 74, PC. A similar conservatism is at work with regard to restitutionary claims in *Westdeutsche Landesbank Girozentrale v Islington London BC* [1996] AC 669, HL, *per* Lord Browne-Wilkinson, but proprietary restitutionary claims in cases like *Lord Napier and Ettrick v Hunter* [1993] AC 713, HL, and *FHR Ventures LLP v Cedar Capital Partners LLC* [2014] UKSC 45, [2015] AC 250 have implications for insolvency distribution.

[135] Direct payment clauses are discussed at 9.96–9.97.

[136] *Re Ashby* [1892] 1 QB 872.

[137] *Re Smith* [1916] 1 Ch 369.

[138] See *Money Markets International Stockbrokers Ltd v London Stock Exchange Ltd* [2002] 1 WLR 1150; *British Eagle International Airlines Ltd v Cie Nationale Air France* [1975] 1 WLR 758, HL. This subject is discussed in greater detail at 9.95.

[139] According to Neuberger J in *Money Markets International Stockbrokers Ltd v London Stock Exchange Ltd* [2002] 1 WLR 1150, 1182: '[I]t is not possible to discern a coherent, or even an entirely coherent set of rules, to enable one to assess in any particular case whether . . . a provision falls foul of the principle' that a clause transferring property on an insolvency is void.

[140] [2011] UKSC 38, [2012] 1 AC 383.

[141] The anti-deprivation rule is considered in greater detail below in connection with the *pari passu* distribution principle: see 9.94 et seq.

[142] Also excluded are certain types of tenancy (s 283(3A)) though the trustee may require them by notice to be vested (s 308A).

[143] *Patel v Jones* [2001] EWCA Civ 779, [2001] BPIR 919; *Re Rae* [1995] BCC 102, 111.

So that the bankrupt and his family will not be a burden on state provision, the Insolvency Act excludes certain personal effects[144] as well as items used personally by the bankrupt in his employment, business or vocation.[145] In assessing the bankrupt's position, it is useful to distinguish property that vests initially in the trustee, property later acquired by the bankrupt prior to discharge, and property that will be acquired after discharge. This helps to explain the position concerning personal and occupational pension plans, which has been substantially altered by legislation. Prior to 1999, the insured bankrupt's entitlement, whether it took the form of the capital sum paid under some schemes on taking retirement or the periodic income stream, though payable in the future was treated as a present asset that automatically vested in the trustee at the commencement of the bankruptcy.[146] Pension rights therefore did not have to be the subject of a written claim by the trustee, a procedure which applies to after-acquired property.[147] Furthermore, moneys received under such pensions did not fall within the more limited income payments order system as the pension asset itself had already vested in the trustee,[148] notwithstanding any restrictions on the assignment of pension rights.[149] Discretionary pension rights were a different matter, which is why an income payment order could usefully be applied to such income actually received by the bankrupt.[150] With the passing of the Welfare Reform and Pensions Act 1999, the rights of a bankrupt under an approved pension arrangement were excluded from his estate.[151] The same applies to unapproved pension arrangements where appropriate regulations are made.[152]

9.33 The release of the bankrupt from his due debts justifies the trustee's power, exercised unilaterally and by notice, to claim for the estate after-acquired property falling in after the date of the trustee's appointment.[153] This power does not extend to the bankrupt's income[154] for which special provision is made. An income payment order may be made on the trustee's application so that the excess of the bankrupt's income, including pension payments,[155] vests in the trustee after provision has been made for the reasonable domestic needs of the bankrupt and his family.[156] This latter factor points to a broad interpretation being given to 'income' so that, especially where the bankrupt has little earning capacity, the word includes

---

[144] Section 283(2)(b).

[145] Section 283(2)(a). See also s 308 (trading down for cheaper substitutes).

[146] *Patel v Jones* [1999] BPIR 509 (occupational plan); *Re Landau* [1998] Ch 223 (personal plan); *Krasner v Dennison* [2001] Ch 76, CA. But the vesting was confined to pensionable service occurring before the date of the trustee's appointment: *Patel v Jones* [2001] EWCA Civ 779, [2001] BPIR 919. This was held not to infringe the European Convention on Human Rights in *Malcolm v Benedict Mackenzie* [2004] EWCA Civ 1148, [2005] 1 WLR 1238.

[147] Section 307. Confined to pre-discharge assets by subs (1)(aa) from 2002.

[148] *Krasner v Dennison* [2001] Ch 76, CA (which reviews fully the position regarding pensions of different types).

[149] *Re Landau* [1998] Ch 223; *Krasner v Dennison* [2001] Ch 76, CA.

[150] *Krasner v Dennison* [2001] Ch 76, CA.

[151] Section 11 of the 1999 Act. But see 9.33.

[152] Section 12 of the 1999 Act.

[153] Insolvency Act, s 307. Under previous legislation, after-acquired property automatically vested in the trustee. After-acquired property includes financial loss claims vesting after bankruptcy in the bankrupt, even though these claims would have automatically vested in the trustee under s 306 had they been in existence at that time: *Mulkerrins v Pricewaterhouse Coopers* [2003] UKHL 41, [2003] 1 WLR 1937 (*res judicata* prevented any reopening of the district judge's ruling that an action for damages against financial advisers for being made bankrupt could not vest in the estate).

[154] Section 307(5). Income can include income arising after the bankruptcy order and before the making of the income payment order: *Official Receiver v Baker* [2013] EWHC 4594 (Ch), [2014] BPIR 724.

[155] Section 310(7). See *Raithatha v Williamson* [2012] EWHC 909 (Ch), [2012] 3 All ER 1028, and *Horton v Henry* [2014] EWHC 4209 (Ch), [2015] Pens LR 59, for conflicting views on whether the pensioner should be compelled to draw down a pension not yet in payment. This question is in urgent need of resolution.

[156] Section 310 (amended so as not to entrench upon the guaranteed minimum pension).

redundancy payments, money in lieu of notice and lump sum pension payments.[157] The income payment order runs for three years, which may terminate after discharge,[158] but it cannot be made after discharge.[159] The income payments procedure does not apply where a right to payment of a contingent amount has already vested in the trustee upon his appointment, as occurred in one case where the bankrupt was a member of a society. Although the membership of that society was personal and could not be transferred to the trustee, the right to receive future royalty income from the society, to which the copyright in certain musical works had been assigned, did vest in the trustee on his appointment.[160]

(vi) Bankrupts and litigation

It was stated above that a cause of action for breach of contract vested in the trustee at the date of his appointment. Certain actions in tort are also capable of vesting except in so far as 'damages are to be estimated by immediate reference to pain felt by the bankrupt in respect of his body, mind, or character, and without immediate reference to his rights of property'.[161] For that reason, a cause of action in defamation will not vest,[162] though a judgment debt against the defendant would undoubtedly vest; judgment rendered after the trustee's appointment would give rise to after-acquired property to which the trustee could lay claim.[163] In personal injury cases, the claimant may have a claim for pain and suffering as well as a claim for loss of future earnings. The former type of claim is certainly personal[164] but the latter is not. Yet there is only one cause of action[165] and, though hybrid in nature, it vests in the trustee under section 306 of the Insolvency Act.[166] Nevertheless, there is a separate property right in the bankrupt in the pain and suffering claim, so that any damages recovered by the trustee respecting this claim are to be held on constructive trust terms for the bankrupt.[167]

9.34

The effect of the bankrupt's property vesting in the trustee, coupled with the rule that upon the making of a bankruptcy order a creditor's claim must be submitted to proof and cannot otherwise be asserted against the bankrupt or his property,[168] means that he ceases to have an interest in either his assets or liabilities, apart from any surplus that may become available.[169]

9.35

---

[157] The trustee in *Patel v Jones* [2001] EWCA Civ 779, [2001] BPIR 919 conceded that statutory redundancy pay and pay in lieu of notice did not vest in him.

[158] Section 310(6).

[159] *Chadwick v Nash* [2012] BPIR 70.

[160] *Performing Right Society v Rowland* [1997] 3 All ER 336. But no vesting would occur in respect of songs not yet written. Sums received by the bankrupt in respect of such songs would have to be made the subject of an income payment order (s 310) if the trustee and the creditors were to participate in them.

[161] *Beckham v Drake* (1849) 2 HLC 579, 604, 9 ER 1213, HL. A cause of action for disablement vests in the estate: *Cork v Rawlins* [2001] EWCA Civ 202, [2001] Ch 792.

[162] *Wilson v United Counties Bank* [1920] AC 102, HL. See *Re Campbell* [1997] Ch 14, 21. A cause of action for wrongful dismissal seeking reinstatement will not vest (*Grady v Prison Service* [2003] EWCA Civ 527, [2003] 3 All ER 745), nor will a claim for discrimination or injury to feelings (*Khan v Trident Safeguards Ltd* [2004] EWCA Civ 624, [2004] ICR 1591).

[163] Section 307.

[164] Similarly, a claim under the criminal injuries compensation scheme: *Re a Bankrupt No 145/95*, The Times, 8 December 1995.

[165] Despite the practice of itemizing damages awards instead of awarding a global sum, which began with *Jefford v Gee* [1970] 2 QB 130, CA.

[166] *Ord v Upton* [2000] Ch 352, CA (containing a full review of the authorities). See *Mulkerrins v Pricewaterhouse Coopers* [2003] UKHL 41, [2003] 1 WLR 1937 where Lord Millett (generally supported by Lords Bingham and Scott) saw some merit in the view that a cause of action against financial advisers for being made bankrupt could not vest in the estate, since the object of damages was to put the bankrupt in the position she occupied before the bankruptcy order was made.

[167] *Ord v Upton* [2000] Ch 32, CA

[168] Section 285(3).

[169] *Heath v Tang* [1993] 1 WLR 1421, 1422, CA.

Consequently, the bankrupt no longer has a continuing interest in litigation in which he is the defendant and may not in his own person appeal against a judgment,[170] except where the claimant is seeking personal relief against the bankrupt, for example, by way of injunction.[171] This prevents 'the bankrupt's substance from being wasted in hopeless appeals and protects creditors from vexatious challenges to their claims'.[172] The rule is capable of causing hardship in those cases where the judgment against the bankrupt led to the bankruptcy order and the trustee lacks the means to conduct the appeal, whereas the bankrupt himself might qualify for legal aid.[173]

(b) Effect of insolvency on contracts

9.36 The state of insolvency or the commencement of a winding-up or bankruptcy[174] does not alone amount to a present or anticipatory breach of contract though there is nothing to prevent contracting parties from agreeing upon a right to withdraw from the contract in that event.[175] Similarly, the winding-up of one party does not automatically terminate the contract.[176] As the company's agent,[177] the liquidator has the power to transfer the company's property to a purchaser and to carry on its business so far as may be necessary for its beneficial winding-up.[178] This will include completing those contracts, presumably profitable ones, that he chooses not to disclaim or neglect to the point of breach. In this sense, the liquidator has an option to perform the contract.[179] The solvent co-contractant is protected by his entitlement to exercise any available lien or right of retention under a contract involving the sale of land or goods to the insolvent. If the liquidator elects to complete the contract, this must be done within a reasonable time.[180] Sometimes, the inaction of the liquidator will be treated as an offer of abandonment of the contract to the co-contractant who may accept that offer by declining to perform.[181] As against the liquidator, the co-contractant may apply to the court for the exercise of its discretion to rescind the contract on such terms as it thinks just.[182] This jurisdiction would be most useful where the co-contractant lacks the security of a lien or mutually concurrent performance due from the insolvent, but it appears to be rarely exercised.

9.37 In one respect, a party's insolvency will vary contractual terms. This occurs where goods are due to be supplied on credit terms to a buyer who becomes insolvent before delivery. Should

---

[170] *Heath v Tang* [1993] 1 WLR 1421, 1422, CA. A bankrupt may also not seek judicial review against a tax assessment: *R (on the application of Singh) v HMRC* [2010] UKUT 174 (TCC), [2010] BPIR 933.

[171] *Dence v Mason* [1879] WN 177, CA.

[172] *Heath v Tang* [1993] 1 WLR 1421, 1427, CA.

[173] The court has however a discretion, on the application of the bankrupt (and creditors too) to modify decisions of the trustee: s 303(1).

[174] References below to liquidation will also include bankruptcy unless otherwise indicated.

[175] *Shipton Anderson & Co (1927) Ltd v Micks Lambert & Co* [1936] 2 All ER 1032.

[176] *Griffiths v Perry* (1859) 1 E & E 680, 688, 120 ER 1065.

[177] *Re Silver Valley Mines* (1882) 21 Ch D 381, 386, CA; *Stewart v Engel* [2000] 2 BCLC 528. This is so for both voluntary and compulsory winding-up: *Re Anglo-Moravian Hungarian Junction Railway Co* (1875) 1 Ch D 130, 133, CA.

[178] Insolvency Act, Sch 4 paras 4 and 6. Since he is the company's agent, the liquidator will not in the absence of a contrary intention incur personal liability on any contract. A mere failure to disclaim personal liability will not render him liable: *Stead Hazel & Co v Cooper* [1933] 1 KB 840, 843, but a prudent liquidator will insist upon a disclaimer. Parties dealing with the liquidator look to the assets of the company for payment which counts as an expense of the liquidation: discussed at 9.100–9.102.

[179] Moneys arising from the performance of the contract by the liquidator will not be caught by a pre-insolvency assignment of book debts by the insolvent: *Wilmot v Alton* [1897] 1 QB 517; *Re Collins* [1925] Ch 557. In the case of bankruptcy, there is the further consideration that any property supplied or transferred under the contract will have vested in the trustee.

[180] *Ex p Stapleton* (1879) 10 Ch D 586, 590.

[181] *Morgan v Bain* (1874) LR 10 CP 15.

[182] Section 186 (s 345 for bankruptcy), disapplied by special legislation in money markets and securities settlement systems.

the liquidator choose to proceed with performance, he will have to pay cash on delivery:[183] the seller should not be compelled to supply goods for an insolvency dividend. The amount paid out by the liquidator may be recovered as an expense of the liquidation.[184] The position here is consistent with the seller's right, notwithstanding a sale on credit terms, to recover the goods in transit in the event of the buyer's insolvency.[185]

Insolvency, though not amounting to a repudiation of the contract, may lead the insolvent **9.38** to commit a discharging breach by non-performance. The solvent co-contractant would then be free to terminate the contract.[186] The insolvency might also prevent the insolvent from performing certain future, perhaps contingent, acts, giving rise to a claim for damages, for which a proof would have to be made.[187]

The effect on contracts of a company going into administrative receivership or administration **9.39** is the same as for liquidation. Both administrative receiver and administrator are agents of the company.[188]

(c) Disclaimer of onerous property

(i) General

The Insolvency Act contains provisions on the right to disclaim onerous property for **9.40** winding-up[189] and for bankruptcy,[190] which are essentially the same in their effect.[191]

Onerous property is defined as any property that is unsaleable or not readily saleable or is **9.41** such as to give rise to a liability to pay money or perform any other onerous act.[192] Onerous property will frequently but not necessarily detract from the value of the insolvent's estate. The need to distribute an estate expeditiously, eg, might make it appropriate for a liquidator to disclaim property that has a book value in excess of any costs to be incurred in maintaining it. Onerous property includes some causes of action[193] as well as unprofitable contracts,[194] where the statutory right to disclaim permits the liquidator unilaterally to terminate the contract. An alternative to disclaimer may be to permit the company to breach the contract thus giving the co-contractant a provable claim.

To effect a disclaimer, the liquidator files a notice of disclaimer in court and serves a copy of **9.42** it on, as the case may be, any mortgagee or underlessee of leasehold property, co-contractants and any person he knows claims an interest in, or incurs a liability in respect of, disclaimed property.[195] The liquidator does not need the leave of the court and the property may be disclaimed despite his occupation of the property or exercise of ownership rights over it.[196] Disclaimer, nevertheless, will be disallowed if the liquidator has permitted a period of at least

---

[183] *Ex p Chalmers* (1873) 8 Ch App 289; *Morgan v Bain* (1874) LR 10 CP 15.
[184] Discussed at 9.100–9.102.
[185] Sale of Goods Act 1979, ss 44–46.
[186] *Powell v Marshall Parker & Co* [1899] 1 QB 710, CA; *Sale Continuation Ltd v Austin Taylor & Co* [1968] 2 QB 849, 860.
[187] *Re Asphaltic Wood Pavement Co* (1885) 30 Ch D 216, CA.
[188] Section 44(1)(a) and Sch B1, para 69. But a court-appointed receiver is not an agent of the company and consequently incurs personal liability since the company is not liable: *Burt Boulton & Hayward v Bull* [1895] 1 QB 276, CA.
[189] Sections 178–182.
[190] Sections 315–321.
[191] References to the liquidator below should be read as referring also to the trustee-in-bankruptcy unless otherwise stated.
[192] Section 178(3)(b).
[193] See, eg *Re Ballast Plc* [2006] EWHC 3189 (Ch), [2007] BCC 620.
[194] Section 178(3)(a). See *Re SSSL Realisations (2002) Ltd* [2006] EWCA Civ 7, [2006] Ch 610.
[195] Rules 4.187(1), 4.188(2)–4.188(4). See also r 4.189 (public interest).
[196] Section 178(2).

28 days to expire without responding to an interested party's demand that he disclaim or not.[197] In addition, disclaimer of a contract will not be allowed where it would expropriate a co-contractant's proprietary interest in the subject matter of the contract.[198] An aggrieved party may also petition the court under its general discretionary power to reverse or modify decisions of the liquidator.[199] The court, however, will not sit in the liquidator's chair and will exercise this power only if the liquidator has acted perversely or in bad faith.[200]

9.43 It is not immediately obvious why a statutory power to disclaim is necessary. The mere fact, eg, of the company in liquidation having a leasehold interest in property would not make it equitable to treat the payment of rent as an expense of the winding-up[201] if the liquidator did not retain active possession.[202] In the simple case of a contract being disclaimed, the statutory right to compensation of the co-contractant will be quantified in the same way as an action for damages[203] for breach of contract admitted to proof in the normal way. Nevertheless, disclaimer is important in bankruptcy, given that the assets of the bankrupt vest in the trustee,[204] since it relieves the trustee from personal liability.[205] In contract cases generally, disclaimer prevents the co-contractant from affirming the contract in the face of breach by the insolvent so as to leave open the possibility of future performance leading to a claim for debt.[206] Most importantly, it facilitates the winding-up of the insolvent's affairs by a liquidator dealing with complex matters arising from property interests and long-term contracts. The liquidator is enabled to distribute the estate expeditiously[207] and without fear of personal liability arising out of, eg, a failure to make provision for continuing rent due under a lease not yet (but which might in the future be) brought to an end by the landlord's re-entry or forfeiture of the lease.[208] Disclaimer also accords with the *pari passu* principle of distribution since it obviates the retention of disproportionate amounts to meet future liabilities.[209]

(ii) Disclaimer and leases

9.44 The treatment of leasehold property has posed difficulties when the rent payable under a lease or sublease is higher than the prevailing market rate. Problems can arise at various points in a chain of holdings. Suppose that A leases property to B. B may in turn assign the lease to C or sublet to C instead. The rent payable by B or the rent or subrent payable by C may be guaranteed by D. In the case of an assignment, B may remain liable to A for the payment of rent under the lease. The insolvent party may be B or it may be C.

9.45 If B becomes insolvent and C is an assignee of the lease, then C will be unaffected if B's liquidator disclaims any continuing liability in respect of performance by C of his covenants.[210]

---

[197] Section 178(5).

[198] *Re Bastable* [1901] 2 KB 518, CA (equitable interest of purchaser under contract to sell leasehold property), where however the trustee in bankruptcy could have reached the same result by disclaiming the lease itself (at 530, *per* Romer LJ).

[199] Section 168(5).

[200] *Re Hans Place Ltd* [1993] BCLC 768; cf *Re Katherine et Cie Ltd* [1932] 1 Ch 70, where the court's intervention was explained by its desire to preserve the liability of a surety, which survives today by other means. On the broad discretion given to a liquidator in managing an insolvent's estate, see s 168(4).

[201] Expenses of the winding-up are discussed at 9.100–9.103.

[202] *Re ABC Coupler and Engineering Co Ltd (No 3)* [1970] 1 WLR 702.

[203] *Re Park Air Services plc* [2000] 2 AC 172, HL.

[204] Section 306; cf liquidation: *Re Hans Place Ltd* [1993] BCLC 768.

[205] Section 315(3)(b).

[206] *White & Carter (Councils) Ltd v McGregor* [1962] AC 413, HL (Sc).

[207] See, eg *Re SSSL Realisations (2002) Ltd* [2006] EWCA Civ 7, [2006] Ch 610.

[208] *Re Park Air Services plc* [2000] 2 AC 172, HL.

[209] *Re Celtic Extraction Ltd* [2001] Ch 475, 491, CA.

[210] Since the Landlord and Tenant (Covenants) Act 1995, the assignor is released from covenants that have to be complied with by the tenant.

The position will be the same if there is a default by D, the guarantor of B's obligations. If C, however, is a subtenant, the position is as follows. The starting point is that the rights and obligations of third parties, counterparties and co-contractants are unaffected by the disclaimer except in so far as necessary for the purpose of releasing the company from its liabilities.[211] Upon disclaimer, persons suffering loss in consequence of it are given a statutory right to compensation as though they were creditors of the company.[212] In effect, they are post-insolvency creditors permitted retroactively to prove in the winding-up. In the case of sublet premises, a disclaimer of the lease by B's liquidator terminates C's rights against B. It also terminates B's interest in the property but not so as to affect C, who continues to hold his interest as if B's interest continued.[213] Matters might continue in an indefinite state if C takes the practical course of paying A the rent due under the lease, which C would be advised to do to prevent A from applying for a vesting order,[214] a course of action that C himself might also prudently take if he wishes to assume the lease.

If C becomes insolvent and C's liquidator disclaims, the position in the case of assignment **9.46** is as follows. Where B remains primarily liable to pay the rent,[215] B is not released by C's disclaimer.[216] It was not easy to reconcile this position with the release of D where D had guaranteed payment of the rent by C,[217] a result that accorded with the general rule that the release of a debtor serves also to release a guarantor. The modern position regarding guarantors, that they remain liable notwithstanding the disclaimer of the assigned lease by C, is based upon a straightforward reading of the Insolvency Act that disclaimer affects parties other than the disclaiming party no more than 'is necessary for the purpose of releasing [the disclaiming party] from its liability...'.[218] If C's liquidator disclaims a sublease, then B will remain liable to pay rent due under the head lease in the normal way and the position of D, as guarantor of C's obligations, remains the same.

A further problem arising in the case of leasehold property concerns the claim of a landlord **9.47** when the tenant's liquidator disclaims the lease. The landlord is entitled to claim for the discounted difference between the rent due under the lease and the rent that can be obtained in prevailing market conditions.[219] The landlord's claim is not a debt claim for rent unpaid but rather a new claim arising upon the disclaimer and in the nature of damages.[220] Since damages principles apply, the landlord is treated as having to mitigate and also has to give credit

---

[211] Section 178(4)(b); *Hindcastle Ltd v Barbara Attenborough Associates Ltd* [1997] AC 70, HL, *per* Lord Nicholls; *Shaw v Doleman* [2009] EWCA Civ 283, [2009] BCC 730; *Willmott Growers Group Inc v Willmott Forests Ltd* [2013] HCA 51 (the disclaimer can affect both proprietary and contractual rights arising under the contract).

[212] Section 178(6).

[213] *Hindcastle Ltd v Barbara Attenborough Associates Ltd* [1997] AC 70, 89, HL, *per* Lord Nicholls. In the normal case of a forfeiture of a lease or re-entry, the subtenant would be at liberty to apply for relief which, if granted, would result in the grant of a new lease (Law of Property Act 1925, s 146(4)) or, less commonly, the substitution of the subtenant for the original tenant under the lease (Law of Property Act 1925, s 146(2)).

[214] Insolvency Act, s 181. A surety may seek a vesting order: *Re AE Realisations Ltd* [1987] 3 All ER 83.

[215] See however the Landlord and Tenant (Covenants) Act 1995.

[216] *Hill v East and West India Dock Co* (1884) 9 App Cas 448, HL; *Warnford Investments Ltd v Duckworth* [1979] Ch 127; *Hindcastle Ltd v Barbara Attenborough Associates Ltd* [1997] AC 70, HL.

[217] *Stacey v Hill* [1901] 1 KB 660, CA. For this reason, the result in *Warnford Investments Ltd v Duckworth* [1979] Ch 127 was unsuccessfully challenged in *Smith (WH) Ltd v Wyndham Estates Ltd* [1994] BCC 699.

[218] Section 178(4)(b). See also *Hindcastle Ltd v Barbara Attenborough Associates Ltd* [1997] AC 70, HL (overruling *Stacey v Hill* [1901] 1 KB 660, CA).

[219] *Re Hans Place Ltd* [1992] BCC 737; *Re Park Air Services plc* [2000] 2 AC 172, HL.

[220] Under s 178(6); see *Hindcastle Ltd v Barbara Attenborough Associates Ltd* [1997] AC 70, HL. The landlord is not in the position of a creditor who has released security and has elected to put in a proof instead and r 11.13 has no application: *Re Park Air Services plc* [2000] 2 AC 172, HL.

for the discounted present value of future receipts.[221] The landlord may not therefore claim future rent on the assumption that he will not re-enter or forfeit the lease.

(iii) Disclaimer and waste management licences

9.48   In modern times, acute difficulties have also been presented by waste management licences. The principal question is one of statutory precedence. Environmental legislation provides that a waste management licence, which permits the licensee to carry out certain activities that would otherwise be criminal offences,[222] continues in force until the regulatory authority either revokes it or accepts its surrender.[223] How is this provision to be reconciled with the liquidator's unilateral power of disclaimer? Departing from earlier authority,[224] and rejecting arguments that the 'polluter pays' principle is paramount and that the disclaimer itself can under the environment legislation render criminal the disposal of waste no longer authorized by the terms of the licence, the Court of Appeal has held that the liquidator is entitled to disclaim the licence.[225] The 'polluter pays' principle does not require the unsecured creditors of the polluter to pay by forgoing their right to a *pari passu* distribution. The environmental legislation can be sensibly interpreted as dealing with the termination of licences by acts of the parties as opposed to 'external statutory force'.[226]

(d) Assignment of causes of action

(i) General

9.49   A primary goal of the insolvency process is to maximize the estate so as to give creditors as high a dividend as possible. Gathering in the estate, however, is time-consuming and expensive, especially where it involves litigation. An endemic problem facing liquidators in particular is that they are short of the funds needed to perform their statutory functions.[227] One attempt to deal with this problem of underfunding is the assignment for value of the company's causes of action. This practice is founded on the fact that companies and liquidators representing them are not eligible for legal aid whereas individuals are. The practice has long existed in the case of bankruptcy,[228] where trustees are also ineligible for legal aid, but it has only more recently come into prominence in the field of company liquidations. Such assignments may be set aside if made for inadequate consideration.[229] Furthermore, an assignment for a share of the financial outcome of the assignee's proceedings may leave the trustee or liquidator on risk in respect of a successful defendant's costs claim.[230]

---

[221] *Re Park Air Services plc* [2000] 2 AC 172, HL.
[222] It was treated as 'property' under s 436 in *Re Celtic Extraction Ltd* [2001] Ch 475, CA.
[223] Environmental Protection Act 1990, s 35(11).
[224] *Re Mineral Resources Ltd* [1999] 1 All ER 746.
[225] *Re Celtic Extraction Ltd* [2001] Ch 475, CA. The effect of the disclaimer extends also to any fund set up to meet the company's obligations under the licence: *Environmental Agency v Hillridge Ltd* [2003] EWHC 3023 (Ch), [2004] 2 BCLC 358. cf *Joint Liquidators of the Scottish Coal Co Ltd* [2013] CSOH 108, 2014 SC 372.
[226] *Re Celtic Extraction Ltd* [2001] Ch 475, CA.
[227] The sole purpose of a liquidation is the realization and distribution of assets: *Heis v MF Global Inc* [2012] EWHC 3068 (Ch), at [52].
[228] See *Kitson v Hardwick* (1872) LR 7 CP 473; *Seear v Lawson* (1880) 15 Ch D 426; *Ramsey v Hartley* [1977] 1 WLR 686, CA. The rules for assigning to bankrupts and to former officers of a company in liquidation are the same: *Freightex Ltd v International Express Co Ltd* [1980] CA Transcript 395 with the necessary difference that a cause of action can be assigned to the bankrupt himself: see *Kitson v Hardwick* (1872) LR 7 CP 473 ('any person').
[229] *Faryab v Smith* [2001] BPIR 246, CA.
[230] *Hunt v Aziz* [2011] EWCA Civ 1239, [2012] 1 WLR 317, noting that the assignee might have limited resources. The trustee or liquidator, moreover, though entitled to be indemnified by the estate for costs incurred, will rank behind the successful defendant: *Norglen Ltd v Reeds Rains Prudential Ltd* [1999] 2 AC 1, HL.

A number of other issues are raised by this practice of assignment. The first is whether such **9.50** assignments infringe public policy rendering void contracts for champerty and maintenance,[231] with the related issue whether an exception to this rule exists for insolvency. A second issue is, if such assignments are permissible, whether all causes of action available to the liquidator or the fruits of a recovery are capable of being assigned in this way. A third issue is whether such assignments abuse the system of legal aid.

(ii) Public policy

The definition of property of the company as including 'every thing in action...and every **9.51** description of property...and also obligations' is more than wide enough to embrace causes of action as well as the fruits of recovery.[232] It is capable of including a cause of action in tort, provided that the cause of action is not so personal to the assignor as to be unassignable.[233] It includes also the net balance in favour of the insolvent reached after a set-off.[234] Since the liquidator has the statutory power to 'sell any of the company's property...with power to transfer...it to any person...',[235] assignments[236] are permitted that would otherwise amount to unlawful champerty or maintenance.[237] The statute therefore trumps public policy. Even in the absence of such statutory legitimation, an assignment would not be void as against public policy if the assignee had a genuine commercial interest in the enforcement of another's claim.[238] This requirement was not fulfilled in one case where the estate stood to gain nothing from the assignment because it had no interest in the recovered proceeds.[239]

(iii) Causes of action as property

With regard to the second issue, a close examination has to be made of what constitutes the **9.52** property of the insolvent company.[240] The practical question is whether a liquidator may assign a cause of action against directors and other persons guilty of wrongful and fraudulent

---

[231] Maintenance is supporting litigation in which one has no interest and champerty is maintenance where the maintainer also takes a share of the proceeds of recovery: *Re Oasis Merchandising Services Ltd* [1998] Ch 170, CA.

[232] See *Re Oasis Merchandising Services Ltd* [1998] Ch 170, CA, disapproving the contrary view of Lightman J in *Grovewood Holdings plc v James Capel & Co Ltd* [1995] Ch 80, 86, concerning the fruits. A liquidator assigning the fruits may not however also assign the fiduciary power to conduct proceedings in the name of the company: *Ruttle Plant Ltd v Secretary of State for Environment Food and Rural Affairs* [2008] EWHC 238 (TCC), [2009] 1 All ER 448. For this purpose, an assignment of the cause of action and an assignment of its fruits are to be distinguished: *Rawnsley v Weatherall Green & Smith North Ltd* [2099] EWHC 2482 (Ch), [2010] BCC 406.

[233] *Empire Resolution Ltd v MPW Insurance Brokers Ltd* [1999] BPIR 486 (negligent misstatement), referring to case law dealing with causes of action vesting in the trustee in bankruptcy (discussed at paras 9.25 and 9.35).

[234] *Stein v Blake* [1996] AC 243, 258, HL.

[235] Insolvency Act, Sch 4 para 6. Similarly, the trustee has the power to 'sell any part of the property for the time being comprised in the bankrupt's estate' (Sch 5 para 9) and the administrator and administrative receiver have the power to 'sell or otherwise dispose of the property' (Sch 1 para 2).

[236] The word 'sell' is broad enough to capture assignments of a bare cause of action, although there has to be consideration, which may be the fictitious consideration that reposes in the form of a deed: *Ramsey v Hartley* [1977] 1 WLR 686, 694, CA.

[237] *Guy v Churchill* (1889) 40 Ch D 481, 485 (bankruptcy); *Ramsey v Hartley* [1977] 1 WLR 686, 694, CA. This is why the assignments were attacked on other grounds in *Norglen Ltd v Reeds Rains Prudential Ltd* and *Circuit Systems Ltd v Zuken-Redac (UK) Ltd* [1999] 2 AC 1, HL (conjoined appeals).

[238] *Trendtex Trading Corp v Credit Suisse* [1982] AC 679, HL. An assignment of the fruits of litigation, where the assignee does not influence the conduct of litigation, is just an assignment of future property and does not offend public policy: *Glegg v Bromley* [1912] 3 KB 474, CA.

[239] *Turner v Schindler & Co* [1991] CA Transcript 665; *Circuit Systems Ltd v Zuken-Redac (UK) Ltd* [1997] 1 WLR 721, 733–734, CA, *per* Simon Brown LJ. This argument runs the risk of confusing what amounts to a void agreement with the question whether the assignment represents a proper exercise of the insolvency office holder's powers.

[240] This issue is particularly appropriate to corporate insolvency.

trading[241] as well as the right to challenge disposals of a company's property after the commencement of a winding-up[242] and unregistered charges granted by the company.[243] In order for the liquidator's assignment to shelter behind the statutory power to sell property belonging to the company,[244] the property in question must belong to the company at the commencement of the winding-up.[245] This distinction follows the scheme of the Insolvency Act and is consistent with the rule that recoveries by the liquidator in fraudulent trading actions, eg, are not attached by a charge granted by the company to a secured creditor.[246] Neither the cause of action nor its fruits are property of the company at the critical date, which is the commencement of the winding-up. Since, however, the company itself could have brought proceedings against directors for misfeasance,[247] the liquidator's power to sell the company's property applies here.[248]

9.53 Since any assignment of property that does not belong to the company at the date of the winding-up falls outside the liquidator's statutory power to sell, it has to be considered whether a liquidator[249] may nevertheless lawfully assign those causes of action and their fruits on other grounds. Now, the liquidator may not assign the causes of action themselves since only the liquidator is empowered to bring the proceedings.[250] There is no reason, however, why the fruits of recovery may not be assigned so long as the assignee does not interfere in the conduct of the proceedings so as to invalidate the assignment on the ground of maintenance.[251] Such interference would be offensive for the further reason that it could impede the liquidator in the exercise of his statutory functions by preventing him from applying to the court for directions in respect of any matter arising during the course of the winding-up.[252]

(iv) The legal aid system

9.54 The final issue concerns the matter of the legally aided claimant and the integrity of the legal aid system. It is clear that this is not a matter of insolvency law at all and therefore does not invalidate an assignment that otherwise complies with insolvency law principles.[253] Regulations dealing with legal aid are apt to deal with abuses in the system.

(e) Embargo on proceedings against the insolvent

(i) General

9.55 In the case of a compulsory winding-up, the leave of the court is required for an action or proceeding against the company or its property to be commenced or continued after the making of a winding-up order or the appointment of a provisional liquidator.[254] This follows

---

[241] Sections 213–214.
[242] Section 127.
[243] Companies Act 2006, s 859H.
[244] Insolvency Act, Sch 4 para 6. For trustees, see Sch 5 para 9.
[245] *Re Oasis Merchandising Services Ltd* [1998] Ch 170, CA; *Re Ayala Holdings Ltd (No 2)* [1996] 1 BCLC 467.
[246] *Re Yagerphone Ltd* [1935] Ch 392.
[247] Section 212.
[248] *Re Park Gate Waggon Works Co* (1881) 17 Ch D 234, CA; *Re Oasis Merchandising Services Ltd* [1998] Ch 170, CA.
[249] The court in *Re Oasis Merchandising Services Ltd* [1998] Ch 170, CA, expressed considerable doubt about whether an administrator or administrative receiver could assign the fruits of a future action brought by the *liquidator*. This should not be possible if it diverts assets from the unsecured creditors of the company to the secured debenture holder.
[250] *Re Oasis Merchandising Services Ltd* [1998] Ch 170, CA.
[251] *Re Oasis Merchandising Services Ltd* [1998] Ch 170, CA.
[252] Section 168(3).
[253] *Norglen Ltd v Reeds Rains Prudential Ltd* [1999] 2 AC 1, HL.
[254] Section 130(2).

on from another provision that, between the presentation of a winding-up petition and the making of a winding-up order, the company or any creditor or contributory may apply to the court for any further proceedings to be restrained or stayed.[255] For both provisions, the action may be permitted or stayed, as the case may be, on such terms and conditions as the court thinks fit. The action or proceeding in question is commonly distress by a landlord[256] or by a creditor entitled to similar relief.[257] An ordinary creditor facing a bleak prospect of recovery will need little further discouragement to discontinue pending litigation and is unlikely to commence litigation once an insolvent winding-up supervenes. There are similar special provisions dealing with executions and attachments.[258]

The purpose of these various provisions[259] is to maintain the integrity of the company's estate **9.56** so that it may be rateably distributed in the usual *pari passu* way, a process that is at odds with a judgment creditor's right to enforce a money judgment.[260] Upon the commencement of a winding-up, the individual process of debt collection gives way to a collective, solidary procedure in which creditors are treated as a class. Individual creditors of the company may not therefore act unilaterally to improve their position even if, like execution creditors, they have invested significant time and assets in the collection of what is owed to them and have been vigilant and energetic when other creditors may not have been. This result is consistent with the assets of a company in liquidation being held on the terms of a notional trust in favour of its creditors.[261]

(ii) Distress

Taking first the general provisions as they relate to actions and proceedings begun before the commencement of a winding-up, the discretion will be exercised so as to allow the distress,[262] **9.57** or other action or proceeding, to continue, unless special circumstances are shown rendering such continuance inequitable, since the general creditors have no intrinsic right to be preferred to the creditor taking action.[263] Once the winding-up has commenced, however, the general position is reversed and the landlord will not be allowed to distrain.[264] The burden of persuasion thereupon switches from the liquidator to the landlord, and the landlord would be compelled to show special reasons in the nature of fraud or unfair dealing if the distress were to be allowed to continue.[265] In the exercise of its discretion, the court conducts a balancing exercise, considering the interests not of one particular class of creditor but of 'each' of them.[266] In an execution case involving a similar discretion, the court declined to draw a

---

[255] Section 126.

[256] It is now settled beyond challenge that distress is a 'proceeding': *Re Herbert Barry Associates Ltd* [1977] 1 WLR 1437, HL; *Re Memco Engineering Ltd* [1986] Ch 86. Distress has now been superseded by a new statutory remedy; see 9.57.

[257] Other examples include an application for the appointment of a receiver: *Croshaw v Lyndhurst Ship Co* [1897] 2 Ch 154.

[258] Sections 183–184. These apply to goods, land and debts.

[259] The corresponding provisions for bankruptcy are ss 285 and 346–347. There are no such specific provisions for voluntary liquidation, but the same effect is reached under s 112, which permits a liquidator to apply to the court to exercise any powers that the court itself might exercise in a compulsory winding-up.

[260] *Roberts Petroleum Ltd v Bernard Kenny Ltd* [1983] 2 AC 192, HL.

[261] See *Ayerst v C&K (Construction) Ltd* [1976] AC 167, HL; *Re Yagerphone Ltd* [1935] Ch 392; *Re MC Bacon Ltd* [1991] Ch 127.

[262] Common law distress was superseded by a new statutory remedy, commercial rent, arrears recovery, the Tribunals, Court, and Enforcement AC 2007, s 71 and Sch 12. The contents of this paragraph may be taken for present purposes as applicable to the new remedy.

[263] *Re Great Ship Co Ltd* (1862) 4 De GJ & S 63, 69, 46 ER 839; *Re Roundwood Colliery Ltd* [1897] 1 Ch 373, 381, CA.

[264] *Thomas v Patent Lionite Co* (1881) 17 Ch D 250, CA, where a compulsory winding-up succeeded a voluntary winding-up, with the landlord distraining between the dates of commencement of each winding-up.

[265] *Venner's Electrical Cooking and Heating Appliances Ltd v Thorpe* [1915] 2 Ch 404, CA.

[266] *Re Great Ship Co Ltd* (1862) 4 De GJ & S 63, 69, 46 ER 839; *Re Roundwood Colliery Ltd* [1897] 1 Ch 373, 381, CA; *Venner's Electrical Cooking and Heating Appliances Ltd v Thorpe* [1915] 2 Ch 404, 407, CA.

distinction between trade creditors and loan creditors on the ground that the latter were a less deserving class.[267]

(iii) Executions

9.58   In the case of executions[268] against land or goods and attachments of debts, a creditor is not entitled to retain as against the liquidator the 'benefit of the execution' or attachment unless the execution or attachment has been completed before the commencement of the winding-up.[269] In cases where the execution is not completed by the relevant time, the court has a broadly stated discretion to set aside the rights of the liquidator,[270] when formerly its discretion was confined to trickery or dishonesty by the judgment debtor.[271] When exercised, the discretion can lead to a division of moneys between creditor and liquidator and may be invoked against impropriety and undue pressure by the debtor.[272] The conduct of the debtor leading up to judgment and up to the completion of execution are equally open to review.[273] The present statutory discretion, though not limited to an abuse of process by the debtor, will nevertheless be exercised with caution and only in special circumstances[274] since the execution creditor's gain is the loss, not of the debtor, but of the other creditors. It is possible that the discretion will be more liberally exercised in respect of the debtor's behaviour after judgment,[275] given the obvious judicial reluctance to interfere with the conduct of a defence in litigation. Delay on the part of an execution creditor and its advisers will be harmful to the prospects of the discretion being exercised.[276] It will not be enough for an execution creditor to show that it stayed its hand at the request of the debtor, for this would deny to other creditors the chance to show that they too had stayed their hand where the debtor had adopted a broad policy of stalling all of its creditors. Furthermore, the process of winding-up might have been accelerated anyway if the execution creditor had not stayed its hand.[277]

9.59   Completion of an execution against land occurs when it is seized, a receiver is appointed or a charging order[278] is made against it.[279] The attachment of a debt is completed by the receipt

---

[267] *Re Caribbean Products (Yam Importers) Ltd* [1966] Ch 331, 347–348, 351, CA, where the proposal was to divide the fruits of execution with other trade creditors to the exclusion of loan creditors who had anticipated becoming members of the company. The court was also reluctant to reward the execution creditor merely on the ground of his 'extra vigilance': at 347.

[268] A distress, such as one for unpaid taxes, is not an execution: *Re Modern Jet Support Centre Ltd* [2005] EWHC 1611 (Ch), [2005] 1 WLR 3880.

[269] Section 183 (compulsory and voluntary winding-up). For bankruptcy, the execution must be completed before the bankruptcy order is made: ss 278 and 346(1). If the creditor has notice of the calling of a meeting at which a voluntary winding-up resolution is to be proposed, the date of such notice is substituted for the date of commencement of the winding-up: s 183(2)(a).

[270] Section 183(2)(c).

[271] *Armorduct Manufacturing Co Ltd v General Incandescent Co Ltd* [1911] 2 KB 143, CA.

[272] *Re Grosvenor Metal Co Ltd* [1950] 1 Ch 63.

[273] *Re Suidair International Airways Ltd* [1951] Ch 165, 172; *Landau v Purvis* (High Ct, 15 June 1999).

[274] *Re Buckingham International plc (No 2)* [1998] BCC 943, 962. See *Tagore Investments SA v Official Receiver* [2008] EWHC 3495 (Ch), [2009] BPIR 392, where the debtor presented his own petition with the aim of frustrating the charge.

[275] *Landau v Purvis* (High Ct, 15 June 1999), distinguishing *Re Buckingham International plc (No 2)* [1998] 2 BCLC 369.

[276] *Landau v Purvis* (High Ct, 15 June 1999).

[277] *Re Redman (Builders) Ltd* [1964] 1 WLR 541, 552.

[278] Under the Charging Orders Act 1979. The fact that the debtor is insolvent and will inevitably go into liquidation is no ground for refusing to make final an interim charging order. There would have to be some additional significant factor present, such as a scheme of arrangement set on foot by the main body of creditors with a reasonable prospect of success: *Roberts Petroleum Ltd v Bernard Kenny Ltd* [1983] 2 AC 192, CA. Although the court has a discretion to stay an execution when bankruptcy proceedings are pending (s 283(1)), it will not set aside an execution completed before the bankruptcy order is made merely because of the making of that order. See *Nationwide Building Society v Wright* [2009] EWCA Civ 811, [2010] Ch 318, where the court noted the limited survival of the doctrine of relation back in s 284.

[279] Insolvency Act, s 183(3)(c).

of the 'debt' or rather its proceeds,[280] and an execution against goods when the goods are seized and sold[281] and the proceeds remitted to the creditor.[282] The position regarding goods is reinforced by a duty placed on the sheriff, as and when he has notice of the commencement of the winding-up,[283] to make over to the liquidator the goods as well as any money received or seized in part satisfaction of the judgment.[284] Further, a sheriff receiving moneys to avoid sale, or as a result of selling certain goods, must retain the moneys for 14 days. If within that time he is served with notice of a winding-up petition or of the calling of a meeting at which a winding-up resolution is to be proposed,[285] and there consequently follows a winding-up,[286] the sheriff must pay the moneys over to the liquidator.[287] This provision makes it very difficult for a major unsecured creditor to sue to judgment and complete an execution if the company's financial state is a parlous one. If the 14-day period elapses and moneys received in part execution have not been paid to the creditor, the liquidator is not entitled to them if execution remains uncompleted at the date of commencement of the winding-up. This is because the 'benefit of the execution'[288] means the charge created by the issue of execution and not any moneys paid over to avoid execution.[289]

This same view, that the benefit means the charge and not moneys received, underpinned **9.60** the decision in one case[290] where a debtor paid certain sums directly to an execution creditor in order to avoid a sale. He failed to keep up the agreed schedule of payments. Execution was recommenced but was incomplete at the commencement of his bankruptcy. If the court had interpreted the benefit of the execution to mean moneys received, the debtor would, subject to any discretion and to any limitations defence, have had to pay over the sums he had received to the trustee no matter how long before the bankruptcy the moneys had been paid. The execution may not have been completed by the time of the commencement of the bankruptcy but the sums were paid outside the execution process altogether. Any other result would have discouraged forbearance by creditors where this is as much for the benefit of debtors as for creditors themselves.[291] A different view of the 'benefit of the…attachment' was, however, taken in another case[292] where a garnishee[293] paid only a part of the garnished debt before the commencement of a winding-up. In this conventional example of an incomplete attachment, the liquidator, subject to any discretion to the contrary, was entitled to recover moneys received by the debtor. The court also dismissed the creditor's argument that the absence of any statutory provision dealing with an action by the liquidator to recover money from the creditor indicated an intention that the creditor should retain moneys in hand. The

---

[280] Section 183(3)(b).
[281] Section 183(3)(a) (or a (rare) charging order made under the Charging Orders Act 1979).
[282] *Bluston & Bramley Ltd v Leigh* [1950] 2 KB 548 (even though, prior to any divestment effected under s 183, the sheriff holds moneys received from the sale to the use of the judgment creditor).
[283] Section 184(1) (or of the appointment of a provisional liquidator).
[284] Section 184(2).
[285] As a provision divesting rights, this is to be construed against the liquidator: *Re Walton (TD) Ltd* [1966] 1 WLR 869 (notice adverting to the possibility of liquidation but making no mention of a winding-up resolution). But see *Bluston & Bramley Ltd v Leigh* [1950] 2 KB 548 (sufficient for notice to refer generally to the statutory provision and not its contents).
[286] For present purposes, a proposal for a voluntary winding-up resolution cannot be followed by a resolution for a compulsory winding-up: *Bluston & Bramley Ltd v Leigh* [1950] 2 KB 548.
[287] Section 184(3), (4). There is a first charge over the moneys for the costs of the execution. These provisions dealing with sheriffs are also subject to a broadly stated discretion in favour of the creditor: s 184(5).
[288] Section 183(1).
[289] *Re Walkden Sheet Metal Co Ltd* [1960] Ch 170.
[290] *Re Andrew* [1937] 1 Ch 122, CA. See also *Re Samuels* [1935] Ch 341.
[291] *Re Andrew* [1937] 1 Ch 122, 133–134, CA, criticizing *Re Kern (PE and BE)* [1932] 1 Ch 555, 560.
[292] *Re Caribbean Products (Yam Importers) Ltd* [1966] Ch 331, CA.
[293] Here and in 9.68, references to the former garnishee order should now be to a third party debt order and garnishor and garnishee should be adapted accordingly.

same result should also apply to an incomplete execution against goods. Nevertheless, as seen above, these cases of incomplete execution and attachment are to be distinguished from cases where an incomplete payment is made outside the execution and attachment processes.

(iv) Administrators: general

9.61 In the case of administration, there is an equally compelling reason for constraining execution, attachments and related actions and proceedings by individual creditors. Indeed, the justification for restraint may be even more compelling given that administration may last longer than a winding-up, and that the administrator during that time carries on the company as a going concern while a liquidator exercises limited powers of management. Prior to 2002, the administrator was not charged with *pari passu* distribution[294] since administration was only an interim process, yielding to a winding-up in those cases where the company could not be saved. The administrator may now make distributions[295] compliant with the *pari passu* principle.[296] The administrator is charged with designated statutory purposes[297] and is supported by the Insolvency Act which prevents individual creditors from interfering with the attainment of those purposes. Hence, as soon as an administration application is made, there is a 'moratorium on other legal process' so that no 'legal proceedings, execution, distress...may be instituted or continued against the company'[298] without the leave of the court.[299] The same embargo continues upon the appointment of the administrator except that the administrator also may grant leave for the action or proceedings to continue.[300]

(v) Proceedings against a company in administration

9.62 In the case law, the difficulties have centred on the meaning of 'other legal process' and related expressions, mention of which is made immediately after similar prohibitions on the passing of a resolution and the making of an order for a winding-up,[301] and on repossession under a title retention agreement and the enforcement of security.[302] The question is whether the list of actions and proceedings constitutes a genus so as to confine the generality of the words 'proceedings' and 'process'. A Scottish court has given support for the view that there is a genus exercising a limiting effect on the meaning of 'proceedings'.[303] These proceedings have to be in the nature of claims by creditors against the company. Hence, an application by a competitor airline to the Civil Aviation Authority for the revocation of the operating licence of the company in administration fell outside the prohibition.

9.63 This approach, however, is too narrow, given that the prohibition explicitly applies earlier in the Schedule to winding-up petitions and resolutions. These are not proceedings 'against' the company. Consequently, the word 'other' in 'other legal process' is deprived of any significant meaning and there is no restrictive genus. Hence, the prohibition has been held applicable to industrial tribunal proceedings and specifically to an action by a dismissed employee for

---

[294] Powers are conferred by the Insolvency Act on the administrator for the running of the company: see *Bristol Airport plc v Powdrill* [1990] Ch 744, CA; *Smith v Bridgend County Borough Council* [2000] 1 BCLC 775, CA, reversed on other grounds [2001] UKHL 58, [2002] 1 AC 336.

[295] Insolvency Act, Sch B1 para 65.

[296] Insolvency Rules, r 2.69.

[297] Insolvency Act, Sch B1, para 3(1).

[298] A statutory right of detention exercised under the Civil Aviation Act 1982, s 88(1), is not a right of distress for present purposes: *Bristol Airport plc v Powdrill* [1990] Ch 744, CA.

[299] Insolvency Act, Sch B1, paras 43(6) and 44(5).

[300] Insolvency Act, Sch B1, paras 43(6) and 44(5). The exercise of the discretion to grant leave is discussed below.

[301] Insolvency Act, Sch B1, para 42.

[302] Schedule B1, para 43(2), (3). The position of secured creditors and title retainers is dealt with below.

[303] *Air Ecosse Ltd v Civil Aviation Authority* 1987 SC 285, 291–292, 294–295, 298–299, Inner House.

reinstatement,[304] to criminal proceedings under the Environmental Protection Act 1990,[305] and to proceedings in the Patent Court for the revocation of the company's patent.[306] This does not mean that the word 'proceedings' should be given an expansive interpretation: it should not, eg, extend to the acceptance of a repudiatory breach of contract by the company in administration.[307] The proceedings have to be legal or quasi-legal. Further, the word 'process' suggests a recognizable procedure with a defined beginning and outcome, in some way involving the compulsive power of the law, but not including regulatory review,[308] where the regulator may have broader public interest responsibilities that override the moratorium.[309] The proceedings subject to restraint do not include the exercise of a unilateral right of detention of an aircraft for unpaid airport charges.[310] The word 'proceedings' also excludes an application to register a company charge out of time. The company itself is capable of making the application.[311]

(vi) Proceedings against a company in administrative receivership

There are no similar provisions interfering with actions or the exercise of rights against the company in the case of administrative receivership, which, since the Enterprise Act 2002, arises only in a limited number of cases. Unsecured creditors are free to sue the company to judgment and to seek execution but this is normally futile as it would simply precipitate the company into insolvency. It is a different matter if the creditor obtains a proprietary interest under a contract with the company, for receivership does not override this interest.[312] Furthermore, a creditor may be able to take action so as to prevent a non-proprietary claim against the company from arising. For example, a creditor may be entitled to injunctive relief restraining the administrative receiver from acting to bring about a breach of contract by the company where the receiver would not by so acting be preferring the interests of the debenture holder to those of the company.[313] Nevertheless, in the case of subsisting contracts, the receiver does not on his appointment incur personal liability so as to give the creditor a practical alternative to a hopeless action against the company.[314] Landlords, however, are in a better position than ordinary unsecured creditors since if rent remains unpaid they may re-enter the premises. The threat of this will often bring about an arrangement between the landlord and the administrative receiver for the payment of current and even accrued rent.

9.64

(vii) Execution, administration and administrative receivership

Under the Insolvency Act, the moratorium instituted in the event of an administration prevents an execution from being 'continued' without the consent of the administrator or the

9.65

---

[304] *Carr v British International Helicopters Ltd* [1994] 2 BCLC 474 (EAT).

[305] *Re Rhondda Waste Disposal Ltd, sub nom Environment Agency v Clark* [2001] Ch 57, CA.

[306] *Biosource Technologies Inc v Axis Genetics Plc* [2000] 1 BCLC 286 (reviewing the authorities).

[307] *Bristol Airport plc v Powdrill* [1990] Ch 744, 766, CA, *per* Browne-Wilkinson VC. Also excluded is the service of a time of the essence notice (*Re Olympia & York Canary Wharf Ltd* [1993] BCLC 453).

[308] *Re Frankice (Golders Green) Ltd* [2010] EWHC 1229 (Ch), [2010] Bus LR 1608.

[309] *Re Railtrack plc* [2002] EWCA Civ 955, [2002] 1 WLR 3002.

[310] *Bristol Airport plc v Powdrill* [1990] Ch 744, CA, disagreeing on the width of 'proceedings' with the trial judge (Harman J) at [1990] BCC 130, 139 ('every sort of step against the company').

[311] *Re Barrow Borough Transport Ltd* [1989] Ch 227.

[312] *Freevale Ltd v Metrostore (Holdings) Ltd* [1984] Ch 199.

[313] *Ash and Newman Ltd v Creative Devices Research Ltd* [1991] BCLC 403. In the case of a court-appointed receiver, creditors may also be protected indirectly if the court declines to permit the receiver to repudiate contracts of the company on the ground that such action will damage the company's goodwill: *Re Newdigate Colliery Ltd* [1912] 1 Ch 468, CA. An insolvent company in receivership, however, may have no appreciable goodwill (but see *Airline Airspares Ltd v Handley Page Ltd* [1970] Ch 193 where damage to goodwill would seriously have affected the realization of net assets).

[314] But an administrative receiver may incur personal liability on contracts of employment that he adopts and will also incur liability on contracts he enters into unless he disclaims personal liability: s 44(1)(b).

leave of the court.[315] Such leave or consent is unlikely to be given in those cases where an administrator is appointed out of court under a qualifying charge. In the great bulk of cases, administrative receivers have now been superseded by such administrators. The law on the completion of an execution for administrative receivership should therefore still be relevant for the purpose of determining when, for the purposes of administration, an execution has not yet been completed. The case law involving administrative receivers and other receivers has, for the purpose of priority against the debenture holder, centred on whether the execution or attachment was complete before the crystallization of a floating charge, which commonly occurs upon the appointment of a receiver. It is difficult to state the precise law in this area, which is bedevilled by the use of loose proprietary language and by statutory changes to the insolvency position that may to some extent spill over into receivership. A writ of *fieri facias* (or other writ of execution) binds the goods of the execution debtor as soon as the writ is delivered to the sheriff.[316] This means that the sheriff, on behalf of the execution creditor, has a right to seize the goods while they remain in his bailiwick; he does not as such have a proprietary interest in them.[317] The sheriff acquires a special or qualified property in the debtor's goods as from the date of actual seizure, which allows him to sue a third party tortfeasor in conversion.[318] Nevertheless, this property right is liable to be overridden by the fixed charge that is subsequently created upon the crystallization of a pre-existing floating charge, for the sheriff acquires his special property subject to existing equities.[319] For this reason, the floating chargee takes precedence over the execution creditor when the charge crystallizes and the goods remain in the sheriff's hands.[320]

9.66 What the position is if the charge crystallizes before the proceeds of a sale by the sheriff are paid to the execution creditor is unclear.[321] The statutory provisions regarding incomplete executions in insolvency, where the liquidator in those circumstances would prevail over the execution creditor, appear to have modified the common law[322] and anyway do not extend to receivership. In favour of the view that the floating chargee should prevail in such a case is that it avoids an invidious distinction being drawn between insolvency and receivership. In the event of a winding-up, the secured debenture holder ranks ahead of unsecured creditors whose representative, the liquidator, would in the absence of the floating chargee be entitled to demand the proceeds from the sheriff. It would be odd if the positions of floating chargee and sheriff should be reversed just because a winding-up has not supervened. Nevertheless, it is unlikely that any court would require a garnishor to pay part of the proceeds of a debt to the floating chargee whose charge crystallizes before the debt has been paid in full. For the sake of consistency, an execution creditor should also prevail where goods are sold and the proceeds are still in the sheriff's hands at the time of crystallization.

9.67 Two further points need to be made. First, as long as the floating charge remains uncrystallized, the floating chargee may not selectively intervene in the affairs of the company so as to impede the payment of a judgment debt.[323] Secondly, the courts with a paucity of reasoning have, in the case of payments made to avoid a sale by the sheriff, approximated the position in winding-up and

---

315 Schedule B1, para 43(6).
316 Supreme Court Act 1981, s 138(1).
317 *Ex p Williams* (1872) 7 Ch App 314, 316.
318 *Ex p Williams* (1872) 7 Ch App 314, 317–318.
319 *Re Standard Manufacturing Co* [1891] 1 Ch 627, 641, CA.
320 *Re Standard Manufacturing Co* [1891] 1 Ch 627, CA; *Re Opera Ltd* [1891] 3 Ch 260, CA; *Taunton v Sheriff of Warwickshire* [1895] 2 Ch 319, CA.
321 The point was left open by Lindley LJ in *Taunton v Sheriff of Warwickshire* [1895] 2 Ch 319, 322, CA, and in *Re Opera Ltd* [1891] 3 Ch 360, CA.
322 See *ex p Williams* (1872) 7 Ch App 314.
323 *Evans v Rival Granite Quarries Ltd* [1910] 2 KB 979, CA; *Robson v Smith* [1895] 2 Ch 118, CA.

receivership. Just as such payments may not be recovered by a liquidator or trustee from an execution creditor,[324] so when payment of the entire sum due [325] or part of it [326] is made directly to the sheriff, receiving it as agent for the execution creditor, it may not be recovered by or on behalf of a floating chargee appointing a receiver before the sheriff accounts to the execution creditor.

Where the execution creditor attaches a debt through garnishee proceedings, the debt must **9.68** actually be paid to the garnishor if the garnishor is to prevail against a chargee whose floating charge has crystallized. The garnishee order, even when it becomes absolute, merely attaches the debt owed; it does not assign or transfer it to the garnishor. The debt remains owing to the company granting the charge that has now crystallized, and the effect of the order absolute is merely to empower the garnishor to give a good discharge of the debt to the garnishee upon payment being received.[327]

(f) Dispositions of the insolvent's property

(i) General

Upon the commencement of a compulsory winding-up, section 127 of the Insolvency Act **9.69** provides that any disposition of the company's property is void unless the court otherwise orders.[328] The section treats in the same way transfers of shares and alterations in the status of the company and its members. The simple effect of the section is to avoid dispositions of the company's property. Its limitations are exposed where the company's property cannot be traced by common law or equitable means.[329] In the past, banks operating current accounts have been at some considerable risk of exposure to a claim for the recovery of moneys whose payment they could have prevented, since a disposition occurs in favour of the bank whenever the bank's indebtedness to the company account holder is diminished by the payment of cheques drawn on an account in credit.[330] More recently, the Court of Appeal has held that section 127 is not concerned with the bank's mandate to honour cheques and does not 'impinge on the legal validity of intermediate steps...which are merely part of the process by which dispositions of the company's property are made'. The section goes directly to the 'end result of the process of payment', namely, the payee's receipt of the proceeds of the collected cheque.[331]

The object of section 127 is to protect the estate of the insolvent[332] from improper **9.70** dissipation[333] pending the appointment of a liquidator to take control and the eventual distribution of the estate in the usual way. A compulsory winding-up normally commences with

---

[324] See discussion at 9.59 and 9.60.

[325] *Heaton and Dugard Ltd v Cutting Bros Ltd* [1925] 1 KB 655.

[326] *Robinson v Burnell's Vienna Bakery Co Ltd* [1904] 2 KB 624.

[327] *Norton v Yates* [1906] 1 KB 112; *Cairney v Back* [1906] 2 KB 746; *Relwood Pty Ltd v Manning Homes Pty Ltd (No 2)* [1992] 2 Queensland R 197.

[328] A similar provision introduced in the 1980s applies in bankruptcy between the date the bankruptcy petition is presented and the date that the bankrupt's property vests in the trustee: s 284. The discretion is exercised in broadly the same way as the discretion under s 127: *Re Flint* [1993] Ch 319. Under the previous law, the title of the trustee to the bankrupt's assets related back to the commission of an act of bankruptcy, so that the preservation of the estate for *pari passu* distribution was achieved by other means.

[329] *Re Leslie (J) Engineers Co Ltd* [1976] 1 WLR 292. The difficulty of tracing payments *out of* a company's bank account has had the effect of challenges also being made in respect of payments *into* its account by the bank collecting cheques on behalf of the company payee: see 9.78.

[330] *Re Gray's Inn Construction Co Ltd* [1980] 1 WLR 711, 716, CA.

[331] *Hollicourt (Contracts) Ltd v Bank of Ireland* [2001] Ch 555, 563, CA, reversing the court below at [2000] 1 WLR 895 and disapproving on this point *Re Gray's Inn Construction Co Ltd* [1980] 1 WLR 711, CA (where the relevant account was overdrawn).

[332] If the s 127 proceedings involve a company, it may not be insolvent. The expression 'insolvent' conveniently unites companies and individuals.

[333] *Re Wiltshire Iron Co* (1868) 3 Ch App 443, 446–447.

the petition to wind up and not with the making of a winding-up order or the appointment of a provisional liquidator.[334] The date of commencement for a voluntary winding-up is the passing of the resolution,[335] whereupon the rules regarding the distribution of the estate come into effect[336] and the company ceases to carry on trading except for the purpose of a beneficial winding-up.[337] The directors' powers cease as soon as the liquidator is appointed.[338] In a voluntary winding-up, there is no backdating measure corresponding to section 127 that bars dispositions of property between the notice of a meeting at which a winding-up resolution is proposed and the passing of the resolution. The safety valve for creditors apprehensive about the directors' behaviour is to petition for the compulsory winding-up of the company instead. A further reason for the presence of backdating only in a compulsory winding-up is that transactions entered into by the company cannot be challenged as preferences or undervalue transactions if entered into after the date of the winding-up petition;[339] but in the case of a voluntary winding-up, they may be challenged if entered into at any time before the date of the winding-up resolution itself.[340]

9.71 Section 127 is a very wide provision. It extends to any disposition[341] of the company's property,[342] which for present purposes includes property the subject of a charge.[343] The company's hands are therefore completely tied. As from the commencement of the winding-up it is not at liberty to trade without the sanction of the court. Particular difficulties are posed with regard to the operation of the company's bank accounts,[344] which the bank will freeze only when it learns of a winding-up petition. All that stands between paralysis and continued trading is that the court's discretion to allow the disposition is stated in the section in the broadest terms and is, moreover, broadly exercised.[345] Furthermore, the court's sanction need not be sought in advance but can be given retrospectively, though prudence dictates a preliminary application, at least in the case of substantial or unusual transactions. Indeed, it may be desirable that an application be made even before the winding-up order is made by the court, which despite the language of section 127 is permissible, given that the section exists to protect creditors during the pendency of the petition.[346]

9.72 It is not always the case that the company is insolvent when a petition is presented to wind it up. A compulsory winding-up may be the outcome of unresolvable deadlock in a closely held company. Furthermore, it is by no means inevitable that a petition will actually lead to the winding-up of the company. It may be possible to sell the company as a going concern. Consequently, it may be for the good of all parties interested in the assets of the company that it be permitted to trade on.[347]

---

[334] Section 129(2).

[335] Section 86.

[336] Section 107.

[337] Section 87(1).

[338] Sections 91(2) and 103. Transfers of shares after the winding-up resolution are also avoided: s 88.

[339] Sections 129(2), 238(2), 239(2) and 240(3)(b).

[340] Sections 86, 238(2), 239(2) and 240(3)(e).

[341] Its companion provision, s 284, has been applied to reverse a court order vesting the matrimonial home in the wife of the bankrupt, counsel for the trustee not basing his submissions on the fact that the order was a consent order: *Re Flint* [1993] Ch 319.

[342] It therefore does not operate to strike down assumptions of liability or the consumption or exhaustion of the company's assets: *Coutts & Co v Stock* [2000] 1 WLR 906.

[343] *Mond v Hammond Suddards (No 1)* [1996] 2 BCLC 470.

[344] Discussed at 9.78.

[345] *Re Wiltshire Iron Co* (1868) LR 3 Ch App 443; *Re Steane's (Bournemouth) Ltd* [1950] 1 All ER 21; *Re Levy (AI) Holdings Ltd* [1964] Ch 19.

[346] *Re Levy (AI) Holdings Ltd* [1964] Ch 19; *Re Burton & Deakin Ltd* [1977] 1 WLR 390.

[347] *Re Wiltshire Iron Co* (1868) LR 3 Ch App 443, 446.

(ii) The court's discretion

In exercising its discretion with regard to dispositions of the insolvent's property, the court **9.73** is principally guided by a concern for unprotected creditors who would be harmed by a preferential disposition.[348] Where, exceptionally, the disposition is challenged by a secured creditor, the outcome is that the recovered property is impressed with the security and is not distributed in favour of the unsecured creditors.[349] This may seem odd when a transaction entered into before the commencement of the winding-up cannot be challenged by the secured creditor as a preference or as an undervalue transaction, which grounds of challenge are available only to administrators and insolvency officers, with the fruits of recovery being held for all the creditors of the company.[350] Section 127 appears therefore to provide that secured creditor with something of a windfall. Assets of the company disposed of with that secured creditor's express or implied permission may as a result of a disposition being void fall back into a continuing security, whether of a fixed or floating kind.[351] The exercise by the court of its discretion to uphold the disposition would avoid such an anomaly. If the company has disposed of fixed charge assets without permission or of floating charge assets outside the ordinary course of business, the secured creditor may, subject to the rights of a *bona fide* purchaser of the legal estate, take proceedings to recover the assets. The court's discretion to uphold the disposition, it is submitted, ought not to be exercised in such a case.

The court's discretion under section 127 depends upon two principal variables: there is the **9.74** effect of the disposition upon the company's business and its creditors, and there is also the state of mind and judgment of the parties to the disposition. There is no requirement that the disposition actually succeed in having a beneficial effect on the company[352] but it is highly probable that the approval of the court will retrospectively be given where the company has benefited from the disposition.[353] The court will sanction a disposition that is *apt* to benefit the company, a test that avoids a needlessly expensive and 'massive investigation' into the company's affairs.[354] It is not enough, however, that the disposition be shown merely to have no injurious effect.[355] Consequently, as the cases demonstrate, the court's discretion is widely exercised to ensure, not just the rateable distribution of the insolvent's estate, but also its maximization. The sale at arm's length of the company's property at the prevailing market rate would have no injurious consequences for the creditors, especially given the impending liquidation of the company; a sale at an undervalue would damage the estate and harm creditors.

Transactions that have given rise to dispositions approved under section 127 include pay- **9.75** ments arising from trade that are paid into a bank account to maintain an overdraft facility,[356] the speedy sale of property that commands an exceptionally good price,[357] the grant of security to a director injecting fresh capital into a company to help it pay its wages bill[358] and the payment of outstanding trade debts to a supplier whose goods are vital to the continuing

---

[348] *Re Gray's Inn Construction Co Ltd* [1980] 1 WLR 711, CA; *Denney v Hudson (J) & Co Ltd* [1992] BCLC 901, CA; *Re Leslie (J) Engineers Co Ltd* [1976] 1 WLR 292.
[349] *Mond v Hammond Suddards (No 1)* [1996] 2 BCLC 470 (where a floating charge crystallized upon the appointment of receivers after the void disposition had taken place).
[350] *Re Yagerphone Ltd* [1935] Ch 392.
[351] See *Mond v Hammond Suddards (No 1)* [1996] 2 BCLC 470; cf *Campbell v Michael MountPPB* (1996) 14 ACLC 218.
[352] *Re Clifton Place Garage Ltd* [1970] Ch 477, CA.
[353] See *Re Park Ward and Co Ltd* [1926] Ch 828, 832.
[354] *Denney v Hudson (J) & Co Ltd* [1992] BCLC 901, 907–908, CA.
[355] *Re Webb Electrical Ltd* (1988) 4 BCC 230.
[356] *Re Construction (TW) Ltd* [1954] 1 WLR 540.
[357] *Re Gray's Inn Construction Co Ltd* [1980] 1 WLR 711, 717, CA.
[358] *Re Park Ward and Co Ltd* [1926] Ch 828.

trading prospects of the company.[359] The *object* of the section is the benefit of creditors that comes from preventing the dissipation of the estate for the purpose of *pari passu* distribution. But the *pari passu* principle may have to yield to the need to maximize the estate, which is why the discretion may exceptionally be exercised in favour of a creditor disponee whose debts are paid in full when other creditors receive no more than a dividend.[360] Creditors benefit more from a larger dividend and some measure of inequality than they do from equality and a smaller dividend.

9.76 The state of mind of the parties to the disposition, as well as the judgment of the company's directors, is relevant to the court's discretion. A disposition of property may be caught by the legislation even though neither the insolvent nor the disponee was aware that a bankruptcy or winding-up petition had been presented. This makes a broad judicial discretion all the more necessary to avoid confounding reasonable expectations.[361] A creditor's ignorance of the presentation of a winding-up petition has been described as 'a very powerful factor' in the court's consideration, but it is not conclusive.[362] In particular, it cannot improve the position of a pre-existing creditor who receives a preferential payment[363] especially when, as seen above, the provisions dealing with preferences do not apply after the commencement of the winding-up.[364] Knowledge by the disponee of the existence of a winding-up petition is no bar to the court's approval of a disposition when the transaction under which the disposition took place was beneficial,[365] or perceived to be beneficial,[366] to the company. The court's approval of a disposition has been stated to depend on the existence of good faith[367] but this of itself is not enough. There must also be a judgment, reasonably entertained, that the disposition will be beneficial to the company.[368]

9.77 Section 127 does not list the persons eligible to seek approval for the disposition but the usual applicant will be the company or the disponee. In one case, however, the successful applicant was a bank to which the disponee of land had granted a mortgage. Stressing the flexibility of the statutory discretion, the court upheld the transaction to a limited extent, namely, the extent of the bank's mortgage interest.[369] Section 127 also fails to list those who may challenge the disposition. As seen above, a secured creditor may invoke the provision. In one case of corporate deadlock, the court ruled that an individual shareholder had standing to bring the proceedings (though it gave no opinion as to whether a director could do the same).[370] No good reason existed in the case of dispositions to introduce an implied limitation on eligible applicants into section 127 that was not present for the other instances of its application. It was, however, one thing to say that a shareholder could bring proceedings but quite another to say that all proceedings were brought with equal weight, regardless of the applicant. In particular, while the burden of persuasion properly falls upon the applicant seeking to have a transaction upheld, where a shareholder challenges a transaction authorized

---

[359] *Denney v Hudson (J) & Co Ltd* [1992] BCLC 901.

[360] *Denney v Hudson (J) & Co Ltd* [1992] BCLC 901; *Re Gray's Inn Construction Co Ltd* [1980] 1 WLR 711, 718, CA.

[361] See *Re Steane's (Bournemouth) Ltd* [1950] 1 All ER 21.

[362] *Re Leslie (J) Engineers Co Ltd* [1976] 1 WLR 292, 304.

[363] *Re Leslie (J) Engineers Co Ltd* [1976] 1 WLR 292, 304.

[364] For present purposes, it is submitted that a court should take a broad view of what amounts to a preference and not the narrow view that has been taken under s 239: see discussion at 9.156–9.158.

[365] *Re Park Ward and Co Ltd* [1926] Ch 828.

[366] *Re Clifton Place Garage Ltd* [1970] Ch 477 (receiver misled by director of state of company's indebtedness).

[367] See *Denney v Hudson (J) & Co Ltd* [1992] BCLC 901; *Re Gray's Inn Construction Co Ltd* [1980] 1 WLR 711, 718, CA.

[368] *Re Clifton Place Garage Ltd* [1970] Ch 477. See also *Re Burton & Deakin Ltd* [1977] 1 WLR 390.

[369] *Royal Bank of Scotland Plc v Bhardwaj* [2002] BCC 57.

[370] *Re Argentum Reductions (UK) Ltd* [1975] 1 WLR 186.

by the company's managers it is the shareholder who will have to show compelling evidence that the transaction was likely to injure the company.[371]

(iii) Bank accounts

Finally, as stated above, the position of the company and its bankers has caused difficulties **9.78** under section 127 with particular reference to defining what is the company's property and whether a disposition of it is taking place. The first difficulty arises when payments are made into a company's account. When a bank collects cheques on its customer's behalf and pays the proceeds into an overdrawn account, a disposition of the company's property has been said to be made since the effect of this payment in is *pro tanto* to diminish the customer's liability on the overdraft.[372] This view is not without its difficulties in that the effect of the bank's action is to exchange the customer's beneficial interest in the proceeds of the cheque for a reduction of the customer's indebtedness to the bank. The bank may be dealing away its corporate customer's property but it is replacing that property with an item of equal value. The customer's estate is not thus reduced yet the prospects of recovery of the customer's other creditors may be sensibly diminished. The object of section 127, which is to avoid the dissipation of the company's assets, at this point diverges from the principle of *pari passu* distribution, just as it does in a few other instances mentioned above. The Court of Appeal in *Re Gray's Inn Construction Co Ltd*[373] stated that the proper exercise of its discretion under section 127 was to freeze the company's account at the date of the petition, with subsequent dealings, when necessary for the conduct of the company's business, being carried out in a new account. This would avoid the preferential discharge of the company's overdraft with the bank.[374]

Where the customer's account is at all material times in credit, the payment of the proceeds of **9.79** collected cheques into a bank account has been held not to be a disposition of the company's property.[375] Nevertheless, there has equally been a substitution of the company's property, namely the proceeds of the collection, for an increased indebtedness of the bank to the customer. In this instance, however, there has occurred no divergence of the *pari passu* principle and the preservation of the company's estate. Since a disposition is a proprietary transfer, it is present in both cases of accounts in credit and overdrawn accounts and is not negatived by the receipt of property in exchange.[376] The grounds for exercising the court's discretion under section 127 to uphold the disposition are stronger, however, where the account is in credit.

The second area of difficulty concerns payments out of the company's account. According **9.80** to dicta of the Court of Appeal in *Re Gray's Inn Construction Co Ltd*, all payments out of the company's account are dispositions of its property and not just any excess of payments out over payments in.[377] The same view that a disposition had occurred was rejected in a case where the account from which the payments were made was overdrawn.[378] The court held there had been no disposition but rather, as a result of the loan made by the bank when the overdraft was increased upon the payment out of the account, an increase in the company's

---

[371] *Re Burton & Deakin Ltd* [1977] 1 WLR 390.

[372] *Re Gray's Inn Construction Co Ltd* [1980] 1 WLR 711, 715–716, CA. See also *Rose v AIB Group (UK) Plc* [2003] EWHC 1737 (Ch), [2003] 1 WLR 1791.

[373] [1980] 1 WLR 711, CA.

[374] [1980] 1 WLR 711, 719, CA.

[375] *Re Barn Crown Ltd* [1995] 1 WLR 147.

[376] Notwithstanding the reasoning in *Re Barn Crown Ltd* [1995] 1 WLR 147, 152–156, the customer is lending money to the bank when it causes its account to be credited with the proceeds of a cheque collected on its behalf by the bank, its agent.

[377] [1980] 1 WLR 711, 719–720, CA.

[378] *Coutts & Co v Stock* [2000] 1 WLR 906 (noting that the point had been conceded in *Re Gray's Inn Construction Co Ltd* [1980] 1 WLR 711, CA, that all payments out were dispositions of the company's property).

liabilities. The dicta in *Re Gray's Inn Construction Co Ltd* were disapproved of in the case of an account in credit in *Hollicourt (Contracts) Ltd v Bank of Ireland*,[379] where as stated above the Court of Appeal focused on the end result of the payment, dismissing the relevance for the purpose of section 127 of intermediate steps taken by the bank pursuant to its mandate to honour cheques drawn on the account.

(2) Secured Creditors in the Insolvency Process

(a) Recognizing security

9.81 The assets available for distribution to unsecured creditors do not include assets that are subject to a charge or other security granted by the insolvent[380] or that are still owned by a creditor seller supplying them under the terms of a valid reservation of title clause. Title reservation is more effective even than security, for the seller need not procure the registration of his reserved interest under the Companies Act 2006.[381] Moreover, title reservation defeats at source an earlier security, granted by the buyer and extending to future assets, whose description covers the goods supplied by the seller, since that security only attaches to assets of the buyer.

9.82 The strength of the secured creditor's hand is further revealed by the rule that a security over future assets will attach to assets embraced by the security even if they fall into the estate of an insolvent during the bankruptcy or winding-up process. In that event, the assets fall in already encumbered and, to the extent of the encumbrance, are not subject to the trust in favour of unsecured creditors.[382] This is because an assignment by way of security over future assets is by a fiction treated as conferring 'an actual interest in the assignee as if the assignor had been possessed of the property at the date of the assignment'.[383] For the same reason, the payment of the proceeds of assets subject to a floating charge into an account with the creditor bank is not a disposition of the company's property for the purposes of section 127.[384]

9.83 Although assets caught by a security are not generally available for distribution, this does not mean that the secured creditor has first call on all such assets. In the case of assets the subject of a charge that, as created, was a floating charge, preference creditors, followed by unsecured creditors up to a stated money limit,[385] have priority in a winding-up ahead of the secured creditor.[386] Where an administrative receiver is appointed to enforce such a floating charge, the preference creditors' priority is expressed as a rule that, where other assets of the company are insufficient to pay the preference creditors,[387] a receiver is bound first to pay them before the secured creditor.[388] The same rule now applies to administrators too since they were empowered to make distributions.[389] A similar rule prevents a secured creditor who enters into possession from paying himself off before the preference creditors.[390]

---

[379] [2001] Ch 555, CA.

[380] Except to the extent that the security can be overturned as a transaction concluded in the twilight period: see 9.149.

[381] Section 859A.

[382] On which, see 9.28 and 9.94 et seq.

[383] *Re Lind* [1915] 2 Ch 345, 355, CA, following *Tailby v Official Receiver* (1888) 13 App Cas 523, HL; *Re Margart Pty Ltd* [1985] BCLC 314, New South Wales; *Foamcrete (UK) Ltd v Thrust Engineering Ltd* [2002] BCC 221, at [30], CA. cf *Collyer v Isaacs* (1881) 19 Ch D 342, CA.

[384] *Re Margart Pty Ltd* [1985] BCLC 314 (NSW equivalent provision). Future assets clauses will not extend, however, to certain recoveries made by liquidators pursuant to proceedings taken under, for example, s 214 (wrongful trading): see 9.167.

[385] See 9.111. Expenses of the liquidation may also be paid out of floating charge assets: 9.103.

[386] Section 175(2)(b).

[387] Section 40(3).

[388] Section 40(2). This provision, together with s 175(2)(b) will be discussed in more detail at 9.108.

In those cases where registration of a security interest by way of charge or mortgage is required **9.84** under the Companies Act 2006, but registration is not effected within 21 days of the creation of the charge, the charge will remain effective as between company and debenture holder[391] but will be void against liquidators and administrators.[392] In consequence, a secured creditor who has realized the security and no longer has it in his possession need not fear the later appointment of an administrator who cannot retrospectively claim the right to immediate possession needed to maintain an action in conversion against the creditor.[393] There is a judicial discretion to allow late registration outside the 21-day period,[394] but the commencement,[395] even the imminence,[396] of a winding-up may be a ground for refusing to exercise it. In the case of individuals and partnerships, a narrower range of security bills of sale have to be registered under the Bills of Sale Acts 1878–91 to avoid the same consequences against a trustee-in-bankruptcy.[397]

The fact that a creditor is secured does not prevent that creditor from putting in a proof where **9.85** the security is insufficient to meet the claim. The Insolvency Rules provide that a creditor may prove for the balance after account has been taken of the security. The balance may be quantified by the secured creditor realizing the security.[398] It may also be quantified by means of valuing the security[399] (though surprisingly there is no provision in the Rules expressly allowing for a proof for the balance after valuation). The secured creditor himself may put a value on his security, which value may later be altered only with the leave of the liquidator or of the court.[400] If the liquidator is dissatisfied with the value placed on the security, he may require the security or any part of it to be offered for sale.[401] A secured creditor may be prompted to have the security revalued where, before it is realized, the liquidator gives notice of his intention to redeem the security at the value placed upon it by the secured creditor.[402] Finally, there will be rare cases where a secured creditor may wish to forgo the security and put in a proof instead.[403] The reference in this case to proving for the 'whole' of the debt means that the creditor might not sever both the security and the debt and thus participate as both secured and unsecured creditor.

---

[389] Insolvency Act, Sch B1, para 65(2).

[390] Companies Act 2006, s 754(2).

[391] See *Independent Automatic Sales Ltd v Knowles & Foster* [1962] 1 WLR 974.

[392] Companies Act 2006, s 859H. It is also liable to be postponed in favour of a subsequent charge even where the chargee has actual notice of the earlier unregistered charge: *Re Monolithic Co* [1915] 1 Ch 643, CA.

[393] *Smith v Bridgend County Borough Council* [2000] 1 BCLC 775, CA.

[394] Under Companies Act 2006, s 859M.

[395] *Re Mechanisations (Eaglescliffe) Ltd* [1966] Ch 20.

[396] *Re Ashpurton Estates* [1983] Ch 110, CA; *Re Braemar Investments Ltd* [1989] Ch 54.

[397] The requirement of registration is extended by s 344 of the Insolvency Act from chattels in possession to book debts, more specifically to general assignments of book debts that are not assignments by way of charge.

[398] Rules 2.83(1), 4.88(1) and 6.109(1). The secured creditor may call upon the liquidator or trustee to elect whether to exercise a power to redeem the security: rr 2.92(4), 4.97(4) and 6.117(4).

[399] The value placed on the security will be overridden by the amount of a subsequent realization: rr 2.94, 4.99 and 6.119.

[400] Rules 4.95(1). Or the administrator or trustee-in-bankruptcy: rr 2.90(1) and 6.115(1). The leave of the court is necessary for revaluation if the secured creditor was the petitioner or has voted in respect of the unsecured balance of the debt: rr 2.90(2), 4.95(2) and 6.115(2). On the effects of revaluing security, see r 11.9.

[401] Rules 4.98. For administration and bankruptcy, see rr 2.93 and 6.118.

[402] Rules 4.97. For administration and bankruptcy, see rr 2.92 and 6.117.

[403] Rules 2.83(2), 4.88(2) and 6.109(2). A creditor with only a floating charge and little prospect of any realization from the charge may take this step in order to participate in the s 176A fund; see 9.111.

(b) Dealing with secured assets

(i) General

9.86 The onset of a winding-up or bankruptcy does not prevent the secured creditor from taking practical steps to enforce the security since there is no moratorium equivalent to the moratorium that takes place when the company goes into administration. The enforcement of security rights does not amount to actions or proceedings against the company requiring the leave of the court.[404] Nor does the termination of an administrative receiver's agency to act in the name of the company borrower, occurring when the company goes into liquidation,[405] prevent the receiver from enforcing the security in favour of the secured creditor who procured his appointment by the company.[406] In such a case, the liquidator of the company is in practical terms powerless to move in and distribute the estate if only because the contents of the estate cannot be defined until the receiver has carried out the responsibilities of the receivership. A novel attempt was made by an unsecured creditor in one case to have the receiver ousted by the appointment of a provisional liquidator, on the ground that the receiver's imposition of harsh trading terms upon that creditor, who was a trading partner heavily dependent upon supplies from the company in receivership, amounted to blackmail. The court dismissed the application, holding that the receivers were entitled to exploit the company's only real asset, namely, its bargaining position against the creditor.[407] If, however, it should be necessary for a secured creditor to take legal proceedings to enforce his security, as might eg happen if a liquidator disputes the creditor's right to take possession, the creditor will need the leave of the court to take proceedings,[408] which should without undue difficulty be granted.[409]

(ii) Administration

9.87 Although the secured creditor is free to realize his security notwithstanding winding-up or bankruptcy, there is a moratorium on such action if the company enters into administration.[410] Once a company enters into administration,[411] '[n]o step may be taken to enforce any security over the company's property' without the consent of the administrator or the leave of the court.[412] Security has the conventional meaning of 'any mortgage, charge, lien or other security'.[413] It includes a solicitor's lien,[414] a carrier's lien[415] and a statutory right of detention akin to a lien conferred over aircraft in respect of unpaid airport charges.[416] Equally,

---

[404] Section 130(2). For the meaning of 'proceedings', see discussion in 9.62–9.63.

[405] Section 44(1)(a).

[406] *Sowman v Samuel (David) Trust* [1978] 1 WLR 22. The equivalent issue does not arise in administration because of the moratorium on insolvency proceedings: Insolvency Act, Sch B1, paras 40, 42.

[407] *Ford AG-Werke AG v TransTec Automotive (Campsie) Ltd* [2001] BCC 403.

[408] Sections 130(2) and 285(1).

[409] *Re Lloyd (David) & Co* (1877) 6 Ch D 339, CA.

[410] *Bloom v Harms AHT 'Taurus' GmbH & Co KG* [2009] EWCA Civ 632, [2010] Ch 687.

[411] For the moratorium that arises where the directors of a small company seek a voluntary arrangement, see Insolvency Act, Sch A1.

[412] Insolvency Act, Sch B1, para 43(2). This provision is disapplied for financial collateral arrangements: Financial Collateral Arrangements (No 2) Regulations 2003, SI 2003/3226, reg 8(1)(a). In the case of a court-appointed administrator, an earlier, interim moratorium applies from the time notice of the application is filed with the court: Sch B1, para 44(2).

[413] Section 248. The decision in *Re Park Air Services plc* [2000] 2 AC 172, HL, that security did not include a landlord's power of re-entry under a lease, was overtaken by the separate listing of re-entry as a step requiring the administrator's permission or the leave of the court: Insolvency Act, Sch B1, para 43(4).

[414] *Re Carter Commercial Developments Ltd* [2002] BCC 803.

[415] *Re Sabre International Products Ltd* [1991] BCLC 470. Enforcement will be allowed where the administrator's proposals are inadequate to protect the carrier's rights: *Re La Senza Ltd* [2012] EWHC 1190 (Ch).

[416] *Bristol Airport plc v Powdrill* [1990] Ch 744, CA.

'[n]o step may be taken . . . to repossess goods in the company's possession under a hire-purchase agreement'.[417] Hire purchase is defined expansively so as to include title-retention sales agreements, conditional sales and chattel leasing agreements.[418] If a receiver of part of the company's property is appointed before an administrator, then that receiver is required to vacate office.[419] Formerly, the appointment of an administrator could be blocked by a floating chargee able to secure the appointment of an administrative receiver, but the replacement in the great bulk of cases of the administrative receiver by an administrator appointed out of court has dispensed with the need for such a provision.[420] In consequence, the moratorium on the enforcement of security and related rights will now serve mainly secured creditors with a qualifying floating charge at the expense of other creditors. This moratorium on creditors' rights does not expunge them. Consequently, if an administrator abusively withholds his consent to the enforcement of a security right, a creditor with a continuing right to immediate possession of goods has standing to sue in the tort of conversion.[421]

Apart from security and related rights, the moratorium can affect third parties in other ways. **9.88** A landlord needs the consent of the administrator or the permission of the court to forfeit a lease by peaceable re-entry, which consent or permission is also required in the case of legal process, including execution, against the company.[422] Permission will be refused if there is no good reason for separating the applicant from other creditors.[423] Similarly, when the company is in administration, no administrative receiver may be appointed[424] and no resolution may be passed or order made for the winding-up of the company.[425]

In *Re Atlantic Computer Systems plc*,[426] the court's discretion to grant leave to enforce a security **9.89** received an authoritative exposition. The case concerned the lease and sub-lease of computer equipment, the lessee being in administration. The lessor unsuccessfully argued that the administrator was bound to pay rentals due under the head lease as expenses of the administration, in the same way that a liquidator would have to pay expenses of the winding-up. The amounts in question were significantly larger than the amount of sub-rentals paid under the various sub-leases since the latter had been entered into on disadvantageous terms and because, in some cases, sub-rentals had been withheld by the sub-lessees. Instead, the lessor was awarded the hollow victory of repossessing computer equipment adapted to the needs of the sub-lessees. The administrator was not entitled to retain the equipment in the cause of shoring up the lessee's client base, the lessee's only substantial asset. A balancing exercise[427] had to be conducted and the prejudice that the lessor would suffer as a result of the administrator retaining the equipment meant that the court exercised its discretion in favour of the lessor.

---

[417] Insolvency Act, Sch B1, para 43(3).

[418] Schedule B1, para 111(1). A delay in seeking consent or permission may injure the prospects of a successful administration, so that the court will refuse permission: *Re Fashoff (UK) Ltd v Linton* [2008] EWHC 537 (Ch), [2008] BCC 542 (retention of title).

[419] Schedule B1, para 41(2).

[420] Former s 9(3)(a) of the Insolvency Act.

[421] *Barclays Mercantile Business Finance Ltd v Sibec Developments Ltd* [1992] 1 WLR 1253 (*semble*, both administrator and company might be liable).

[422] Schedule B1, para 43(4), (6). For the denial of the court's permission to a landlord where premises were needed for the business of the company, see *Innovate Logistics Ltd v Sunberry Properties Ltd* [2008] EWCA Civ 1312, [2009] BCC 164. Leave will normally be given if the purposes of the administration will not be impeded: *Metro Nominees (Wandsworth) (No 1) Ltd v Rayment* [2008] BCC 40.

[423] As in the case of employees with monetary claims arising from non-performance of employment contracts, see *Re Nortel Networks Ltd* [2010] EWHC 826 (Ch), [2010] BCC 706.

[424] Schedule B1, para 43(6A).

[425] Schedule B1, para 42 (2), (3) (with exceptions).

[426] [1992] Ch 505, CA.

[427] See also *Re ARV Aviation Ltd* [1989] BCLC 664; *Innovate Logistics Ltd v Sunberry Properties Ltd* [2008] EWCA Civ 1312, [2009] BCC 164.

9.90 Besides the embargo on enforcing security without leave during an administration, secured creditors' rights are affected in other ways during the conduct of an administration. The administrator may deal with and dispose of property subject to a floating charge[428] without leave of the court,[429] but the chargee's priority is transferred to the proceeds.[430] Since, however, the administrator himself ranks ahead of the floating chargee (but not a fixed chargee) in respect of his remuneration and expenses, recoverable from property in his control or custody immediately before the cessation of his appointment,[431] and since sums payable in respect of debts or liabilities incurred by the administrator under contracts made, or contracts of employment adopted,[432] during the conduct of the administration rank ahead of the administrator's personal claim,[433] the priority standing of a secured creditor with a floating charge is considerably diminished during administration.[434]

9.91 The administrator may also deal with and dispose of property subject to a fixed charge or hire purchase agreement with the leave of the court.[435] If the proceeds of disposal are less than the value of the property in the open market when sold by a willing vendor, then the administrator, in addition to paying over the actual proceeds, must also make good any deficiency out of company assets.[436]

(iii) Administrative receivership

9.92 Administrative receivership does not have the same capacity for interfering with the rights of secured creditors. Nevertheless, the administrative receiver may apply to the court under section 43 for permission to dispose of charged property where this 'would be likely to promote a more advantageous realization of the company's assets than would otherwise be effected'. This power would be appropriately exercised where the administrative receiver wants to dispose of a block of integrated assets or to hive down some or all of the assets of the company to another company. It is not needed if the secured creditor for whom he acts ranks ahead of any other secured creditor with an interest in the same assets. Typically, it will be needed where the floating charge, created by the debenture under which the administrative receiver was appointed, is subordinate in respect of one or more assets to a fixed charge or mortgage granted in favour of another creditor. This latter creditor has the first call on the proceeds of realization of the assets in question: section 43 does not alter priorities.

---

[428] Defined as such at the date of creation and ignoring subsequent crystallization: s 251. The floating chargee at risk here is not a floating chargee able itself to procure the appointment of an administrator in the first place.

[429] Insolvency Act, Sch B1, para 70(1).

[430] Insolvency Act, Sch B1, para 70(2).

[431] Insolvency Act, Sch B1, para 99(3). For the list of such expenses, broadly in line since 2003 with liquidation expenses, see r 2.67.

[432] Confined to 'wages or salary' (para 99(5)(c)) and therefore not including redundancy or unfair dismissal payments: *Re Allders Department Stores Ltd* [2005] EWHC 172 (Ch), [2005] BCC 289. For a discussion of the difficult issues concerning 'wages or salary' and arising under para 99(5), (6), see *Re Huddersfield Fine Worsteds Ltd* [2005] EWCA Civ 1072, [2005] BCC 915.

[433] Insolvency Act, Sch B1, para 99(4), (5).

[434] The above provisions of Sch B1 apply at the end of the period of administration: *Re A Company No 005174 of 1999* [2000] 1 WLR 502, though in practice the administrator will make payments in the ordinary course during the conduct of the administration. The implications of administration for the limitations rule are displayed in *Re Maxwell Fleet and Facilities Management Ltd (No 1)* [2001] 1 WLR 323.

[435] Insolvency Act, Sch B1, para 71, *O'Connell v Rollings* [2014] EWCA Civ 639. Disapplied under Financial Collateral Arrangements (No 2) Regulations 2003, SI 2003/3226, reg 8(1)(b). An administrator making an unreasonable and irrational application without consulting the chargee may have to pay the chargee's costs on an indemnity basis: *Re Capitol Films Ltd* [2010] EWHC 3223 (Ch), [2011] BPIR 334.

[436] Schedule B1, para 71(3).

Unlike the case of administration, administrative receivership does not involve the freezing of **9.93** secured creditors' and title retainers' rights of enforcement. Nevertheless, in one decision,[437] the court ingeniously manufactured such a power in the interest of permitting the receivership to work. The title retainer sought an interlocutory injunction to prevent further dealings by the administrative receiver with the disputed goods, despite the latter's personal undertaking that the title retainer's rights would be respected by a later payment, but was denied it on the balance of convenience. The risk of non-payment of the title holder was too slight to justify an interlocutory injunction.

(3) Distributing the Insolvent's Assets

(a) The *pari passu* principle

(i) General

It is a fundamental principle of insolvency law that the assets of the insolvent are to be dis- **9.94** tributed *pari passu*, ie rateably, amongst the creditors of the insolvent.[438] Not stated in general legislative terms is another fundamental principle, the so-called anti-deprivation principle, that assets should not be removed from the estate of the insolvent in the event of insolvency. Particular applications of this principle, dealt with in the legislation, are the rules dealing with fraudulent transfers and undervalue transactions,[439] which exist to hold the estate together pending its distribution on a *pari passu* basis. Although the two principles are different, they may sometimes coincide in their application, as in the treatment of preferences, where the estate is both diminished prior to insolvency proceedings and a particular creditor is singled out for special treatment. Neither the *pari passu* nor the anti-deprivation principle guarantees an appreciable estate for distribution. Creditors able to take security do so and, apart from the rules on preferences and late floating charges,[440] there is nothing to stop them from encumbering the assets of the future insolvent so that in the event of bankruptcy or winding-up there is nothing or very little left for distribution. Insolvency is the very event when the security is most needed. Since the grant of security has already abstracted assets from the estate prior to the insolvency process, it does not fall foul of the anti-deprivation principle. Further, the *pari passu* principle applies only to the contents of the estate at the relevant time in insolvency proceedings, so assets the subject of security are not in the distribution pool in the first place.[441]

The anti-deprivation principle renders unlawful the forfeiture of property rights upon **9.95** insolvency[442] and has been explained as denying any right to bargain for an additional advantage upon insolvency.[443] A clause in a partnership deed transferring one partner's share in a mining lease to the other partner upon his bankruptcy is therefore void.[444] Where the owner of patent rights was indebted to the licensee, the diversion upon the owner's bankruptcy of royalty payments, so as to pay down the debt owed to the licensee, was also void.[445] An unlawful forfeiture also occurred in a case where, under a settlement agreement between an insurer and

---

[437] *Lipe Ltd v Leyland Daf Ltd* [1993] BCC 385.

[438] Sections 107 and 328(3); rr 2.69 and 4.181. See G McCormack, *Proprietary Claims in Insolvency* (1997) ch 2; F Oditah, 'Assets and the Treatment of Claims in Insolvency' (1992) 108 LQR 459.

[439] Discussed at 9.147–9.155.

[440] Discussed at 9.162–9.164.

[441] For part of the distribution process, however, the assets covered by a floating charge are removed from the chargee: see 9.104.

[442] To be distinguished from clauses in a proprietary transfer that *determine* interests upon an insolvency: discussed at 9.31. The property rights must have value for this rule to be applied: *Money Markets International Stockbrokers Ltd v London Stock Exchange Ltd* [2002] 1 WLR 1150.

[443] *Higinbotham v Holme* (1812) 19 Ves 88, 92, 34 ER 451, *per* Lord Eldon.

[444] *Whitmore v Mason* (1861) 2 J & H 204, 70 ER 1031.

[445] *Re Jeavons* (1873) 8 Ch App 643.

an insured that concerned a disputed claim under a liability policy, moneys paid to the insured reverted to the insurer if the moneys were not paid to third party claimants prior to the insured's entry into winding-up proceedings.[446] It has been held that a clause is valid if bankruptcy is only one of a number of events empowering a forfeiture in the event of default.[447] This case has long been considered controversial. In *Money Markets International Stockbrokers Ltd v London Stock Exchange Ltd*,[448] the court disapproved of this reasoning in *Re Garrud* on the ground that this was inconsistent with the decision of the House of Lords in *British Eagle International Airlines Ltd v Cie Nationale Air France*.[449] Prior to recent developments, it was hard to define the scope of the anti-deprivation principle in certain cases and fine distinctions were sometimes drawn.[450] In *Belmont Park Investments Pty Ltd v BNY Corporate Trustee Services Ltd*,[451] the Supreme Court, while it did not reconcile past authority, laid down a broad approach to the application of the anti-deprivation principle in commercial transactions. The case concerned a complex securitization programme attached to a credit default swap, and the disputed event was the reversal of priorities between two creditors on the occurrence of an event of default respecting one of them. The transaction was upheld. So long as a transaction was a bona fide, commercially sensible transaction, where there was no fraudulent intent, it would not be struck down on the ground of unlawful forfeiture. The majority of the court was not, however, prepared to go the extra distance of accepting a general exception to the principle based upon the idea of flawed assets, namely, that a contractual right might from inception be defined as to be determined upon insolvency. Yet the *Belmont* case signals an important retrenchment of the anti-deprivation principle. An *ex post facto* test of the sort that was approved, however, does not provide the *ex ante* certainty that contracting parties need in complex and volatile financial markets. In the result, apart from the uncertainty point, there is little difference between the court's conclusion and a limitation of the principle to cases where it is explicitly recognized in the Insolvency Act, eg, fraudulent transfers.[452]

(ii) The building industry

9.96 The building industry provides a useful illustration of the anti-deprivation principle at work. In that industry, the tiered structure of separate contracts isolates the employer from the sub-contractor, the intervening main contractor being bound to each of them separately. The employer has a strong interest in the continuation of the building project notwithstanding the insolvency of the contractor, and is at risk if an unpaid sub-contractor declines to continue. One method of protection is for the employer to hold a portion of moneys received in trust for the sub-contractor. Another is for the employer to reserve the right to pay the sub-contractor directly in the event of the contractor's insolvency.

---

[446] *Folgate London Market Ltd v Chaucer Insurance Plc* [2011] EWCA Civ 328. See also *Re Brewer's Settlement* [1896] 2 Ch 503 (bankrupt settled property on himself with a remainder on his bankruptcy); *Re Harrison* (1880) 14 Ch D 19, CA (forfeiture of bankrupt's building materials to landlord); *Fraser v Oystertec plc* [2004] EWHC 2225 (Ch), [2004] BCC 233 (forfeiture of patent rights).

[447] *Re Garrud* (1881) 16 Ch D 522, CA. See also *Re Waugh* (1876) 4 Ch D 524. cf *Re Walker* (1884) 26 Ch D 510, CA.

[448] [2002] 1 WLR 1150.

[449] [1975] 2 All ER 390, HL. Discussed at 9.98.

[450] eg, in *Smith v Bridgend County Borough Council* [2001] UKHL 58, [2002] 1 AC 336, Lord Scott distinguished between a seizure of an insolvent contractor's machinery on account of the local authority's claim (not an unlawful forfeiture) from a seizure in satisfaction of the claim. A clause that imposes certain restrictions on, or even prohibits, assignment will not however prevent property from vesting in a trustee-in-bankruptcy, since a vesting in this way will not be treated as a prohibited assignment: *Re Landau* [1998] Ch 223; *Patel v Jones* [2001] EWCA Civ 779, [2001] BPIR 919 (regulations governing a pension scheme could have prevented a vesting in the trustee but were never made).

[451] [2011] UKSC 38, [2012] 1 AC 383.

[452] Sections 423–425.

Direct payment clauses have in the past been upheld in England where they have not referred **9.97**
specifically to insolvency.[453] New Zealand authority, taking its cue from the decision of the
House of Lords in *British Eagle International Airlines Ltd v Cie Nationale Air France*,[454] took
a different view.[455] The New Zealand court's reasoning was that, upon insolvency, the main
contractor had a vested chose in action representing its right to be paid for work already done.
Thus the court did not accept the conditional, flawed quality of the company's right to be paid
arising out of the shaping of the employer's payment duty at the date of the contract.[456] One
difficulty with the flawed asset analysis, however, is that it leaves suspended the ownership of
any debt owed until the contractor exercises its election, and in any case great care would have
to be taken that there is a genuine election and not merely a duty to pay the contractor which
is defeasible. Apart from this, the direct payment clause seems to be a good example of a bona
fide commercial transaction that would now be upheld after the *Belmont* decision.[457] The site
owner asserted its own interests in the bargaining process and had indeed a legitimate interest
in the continuation of the building project that the payment of the sub-contractor would do
much to safeguard. The issue here does not concern the *pari passu* principle, because it is not
a case of one creditor of the main contractor being preferred to others. The employer is taking
steps to avert a liability on the part of the main contractor.

(iii) Settlement systems

British Eagle International Airlines Ltd v Cie Nationale Air France[458] concerned settlement arrange- **9.98**
ments amongst the various airline members of IATA, which had performed various services for
each other. At the end of each settlement period, net debtor airlines paid over their net indebtedness to the settlement authority which in turn paid over these sums to net creditor airlines. In the
present case, the airline in liquidation, British Eagle, was overall a net debtor but, in its bilateral
dealings with Air France, was a net creditor. Could it avoid the settlement system and claim
directly from Air France? The House of Lords held by a bare majority that the system of netting
adopted in the present case, by diverting funds from Air France to British Eagle's airline creditors,
preferred those creditors to British Eagle's other creditors.[459] The settlement process amounted to
a mini-liquidation process carried out before the main liquidation of British Eagle. The airlines
participating in the process were behaving as though they had charges over British Eagle's book
debts, which was not the case. Though presented as an application of the *pari passu* principle, the
case may more accurately be seen as an application of the anti-deprivation principle.

Though concerned with airlines, the *British Eagle* case demonstrated the vulnerability of set- **9.99**
tlement systems in the money markets. In particular, the insolvency of one member could
not be isolated in the way that the settlement system promised, which gave rise to the threat

---

[453] *Re Wilkinson* [1905] 2 KB 713; *Re Tout and Finch Ltd* [1954] 1 WLR 178.

[454] [1975] 1 WLR 758, HL.

[455] *A-G v McMillan & Lockwood Ltd* [1991] 1 NZLR 53. See also *Mullan (B) & Sons (Contractors) Ltd v Ross* (NI High Ct, 7 December 1995).

[456] The liquidator takes the company's property subject to the same restrictions that lay upon it in the company's hands: *Glow Heating Ltd v Eastern Health Board* (1988) 6 ILT 237 (Ireland).

[457] [2011] UKSC 38, [2012] 1 AC 383. Concerns in the building industry about the effectiveness of direct payment clauses after the *British Eagle* case, however, resulted in the clause being dropped from the JCT 1980 form.

[458] [1975] 1 WLR 758, HL.

[459] See also *North Atlantic Insurance Co Ltd v Nationwide General Insurance Co Ltd* [2004] EWCA Civ 423, [2004] 1 CLC 1131 (an arrangement among members of an underwriting pool about the proceeds of reinsurance could not affect the liquidator of a member from collecting that member's assets to distribute them to its creditors). When the IATA scheme was slightly revised after *British Eagle*, this resulted in the valid-ity of the clearing scheme being upheld in *International Air Transport Association v Ansett Australia Holdings Ltd* (2008) 234 CLR 151, Australian HC.

of cascading insolvencies produced as one member brought down the next and so on. The threat was considered real enough for a system of mini-liquidation to be introduced by statute for designated money markets.[460]

(b) Expenses of the insolvency process

9.100   Various expenses are incurred in the conduct of a winding-up, bankruptcy or administration that have to be paid before the balance of the insolvent's assets is distributed. The Insolvency Act and Insolvency Rules make provision for the priority treatment of expenses incurred by liquidators,[461] administrators,[462] and trustees-in-bankruptcy.[463] In putting the expenses claim ahead of preference creditors, these rules introduce complexities in the ranking of expenses, preference creditors, fixed chargees and floating chargees. They also require a careful distinction to be drawn between pre-insolvency process expense claims, provable in a winding-up, administration or bankruptcy, and expenses of the insolvency process, which occupy a preferential position.[464] The distinction drawn here has proved particularly troublesome in the case of administration, especially in the case of contingent claims where the courts have striven to prevent certain claims from falling in a black hole between provable claims and expenses of the administration so as to be wholly irrecoverable.[465] A too-ready willingness to classify claims as expenses of the administration would imperil the objectives of the administration process as a whole and introduce a degree of unfairness in the ranking of unsecured claims.

9.101   Further difficulties arise because of the draftsman's varied terminology when referring to expenses.[466] Taking liquidation as an example, recoverable expenses are specifically listed so as to include numerous items, such as the expenses of getting in the insolvent's assets; necessary disbursements[467] made by the liquidator; the liquidator's fees and remuneration; and the remuneration of those employed by a liquidator to perform services for the company. Formerly, the costs of a liquidator's unsuccessful action taken to recover assets transferred

---

[460] Part VII of the Companies Act 1989. Though it is not entirely clear, the exemption from insolvency legislation accorded to close-out netting schemes concerning financial collateral would seem not to apply in the case of multilateral schemes (the IATA scheme did not concern financial collateral): Financial Collateral Arrangements (No 2) Regulations 2003, SI 2003/3226, reg 12.

[461] Section 175(2)(a); see also ss 107, 115 and 156, Sch 8 para 17 and rr 4.218–4.220 and 12.2.

[462] Schedule B1, para 65(2) and rr 2.67 and 12.2. See *Exeter City Council v Bairstow* [2007] EWHC 400 (Ch), [2007] BCC 236 (business rates); *Laverty v British Gas Trading Ltd* [2014] EWHC 2721 (Ch) (gas and electricity supplies provable debt, not expenses, when the company has vacated the premises). Rent payable for the occupation of premises during an administration will count from day to day as an expense of the administration even if the rent for a stipulated period, say a month, is payable in advance before the company enters into administration: *Pillar Denton Ltd v Jervis* [2014] EWCA Civ 180, [2015] Ch 87. For the recovery of pre-administration expenses, for which an administrator may ultimately have recourse to the court if dissatisfied with the amount permitted by creditors, see r 2.67A.

[463] Section 328(2) and Sch 9 para 22 and rr 6.202, 6.224 and 12.2.

[464] *Re Toshoku Finance plc* [2002] UKHL 6, [2002] 1 WLR 671. See *Mackay v Kaupthing Singer & Friedlander Ltd* [2013] EWHC 2553 (Ch), [2013] BCC 752, where the balance of the sale price due under sale and leaseback transactions by a company in administration was not an expense of the administration but a pre-administration claim provable in the ordinary way.

[465] See *Re Nortel GmbH* [2013] UKSC 52, [2014] AC 209, where the liability of a company to render financial support for an under-funded pension scheme was not an expense of the administration but a provable debt in the administration, ranking pari passu with other debts in the usual way.

[466] Section 115 ('expenses properly incurred'); s 156 ('expenses incurred'); s 175(2) ('expenses of the winding-up'); r 4.218 ('expenses of the liquidation' with various sub-formulations, eg, 'expenses properly chargeable', 'necessary disbursements'). See *Mond v Hammond Suddards (No 2)* [2000] Ch 40, CA (the language in ss 115 and 156 being narrower than the language in s 175(2) and r 4.218).

[467] eg, tax liabilities: *Re Mesco Properties Ltd* [1980] 1 WLR 96, CA; *Re Toshoku Finance plc* [2002] UKHL 6, [2002] 1 WLR 671.

by means of a preference did not rank as expenses of the liquidation,[468] essentially because an unsuccessful liquidator could assert priority for his costs against the very chargee who had successfully defended the action. The position now is that a liquidator bringing various proceedings, including undervalue, preference, fraudulent trading, and wrongful trading proceedings, must first obtain the approval of preferential creditors and floating chargees, otherwise he is not allowed to assert the priority of those expenses over those two classes of creditor.[469] The statutory list of liquidation expenses is a definitive one. Language in the Insolvency Act appearing to create a general, open-ended category of liquidation expenses does not in fact have this effect, since the relevant provisions are concerned with priority amongst expenses claimants and not with the eligibility of expenses as expenses of the liquidation.[470] There is, nevertheless, an exception to the definitive listing of liquidation expenses in the Act. On just and equitable grounds, certain pre-liquidation expenses, such as the liability to pay rent under a continuing lease, are treated as if they were expenses of the liquidation.[471] The reason is that those for whose benefit the estate is being administered should bear the burden of debt incurred in the process.[472]

9.102 Recoverable expenses are paid out in the order of priority laid down by the Insolvency Rules,[473] with the cost of getting in the assets at the head of the list, except that in the case of compulsory winding-up the court has a discretion to order payment in such order of priority as it thinks just if the company's assets are insufficient to meet its liabilities.[474]

(c) Priority: expenses, preferential creditors, unsecured creditors and members

9.103 Another critical difficulty is to determine whether the expenses properly recoverable by a liquidator or administrator, and therefore ranking ahead of preference and other unsecured creditors, should be recoverable at the expense of secured creditors with a floating charge. The scheme of the Insolvency Act invites the assumption that, because expenses rank ahead of preferential creditors,[475] who in turn rank ahead of secured creditors with a floating charge, it therefore follows that expenses rank ahead of floating chargees. The order of distribution in the case of insolvent companies would therefore be as follows: fixed chargees, expenses of the insolvency process, preferential creditors, floating chargees, unsecured creditors and members. Subject to the special provision made for unsecured creditors by the Enterprise Act 2002, this ranking is confirmed by section 176ZA of the Insolvency Act, which overturned a House of Lords decision[476] that had altered the previous understanding of the law.[476a]

(i) Floating charges

9.104 Distribution takes place out of the assets of the company. It is particularly important to determine what those assets are in the case of preferential creditors and, since the Enterprise Act 2002, unsecured creditors participating in the special fund created by amendment to the Insolvency

---

468 *Re MC Bacon Ltd* [1991] Ch 127; *Mond v Hammond Suddards (No 2)* [2000] Ch 40, CA.
469 Rule 4.218A(1)(c). See also r 4.220(2) (discretionary power to order liquidator to pay costs).
470 *Re MC Bacon Ltd* [1991] Ch 127; *Mond v Hammond Suddards (No 2)* [2000] Ch 40, CA.
471 *Re Lundy Granite Co* (1871) 6 Ch App 462; *Re Toshoku Finance plc* [2002] UKHL 6, [2002] 1 WLR 671. For the applicability of this principle to administration, see *Pillar Denton Ltd v Jervis* [2014] EWCA civ 180, [2015] ch 1587.
472 *Re Atlantic Computer Systems plc* [1992] Ch 505, 522, CA.
473 Rules 2.67–2.67A, 4.218–4.220 and 6.224.
474 Section 156 and r 4.220(1). See *Re MC Bacon Ltd* [1991] Ch 127; *Re Toshoku Finance plc* [2002] UKHL 6, [2002] 1 WLR 671.
475 Sections 115 and 175(2)(a).
476 *Buchler v Talbot* [2004] UKHL 9, [2004] 2 AC 298.
476a The order of distribution and the length of the distribution list can in rare cases give rise to considerable complexity: see *Re Lehman Brothers International (Europe)* [2015] EWCA Civ 485.

Act.[477] These assets do not include assets the subject of a fixed charge or mortgage[478] but they do include assets subject to a floating charge.[479] Nevertheless, before changes were made to insolvency legislation in the 1980s, it was held that preference creditors were not entitled to be paid out of assets subject to a floating charge that had crystallized between the dates of the winding-up petition and order.[480] The assets at the relevant time had become the subject of a fixed charge. When the law was subsequently changed so that preferential creditors were to be paid ahead of floating chargees, regardless of whether or when the charge had crystallized,[481] this gave rise to the modern problem of resolving the competing claims of liquidators, for the reimbursement of expenses of the liquidation, and of floating chargees. The position taken in *Re Barleycorn Enterprises Ltd*[482] was that, since floating charge assets were assets of the company, it followed that the order of distribution was, in respect of them, first, expenses of the liquidation, secondly, preferential debts, and thirdly, the claim of the floating chargee. Nevertheless, the House of Lords asserted in *Buchler v Talbot*[483] that the position was altogether different. There were two funds each bearing its own costs. The first fund consisted of the free assets of the company in liquidation, out of which the expenses of the liquidation were to be paid, ahead of any claim of the preferential creditors. The second fund, administered by a receiver (or administrator appointed out of court), would be charged with the expenses of the receivership or administration after the preferential creditors had been paid but before the floating chargee was paid.[484] The expenses of the liquidation would not be charged against this fund. *Buchler v Talbot* had hardly settled the law before it was overturned by section 176ZA of the Insolvency Act as follows: '(1) The expenses of winding up in England and Wales, so far as the assets of the company available for payment of the general creditors of the company are insufficient to meet them, have priority over any claims to property comprised in or subject to any floating charge created by the company and shall be paid out of any property accordingly.' Sub-section (2) goes on to make it clear that expenses rank ahead of any claim of preferential creditors to those same assets,[485] while preferential claims rank ahead of section 176A creditors.[486]

(ii) Preferential claims

9.105 In response to the recommendation of the Cork Committee,[487] the insolvency reforms of the 1980s drastically reduced the number of preferential claims. For example, local authorities' claims for unpaid rates lost their preferential status. When first enacted, the Insolvency Act listed six types of preference claim, but the number has now been reduced to three.[488]

---

[477] See Insolvency Act, s 176A, discussed at 9.111.

[478] The court has no inherent jurisdiction to interfere with the rights of secured creditors: *Re MC Bacon Ltd* [1991] Ch 127, 140. The company's equity of redemption in the assets would be subject to distribution in the normal way.

[479] *Re Barleycorn Enterprises Ltd* [1970] Ch 465, CA (in the light of legislative changes of 1888 and 1897 introducing the special category of preferential claims and ranking them ahead of floating chargees); *Re MC Bacon Ltd* [1991] Ch 127.

[480] *Re Christonette International Ltd* [1982] 1 WLR 1245, relying upon *Re Griffin Hotel Co Ltd* [1941] Ch 129.

[481] Sections 40 and 175, and Sch B1, para 65(2), of the Insolvency Act; s 754(2) of the Companies Act 2006.

[482] [1970] Ch 465, CA, followed in *Re Portbase (Clothing) Ltd* [1993] Ch 388.

[483] [2004] UKHL 9, [2004] 2 AC 298.

[484] See Insolvency Act, ss 40(2), 45(3) and 175(2)(b), Sch B1, paras 65(2) and 99(3). Preferential creditors are expected to look first to the general fund before turning to the floating charge fund: ss 40(3) and 175(2)(b), Sch B1, para 65(2).

[485] Section 176ZA does not apply to administration, but the position should be the same: see Sch B1, paras 70 and 99(3).

[486] Section 176A(6).

[487] Cmnd 8558 (1982), ch 32.

[488] Enterprise Act 2002, s 251 (amending as necessary the Insolvency Act).

In the event of a bankruptcy or winding-up, preferential claims rank equally and therefore abate equally if there are insufficient assets to satisfy them all.[489] Since they are a closed list, there is no judicial discretion to create others, eg, by authorizing payments made to selected creditors under section 127.[490]

9.106 The three remaining preferential claims[491] are for all unpaid contributions to contributory pension schemes, remuneration up to £800 in amount[492] owed to employees in respect of the preceding four months, and ECSC coal and steel levies.[493] The time provisions are based on the 'relevant date', which is defined by reference to the particular circumstances of company and individual voluntary arrangements, voluntary and compulsory winding-up, winding-up preceded by an administration order and bankruptcy.[494] For example, the date for a voluntary winding-up is the passing of the resolution, for compulsory winding-up the date of the winding-up order or (where relevant) of the appointment of a provisional liquidator, and for bankruptcy the date of the order or (where relevant) of the appointment of an interim receiver.

9.107 A particular difficulty has arisen in defining preferential claims when a company is wound up after an administration. In the case of a compulsory winding-up, the claims are dated from the making of the administration order, while in the case of a voluntary winding-up the date is that of the winding-up resolution. Preferential claims will often be greater at the date of the order than at the date of the resolution, in which case preferential creditors will be reluctant to accede to a voluntary winding-up after administration, though this may be a less expensive and speedier option than compulsory winding-up and therefore beneficial to creditors as a whole. It is therefore sensible to proceed to a voluntary winding-up while safeguarding the interests of preferential creditors as at the date of the administration order. In one case,[495] regrettably, Lightman J was of the view that it was not possible, upon the administrator's application,[496] for the liquidator in the consequent voluntary winding-up to be directed to pay preferential creditors as at the date of the administration order instead of in accordance with the statutory scheme. Furthermore, a direction to the administrator to pay those preferential creditors could not be given[497] since it was not consonant with the purpose of the administration order in the present case, which was to secure the more advantageous realization, as opposed to distribution, of the company's assets. More recently, however, it has been held that the court may exercise its inherent jurisdiction over administrators to authorize them to make payments,[498] which appears to solve the problem.

(iii) Preferential creditors and receivership

9.108 Preferential creditors are advanced not only in the event of bankruptcy or winding-up. Where a company is not in the course of being wound up, section 40 requires receivers,[499] out of

---

[489] Sections 175(2)(a) and 328(2).

[490] *Re Rafidain Bank (No 1)* [1992] BCLC 301.

[491] The three preferential claims abolished by the Enterprise Act 2002 were claims for PAYE tax deducted in the preceding 12 months, VAT and certain other taxes referable to the preceding six months, and social security contributions due in the preceding six months.

[492] Insolvency Proceedings (Monetary Limits) Order 1986, SI 1986/1996.

[493] Schedule 6.

[494] Section 387.

[495] See *Re Powerstore (Trading) Ltd* [1997] 1 WLR 1280.

[496] Pursuant to s 18(3).

[497] Under s 14(3).

[498] *Re Mark One (Oxford Street) plc* [1999] 1 WLR 1445. See also *Re UCT (UK) Ltd* [2001] 1 WLR 436; *Re Beauvale Group Ltd* [2006] BCC 912.

[499] And not merely administrative receivers. The position is the same for administrators: Insolvency Act, para 65(2).

the assets coming into their hands, to pay preferential creditors before payments are made to debenture holders[500] whose debentures are secured by a charge that as created was a floating charge.[501] The 'relevant date'[502] is the date of the appointment of the receiver.[503] So far as possible, the receiver should pay the preferential creditors out of assets available for the payment of general creditors.[504] The receiver is not bound to pay preferential creditors ahead of debenture holders with a floating charge where and to the extent that those debenture holders have a fixed charge over assets of the company.[505]

(iv) Preferential creditors and priority agreements

9.109   The interposition of preferential creditors between fixed and floating chargees has created a difficulty arising out of priority agreements where the fixed chargee surrenders priority to the floating chargee. For reasons stated, the fixed chargee ranks ahead of the preferential creditor who ranks ahead of the floating chargee who now, as a result of the priority agreement, ranks ahead of the fixed chargee, closing the circle. Problems of circular priority need to be solved by breaking the circle at some point in a principled way. Since the rights of preferential creditors amount to a statutory expropriation of secured creditors, then the legislation should not be given an expansive interpretation. At first sight, the natural order of distribution is to rank the floating chargee first, by way of subrogation and to the extent of the fixed chargee's rights, followed by the preferential creditors, then by the floating chargee for the balance (if any) of its secured claim, and finally by the fixed chargee.[506]

9.110   Nevertheless, as sensible as the above approach is, it was not adopted in one case[507] where the priority agreement was construed as making the agreement creating the fixed charge subject to the agreement creating the floating charge. Since the legislation stated that the preferential creditors 'shall be paid' ahead of the floating chargee, this meant that the preferential creditors finished on top, thus receiving an undeserved windfall benefit as an accidental by-product of a priority agreement between parties who intended no such effect. If, instead of subsuming the fixed charge agreement under the floating charge agreement, there had been an assignment to the floating chargee of the fixed chargee's right to payment, the priority agreement should have been successful. The extraordinary promotion of preferential creditors can thus be avoided by competent drafting.

(v) The special fund for unsecured creditors

9.111   The disadvantageous position of unsecured creditors in insolvency has attracted adverse judicial comment[508] and was responsible for the creation of preferential claims in the first place. A new section 176A of the Insolvency Act was added by the Enterprise Act 2002,[509] at the time when the ranks of preferential creditors were being reduced, to improve the position of unsecured creditors. Under section 176A, a prescribed part of the company's 'net property' is set aside to be applied by liquidators, administrators and receivers to unsecured claims. Net

---

[500] Who need not be the debenture holders at whose behest the receiver was appointed: *Re H & K Medway Ltd* [1997] 1 WLR 1422 (cf *Griffiths v Yorkshire Bank plc* [1994] 1 WLR 1427).

[501] See *Re Pearl Maintenance Services Ltd* [1995] 1 BCLC 449.

[502] For the purpose of identifying preferential debts.

[503] Section 387(4)(a).

[504] Section 40(3). Conceivably, a receiver enforcing a narrowly based floating charge might not have unencumbered assets coming into his hands.

[505] *Re Lewis Merthyr Consolidated Collieries Ltd* [1929] 1 Ch 498, CA.

[506] This was the uncontested order of distribution in *Re Woodroffes (Musical Instruments) Ltd* [1986] Ch 366.

[507] *Re Portbase Clothing Ltd* [1993] Ch 388.

[508] *Saloman v A Saloman & Co Ltd* [1897] AC 22, 53, HL (Lord Macnaghten); *Borden v Scottish Timber Products Ltd* [1981] Ch 25, 42 (Templeman LJ).

[509] Section 252.

property includes assets the subject of a floating charge. The prescribed part of the company's property constituting the fund is not linked to the loss of the Crown's status as preferential creditor. Instead, given a minimum net property value of £10,000, 50 per cent of the first £50,000 is set aside for unsecured creditors, followed by 20 per cent of the remainder of the net property. The total amount constituting the fund, however, is capped at £600,000.[510] Access to the fund is denied to secured creditors even in respect of a shortfall arising after the realization of their security.[511] There is no duty on liquidators, administrators, and receivers to set up a fund where the cost of the distribution would be disproportionate to the benefits of the distribution,[512] but this discretion does not permit the exclusion of particular creditors whose claims would be disproportionately expensive to recognize.[513]

(vi) Final claimants

9.112 Last in the distribution list come unsecured creditors who have put in a proof of debt,[514] so far as they have not been paid in full out of the special fund, followed by members,[515] in the case of winding-up, and spouses,[516] in the case of bankruptcy. Furthermore, members may be liable as contributories[517] to contribute to the assets of the company in a winding-up,[518] eg, where their shares are not fully paid up.

(d) Set-off (insolvency and receivership)

(i) General

9.113 An unsecured creditor who is also indebted to the insolvent is in a better position than an unsecured creditor who is not. The former may take advantage of set-off rights which, if the claim of the insolvent matches the claim of the creditor, permits the creditor to recover in full instead of receiving only the very limited dividend that would otherwise be paid. Set-off in fact operates as a form of security,[519] though it will often arise as a windfall benefit if insolvency supervenes at a time when the creditor happens to owe money to the insolvent. Indeed, it is more effective in that it can be exercised passively by the creditor and does not require any particular formalities or notice.

9.114 Insolvency set-off[520] exists to work justice between creditor and insolvent. Unlike legal (or statutory) set-off, it is not a matter of accounting between two liquidated claims or debts in the cause of avoiding circuity of actions. Unlike equitable set-off, which is not confined to liquidated claims or debts, it is not a matter of one party's 'legal' title to a claim being undermined by the persuasive equity of the other party's closely connected cross-claim. Insolvency set-off applies to all claims and cross-claims, whether they are connected or not and whether

---

[510] The Insolvency Act 1986 (Prescribed Part) Order 2003, SI 2003/2097.

[511] *Re Permacell Finesse Ltd* [2007] EWHC 3233 (Ch), [2008] BCC 208; *Re Airbase Services (UK) Ltd* [2008] EWHC 3233 (Ch), [2008] BCC 208. It is uncertain whether a qualifying chargee, having taken advantage of its floating charge in appointing an administrator out of court, might then disclaim its floating charge so as to seek participation in the fund. In general, a secured creditor surrendering its security is entitled to participate: *Re PAL SC Realisations 2007 Ltd* [2010] EWHC 2850 (Ch), [2011] BCC 93.

[512] Section 176A(5). See *Re Hydroserve Ltd* [2007] EWHC 3026 (Ch), [2008] BCC 175. cf *Re International Sections Ltd* [2009] EWHC 137 (Ch), [2009] BCC 574.

[513] *Re Courts plc* [2008] EWHC 2339 (Ch), [2009] 1 WLR 1499.

[514] A debt can also include any liability, including liability in tort: Insolvency Rules (as amended by SI 2006/1272), r 13.12.

[515] Section 107.

[516] Section 329.

[517] Section 79.

[518] Section 74.

[519] *Stein v Blake* [1996] AC 243, 251, HL, *per* Lord Hoffmann.

[520] See generally R Derham, *Set-Off* (4th edn, 2010); R Goode, *Principles of Corporate Insolvency Law* (4th edn, 2011) ch 9.

they are liquidated or not. There are however certain limitations on the availability of insolvency set-off of which account has to be taken.

9.115 Insolvency set-off is provided for in section 323 for bankruptcy and rule 4.90 for winding-up. Section 323 re-enacts, with only slight changes, section 31 of the Bankruptcy Act 1914. In the case of companies, set-off was first applied in winding-up as a result of the Judicature Act 1873,[521] the language of the bankruptcy section being extended by analogy to companies before language apt for companies was created in rule 4.90,[522] which is *mutatis mutandis* identical to section 323. Nevertheless, rule 4.90 is expressed so that it applies in solvent and insolvent windings-up alike; section 323 is obviously confined to bankruptcy.

(ii) Scope of set-off

9.116 According to rule 4.90, an account has to be taken of what is due from creditor to company and company to creditor where, before the company goes into liquidation, there have been 'mutual credits, mutual debts or other mutual dealings'. This results in the extinguishment of the two claims in favour of one net claim so that neither of the previous claims may thereafter be assigned.[523] A balance due to the company has to be paid to the liquidator; a balance in favour of the creditor is the subject of a proof. The cut-off date for amounts due from the company is the date when the creditor had notice that a meeting of creditors had been called or that a winding-up petition was pending, as the case may be.[524] Otherwise, an incentive would arise for debtors of the insolvent company to purchase claims against the company, which is impermissible.[525]

9.117 Set-off can take place only where the claim and cross-claim are monetary claims. In one case, the notion of a monetary claim was given an extended meaning where one of the claims was not immediately money-based but was for the return of goods that were subject to a direction to the recipient that they be sold.[526] Otherwise, an obligation to deliver non-monetary assets, even assets with a definable market value, may not be included in insolvency set-off. Close-out netting, which involves accelerating asset delivery obligations so as to commute them into monetary obligations, on an event of default such as insolvency, therefore falls outside the insolvency set-off rule. For close-out netting to take effect on insolvency, it therefore needs the sanction of special legislation.[527]

9.118 Mutuality is present even though the two claims are completely unrelated to each other.[528] Moreover, one claim may be a debt and the other for unliquidated damages.[529] At one time it was thought that a claim in tort could not be the subject of set-off in insolvency.[530] Subsequent case law justified this approach on the ground that a tort claim was not provable under the Bankruptcy Act 1914.[531] Since, under section 322, a tort claim is now provable,

---

[521] Section 10.
[522] Modified in significant respects by the Insolvency (Amendment) Rules 2005 (SI 2005/527), reg 23.
[523] *Stein v Blake* [1996] AC 243, HL.
[524] Rule 4.90(2), which also cuts off claims arising during administration and claims acquired by assignment after the cut-off date. See *Re Eros Films Ltd* [1963] Ch 565; *Re Gray's Inn Construction Co Ltd* [1980] 1 WLR 711, CA.
[525] *Re Charge Card Services Ltd* [1987] Ch 150.
[526] *Rolls Razor Ltd v Cox* [1967] 1 QB 552, CA (confined to goods held by a salesman for sale as opposed to demonstration purposes).
[527] Financial Collateral Arrangements (No 2) Regulations 2003, SI 2003/3126, reg 12.
[528] *Re Daintrey* [1900] 1 QB 546, CA.
[529] *Mersey Steel and Iron Co v Naylor Benzon & Co* (1884) 9 App Cas 434, HL.
[530] *Re Mid-Kent Fruit Factory* [1896] 1 Ch 567; cf *Tilley v Bowman* [1910] 1 KB 745.
[531] *Re DH Curtis (Builders) Ltd* [1978] Ch 162.

it follows that it may be the subject of a set-off, like any other provable claim consisting of a pecuniary demand.[532]

Mutuality of claim and cross-claim is absent where money has been paid by the insolvent **9.119** for a purpose that can no longer be accomplished. The insolvent's representative may recover the money without giving credit for a claim against the insolvent[533] since the dedication of money to a purpose takes it 'out of the course of accounts between the parties to be held…in suspense between them'.[534] Moneys held on the terms of a *Quistclose* trust will thus fall outside the bounds of mutuality. Indeed, since money is always paid for one purpose or other, it would be preferable to confine special purposes cases to the existence of such a trust or, at least, to cases where it would be a 'misappropriation' of the money to use it other than for the purpose for which it was paid.[535]A further restriction on set-off arises in respect of a contributory's claim against an insolvent limited liability company. As a contributor to the insolvency fund,[536] the contributory may not set off any claim he has against the company against his indebtedness as a contributory[537] unless the creditors of the company have been paid in full.[538] The absence of mutuality may go to the personalities of claimant and cross-claimant. A claim asserted by one party as trustee for a third party is not bound by mutuality to a cross-claim against the former party in his personal capacity.[539] The Crown may be seen as presenting a special case. Since the Crown in its various emanations is the beneficial owner of all central funds, a company may set off a claim against Customs and Excise for overpaid VAT against a subrogated Crown claim for the company's failure to make redundancy payments.[540]

(iii) Directors, companies, and set-off

The case of bank insolvency has sharply pointed the features of mutuality where directors of **9.120** a corporate borrower have given security over personal deposits with the bank for moneys advanced by the bank to the company. The question is whether the bank may enforce payment by the company despite its indebtedness to the director. If the bank's indebtedness to the director were to be taken into account, the director would benefit in his personal capacity as shareholder of the company. On the face of it, there is no mutuality present for set-off since director and company are separate personalities and '[i]t is not the function of insolvency set-off to confer a benefit on a debtor of the insolvent who has not been a party to the mutual dealing',[541] the debtor in this case being the company and the dealing that between bank and director.

---

[532] *Re Bank of Credit and Commerce International SA (No 8)* [1998] AC 214, HL; *Eberle's Hotels and Restaurant Co Ltd v Jonas (E) & Bros* (1887) 18 QBD 459, CA.

[533] *Re Pollitt* [1893] 1 QB 455, CA; *Re City Equitable Fire Insurance Co Ltd* [1930] 2 Ch 293, CA.

[534] *Re City Equitable Fire Insurance Co Ltd* [1930] 2 Ch 293, 312, CA.

[535] *National Westminster Bank Ltd v Halesowen Presswork and Assemblies Ltd* [1972] AC 785, 808, HL, *per* Lord Simon.

[536] *Cherry v Boultbee* (1839) 4 My & Cr 442, 41 ER 171 gives its name to the rule that contributors to a fund must first make their contribution to that fund before being able to assert a claim against it. Where the rule applies exceptionally in insolvency cases, as it does where the rule against double proof ousts insolvency set-off, the rule in *Cherry v Boultbee* is likewise subjected to the rule against double proof: *Re Kaupthing Singer and Friedlander Ltd* [2011] UKSC 48, [2012] 1 AC 804. According to the rule against double proof, a single debt may not be the subject of more than one claim on the estate.

[537] *Re Overend Gurney* (1866) 1 Ch App 528; *Re West Coast Gold Fields Ltd* [1905] 1 Ch 597, 602, aff'd [1906] 1 Ch 1, CA.

[538] Section 149(3).

[539] *Re ILG Travel Ltd* [1995] 2 BCLC 128.

[540] *Secretary of State for Trade and Industry v Frid* [2004] UKHL 24, [2004] 2 AC 506.

[541] *Re Bank of Credit and Commerce International SA (No 8)* [1996] Ch 245, 257, CA, *per* Rose LJ.

9.121 Nevertheless, the answer to this question turns upon whether the director has incurred personal liability on the loan by the bank to the company. Where the director undertakes liability to the bank as 'principal debtor', set-off will take effect automatically as between the director's claim against the bank and the bank's claim against the director.[542] Consequently, to the extent of the satisfaction of the debt to the bank arising out of the set-off, the bank's claim against the company is abated. If, however, the director charges his rights against the bank in favour of the bank[543] as security for the loan to the company, without undertaking a personal liability to the bank, there can be no set-off since there are no 'mutual credits, mutual debts or other mutual dealings' between the director and the bank.[544] Although insolvency set-off may not be excluded by agreement,[545] the parties are not prevented from defining their relationship in such a way as to place the director at financial risk without incurring personal liability. The intermediate case is that of the director who undertakes as surety secondary liability on the loan in such a way as not to become liable until a demand is made on him by the bank.[546] Set-off can be effected in respect of the bank's contingent claim against the director[547] but this holds little comfort for the director. The reason is that a solvent corporate borrower will be able to pay in full and the bank's liquidator will not call upon the director in such a case, or indeed in any case where the amount unrecovered from the company is less than the amount deposited by the director with the bank.

(iv) Security and set-off

9.122 Another difficult aspect of set-off is provided by secured credit. The insolvency set-off rule applies in the case of 'any creditor . . . proving or claiming to prove for a debt' in the winding-up or bankruptcy.[548] It has been held that a secured creditor not proving in the winding-up[549] should therefore be able to enforce the security unabated by the insolvent's cross-claim.[550] This is inconsistent with the view that set-off applies to claims that are provable, whether proved or not.[551] The latter view is preferable, since it results in an even-handed outcome: set-off is available where it is the insolvent party who has the security.[552]

(v) Contingent claims and set-off

9.123 Difficulties in applying set-off have arisen in the case of contingent claims. If the contingent claim is that of the creditor, then it is usually a relatively simple matter of the insolvency officer putting a value on the claim in the same way that this is done in the case of any contingent claim outside set-off.[553] This position has now been explicitly confirmed by the Insolvency

---

[542] *MS Fashions Ltd v Bank of Credit and Commerce International Ltd (No 2)* [1993] Ch 425, CA.

[543] It is now settled that a bank may take a charge over its own indebtedness to an account holder: *Re Bank of Credit and Commerce International SA (No 8)* [1998] AC 214, HL.

[544] *Re Bank of Credit and Commerce International SA (No 8)* [1998] AC 214, HL.

[545] See 9.125.

[546] *Bradford Old Bank Ltd v Sutcliffe* [1918] 2 KB 833, CA.

[547] See *MS Fashions Ltd v Bank of Credit and Commerce International Ltd (No 2)* [1993] Ch 425, CA.

[548] Section 323(1); r 4.90(1).

[549] A secured creditor can petition for bankruptcy only if he waives the security or confines his petition to unsecured debt: see s 269. No similar provision exists for corporate insolvency.

[550] *Re Norman Holding Co Ltd* [1991] 1 WLR 10.

[551] *Re Bank of Credit and Commerce International SA (No 8)* [1998] AC 214, HL.

[552] *Ex p Barnett* (1874) 9 Ch App 293; *Hiley v People's Prudential Assurance Co Ltd* (1938) 60 Commonwealth LR 468, 498, Australian High Ct; *MS Fashions Ltd v Bank of Credit and Commerce International Ltd (No 2)* [1993] Ch 425, 446, CA; *Re ILG Travel Ltd* [1995] 2 BCC 128.

[553] Section 322(3); r 4.86(1). This is now explicitly permitted by r 4.90(4) (which has no bankruptcy counterpart). See *Re Asphaltic Wood Pavement Co* (1885) 30 Ch D 216, CA; *Baker v Lloyds Bank Ltd* [1920] 2 KB 322; *Re Danka Business Systems Plc* [2013] EWCA Civ 92, [2013] Ch 506 (allowing further proof out of time if contingency materializes before distribution).

Rules.[554] Sometimes, however, the contingency affects not merely the quantum of a claim against the insolvent but the very possibility that a claim against the company will eventuate,[555] which before the change to the rules posed a problem in that the set-off rules refer to amounts that are 'due' between the parties. Where the contingent claim was that of a surety against the principal debtor, set-off had in the past been refused when no claim has yet been made against the surety by the creditor.[556] Later case law established, however, that set-off applied in the case of claims that were contingent and not merely claims whose exact quantum was determined by a contingent event. Hence, set-off was been permitted so that a factor might set off its contingent claim against the insolvent assignor to buy back receivables, if called upon to do so, against its indebtedness to that assignor under a retention fund.[557] The reference in the Insolvency Rules to the 'claim' being contingent confirms this later case law.

Where the contingent claim is that of the insolvent against the creditor, until recently the **9.124** position was as follows. No statutory machinery existed to effect a quantification of the claim since it 'would be unfair upon [the creditor] to have his liability to pay advanced merely because the trustee wants to wind up the bankrupt's estate'.[558] Nevertheless, quantification could sometimes be made with the benefit of hindsight in the light of events occurring after the making of the bankruptcy or winding-up order,[559] which is the date when the accounts have to be settled.[560] In other cases, where a company was finally wound up before the contingency was ascertained, proceedings might be brought to restore the company to the register[561] for the purpose of bringing proceedings against the creditor. If this were to happen, the creditor would be entitled to set off his full claim, minus the dividend received, against the company's claim.[562] There would be little incentive to take this action if the dividend were only a modest one. If subsequent events demonstrated that the claim against the creditor was overvalued, the creditor would have no recourse if the estate of the company had been distributed. In the case of companies, since 2005 the company's contingent claim against the creditor may be set off against the creditor's claim and that contingent claim can be quantified by the liquidator in the same way as the liquidator quantifies contingent claims against the company.[563] The company's contingent claim is accelerated only to the extent necessary to effect a set-off.[564]

(vi) Set-off mandatory

The final aspect of insolvency set-off concerns its mandatory character. It may not be excluded **9.125** between the parties.[565] One reason is that the legislation requires that an account 'shall' be

---

[554] Rule 4.90(4), (5).

[555] See *Carreras Rothmans Ltd v Freeman Mathews Treasure Ltd* [1985] 1 Ch 207.

[556] *Re a Debtor (No 66 of 1955)* [1956] 1 WLR 1226, CA. See also *Re Fenton* [1931] 1 Ch 85, CA, *per* Lord Hanworth MR. These and similar cases raised formidable problems concerning the rule against double proof, in that the creditor has a claim against the insolvent debtor whilst a guarantor of that debt also has a claim contingent on the guarantee being called in.

[557] *Re Charge Card Services Ltd* [1987] Ch 150. See also *Stein v Blake* [1996] AC 243, 252–253, HL.

[558] *Stein v Blake* [1996] AC 243, 253, HL.

[559] *Sovereign Life Assurance Co v Dodd* [1892] 2 QB 573, HL; *MS Fashions Ltd v Bank of Credit and Commerce International Ltd (No 2)* [1993] Ch 425, 432 et seq, CA, *per* Hoffmann LJ.

[560] *Re Daintrey* [1900] 1 QB 546, CA; *Re Charge Card Services Ltd* [1987] Ch 150, 177; *Re Dynamics Corp of America* [1976] 1 WLR 757, 762; *Stein v Blake* [1996] AC 243, HL. It will be the date of the resolution in the case of a voluntary liquidation: *Barclays Bank Ltd v TOSG Trust Fund Ltd* [1984] BCLC 1, 25, CA.

[561] Discussed at 9.13.

[562] *MS Fashions Ltd v Bank of Credit and Commerce International Ltd (No 2)* [1993] Ch 425, 435, CA, *per* Hoffmann LJ.

[563] Rules 4.86(1), 4.90(4), (5). In the case of administrators distributing the estate, see to the same effect r 2.85(4)(b).

[564] *Re Kaupthing Singer and Friedlander Ltd* [2010] EWCA Civ 518, [2011] BCC 555 (administration).

[565] *National Westminster Bank Ltd v Halesowen Presswork and Assemblies Ltd* [1972] AC 785, HL.

taken and the sums due 'shall' be set off against each other.[566] If the only reason for the legislation was to confer a benefit on the creditor of the insolvent, the legislation could be read as subject to contrary agreement on the ground that those for whose exclusive benefit a protective provision is introduced are entitled to surrender the benefit of that protection.[567] Nevertheless, the rule against contracting out of insolvency set-off, which does not apply to other types of set-off, has been justified on the somewhat unpersuasive ground that the set-off rules were introduced so that insolvents' estates 'are to be administered in a proper and orderly way' which 'is a matter in which the commercial community generally has an interest...'.[568] This has in the past been thought to pose problems for subordination agreements.[569]

(vii) Receivership and administration

9.126 Insolvency set-off is confined to the distribution of estates. It does not apply to receivership and has only quite recently been extended to administrators when exercising their distribution powers.[570] For receivership, legal and equitable set-off have a part to play. In the case of receivership, particular problems have arisen in connection with the assignment of a borrower's assets in favour of the secured lender that takes place when a floating charge crystallizes. Like any other assignment, this takes effect subject to existing equities and defences at the time of notice of the assignment.[571] Consequently, those indebted to the borrower may not, upon receipt of notice of the appointment of a receiver, which is tantamount to notice of the assignment, acquire set-off rights by purchasing debts owed by the borrower to third parties.[572] This corresponds to the rule that notice of a winding-up or a bankruptcy petition is the cut-off date for the acquisition of new set-off rights against the insolvent.[573]

9.127 In the case of legal set-off, the claim in question must have accrued due, though it need not be payable, at the time when the cross-claim is assigned if it is to be set off against a demand for payment by the assignee.[574] Consequently, in one case[575] where A owed money to B for television sets the subject of a sale contract, and B in turn owed money to A for computer equipment supplied by A on hire-purchase terms, A could set off hire-purchase instalments that had fallen due at the time when A was notified of the appointment of a receiver of B. A could not, however, set off amounts subsequently due after accelerating future instalments, since A invoked its rights of acceleration only after notice of the assignment. Nor could A have fallen back on equitable set-off, the reason being that the sale and hire-purchase contracts were unrelated so that there was no sufficient connection between the amounts owed under both contracts for B's receiver to have to give credit to A for all sums owed under the hire-purchase contract.

(e) Subordination agreements

9.128 The position of preferential creditors in the event of a priority agreement between a fixed chargee and a floating chargee was discussed above. The issue now is a different one and

---

[566] Section 323(2); r 4.90(2). The language of 'may' in the Bankruptcy Act 1849, s 171, became 'shall' in the Bankruptcy Act 1869, s 39.
[567] *National Westminster Bank Ltd v Halesowen Presswork and Assemblies Ltd* [1972] AC 785, HL.
[568] *National Westminster Bank Ltd v Halesowen Presswork and Assemblies Ltd* [1972] AC 785, 809, HL (Lord Simon). See also the analysis of this decision in *Re Maxwell Communications Corp* [1993] 1 WLR 1402.
[569] Discussed at 9.128–9.131.
[570] Insolvency Rules, r 2.85 (as added by SI 2003/1730).
[571] Section 136 of the Law of Property Act 1925.
[572] *Robbie (NW) & Co Ltd v Witney Warehouse Co Ltd* [1963] 1 WLR 1324, CA (trading in debts between associated companies).
[573] Discussed at 9.116.
[574] *Watson v Mid-Wales Railway Co* (1867) LR 2 CP 593; *Re Pinto Leite and Nephews* [1929] 1 Ch 221.
[575] *Business Computers Ltd v Anglo-African Leasing Ltd* [1977] 1 WLR 578.

concerns an agreement or agreements by which one unsecured creditor subordinates itself to another in the event of the debtor's insolvency. Subordination arrangements of various kinds are valid, despite their apparent disturbance of the *pari passu* principle of distribution. Furthermore, they are not treated as running counter to the state's interest in the orderly distribution of insolvents' estates.

Subordination agreements may take various forms. First of all, a creditor may under a turno-   **9.129**
ver trust declare itself trustee, for the benefit of one or more named creditors, of any dividend distributed by the liquidator. The practical effect of this is to give the latter an added dividend but, since the trust attaches to money in the hands of the creditor after the estate has been distributed in the way sanctioned by the Insolvency Act, there is no reason to strike down this transaction any more than any other trust.[576] Turnover trusts have been stated not to be regis-trable charges granted by the subordinated creditor,[577] which sensibly diminishes insolvency risk associated with that creditor. A possibility similar to the turnover trust is the assignment by the subordinated creditor of the benefit of a future dividend.[578]

A different technique is contractual subordination which exists where, under the terms of the   **9.130**
loan, creditor and debtor agree[579] that, in the event of the debtor's insolvency, the creditor will not receive a dividend until a favoured creditor or creditors have been paid in full.[580] The debt owed to the subordinated creditor is therefore a type of flawed asset. In this case, a further distinction might be drawn between the simple surrender of a dividend, the effect of which would be to prefer *all* other creditors of the debtor, and the surrender of a dividend in favour of one or a limited number of other creditors. As regards the former, there is no reason in law why a creditor might not waive a debt owed by an insolvent or decline to submit a proof. On this reasoning, an agreement of this kind is lawful and does not infringe the *pari passu* principle. That principle prevents a creditor from bargaining for an advantage on the distribution of an insolvent's assets, which is not the case with a subordination agreement of this kind.[581] To strike down such a contractual subordination could have a prejudicial effect on the continued existence of companies that carry on with an infusion of funds from parent and associate companies that are prepared to accept subordination.[582]

A more questionable type of contractual subordination occurs where the subordination is   **9.131**
expressed to benefit fewer than all of the remaining creditors. The favoured creditors them-selves may not have contracted for the extra dividend, in the sense that they may not be parties to the subordination contract, but an apparent stumbling block is the payment of differential dividends by a liquidator.[583] On the other hand, it is arguable that, if turnover trusts and assignments of the benefit of a dividend are permissible, then to strike down a subordination contract that produces the same effect would amount to the triumph of form over substance.[584] Apart from the subordinated creditor, no other creditor is any worse off as

---

[576] *Re NIAA Corp Ltd* (1994) 12 Australian Corporations and Securities Reports 141, New South Wales.
[577] *Re SSSL Realisations (2002) Ltd* [2006] EWCA Civ 7, [2006] Ch 610.
[578] *Re Maxwell Communications Corp* [1993] 1 WLR 1402, 1416.
[579] The possibility of enforceable rights under this agreement on the part of the favoured creditor now arises in light of the Contract (Rights of Third Parties) Act 1999.
[580] This is a common practice in sophisticated lending transactions where there are tranches of different classes of creditor with 'waterfall' clauses dictating the order of payment.
[581] *Re Maxwell Communications Corp* [1993] 1 WLR 1402. See also *Re British and Commonwealth Holding plc (No 3)* [1992] 1 WLR 672, where the subordinated holders of loan stock had no right to vote on a pro-posal for a scheme of arrangement at a meeting of unsecured creditors when the company's assets would be consumed in full by the claims of the favoured creditors.
[582] *Re Maxwell Communications Corp* [1993] 1 WLR 1402, 1416.
[583] But see *Horne v Chester and Fine Property Developments Pty Ltd* [1987] VR 913.
[584] *Re Maxwell Communications Corp* [1993] 1 WLR 1402, 1416; *Re NIAA Corp Ltd* (1994) 12 ACSR 141, 156.

a result of the agreement.[585] This amounts to a forceful case in favour of this type of subordination contract,[586] yet there are plentiful examples of the triumph of form over substance in the pages of the law reports.

C. Powers and Liabilities of Liquidators, Trustees-in-Bankruptcy, Administrators, and Administrative Receivers

(1) Dealing with the Estate

(a) Business, assets, and creditors

(i) Powers of the liquidator

9.132   Schedule 4 to the Insolvency Act 1986 contains in Part I those powers of the liquidator that may be exercised with sanction, which will be the sanction of an extraordinary resolution for a members' voluntary winding-up and of the court or a liquidation committee for a creditors' voluntary winding-up. The remaining powers in Parts II and III of the Schedule may be exercised without sanction in a voluntary winding-up.[587] For a compulsory winding-up, the liquidator needs the sanction of the court or liquidation committee to exercise the powers in Parts I and II but needs no sanction to exercise the powers in Part III.[588] In the case of a creditors' voluntary winding-up, where the creditors have not yet met,[589] the sanction of the court is needed in all cases before the liquidator's powers may be exercised. This control is in place to counter the evil of 'centrebinding',[590] which consists of the members of a company appointing their own complaisant liquidator who acts to the disadvantage of creditors by stripping the company of its remaining assets before a deferred creditors' meeting is called.[591] There are other powers contained in the main body of the Act, relating to the settling of the list of contributories,[592] the making of calls,[593] the payment of debts[594] and the calling of meetings.[595] The liquidator may apply to the court for directions concerning matters arising in the course of the winding-up.[596] The court also exercises a continuing supervisory jurisdiction over his actions.[597]

9.133   The powers contained in Part I apply to actions concerning the assets of the company and the paying and composition of the company's debts. Part II deals with bringing or defending legal proceedings in the name of the company and carrying on the business of the company so far as necessary for its beneficial winding-up. Part III includes selling the company's property, putting in a proof in the name of the company in someone else's bankruptcy or winding-up, executing documents, becoming party to bills of exchange in the name of the company, granting security over the assets of the company, authorizing another agent to act

---

[585] *Re NIAA Corp Ltd* (1994) 12 ACSR 141.
[586] *Horne v Chester and Fine Property Developments Pty Ltd* [1987] VR 913.
[587] Section 165.
[588] Section 167.
[589] For the company's duty to call a meeting, see s 98.
[590] The name comes from *Re Centrebind Ltd* [1967] 1 WLR 377.
[591] At least as effective a control is the requirement that liquidators and other insolvency professionals be accredited insolvency practitioners: s 388 et seq.
[592] Section 165(4)(a) (voluntary winding-up).
[593] Section 165(4)(b) (voluntary winding-up).
[594] A duty: s 165(5) (voluntary winding-up).
[595] Sections 165(4)(c) and 168(2).
[596] Sections 112 and 168(3).
[597] Sections 112 and 167(3).

on behalf of the company and doing anything else that is necessary for winding up the company and distributing its assets.

(ii) Powers of the trustee-in-bankruptcy

A similar structure of powers applies in the case of bankruptcy. There is a division between **9.134** powers that may be exercised without sanction and powers that may be exercised with the sanction of the court or the creditors' committee.[598] Provided the court or the creditors' committee agrees, the trustee may employ the bankrupt to carry on his business or otherwise assist the trustee.[599] The trustee also has power to summon a general meeting of creditors.[600]

(iii) Powers of the administrator and the administrative receiver

The powers of an administrator and of an administrative receiver are both expansive and **9.135** more or less identical,[601] except for the moratorium on enforcing rights and taking action.[602] The powers of an administrative receiver may be increased by agreement, which however is unlikely to exceed the administrator's power to do 'anything necessary and expedient for the management of the affairs, business and property of the company'.[603] As befits the condition of the company, the powers in Schedule 1 go beyond conventional management. The prospect of insolvent liquidation bulks large, even though administrative receivers do not as such distribute assets[604] and perform the other functions of a liquidator. Administrators may, eg, present a petition for the winding-up of the company.[605] Both administrator and administrative receiver present proposals or report to a meeting of the company's creditors.[606] This meeting may establish a creditors' committee.[607] Administrators and administrative receivers[608] may apply to the court for directions.[609]

(b) Rights of those dealing with the insolvent

In managing the affairs of the insolvent, liquidators, trustees-in-bankruptcy, administrators, and **9.136** administrative and other contractual receivers act as agents of the insolvent. The position at common law is that agents do not in normal circumstances incur personal liability on contracts they negotiate on behalf of their principal, providing that the principal is disclosed. Consequently, the co-contractants of an insolvent company or individual cannot assume that they can look to the financial integrity of a liquidator or other insolvency agent as an earnest of due performance by the insolvent. Their rights depend upon the particular insolvency regime in operation.

(i) Winding-up and bankruptcy

In the case of a winding-up, co-contractants are protected largely by the priority standing of **9.137** their claims to be paid as expenses of the liquidation ranking ahead of preferential claims.[610] Sums owed to persons doing business with the company, and to landlords for rent arising

---

[598] Section 314. The powers are contained in Sch 5.
[599] Section 314(2).
[600] Section 314(7).
[601] Schedule 1; s 42 and Sch B1, paras 59–60. The powers of a contractually-appointed receiver are purely a matter of contract.
[602] Discussed at 9.86–9.89
[603] Schedule B1, para 59(1).
[604] The administrator may now distribute: Sch B1, para 65(1), (3).
[605] Schedule 1 para 21.
[606] Section 48 and Sch B1, paras 49–54. But an administrator may make disposals in advance of the meeting: *Re Transbus International Ltd* [2004] EWHC 932 (Ch), [2004] 1 WLR 2654.
[607] Section 49 and Sch B1, para 57.
[608] In their general character as receivers or managers of the company's property.
[609] Section 35 and Sch B1, para 63.
[610] Section 175(2)(a).

out of the company's continuing occupation of premises,[611] are recoverable expenses even if the liquidator refuses to pay them. Moreover, as far as they are 'necessary disbursements' they rank ahead of the liquidator's own claim for remuneration.[612] It is no doubt open to co-contractants to require the liquidator to undertake personal liability on contracts concluded with the company in liquidation. Indeed the Insolvency Act expressly contemplates that utility suppliers of water, electricity, gas and telecommunications will require this of liquidators in the case of continuing supplies, though it prohibits demands for payment for past supplies as the condition for continuing to supply.[613]

9.138   Given the provision now made for expenses of the administration,[614] the position in administration is broadly the same as for liquidation, except that the more active powers of administrators will entail a greater number of pre-preferential creditors with claims arising during the conduct of the administration,[615] in addition to the recoverable costs of the administration itself. The position in bankruptcy is very similar to that in a winding-up. Section 324(1) requires the trustee when distributing dividends to retain such sums as are necessary for the expenses of the bankruptcy, and the priority order ranks 'necessary disbursements' ahead of the trustee's own claim for remuneration.[616]

(ii) Administration and receivership: personal liability

9.139   Administrators and receivers, though agents of the company, are capable of incurring personal liability on contracts during their period of office. Taking first receivership, court-appointed receivers, who are not agents of the company, have always been personally responsible on contracts they conclude,[617] even if they make their status clear in documents addressed to the other contracting party. They are expected to look to the assets of the company for indemnification, though they may stipulate special terms excluding that liability with the other contracting party. Initially, the position was quite different with contractual receivers. Starting with legislation dating back 70 years,[618] those receivers are now personally liable on all contracts entered into by them in the performance of their functions, as well as on contracts of employment that they have adopted, in return for which they are indemnified from the assets of the company.[619] The indemnity has the practical effect of a security. The personal liability of administrators is organized on the same basis.[620] Statements concerning administrative receivers below apply also to administrators, unless otherwise stated, though the statutory recognition of expenses of the administration has greatly detracted from the importance of an administrator's personal liability.

(iii) Administrative receivers and contracts of employment

9.140   Besides liability for contracts concluded personally,[621] the administrative receiver is also liable for contracts of employment that he 'adopts'. Case law of the 1990s was considered to pose

---

[611]   *Re ABC Coupler and Engineering Co Ltd (No 3)* [1970] 1 WLR 702.
[612]   Rule 4.218(1)(m),(o); *Re Linda Marie Ltd* [1989] BCLC 46.
[613]   Section 233 (s 372 for bankruptcy). The position under the section is the same for administrators, administrative receivers, provisional liquidators and the supervisors of voluntary arrangements.
[614]   Rules 2.67 and 2.67A.
[615]   Schedule B1, para 99(4).
[616]   Rule 6.224(1)(m), (o).
[617]   *Burt Boulton & Hayward v Bull* [1895] 1 QB 76, CA.
[618]   For the development of the law, see Lord Browne-Wilkinson in *Powdrill v Watson* [1995] 2 AC 394, HL.
[619]   Sections 37(1), (2) (receivers) and 44(1)(b) (administrative receivers).
[620]   Schedule B1, para 99(4)–(6).
[621]   The receiver is free to exclude liability as a matter of contract: ss 37(1)(a), 44(1)(b); *Re Ferranti International plc* [1994] BCC 658 (otherwise varied on appeal *sub nom Powdrill v Watson* [1995] 2 AC 394, HL).

such a grave threat to the rescue culture that emergency legislation had to be passed to alleviate the position of administrative receivers.

The adoption of a contract of employment by an administrative receiver does not occur **9.141** because of anything done or omitted within 14 days of his appointment.[622] Overturning earlier authority that a statement to employees that their contracts were not being adopted would negative adoption,[623] the House of Lords in *Powdrill v Watson* held that administrative receivers (and administrators) may by their actions adopt contracts of employment even if they deny it.[624]

Consequently, those employees who were kept on did better than those dismissed, who had **9.142** the rights only of preferential creditors.[625] Nevertheless, *Powdrill v Watson* is authority that administrative receivers should be bound only in respect of liabilities 'incurred' during the receivership. This word, formerly present in the case only of administrators,[626] was read into the section dealing with administrative receivers.[627] On the facts, the significance of 'incurred' was that it protected administrative receivers from liability for employment benefits accruing for periods of service before their appointment. The House of Lords had thus gone some way to easing the particular predicament of administrative receivers who, unlike administrators,[628] are not discharged from liability once their work is done.[629] As regards salary and pension benefits, however, administrative receivers still remained highly vulnerable after *Powdrill v Watson*, since employees whose contracts were adopted carried forward from earlier service their entitlement to notice, which could be very lengthy indeed in the case of a senior employee with many years' service.

Before *Powdrill v Watson* was decided in the House of Lords, hastily enacted legislation[630] **9.143** went further by limiting the employment liability of administrative receivers to wages and pension contributions incurred during the period in which they held office and in return for services rendered wholly or partly after the adoption of the contract of employment in question. The legislation was not made retrospective and, for unexplained reasons, did not extend to contractually appointed receivers.[631]

(iv) Administrative receivers and rates

Besides contracts of employment adopted, and other contracts entered into, by the admin- **9.144** istrative receiver, difficulties have arisen in connection with rates, which since the reforms of the 1980s are no longer preferential debts. The question that arose in one case[632] was whether a receiver could refrain from selling a building in the expectation of the market rising, whilst not paying even the reduced rates due on an unoccupied building. A rating authority pursuing litigation against the company would merely precipitate a liquidation in which it would rank only as an unsecured creditor. The authority was not providing a service, like the supply

---

[622] Sections 37(2) and 44(2).
[623] *Re Specialised Mouldings* (High Ct, 1987).
[624] [1995] 2 AC 394, HL.
[625] The extent of whose claims are set out in ss 386–387 and Sch 6.
[626] Section 19(4) (now replaced by Sch B1, para 99(3)).
[627] The pre-1994 text of s 44.
[628] Schedule B1, para 98(1).
[629] Changes in the law occurring after they had accounting for all dealings with the assets of the company posed a particular risk for them.
[630] Insolvency Act 1994, adding s 44(2)(A)–(D) to the Insolvency Act.
[631] Significant liabilities could still exist in their case from the running of a particular major business, eg, a hotel.
[632] *Re Sobam BV* [1996] 1 BCLC 446 (not an administrative receivership case, but the same would there apply).

of electricity, that would give it leverage against the receiver, so it asserted that the receiver had become personally liable to pay the rates under the relevant legislation as the person in possession of the building. The argument failed on the familiar ground that the receiver was only the agent of the company: it was the company itself that was in possession. The company's liability to pay rates was akin to its liability to perform pre-receivership contracts, for which the receiver would not be liable.[633]

(2) Bringing Proceedings

(a) Vulnerable transactions and fraudulent transfers

(i) Distributable assets

9.145   It is only the assets of the insolvent at the time of the bankruptcy or winding-up order or resolution that are distributed. There is, however, a major exception that arises in the case of dispositions of the insolvent's assets occurring in the run up to bankruptcy or winding-up. In that period, certain transactions are vulnerable to challenge by insolvency officers[634] and administrators, but not by receivers. These challenges may be made under different heads, but their broad purpose, taken together, is to reinforce the *pari passu* principle by preserving the insolvent's assets for distribution and by preventing one creditor from being singled out for favourable treatment at the expense of the others. This is consistent with the principle that the directors owe a duty to the company in its final stages to run it for the benefit of its creditors.[635] That said, the various heads suffer as a result of their heterogeneity and a certain incoherence of overall purpose. It is by no means certain that their broad purpose is served well by existing legislation.

9.146   In consequence of the purpose served by these heads of challenge and their confinement to liquidators, trustees-in-bankruptcy, and administrators, the moneys recovered are, correctly it is submitted, 'impressed ... with a trust' for the benefit of the unsecured creditors, who are the eventual victims of the transactions in question. They are not assets of the company so as to be caught by a security given to one of its creditors.[636] Money paid under the impugned transactions ceases to be the property of the company. Consequently, there is no proprietary claim for its recovery. The conclusion that the unsecured creditors benefit from the liquidator's action means that an office-holder is not pointlessly bringing proceedings that can only benefit a secured creditor. On the other hand, so the argument runs, any inflation of the assets embraced by the security would have the kinetic effect of releasing other assets for the unsecured creditors, at least where the chargee is not undersecured.[637]

(ii) Undervalue transactions

9.147   The first head of challenge arises under section 238 and concerns transactions [638] entered into at an undervalue.[639] This head, introduced for companies by the Insolvency Act 1985,

---

[633] For administration, rates are now recognized expenses under r 2.67.

[634] The sanction of the court is needed for actions to be brought by liquidators and trustees: Insolvency Act, Sch 4, para (3A) and Sch 5, para (2A).

[635] *West Mercia Safetywear Ltd v Dodd* (1988) 4 BCC 30, CA; *Stone & Rolls Ltd v Moore Stephens* [2009] UKHL 39, [2009] 1 AC 1391.

[636] *Re Yagerphone Ltd* [1935] 1 Ch 352; *Re Oasis Merchandising Services Ltd* [1998] Ch 170, CA.

[637] On the proceeds of actions brought by the liquidator under ss 212–214, see the discussion in 9.168.

[638] Section 436 defines 'transaction' as 'gift, agreement or arrangement', which is a broad definition: *Phillips v Brewin Dolphin Bell Lawrie Ltd* [1999] 1 WLR 2052, CA, aff'd on different grounds at [2001] UKHL 2, [2001] 1 WLR 143 where the word 'transaction' meant connected contracts in a complex business sale and permitted the value of the consideration to be drawn from a connected contract. See also *Feakins v DEFRA* [2005] EWCA Civ 1513, [2007] BCC 54. cf *National Westminster Bank plc v Jones* [2001] EWCA Civ 1541, [2002] 1 BCLC 55.

[639] For bankruptcy, the provision is s 339.

was developed from earlier bankruptcy legislation.[640] An undervalue transaction exists either where the insolvent makes a gift,[641] or where the insolvent receives either no consideration[642] or a consideration that is worth 'significantly' less in money terms than the consideration provided in return.[643] The adequacy of consideration is calculated in terms of what a reasonably informed buyer would pay in an arm's length transaction.[644] These provisions are confined to transactions[645] that deplete or reduce the value of the transferor's assets. On one view, an undervalue transaction was not concluded where a company granted a security to one of its existing creditors, a bank. Although this transaction 'adversely affect[ed] the rights of other creditors in insolvency', the only thing that the company lost as a result of the transaction was 'the right to apply the proceeds [of the charged assets] otherwise than in satisfaction of the secured debt',[646] which could not be valued in monetary terms. Nevertheless, the opposite view that section 238 does apply to the grant of security has been firmly and authoritatively expressed.[647]

For the transaction to be open to challenge, the insolvent must either be unable to pay its debts at that time or become so as a result of the transaction.[648] This financial state of affairs is presumed to exist where the other party is an associate of the bankrupt or connected to the company in winding-up.[649] Otherwise, the burden of proof will be on the administrator or liquidator. **9.148**

The date of the transaction is relevant if it is to be challenged. In the case of companies, the transaction has to be entered into two years before the 'onset of insolvency',[650] which is the date of commencement of the winding-up.[651] In the case of individuals, the period is five years.[652] Where the company going into liquidation has been in administration, care has to be taken that the winding-up follows directly on from the administration or else **9.149**

---

[640] Section 42 of the Bankruptcy Act 1914.

[641] *Re Barton Manufacturing Co Ltd* [1999] 1 BCLC 740.

[642] Past consideration is no consideration: *Re Bangla Television Ltd* [2006] EWHC 2292 (Ch), [2007] 1 BCLC 609.

[643] Sections 238(4) and 339(3). The latter, bankruptcy provision also lists transactions in consideration of marriage. An example of undervalue would be the transfer by husband to wife of an interest in the matrimonial home that exceeds in value the mortgage commitments assumed by the wife: *Re Kumar* [1993] 1 WLR 224.

[644] *Phillips v Brewin Dolphin Bell Lawrie Ltd* [2001] UKHL 2, [2001] 1 WLR 143, at [30] (Lord Scott), HL, On the process of valuation, see *Agricultural Mortgage Corp plc v Woodward* [1995] 1 BCLC 1; *Jones v National Westminster Bank plc v Jones* [2001] EWCA Civ 1541, [2002] 1 BCLC 55; *Ramlort Ltd v Reid* [2004] EWCA Civ 800, [2005] 1 BCLC 331.

[645] On various dealings amounting to a transaction, see *Phillips v Brewin Dolphin Bell Lawrie Ltd* [2001] UKHL 2, [2001] 1 WLR 143; *Ailyan v Smith* [2010] EWHC 24 (Ch), [2010] BPIR 289.

[646] *Re MC Bacon Ltd* [1991] Ch 127. See also *Re Lewis's of Leicester Ltd* [1995] 1 BCLC 428. On a sale of the secured asset, the value for undervalue purposes has been held to be the value of the asset minus the security: *Re Brabon* [2001] 1 BCLC 11.

[647] *Hill v Spread Trustee Co Ltd* [2006] EWCA Civ 542, at [93], [2007] 1 WLR 2404 (Arden LJ), noting that a security granted for no consideration at all would be a gift under s 238.

[648] Sections 240(2) and 341(2), (3); *Re Casa Estates (UK) Ltd* [2014] EWCA Civ 383, [2014] BCC 269. An apparent difference exists between bankruptcy and liquidation in that the bankruptcy provision is not confined to cash flow insolvency (inability to pay debts as they fall due) but extends also to balance sheet insolvency (assets exceeded by liabilities). Nevertheless, balance sheet insolvency is deemed elsewhere (s 123(2)) to amount to cash flow insolvency.

[649] Sections 240(2) and 341(2).

[650] Section 240(1)(a).

[651] Discussed in 9.11 and 9.12. Where the winding-up is preceded by an administration, see s 240 for the relevant dates.

[652] Section 341(1)(a) (substituting the former period of ten years).

the passage of time during the administration will prevent the liquidator from challenging pre-administration transactions.[653]

9.150 In the case of companies, an order will not be made by the court if, despite the undervalue, the company carried out the transaction in good faith and for the purpose of carrying on its business, and if at the time of the transaction there were reasonable grounds for believing that the transaction would benefit the company.[654] The order made by the court is designed to restore the *status quo ante*, but the court has a discretion as to how this should be accomplished[655] and may indeed make no order at all[656] or an order on terms.[657]

(iii) Undervalue transactions and third parties

9.151 The order made may in certain cases affect the property of, or subject to liability, third parties subsequently acquiring assets from the other party to the undervalue transaction.[658] The central idea is that *bona fide* third parties purchasing former company property should be put beyond the reach of a court order.[659] Prior to the Insolvency (No 2) Act 1994, the position was that the broad sweep of the opening words of section 241(2),[660] allowing for the recovery of property and benefits from such third parties, was qualified by a defence available to those third parties. They had to show that they had acted in good faith, given value and had had no notice of the relevant circumstances. The relevant circumstances were the entry of the company into an undervalue transaction. The danger, which prompted the legislation, was that purchasers of unregistered land could be put upon notice when investigating a root of title over the preceding years, since they would discover the price at which the land had previously been sold. This would disqualify them from claiming the above defence.

9.152 The solution of the amended section 241, was to make notice a sub-category of good faith, and to expand notice of the relevant circumstances so that it had to include notice of the relevant proceedings. Proceedings are defined to include winding-up, administration and administration leading into winding-up.[661] Section 241(2) makes the defence available to third parties acting in good faith and giving value. A third party with notice of the relevant circumstances *and* the relevant proceedings is now presumed to have acted otherwise than in good faith.[662] This same presumption arises against persons connected or associated with the company or individual transferor even in the absence of such notice. In the case of the purchaser of unregistered land, notice of the relevant proceedings will thus not arise from searching title. The title that that purchaser acquires upon the conveyance ought therefore to be safe from the attentions of the administrator or insolvency officer. The third party defence of good faith purchase has thus become significantly easier to establish.

---

[653] For the procedure to overcome the various difficulties, see *Re Powerstore (Trading) Ltd* [1997] 1 WLR 1280; *Re Mark One (Oxford Street) plc* [1999] 1 WLR 1445; *Re Norditrack (UK) Ltd* [2000] 1 WLR 343.

[654] Section 238(5). No equivalent provision exists for bankruptcy.

[655] Sections 238(3) and 339(2).

[656] *Re Paramount Airways Ltd* [1993] Ch 223, 239; *Singla v Brown* [2007] EWHC 405 (Ch), [2008] Ch 357; *Re MDA Investment Management Ltd* [2003] EWHC 227 (Ch) and [2004] EWHC 42 (Ch), [2005] BCC 783 (company worse off without the undervalue transaction).

[657] See, eg, *Weisgard v Pilkington* [1995] BCC 1108.

[658] Sections 241(2) and 342(2).

[659] The burden of proof of good faith is on the third party: *Re Sonatacus Ltd* [2007] EWCA Civ 31, [2007] BCC 186.

[660] For bankruptcy, s 342(2).

[661] Section 241(3A), (3B), (3C).

[662] Sections 241(2A) and 342(2A).

(iv) Transactions defrauding creditors

The provisions dealing with undervalue transactions[663] are similar in scope to section 423, **9.153**
which concerns transactions defrauding creditors.[664] The transaction must be at an undervalue, which is defined in the same way as it is for undervalue transactions in bankruptcy
in section 339,[665] and any order made by the court will be made on similar principles.[666]
Furthermore, there has to be present an intended purpose of putting assets beyond the reach
of present or future claimants or of otherwise prejudicing their interests, the burden of proof
being on the person challenging the transaction though it can be inferred from the circumstances of the undervalue transaction.[667] This purpose need not be the only purpose[668] but
it has to be a 'substantial' one.[669]

One example of a fraudulent transfer is that of the lease of agricultural land by a farmer to his **9.154**
sons at an annual rent payable (unusually) in arrears, the effect of which was to place the sons
in a 'ransom position' against the bank which had a charge over the land.[670] Consequently,
the bank's interests had been prejudiced for the purpose of section 423. Moreover, it did not
matter that, after the transaction, the bank still held security exceeding in value the debt
owed. There was no realistic possibility of the bank being able to realize the freehold land
and the debt was mounting from day to day. In another case,[671] the claimant financed the
defendant's business by leasing coaches and aircraft to the defendant which in turn sub-leased
them to end users. Fearing prospective litigation, the defendant transferred its business and
assets, including the benefit of certain leases with the claimant, to an undercapitalized shell
company. The shell company acquired the benefit of these leases for the same sum that
the defendant had to pay under the various leasing agreements, but it paid for these benefits quarterly and in arrears. Furthermore, the shell company was paid by the defendant
an annual management fee of £1.5 million. The receipt of deferred payments in return for
its income stream would itself have been enough to mark out the transfer as an undervalue
transaction. Even legal advice to the effect that the transaction was a proper one did not preclude the existence of the purpose forbidden under section 423.

Certain differences exist between section 423 and section 238. The former provision is not **9.155**
subject to a qualifying period at all. Indeed, calculating the commencement of a limitation period, especially for a transaction transferring both present and future assets, is no

---

[663] On the meaning of transaction, see *Ailyan v Smith* [2010] EWHC 24 (Ch), [2010] BPIR 289; *DEFRA v Feakins* [2005] EWCA Civ 1513, [2007] BCC 54.

[664] Section 423 applies to both companies and individuals. Legislation of this type dates from the time of Elizabeth I. It has long been the practice to refer to such transactions as fraudulent conveyances (or transfers), though there is no requirement of fraud in the text of s 423 (see *Arbuthnot Leasing International Ltd v Havelet Leasing Ltd (No 1)* [1992] 1 WLR 455). The mental state of the transferor comes into play at the remedial stage: *4Eng Ltd v Harper* [2009] EWHC 2633 (Ch), [2010] BCC 746.

[665] Akin to the rules in s 423 are ss 342A to 342C, which give the court power to make such order as it thinks fit where a bankrupt has previously made excessive contributions to a pension scheme so as unfairly to prejudice his creditors. The individual's purpose in putting assets beyond the reach of his creditors is relevant in determining whether excessive contributions have been made. Amounts are excessive in the light of the individual's circumstances when the contributions were made.

[666] See *Arbuthnot Leasing International Ltd v Havelet Leasing Ltd (No 1)* [1992] 1 WLR 455. A compen-
sation order will reflect the value of the assets as a going concern at the time of the assignment, which may involve a measure of hindsight: *Watchorn v Jupiter Industries Ltd* [2014] EWHC 3003 (Ch).

[667] See *Barclays Bank plc v Eustice* [1995] 1 WLR 1238, CA.

[668] *Chohan v Saggar* [1992] BCC 306, 321, CA.

[669] *Hashmi v IRC* [2002] EWCA Civ 981, [2002] BCC 943; *Royscot Spa Leasing Ltd v Lovett* [1995] BCC 502, CA (disapproving of 'dominant' in *Chohan v Saggar* [1992] BCC 306, CA).

[670] *Barclays Bank plc v Eustice* [1995] 1 WLR 1238, CA. See also *National Westminster Bank plc v Jones* [2001] EWCA Civ 1541, [2002] 1 BCLC 55.

[671] *Arbuthnot Leasing International Ltd v Havelet Leasing Ltd (No 1)* [1992] 1 WLR 455.

easy matter.[672] Furthermore, a challenge to a transaction may be mounted, not just by insolvency officer and administrator, but by 'any victim',[673] who is treated as acting representatively on behalf of other victims too. The leave of the court is nevertheless required if a victim wishes to challenge a transaction entered into by a company in winding-up or administration.[674]

(v) Preferences

9.156 The provisions dealing with undervalue transactions[675] are also related to the provisions dealing with preferences. A number of sections of the Act apply to both, notably those dealing with the qualifying period, the order of the court and the protection given to good faith purchasers. The period of vulnerability, however, is in the case of preferences six months for both winding-up and bankruptcy except in the case of connected persons or associates where it is extended to two years.[676]

9.157 The preference itself exists where the insolvent 'does anything or suffers anything to be done which...has the effect of putting that person into a position which, in the event of the company going into an insolvent winding-up, will be better than the position he would have been in if that thing had not been done'. This will certainly include the giving of security, which does not constitute an undervalue transaction. An example of a preference was the payment of £2,000 to a 17-year-old management trainee (the son of the majority shareholder) a month before the company went into liquidation. It exceeded the amount that the trainee could have recovered in a breach of contract action.[677]

9.158 A preference is not enough of itself for the transaction to be struck down. The person conferring the preference has to be 'influenced' by a 'desire' to bring about the preferential effect. The provisions in the Insolvency Act 1986 replaced earlier legislation striking down transactions in favour of certain creditors 'with a view of giving such creditor...a preference over the other creditors'. This was interpreted to require 'the dominant intention to prefer' the chosen creditor. The radical change in language in the current provisions means that authorities on the intention element in the old provision cannot be considered.[678] The preference need now only be influenced by the requisite desire and not dominated by it, and the intention to prefer must not merely have been intended but positively desired. The latter change seems to have made it almost impossible to prove an unlawful preference given that: 'Intention is objective, desire is subjective. A man can choose the lesser of two evils without desiring either.'[679] Where a company is pressed by a bank to give security,[680] or a store sets up a trading account on *Quistclose* terms in favour of concessionaires in order to keep them in the store in the run up to Christmas,[681] the necessary desire will not be present. Practical compulsion does not amount to desire.

---

[672] See *Hill v Spread Trustee Co Ltd* [2006] EWCA Civ 542, [2007] 1 WLR 2404 (the period itself is 12 years).

[673] Anyone prejudiced by the transaction whether contemplated by the transferor or not: *Sands v Clitheroe* [2006] BPIR 1000.

[674] *National Bank of Kuwait plc v Menzies* [1994] 2 BCLC 306, CA; *Re Simon Carves Ltd* [2013] EWHC 685 (Ch), [2013] 2 BCLC 100. See the discussion above on proceedings against companies in administration and liquidation.

[675] Sections 239 and 340.

[676] Sections 240(1)(a), (b) and 341(1)(b), (c).

[677] *Re Clasper Group Services Ltd* [1989] BCLC 143.

[678] *Re MC Bacon Ltd* [1991] Ch 127.

[679] *Re MC Bacon Ltd* [1991] Ch 127.

[680] *Re MC Bacon Ltd* [1991] Ch 127.

[681] *Re Lewis's of Leicester Ltd* [1995] 1 BCLC 428.

In the case of preferences in favour of associates or connected persons, there exists a rebut- **9.159**
table presumption of a desire to prefer.[682] It is only in such cases that the legislation has
real teeth, since the absence of desire may be nearly as hard to prove as its presence. In one
case,[683] a publishing company granted a debenture to one of its directors who provided in
return a borrowing facility to the company. The immediate purpose of the transaction was
to reduce the bank overdraft to below its permissible ceiling. The director was a guarantor
of this overdraft. Payments were made directly into the company's account, thus benefiting
the director who had a security for the sums advanced at the same time as he commensu-
rately reduced his liability as guarantor. The presumption was rebutted because the company
was actuated by proper commercial considerations, namely the need to obtain finance from
someone other than the bank, while it kept going the publication of a 'valuable title' that it
was seeking to sell.

(vi) Extortionate credit

A further head under which a transaction may be struck down at the behest of an insolvency **9.160**
officer or administrator is where the insolvent is a party to an extortionate credit transaction.[684] The relevant provisions in the Insolvency Act 1986 take their inspiration from provisions in the Consumer Credit Act 1974,[685] repealing the old Moneylenders Acts 1900–27,
which struck down certain oppressive loans. They replace a provision that limited the rate of
interest that could be applied for in bankruptcy and winding-up.

An extortionate credit transaction can be challenged in a three-year twilight period preceding **9.161**
the commencement of bankruptcy, the making of an administration order or the company
going into a winding-up. The terms have to be 'grossly exorbitant' or otherwise 'grossly contravene ordinary principles of fair dealing'. There is a presumption of extortion and the court
has a discretion to set aside or vary the transaction.

(vii) Late floating charges

The final head of challenge arises under section 245 of the Insolvency Act 1986[686] and con- **9.162**
cerns late floating charges granted by a company in the 12 months[687] preceding the onset of
insolvency or at any time between the petition for an administration and the making of an
administration order. Such charges are valid[688] only to the extent of the value of the money,
goods or services supplied in consideration for the charge[689] 'at the same time as, or after, the
creation of the charge'. The purpose of the section as to hold the ring embracing a company's
unsecured creditors is thus manifest.

The formula concerning the timing of a charge departs slightly from earlier legislation, which **9.163**
was interpreted flexibly to cover advances made before the granting of the charge and in
contemplation of the grant of the charge,[690] which accommodated the advance of emergency

---

[682] Sections 239(6) and 340(5).

[683] *Re Fairway Magazines Ltd* [1993] BCLC 643.

[684] Sections 244 and 343. The test of an extortionate transaction is hard to satisfy where the terms have
been clearly spelt out: *White v Davenham Trust* [2010] EWHC 2748 (Ch), [2011] BCC 77.

[685] Sections 137–140, now repealed by the Consumer Credit Act 2006 (Sch 4), which modifies to a minor
extent s 343(6).

[686] Disapplied by the Financial Collateral Arrangements (No 2) Regulations 2003, SI 2003/3226, reg
10(5), but see *Gray v G-T-P Group Ltd* [2010] EWHC 1772 (Ch), [2011] BCC 869.

[687] Two years for those connected with the company.

[688] Section 245 invalidates only the charge: see *Re Mace Builders (Glasgow) Ltd* [1985] BCLC 154.

[689] The phrase 'in consideration for' means 'as a result of', so that a bank's later factual forbearance from
calling in a loan will suffice: *Re Yeovil Glove Co Ltd* [1965] Ch 148, CA.

[690] *Re Stanton (F and E) Ltd* [1929] 1 Ch 180. See also *Re Columbian Fireproofing Co* [1910] 2 Ch
120, CA.

funds.[691] The current, literalist position is that even a minimal time gap between the giving of value and the grant of the charge will be fatal,[692] though an informal charge granted at the time or before the value is given should not be invalidated by its subsequent reduction to writing.

9.164 In calculating the value given for the charge, some difficulties have been presented where a portion of the value has found its way back to the secured creditor. Where there have been solid business reasons for the transaction, the courts have resisted invalidating the charge. Consequently, where moneys advanced to a company were used to pay off an unsecured debt owed to another creditor in which the secured creditor had an interest, the charge was upheld because the payment to that other creditor preserved goodwill and future supplies to the company.[693] No such judicial generosity will be shown if the company is merely a conduit through which the secured creditor repays himself money advanced to the company in return for the charge.[694] Finally, value granted later than the charge will be found in the case of a bank where the company maintains a current account so that, in accordance with the rule in *Clayton's Case*,[695] payments into the account discharge existing debts in order of seniority. If, eg, an overdraft limit of £20,000 before the charge remains £20,000 afterwards, the bank will nevertheless be able to rely upon the charge to the extent that any sum outstanding represents new debt coming into existence after the charge as a result of payments out of the account.[696] Payments into the account, which keep the overdraft down to the agreed limit, are offset against old debt. Eventually, the whole of the debt will represent advances made after the grant of the charge.

(b) Misfeasance and fraudulent and wrongful trading

(i) Misfeasance

9.165 A series of provisions in the Insolvency Act 1986 deals with misfeasance by directors[697] and officers of a company and with wrongful and fraudulent trading in the run up to liquidation. Under section 212, a summary remedy for misfeasance lies in the course of winding up a company if there has been, on the part of directors and other persons taking part in the 'formation, promotion or management of the company',[698] conduct that amounts to the misapplication or retention of, or refusal to account for, the company's property or money, or to misfeasance[699] or a breach of any fiduciary or other duty owed to the company.[700] The breach of a duty owed to the company now extends under the current provision to a breach of the duty of care in negligence[701] but otherwise the section merely creates a summary remedy without altering the law. The court may require restitution of the money or property and has a broad discretion to make a compensatory award.[702]

---

[691] See *Re Fairway Magazines Ltd* [1993] BCLC 643.

[692] *Power v Sharp Instruments Ltd* (orse *Re Shoe Lace Ltd*) [1994] 1 BCLC 111, CA.

[693] *Re Ellis (Matthew) Ltd* [1933] Ch 458, CA.

[694] *Re Destone Fabrics Ltd* [1941] 1 Ch 319, CA.

[695] (1816) 1 Mer 572, 35 ER 781.

[696] *Re Yeovil Glove Co Ltd* [1965] Ch 148, CA.

[697] While de facto directors are included, shadow directors are not: *Revenue and Customs Commissioners v Holland* [2010] UKSC 51, [2010] 1 WLR 2793. On de facto directors, see *Re Idessa (UK) Ltd* [2011] EWHC 804 (Ch), [2012] BCC 315.

[698] The section extends also to the conduct of liquidators, administrators and administrative receivers: see 19.171.

[699] Under the antecedent provision in companies legislation, misfeasance meant conduct in the nature of a breach of trust: *Coventry and Dixon's Case* (1880) 14 Ch D 660, CA.

[700] A developing case law requires directors of an insolvent company to treat the interests of creditors as paramount: *Colin Gwyer and Associates Ltd v London Wharf (Limehouse) Ltd*, [2002] EWHC 2748 (Ch), [2003] 2 BCLC 153; *Miller v Bain* [2002] 1 BCLC 266.

[701] *Re D'Jan of London Ltd* [1994] 1 BCLC 561.

[702] Section 212(3).

The Insolvency Act 1986 also sets out a series of criminal offences arising out of fraud on the part of a company's officers in the period preceding a winding-up.[703]

(ii) Fraudulent trading

Like the misfeasance provision, the fraudulent and wrongful trading provisions also deal **9.166** with the emergence of prior wrongdoing in the course of winding up a company. Fraudulent trading, according to section 213,[704] arises where the business of a company has been carried on with an intent to defraud creditors or for any other fraudulent purpose.[705] The test of fraud is a very difficult one to satisfy[706] and is not met just because the company's indebtedness arises at a time when it is known by its directors to be insolvent.[707] Only the liquidator can bring proceedings under the section,[708] which may be brought against outsiders.[709] In the unlikely event of those proceedings being successful, the court has a broad discretion to require defendants to make a contribution to the assets of the company.

(iii) Wrongful trading

The wrongful trading provision, section 214, was conceived by the Cork Committee as an **9.167** objective replacement for the subjective fraudulent trading provision.[710] Wrongful trading concerns conduct that the section never defines: the word trading appears only in the title of the section. It exists whenever a person does the prohibited thing (whatever it is)[711] at a time when that person was a director of a company[712] and should have known that there was no reasonable prospect of the company avoiding the insolvent liquidation that subsequently occurred. Section 214 is laconic also to the point of not expressly requiring that the prohibited thing cause anyone loss,[713] except that an order shall not be made against the director if the court is satisfied that he took 'every step' to 'minimize' the 'potential loss' to the company's creditors.[714] The draftsmanship seems makeshift but its broad purpose is to wave the prospect of liability before directors in order to restrain them from trading on irresponsibly when they should be appointing an administrator or inviting the bank to do so, or taking steps to wind up the company. The objective test of liability takes account of the director's general knowledge, skill and experience.[715] If liable, the director is required to contribute to the company's assets,[716] which points to a jurisdiction that is primarily compensatory rather than penal.[717]

---

[703] Section 206 et seq.

[704] The section has extraterritorial application: *Bilta (UK) Ltd v Nazir* [2012] EWHC 2163 (Ch).

[705] It is not enough that individual creditors were defrauded in the course of a business: *Morphitis v Bernasconi* [2003] EWCA Civ 289, [2003] Ch 552.

[706] But the knowledge of an employee can be attributed to an employer: *Bank of India v Morris* [2005] EWCA Civ 693, [2005] 2 BCLC 328.

[707] *Re Patrick and Lyon Ltd* [1933] Ch 786. Proceedings may be taken against anyone who knowingly is party to the carrying on of the business in a fraudulent manner: s 213(2). For the requirement of knowledge, see *Morris v Bank of America National Trust* [2000] 1 All ER 954, 963, CA.

[708] The sanction of the court is required for this and for wrongful trading actions: Insolvency Act, Sch 4, para (3A) (as added by s 253 of the Enterprise Act 2002).

[709] *Bank of India v Morris* [2005] EWCA Civ 693, [2005] BCC 739.

[710] Cmnd 8558 (1982), para 1775 et seq.

[711] Parliament rejected the Cork Committee's proposal that the conduct consist of incurring 'further debts or other liabilities': Cmnd 8558 (1982), para 1806.

[712] This includes shadow directors (ss 214(7) and 251) and de facto directors (*Re Hydrodan (Corby) Ltd* [1994] BCC 161).

[713] According to *Marini Ltd v Dickenson* [2003] EWHC 334 (Ch), [2004] BCC 172 a net deficiency must exist in the company's estate between the time the directors realized liquidation was inevitable and the occurrence of liquidation.

[714] Section 214(3).

[715] Section 214(4).

[716] Section 214(1).

[717] *Re Produce Marketing Consortium Ltd* [1989] BCLC 520.

(iv) Proceeds of actions

9.168 As in actions dealing with vulnerable transactions, the proceeds of wrongful and fraudulent trading actions are held for the general body of creditors.[718] The sections do speak of the orders made contributing, in the present tense, to the assets of the company, which are impressed with the statutory trust in favour of the general creditors. Furthermore, it has to be asked why a liquidator should wish to bring proceedings in actions that cannot be assigned to third parties, and which can only be brought by liquidators, if the proceeds are going to be scooped up by creditors with a charge over the future assets of the company. Nevertheless, in a misfeasance case,[719] it was held that the sum recovered could not be used to recoup the costs of the winding-up. In so far as the action leads to the recovery of property that ought not to have been alienated, there is good reason for it to be returned so that it falls within a secured creditor's charge, especially as misfeasance proceedings can be brought by any creditor and not just by a liquidator.

(c) Powers of investigation and examination

9.169 The liquidator has powers of investigation and examination to assist him in determining whether to challenge pre-liquidation transactions or to take proceedings against officers of the company. These powers assist also in gathering in the assets of the company. Under section 133,[720] the compulsory liquidator may apply to the court for the public examination of former officers of the company and of receivers and administrators, as well as of those involved in the promotion, formation or management of the company.[721] A sufficient number of creditors or members may require an application to be made unless the court rules otherwise. A similar process of public examination applies to bankrupts.[722]

9.170 The Insolvency Act also contains duties on the part of identified individuals such as promoters, employees and officers of the company[723] to co-operate with office holders, namely the official receiver, the liquidator, the administrator and the administrative receiver, by supplying information and making themselves available.[724] This is backed up by a further provision for a judicial inquiry into a company's dealings calling for affidavits, books, papers and company records as well as for attendance by officers, promoters and persons suspected of having in their possession company property.[725] Books, papers and records will have to be surrendered even if the holder has a lien over them.[726] The inquiry must be necessary and must not oppress those who are summoned to appear.[727] Its purpose has been said to be to reconstitute the company's knowledge in the event of, eg, an ensuing winding-up[728] but the reason for it has also been put more broadly as the facilitation of the work of an office holder.[729] The

---

[718] *Re Oasis Merchandising Services Ltd* [1998] Ch 170, CA; *Re MC Bacon Ltd* [1991] Ch 127.

[719] *Re Anglo-Austrian Printing Co* [1895] 2 Ch 891, CA.

[720] This may be extended to voluntary liquidation with the aid of s 112.

[721] See *Re Richbell Strategic Holdings Ltd* [2000] 2 BCLC 794. For voluntary liquidation, see *Bishopsgate Investment Management Ltd v Maxwell Mirror Group Newspapers Ltd* [1993] Ch 1, CA.

[722] Section 290.

[723] Also administrators and administrative receivers.

[724] Section 235. The equivalent provisions for bankruptcy are ss 291(4) and 333.

[725] Section 236. The order will require the surrender of documents as opposed to the provision of information, for which other procedures such as interrogatories are appropriate: *Re Comet Group Ltd* [2014] EWHC 3477 (Ch), [2015] BPIR 1.

[726] Section 246. See *Akers v Lomas* [2002] 1 BCLC 655. For a demand made by an administrative receiver, see *Re Aveling Barford Ltd* [1989] 1 WLR 360.

[727] *Re British and Commonwealth Holdings plc (No 2)* [1993] AC 426, CA. The need for speed may outweigh the avoidance of oppressive conduct: *Shierson v Rastogi* [2002] EWCA Civ 1624, [2003] 1 WLR 586.

[728] See eg *Re Cloverbay Ltd (No 2)* [1991] Ch 90, CA.

[729] *Re British and Commonwealth Holdings plc (No 2)* [1993] AC 426, HL.

inquiry should not take place where the decision to take proceedings against individuals has already been firmly taken[730] But it is permissible if the purpose is to gather evidence to determine if directors disqualification proceedings should be taken.[731] Nevertheless, persons summoned to appear are not protected by a privilege against self-incrimination.[732]

(3) *The Conduct of Insolvency Officers, Administrators, and Receivers*

(a) Personal liability

The Insolvency Act provides for actions against liquidators who act in breach of certain duties. **9.171** Section 212, the summary misfeasance provision,[733] applies also to liquidators.[734] The liquidator's misfeasance may consist of negligence in admitting to proof claims against the estate without making proper inquiry.[735] Proceedings may be launched by the official receiver, a creditor or a contributory.[736] Further control over the conduct of liquidators in office can be exercised by an application to the court to remove the liquidator 'on cause shown',[737] which is a broadly stated discretion that can be employed to deal with dilatory liquidators for the general advantage of those interested in the assets of the company.[738] Administrators and administrative receivers[739] are also open to misfeasance proceedings.[740] Administrators who unfairly harm the interests of a creditor may be the subject of an application to the court, which may make any appropriate order, including a compensation order.[740a] The leave of the court is required if proceedings are to be taken against liquidators and administrators after their release.[741] Administrators may be removed from office at any time by an order of the court.[742] The same applies to administrative receivers.[743] Liquidators, administrators and receivers are all exposed to public examination under section 133. Under section 235, liquidators, administrators and administrative receivers[744] are all under a duty to co-operate with the office-holder.

There is no statutory misfeasance provision for receivers but, when dealing with company **9.172** assets, the question has arisen whether they may incur liability outside the Insolvency Act to

---

[730] *Re Cloverbay Ltd (No 2)* [1991] Ch 90, CA.

[731] *Re Pantmaenog Timber Co Ltd* [2003] UKHL 49, [2004] 1 AC 158.

[732] *Re Levitt (Jeffrey S) Ltd* [1992] Ch 457. Whether the process infringes the European Convention on Human Rights (Art 6: right to a fair trial) depends on various factors, such as the nature of the proceedings and the level of coercion required for different proceedings: *Official Receiver v Stern* [2000] 1 WLR 2230. See also *Saunders v United Kingdom* [1997] EHRR 313; *Shierson v Rastogi* [2002] EWCA Civ 1624, [2003] 1 WLR 586.

[733] Discussed in 9.165.

[734] The misfeasance provision for trustees-in-bankruptcy, who are liable on the same principles as liquidators, is s 304.

[735] *Re Windsor Steam Coal Co* [1929] 1 Ch 151, CA; *Re Home and Colonial Insurance Co Ltd* [1930] 1 Ch 102 (a high standard of care and diligence is required).

[736] Leave of the court is required in the case of a contributory: s 212(5).

[737] Section 108(2).

[738] *Re Keypak Homecare Ltd* [1987] BCLC 409. The removal of trustees-in-bankruptcy is stated simply as occurring when the court so orders or a general meeting of the creditors so decides: s 298(1). Further provision is made for control of the trustee by the creditors' committee and by the court: ss 301 and 303.

[739] But not other receivers except insofar as they have been involved in managing the company: s 212(1)(c).

[740] In their case, the proceedings may be started by the liquidator. In the absence of a special relationship, an administrator owes no common law duty of care to creditors: *Kyrris v Oldham* [2003] EWCA Civ 1506, [2004] 1 BCLC 305.

[740a] Insolvency Act, Sch B1, para 74; *Re Coniston Hotel (Kent) LLP* [2013] EWHC 93 (Ch), [2013] 2 BCLC 405.

[741] Section 212(4).

[742] Schedule B1, para 88.

[743] Section 45(1).

[744] But not other receivers.

the company and to others. A court-appointed receiver is under a duty to preserve the assets and goodwill of the company,[745] but there is no true corresponding and unqualified duty on contractual receivers.[746] The primary duty of the contractual receiver is owed to the debenture holder who procured his appointment and not to the company as such, which is not entitled to expect of him the performance of its own directors and managers.[747]

9.173 Yet there is a duty owed by the receiver. The starting point is the position of the mortgagee who enforces a security directly without procuring the appointment of a receiver. That mortgagee is not a trustee of his power of sale for the mortgagor but may exercise it exclusively in his own interests without however fraudulently or recklessly sacrificing the interests of the mortgagor.[748] This is consistent with the rule that a debenture holder is not obliged to consult the interests of the company when deciding to send in a receiver.[749] Over the years, attempts have been made to introduce an element of due care into the performance by the receiver of his responsibilities. The fundamental issue that has arisen is whether a duty to take care, going beyond a duty to abstain from acting fraudulently, can sit with the receiver's right to place the interests of the debenture holder first. A secondary issue, whose late resolution has clouded the debate, has been the largely taxonomic one of determining whether the provenance of the receiver's duty lies in equity or in the tort of negligence.

9.174 In one important case, the Court of Appeal held that a mortgagee taking possession and exercising a power of sale owed a duty to the mortgagor to obtain a proper price.[750] The same approach was adopted in the case of a receiver when the matter arose collaterally as between the debenture holder and guarantor of the company's obligations.[751] Nevertheless, the Privy Council has trenchantly asserted that the law of tort has no part to play and that a receiver's duties lie only in equity,[752] stressing that the receiver's duty to others must not be allowed to conflict with the duty owed to the debenture holder.[753] In equity, the receiver must act in good faith and refrain from wilful default. More recently, however, the equitable duty has been held to encompass an obligation on the part of a receiver to manage the affairs of a company with care when there is no conflict with the essential duty owed to the debenture holder.[754] Since the tort of negligence is sophisticated enough to tailor due care to the exigencies of the receiver's position, it hardly matters, as far as the company is concerned,[755] whether the duty is classified as equitable or tortious.

---

[745] *Re Newdigate Colliery Ltd* [1912] Ch 468, CA.

[746] But see the attempt to move towards this position in *Astor Chemical Ltd v Synthetic Technology Ltd* [1990] BCC 97. The receiver's entitlement to act against the interests of the company's co-contractants is recognized in *Airlines Airspares Ltd v Handley Page Ltd* [1970] Ch 193 but he may be enjoined from disregarding contracts of the company to the extent that he is not preferring the interests of the debenture holder: *Ash and Newman Ltd v Creative Devices Research Ltd* [1991] BCLC 403.

[747] *Re B Johnson & Co* [1955] Ch 634, 661–2, CA.

[748] *Kennedy v de Trafford* [1896] 1 Ch 762, 772, CA.

[749] *Shamji v Johnson Matthey Bankers Ltd* [1991] BCLC 36, CA.

[750] *Cuckmere Brick Co Ltd v Mutual Finance Ltd* [1971] 1 Ch 949, CA. The creditor's freedom to choose the time to sell is not always easily reconciled with the duty to conduct a sale in a competent manner: see *Den Norske Bank ASA v Acemex Management Co Ltd* [2003] EWCA Civ 1559, [2004] 1 Lloyd's Rep 1.

[751] *Standard Chartered Bank v Walker* [1982] 1 WLR 1410, CA.

[752] *China and South Seas Bank v Tan* [1990] 1 AC 536, PC. See also *Silven Properties Ltd v Royal Bank of Scotland plc* [2003] EWCA Civ 1409, [2004] 1 WLR 997; *Raja v Austin Gray* [2002] EWCA Civ 1965, [2003] BPIR 725.

[753] *Downsview Nominees v First City Corporation Ltd* [1993] AC 295, PC.

[754] *Medforth v Blake* [2000] Ch 86, CA.

[755] Guarantors, eg, may well be a different matter.

(b) Officers of the court and *ex p James*

Official receivers, compulsory liquidators, trustees-in-bankruptcy and administrators, all **9.175** officers of the court,[756] are bound by a particular rule of ethical conduct to behave in a high-minded fashion and abstain from shabby conduct.[757] This is known as the rule in *ex p James*[758] which goes beyond any legal duties owed by the insolvent individual or company and concerns essentially the undue enrichment of the insolvent's estate.[759] There is no true proprietary claim against the officer and the estate,[760] but rather an application to the court to control the conduct of one of its own officers so as to nullify the effect of the enrichment.[761] Early cases concerned the officer's receipt of money paid over under a mistake of law.[762] The recoverability now of money paid in such circumstances[763] abridges the scope of the rule in *ex p James*, which however is not confined to mistake of law.[764] It is a matter of no small difficulty to estimate the reach of the rule, for 'questions of ethical propriety...will always be...the subject of honest difference among honest men'.[765] It does not, eg, prevent a trustee from bringing an action to recover the proceeds of collected cheques drawn by the bankrupt when paying gambling debts.[766] Moreover, the availability of an alternative remedy will result in the rule not being brought into play.[766a]

---

[756] The rule therefore does not apply to voluntary liquidators (*Re TH Knitwear (Wholesale) Ltd* [1988] 1 Ch 275, CA) and contractual receivers (*Triffit Nurseries v Salads Etcetera Ltd* [2000] 1 BCLC 262). For its applicability to receivers, see *Wallace v Shoa Leasing (Singapore) PTE Ltd* [1999] BPIR 911. Insolvents receiving money for services they know they cannot provide may hold those moneys on constructive trust terms (*Neste Oy v Lloyds Bank plc* [1983] 2 Lloyd's Rep 658), which may be a more promising avenue in some cases than the rule in *ex p James*.

[757] Criticized as an 'anomalous' rule by Harman J in *Re Bateson (John) & Co* [1985] BCLC 259, 262.

[758] (1874) 9 Ch App 609.

[759] The rule appears to be confined to cases of enrichment: *Government of India v Taylor* [1955] AC 491, 513, HL; *Re Clark* [1975] 1 WLR 559, 563.

[760] *Re Tyler* [1907] 1 KB 865, 869, CA, explaining James LJ's reference to 'equity' in *ex p James*, but see *Re Nortel GurbH* [2013] uksc 1352 at [122], [2014] Ac 209 (referring to the continued existence of the principle but voting that it cannot be applied so as to compel a liquidator or administrator to alter the ranking of a claim).

[761] *Re Clark* [1975] 1 WLR 559, 564 (and not to restore the claimant to the *status quo ante*).

[762] *Ex p James* (1874) 9 Ch App 609; *ex p Simmonds* (1885) 16 QBD 308, CA.

[763] *Kleinwort Benson Ltd v Lincoln City Council* [1999] 2 AC 349, HL.

[764] *Re Thellusson* [1919] 2 KB 735, CA; *Re Tyler* [1907] 1 KB 865, CA.

[765] *Re Wigzell* [1921] 2 KB 835, 845, CA.

[766] *Scranton's Trustee v Pearse* [1922] 2 Ch 87, CA.

[766a] *Re London Scottish Finance Ltd* [2013] EWHC 4047 (Ch), [2014] Bus LR 424 (remedy available under Consumer Credit Act 1974).

INDEX